Private Saving and Public Debt

Private Saving and Public Debt

Edited by
Michael J. Boskin, John S. Flemming
and
Stefano Gorini

Basil Blackwell

First published 1987
First published in USA 1987

Basil Blackwell Ltd
108 Cowley Road, Oxford, OX4 1JF, UK

Basil Blackwell Inc.
432 Park Avenue South, Suite 1503
New York, NY 10016, USA

British Library Cataloguing in Publication Data

Private saving and public debt.
1. Finance, Personal 2.Saving and thrift
3. Fiscal policy
I. Boskin, Michael J. II. Flemming, John S. III. Gorini, Stefano
339.4'3 HG7920
ISBN 0-631-15142-7

Library of Congress Cataloging in Publication Data

Private saving and public debt.
Includes index.
1. Saving and investment. 2. Debts, Public.
I. Boskin, Michael J. II. Flemming, John Stanton, 1941. III. Gorini, Stefano.
HC79.S3P75 1987 332'.0415 86-17612
ISBN 0-631-15142-7

Typeset in 10 on 12 pt Times
by Photo·Graphics, Honiton, Devon
Printed in Great Britain by T J Press Ltd, Padstow, Cornwall

Contents

List of Contributors vii
Preface viii
Acknowledgements xi

Part I Comparative Analysis of Recent Trends

1 Sectoral Saving and Investment Patterns in 16 OECD Countries, 1965–82 3
Hans Tson Söderström

2 Rising Public-sector Indebtedness: Some More Unpleasant Arithmetic 40
J.A. Bispham

3 The Link between Budget Deficits and Inflation: Some Contrasts between Developed and Developing Countries 72
Tim G. Congdon

Part II Case Studies

The USA

4 Appraising the American Fiscal Stance 95
Edmund S. Phelps

5 Government Deficits: The Case of the United States 105
Rudolph G. Penner

Italy

6 Fiscal Policy and Saving in Italy since 1860 126
Franco Modigliani and Tullio Jappelli

7 Four Arguments for Fiscal Recovery in Italy 171
Rainer S. Masera

The UK: Keynes and Keynesian and later Views of Deficit Finance

8 Keynes on British Budgetary Policy, 1914–46 208
N.H. Dimsdale

9 Deficit Financing: Keynes, the Keynesians and the New Approach, with Special Reference to the UK 234
M.J. Artis

Part III Empirical and Theoretical Issues

Debt and Savings

10 Deficits, Public Debt, Interest Rates and Private Saving: Perspectives and Reflections on Recent Analyses and on US Experience 255
Michael J. Boskin

11 Debt Neutrality and Fiscal Illusion: Theoretical Underpinnings and Empirical Studies. A Comment 287
Michele Bagella

Deficits and the Supply Side

12 Public Debt, Private Savings and Supply-side Policies 298
Luigi Paganetto

13 Some Implications of Deficit-financed Tax Cuts: These Will Always Increase Demand, but Will They Reduce Supply? 318
Walter Eltis

Debt in Steady and Stochastic States

14 The Neoclassical Theory of Public Debt and the Theory of a Long-run Full-employment Deficit 347
Stefano Gorini

15 Debt and Taxes in War and Peace: The Case of a Small Open Economy 373
John S. Flemming

Part IV Overview

16 A Survey of the Debate 395
Michael V. Posner

Index 415

List of Contributors

Michael J. Artis, University of Manchester, UK
Michele Bagella, University of Sassari, Italy
John A. Bispham, Bank for International Settlements, Basle, Switzerland
Michael J. Boskin, Stanford University and NBER, USA
Tim G. Congdon, L. Messel & Co., London, UK
Nicholas H. Dimsdale, University of Oxford, UK
Walter A. Eltis, University of Oxford, UK
John S. Flemming, Bank of England, London, UK
Stefano Gorini, University of Sassari, Italy
Tullio Jappelli, University of Palermo, Italy
Rainer S. Masera, Banca d'Italia, Rome, Italy
Franco Modigliani, Sloane School of Management, MIT, Cambridge, USA
Luigi Paganetto, University of Rome 'Tor Vergata', Italy
Rudolph G. Penner, Congressional Budget Office, Washington DC, USA
Edmund S. Phelps, Columbia University, New York, USA
Michael V. Posner, National Economic Development Office, London, UK
Hans Tson Söderström, SNS – Center for Business and Policy Studies, Stockholm, Sweden

Preface

The Conference papers in this volume reflect a major shift that has taken place in macro-public finance in recent years. This is a field in which the views of theorists, policy advisers and policy makers interact with the perception of problems emerging from past decisions and present events. These essays contribute to that continuing process by which collective understanding may be refined.

There are several strands in the explanation of the change of view of the public sector debt and deficits; one is the shift away from Keynesian emphasis on flows to a greater recognition of the importance of stocks and balance sheets; associated with this is the loss of confidence in fine-tuning aspects of demand management and its replacement by medium-term strategies and the consequent emphasis on their longer-term implications and the longer-term properties of models. A third strand is due to the effect of swings in real interest rates associated with changes in inflation trends relative to expectations.

The condition that at constant tax rates the debt will grow as a proportion of the (non-interest) tax base if government expenditure (excluding debt interest) exceeds tax revenues (excluding those on debt interest), and if the (net of tax) interest rate exceeds the growth rate of the tax base, recurs throughout the volume. This 'sustainability' condition discriminates sharply between periods of recent history in many countries, but it does not necessarily separate Mr Micawber's states of happiness and misery quite so strongly. If the growth rate of the tax base exceeds the relevant interest rate, a large deficit may be 'sustainable' in the sense that the debt to income ratio rises towards a finite limit, but that mathematical limit may exceed the actual capacity of the government to borrow or the willingness of lenders to hold government debt.

The final element is the growing perception of the distorting effects of the high marginal tax rates required to finance high public expenditure while servicing a large debt at high real interest rates if the debt is not to grow. While academic economists have typically been cautious in their claims for supply-side measures, there is a long tradition, represented here, of concern about the welfare effects of marginal tax rates.

Nearly all these papers involve getting to grips with the contributions of Robert Barro in this field. In 1974 he resuscitated an argument presented, but not endorsed, by David Ricardo that it made no difference whether the government financed expenditure by lump-sum taxes raised today or by borrowings secured on the receipt of future lump-sum taxes. This proposition implies that government borrowing (dissaving) will be offset by additional private saving – to provide against the future tax liabilities. Econometric work reported here both for Italy and the US lends it little support.

In a later paper Barro (1979) relaxed the assumption of lump sum taxation. Where taxes distort, their deadweight burden typically rises more than proportionately with revenue which rises less than proportionately to the tax rate. Thus if required revenue rises temporarily the total deadweight burden may be reduced if the marginal tax rate fluctuates little, if at all, and the budget goes through successive phases of surplus and deficit – requiring resort to debt and the capital market. This theoretical result is not likely to be more successful in explaining the variations of debt and taxes over time than are static welfare results in explaining observed tax structures, rates and exemptions.

There is not a simple relationship between these various elements and the structure of this book; several of the papers bear witness to the breadth of the authors' concerns across the different strands and over both space and time. The first three papers are explicitly comparative, largely across OECD countries but also with some reference to the interactions of fiscal and monetary policy in the inflation-prone economies of South America. These papers lay a valuable foundation of facts and the shared analysis of the role of the crucial interest/growth inequality condition.

The second section consists of three pairs of case studies, of the US, Italy and the UK respectively. These countries, which were well represented at the conference, differ in their position in terms of the history of debt, deficits and inflation, as is reflected in these papers. The papers also differ in their historical dimension with one of the Italian ones covering a hundred years while the British ones, perhaps because the problem there seems now less acute, have a strong emphasis on the historical development of ideas, notably those of Keynes both in his own lifetime and in the hands of his successors.

The third section also consists of three pairs of papers, two concentrating on effects of debt on savings and thus on the supply of capital, two on supply-side effects more generally, and two more abstract papers on debt in deterministic models and in models where there is a major role for debt to contribute to the smoothing of marginal tax rates.

The final contribution reflects the discussion more explicitly in its summary of one participant's reaction to the exposure of these themes at the conference.

Acknowledgements

The contributions included in this volume are the texts, some of them extensively revised, of a number of papers presented at an international conference on 'Private Saving and Public Debt' held at Alghero, Sardinia, from 9 to 13 September 1985. The Conference was organized jointly by the University of Sassari, Dipartimento di Economia Istituzioni e Società and Istituto Giuridico, and by the Banco di Sardegna. The organizing committee was composed of Michele Bagella, Stefano Gorini and Antonio Serra, all from the University of Sassari, and by Ferdinando Buffoni of the Banco di Sardegna. The financial burden of the conference was borne by the Banco di Sardegna, which provided by far the largest contribution, and by the Consiglio Nazionale delle Ricerche, the SIR (Società Italiana Resine) spA and the Camera di Commercio Industria Artigianato e Agricoltura di Sassari.

The editors wish to thank the organizers of the conference; the Rector of the University of Sassari, Professor Antonio Milella, for his active endorsement of the initiative; the President of the Associazione Bancaria Italiana, Professor Giannino Parravicini, for his stimulating opening address; and the Institutions which bore the financial burden. The editors express their special appreciation to the Banco di Sardegna, in the persons of its President Dr Angelo Solinas and its Director General Dr Angelo Giagu De Martini, for its most generous support. Its sponsorship of the initiative belongs to a tradition of cultural promotion in the Region, and of co-operation with Sassari's ancient University.

PART I
Comparative Analysis of Recent Trends

1
Sectoral Saving and Investment Patterns in 16 OECD Countries, 1965–82

HANS TSON SÖDERSTRÖM

I INTRODUCTION

The period after the first oil price shock saw a dramatic deterioration in the financial position of the public sector in most OECD countries. Timing, duration and magnitude has varied between countries, but the trend has been almost pervasive. In a closed economy it must hold as a matter of national accounting identity that a public sector deficit must be precisely matched *ex post* by a private sector financial surplus. In an open economy, on the other hand, a public sector deficit which is not matched by a financial surplus in the private sector must be accompanied by a deficit on current account. The channels by which these *ex post* identities are fulfilled, at what level of nominal and real national income, how this depends on the nature of public spending, taxation, and on the mode of financing the deficits are questions which have aroused much theoretical and empirical controversy in the last decade or two (for some recent surveys, see e.g. Buiter and Tobin, 1979; Friedman, 1985; Koskela and Virén, 1983; McCallum, 1985; OECD, 1983).

The purpose of this chapter is to present a set of comparable saving and investment data for a large number of OECD countries in such a way that empirical regularities between countries and over time can be studied. We are particularly interested in the relation between

I wish to thank Stefan Ackerby, Håkan Nordström and Peter Sellin for competent and expedient assistance with data collection and compilation. Helpful comments on an earlier version of the paper have been received from many conference participants, notably Walter Eltis, Tom Congdon and John Bispham.

government budget deficits and private sector saving and investment behaviour. Data are therefore presented in a form which can throw some light on this issue.

This chapter is organized as follows. The next section presents the national accounting framework in which the data are presented. After a brief review of some theoretical issues involved, we then proceed to a presentation of the empirical evidence. Finally, in the concluding section, some 'stylized facts' are extracted from the data material. Such stylized facts may be a useful input into further theorizing in this area.

II A NATIONAL ACCOUNTING FRAMEWORK

The macroeconomic aggregates with which we deal in this paper are all derived from the basic national income identity

$$Y \equiv C + I + G + X - M$$

where Y is the national income, C is private consumption, I is total domestic capital formation, G is government consumption expenditure, and $X - M$ is net exports of goods and services. Separating private from public investment

$$I \equiv I^{P} + I^{G}$$

and substituting in definitions of private and public gross saving

$$S^{P} \equiv Y - T - C$$

and

$$S^{G} \equiv T - G$$

where T is tax income, we can rearrange these equations to obtain the familiar savings–investment relation

$$(S^{G} - I^{G}) + (S^{P} - I^{P}) \equiv (X - M)$$

One way of interpreting this identity is to say that the excess absorption of goods and services by the public sector must be provided by either the private or the foreign sector. Another is to say that the bonds (or money) used to finance a public sector deficit must be placed in the hands of either the domestic private sector or the foreign sector. The excess of saving over investment in a sector is called the sector's financial saving. If we exclude public lending to other sectors and some other financial items from public spending, the budget deficit (government expenditure minus income) will be equal to the financial dissaving of the public sector.

The saving–investment view of budget deficits helps us to understand that a deficit does not necessarily mean a decline in the net wealth position of the public sector. If the government wants to hold its net wealth constant, it should in principle debt-finance all public net investment.[1] Only if government net saving (gross saving minus depreciation on the public capital stock) is negative is the net wealth of the public sector declining and future taxes will have to be raised to restore it to the original level (if that is regarded as desirable). The much-debated Ricardian effects of budget deficits (see e.g. Barro, 1974; Buiter and Tobin, 1979; McCallum, 1985) thus crucially depend on three factors: (a) the initial net wealth position of the public sector; (b) what level of public net saving is reflected in the budget deficit; (c) the desired future net wealth position of the public sector. For a country like Sweden all three factors must be considered in a discussion of the effects of budget deficits on private saving. First, the net financial wealth of the public sector was very large in the mid 1970s as a result of accumulation in government controlled pension funds. Second, since public lending and investment are large items by international standards in Swedish government expenditure, the cash deficit is much bigger (and hence occurred much earlier) than negative net public saving. Finally, *some* part of the budget deficit most likely represented a change in the revealed preference of the general public regarding the target level of public net wealth – a change of opinion also reflected in the outcome of general elections in 1976, when the Social Democrats lost power for the first time in 44 years.

The saving–investment view of budget deficits also leads us to the interrelations between the markets for goods and services on the one hand and the markets for financial assets on the other. These interrelations are best illustrated by a flow-of-funds matrix as presented in table 1.1.

Here the economy has been condensed into the three sectors just discussed. The first row shows how the financial saving of the private sector can go into increased claims on the government sector (ΔB^{P}), on the foreign sector (ΔF^{P}), or into reductions of the private debt to these sectors ($-\Delta D^{G}$, $-\Delta D^{F}$). Similar adding-up exercises can be carried out along the rows for the two other sectors. Adding up columns we get the financial *dis*saving of the sectors. The sum of financial saving and dissaving for the economy as a whole – including the foreign sector (the rest of the world) – must of course be equal to zero.

We have abstracted here from a banking sector and a corresponding asset – money – which normally occur in traditional flow-of-funds matrices (see e.g. Brainard and Tobin, 1968). Still, with only three

Table 1.1 *Flow-of-funds matrix*

Sources of funds	Uses of funds Change in financial claim on/liabilities to sector P	G	F	Σ
P	0	$\Delta B^{P} - \Delta D^{G}$	$\Delta F^{P} - \Delta D^{F}$	$S^{P} - I^{P}$
G	$\Delta D^{G} - \Delta B^{P}$	0	$\Delta F^{G} - \Delta B^{F}$	$S^{G} - I^{G}$
F	$\Delta D^{F} - \Delta F^{P}$	$\Delta B^{F} - \Delta F^{G}$	0	$X - M$
Σ	$I^{P} - S^{P}$	$I^{G} - S^{G}$	$M - X$	0

Sectors: P = Private; G = Public; F = Foreign.
Assets: D = Claims on private sector (private debt)
B = Claims on public sector (government bonds)
F = Claims on foreign sector (foreign bonds)
(Example: ΔB^{P} = Change in private sector claims on the public sector (private sector holdings of government bonds)).
Real transactions: S^{P} = Private savings ($Y - T - C$)
I^{P} = Private investment
S^{G} = Public saving (T − G)
I^{G} = Public investment
X = Exports of goods and services
M = Imports of goods and services.

sectors and three assets, the matrix should help us to keep in mind two important relations:

1 The budget constraint, linking the excess absorption of goods and services of a sector to that sector's decumulation of net financial claims on other sectors during any particular period of time.
2 The balance sheet constraint, linking the change in claims and liabilities between sectors to each other at any moment of time $((S^{P}-I^{P}) + (S^{G}-I^{G}) + (X-M) = 0)$.

In addition, the matrix is composed so as to draw our attention to a fact which is not always noted in this connection: there is not necessarily any one-to-one relation between the financial dissaving of a sector and a change in the volume outstanding of any particular debt *instrument*. A distinction between money-financed and bond-financed budget deficits is always made, of course. But in a situation where all sectors of the economy initially hold gross claims on each other, excess real absorption in a sector can be financed by a decumulation of such claims rather than by an increase in the amount of outstanding debt instruments of that particular sector. So, for instance, in table 1.1, a budget deficit can be financed not only by $\Delta B^{P}+\Delta B^{F}$ but also by $-\Delta D^{G}$ and/or $-\Delta F^{G}$.

If the government initially holds a significant amount of public sector bonds (as was the case in Sweden), a budget deficit does not *necessarily* mean an increased amount of government bonds outstanding (even though this proved to happen in practice). Also – in a case not covered by our matrix – a budget deficit can be financed by transfers of claims on real capital from public to private sector, as we have recently witnessed in the UK.

III THEORETICAL ISSUES

Should we expect a budget deficit to be matched primarily by higher private financial saving or by a current account deficit? If higher private financial saving is involved, should we expect this to be due to higher private saving, lower private investment, or both? The economist's answer to these questions is 'It depends'.

A brief review of the main theoretical issues involved may help to explain the complexity of the matter. There are at least four issues that have to be straightened out before we can even start to approach an answer to the questions raised above. These four matters are: the nature of the deficit itself, the channels through which we are tracing the effects, the structure of the economy, and the assumptions we make regarding private sector behaviour.

The Nature of the Deficit

A first natural question to ask is: How did the deficit arise? Is it exogenous – that is a result of discretionary changes of public expenditures or tax rates – or is it endogenous – a result of a decline in private economic activity at tax and expenditure rules which would lead to budget balance at full capacity utilization? The latter type of deficits are often called 'cyclical', a result of 'built-in stabilizer' effects. Cyclical deficits can be caused by autonomous declines in private investment and exports, or by autonomous increases in private saving and import propensities and their multiplier effects. We must be careful not to confound such *causes* of budget deficits with their effects. Cyclical deficits are contrasted to 'structural' deficits, which are not eliminated by a return to full capacity utilization, but which require discretionary changes in tax rates and/or spending rules for the budget to balance at full employment.

It goes without saying that the distinction between cyclical and structural deficits must by necessity be quite imprecise. One main reason for this is that the concepts of capacity and capacity utilization are fuzzy in situations where the structure of demand and relative prices are rapidly changing. Another reason is that the distinction between automatic effects and discretionary changes is not always self-evident. For instance, one government may index tax schedules via an automatic formula. Another government may also be committed to indexation, but tax schedules may formally be adjusted by parliamentary decision every year.

Even so, it is interesting to note that – out of a total budget balance deterioration of 4.1 per cent of GNP in the OECD 'major seven' between 1971 and 1982 – a full 3.1 per cent has been calculated by the OECD (1983) to be the result of built-in stabilizers. Only one percentage point remains to be explained by discretionary change. No matter what conceptual and statistical ambiguities are involved, these relative magnitudes must imply that it would be a serious mistake to regard private sector developments solely as *effects* of deficits, and to no extent as their *causes*.

Deficits caused by discretionary changes in the government budget will obviously have different effects depending on which budget item is subject to change. Is the deficit due to tax cuts or spending increases? If tax cuts, is it household taxes or corporate taxes? Is it income taxes or expenditure taxes? Is it marginal taxes or average taxes at a given degree of progressivity? If spending increases, is it transfer payments or public expenditure on goods and services? Transfers to households or corporations? Public consumption or public investment? Are public expenditures substitutes or complements to private expenditure? Substitutes – like public dental care – may obviously crowd out private sector production. Complements – like public infrastructure investment – may similarly 'crowd in' private sector activity.

A final question regarding the nature of the deficit regards the mode of financing. We have an abundant literature on the different economic effects of *money* financed versus *bond* financed budget deficits. According to current doctrine (see e.g. Gordon, 1981; Barro, 1984; Friedman, 1985; McCallum, 1985) an unexpected money financed budget deficit will have an expansionary wealth effect on aggregate demand, and an expansionary 'surprise inflation' effect on aggregate supply. A bond financed deficit will have a smaller wealth effect on aggregate demand, and its effects on saving and investment will depend on relative asset substitutabilities and the maturity structure of government bonds.

The Channels of Effects

We have just made a distinction above between demand-side and supply-side effects. Obviously, effects on both aggregate demand and aggregate supply must be taken into account in order to trace the overall effects of budget deficits on the economy. On this point there has been a healthy shift of emphasis away from the one-sided study of demand-side effects of the early Keynesian literature to a more balanced view in more recent work where also effects on the supply of labour and capital are observed. Clearly, the *aims* of budgetary measures must not be confounded with their *effects*. So-called supply-side measures may have by far their largest effects on the demand side of the economy as recent American experience has taught us.

We have also already touched upon the distinction beween real and financial effects of budget deficits. There is no established taxonomy here. We may call 'real' those effects that emanate from public expenditure and taxation. That would reserve the term 'financial' for those effects which emanate from the mode of financing the deficit. With this taxonomy we could say that the pendulum of emphasis in the economics literature on the effects of deficits has swung very far from the real to the financial side. A problem with this taxonomy is, however, that real effects may be largest on the financial markets (like, for example, effects of changes in capital income taxation on relative asset demands), whereas financial effects may be most important on the markets for goods and services (like, for example, wealth effects of government bonds on consumption demand).

This leads on to another important distinction, which must be made between channels of effects on the financial side: the distinction between *wealth* effects and *portfolio* effects of budget deficits. The magnitude – or even existence – of wealth effects of bond financed budget deficits in an economy with forward-looking agents has been a much debated issue ever since the appearance of Barro's (1974) by now classical paper. Still, there will always be portfolio effects of an increased supply of government bonds. They may 'crowd out' or 'crowd in' other assets in private portfolios, depending on relative asset substitutabilities and maturity structure, as mentioned above. The predicted effect of a given bond financed budget deficit on saving and investment will be different depending on if only wealth effects, only portfolio effects or both are taken into account.

The Structure of the Economy

The effects of identical deficits on the private sector will be different depending on the structure of the economy in at least two important respects. First, the initial conditions when the deficit appears have to be specified in a number of dimensions. We have to know, of course, whether or not the economy is at full capacity utilization initially. It is reasonable also to assume that the effects on, for example, the labour force participation rate and the private savings rate will depend on the initial levels of these variables. As was discussed in the previous section of the paper it is furthermore important to specify the initial financial structure of the economy. What it the financial net wealth position of the private and public sectors? What proportion of government bonds do private sector portfolios contain initially? The effects of deficits on private savings and investment will be contingent on the answer to these questions.

Another respect in which it is important to specify the structure of the economy refers to its degree of openness both on commodity markets and on the markets for financial capital. Openness can be specified in terms of the degree of substitutability between domestic and foreign goods or assets. On commodity markets a simplification is often made whereby one type of goods – tradables – are assumed to be perfectly substitutable, and another type of goods – nontradables – are assumed to be entirely nonsubstitutable. We call 'open' those economies which have a relatively large tradables sector and a high degree of substitutability between foreign and domestic financial assets.

In order to determine the effects of budget deficits in open economies it is essential to specify also the exchange rate regime under which the economy is operating. In an economy under a fixed exchange rate with all goods tradable and perfect substitutability between domestic and foreign bonds a budget deficit will have no effect on total output or interest rates, and will therefore spill over into the current account independent of the level of capacity utilization. With imperfect asset substitutability there will be interest rate effects, portfolio adjustments and consequently some effects on saving and investment. With the existence of non-tradable goods there will also be effects on private investment and saving via the commodity and labour markets. Under flexible exchange rates, finally, budget deficits will affect saving, investment and the current account also via exchange rate adjustments in response to changing asset supplies and yield structures.

Behavioural Assumptions

The effect of budget deficits on saving and investment will depend not only on the structure of the economy in the respects just mentioned, but also on the behavioural responses in various sectors of the economy. One crucial area for behavioural assumptions concerns wage and price formation. With perfect wage flexibility the labour market will be cleared at all times and there is not much need for budget policy in the first place. Imperfect wage flexibility may create a need for budget policy in order to maintain full employment, but it also makes it necessary to take the wage formation responses to budget policy into account. Is there real or nominal wage rigidity? Are there implicit employment contracts? Are wages formed atomistically or by unions? Is there strategic behaviour in the wage formation process? The answers to such questions condition the expected response of saving and investment to budget deficits.

Behavioural assumptions are no less crucial on financial markets. A higher yield on financial assets will increase private saving only if the intertemporal substitution effect dominates the income effect. This in turn depends on the relative importance of different savings motives in private behaviour. Also, we need to have some idea about portfolio preferences in order to make predictions regarding the effect of budget deficits on private portfolios.

Perhaps the most important area for behavioural assumptions concerns expectations formation. How far-sighted are private agents? Do they anticipate the future tax burden of current deficits? Do they fully understand the functioning of the economy? Do they know the policy rule which is guiding budgetary policy?

Such behavioural assumptions can be more or less supported by econometric testing. But the empirical study of the effects – as distinct from the causes – of budget deficits becomes a very intricate matter when the question of causality must remain open. In principle, it is necessary to specify and test a complete macro model with behavioural relations for both the private *and* public sectors, and with the effects of exogenous changes on government expenditure and revenue specified in detail. The empirical difficulties are aggravated by the fact that *both* the government and agents in the private sector can be assumed to act in anticipation of changes in the other sector and in the rest of the world. The explanatory variables are therefore not directly observable except in the special case of a rational expectations equilibrium, when they coincide with realized values.

This brief theoretical survey should have made clear that it is difficult to hold with conviction many operational a priori beliefs about the aggregate relations between budget deficits and private saving and investment. Given the many potential constellations of a priori assumptions it is possible to defend theoretically almost any specification of these relations. The purpose of this paper is not to add to the theoretical discussion, but rather to present some data on the matter in an accessible way, and to extract from them some stylized facts about the behaviour of public deficits and private saving and investment behaviour in the more important OECD countries over the last two decades. Such stylized facts might at least help us to put the relevant questions in future theoretical and empirical research.

IV EMPIRICAL EVIDENCE

In order to get a general overview of actual developments, I have gathered data on sectoral savings and investment in the more important OECD countries for a period extending over approximately a decade before and after the first oil price shock. The data cover all the major OECD countries for which data are available. Countries not included are Greece, Iceland, Ireland, Luxemburg, Portugal, Switzerland, Turkey and New Zealand. The time period covered is 1965 through 1982. This should give an adequate representation of conditions before and after the first oil price shock. Data for 1983 and later were not available at the time of data collection.

The data are presented in figures 1.1 to 1.16 for each country separately. The top left panel in each country diagram shows the financial savings ratio for the public sector $(S^G - I^G)/Y$, the private sector $(S^P - I^P)/Y$, and for the country as a whole $(X - M)/Y$. The national income identity $(S^P - I^P) + (S^G - I^G) = X - M$ is not automatically fulfilled by the OECD statistics, as data on saving and investment derive from different sources than the foreign trade statistics. The statistical discrepancy cannot be allocated between variables on a priori grounds. It has been added to private investment, I^P, for the single reason that it is the largest aggregate, variations in which should therefore be least affected by changes in the statistical discrepancy. For those countries where a subdivision of the private sector into corporate and household sector has been available the discrepancy has been added to corporate investment, I^C, for the same reason.

The top middle panel of figures 1.1 to 1.16 presents aggregate saving, investment and depreciation ratios for the different countries, where the difference between saving and investment is identically equal to the current account. Financial saving in the public and private sector respectively is decomposed into saving and investment in the top right and bottom left panels. Finally, private sector saving and investment ratios are decomposed into corporate and household sectors for those countries where such a decomposition is available (not available for Germany, Austria, Belgium, Denmark, Netherlands, Norway, Spain and Australia). The data presented in the country diagrams give a first

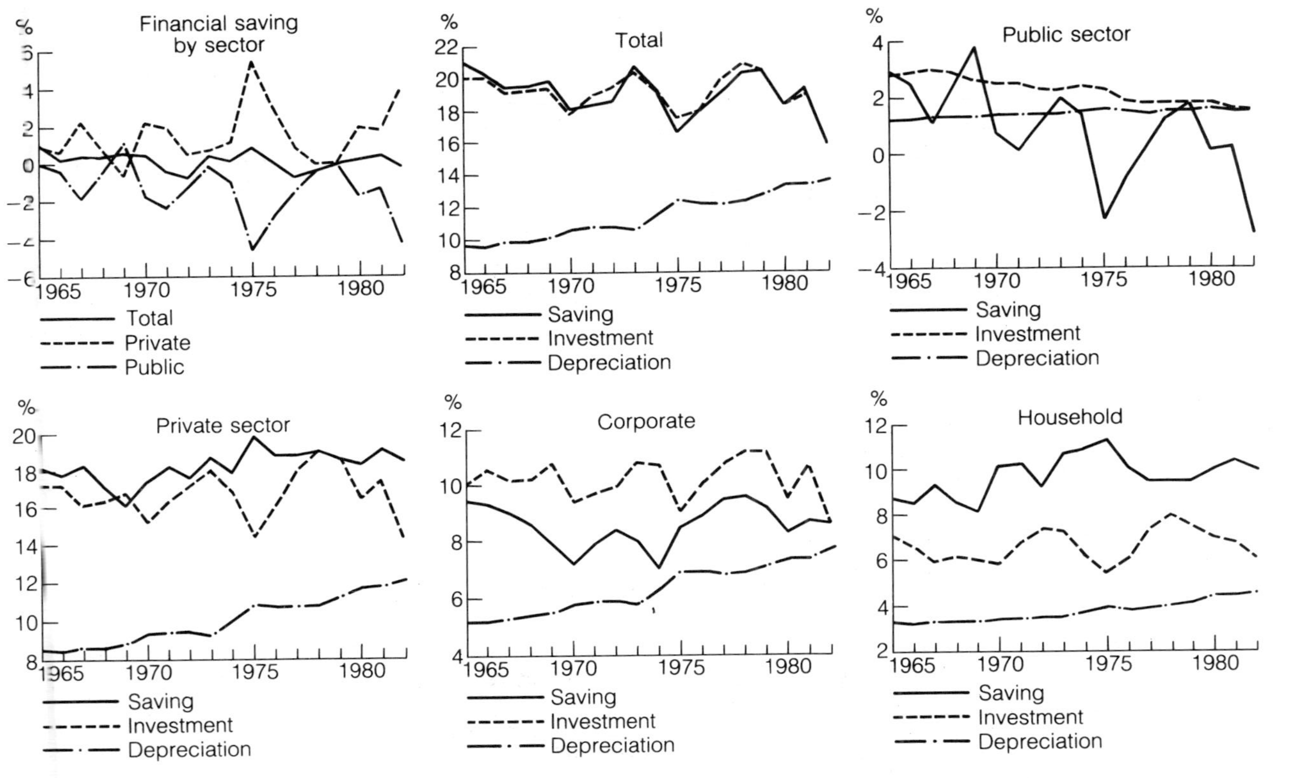

Figure 1.1. The USA

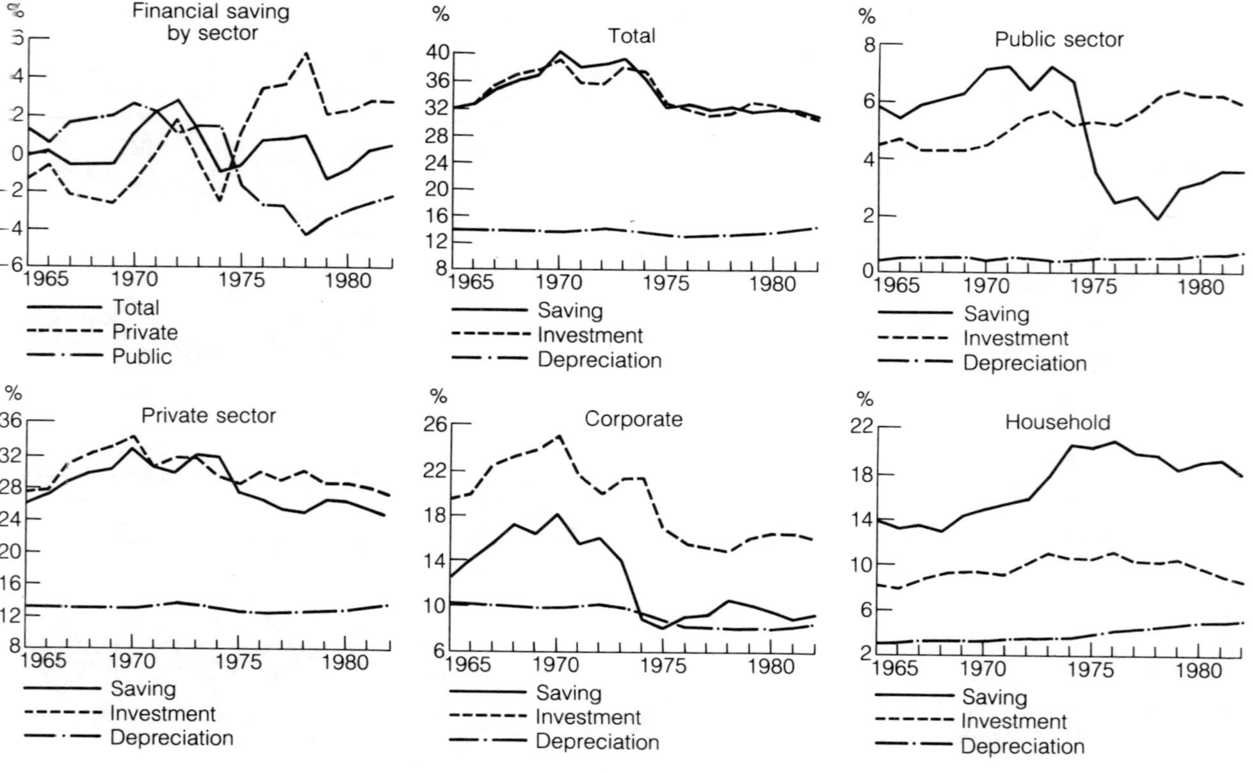

Figure 1.2 Japan

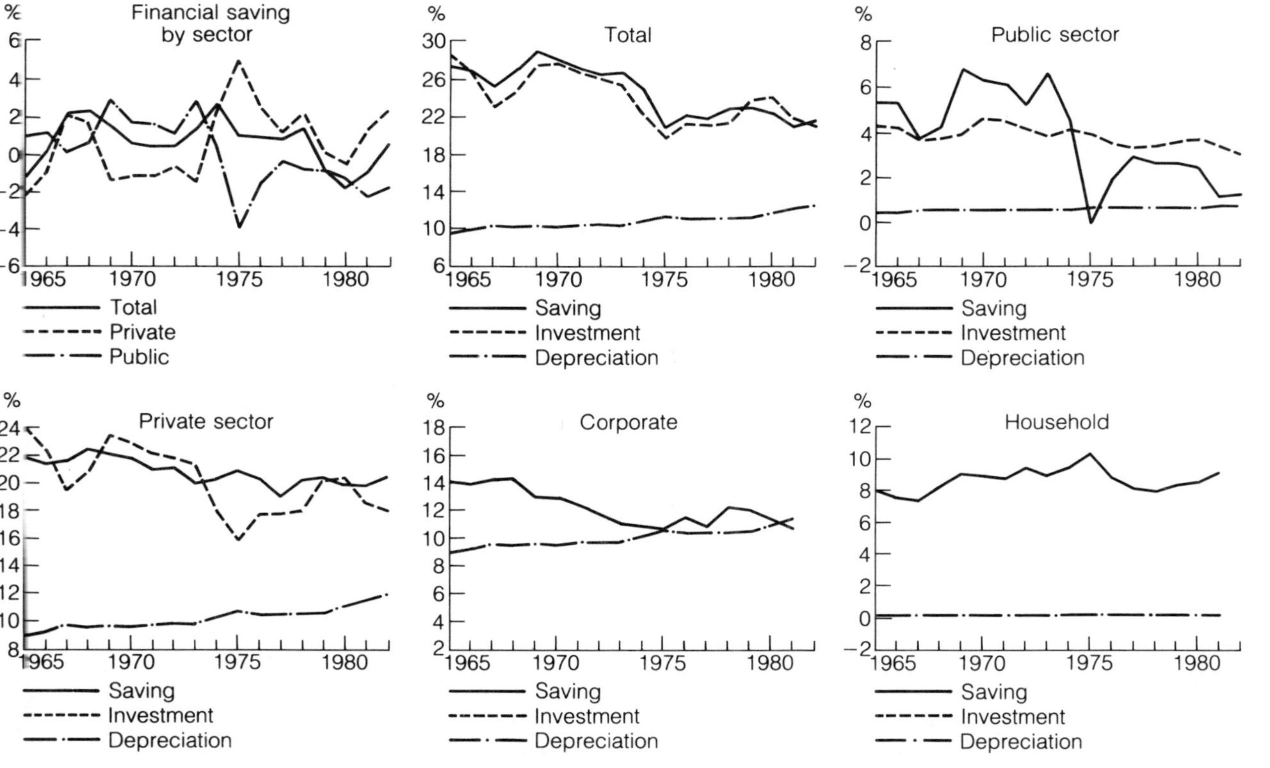

Figure 1.3 Germany

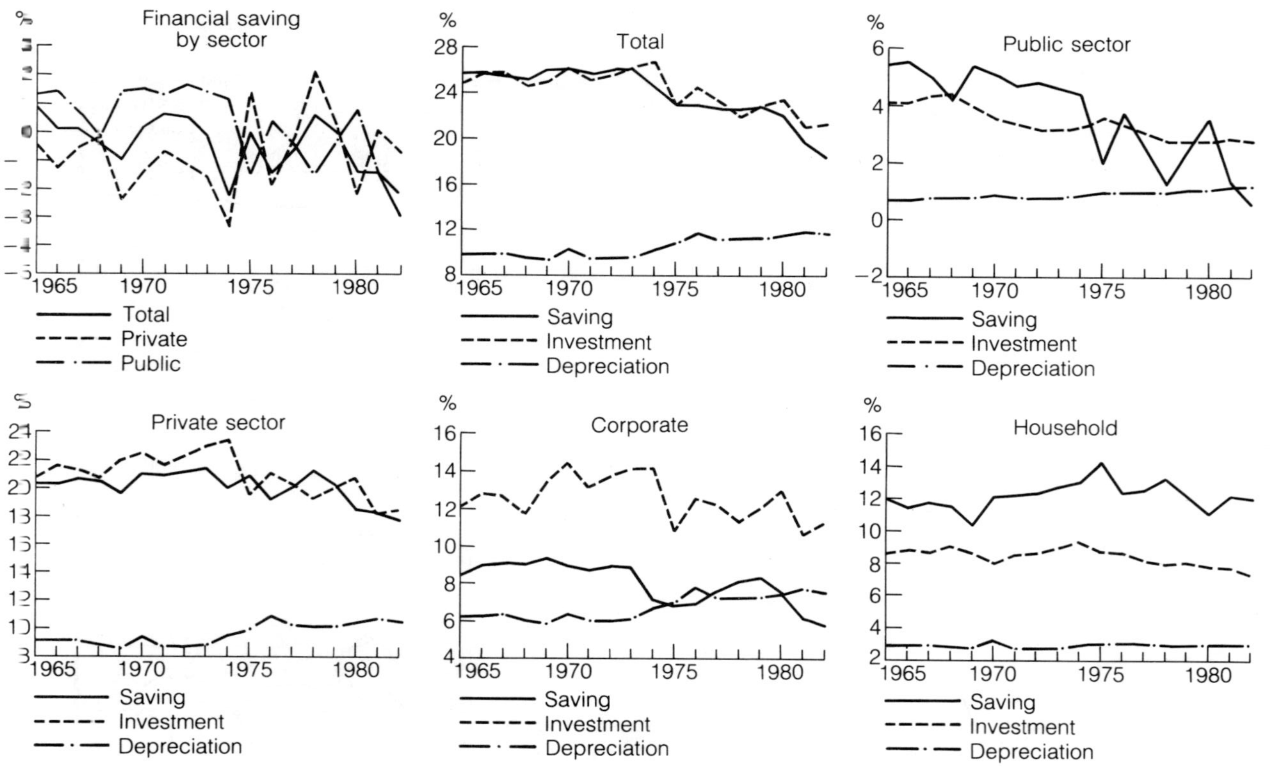

Figure 1.4 France

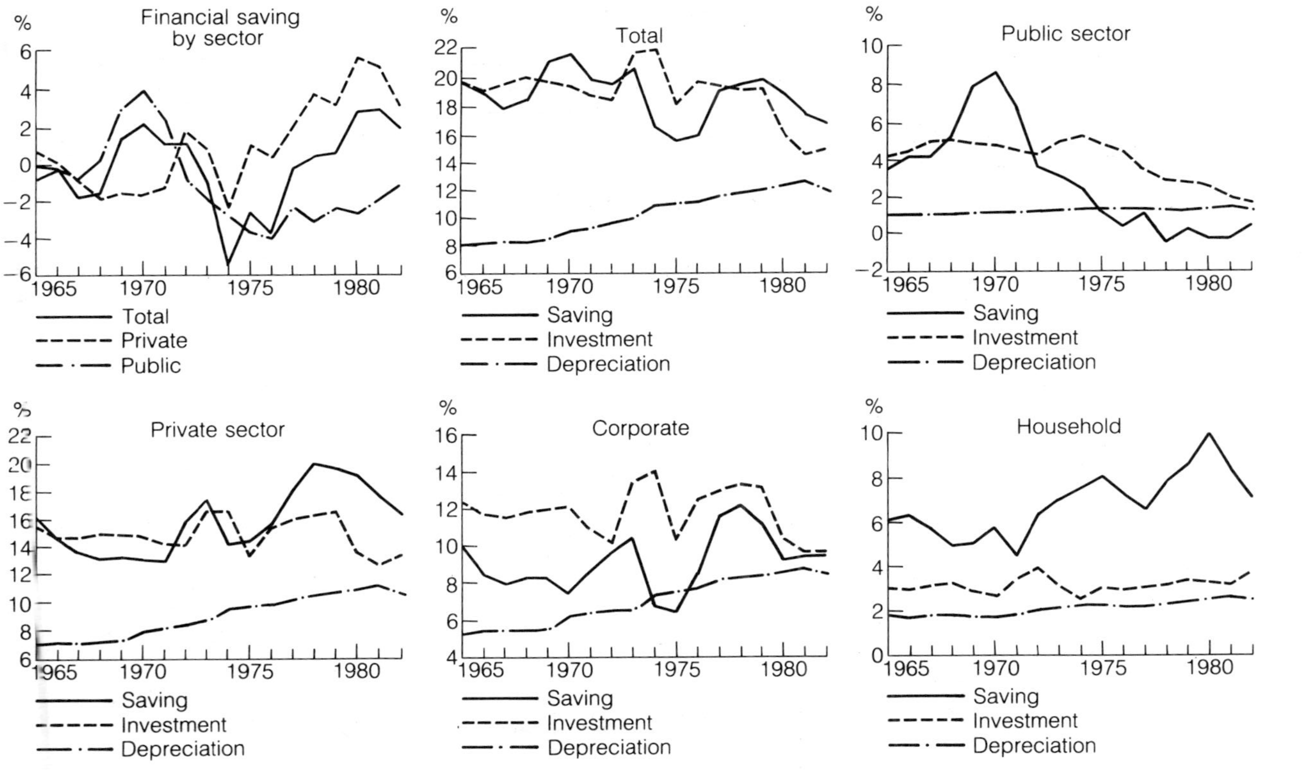

Figure 1.5 The UK

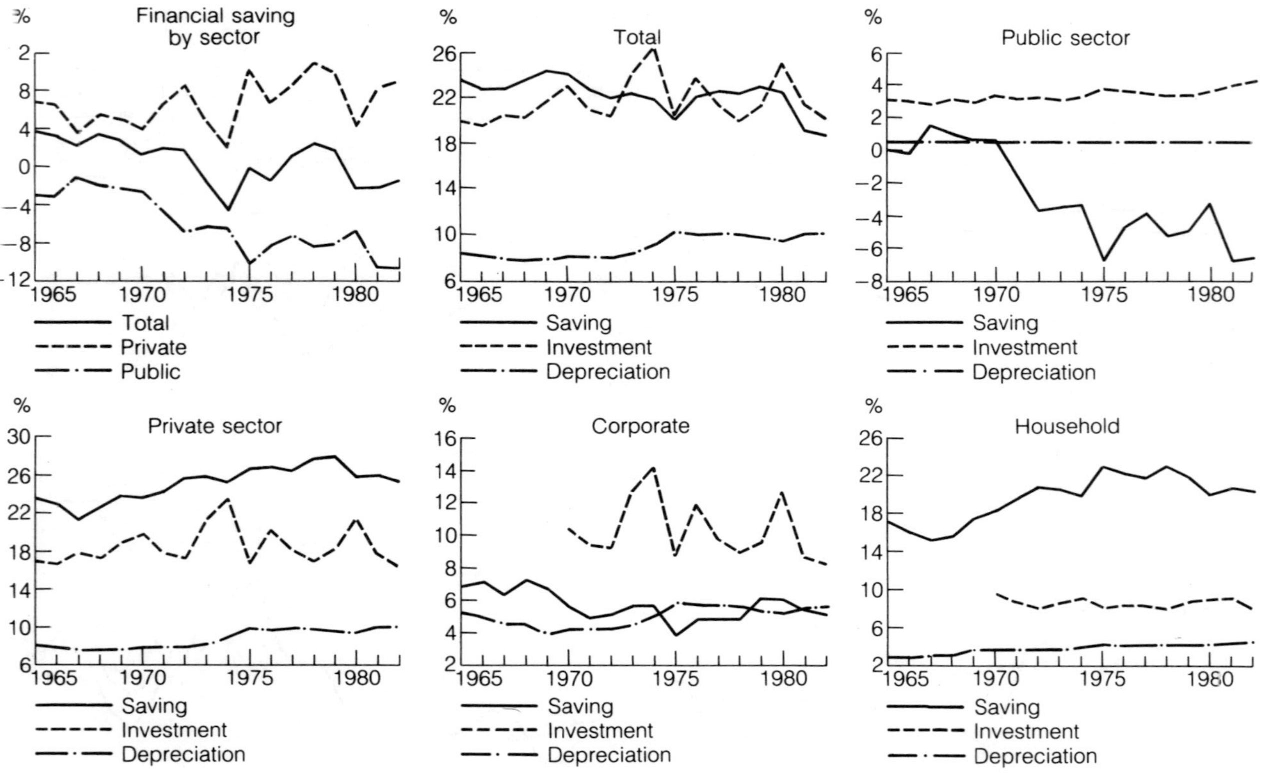

Figure 1.6 Italy

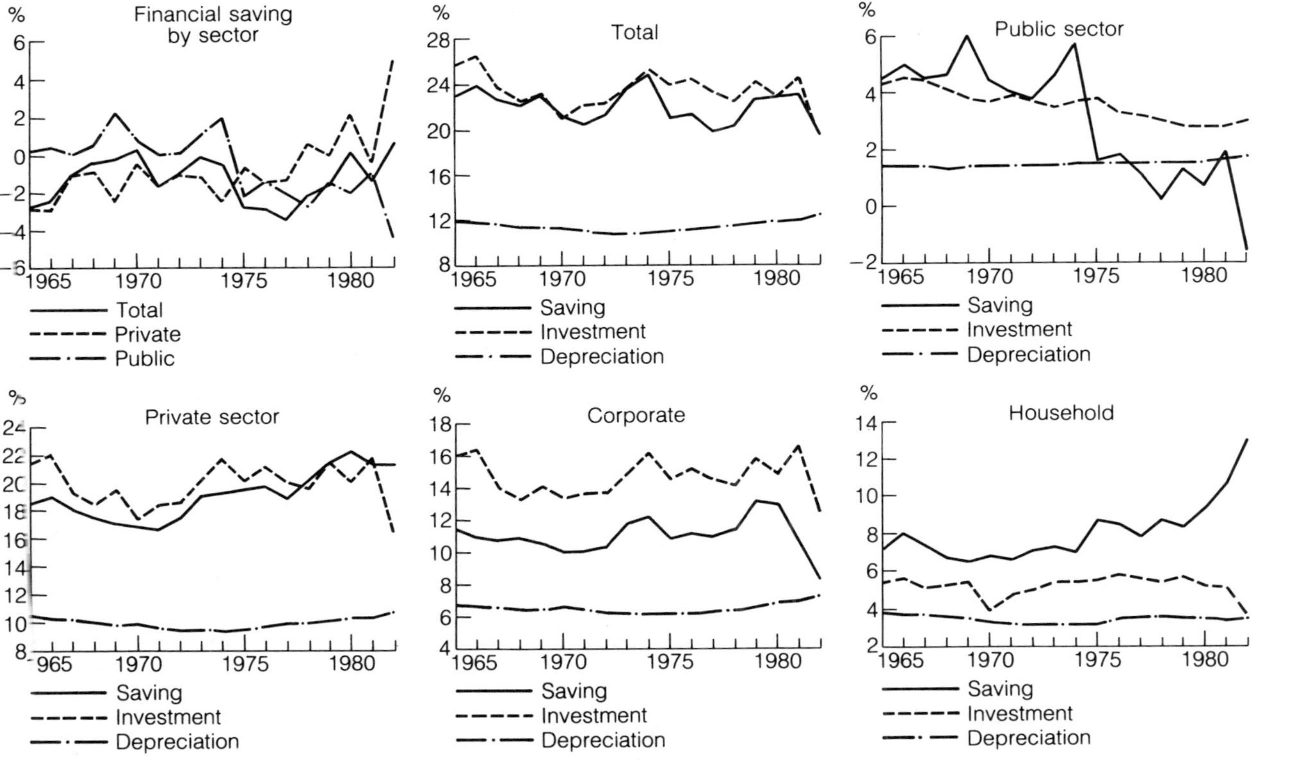

Figure 1.7 Canada

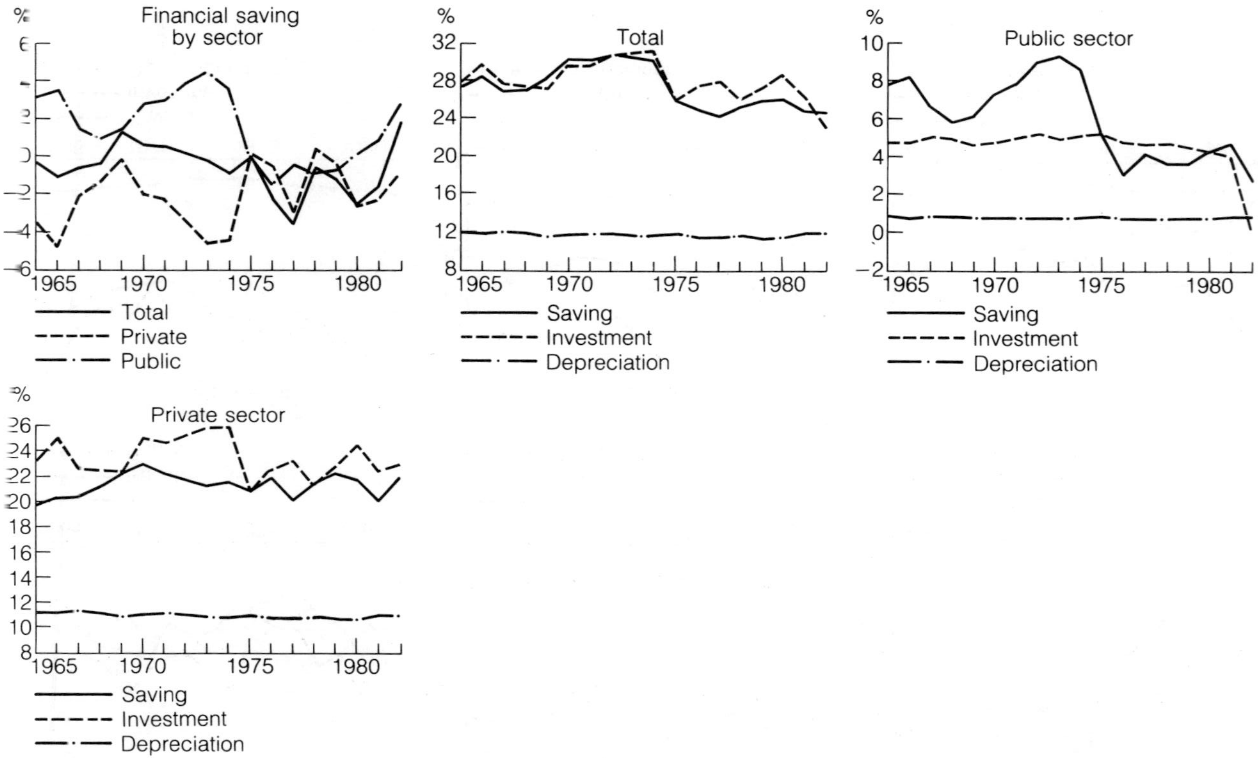

Figure 1.8 Austria

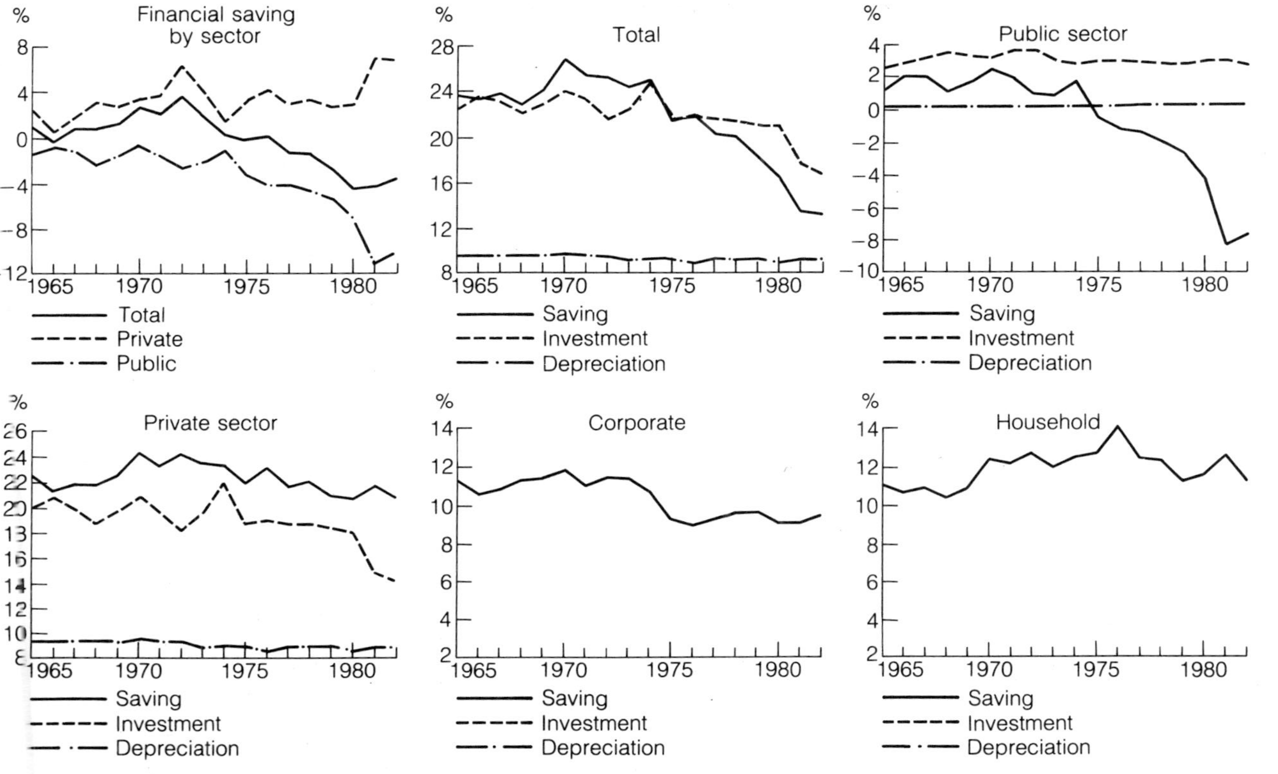

Figure 1.9 Belgium

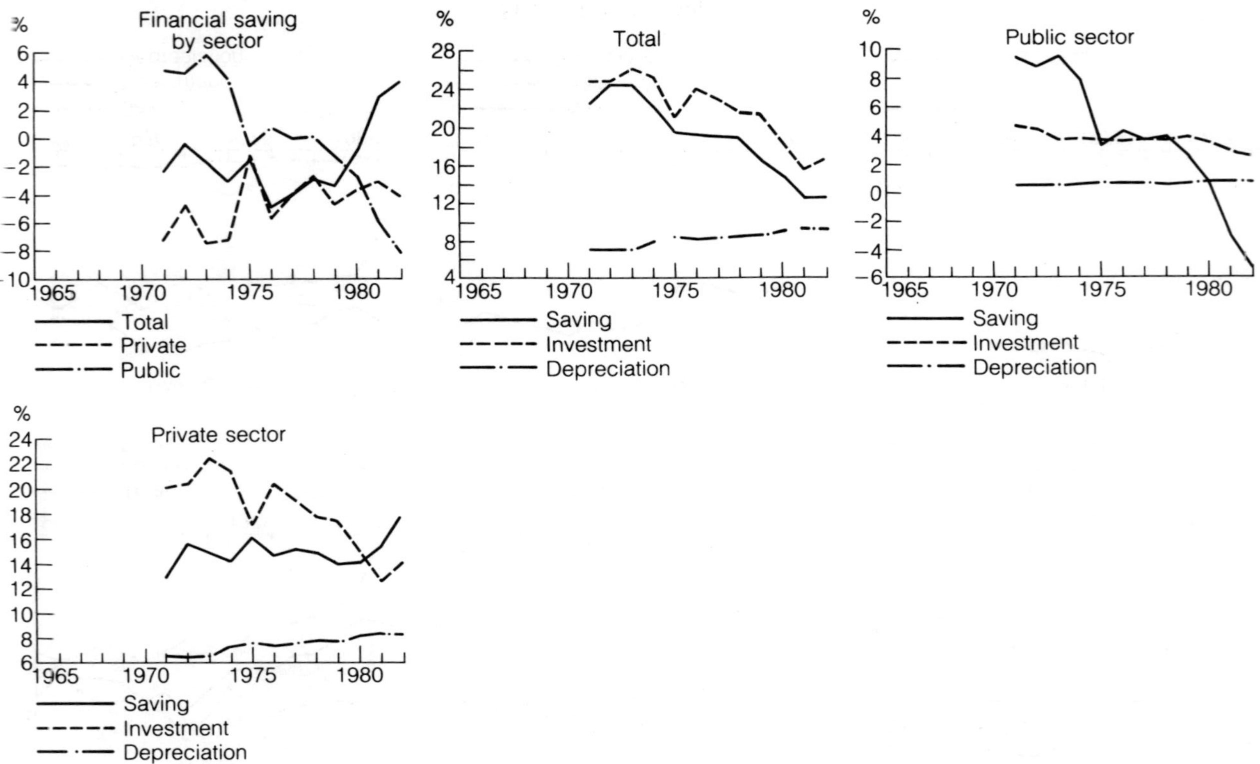

Figure 1.10 Denmark

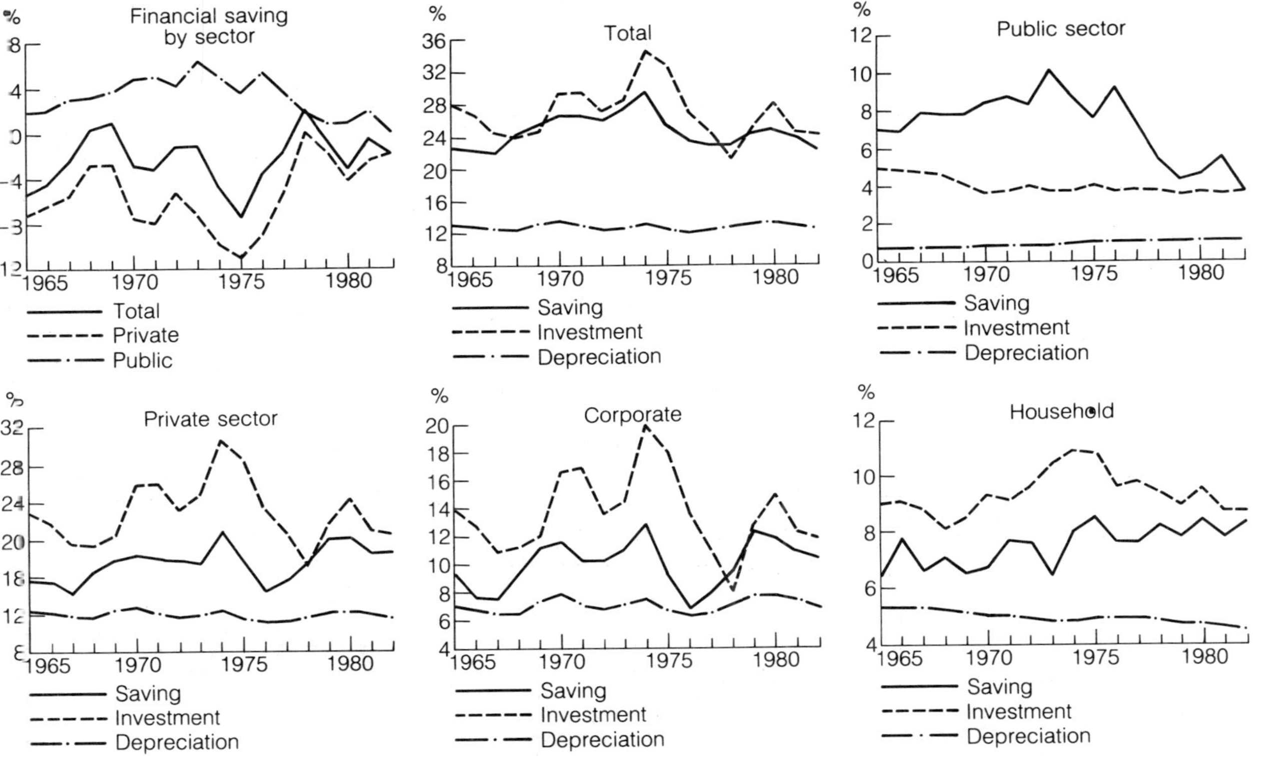

Figure 1.11 Finland

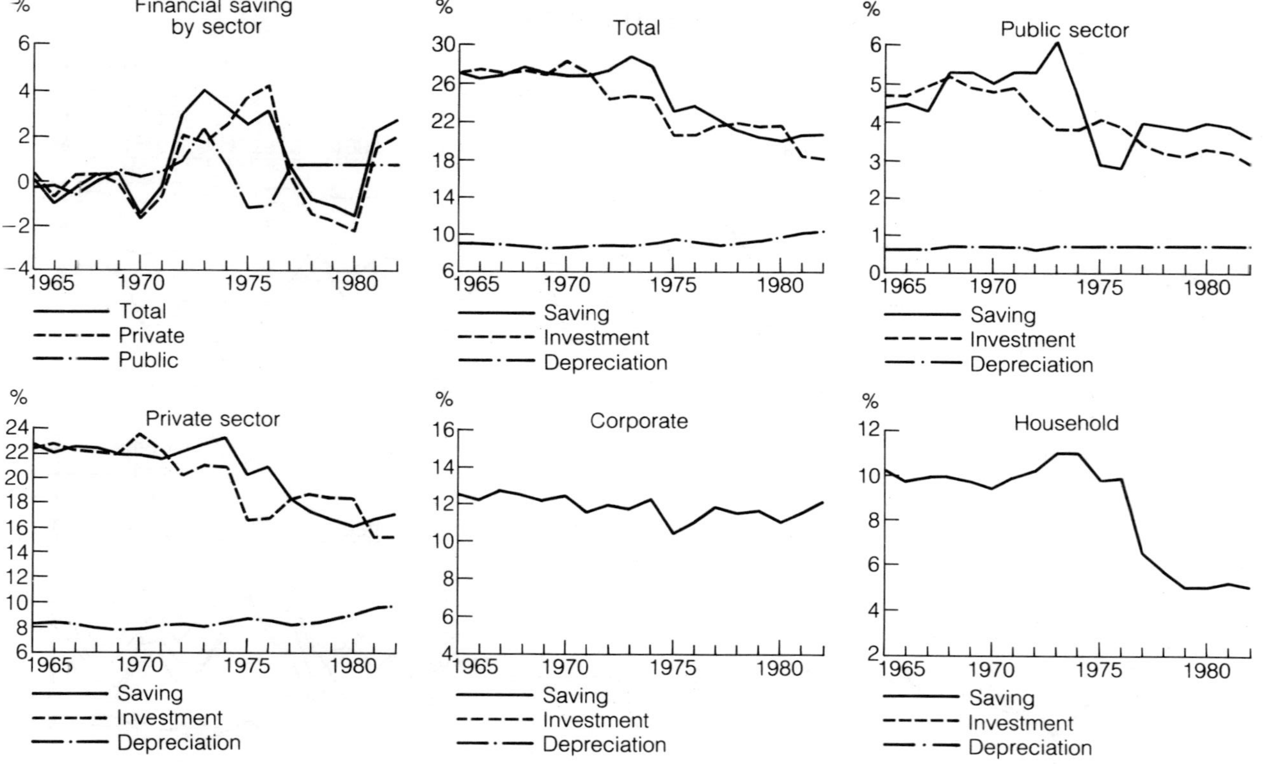

Figure 1.12 The Netherlands

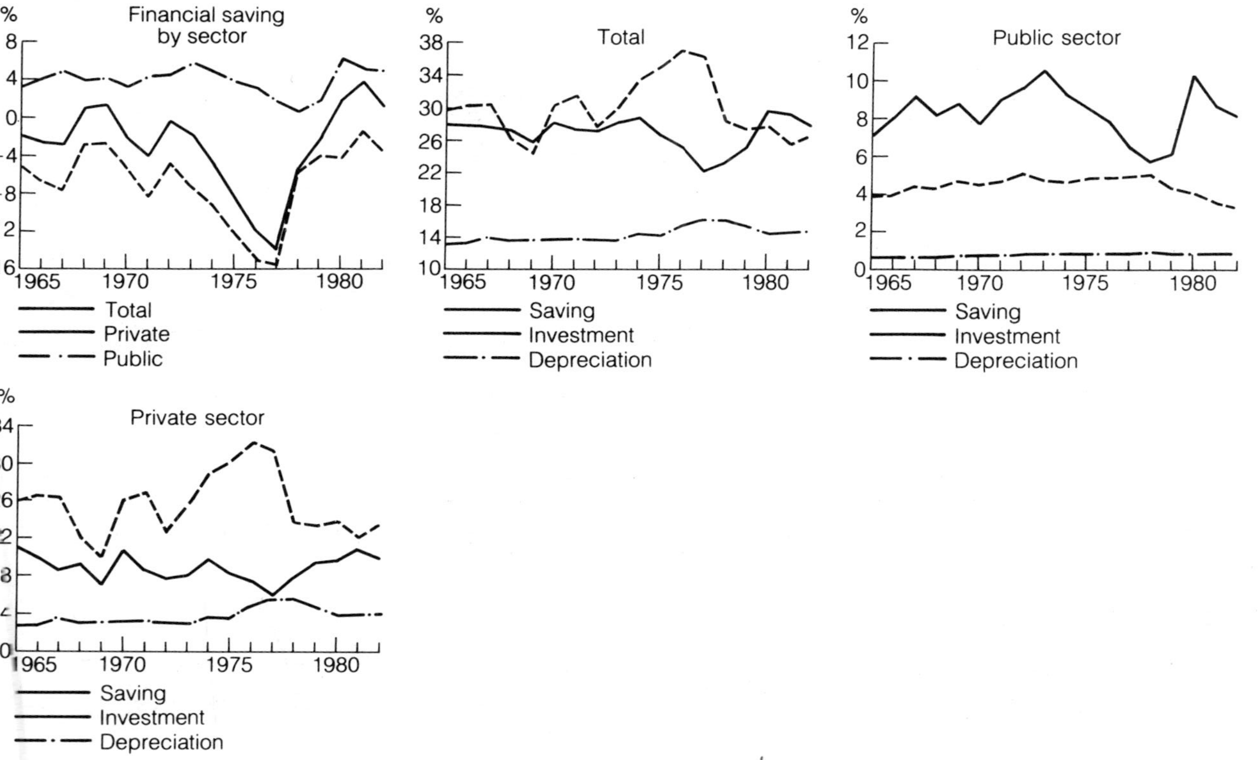

Figure 1.13 Norway

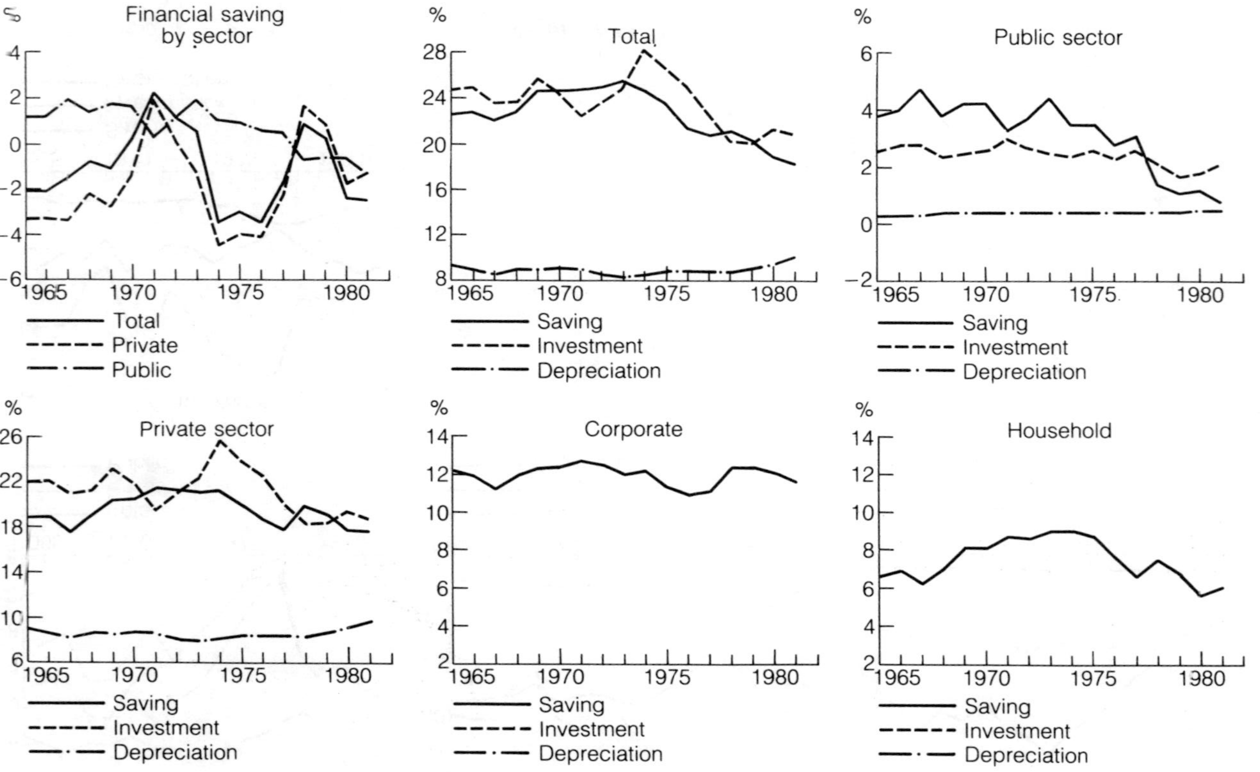

Figure 1.14 Spain

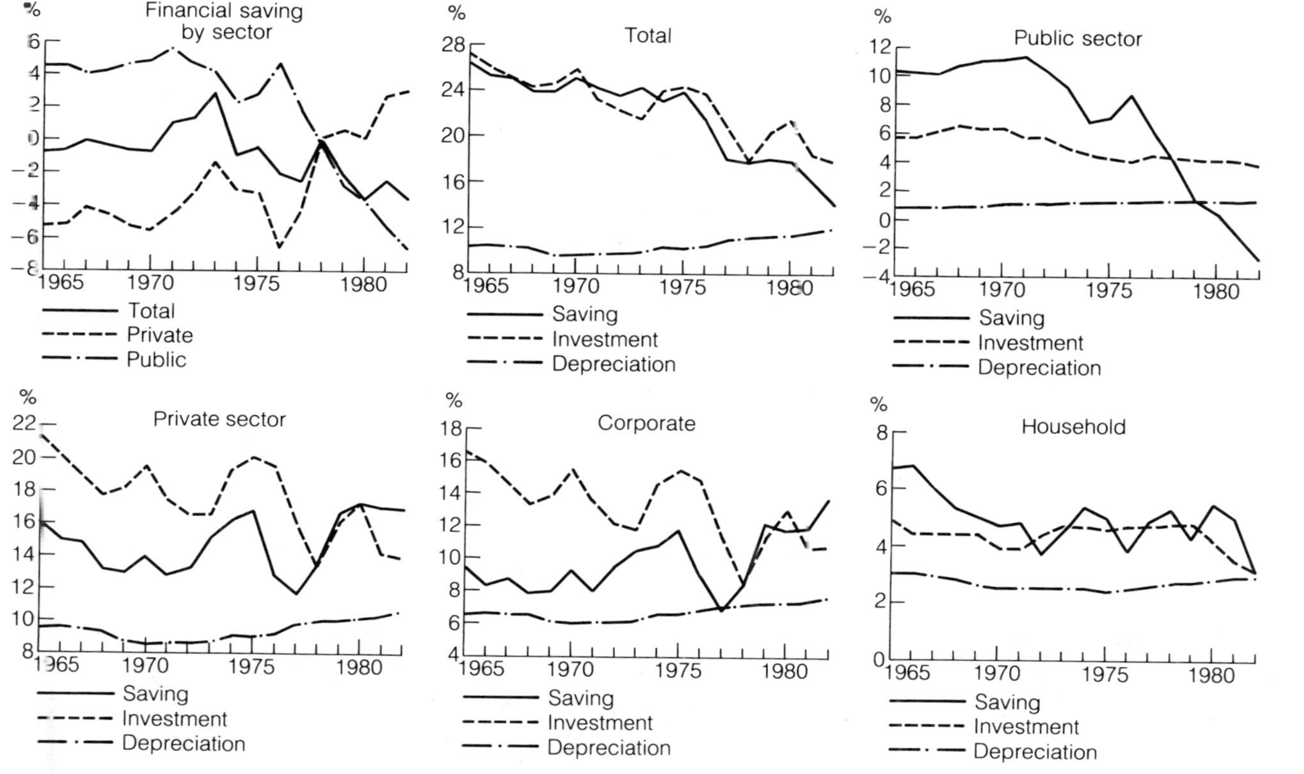

Figure 1.15 Sweden

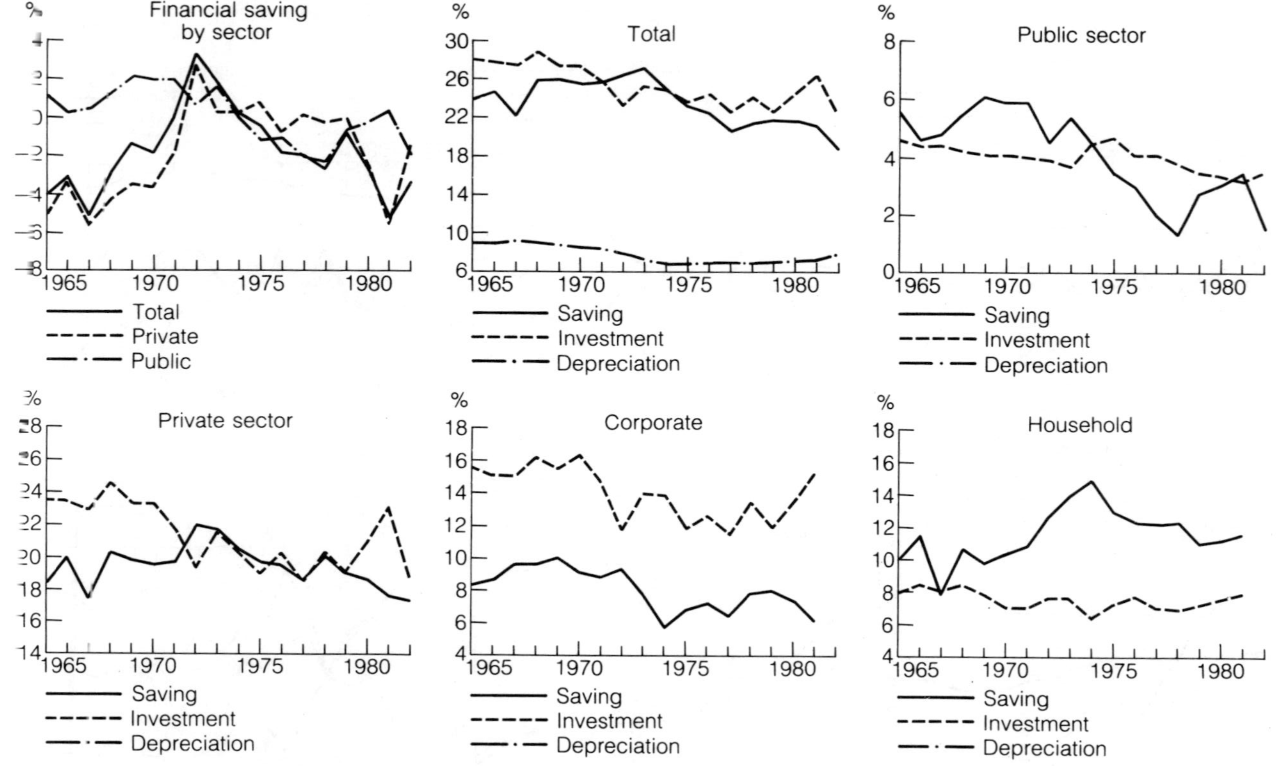

Figure 1.16 Australia

overview of those changes in saving and investment that occurred after the first oil price shock.

In table 1.2 countries have been ranked according to the magnitude of the deterioration of the public (gross) saving ratio after 1973. The beginning year varies from country to country depending on when the decline started. We can then see how the decline in public saving has been associated with changes in other saving and investment ratios, where of course the adding-up properties of national accounting identities must hold also for percentage point changes in the ratios.

In table 1.3 a similar ranking has been made on the basis of changes in *average* public savings ratios and associated changes in other average ratios between the average 1964–73 level and the average 1974–82 level. It should be noted that the adding-up properties of average ratios do not necessarily hold. Naturally enough the deterioration of public saving between the two period averages is not normally as dramatic as the deterioration from a single peak value to the end of period in 1981/82. Still, there is a clear deterioration in average government saving in the period after the first oil price shock.

Table 1.4 reports regression coefficients for simple regressions based on pooled time series and cross-section data using $(S^G - I^G)/Y$ and S^G/Y as explanatory variables and other saving and investment ratios as dependent variables. The regressions should of course not be regarded

Table 1.2 *Deterioration of the government saving ratio and associated changes in other saving and investment ratios*

Country	Period	$\Delta(S^G/Y)$	$\Delta(I^G/Y)$	$\Delta(I^P/Y)$	$\Delta(S^P/Y)$	$\Delta[(X-M)/Y]$
Denmark	73–82	−14.9	−1.1	−8.3	+3.0	−2.4
Sweden	76–82	−11.5	−0.3	−5.6	+4.1	−1.5
Belgium	74–82	−9.2	−0.1	−7.8	−2.6	−3.9
Canada	74–82	−7.3	−0.7	−6.4	−2.0	+1.8
Germany	73–82	−5.4	−0.8	−3.4	+0.4	−0.7
Austria	73–81	−4.6	−1.0	−3.5	−1.2	−1.4
USA	74–82	−4.2	−0.9	−2.1	+0.6	−0.6
Finland	75–82	−3.8	−0.3	−8.3	−1.0	+5.8
Australia	73–81	−3.8	−0.2	−4.7	−4.4	−3.3
France	74–82	−3.8	−0.5	−5.0	−2.3	−0.6
Spain	73–81	−3.6	−0.4	−3.6	−3.4	−3.1
Italy	74–82	−3.2	+1.0	−7.2	0.0	+3.0
Japan	74–82	−3.1	+0.7	−7.9	−2.3	+1.7
The Netherlands	73–82	−2.5	−0.9	−5.8	−5.6	−1.3
United Kingdom	74–82	−2.0	−3.7	−2.6	+2.2	+6.5
Norway	76–82	+0.2	−1.6	−8.8	+2.5	+13.1

Table 1.3 *Changes in average saving and investment ratios between 1964–73 and 1974–82*

Country	$\Delta(S^G/Y)$	$\Delta(I^G/Y)$	$\Delta(I^P/Y)$	$\Delta(S^P/Y)$	$\Delta[(X - M)/Y]$
Denmark	−7.2[a]	−0.8[a]	−2.4	−5.2	−1.5[a]
Sweden	−6.8	−1.6	−2.1	+0.9	−2.2
Italy	−4.9	+0.4	+0.4	+3.0	−2.7
United Kingdom	−4.5	−1.4	−0.5	+2.7	+0.1
Belgium	−4.5	−0.3	−1.8	−0.9	−3.4
Germany	−3.6	−0.7	−3.9	−1.4	−0.4
Canada	−3.1	−0.8	+1.2	+2.5	−1.0
Austria	−3.1	−0.2	−1.0	+0.1	−1.3
Japan	−3.0	+1.0	−4.3	−1.3	+0.9
Australia	−2.6	−0.3	−2.5	−0.9	−0.8
France	−2.5	−0.7	−1.6	−1.0	−1.6
USA	−2.0	−0.8	+0.1	+1.1	−0.3
Spain	−1.8	−0.5	−0.8	−0.9	−1.7
Finland	−1.7	−0.6	+0.7	+1.4	−0.3
The Netherlands	−1.2	−1.3	−4.6	−3.7	+0.7
Norway	−0.7	−0.1	+2.1	−0.3	−2.9

[a] 1971–73 to 1974–82.

Table 1.4 *Regression coefficients: pooled time series and cross-section data, 16 OECD countries 1965–82*

	$(X - M)/Y$	$(S^P - I^P)/Y$	I^P/Y	I^{PC}/Y	I^{PH}/Y	S^P/Y	S^{PC}/Y	S^{PH}/Y
$(S^G - I^G)$	0.34[a]	−0.66[a]	0.36[a]	0.48[a]	0.10[a]	−0.30[a]	−0.07	−0.16[b]
S^G/Y	0.24[a]	−0.74[a]	0.35[a]	0.32[a]	0.11[a]	−0.39[a]	−0.32[a]	−0.04

[a] Significant at 0.01 level.
[b] Significant at 0.05 level.

as attempts to estimate structural relations but rather as simple measures of the correlation between large aggregates. No parameter restrictions have been imposed on the regressions. Still, however, the adding-up properties do hold for the more important regression coefficients.[2] The pooled regression included dummy variables for all countries and years except USA and 1965. Estimated coefficients for these country and year dummies are presented – if significant – in table 1.5. Table 1.6 reports regression coefficients for identical regressions on time series data for each country separately.

Table 1.5 Significant dummy parameter estimates in pooled regressions

Explanatory variable		$(I^G - S^G)/Y$	
Dependent variable	$(X - M)/Y$	I^P/Y	S^P/Y
Dummy for			
Japan		11.38[a]	11.61[a]
Germany		2.96[a]	2.30[a]
France		3.58[a]	2.40[a]
United Kingdom		−1.99[a]	−2.29[a]
Italy	2.04[a]	3.53[a]	5.57[a]
Canada	−1.62[a]	2.68[a]	1.07[b]
Austria	−1.78[a]	5.78[a]	4.00[a]
Belgium		2.96[a]	3.39[a]
Denmark	−3.69[a]		2.74[a]
Finland	−3.91[a]	4.49	
The Netherlands		2.45[a]	2.61[a]
Norway	−4.86[a]	6.95[a]	2.09[a]
Spain	−1.88[a]	3.65[a]	1.77[a]
Sweden	−2.14[a]		−2.49[a]
Australia	−3.05[a]	4.69[a]	1.65[a]
1972	1.69[a]		
1973			1.26[b]
1974		1.66[b]	
1977			−1.12[b]
1978		−1.52[b]	
1981		−1.67[b]	
1982		−2.30[a]	

No dummy variables for USA and 1965.
[a] Significant at 0.01 level.
[b] Significant at 0.05 level.

V STYLIZED FACTS

Of course one must be extremely careful in interpreting relations between macroeconomic aggregates at this level where the underlying structural relationships remain obscure. Still, it seems that some interesting patterns emerge from the compilations and correlations. I shall venture a few observations in the form of stylized facts that can be extracted from the data:

1 (Tables 1.2 and 1.3) Public financial saving underwent a significant decline in nearly all net oil importing OECD countries in the period following the first oil price shock. Peak to trough

Table 1.6 *Regression coefficients: 16 OECD countries 1965–82*

Country	Explanatory variable	Dependent variable							
		$(X - M)/Y$	$(S^P - I^P)/Y$	I^P/Y	I^{PC}/Y	I^{PH}/Y	S^P/Y	S^{PC}/Y	S^{PH}/Y
USA	$(S^G - I^G)/Y$	−0.05	−1.05[a]	0.72[a]	0.49[a]	0.22[b]	−0.33[b]	0.03	−0.37[a]
	S^G/Y	0.0	−0.83[a]	0.51[a]	0.38[a]	0.13	−0.33[b]	0.0	−0.33[a]
Japan	$(S^G - I^G)/Y$	0.10	−0.90[a]	1.17[a]	1.31[a]	−0.14	0.27	1.15[a]	−0.88[a]
	S^G/Y	0.10	−1.15[a]	1.55[a]	1.70[a]	−0.14	0.40	1.41[a]	−1.01[a]
Germany	$(S^G - I^G)/Y$	0.16	−0.84[a]	1.07[a]	na	na	0.23	na	na
	S^G/Y	0.11	−0.74[a]	0.96[a]			0.22[b]		
France	$(S^G - I^G)/Y$	0.28	−0.72	1.05[a]	0.80[a]	0.25[a]	0.33	0.60[a]	−0.27
	S^G/Y	0.26	−0.50[b]	0.78[b]	0.55[a]	0.24[a]	0.29	0.52[a]	−0.24
United Kingdom	$(S^G - I^G)/Y$	0.31	−0.69[a]	0.02	0.03	0.0	−0.67[a]	0.19	−0.48[a]
	S^G/Y	0.30	−0.70[a]	0.04	0.06	−0.02	−0.66[a]	−0.25	−0.41[a]
Italy	$(S^G - I^G)/Y$	0.47[a]	−0.53[a]	0.04	0.34	0.11	−0.50[a]	0.10	−0.41[b]
	S^G/Y	0.50[a]	0.59[a]	0.03	0.35	0.13	−0.56[a]	0.11	−0.49[a]
Canada	$(S^G - I^G)/Y$	0.14	−0.86[a]	0.23	0.17	0.06	−0.63[a]	0.12	−0.75[a]
	S^G/Y	0.10	−0.71[a]	0.13	0.08	0.05	−0.57[a]	0.05	−0.63[a]

Austria	$(S^G - I^G)/Y$	0.37[b]	−0.63[a]	0.61[a]	na	na	−0.02	na	na
	S^G/Y	0.18	−0.55[a]	0.50[a]			−0.05		
Belgium	$(S^G - I^G)/Y$	0.63[a]	−0.37[a]	0.57[a]	na	na	0.20[a]	na	na
	S^G/Y	0.63[a]	−0.34[a]	0.54[a]			0.20[a]		
Denmark	$(S^G - I^G)/Y$	0.16	−0.84[a]	0.67[a]	na	na	−0.17[b]	na	na
	S^G/Y	0.15	−0.75[a]	0.59[a]			−0.16[b]		
Finland	$(S^G - I^G)/Y$	0.26	−1.26[a]	1.05[b]	0.83[b]	0.21[b]	−0.22	−0.06	−0.16
	S^G/Y	0.36	−1.32[a]	0.91	0.74	0.17	−0.41	−0.2	−0.21[b]
The Nether-lands	$(S^G - I^G)/Y$	0.42	−0.58	0.03	na	na	−0.55	na	na
	S^G/Y	0.07	−0.62	2.24[a]			−1.61[b]		
Norway	$(S^G - I^G)/Y$	1.80[b]	0.80	−0.49	na	na	0.31	na	na
	S^G/Y	1.34	0.32	−0.26			0.06		
Spain	$(S^G - I^G)/Y$	0.03	−0.97[b]	1.42[a]	na	na	0.45	na	na
	S^G/Y	0.08	−0.69	1.08[a]			0.38		
Sweden	$(S^G - I^G)/Y$	0.30[a]	−0.70[a]	0.41[a]	0.35[a]	0.06[b]	−0.29[a]	−0.36[a]	0.07
	S^G/Y	0.25[a]	−0.58[a]	0.33[a]	0.29[a]	0.04	−0.25[a]	−0.31[a]	0.07
Australia	$(S^G - I^G)/Y$	0.31	−0.69	0.97[a]	na	na	0.28	na	na
	S^G/Y	0.32	−0.57	0.86[a]			0.29		

[a] Significant at 0.01 level.
[b] Significant at 0.05 level.

changes ranged from 3 to 14 per cent of GDP, with Japan at the low end and Denmark, Sweden and Belgium at the high end. The increase in the *average* budget deficit for approximately a decade before and after the first oil price shock is less dramatic but still significant, being around 3 per cent of GDP for a typical OECD country.

2 (Tables 1.2 and 1.3) The increase in budget deficits was *not* the result of higher public investment as one might have expected assuming a divergence of views between the public and private sectors regarding the permanence of the oil price shock (Sachs, 1981). Rather, public investment typically declined, implying an even larger deterioration in gross public saving (public income minus public consumption) than in the budget deficits.

3 (Tables 1.3 and 1.4) The changes in other saving and investment ratios which have been associated with the decline in the public savings ratio have been as follows for a typical OECD country.[3] A decline in the public (gross) savings ratio by an average four percentage points of GNP has typically been accompanied by a reduction in the public (gross) investment ratio by around one percentage point. The decline in public sector financial saving ('the increase in the budget deficit') has therefore been limited to 3 per cent of GNP. Of these three percentage points no more than one has on average spilled over into the current account. This leaves two percentage points that have corresponded to an increase in private sector financial saving. This increase, in turn, has been fairly evenly divided between an increase in the private sector savings ratio and a decline in the private sector investment ratio.

4 (Table 1.5) All reported OECD countries except the UK, Sweden and Denmark had higher private investment ratios than the US as an average over the whole period. The higher investment ratios were normally matched by higher private savings ratios, implying that the current account did not reflect these differences for any given level of the budget deficit (cf. Feldstein and Horioka, 1980). Four countries, i.e. Austria, Finland, Norway and Australia, had structural deficits on current account in the sense that a relatively high private investment ratio was not fully reflected in a high private savings ratio. Two countries, notably Denmark and Sweden, had a structural deficit in the sense of an unusually low private savings ratio without a significantly lower investment ratio

than the US. Only Italy demonstrates a structural current account surplus.

It is interesting to note that no individual year demonstrates a significant current account deficit for the (unweighted) country group as a whole, once the association with budget deficits has been eliminated. The large deterioration of OECD current account deficits in connection with the first oil price shock can find a complete explanation in (a) an unusually *strong* current account in 1972; (b) an unusually high private investment ratio in 1974; (c) the considerable weakening of public saving between 1972 and 1974.

It is also interesting to note that in the early 1980s the private investment ratio has fallen more than could have been expected by reference to the continued weak financial position of the public sector.

5 (Table 1.6) On a country-by-country basis we do *not* find a significant association between the budget deficit and the current account, except in the cases of Italy, Belgium and Sweden. On the other hand, we *do*, for most countries, find a strongly significant association between budget deficits and private financial saving (the exceptions being the oil/gas exporting countries, The Netherlands and Norway plus Spain and Australia). Since the adding-up constraints hold in all cases we can also take the current account estimates seriously and make a comparison between countries as to the division of the budget deficit between the current account and private financial saving. We can also make a division of the change in private financial saving into change in private investment and change in private saving. These figures are reported, for those countries where significant coefficients have been obtained, in table 1.7.

With the USA and Japan at the top of the table and Sweden, Austria and Belgium at the bottom, one might expect it to be held as an empirical regularity that budget deficits are more closely associated with current account deficits in small economies than in large. However, Finland, Denmark and Italy are exceptions to this rule. It is notable also to what extent improvements in private financial saving have been associated with a decline in private investment: in countries like Spain, Japan, Germany, France, Finland and Australia, budget deficits have been matched more or less dollar for dollar by declines in private investment. On the other hand there are countries such as the UK, Italy and The Netherlands

Table 1.7 Changes in the current account and the private sector ratios associated with an increase in the budget deficit of 1 per cent of GNP 1965–82

Country	Change in			
		Private sector		
			Whereof:	
	Current account $(X - M)/Y$	Financial saving $(S^P - I^P)/Y$	Investment I^P/Y	Saving S^P/Y
Finland	0.26	1.26[a]	−1.05[b]	0.22
USA	0.05	1.05[a]	−0.72[a]	0.33[b]
Spain	−0.03	0.97[b]	−1.42[a]	−0.45
Japan	−0.10	0.90[a]	−1.17[a]	−0.27
Canada	−0.14	0.86[a]	−0.23	0.63[a]
Denmark	−0.16	0.84[a]	−0.67[a]	0.17[b]
Germany	−0.16	0.84[a]	−1.07[a]	−0.23
France	−0.28	0.72[a]	−1.05[a]	−0.33
Sweden	−0.30[a]	0.70[a]	−0.41[a]	0.29[a]
Australia	−0.31	0.69	−0.97[a]	−0.28
United Kingdom	−0.31	0.69[a]	−0.02	0.67[a]
Austria	−0.37[b]	0.63[a]	−0.61[a]	0.02
The Netherlands	−0.42	0.58	−0.03	0.55
Italy	−0.47[a]	0.53[a]	−0.04	0.50[a]
Belgium	−0.63[a]	0.37[a]	−0.57[a]	−0.20[b]
Norway	−1.80[b]	−0.80	0.49	−0.31
'Typical OECD country' (pooled regression)	−0.34[a]	0.66[a]	−0.36[a]	0.30

[a] Significant at 0.01 level.
[b] Significant at 0.05 level.

where we can discern no association between budget deficits and private investment. Of course, two of the latter countries became net oil/gas exporters during the 1970s.

6 (Table 1.6) As far as private savings ratios are concerned it is most natural to look at their relation to public savings ratios rather than public deficits. The regression coefficients are reported in table 1.8.

In the UK, Canada, Italy, USA and Sweden the decline in public saving ratios has been significantly offset by increases

Table 1.8 *Changes in private savings ratios associated with a decline in the* public savings *ratio by 1 per cent of GNP 1965–82*

	Change in		
		Whereof:	
Country	Private savings ratio (S^P/Y)	Corporate	Household
The Netherlands	1.61[b]	na	na
United Kingdom	0.66[a]	0.25	0.41[a]
Canada	0.57[a]	−0.05	0.63[a]
Italy	0.56[a]	−0.11	0.49[a]
Finland	0.41	0.20	0.21[b]
USA	0.33[a]	0.00	0.33[a]
Sweden	0.25[a]	0.31[a]	−0.07
Denmark	0.16[b]	na	na
Austria	0.05	na	na
Norway	−0.06	na	na
Belgium	−0.20	na	na
Germany	−0.22[b]	na	na
France	−0.29	−0.52[a]	0.24
Australia	−0.29	na	na
Spain	−0.38	na	na
Japan	−0.40	−1.41[a]	1.01[a]
'Typical OECD country' (pooled regression)	0.39[a]	0.32[a]	0.04

[a] Significant at 0.01 level.
[b] Significant at 0.05 level

in private sector saving to an extent varying between one-fourth (Sweden) and two-thirds (UK) of the decline. For most countries, however, we do not find a statistically significant association between public and private saving ratios. In many of these countries the association must come out negative when account is taken of the significant relation between the public savings ratio on the one hand and the private financial saving and investment ratios on the other. In these cases the relation between the public and private savings ratios is not statistically significant, however.[4]

A disaggregation of private saving into the corporate and household sectors reveals some interesting observations. In all countries but one with a significant negative relation between public and private saving, it is the household sector which brings about the offsetting changes in private saving. This is true for Canada, Italy, the UK and the USA in declining order of the strength of the offsetting tendency. The exception is Sweden, where the corporate sector (with the help of a sequence of devaluations) has increased its savings ratio in conjunction with declining public saving (for further details, see Söderström, 1984).

The only case where some kind of Ricardian equivalence seems to be at hand is Japan, where declining public saving has been offset one-to-one by higher household saving. This presupposes, however, that households pierce the public but not the corporate veil: the decline in corporate saving has been even stronger than the decline in public saving.

In general, we should avoid interpreting these simple correlations in terms of structural relations. For some countries (like e.g. Italy and the UK) the negative association between public and household saving probably goes via inflation and real balance effects rather than via Ricardian equivalence. In other cases causality may run from private to public sector as underlined throughout this chapter. The purpose of this data compilation, the graphs and tables, is to help us to ask relevant questions on public deficits and private savings, not to answer them.

NOTES

1 This presupposes that the nominal rate of return on the public capital stock is equal to the rate of interest in government bonds.

2 The adding-up properties do not hold, however, for the subdivision of private saving and investment ratios into corporate and household sectors.

3 Regressions have been run on ratios without GDP weights. The results therefore refer to 'a typical OECD country' rather than the average for the OECD area.

4 The exception is Germany, where a negative relation is statistically significant at the 5 per cent level.

REFERENCES

Barro, R.J. 1974: Are government bonds net wealth?, *Journal of Political Economy*, 82, 1095–1117.

Barro, R.J. 1984: *Macroeconomics*, Wiley, New York.

Brainard, W.C.and Tobin, J. 1968: Pitfalls in financial model building, *American Economic Review*, LVIII, May, 99–149.

Buiter, W.H. and Tobin, J. 1979: Debt neutrality: A brief review of doctrine and evidence. In G.M. von Furstenberg (ed.), *Social Security versus Private Saving*, Ballinger, Cambridge, Mass.
Feldstein, M. and Horioka, C. 1980: Domestic saving and international capital flows, *Economic Journal*, 90, June, 314–29.
Friedman, B. 1985: Crowding out or crowding in? Evidence on debt–equity substitutability, *NBER Working Paper*, No. 1565, February.
Gordon, R.J. 1981: Output fluctuations and gradual price adjustment, *Journal of Economic Literature*, XIX, June, 493–530.
Koskela, E. and Virén, M. 1983: National debt neutrality: Some international evidence, *Kyklos*, 36(4), 575–88.
McCallum, B.T. 1985: Monetary vs fiscal policy effects: A review of the debate, *NBER Working Paper*, No. 1556, February.
OECD, 1983: Public sector deficits: Problems and policy implications, *Occasional Studies*, June.
Sachs, J, 1981: The current account and macroeconomic adjustment in the 1970s, *Brookings Papers on Economic Activity*, 1.
Söderström, H.T. 1984: Imbalances in the Swedish economy from a financial perspective, *Skandinaviska Enskilda Banken*, Quarterly Review, No. 2.

2

Rising Public-sector Indebtedness: Some More Unpleasant Arithmetic

J.A. BISPHAM

I INTRODUCTION AND OVERVIEW

This chapter is concerned with a paradox and a dilemma. The paradox is compounded of two parts. There is, firstly, the fact that many countries, especially in Europe, have in recent years undoubtedly been pursuing policies of fiscal retrenchment. At the same time, however, the ratio of the outstanding stock of public sector debt to national income has been rising virtually universally and for some time. Previously – and even during periods of more active manipulation of fiscal policy – this ratio had been relatively stable or even, in some cases, following a trend decline.

This situation is clearly not likely to be sustainable indefinitely, if for no other reason than that increases in debt servicing costs can only increase further the tensions already inherent in the present fiscal situation.[1] The dilemma arises, however, over what measures to take to halt the seemingly relentless rise of public debt. The obvious attack would be on the budget itself – taking further the expenditure retrenchment measures already enacted. But would not this have adverse effects on the economy in terms of a reduction in aggregate demand, even if it strengthened further the attempt to revitalize supply? This would seem to be the core of the dilemma, a dilemma which seems to be the more severe in Europe. For there, despite some favourable signs – most notably a long-running decline in inflation even in the face of

T.R.G. Bingham and E.P. Davis of the BIS Monetary and Economic Department made extensive and helpful comments on an earlier draft of this paper, as did G. Midgley, P.D. Mortimer-Lee and C.T. Taylor of the Bank of England. I would also like to acknowledge the contribution of J.S. Flemming in his editorial capacity. H.J. Bernard of the BIS provided helpful assistance with the computations.

dollar strength – the recovery in output growth has (at the time of writing) not been sufficient generally to turn the unemployment trend downwards. What is more, few, if any, forecasters expect any material change in this situation, at least over the relatively short term.

This makes the European policy dilemma the more acute. It is one thing to risk some withdrawal of demand in a reasonably fully employed economy; it is quite another matter to take that risk when unemployment is at record levels, even when there are such obviously pressing reasons for action as in the present case.

Against this background, this chapter sets out firstly to review the analytics of the determination of debt/income ratios, and then to apply the results to recent data on general government budget deficits, interest rates, public debt ratios and the growth of national income. It has become a commonplace that one important analytical distinction concerns the relationship between the rate of interest and the economy's growth rate. With the effective interest rate on government debt greater than, or equal to, the growth rate, the public debt situation tends to become explosive.

The chapter records that, in recent years, potentially explosive debt situations seem to have been widespread. Less well known, however, is its demonstration that even at more 'reasonable' rates of growth and interest, the underlying fiscal situation seems to be tending towards equilibrium debt/income ratios which, although they may be finite, are also likely to be considered too high.

Finally, the chapter turns to an examination of the policy dilemma thrown up by this situation. This examination is facilitated by some purely mechanical, but hopefully not too unrealistic, simulation calculations of policy options. It strongly suggests that, if real interest rates could be reduced somewhat from their recent exceptionally high levels, then a resumption of rather faster trend growth – especially if accompanied by some reduction in unemployment – could go a long way towards resolving the fiscal problem in many countries. The problem, particularly in Europe, would seem to be how such an improvement in 'real' economic performance could be brought about in a sustainable way, especially against the background of a slow-down of growth in the United States. As already noted, further fiscal tightening, while addressing the public debt problem directly, might nevertheless prejudice the attainment of better 'real-side' outcomes from the demand side. Fiscal relations would, on the other hand, involve running obvious risks with public debt ratios. Calling in aid monetary policy, the question might become that of whether a sufficiently tight fiscal/low interest rate policy mix could be devised such that the fiscal problem could be addressed directly, but in the context of better 'real-side' developments.

II DEBT RATIO DYNAMICS: RELATIONSHIPS BETWEEN DEBT, BUDGET DEFICITS, GROWTH AND INTEREST RATES

The mathematical (as opposed to the economic) interaction of the debt stock, budget deficits, GNP changes and interest rates is set out formally in the appendix. Here it might be helpful for the discussion which follows to draw out some of the more important implications of that analysis in a more accessible form.

One of the most crucial distinctions to result from the analysis is that between situations in which the rate of interest on government debt is less than the growth rate of nominal GNP, and those in which it is greater than or equal to the nominal growth rate. (It is important to note here that 'the interest rate' is from now on to be taken as the *net of tax rate*. That is, it is the rate net of any tax paid by bond holders on interest income received. Clearly, for calculations of net budgetary effects, this is the appropriate concept to use, though it may well differ from the 'net of tax' concept as normally employed when analysing the behaviour of borrowers and investors in fixed capital, i.e. *payers* of interest.) Provided the same price index is used to deflate nominal GNP as that used to calculate the real interest rate (as just defined), the distinction may be made in exactly the same way between situations in which the *real* rate of interest is less than the economy's *real* growth rate, and those in which it is not. It will be convenient to begin by analysing cases in which interest rates are below growth rates, nominal and/or real.

The Notion of an Upper Limit to the Debt Ratio in Non-explosive Cases

Probably the most important result to emerge from the analysis under this heading is the fact that an increase in the budget deficit does not imply an ever-expanding ratio of outstanding debt to GNP, even when the deficit is entirely debt-financed.

Taking first the simple case where no interest is paid on debt, any given budget deficit ratio, q,[2] will be associated with an upper limit of the debt ratio, D_{MAX}, a limit which varies with the rate of growth of nominal GNP. This limit is given by the formula

$$D_{MAX} = \frac{q(1 + y)}{y}$$

where y is the rate of growth of nominal GNP and all quantities are measured as simple proportions (e.g. a growth rate of 5 per cent per annum is represented by 0.05).

The dotted line in figure 2.1(a) illustrates the case where, starting from a zero stock of debt outstanding, the budget deficit is 2 per cent of GNP and nominal GNP grows at 8.15 per cent per annum (equivalent to 3 per cent real growth with 5 per cent inflation). The figure shows the time profile of the ratio of debt to GNP as it asymptotically approaches 0.265 ($26\frac{1}{2}$ per cent).

Where interest is paid on the debt and the resulting expenditures are not offset by changes in the noninterest budget deficit (the *primary* deficit) the asymptotic debt ratio is

$$D_{\mathrm{MAX}} = \frac{q(1 + y)}{y - r}$$

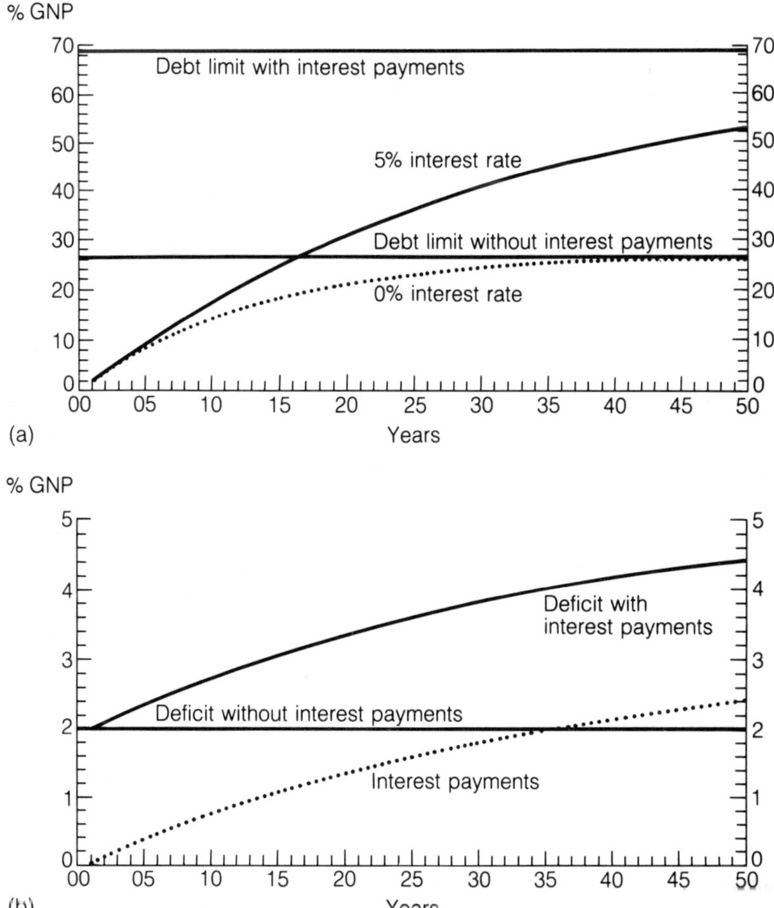

Figure 2.1 Debt ratio ceilings and budget deficits (a) with and without interest payments (b) budget deficits as proportion of GNP

where r is the rate of interest, again expressed in ratio, rather than percentage, form, and q is the primary deficit ratio.

Clearly, for any positive interest rate (less than y) the debt ratio limit will now be higher. In the example shown in figure 2.1(a), nominal growth is again 8.15 per cent per annum, the primary budget deficit is 2 per cent of GNP and the interest rate is set at 5 per cent. At 0.687, the long-run asymptotic debt ratio is now much higher. It also takes much longer for the actual debt ratio to approach this level.

In addition, with the total deficit itself now affected as the debt rises (at constant interest rates), the budget deficit no longer remains a constant proportion of GNP (see figure 2.1(b)). Clearly, the deficit itself is also heading for some new equilibrium level, where it will equal the sum of the constant primary deficit plus a 5 per cent effective interest charge on the equilibrium stock of debt. Expressed as a ratio to GNP, the total deficit will thus approach a maximum of $0.687 \times 0.05 + 0.02 = 0.0543$, or 5.43 per cent of GNP.

Two points thus stand out so far from this highly simplified form of analysis. Firstly – so long as interest rates remain below the growth rate of national income – an increase in the primary budget deficit does not result in an explosion of the ratio of public debt to GNP. It does, however, move the long-run equilibrium ratio to a higher level. (In the real world, of course, a rise in interest rates might also occur.) Secondly, and at least for the case where interest rates remain constant, the debt ratio can take some considerable time to reach its new, and higher, level. As figure 2.1 shows, even after fifty years, in the non-zero interest case, the debt ratio is still well short of its long-run equilibrium. The practical import of this is that one may in practice observe rising debt ratios for some time without the situation necessarily having become explosive.

Of course, as figure 2.2 shows, any rise in interest rates relative to nominal GNP growth raises the debt ratio ceiling, and it does so increasingly sharply as the interest rate approaches the nominal income growth rate – the latter taken to be 8 per cent per annum in this case. The three lines shown on the diagram are for the cases where the primary deficit, q, is 1, 3 and 5 per cent of GNP respectively.

Potentially Explosive Cases: The Speed of Explosion

Once the rate of interest is equal to, or greater than, the economy's nominal growth rate, the debt situation is potentially unstable (except for unlikely cases – for example where no previously accumulated debt exists and where the primary deficit is always exactly zero). Then the only question is what conditions determine the speed at which the

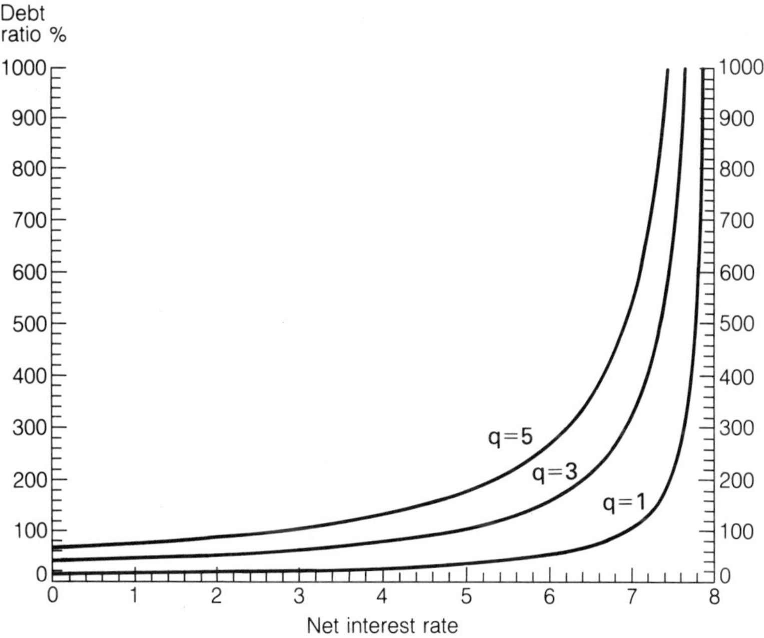

Figure 2.2 Long-term equilibrium debt ratios, the rate of interest and the net budget deficit (q is the budget deficit, net of interest payments (per cent of GNP))

situation deteriorates. Or, to look at it from the opposite angle, what factors determine the room for manoeuvre once the situation has become fundamentally unstable?

Figure 2.3 shows first the progress of the debt ratio under the assumption of a primary deficit of 2 per cent of GNP, a nominal growth rate of just over 8 per cent and an interest rate of 12 per cent (figure 2.3(a)). Clearly, as time passes, the line steepens. This demonstrates that the situation worsens faster the higher the level of debt. (It is true that the proportional rate of increase of the debt ratio slows down progressively. However, it is more likely to be the absolute rate of increase which will be relevant for policy makers in real situations.)

Figure 2.3 then shows two variants of this basically unstable state of affairs. Firstly, the effects of a lower (in this case, zero) and of a higher primary deficit are examined (figure 2.3(b)). Not surprisingly, the rate of explosion (for given interest and nominal growth rates) increases with the primary deficit.

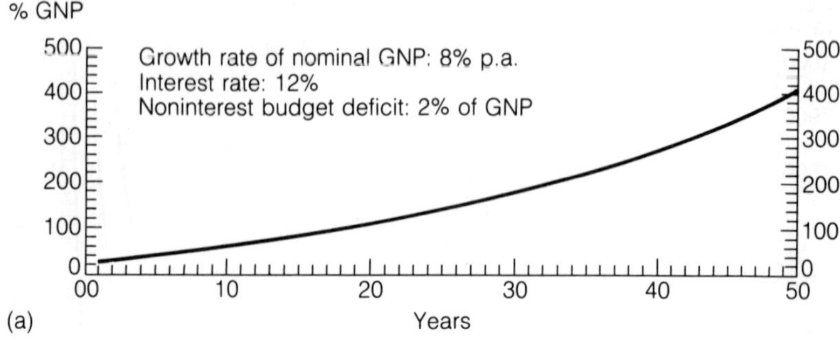

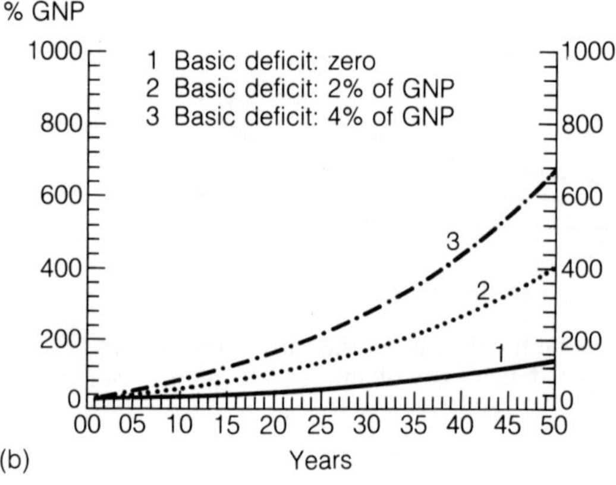

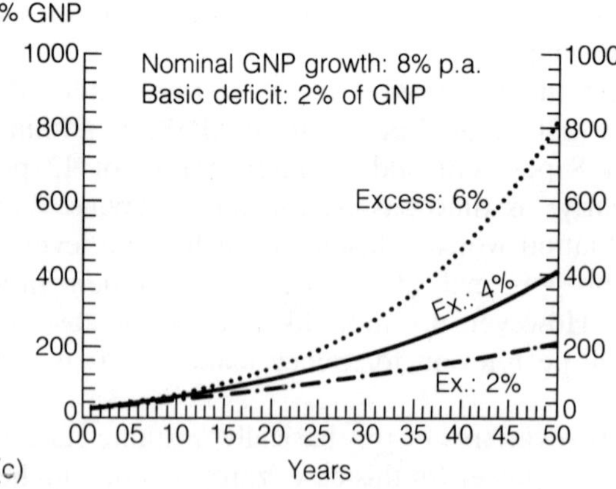

Figure 2.3 Speeds of debt explosion against (a) debt level (b) noninterest deficit (c) interest rate excess (defined as excess of interest rates over nominal GNP growth)

Similarly, as the excess of interest rates over nominal income growth varies from 2, through 4, to 6 percentage points, the rate of debt explosion accelerates. As figure 2.3(b)) shows, however, the three lines diverge relatively slowly at low levels of debt. But as debt accumulates, excess interest differences come to play a larger and larger role in the speed of debt accumulation. The effects of the size of the existing debt stock and of excess interest rates are thus interconnected.

Real Interest Rates and the Composition of Nominal GNP Growth

Instead of measuring 'excess' interest rates against total nominal income growth, it is perhaps more relevant to measure them against inflation only – thus giving an indication of 'real' interest rates as commonly understood. When this is done, and when some standard is then set for real interest rates so measured, the 'split' of nominal GNP growth between its 'real' and inflationary components is found to have important implications for the behaviour of the debt ratio. This is because the excess interest rate, as used so far (i.e. measured with reference to overall nominal GNP growth) will now vary with the GNP split, even if overall nominal growth remains unchanged. Indeed, as illustrated in figure 2.4, it is possible to construct an entirely feasible example in which the GNP split is the deciding factor between an equilibrium debt ratio case and an explosive one.

For both cases, nominal GNP growth is set at 5 per cent per annum and the primary budget deficit at 2 per cent of GNP. But, instead of the nominal interest rate being fixed, say, at 7 per cent, the nominal interest rate is set two percentage points above the rate of inflation. Hence, in case 1, where real growth is 5 per cent and inflation is zero, the nominal interest rate is only 2 per cent. The situation is thus basically stable and the debt ratio rises gradually towards its equilibrium level. In the second case, however, inflation is assumed to account for the whole of nominal income growth. Thus the nominal interest rate, at 7 per cent, exceeds the nominal growth rate and the situation is unsustainable in the medium to longer run.

The Possibility of Knife-edge Cases

While cases where interest rates exceed nominal growth are virtually certain to be explosive, the direction of explosion can in theory, of course, be in either direction. In particular, it would be entirely feasible for the primary budget deficit to be negative – i.e. for there to be a primary surplus. Less realistically, though still theoretically possible,

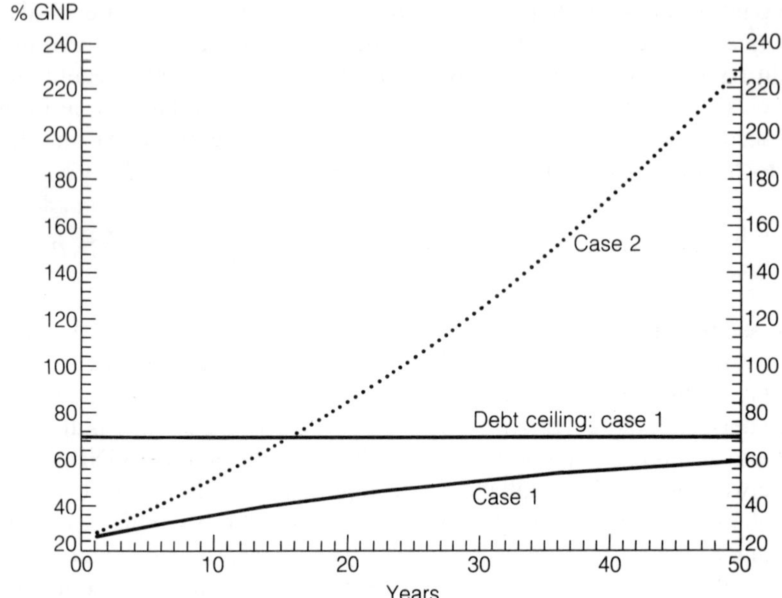

Figure 2.4 The composition of nominal GNP growth and the debt ratio (case 1: 5 per cent real growth, zero inflation; case 2: zero per cent real growth, 5 per cent inflation, in both cases, real interest rate of 2 per cent)

the initial situation may be one in which the public debt is negative – i.e. the government is a net holder of financial assets. In both these cases, there is the possibility of explosion towards infinite net worth, rather than to infinite indebtedness.

The conditions for this are examined rigorously in the appendix. The purpose of mentioning the point here is that, combined with the relative slowness of the initial pick-up in debt ratios, a situation of 'excess' interest rates may be sustainable for longer than otherwise if the primary deficit stays close to the knife-edge point. More realistically, the primary deficit may vary from year to year around the knife-edge, first exceeding it and then falling short of it. In this way, the *actual* debt situation may stay more balanced than the underlying factors might at first sight suggest.

Debt and the Process of Disinflation

The simple analytical apparatus set out above may also be used to investigate qualitatively the debt implications of a process of disinflation, and, in particular, the implications of the form of disinflationary policies applied. It should be stressed, however, that the examples given are purely arithmetic. Although the selection of assumptions for growth rates, inflation rates, etc. seems reasonable in the light of experience, they are basically *ad hoc* assumptions not based on detailed behavioural analysis.

Figure 2.5 attempts to portray the kind of experience many countries have been going through in recent years. The initial situation is one of relatively high inflation, budget deficit and debt ratio, a situation which begins to deteriorate as inflation is assumed to accelerate from 10 to 15 per cent per annum. An important part of the policy response is assumed to be on the monetary side with real interest rates moving from initially negative rates and reaching a peak of plus 7½ per cent before declining somewhat, but still remaining positive. On the fiscal side there is initially relatively little response. Indeed, with the economy falling into recession as the growth rate falls from 4 per cent per annum to a low point of minus 1 per cent, the automatic stabilizers are assumed to come into effect. Hence, initially, the actual budget deficit increases quite alarmingly and the debt ratio, which had been slowly declining, turns upward from a low point of about 30 per cent to 70 per cent of GNP.

However, for one reason or another, inflation is assumed to respond to the monetary treatment, and as it is reduced so the economy recovers. As it does so, the budget deficit problem is dealt with – partly by virtue of the automatic stabilizers – and the primary deficit is assumed to fall to only ½ per cent of GNP. With real interest rates remaining positive, however, the overall deficit, now including interest on a higher level of debt, is still running at about 3 per cent of GNP compared with the 4 per cent from which the process was assumed to begin. Nevertheless, so long as the real growth rate of the economy can be held at its assumed new equilibrium rate of 3 per cent, both the total deficit ratio and the debt ratio will tend to decline, though very slowly. Indeed, the new equilibrium debt ratio towards which the economy will then be tending will be virtually identical with the 50 per cent with which the example started.

In sum, however, a fairly successful process of disinflation, conducted along the lines assumed here, still leaves the economy with a considerably enlarged (though not explosive) debt for a very long period. With real interest rates requiring adjustment too – towards being positive – the implication is that the primary budget has been put under greater pressure, some of the increase being permanent. Looked at more positively, the example suggests that, while at the height of the disinflationary process the fiscal situation may appear frightening, if not hopeless, it need not necessarily be so in the longer run.

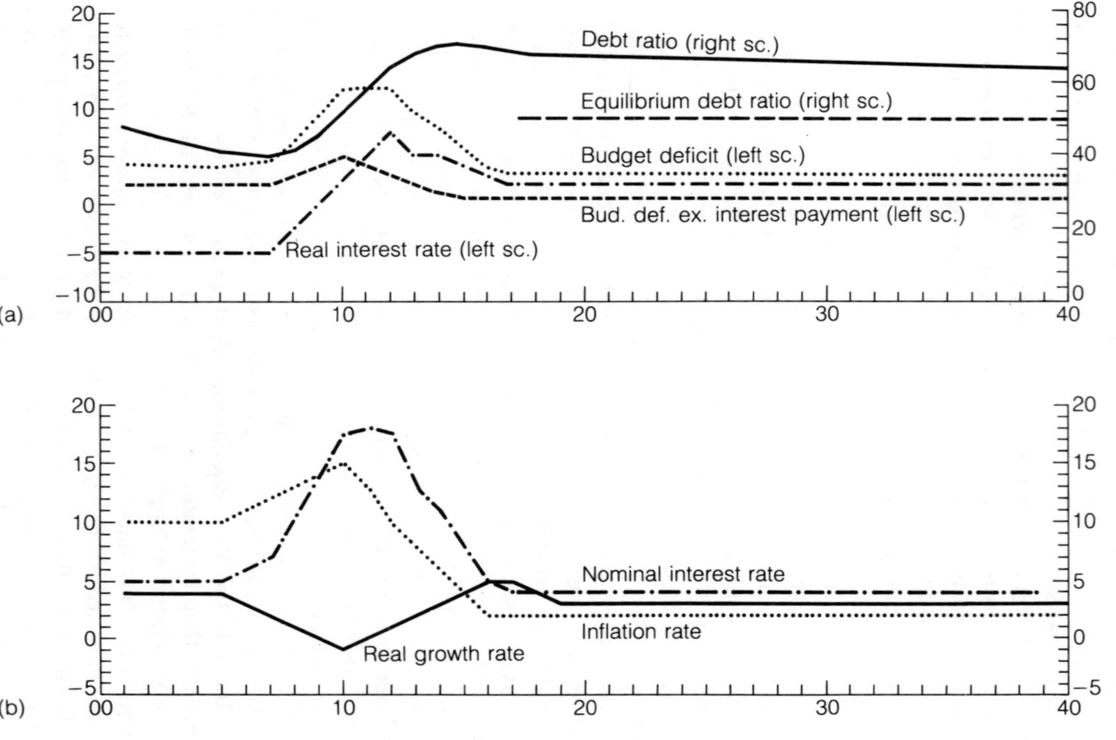

Figure 2.5 Disinflation: primary reliance on monetary policy (a) the debt/budget situation (b) the economy

There is also the question of what might have happened had the mix of disinflationary policies been different, that is, if more weight had been borne by fiscal tightening. Figure 2.6 shows an inherently more speculative version of 'events', assuming that the growth and inflation – and thus nominal GNP – outcomes would have been exactly the same as in the first example. The difference is that real interest rates are now assumed to remain negative, and constant, throughout the period of disinflation, and only to become positive in the recovery phase. At the same time, the primary budget deficit is also assumed to remain unaltered through the recession. Implicitly, the automatic stabilizers are being overridden as the main 'nonaccommodating' response to the price shock.

Again, however, the successful reduction of inflation is assumed to bring a sufficiently robust recovery to permit both a rise in real interest rates and the *same ultimate degree of primary budget retrenchment* as in the first example. The – *purely arithmetic* – result is that the debt ratio never rises significantly through the disinflationary process, while the total budget deficit, which did rise slightly during the pre-recession period, is soon reduced to about 2 per cent of GNP.

Hence, the suggestion of these exercises is that disinflation may or may not be accompanied by an apparent public debt problem, depending on the way in which it is carried out. Even in the former case, however, it need not necessarily lead to a wholly unsustainable fiscal situation. In both cases, however, it is crucial that the disinflationary process be successful, not only in terms of reducing inflation, but also in terms of its leading to a sustainable recovery. These, however, can only be suggestions: it cannot be over-stressed that the calculations are purely arithmetic exercises. Their value rests almost entirely on the plausibility of the assumptions underlying them.

It is also worth noting, finally and parenthetically, that one of the assumptions underlying this analysis was that nominal GNP growth, rather than money supply growth, was held constant between the two cases considered. In fact, it is likely that, in order to achieve the difference in interest rates (some 10 percentage points at the peak) assumed between the two simulations, higher monetary growth would have been required in the case where more of the disinflationary pressure came from the fiscal side.[3] Put another way, unless crowding out/crowding in were complete (something normally considered unlikely, at least in the relatively short run), reduction of the budget deficit would need to be accompanied by rather faster monetary growth if the growth of nominal (and, implicitly, real) GNP was to be maintained. The above results should therefore not be read as implying that, *given the monetary growth rates actually set and/or achieved* during

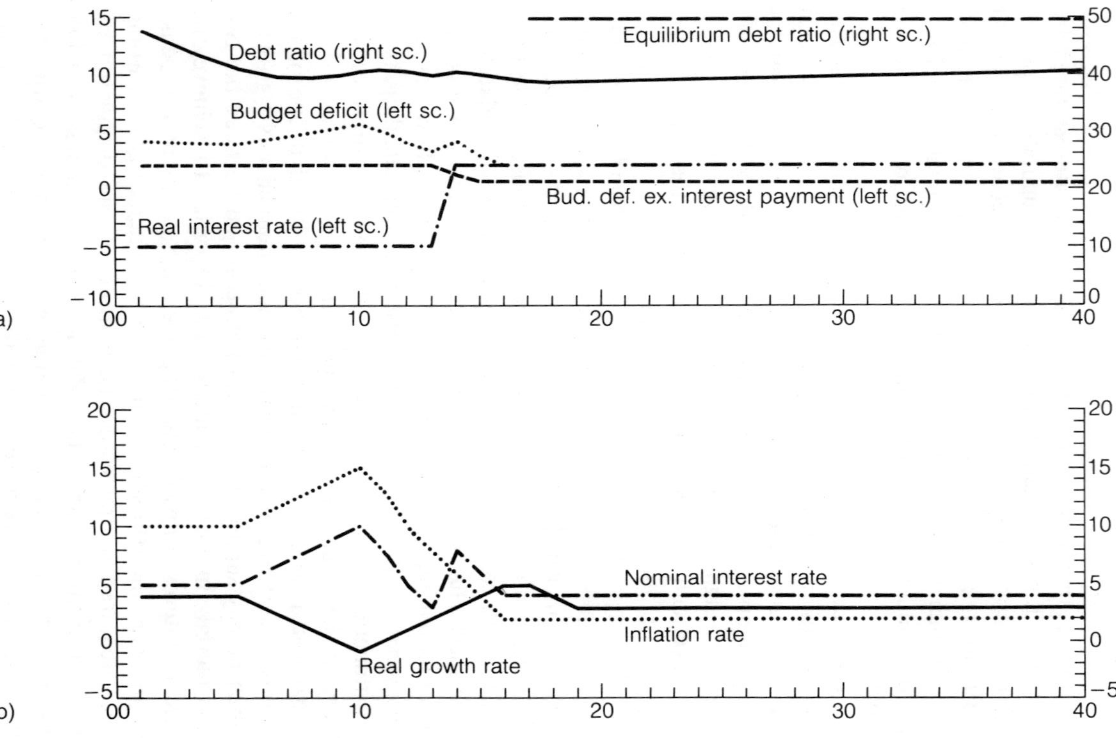

Figure 2.6 Disinflation: primary reliance on fiscal policy (a) the debt/budget situation (b) the economy

the disinflation process of 1980–83, a unilateral tightening of fiscal stance would not have imposed further downward demand pressures on the world economy. Rather, they suggest that a different policy mix – defined more generally – could conceivably have been more appropriate.

Put provocatively, they raise the intriguing question as to whether – given the apparent limits to the acceptable 'real' consequences of disinflation – the monetary targets actually set were not inadvertently *too* tight to permit a more desirable degree of fiscal retrenchment. For, given the monetary targets set, the feared real demand effects of further fiscal tightening may well have inhibited policy makers from taking additional action. Against this, however, some might argue that earlier and more convincing fiscal restraint might have facilitated the earlier attainment of the fundamental goals of disinflationary policy.

III RECENT FISCAL AND ECONOMIC PERFORMANCE AND ITS APPARENT LONG-RUN IMPLICATIONS FOR PUBLIC DEBT

Interest Rates and Growth: the Development of Debt Instability

The previous analysis highlighted the crucial importance of the relationship between interest rates and GNP growth for the longer-run behaviour of the public debt ratio. In particular, it was noted that any tendency for interest rates to equal or exceed nominal income growth made the situation potentially unstable. Table 2.1 shows, for recent years, the cases in which such a situation may have existed.

Two points should be made immediately. Firstly, the interest rate used to make the comparison with the nominal growth rate is the current rate on long-term government bonds (as recorded in the IMF's International Financial Statistics). At any particular time, of course, this is likely to misrepresent the *de facto* average cost of servicing the total debt both because of maturity structure effects and because only a small part of the debt may have been contracted at the current interest rate. On the other hand, should the current rate persist for some time, then sooner or later actual debt service costs would tend to move closer to that rate. In addition, the greater the rise in the debt ratio, the more might interest rates themselves begin to rise further. For our present purposes, it may thus be that we are not running too great a risk of overdramatizing the public debt problem by using the interest rate statistics as just defined.

Secondly, and perhaps more seriously, there are no readily available estimates across countries of the net-of-tax interest rate which, as

Table 2.1 *Incidence of interest rates in excess of nominal GNP growth 1979–85*[a]

Country	*1979*	*1980*	*1981*	*1982*	*1983*	*1984*	*1985*[b]
Belgium	**	**	**	**	**	**	**
Germany		*	**	**	**	**	**
France			*	*	*	**	**
United Kingdom			**	**	*	**	**
Italy[c]			*	*	*	*	*
The Netherlands	**	**	**	**	**	**	**
Sweden			**	**	*	*	**
Ireland					*	**	**
Denmark	*	**	**	*	**	**	**
Japan		*	*	**	**	*	
Canada			*	**	**	**	**
United States		*	*	**	**	*	**

[a] ** = cases in which post-tax interest rates exceeded nominal income growth (uniform tax rate of 25 per cent assumed). * = cases in which only pre-tax interest rates exceeded nominal income growth.
[b] Estimated. Nominal GNP growth estimates taken from *OECD Economic Outlook*, June 1985.
[c] In the case of Italy, little or no taxation is levied on public debt interest receipts. Hence a single star here indicates a considerably greater risk of debt explosion than in other cases.

has been explained, is the relevant rate for calculating long-run debt implications. The greater the proportion of interest outlays which automatically returns to the government in the form of tax on interest received, the less serious (in this context) is any given gross interest rate. At times and in certain countries, private interest receipts have been subject to relatively penal rates of taxation, while conversely, there are cases, notably where insurance companies and pension funds are concerned, in which particularly favourable tax treatment is accorded to personal income from capital – especially when that capital takes the form of public sector bonds. The net effect is thus very difficult to discern. Only in the case of Italy, among the countries considered here, is interest on virtually all public debt holdings specifically exempt from explicit taxation.[4]

The approach taken in table 2.1 is to show the situation in two lights – one assuming no tax is paid on interest income, the other assuming that the effective tax rate on such income is at all times and in all cases, bar Italy, 25 per cent. At the very least this ensures that the test being applied is more rigorous than that which assumes a zero effective tax rate. Nevertheless, it will be well to bear in mind in the reported calculations which follow, that this particular house has at least one wing built on somewhat sandy foundations.

Table 2.1 shows, broadly, the growing spread of the problem over the period since 1979. The two Low Countries seem to have had an unfavourable interest rate/nominal growth relationship over the whole period. But for the rest, it is a problem which began to surface in 1980–81. And, at least up to 1983, there was little sign of any improvement. Indeed, in that year three European G–10 countries (plus Italy, *de facto*) remained in a potentially explosive situation on the stronger criterion, as did Denmark, Japan, Canada and the United States. For the rest, at least the gross interest rate was higher than the nominal growth rate. The case of the United Kingdom was also potentially explosive in 1981 and 1982 even though fiscal retrenchment had been carried to the point where the general government budget net of estimated net interest payments had moved into surplus. However, the weight of net interest payments on a relatively high pre-existing level of debt was still sufficient to ensure an explosive tendency in a positive direction (i.e. in the direction of increasing net indebtedness). The same may have become true again in 1985 as inflation-adjusted interest rates rose further.

The Situation in 1983

Much of the period since 1979, we may assume, has been somewhat exceptional. That is to say, part of the unnerving fiscal picture which has emerged above may have been due to factors – in particular the effects of the disinflation process – which might reasonably be expected to be once-for-all. This would probably be reinforced if the automatic budgetary effects of recession had been brought into the picture as well. Hence, to some extent, part of the fairly general fiscal problem may now be 'water under the bridge'. If so, it would seem sensible to concentrate attention on a more recent year. 1983 has been chosen, partly because at the time of writing it was the latest year for which full figures were available, but also, and more importantly, because it is perceived in many countries to have been the first year of the recovery – albeit, a large amount of slack still remained to be taken up at the end of it.

Table 2.2 sets out the relevant basic data for 1983 while table 2.3 proceeds to some more detailed analytical treatment. Again it should be stressed that one of the crucial assumptions necessary for a meaningful analysis – namely the effective tax rate on interest income received – has been rather arbitrarily put at 25 per cent in all cases bar one.[5]

Table 2.2 Deficits, debt, interest rates and growth: the 1983 situation

Country	*Actual budget deficit*[a]	*Net debt ratio*[b]	*Nominal interest rate*[c]	*Nominal GNP growth*	*Real GNP growth*	*Inflation rate*[d]	*Real interest rate*[e]
Belgium	−11.1	96.8	11.9	6.2	0.3	5.9	6.0
Germany	− 2.7	21.5	7.9	4.5	1.3	3.2	4.7
France	− 3.2	15.0	13.6	10.9	1.0	9.8	3.8
United Kingdom	− 3.7	49.0	10.8	9.0	3.4	5.4	5.4
Italy	−11.8	78.5	18.0	13.9	−1.2	15.3	2.7
The Netherlands	− 6.6	61.2	8.6	2.4	1.3	1.1	7.5
Sweden	− 5.0	11.0	12.3	11.6	1.2	10.3	2.0
Ireland	−13.6	92.8	13.9	11.3	0.6	10.6	3.3
Denmark	− 7.8	34.4	14.5	10.3	2.5	7.6	6.9
Japan	− 3.1	25.8	7.4	3.8	3.1	0.7	6.7
Canada	− 5.9	24.0	11.8	8.9	3.2	5.5	6.3
United States	− 3.9	26.3	11.3	7.7	3.7	3.9	7.4

[a] General government net lending as a percentage of GNP. Source Muller and Price (1984).
[b] Ratio to GNP; percentage. Source: Muller and Price (1984).
[c] Long-term government bond yield. Source: IFS.
[d] GNP deflator.
[e] Pre-tax; measured using change in GNP deflator.

Table 2.3 The potential debt implications of the 1983 situation

Country	Assumed after-tax interest rate[a]	Real after-tax interest rate	Assumed primary deficit[b]	Equilibrium debt ratio[c]	Change in nominal growth rate required to limit debt ratio to 100%[d]	Net interest rate required to limit debt ratio to 100%[e]	Number of years before debt ratio reaches 100%[f]
Belgium	8.9	3.0	−5.3	∞	7.3 (7.6)	0.6 (−5.1)	< 1
Germany	5.9	2.7	−1.5	∞	2.8 (4.1)	2.9 (0.7)	36
France	10.2	0.4	−2.3	364.4	1.3 (2.3)	8.3 (1.3)	45
United Kingdom	8.1	2.7	−0.4	48.4	−0.5 (2.9)	8.6 (6.1)	∞
Italy	18.0	2.7	−2.8	∞	7.5 (6.3)	10.7 (−3.2)	4
The Netherlands	6.5	5.4	−1.4	∞	5.4 (6.7)	1.0 (0.2)	9
Sweden	9.2	−1.1	−4.1	190.7	1.2 (2.4)	7.0 (−1.0)	32
Ireland	10.4	−0.2	−7.5	927.5	5.4 (6.0)	3.0 (−6.6)	2
Denmark	10.9	3.3	−4.5	∞	4.4 (6.9)	5.3 (−0.5)	14
Japan	5.6	4.9	−1.8	∞	3.5 (6.6)	1.9 (1.8)	27
Canada	8.9	3.4	−3.6	∞	3.2 (6.4)	5.0 (2.2)	22
United States	8.5	4.6	−2.3	∞	2.9 (6.6)	5.2 (3.0)	28

[a] After deducting tax at a 25% rate.

[b] Equals recorded deficit minus 0.75 times net interest payments of general government as a percentage of GNP. Source: Muller and Price (1984).

[c] Eventual debt ratio implied by the interest rates, growth, inflation and budget position of 1983. ∞ = infinite, i.e. explosive.

[d] Figures in parentheses show the real growth rate implied when all the required change in nominal GNP growth is accounted for by output.

[e] Figures in parentheses show the corresponding *pre-tax real* interest rate.

[f] Assuming interest rates, net budget deficits and nominal growth remained at their 1983 levels.

On this assumption table 2.3 shows that real after-tax interest rates in 1983 were in many cases not inordinately high. The Netherlands, Japan and the United States might be exceptions to some degree, though in two other countries, Sweden and Ireland, real net rates may have been negative. In addition, although 1983 was on average a year of recovery, the first part of the table shows that that was not universally true, even if one must nowadays reckon with lower underlying growth rates of productive potential than used to be the case some years ago. Particularly weak growth rates were, in addition, concentrated among the European countries, with Italy, Belgium, Ireland and possibly France being the most noteworthy cases.

Even so, the long-run public debt implications of the 1983 situation remained almost universally unsatisfactory. Even where recovery was reasonably well under way, in North America and Japan, the situation was apparently still potentially unstable, as can be seen from column 4 of table 2.3. And in Europe, although there were some non-explosive cases, these nevertheless implied – with the possible exception of the United Kingdom – equilibrium debt ratios likely to be too high for comfort.

Table 2.3 also shows the real growth rates and, alternatively, the net interest rates, which would be required even to limit the long-run debt ratio to 100 per cent of GNP – a figure which many countries might not find tolerable. As can be seen, for some of the more severe cases, such as Italy, Belgium and The Netherlands, and also for Ireland and Denmark, the required real growth rates – in the 6 to 7½ per cent range – are far higher than are likely to be feasible in anything but the very short run. But a solution along these lines – i.e. without either specific action on the budget itself or powerful automatic stabilizer effects[6] – necessarily implies the continuation of such growth rates well beyond the short term. Similarly, for a 'solution' – i.e. a debt ratio limit of 100 per cent – to be achieved in continental Europe solely via a fall in interest rates would require unreasonably low real rates to be held at least until such time as more direct action on the budget proved possible. Whether such negative real rates would or would not be desirable *per se*, it is doubtful whether they could in fact be engineered either because of a greater degree of sophistication now amongst financial market participants, or because they would require an unacceptable, and possibly continuing, acceleration in inflation.

On the face of it, then, by one means or another, direct action on the primary budget itself seems to be the inescapable conclusion of the analysis so far. For some countries, as the final column of the table shows, there is at least some time to play with, as the growth of the debt ratio is a fairly prolonged process. By the same token, though, it could also prove a lengthy process to try to reduce debt ratios significantly.

For other countries, however, time is rapidly running out if they are to prevent the net public debt from exceeding one year's GNP. Belgium, Italy, Ireland and, to a lesser extent, The Netherlands, are apparently in this position. (Only the United Kingdom has literally 'all the time in the world' – its equilibrium debt ratio in 1983 was less than 50 per cent.)[7] The next table thus presents an attempt to calculate the required degree of fiscal retrenchment.

The Possible Implications of a 3 per cent Growth Assumption

Firstly, however, all countries are put on to a common, but modest, base as regards growth performance. That is, the required degree of retrenchment is calculated assuming real growth running at a moderate 3 per cent per annum everywhere. Especially for those countries which were lagging in the recovery process this seems a more realistic basis for calculation. At the other end of the spectrum it also prevents an optimistic bias arising from calculating on the basis of what might be above-trend, purely cyclical, rates of growth.

At the same time, however, a uniform post-tax real interest rate of 2 per cent is introduced as a constraint for those countries whose debt problems may not be fully apparent on account of low, or even negative, real rates. For those suffering from 'excessively high' real rates, on the other hand, the imposition of this assumption may remove what is possibly a relatively temporary exacerbation of their long-run fiscal problem.

It will be noticed that, in choosing a real growth rate higher than the real interest rate, we have imposed on all countries the existence of a finite debt ratio limit. Potentially explosive cases are, in other words, ruled out by assumption. Even so, no country other than the United Kingdom has an equilibrium debt ratio on this basis of less than 100 per cent. Many, if not most, are still far in excess of such a limit. What is more, for two out of the four countries which were previously about to cross the 100 per cent figure very shortly, the situation has not changed materially. For The Netherlands, however, the combination of raising the real growth rate from 1 to 3 per cent, and of reducing the post-tax real interest rate from 5½ to 2 per cent, has a dramatic effect. The equilibrium ratio is now less than 150 per cent, while even the 100 per cent barrier would not be crossed for more than half a century – a time horizon which may be reasonably well beyond that of even the most forward-looking policy maker. In Italy, too, the assumption of 3 per cent growth as against the −1.2 per cent recorded in 1983, has a sizeable effect on the equilibrium debt ratio and on the time taken to reach 100 per cent.

For most countries, however, there might seem a reasonable case for considering what size of action might be required to keep the debt ratio within a 100 per cent limit. The results are shown in the penultimate column of table 2.4 in terms of change required in the primary General Government budget deficit as a percentage of GNP – assuming all other conditions remain unchanged. These are shown next to recent OECD estimates of the automatic stabilizer consequences of economies being somewhat below their full employment potential in 1983 (see Muller and Price, 1984).

Countries which stand out as being in apparent need of fairly major policy changes are Belgium, Sweden, Ireland and Denmark. What is more, in all these cases (though only marginally so for Belgium) the required adjustment is more than would come about automatically should the economy take up its estimated degree of slack.

At the other extreme, the United Kingdom appears to be relatively favourably placed: an actual relaxation of fiscal stance would have been necessary under 1983 conditions, were the authorities to have 'aimed' for a 100 per cent debt ratio.[8] Perhaps more relevantly, the amount of budgetary correction waiting, as it were, 'in the wings', if and when slack comes to be taken up, is large enough for public debt fears to be kept to a minimum. In Germany, The Netherlands and, to a lesser extent, France and Italy, the situation appears to call for a relatively modest further adjustment, comfortably within the margin provided by the automatic stabilizers.

Finally, it should be noted that the comparatively comfortable position of the United States has to be interpreted with care. It underlines the fact that the calculations assume the continuation of the underlying primary budgetary situation as recorded in 1983. For the United States, of course, we know that, without correction, this underlying situation was programmed to worsen as the structural budget deficit was generally believed likely to increase further compared with 1983. Conversely, for European countries, the calculations do not make allowance for further fiscal tightening which may already be in the policy 'pipeline'.

IV THE POLICY DILEMMA

Taking for the moment the fiscal situation *per se*, there are in principle three routes by which the looming debt problem could at least be eased, if not solved. Firstly, a lower real stock of debt would itself

Table 2.4 *Public debt implications of 3 per cent real growth and 2 per cent post-tax real interest rates*

Country	*Primary budget deficit in 1983*	*Nominal post-tax interest rate required*	*Nominal GNP growth required (given 1983 inflation rate)*	*Equilibrium debt ratio (percentage of GNP)*	*Number of years to debt ratio of 100%*	*Change in budget balance required to limit debt ratio to 100%*	*Difference between actual and cyclically-adjusted budget balance in 1983*[c]
Belgium	−5.3	7.9	9.1	481.9	<1	4.2	4.1
Germany	−1.5	5.2	6.3	145.0	>50	0.5	3.2
France	−2.3	11.8[a]	13.1	200.1	>100	1.2	2.5
United Kingdom	−0.4	7.4	8.6	36.2	..	−0.7[b]	5.3
Italy	−2.8	17.3	18.8	221.8	13	1.3	2.1
The Netherlands	−1.4	3.1	4.1	145.7	>50	0.4	5.5
Sweden	−4.1	12.3[a]	13.6	358.3	26	3.0	3.4
Ireland	−7.5	12.6[a]	13.9	657.1	2	6.4	3.0
Denmark	−4.5	9.6	10.8	415.5	18	3.4	2.3
Japan	−1.8	2.7	3.7	186.7	>50	0.8	0.9
Canada	−3.6	7.5	8.7	326.1	26	2.5	4.0
United States	−2.3	5.9	7.0	223.7	46	1.2	3.7

[a] Rise in interest rate required.
[b] Relaxation.
[c] Source: Muller and Price (1984).

reduce budgetary pressures, at least for a time. Secondly, lower interest rates could in theory be of more permanent assistance, and thirdly, and probably most importantly, a lowering of the primary deficit would, *ceteris paribus*, be the surest route to a more lasting solution. In practice, of course, these three routes will not be independent.

As a way into the problem, a unilateral lowering of the existing debt ratio would almost certainly involve unacceptable side effects and might, in any case, be impossible. A rise in the inflation rate is anyway ruled out for other, overriding reasons. But, even if it were not, it is not clear that a move to very low, or negative real interest rates would be possible. For, while such an event might accompany a sharp external price shock it is difficult to see how it could be deliberately engineered by domestic policy changes, without inflaming inflationary expectations. In turn, such revived expectations could well, in today's financial markets, put upward pressure on interest rates – certainly in nominal, and possibly also in real, terms.

A lowering of interest rates seems a more promising candidate for inclusion in any convincing package of measures to ease the fiscal problem. In most countries interest rates remain unusually high in relation to current rates of inflation – especially given the depressed state of many economies.

To the extent that interest rates in Europe are appreciably affected by the international effects of the mix and stance of monetary and fiscal policies in the United States, the hands of European policy makers are tied. This is especially so, the greater the reluctance to risk another period of exchange rate weakness. The latter would, of course, have inflationary implications. It might also not result in much further net demand stimulus from the external sector. To the extent that European businessmen believe that the recent exchange rate configuration was not tenable in the longer run, they will be unwilling to react to further demand stimulus from this source by raising investment – investment which might well not be profitable at more 'reasonable' exchange rate levels.

In this sense, at least part of the desired reduction in European interest rates may have to wait on a resolution of the US policy problem and/or a further change in sentiment about the dollar. For the exchange rate reason already mentioned it can probably also not be brought about by substantial changes in the European monetary stance. But what of the fiscal position itself? Would not further surgery here attack the public debt problem from two angles simultaneously – by both a direct and an indirect (interest rate) route?

This leads us into the wider discussion of direct fiscal action. Two headings may be distinguished: firstly, further fiscal retrenchment, and, secondly, a temporary reversal of the restrictive stance.

Further Retrenchment

Figures 2.7 and 2.8 show that further retrenchment is, not surprisingly, entirely compatible – in a purely arithmetic sense – with a solution of the public debt problem, that is, with preventing any further rise in the debt ratio. They also show, however, that the economy's growth performance is crucial to the success of the operation. (In this and subsequent arithmetic simulations the real post-tax interest rate is fixed at 2 per cent throughout and inflation is assumed to remain under control at the low level of 3 per cent per annum.)

Figure 2.7 shows first the hypothesized policy action which reduces the primary budget deficit from 1 per cent of GNP to zero. Shortly thereafter economic recovery is assumed to intensify, the growth rate of output rising from a stagflationary 2 per cent to a temporary peak of 5 per cent as slack is taken up, and then settling back to an underlying 'equilibrium' rate of 3 per cent per annum. As the graph shows, the debt ratio is thereby held under control and indeed begins to decline very gently to below the 25 per cent figure from which the simulation was assumed to begin. Likewise, the overall budget deficit is reduced from over 2 per cent of GNP to around 1 per cent, and, implicitly,

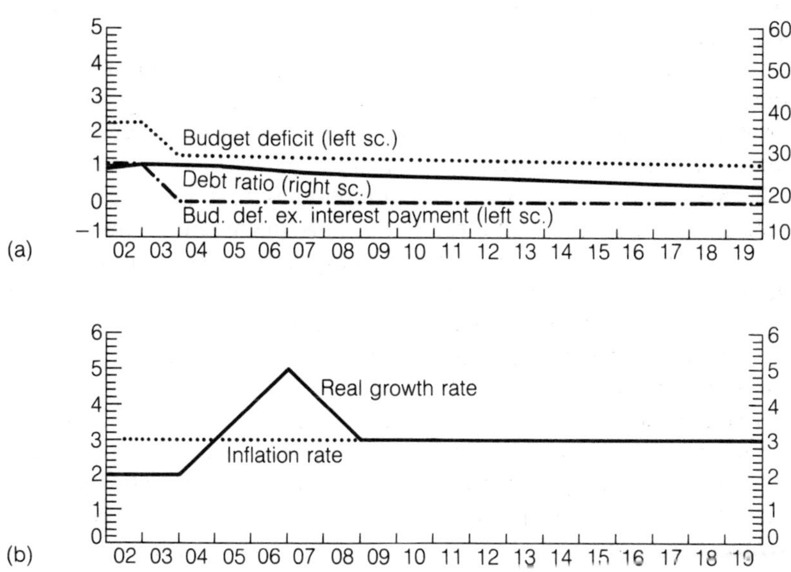

Figure 2.7 Successful further retrenchment (a) the debt/budget situation (b) growth and inflation

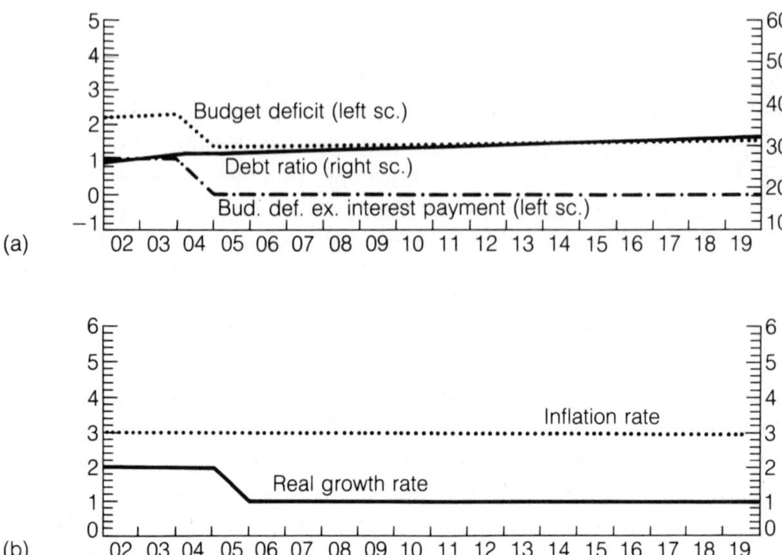

Figure 2.8 Unsuccessful further retrenchment (a) the debt/budget situation (b) growth and inflation

some of the hidden fiscal tensions are alleviated as the automatic stabilizers come to play a helpful role.

A crucial assumption underlying this outcome is clearly that involving the recovery of output, even in the face of further retrenchment. Put another way, the *ex ante* reduction in public sector dissaving has to be more than offset by a decline in private sector financial saving.[9] A subsidiary, but still important, assumption is that no resurgence of inflation occurs during the recovery. This might either damage the recovery process *per se*, or, perhaps more realistically, cause it to be aborted as the assumed commitment to a continued anti-inflationary stance of monetary policy began to act as a constraint – in which case real interest rates might also begin to rise again, and add further to the debt problem.

Even without a resurgence of inflation, however, figure 2.8 demonstrates how a failure of recovery to materialize could be potentially fatal to the public finance problem even under a policy of further fiscal cutbacks. Indeed, with growth assumed actually to fall to 1 per cent – perhaps because of the demand effects of intensified budgetary restraint the situation becomes technically explosive, although the acceleration in debt growth is very slow over the period shown.

A Temporary Relaxation of Fiscal Stance

The possibility of such an adverse outcome, of course, leads one logically to consider the possible effects of moving the fiscal levers in precisely the opposite direction – at least for a time. Past history suggests that temporary demand effects were often obtained in this way. Recent transatlantic experience seems to corroborate earlier history, at least in the context of strong supply-side, as well as demand-side, stimuli.

Unfortunately, however, there can again be no a priori certainty of success. On the one hand, past experience suggests to many that a resurgence of inflation was also a concomitant of fiscal reflation. On the other, much recent theoretical reasoning seems to lead to the conclusion that – via strong and immediate expectational effects – the recovery of output does not occur even temporarily. 'Crowding-out' is complete and, for all practical purposes, instantaneous.

If this is true, of course, then – as figure 2.10 illustrates – fiscal stimulus will actually worsen the debt situation, possibly quite materially if interest rates rise too. Even during a successful policy initiative along these lines – as figure 2.9 shows – there may well be some further,

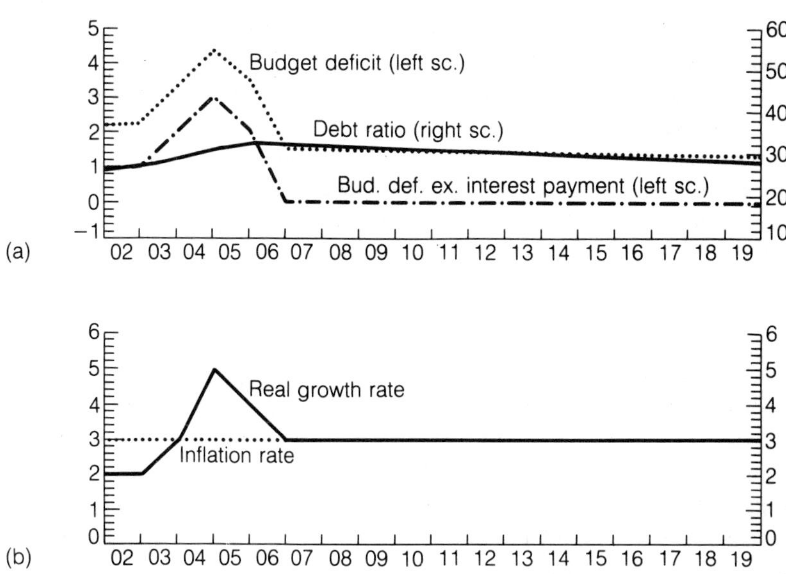

Figure 2.9 Successful fiscal stimulus (a) the debt/budget situation (b) growth and inflation

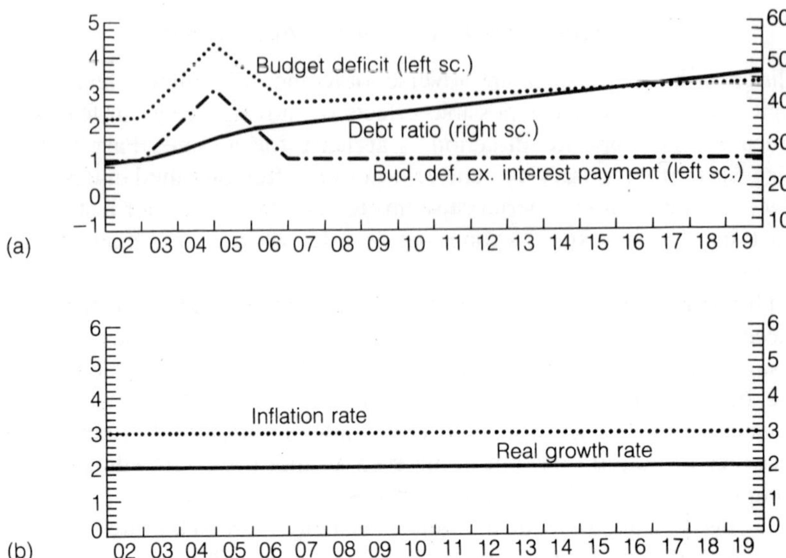

Figure 2.10 Unsuccessful fiscal stimulus (a) the debt/budget situation (b) growth and inflation

though temporary, increase in the debt ratio before an underlying decline begins to assert itself. On the other hand, any success in terms of a reduction in slack pays a kind of 'bonus' here through the automatic stabilizers, which are assumed to permit the eventual elimination of the primary deficit without prejudice to the maintenance of the underlying trend rate of growth. The main prerequisite for this is that the 'pump' of private sector spending/reduced financial saving should have been effectively (but also sustainably) 'primed'.

V CONCLUSION

The conclusion of all this seems to be that there is no early and satisfactory way out of the European public debt problem unless one of two things happens. Firstly, the economic recovery could spontaneously intensify and spread out – in response to policies already in place – more than is allowed for in current forecasts. Or, secondly, further policy measures could be taken. However, such measures – in whatever direction – would ideally have to be 'successful' in the sense that they brought on, or were at least accompanied by, some quickening in the pace of recovery and some taking up of slack; at the very least, further fiscal retrenchment would need to exert no major adverse effect on growth performance. Otherwise, the public debt problem – as well as the overall problem of economic performance – would seem likely to get worse, rather than better.

APPENDIX THE BUDGET DEFICIT, NATIONAL INCOME GROWTH AND THE RATE OF INTEREST

Ratio of Government Debt to GNP

For any given growth rate of nominal national income the ratio of outstanding debt to GNP tends to a finite constant, given that the budget deficit remains a constant proportion of GNP.

Let nominal GNP grow at a constant annual percentage rate, $y \times 100$. Let the budget deficit, BD, be a constant proportion, q, of nominal GNP. Then, at any time, t,

$$\begin{aligned} \mathrm{BD}_t &= q\mathrm{GNP}_t & t > 0 \\ \mathrm{GNP}_t &= \mathrm{GNP}_0 (1+y)^t & t > 0 \end{aligned}$$

The outstanding stock of government debt, DBT – assuming either that all deficits are bond financed, or that the definition of debt includes monetary financing – is then

$$\mathrm{DBT}_t = \sum_{k=1}^{t} \mathrm{BD}_k + \mathrm{DBT}$$

$$= q \sum_{k=1}^{t} \mathrm{GNP}_k + \mathrm{DBT}_0$$

$$= q\mathrm{GNP}_0 \sum_{k=1}^{t} (1+y)^k + \mathrm{DBT}_0$$

$$= q\mathrm{GNP}_0 \left\{ \frac{(1+y)\,[(1+y)^t - 1]}{(1+y) - 1} \right\} + \mathrm{DBT}_0$$

$$= \frac{q}{y} \mathrm{GNP}_0 \{(1+y)\,[(1+y)^t - 1]\} + \mathrm{DBT}_0$$

$$\therefore \quad \frac{\mathrm{DBT}_t}{\mathrm{GNP}_t} = \frac{q}{y} \mathrm{GNP}_0 \left\{ \frac{(1+y)\,[(1+y)^t - 1]}{\mathrm{GNP}_0 (1+y)^t} \right\} + \frac{\mathrm{DBT}_0}{\mathrm{GNP}_t}$$

$$= \frac{q}{y} \frac{[(1+y)^t - 1]}{(1+y)^{t-1}} + \frac{\mathrm{DBT}_0}{\mathrm{GNP}_t}$$

$$= \frac{q}{y}(1+y) - \frac{q/y}{(1+y)^{t-1}} + \frac{\mathrm{DBT}_0}{\mathrm{GNP}_t}$$

As $t \to \infty$ the first term only remains. Hence as $t \to \infty$

$$\frac{\mathrm{DDT}_t}{\mathrm{GNP}_t} \to \frac{q}{y}(1+y) \tag{2.1}$$

Explosive Debt Ratios

If the budget deficit is not necessarily constant but can be affected by changes in interest relates on accumulated debt, then the possibility of explosive debt (and deficit) ratios appears. The simplest case is that where the budget excluding interest payments is assumed to be balanced. Then the deficit is equal to interest payments. Clearly, if the interest rate equals the rate of growth of GNP, the debt ratio remains constant as both GNP and outstanding debt grow at the same rate. Similarly, if the interest rate exceeds the rate of income growth the debt and deficit ratios will rise indefinitely. More realistically, with interest receipts being taxable, the relevant interest rate should rather be the nominal interest rate less the average rate of tax on interest incomes.

The general case would also allow for some deficit in the budget excluding interest (the *primary* deficit), and may be analysed as follows. Suppose

$$BD_0 = pGNP_0 \ (=DBT_0)$$

i.e. p is the initial debt ratio.

$$BD_t = qGNP_t + rDBT_{t-1} \quad t > 0$$

where $r \times 100$ = the rate of interest per cent.

$$BD_t = DBT_t - DBT_{t-1} = qGNP_t + rDBT_{t-1} \quad t > 0$$

$$DBT_t = qGNP_t + (1+r)DBT_{t-1} \quad t > 0$$

$$DBT_{t-1} = qGNP_{t-1} + (1+r)\,DBT_{t-2}$$

Substituting

$$\begin{aligned} DBT_t &= qGNP_t + (1+r)\,[qGNP_{t-1} + (1+r)DBT_{t-2}] \\ &= q[GNP_t + (1+r)GNP_{t-1} + (1+r)^2GNP_{t-2} + \ldots \\ &\quad + (1+r)^{t-1}\,GNP + (1+r)^tDBT_0] \\ &= q\sum_{k=0}^{t-1}(1+\mathrm{r})^kGNP_{t-k} + (1+r)^t\,pGNP_0 \end{aligned}$$

But

$$GNP_{t-k} = (1+y)^{t-k}GNP_0$$

$$\therefore\ DBT_t = qGNP_0\sum_{k=0}^{t-1}(1+r)^k\,(1+y)^{t-k} + (1+r)^t\,pGNP_0$$

$$\begin{aligned} \frac{DBT_t}{GNP_t} &= \frac{qGNP_0}{(1+y)^tGNP_0}\left[\sum_{k=0}^{t-1}(1+r)^k\,(1+y)^{t-k}\right] + p\left[\frac{(1+r)}{(1+y)}\right]^t \\ &= q\sum_{k=0}^{t-1}(1+r)^k\,(1+y)^{t-k}\,(1+y)^{-t} + p\left(\frac{1+r}{1+y}\right)^t \\ &= q\sum_{k=0}^{t-1}\left(\frac{1+r}{1+y}\right)^k + p\left(\frac{1+r}{1+y}\right)^t \end{aligned}$$

But

$$\sum_{k=0}^{t-1} x^k = \frac{x^t - 1}{x - 1}$$

Hence

$$\frac{\text{DBT}_t}{\text{GNP}_t} = q\left\{\left[\left(\frac{1+r}{1+y}\right)^t - 1\right]\Big/\left[\left(\frac{1+r}{1+y}\right) - 1\right]\right\} + p\left(\frac{1+r}{1+y}\right)^t \quad r \neq y$$

or

$$\frac{\text{DBT}_t}{\text{GNP}_t} = q\left(\frac{1+y}{r-y}\right)\left[\left(\frac{1+r}{1+y}\right)^t - 1\right] + p\left(\frac{1+r}{1+y}\right)^t \tag{2.2}$$

for all r, $r \neq y$. For $r = y$,

$$\frac{\text{DBT}_t}{\text{GNP}_t} = q\sum_{k=0}^{t-1}\left(\frac{1+y}{1+r}\right)^k + p\left(\frac{1+r}{1+y}\right)^t$$

or

$$\frac{\text{DBT}_t}{\text{GNP}_t} = tq + p \quad r = y \tag{2.3}$$

As $t \to \infty$, what happens to the debt ratio is then crucially dependent on the relationship between r and y.

1 For $r = y$,

$$\frac{\text{DBT}_t}{\text{GNP}_t} = tq + p \to \infty \text{ as } t \to \infty$$

the direction of explosion depending on the sign of q.

2 For $r > y$,

$$\left(\frac{1+r}{1+y}\right) > 1$$

$$\therefore \frac{\text{DBT}_t}{\text{GNP}_t} \to \infty \text{ as } t \to \infty$$

The direction of the explosion here will, however, depend on the signs of p and q, as well as on their relative magnitudes; see 4 below.

3 For $r < y$,

$$\frac{(1+r)}{(1+y)} < 1$$

$$\therefore \left(\frac{1+r}{1+y}\right) \to 0 \text{ as } t \to \infty$$

$$\therefore \frac{\text{DBT}_t}{\text{GNP}_t} \to -q\left(\frac{1+y}{r-y}\right) + 0 = q\frac{(1+y)}{(y-r)}$$

For $r = 0$, this gives us the simple case discussed earlier. The net result is that for $r \geqslant y$, the debt ratio tends to increase indefinitely.

4 Returning to the case where $r > y$, the relevant basic equation (equation 2.2) shows that more than one version of the explosive debt case is possible.

Equation 2.2 can be rewritten as

$$\frac{\text{DBT}_t}{\text{GNP}_t} = q\left(\frac{1+y}{r-y}\right)\left(\frac{1+r}{1+y}\right)^t - q\left(\frac{1+y}{r-y}\right) + p\left(\frac{1+r}{1+y}\right)^t$$

The middle term is a constant and can therefore be ignored in what follows. As already shown above, with p and q both positive, the debt ratio increases without limit. But suppose q to be negative, i.e. the budget net of interest payments to be in surplus. The two explosive terms in the above expression will then be pulling in opposite directions.

Thus – and again only for the case when $r > y$ – the debt ratio will either explode or implode (towards an infinite net *asset* position) according to whether

$$\left|q\left(\frac{1+y}{r-y}\right)\right| \text{ is } < \text{ or } > |p|$$

Only if the absolute values of the two terms were exactly equal, and were to remain so (something virtually impossible in the real world), would the debt ratio remain constant. Slightly more conceivable might be a situation in which, from year to year, the inequality sometimes reversed, thus avoiding a debt ratio explosion in practice, even while r remained greater than y.

NOTES

1 This paper focuses only on the net *financial* liabilities of the general government sector. Many observers – including J.S. Flemming and M. Posner at the conference itself – have pointed out that public sectors are typically also owners of real assets which should in some way be brought in to any balance-sheet type of assessment. This would be particularly relevant where a sizeable proportion of such assets produce a return, *in cash*, to the budget itself, e.g. in countries where the public sector is a large provider of housing.

A case in point would be that of the United Kingdom, where according to OECD estimates (Muller and Price, 1984), the net financial indebtedness of the general government sector stood at around £125 billion in 1983. At the same time the *replacement-cost* valuation of the general government's net capital stock was nearly £200 billion of which some £150 billion represented the local authority housing stock (UK National Accounts, 1984).

It may be noted, however, that the cash return on the latter is already taken account of in the analysis which follows, in the sense that it is an item on the receipts side of the budget deficit. The same kind of point is true, more indirectly, of other public sector assets to the extent that they affect the tax base favourably, even though no direct rental charges are levied.

Also important, to some observers, is the implicit and often growing present value of public sector liabilities resulting from the institution of unfunded pension and other social security schemes. See, for example, Boskin's contribution to the present volume.

2 Strictly, the ratio of the *debt-financed* deficit to GNP. The proportion of the budget of deficit financed by base money creation may be expected to be typically small on average, especially under policy regimes involving monetary targeting.

3 If so, the growth of interest-bearing public debt might also have been somewhat smaller, more of the budget deficit being financed, implicitly, by monetary means.

4 See Tanzi (1984, chapter I, pp. 52–8) for a useful, but still not quantitative, international summary of how varied and complex is the tax treatment of interest.

5 The calculations also ignore the role of central-bank financing of budget deficits. Along with the use of long-term interest rates, as opposed to actual debt interest costs, this implies that the figures are likely, if anything, to overstate the debt problem to some degree. Against this – as already noted – it could, however, be argued that, if the situation remains substantially uncorrected, real interest rates might themselves rise further.

6 In fact, of course, the latter would be very likely to come into play at the kind of growth rates mentioned.

7 Care should, however, be taken in interpreting this result, which applies to one year only. The analysis of knife-edge cases (page 47) is particularly relevant to the UK case. In 1984 and 1985 the situation was again looking (just) potentially explosive as real interest rates rose further but growth had not accelerated noticeably compared with 1983. The implied rate of increase of the debt ratio remained, however, very low – thanks in part to continued relatively tight control over the primary budget deficit.

8 See, however, the qualifying note 7.

9 Logically, one can also envisage a situation in which the budget deficit and private savings were reduced *pari passu*, without any effect on output. Whether this could be brought about in the real world, and whether it would be desirable, are matters for debate.

REFERENCES

Muller, P. and Price, R.W.R. 1984: Structural budget deficits and fiscal stance, *Economics and Statistics Department, OECD, Working Paper* No. 15, July.

Tanzi, V. (ed.) 1984: *Taxation, Inflation and Interest Rates*, International Monetary Fund, Washington, DC.

3

The Link between Budget Deficits and Inflation: Some Contrasts between Developed and Developing Countries

TIM G. CONGDON

I INTRODUCTION

Although the precise nature of the relationship is debated, there is widespread recognition among economists that the growth of the money supply affects inflation. Less well understood is the link between budget deficits and inflation. Until the 1930s most economists were suspicious of budget deficits on the grounds that sooner or later they had to be monetized. This suspicion was particularly strong among British economists. Bresciani-Turron (1937), in his classic study of the Weimar hyperinflation, contrasted German views with 'the "English" theory, . . . vigorously upheld by the representatives of Great Britain in the Reparations Commission and in the Guarantees Committee, according to which the fundamental cause of the depreciation of the mark was the budget deficit, which provoked continued issues of paper money'. In the early post-war decades concern about the inflationary repercussions of deficit financing abated, perhaps under the influence of the Keynesian revolution. But in the last few years interest in the question has revived. The rapid growth of government debt in the leading industrial countries has raised doubts about the long-run sustainability of current fiscal policies, while in several developing countries inflation has accelerated in the aftermath of the debt crisis.

Recent contrasts between developed and developing countries provide the immediate motive for this chapter. In some of the largest developed countries, notably the USA, declining inflation has been reconciled with unusually high budget deficits. In many developing countries inflation has risen despite harsh programmes of fiscal austerity. The conjunction of rising inflation with fiscal austerity has been most obvious and disturbing in Latin America. How are the differences between developed and developing countries to be explained? And how do they illustrate the linkage between fiscal policy and inflation?

The chapter will start with a simple and general statement of the relationship between the budget deficit and the growth of money national income in a long-run steady state. The relationship does not say much in itself, but it focuses attention on the ratio of public sector debt to national income (the debt to income ratio). Some conjectures on the differing experiences of developed and developing countries are then made. Monetary factors also need to have a role and the next section introduces them by comparing the framework of financial control in developed and developing countries. The message of the concluding section is that in all countries responsible fiscal policies are a condition for price stability.

II BUDGET DEFICITS AND INFLATION: A SIMPLE RELATIONSHIP

In a long-run steady state the debt to income ratio is constant. Let *a* denote the constant ratio of debt to income. Then

$$D = aY$$

and

$$\Delta D = a\Delta Y$$

where D is the national debt, Y national income and Δ signifies changes in the variables. But the change in the debt is the same as the budget deficit (denoted by B), and so

$$\frac{B}{Y} = a\frac{\Delta Y}{Y}$$

Here $\Delta Y/Y$ is, of course, the rate of increase of money national income and is equal to the rate of increase in prices plus the rate of increase in real output, which may be denoted by i (inflation) and g (growth) respectively. We therefore have

$$\frac{B}{Y} = a(i + g) \tag{3.1}$$

As long as the budget deficit to income ratio is kept equal to the right-hand side of this equation year after year, the debt to income ratio will be constant.[1]

Equation 3.1 shows that, in steady state and with an unchanging growth rate, a given budget deficit to income ratio will be associated with higher inflation the lower is the debt to income ratio. The inverse relationship between inflation and the debt to income ratio is critical to our later discussion. It suggests that a country has more scope to run a large budget deficit, without inflationary repercussions, the more extensive is the market in government debt and the more prepared are its citizens to hold claims on government. In other words, a high debt to income ratio gives more room for manoeuvre with fiscal policy than a low debt to income ratio. An analysis of the determinants of the demand for public sector debt is therefore important to policy makers concerned about both the short-run options in demand management and the long-run inflation consequences of fiscal actions.

An extension of these ideas is to differentiate between domestic and external holders of government debt. If in steady state the two categories of debt holder have claims on government which are a constant proportion of domestic income, then

$$D_1 = a_1 Y$$
$$D_2 = a_2 Y$$

where D_1 is debt held by home residents and D_2 is debt held by foreign residents, and

$$D = D_1 + D_2$$

So

$$\Delta D = a_1 \Delta Y + a_2 \Delta Y$$

and

$$\frac{B}{Y} = a_1 \frac{\Delta Y}{Y} + a_2 \frac{\Delta Y}{Y}$$

$(a_2 \Delta Y)/Y$ is the net sale of public sector debt to non-residents as a proportion of national income, which may be denoted by f. Then we have

$$\frac{B}{Y} = a_1(i + g) + f \tag{3.2}$$

Equation 3.2 identifies further long-run trade-offs in the conduct of fiscal policy. If a government is able to attract substantial external finance, it can run a budget deficit without inflation risks. In a steady state the availability of external finance is, of course, only growing in line with national income since the external debt to income ratio is assumed constant.

Neither equation 3.1 nor equation 3.2 is altogether suitable for discussing the passage from one steady-state path to another. However, some observations about the comparison of different steady states are justified. It is evident that the government economy with a strong domestic demand for government debt and considerable external credit-worthiness can, on a sustained basis, run a higher budget deficit to income ratio without inflation than that of an economy with weak domestic demand for government debt and little external credit-worthiness. A buoyant trend rate of economic growth also obviates the inflationary dangers of budget deficits.

III THE DEMAND FOR PUBLIC SECTOR DEBT IN DEVELOPED AND DEVELOPING COUNTRIES

The characteristic assumption in economic analysis is that the government's debt is free from default risk, at any rate to domestic creditors. This assumption has little justification in fact since there are many examples of governmental failure to meet obligations. Even the British government has had its problems. Surprising though it may seem today, part of the rationale for the establishment of the Bank of England was that savers would have more confidence in an independent, privately-owned institution than in the crown itself. In the early 1690s there were still memories of the Stop of the Exchequer in January 1672 when interest payments on Charles II's £1 million debt were suspended.

The belief that government debt is free from default risk stems from the state's right to levy taxes. In principle, this right is absolute and permits government to take all, or at least a very high share, of a nation's income. The ability to capture resources implies that government has a greater ability to service debt than any private-sector agency. However, in reality there are limits to taxable capacity. These limits arise for several reasons. High taxation acts as a drag on initiative and effort, and encourages evasion; the possibility of evasion creates administrative strains for the tax-collecting service; and the ease with which the tax-collecting service can meet these strains depends partly on technology, but also on taxpayer ethics. Taxpayer ethics vary from country to country, but are clearly enhanced if citizens identify their governments with their perception of their nation's interests.

These remarks suggest that potential taxable capacity is likely to be higher in developed than in developing countries, where potential taxable capacity is defined loosely as the proportion of national income the government can extract without excessive administrative cost or economic distortion. Developed countries have a number of advantages. Most obviously, good standards of education and literacy simplify the tax collectors' task. This may seem an unimportant consideration in the modern world, but there is no doubt that many developing countries do not possess the administrative infrastructure for the government to raise taxes equivalent to more than a fifth or a quarter of national income. Kaldor's recommendations for India in the 1950s, that it adopt a sophisticated mixture of an annual wealth tax, capital gains tax, expenditure tax and gifts tax, have been judged 'a transfer of inappropriate technology'. According to Little (1974), 'The Kaldor taxes had a negligible yield'.[2] The administrative difficulties in raising taxes are aggravated by the weak sense of loyalty felt by the citizens of most developing countries towards their political elites. The lack of citizen support can often be blamed on the selfish and corrupt motives of political leaderships, these being particularly transparent in one-party states and military dictatorships.

The broad generalization that potential taxable capacity is higher in developed than in developing countries is surely valid. It follows that acceptable ratios of public sector debt to national income are also higher in the developed countries. This is a key conclusion for our discussion. In essence, developing country governments cannot borrow domestically as much as their developed country counterparts because savers know that their ability to service debt is constrained by taxpayer resistance. A further obstacle is that markets in government debt are usually primitive, with little liquidity and high transactions costs, in developing countries. Considerations similar to those responsible for restricted taxable capacity explain this backwardness. Without good educational standards and recognized ethical codes, it is difficult for markets in government securities to become established.

In many developing countries, governments try to overcome the unwillingness of domestic residents to hold much of their debt by direct intervention in the savings process. These interventions typically bring into stronger relief the competition between public and private sectors for resources and exacerbate citizen distrust. Their long-run effect may therefore, ironically, be to reduce the ratio of domestically-held government debt to national income. A common arrangement is for the government to require savings institutions, notably insurance companies and social security funds, to hold a minimum proportion of their assets in public sector debt. It has been noted that, 'Such practices make it difficult for an active bond market with broad participation by the general public to develop' (Agtmael, 1984). More seriously, the imposition of compulsory investment patterns reduces the attractions of saving through institutions and makes social security contributions indistinguishable from taxation. The eventual effect is to lower the amount of government debt savers voluntarily hold in their portfolios.

Government restrictions on the disposition of bank assets ought to be more effective as a means of channelling resources into the public sector, since there should be an irreducible minimum demand to hold money balances. If people are certain to hold a particular quantity of bank deposits, the government can be equally certain to capture their savings by forcing the banking system to keep part of its assets in public sector instruments. For this reason onerous reserve requirements are widespread in the developing world. There is, however, a limit to such practices. If reserve requirements are excessive by comparison with banks' functional requirements and reserve assets yield a low rate of return, the interest rate of deposits is adversely affected. Money holders react by economizing on the balances they keep in the banks, either shifting funds to non-bank intermediaries (such as the *financieras* so common in Latin America) or storing their wealth in non-monetary form (land, precious metals).[3] Governments' final and most secure base for debt issuance is the stock of high-powered money. People need a means of payment and, however much they run down their bank balances, they must still have a transactions demand for the fiat money issued by the central bank. These central bank liabilities can be matched on the assets side by claims on government. But the ratio of high-powered money to national income is quite low, at perhaps 5 to 10 per cent, in financially undeveloped societies. In consequence, high-powered money does not provide the government with a major avenue for funding budget deficits.

Unhappily, political leaders in developing countries do not always appreciate the severity of the financial constraints they face. They are tempted to use the stock of high-powered money (and so also to some extent the banking system's deposits) not as a base for debt issuance, but as a tax base. Budget deficits may be financed wholly at the central bank, leading to rapid growth in high-powered money and fast inflation. Inflation erodes the real value of the central bank's (and, in effect, the government's) liabilities, transferring control of resources from the private to the public sector. Citizens retaliate by holding a lower proportion of their assets in transactions money form and by switching out of the domestic currency into an internationally convertible currency. The outcome may be a comprehensive 'dollarization' of the economy. Argentina and Israel in recent years illustrate the process. Exchange controls may be introduced or tightened to stop this, but they are of limited effectiveness when the government is behaving with manifest financial irresponsibility. The eventual result is that the ratio of domestically-held public sector debt to national income is lower than if the government had tried to extract resources by more honest and straightforward means.

Suspicion of the political process may, because of bitter experiences in the past, become unduly intense. As a result the debt to income ratio in a developing country may be lower than justified by taxable capacity. This creates an opportunity for foreign investors to lend to the governments concerned. Their loans are usually denominated in the convertible currency of a developed economy, which protects them against the risks of inflation, financial restrictions and exchange control which worry domestic residents. In terms of our equation 3.2 the government of a developing economy may be able partly to neutralize the constraints on fiscal policy imposed by domestic aversion to its debt (i.e low a_1) by running an external payments deficit (i.e. positive f).

Our discussion suggests a schematic contrast between the determinants of the debt to income ratio in developed and developing countries (table 3.1). A warning has to be given that it is perhaps excessively stylized. It should not be taken as precluding intermediate cases which mix the characteristics of 'developed and developing countries' in our sense of those terms. Italy and other Mediterranean countries exemplify the mixing of characteristics.[4] Moreover, although much has been said to explain the differences between developed, intermediate and developing countries, our discussion has not been able to fix debt to income ratios. In steady state this ratio is constant by assumption, but we have not been able to say what precise value it should take.

IV THE RELATIONSHIP BETWEEN THE DEBT TO INCOME RATIO, THE REAL INTEREST RATE AND THE GROWTH RATE

This gap in the analysis reflects the real world, as governments have considerable discretion about the debt to income ratios at which their economies settle. However, it is implicit in our discussion that this discretion is not unlimited, since we have argued that debt to income ratios are systematically lower in developing countries than developed. The contrast between them suggests the presence of a constraint. The constraint could derive from an assumed tendency of the real interest rate to increase with rises in the debt to income ratio. A well-known result in public finance theory is that, if the real interest rate exceeds the growth rate, and the budget deficit (exclusive of debt interest) is zero or positive, interest payments on government debt will explode. This clearly cannot be reconciled with steady state. So an excessive debt to income ratio accompanied by a real interest rate above the growth rate also cannot be reconciled with steady state. The debt to income ratio can take the value at which the real interest rate equals

Table 3.1 Determinants of the debt/income ratio: stylized contrasts between developed and developing countries

	Developed countries	Developing countries
National characteristics	Strong citizen identification with nation-state	Weak citizen identification with nation-state
	High educational attainment and universal literacy	Low educational attainment and literacy rate
Value of debt to income ratio	In range from very low to high (0.05 to 1.25)	In range from very low to high (0.05 to 0.25)
Value of tax to income ratio	Moderate to high (0.30 to 0.70)	Low (0.10 to 0.30)
Characteristics of financial markets	Large, liquid and well-informed market in government debt	Small, primitive and illiquid market in government debt
	Government's high creditworthiness permits:	Government, unable to borrow on large scale, tries to extract resources by:
	(i) Exchange freedom	(i) Exchange control
	(ii) Liberalized banking system	(ii) Regulated banking
	(iii) Low reserve requirements on banks	(iii) High reserve requirements on banks
	(iv) Financial institution free in asset allocation decisions	(iv) Financial institution directed to invest in government debt
	(v) Social security system actuarially sound or subsidized by government	(v) Social security system lends to and subsidizes government
	(vi) Low inflation	(vi) Inflation used as a tax instrument

the growth rate or it can take any value beneath that. But it cannot take any higher value.

This idea can be expressed simply as shown in figure 3.1. The real interest rate r is made a positive function of the debt to income ratio in the curves AA^1, BB^1 and CC^1 below. The curve AA^1 can be thought of as describing the relationship between the real interest rate and the debt to income ratio in a developing country. It is quite flat for very

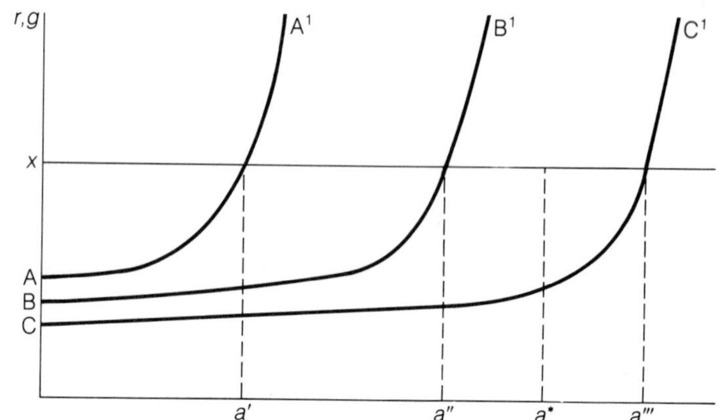

Figure 3.1 Critical debt to income ratios are typically higher in more developed economies

low values of the debt to income ratio, due to the interest-inelastic demand for high-powered money, but then rises steeply at a low value of the debt to income ratio because of the absence of an effective market in government debt. The curve CC^1 – which is much further to the right – is the same relationship in a developed country. As savers have considerable confidence in governments' ability to service debt at low or moderate debt to income ratios, the curve rises gently until a danger zone rightwards of a^* is reached. Here there is increased concern about debt servicing ability and, if the government is to induce savers to hold extra debt, it must increase the real interest rate sharply. The curve BB^1 has roughly the same shape as curve CC^1, but lies between AA^1 and CC^1, and can be regarded as describing the circumstances of an intermediate economy.

Let us suppose, for the sake of expository convenience, that the growth rate is the same in all countries at x per cent a year. Then the values of the debt to income ratio at which the real interest rate equals the growth rate are a' in the developing country, a'' in the intermediate economy and a''' in the developed economy. These could be termed the critical values of the debt to income ratios. Fiscal policy is sustainable if the debt to income ratio stays at or beneath its emergency value; it is unsustainable if it goes any higher. The critical debt to income ratio is the maximum value. We have not said anything to fix the minimum value which could, of course, be negative.

V IMPLICATIONS OF THE DIFFERENCE IN DEBT TO INCOME RATIOS BETWEEN DEVELOPED AND DEVELOPING COUNTRIES

In our discussion of the simple theoretical relationship between budget deficits and inflation we saw that, when comparing steady states, budget deficits are less inflationary the higher is the domestic demand for the government's debt (measured as a proportion of national income) and the greater its external creditworthiness. By contrasting the determinants of debt to income ratios in developed and developing countries we are able to understand the importance of this conclusion for the conduct of fiscal policy. Because debt to income ratios are low in developing countries their governments have little room for deficit financing unless they have access to external funds. In developed countries deficit financing can be pursued on a larger scale, without inflationary repercussions, because of high debt to income ratios. The scope for so-called reflationary measures or supply-side tax cuts in developed countries is also increased by their good reputations in international financial markets. These reputations may enable them to run persistent and substantial payments deficits without much difficulty.

Our analysis also helps in understanding the historical popularity of copy-book maxims for fiscal policy, in particular the balanced budget rule. Large markets in government debt, and the associated high debt to income ratios, are possible only in societies with abundant legal, accounting and financial expertise and with long records of political stability. Until the second half of the nineteenth century there were relatively few such societies. Moreover, powerful international capital markets – able safely to transfer funds in considerable volume between financial centres – are, from an historical standpoint, a recent innovation. Although early small-scale examples could be cited, they also have only existed on a large scale since the second half of the nineteenth century. Low debt to income ratios and limited external finance therefore constrained governments' ability to incur debt. The balanced budget rule was a sensible method of organizing public finances and effectively precluded the use of 'fiscal policy' as an instrument of demand management. The cogency of the balanced budget prescription was reinforced by the low rates of economic growth, usually a mere 1 or 2 per cent a year, which prevailed in most countries until the twentieth century.

It is important to make this point because some economists have urged that Keynesian ideas on fiscal policy have a general applicability to both developed and developing countries.[5] In fact, the conditions for successful programmes of deficit financing on Keynesian lines do not hold in poor and backward countries today, just as they did not hold in poor and backward countries in the past. As Bagehot warned in 1867, 'Many persons have not a distinct perception of the risk of lending to a country in a wholly different state of civilisation . . . They forget that national good faith is a rare and recent thing, and they expect to find it where the condition of its existence cannot be found.[6]

VI RECENT ILLUSTRATIONS OF THE LINK BETWEEN BUDGET DEFICITS AND INFLATION

The Debt Crisis and Accelerating Inflation in Latin American Countries in the early 1980s

Our analytical framework can now be used to throw light on the inflationary process in Latin American countries since the onset of the debt crisis in the summer of 1982. Before the debt crisis, Latin American countries were borrowing heavily abroad, with syndicated credits from the international banking system being the most common form of finance. The ratio of the current account deficit to national income varied between countries, but was typically in the 3 to 7 per cent range. The capital inflow from abroad accrued mainly to the public sector, with the syndicated credits being acceptable to bankers because they were claims on sovereign states, not risky private sector companies. The access to external finance enjoyed by Latin American countries in the late 1970s was a new phenomenon, made possible partly by the recycling of petrodollars, and gave them leeway to widen budget deficits without provoking inflation. By 1982 Brazil, Mexico and Argentina all had public sector deficits amounting to more than 15 per cent of gross national product. In the late 1970s a more typical figure would have been 10 per cent.

The ratios of domestically-held public sector debt to national income are uniformly low in Latin America, because of the profound scepticism with which government is regarded. In Brazil, which is fortunate compared to neighbouring countries because it has never suffered extreme political turmoil, there is a market in government debt. But it is small scale and short term, and is dominated by two instruments, national treasury indexed bonds (ORTNs) and national treasury bills (LTNs). In 1978 their total value was 357.5 billion cruzeiros, equal to about 10 per cent of national income, with 52.5 billion held by the central bank and the publicly-owned Banco de Brasil, and most of the remainder with the banking system. The situation in Brazil was typical and it would be reasonable to take 10 per cent as the debt to income ratio in

Latin American countries before the debt crisis. As a highly simplifed but nevertheless instructive exercise, we can insert the suggested values for the key ratios in our equation 3.2 to derive the steady-state inflation rate in Brazil in the late 1970s. It turns out to have been 42 per cent (see box 3.1 below). Actual inflation rates were similar, increasing from 29.2 per cent in 1975 to 77.2 per cent in 1979 but averaging 46.5 per cent over the five years.

The main effect of the debt crisis for Latin America was to curtail access to external finance. Although foreign creditors were sometimes prepared to add interest to loan principals and even to reschedule old debts, new money was available only in very limited amounts. The interest payments for some countries were so heavy that they continued to run current account deficits despite the achievement of large trade surpluses. But in the cases of Brazil and Mexico the current account was in balance or surplus in 1984. The improvement brought considerable relief to international bankers, many of whom judged that the debt crisis was largely overcome. However, this view was too

Box 3.1 Inflation in Brazil: steady-state outcomes before and after the debt crisis

After rearrangement and assuming the whole of the current account deficit to be financed by foreign purchases of public sector debt equation 3.2 gives

Inflation rate

$$= \frac{\text{Budget deficit to income ratio} - \text{Payments deficit to income ratio}}{\text{Debt to income ratio}} - \text{Growth rate}$$

(i) Inflation in Brazil before the debt crisis

Budget deficit to income ratio	=	10%
Debt to income ratio	=	10%
Current account deficit to income ratio	=	5%
Growth rate p.a.	=	8%

Inserting these values of the variables in the equation, inflation is 42% p.a.

(ii) Inflation in Brazil after the debt crisis

Budget deficit to income ratio	=	20%
Debt to income ratio	=	10%
Current account payments balanced		
Economic growth negligible		

Using these values of the variables in the same way, inflation is 200%

sanguine as it neglected the domestic inflationary consequences of the withdrawal of external finance. In Brazil the budget deficit rose to 20 per cent of national income in 1983 and 1984, mainly because maxi-devaluations to correct the payments deficit led to inflation, and inflation raised the costs of monetary correction on the national debt. We can again calculate the steady-state inflation rate implied by our equation. It is 200 per cent, not far from the actual rate of 220 per cent recorded in late 1984. Of course, comparison of steady-state, formula-derived solutions with real-world situations is rather mischievous. In the dynamics of real life it is not legitimate to treat the ratios as steady-state constants, and the process of change from one set of values of the ratios to another itself affects inflation. Nevertheless, the fit between the answers given by our approach and recorded inflation rates is suggestive. The low debt to income ratios in Latin America help to explain why budget deficits soon led to escalating inflation after the onset of the debt crisis.[7]

Reagonomics and Decelerating Inflation in the USA in the mid 1980s

The behaviour of inflation in the USA in the mid 1980s appears anomalous. The tax cuts associated with Reagonomics have resulted in large budget deficits and these budget deficits might have been expected to generate a higher rate of price increases. In fact, inflation has fallen sharply. How is this case accommodated within our analytical framework? Can the combination of an increased budget deficit and reduced inflation be reconciled with it?

Equation 3.2 shows that a higher budget deficit to income ratio may not lead to more inflation if the debt to income and foreign finance of the public sector (as a proportion of national income) increase. Both developments are to be observed in the USA in recent years. American government debt has risen faster than national income since 1981, with the result that the debt to income ratio has gone up from 30 per cent to over 40 per cent today. The public sector payments deficit is more awkward to handle. As direct foreign purchases of US government debt are a relatively small proportion of gross national product, they are not powerful enough by themselves to have influenced macroeconomic trends. But the net foreign acquisition of claims on the US private sector has been very large and this has made it possible for domestic savings to be channelled towards government debt on a substantial scale. In this indirect sense the whole current account deficit has been available to finance the budget deficit. The current account has moved from small surplus in the late 1970s to a deficit of about 3 per cent of national income today.

It could be argued that the changes in the debt to income ratio and the ratio of the current account deficit to income contribute to understanding the anomalous behaviour of American inflation. When President Carter was in office, low real interest rates, a weak dollar and a current account surplus were associated with 5 to 10 per cent inflation despite a modest budget deficit; under President Reagan high real interest rates, a strong dollar and a current account deficit have been accompanied by low inflation despite a budget deficit which is of record dimensions. But, although the relevance of the debt to income ratio and the payments position in any account of US inflation cannot be in doubt, it would be improper to insert the values of these variables in equation 3.2 to 'explain' changes in inflation between Carter and Reagan (see Box 3.2). The USA is not and never has been in a steady state. Its departure from such a condition is particularly obvious today, when the real interest rate on government debt is above the growth rate.

The most that can be said is that the plight of Latin America and the apparent initial success of Reagonomics can be analysed with the help of the variables highlighted here. The US government, which enjoys the favour of savers both domestically and internationally, can

Box 3.2 Inflation and budget deficits in the USA: President Carter's economics compared with Reaganomics

The same relationship applies as in Box 3.1

(i) Inflation in the USA under President Carter

Budget deficit to income ratio	=	2%
Debt to income ratio	=	30%
Current account deficit to income ratio	=	−1%
Growth rate p.a.	=	3%

Using the same procedure as in Box 3.1, inflation is 7%

(ii) Inflation in the USA under Reagonomics

Budget deficit to income ratio	=	5%
Debt to income ratio	=	40%
Current account deficit to income ratio	=	3%
Growth rate	=	3%

Inflation is 2%

run a large deficit with much less risk to itself than Latin American governments distrusted by their internal and external creditors.

THE MONETARY DIMENSION

The discussion of inflation so far has been very much in fiscal terms. This has been possible because of the trick of steady-state analysis, that – with ratios constant – rates of change become the focus of attention. It is particularly helpful, in considering the relationship between fiscal policy and inflation, to be able to fix the debt to income ratio. In the real world the debt to income ratio is variable and, although much can be said about its determinants, it can take a wide range of values. The more normal approach, which emphasizes the money supply as the main influence on the rate of price increases, gains its cogency from the empirically observed stability of the demand for money. The ratio of the money supply to national income is not constant, but it more closely approximates to constancy than the debt to income ratio.

However, there is not necessarily any conflict between the fiscal and monetary approaches. It can be shown that – if certain conditions are met – changes in the size of the budget deficit should be accompanied by changes in the rate of monetary expansion and that these changes should be in the same direction. The nexus between fiscal and monetary policy is nevertheless different in developed and developing countries.

In developed countries the banking system is technically sophisticated, relatively free from government regulation and frequently used by the majority of the population. Most bank deposits are held not for transactions purposes, but as a form of saving, and interest-bearing deposits are much larger than non-interest-bearing. Although emphases differ between countries, there is an obvious case for basing policy decisions, at least in part, on the behaviour of broad money aggregates. In Britain this has been the practice for almost a decade, with analysis in the City and Whitehall focused on the credit counterparts identity:

$$\Delta M_b = B - \Delta D^* + \Delta L - N - X \qquad (3.3)$$

Where M_b is broad money (sterling M3 in most British discussions), L is bank lending to the private sector, D^* is government debt held by the non-bank public, N is the change in non-deposit liabilities and X measures the impact of a variety of external transactions. N normally has little significance in the British context. (In West Germany it corresponds to the formation of 'monetary capital', such as the sale of bank bonds, and can be very large.) Since most developed countries do not rely on external finance over the long term, X also has no systematic tendency to be positive or negative and can be ignored. Then we have more briefly

$$\Delta M_b = B - \Delta D^* + \Delta L$$

Let D^* and L be constant as proportions a_3 and c respectively of national income. So, after taking differences in D^* and L, and dividing throughout by Y,

$$\frac{\Delta M_b}{M_b}\frac{M_b}{Y} = \frac{B}{Y} - a_3\frac{\Delta Y}{Y} + c\frac{\Delta Y}{Y}$$

If in equilibrium the rate of money supply growth, $\Delta M_b/M$, equals the rate of growth of national income, $\Delta Y/Y$, it follows that

$$\frac{\Delta M_b}{M_b} = \frac{1}{M_b/Y + a_3 - c}\frac{B}{Y} \qquad (3.4)$$

Equation 3.4 shows that the rate of money supply growth is a positive function of the budget deficit to income ratio if

$$\frac{M_b}{Y} + a_3 > c$$

This will always be true since the stock of broad money is higher than the outstanding bank advances total. It is also clear that, if three aspects of an economy's preferences (the money supply to income ratio, the debt to income ratio and the ratio of bank advances to income) are stable, an increase in the budget deficit to income ratio will be associated with an equiproportionate increase in the rate of growth of broad money. For a developed economy, with an advanced banking system and a high ratio of broad money to national income, there is no inconsistency between fiscal and monetary theories of inflation.

However, equation 3.4 is not particularly serviceable in the analysis of inflation in developing countries. As there is usually no meaningful market in government debt outside the banking system, the ratio of such debt to income, a_3, is low or negligible. Banks do, of course, lend to the private sector, but the backwardness of financial institutions – summed up in McKinnon's (1973) term 'financial repression' – prevents it being on a significant scale. As a result the ratio of bank lending to national income, c, is also low and can be quite volatile. Most bank deposits are held for transactions purposes, with narrow money (i.e. non-interest-bearing sight deposits) representing a high proportion of all money balances in the economy. In the poorest developing countries the financial system is so primitive that the central bank is both a major source of funds for the private sector and a dominant participant in the intermediation process. Narrow money is a low and stable multiple of the central bank's liabilities. The analysis of inflation can therefore be pursued by examining the forces behind the growth of these liabilities.[8]

Once again we can state a credit counterparts identity, this time for high-powered money:

$$\Delta H = B - \Delta D^{*} - \Delta D^{**} + \Delta L_h + \Delta R \qquad (3.5)$$

where H is high-powered money (assumed to account for all the central bank's liabilities), D^{**} is sales of government debt to the banking system, L_{h} is lending by the central bank to the private sector and R is the foreign exchange reserve. This can be rearranged in the same manner as the previous credit counterparts identity. Using the equilibrium property that the growth rate of high-powered money equals the growth rate of national income, we have

$$\frac{\Delta H}{H} = \frac{1}{H/Y + a_3 + a_4 - d - r}\,\frac{B}{Y} \qquad (3.6)$$

as the steady-state relationship between the budget deficit to income ratio and the growth of high-powered money, where D^{*}, D^{**}, L_{h} and R are constant as proportions a_3, a_4, d and r respectively of national income. Like its broad money analogue for developed countries, the relationship suggests that fiscal and monetary approaches to inflation are compatible. This is in agreement with some empirical work (Edwards, 1983, pp. 477–85). The link between budget deficits and monetary conditions may nevertheless be less reliable in developing countries than developed because the relevant ratios (of high-powered money, government debt, bank lending and foreign exchange reserves to national income) are more likely to fluctuate than, for example, the ratio of the money supply to national income. Much depends, as always, on the government's creditworthiness. If the reserves have been exhausted and opportunities to lend to the private sector have vanished (i.e. d and r are nil), the inflationary impact of deficit financing is determined by the values of the ratios of high-powered money and government debt to national income. If there is no trust in government, these ratios will be low, particularly by comparison with the money supply to income and debt to income ratios in developed countries. The lower are the ratios, the higher the inflation rate generated by any particular budget deficit to income ratio. This conclusion is in accord with our previous discussion, including the contrast between contemporary Latin America and the USA.[9]

VIII CONCLUSION: THE CASE FOR SOUND FINANCE

The main conclusions of this paper can be summarized briefly. The scope for deficit financing is constrained by medium- and long-term inflation dangers. These dangers can be avoided if a country incurs a payments deficit on current account, but there is a consequent vulnerability to the withdrawal of external finance. Indeed, as the recent experience of Latin America shows, a reduction in capital inflows from abroad may lead not only to a deterioration in living standards, but also – in the absence of effective action to cut budget deficits – to accelerating inflation. It is not misleading to claim that, when a government runs an excessive budget deficit, the choice is between two evils – inflation and a payments deficit.

A large budget deficit is easier to accommodate in a nation where savers, both at home and abroad, have confidence in the government's ability to service debt. For a number of reasons savers' trust in government, which is reflected in the debt to income ratio, is generally greater in developed countries than in developing. It follows that the unwelcome choice between inflation and external imbalance confronts policy makers more immediately in developing countries than in developed. The good fortune of the American government, which has been able to reconcile a large budget deficit with declining inflation because of a high and rising debt to income ratio, could not be enjoyed by the government of any developing country. However, savers' confidence in the governments of developed countries is not preordained and certain. It can be jeopardized by persistent financial irresponsibility. If budget deficits are too large for too long, an increase in the debt to income ratio may cause bondholders' claims to become intolerable to taxpayers and this obliges governments to reduce the real value of the debt by inflation.[10] Memories of inflation then reduce savers' willingness to hold government debt in future. As we have already seen that a low debt to income ratio limits the room for manoeuvre in fiscal policy, the implications are clear. A responsible approach to budgetary decisions is essential to the achievement of stable prices. This is in part because – with no inflation – only a small nominal increase in debt each year is consistent with a given debt to income ratio. But it is also, and perhaps more fundamentally, because inflationary episodes erode saver trust and so lead to a permanent reduction in the debt to income ratio. This drawback to deficit financing applies to both developed and developing countries.

NOTES

1 This relationship and the later one between the budget deficit to income ratio and the growth rate of broad money were discussed by Congdon (1984a).
2 Collection costs, and their implications for tariff regimes, are also discussed by Corden (1974).
3 Congdon (1985, ch. 2) describes this and other features of financial repression in the Latin American context.
4 Monti and Siracusano (1980) describe some features of the Italian situation. Recent developments in Spain (a developed country) and Indonesia (a developing) show how unreliable the schema may sometimes be. In Spain banks have increasingly been subject to 'coeficientes', prescribed ratios of approved public sector investments to total assets, to the point where a senior executive has asked 'Am I a banker at all? I am not allowed to be one' (Burns, 1985). (In 1982 the coeficientes were 31.75 per cent of deposits; in 1985 they had reached 51.5 per cent.) In Indonesia, by contrast, exchange controls have been relaxed and guidance on asset allocation has been eased. In June 1983 the central bank 'abolished ceilings on credit expansion, allowing banks to lend according to availability of funds and their own portfolio decisions' (Sherwell, 1984).
5 See Eshag (1983) for an example.
6 St John-Stevas (1978, p 419). The quotation is from an article on 'The danger of lending to semi-civilised countries' in *The Economist* of 23rd November 1867.
7 The argument here amplifies that by the author (Congdon, 1984b).
8 Many economists believe that in all economies inflation is driven by changes in the stock of high-powered money. The author's view is that this approach is not fruitful in advanced economies where bank deposits are a very high and not particularly stable multiple of high-powered money, and the most important feature of the money supply process is the effect of the extension of bank credit on broad money. See Congdon (1981a; 1981b) for a development of the argument that an integral part of technical progress in the financial system is the attempt to economize on the use of high-powered money. As a general rule, the ratios of high-powered money to national income are higher in developing countries than developed, whereas the ratios of broad money to national income are lower.
9 Or, indeed, the contrast between contemporary Argentina and Italy. In Argentina the ratio of government debt to national income is down to 3 or 4 per cent, but a budget deficit which is lower than Italy's as a share of national income can set in motion an inflation rate of almost 1,000 per cent. Italy is protected by its citizens' willingness to hold a government debt similar in size to national income. On the need for balanced budgets in Latin America, see Congdon (1985, 46–53). It should be mentioned that there is still an apparent conflict between the fiscal and monetary approaches to the determination of the inflation rate. In the fiscal section, $dn/db = 1/a$ where $n = \Delta Y/Y$. In the monetary section,

$$\frac{dn}{db} = \frac{1}{M/Y + a_3 - c}$$

This looks a bit odd. Actually, it is coherent. If we remember that M/Y is not very different from c in most developed economies and that government debt includes debt held by the banks and overseas as well as debt held by the domestic non-bank public (i.e. a is not equal to a_3), the difference between the two answers becomes less puzzling. (Note that, if $M/Y - c = a_4$, where a_4 is the banks' holdings of government debt, $M/Y + a_3 - c = a_4 + a_3 = a_1$.)

10 See Moggridge and Johnson (1972) 'An open letter to the French minister of finance (whoever he is or may be)', pp. 76–82, for Keynes' views on a problem of this kind in France in the 1920s. In Sargent and Wallace (1984), the constraint on the debt to income ratio is imposed by savings behaviour.

REFERENCES

Agtmael, A.W. van 1984: *Emerging Securities Markets*, Euromoney Publications, London, p. 56.

Bresciani-Turroni, C. 1937: *The Economics of Inflation*, tr. Mrs M.E. Sayers, Kelley, New York, pp. 46–7. (First published Italy, 1931.)

Burns, T. 1985: Hamstrung by syphoning of deposits, *Financial Times*, 3 April.

Congdon, T.G. 1981a: First principles of central banking, *The Banker*, 131, April, 57–62.

Congdon, T.G. 1981b: Is the provision of a sound currency a necessary function of the state, *National Westminster Quarterly Review*, August.

Congdon, T.G. 1984a: The analytical foundations of the medium-term financial strategy. In M. Keen (ed.) *The Economy and the 1984 Budget*, Blackwell, Oxford, for Institute of Fiscal Studies, pp. 17–29.

Congdon, T.G. 1984b: The debt crisis is not over, mimeo, Messel, 19 Sept.

Congdon, T.G. 1985: *Economic Liberalism in the Cone of Latin America*, Trade Policy Research Centre, London.

Corden, W.M. 1974: *Trade Policy and Economic Welfare*, Clarendon Press, Oxford, pp. 64–7.

Edwards, S. 1983: The short-run relaton between growth and inflation in Latin America: a comment, *American Economic Review*, 73, June, 477–85.

Eshag, E. 1983: *Fiscal and Monetary Policies and Problems in Developing Countries*, Cambridge University Press, Cambridge.

Little, I.M.D. 1982: *Economic Development*, Basic Books, New York, p. 117.

McKinnon, R.I. 1973: *Money and Capital in Economic Development*, Brookings Institution, Washington, DC, p. 68.

Moggridge, D. and Johnson, E. (eds) 1972: *The Collected Writings of John Maynard Keynes*, vol. 9, *Essays in Persuasion*, Macmillan, London.

Monti, M. and Siracusano, B. 1980: *The Public Sector's Financial Intermediation, the Composition of Credit and the Allocation of Resources*, Société Universitaire Européenne de Réchérches Financières, Tilburg.

St John-Stevas, N. (ed.) 1978: *The Collected Works of Walter Bagehot*, The Economist, London, p. 419.

Sargent, T.J. and Wallace, N. 1984: Some unpleasant monetarist arithmetic. In B. Griffiths and G.E. Woods (eds), *Monetarism in the United Kingdom*, Macmillan, London, pp. 15–40.

Sherwell, C. 1984: Quiet revolution in monetary policy, *Financial Times*, 30 April.

PART II
Case Studies

4
Appraising the American Fiscal Stance

EDMUND S. PHELPS

I INTRODUCTION

The 1980s have seen a massive decrease in world saving, and thus in aggregate world investment. Behind that fact is a variegated pattern: there has been a huge structural decrease in public saving, especially in the United States – an important case because of its large scale – and also, on a smaller scale, in Italy and a few countries in Scandinavia. Most of the deficits elsewhere are cyclical, not structural. (But whether structural or cyclical there has resulted a huge increase in public debt.) Further, there has been no offsetting increase of private saving, despite a rise of the world real interest rate. There has been a cyclical fall of private saving.

What are the consequences of this pattern? What are the benefits and costs for America? For Europe and the others? Ought Europe to imitate America's fiscal policy? These are the questions confronting us. Here I can only throw out some ideas, and express the hope and expectation that many other insights will emerge.

II THE COSTS AND BENEFITS TO AMERICA

For America there have been real benefits, and costs of course, from the deficit spending and also from the tax incentives generously offered for investment by American firms. For America there has probably been a balance of benefits over costs. To endorse that conclusion is not to endorse the theories of the supply-side economists, since *our* reasons for reaching that conclusion might not be *their* reasons and *our* policy prescriptions might differ significantly from *theirs*.[1] (Nor is it implied that their reasons were Reagan's motives.)

The evaluation of the American fiscal stance must recognize the unusual setting in which the tax cuts have developed. There has been a forceful and unremitting attack on inflation by the monetary authorities since late 1980. The tax cut instalments were decided upon in 1981 and later revised or endorsed in 1982 and 1983, years when the tight-money policy was exerting a strong contractionary effect on employment and upon investment.

Reduction of Inflation

One benefit from the fiscal shift is that it seems to have caused a real appreciation of the dollar and a consequent 'setback' in the ascent of the price level. Insofar as this pause of the price level then slowed workers' wage demands, there has resulted a 'permanent' slowing of the wage trend and price trend. Thus less monetary tightening and less unemployment have been required for the disinflation achieved than would otherwise have been needed.

It might be objected that these price-level and inflation reductions are only as permanent as the extraordinary budgetary deficit, and once the deficit is ended the path of the price index and the trend inflation rate will rebound to their former levels. The benefit from the deficit is thus borrowed against the future, not earned. It may well be that the inflation improvement is more fundamental, however. To support this claim I would appeal to the incomplete spread of indexation of wages to prices. The unexpected slow-down, or deceleration, of the price trend causes an unexpected slow-down of the already-negotiated indexed wages; so the unindexed wages when renegotiated will be *cut* to regain their unexpected loss of competitiveness. Thus there is a second round of deceleration of prices and wages. This after-effect is important because it permits the fiscal stance to return to normal without completely undoing its accomplishment![2] However, it may well be that most of the appreciation of the dollar cannot be credited to the general cut of taxes, which accounts for most of the public dissaving; perhaps most of the appreciation was due to the upward pull on American real interest rates from the 1981 investment tax incentives.[3] The 200 billion dollar deficit is not cost-effective in this view.

Replying to the objection that the benefit is borrowed from the future, defenders of the fiscal stimulus can also argue that there *is* a gain provided the stimulus is phased out gradually so as to 'smooth' the costs of the disinflation.

Effect on Labour Supply

Another likely benefit to the United States from the American tax cut involves the supply of labour. Indeed the effect of tax reduction on labour supply was the mainspring in the founding supply siders' original theory as told to Wanniski (1981). We are to suppose that higher pay provides an incentive to work more – that an increase of after-tax wage rates brought by an income tax cut elicits a corresponding increase in the amount of labour supplied; this is the way the world works. Consequently a tax cut will slow down wage rates by boosting the level of unemployment from the supply side of the labour market. (A colossal tax cut might even force a fall of wages, requiring easier money and increased employment, not tighter money, to stabilize prices.) Anyone can see that it would be better to recruit volunteers to wage the war against (wage) inflation than to conscript job holders on some seniority or other discriminatory basis; this way, the voluntary way, the combatants against inflation are self-selecting. But the premise is troubling: what if the supply of labour is, at least locally, quite inelastic with respect to after-tax wage rates or even backward bending? A supply-side answer is that in the Republican world of dynastic families, secure in their ancestral homesteads and buttressed by their faith, there is no income effect from a tax cut which would (taken alone) make people work less: people know they or their heirs must pay their share of the government sooner or later, one way or another. A more plausible answer, in any case, is that the tax cut will be seen as temporary (which, in large part, it probably is), so that people have every reason to take advantage of the *relative* improvement of current rewards, working more now and less later. (It is also true that better after-tax rewards for above-ground jobs will draw people out of underground work, and that will increase the total supply of output.)

Inflation and Disinflation

A third benefit from the tax cut relates to a famous problem concerning inflation and disinflation. In his 1939 study of the German hyperinflation Bresciani-Turroni noted that inflation raises nominal interest rates and reduces real cash balances, while ending the inflation does the reverse. If the Federal Reserve abruptly halted the growth in the supply of money, in order to signal its disinflationary desires, the ensuing drop of nominal interest rates entailed by reduced inflation expectations would (if actually realized immediately) cause a jump in the amount of money demanded – a rush from goods back into money

– and thus force a contraction of income and employment until supply and demand were again equal. A general tax cut (necessarily a temporary one in an essentially stationary economy) meets this problem in two ways. By reducing the tax rate on interest income it helps to hold up the after-tax interest rate of which the demand for money is a function. By creating expectations of 'crowding out', and thus a one-time rise of the price level as a result, it moderates and cushions the fall of before-tax interest rates that would otherwise be entailed by money-supply stabilization. And tax cuts that raise the real interest rates that businesses can pay likewise serve to cushion before-tax nominal interest rates.[4] Of course, the tax cut had better be 'phased out' gradually, not abruptly if the problem of a sudden drop of interest rates is to be surmounted, not merely deferred.

Compensation and Future Generations

A fourth benefit is little discussed. Since the disinflation exercise of the Federal Reserve entailed a big slump in employment and income it is appropriate that the generation suffering this misfortune receive some compensation in the form of deficit-financed tax relief and transfer payments even if that move will come at the expense of future generations. The argument here is similar to that in favour of deficit financing of the public outlays to conduct a war, which goes back at least to Ricardo. I believe the argument is valid under the intergenerational welfare criterion called utilitarian – the Ramsey sum-of-utilities criterion – as well as under the Rawlsian 'maximin' criterion, which in this context calls for equal sharing among the generations. Of course this is not an argument for an indefinite, undiminishing deficit.[5]

Tax Incentives

I would not like to leave this topic without making a point that relates to the 1981 investment tax incentives rather than to tax cuts *strictu sensu*. I never expected I would have a good word for them, but I find now I do. These tax incentives may have played an important role in dampening the recession, or dip, in the capital stock that would otherwise have resulted from the central bank exercise in disinflation. The desirability of that seems an obvious truth: who can be against stabilization of anything, especially the sacred capital stock! Then it seems like an obvious error: doesn't the marketplace (even if only in America) determine the right volume of investment, assuring that the marginal product of capital stays equal to the world cost of capital (or world real interest rate)? But that optimistic view overlooks the side effect of the capital stock on employment in a sticky money-wage or even sticky real-wage open economy: the unemployment first created by the impact of disinflationary monetary policy is magnified by the erosion of the capital stock it precipitates. It was beneficial for the United States to check this decline with tax inducements.

I have identified five benefits to the United States from the loose fiscal stance taken in the early 1980s. Alongside these national benefits stand two national costs. One arises from the loss of national wealth, and hence of 'potential' national income, resulting from the budgetary deficits – especially the personal income tax cuts, less so the fiscal investment stimulants (which operated to back added foreign indebtedness with added domestic capital).[6] The other national cost is less easily measured. It is the worth, or shadow-cost, of the customers lost to American firms in overseas markets resulting from the fiscal stimulus and the associated appreciation of the dollar.[7] I have suggested that the national benefits outweighed the national costs in the early 1980s. But costs intensify and benefits erode, so a gradual phasing out of the fiscal stance is indicated.

III EFFECTS ON THE REST OF THE WORLD

One of the most difficult questions about the American deficit is its effects on the rest of the world. One would guess, at first blush, that the effect of the deficit and particularly of the investment tax incentives on the real rate of interest calculated in terms of the representative basket of goods produced in America has been a great blow to the debtor nations, Mexico, Brazil, Argentina and the rest. In the rosiest scenario this blow will force them to produce with industry and efficiency as never before, almost as if a war had cost them much of their wealth. (Recall the effects on Britain of the loss of its overseas income after the second world war: two decades of saving and hard work until the Beatles.) In the bleakest scenario this blow will destabilize their governments. There is also the resulting appreciation of the dollar, which harms the debtor nations to the extent that their debts are fixed in dollars and to the extent that the real prices (in terms of Latin exports) of the American exports that the debtors import – in short, America's terms of trade – have been driven up as a result. I confess I do not understand the calculation that says the real depreciation of pesos and cruzeiros makes it easier for the debtor countries to export, though I can understand that the contribution of the American deficit to American employment and income is a plus for Latin America.[8] However we come out on these effects, it is beginning to seem rather uncertain that the real interest bill of the debtor nations will be genuinely paid, as distinct from being capitalized, which means borrowing always to 'pay' the interest. The major price paid by the debtor countries may turn out to be the political problems and diversion caused.

For Europe the effects are more problematic. It can be argued that the real appreciation of the dollar resulting from the American fiscal actions, hence the real depreciation in Europe, has raised the wage demands of European labour in terms of European goods – the real wage rigidity hypothesis. Then there is the dollar-price-of-oil rigidity hypothesis, however plausible or implausible it may be. But why should a deficit-caused real appreciation of the dollar be associated with a rise in the real prices, as measured in European goods, of imported goods (final or intermediate) consumed by European workers? A real appreciation of the dollar does not necessarily raise the real price of American exports of consumer goods or other goods. Such a rise could have resulted to the extent that the tax cuts crowded out American exports of some goods – wheat? aircraft? computers? – and in so doing raised appreciably their market-clearing prices. Such a rise could also have resulted to the extent that American exporters operate in customer markets and (like a Phelps–Winter firm) refuse at first to obey the 'law of one price'. It seems likely, however, that the real appreciation of the dollar is in large part a failure of the prices of non-tradable construction and services to fall *pari passu* with the cost of foreign exchange, and to that extent it cannot precipitate new wage demands in Europe.

Another effect works to stimulate European employment. It can be argued that the real interest rate rise caused by the investment tax incentives spells higher nominal interest rates in Europe, given the paths of the European money supplies, and this must cause dishoarding, a rise of the price level and a nominal (even if not real) depreciation in Europe; producers will respond with increased output for export abroad, in part to American firms importing machinery at a faster rate. True, this European 'boom' will be temporary, but natural rate doctrine says that every fluctuation of employment is temporary. More accurately, the effect will only be to speed up recovery in Europe from the slump caused by the monetary disinflation in the United States, a recovery that would have taken place anyway according to natural rate theory; of course the 'speeding up' dwindles as nominal wages adjust.

Perhaps the most serious indictment of the American fiscal stance is that it has artificially diverted capital investment to America (where there would have been none, the incentives being absent) from Europe and elsewhere in the rest of the world. By what rights did the United

States do that? Had the American government established a huge subsidy for purchases of paintings or for world-class performances of grand opera, the rest of the world would have risen up in indignation at the unfair reallocation of resources. There is a 'beggar-thy-neighbour' aspect to the American fiscal manoeuvre.

IV SHOULD EUROPE ADOPT THE AMERICAN FISCAL STANCE?

What is sauce for the goose is sauce for the gander. In its quest to extricate itself from its long slump would there not be large benefits to Europe if it chose to adopt the American fiscal stance? Moreover, turnabout is fair play. So wouldn't it be just to do so?

Before beginning we ought to note that the European countries are not scale replicas of America, in structure and situation, so we should not expect cost–benefit comparisons to yield exactly the American results. A European country that adopted the American fiscal stance could find a lesser appreciation or even no appreciaton of its currency, since investors might attempt a flight from the country's assets in anticipation of the risks of subsequent extraordinary taxation or other terrors. A European country that is not facing inflation would derive less benefit from supply-side measures.

Let us confine our analysis to one choice: either Europe will adopt the 'loose' fiscal stance and America will be encouraged to maintain the same stance, with both phasing it out over several years, or Europe rejects this policy and America proceeds to phase out its present fiscal stance over a brief period of transition.

If all or most countries were to adopt the American fiscal stance, and likewise use monetary policy to keep a tight rein on the money supply or perhaps the money wage level, the fall of national *wealth* in the 'average' country would be approximately matched by a fall of domestic *capital*. Further, the decline in the capital stock located in a country would lower its wage income and thus induce a further fall of its national wealth. So there is a kind of multiplier process. We do not know how much crowding out of world capital a given (temporary) world deficit can do.

The simple analytics of this process are captured by figure 4.1. The diagram there refers to the representative country and shows how its stationary-state desired national wealth – the number of capital shares it owns at home and abroad, denoted by S – is a function of the amount of domestic capital, K, that the international capital has allocated to it. A temporary deficit, by stimulating a higher level of consumption at any level of domestic capital and initial level of national wealth,

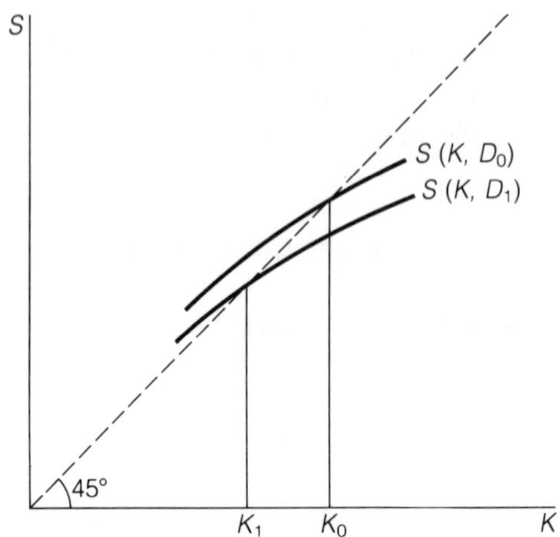

Figure 4.1 Deficit finance in the representative country lowers saving and equilibrium capital

causes national wealth to sink towards a lower steady-state level corresponding to the given *K*; the *S* curve shifts down. But the representative country's *K* must equal its *S*, since it is neither a net creditor nor debtor. So there must follow a movement down the *S* curve, possibly converging to the new intersection point as shown. (The diagram reveals a further possibility. The fall of wealth and capital may fail to be convergent.)

One conclusion, then, is that the adoption, by all, of the American fiscal stance might lead the world much farther down the road to reduced capital. It is better from this perspective that America gradually phase out its deficit than that Europe respond in kind.

Yet this conclusion is unsatisfactory. If the foregoing analysis (section III) is right, phasing out the present fiscal stance in America does not promise a lessening of the unemployment in Europe. On the one hand, the resulting worldwide fall of nominal interest rates would worsen European unemployment. On the other hand, the real appreciation and capital-investment reflux in Europe would tend to shrink European unemployment. So there arises the nagging question of what Europe can do to pull itself out of its long slump. If an exogenous jump of the money supply or a devaluation is excluded as inconsistent with price-level objectives, and if general tax cuts or expenditure increases are not cost-effective, what recourse is left? Are we driven back to a tax cut as the lesser of two evils? A way out of this dilemma, it seems, is a fiscal policy designed to reduce the cost of production for firms. If beggar-my-neighbour investment subsidies (not to mention higher tariffs and export subsidies) are resisted, that leaves employment subsidies paid to firms. By reducing the supply-price of consumer goods, employment subsidies for the hire of low-wage labour would tend to increase real cash balances and thus to permit higher employment with no higher (and perhaps lower) price level. Whatever the particulars, it seems important to get away from conceiving of optimum fiscal policy as the choice of the tax revenue level and thus of the budget deficit. Choosing the structure of tax rates and subsidies is another dimension, and perhaps a more important dimension, of fiscal policy.

NOTES

1 The doctrine was first advanced, though without supporting analysis, by Mundell (1971). There have been subsequent analyses by Rodriguez (1978), Phelps (1982), Hoel (1982) and Sachs (1985).
2 The structure of the argument is the ingenious invention of Jeffrey Sachs (1985), although Sachs's own model makes unindexed wages depend upon price expectations, not wage expectations as here.
3 Phelps (1985) argues that only the investment incentives legislated in 1981 can explain the world-wide rise of real interest rates.
4 Rodriguez (1978) proves that the reverse assignment, in which fiscal policy is assigned to price-level stabilization, does not permit monetary policy to stabilize unemployment.
5 John Flemming in chapter 15 suggests a variation on this theme. The optimum tax rate decreases when the central bank has to wage 'war' against inflation.
6 In this connection it is often said that the stimulative effect upon domestic employment of budget deficits weakens as they transfer a mounting level of national wealth to foreign hands. There may be an element of old-fashioned textbook truth there, provided the enriched foreigners are less disposed to buy the 'domestic goods' than the impoverished nationals. But the weakness or absence of demand-side effects from fiscal stimulus are not generally relevant from the supply-side, or optimum-mix, perspective, since monetary policy can add to them.
7 See Phelps (1984) for a macro model of this phenomenon.
8 The same taxonomy has been reached independently by Dornbusch (1985) with the exception of my last point, which is that Latins selling in American customer markets benefit from increased demand since their prices are not competed down to marginal cost.

REFERENCES

Dornbusch, R. 1985: *Policy and Performance Links (sic) Debtor LDCs and Industrial Countries.* MIT, mimeo, 62 pp., 3 Sept.
Hoel, M. 1982: Short and long-run effects of a tax cut in an open economy

with a sticky real wage, *Scandinavian Journal of Economics*, 84, 555–69.

Mundell, R.A. 1971: The dollar and the policy mix: 1971. In *Essays in International Finance*, No. 85, Princeton University, International Finance Section.

Phelps, E.S. 1982: A fail-safe design for disinflation, *Atlantic Economic Journal*, 10, 41–43.

Phelps, E.S. 1984: 'Customer market' ed effetti delle politiche fiscali in un economia aperta, *Rassegna Economica*, 48, 1911–1210; The significance of customer markets for the effects of budgetary policy in open economies, *Institute for International Economic Studies, Seminar Paper Series No. 315*. University of Stockholm.

Phelps, E.S. 1985: The real interest rate quiz, *Atlantic Economic Journal*, 13.

Rodriguez, C.A. 1978: A simple Keynesian model of inflation and unemployment under rational expectations. *Weltwirtschaftliches Archiv*, 114, 1–11.

Sachs, J.D. 1985: The dollar and the policy mix: 1985, *Brookings Papers on Economic Activity*, 1, 117–97.

Wanniski, J. 1978: *The Way the World Works: How Economics Fails and Succeeds*, Basic Books, New York.

5

Government Deficits: The Case of the United States

RUDOLPH G. PENNER

I INTRODUCTION

In the fiscal year 1984 the United States total unified budget deficit amounted to $185 billion or 5.2 per cent of the GNP. While this figure represents a reduction of $23 billion from the fiscal year 1983, we currently project the deficit will again rise to $210 billion in 1985, or 5.5 per cent of the GNP.[1] Very high deficits have persisted despite the fact that we are in the third year of an economic recovery.

The budget outlook will improve markedly if the three-year plan passed by the Congress in July of 1985 is implemented. Assuming real growth averaging about 3.5 per cent per year from the end of 1985 through the end of 1990 and inflation and interest rates that remain more or less constant through the period, the deficit will fall absolutely, reaching a level of about $120 billion in the fiscal year 1990. The fall relative to GNP is, of course, even more dramatic with the deficit to GNP ratio declining from 5.5 per cent in 1985 to 2.1 per cent in 1990.

Recent very large deficits will leave a legacy of significant long-term costs to the economy. This chapter will argue that it has imposed short-run adjustment costs as well, as the industrial composition of the economy has had to adjust to the pressures created while the deficit absorbed national savings and attracted capital from abroad. Ironically, short-term adjustment costs will accrue again if the recently passed budget plan is implemented. The recent changes in the sectoral composition of the economy will, to some extent, have to be reversed as we return to a more historically normal fiscal policy.

The author would like to thank Kathy Ormiston who collected the data for and drafted considerable portions of the manuscript. Thanks are also due to the staffs of the Fiscal and Budget Analysis Divisions of the Congressional Budget Office who provided valuable assistance. Robert Dennis, Matthew Salomon, C.G. Nuckols, and Andrew Haughwout were particularly helpful.

These conjectures must, however, be put forward with a great deal of uncertainty. Because of the recent disarray in macro-economic theory, it is impossible to document the effects of budget deficits in a precise or a non-controversial manner. Moreover, short-run fluctuations in economic variables during the postwar period are dominantly associated with business cycles. This makes it extremely difficult to isolate the impact of changes in the federal budget deficit which is, itself, strongly affected by the business cycle.

Before discussing changes in the composition of the economy I shall describe the federal spending and receipts trends that led up to the huge deficits of the early 1980s. I shall then discuss movements in some of the major components of the overall public and private savings-investment identity.

Discussions of identities obviously do not lead automatically to conclusions about causality. The trends are, however, highly suggestive and the chapter concludes with some hypotheses regarding the major macro-economic and sectoral forces unleashed as the US budget deficit grew dramatically in the early 1980s.

A Brief History of the Upward Trend in Deficits

In order to show where we are and how we got here it is first necessary to present an overview of the upward trends in federal deficits. It is a short history, because prior to the Great Depression most deficits in the United States were the result of financing wars; in peacetime, surpluses were common and used to retire debt incurred during the war years. According to Ornstein (1985), 'without the deficits caused by the War of 1812, the Mexican War, the Civil War, the Spanish–American War, the federal government would have had a $1.6 billion surplus at the beginning of the twentieth century. Without the deficits caused by the two world wars, it would have had a debt of under $30 billion – or less than 5 per cent of GNP – in 1961.'

The Depression period saw very large federal deficits, more the result of depressed income than of discretionary moves toward fiscal stimulus. After the Korean War, when economic activity was strong and recessions were minor compared with the Depression, there was a marked change from prewar behaviour: deficits became common and, by the 1960s, surpluses were a rare exception. On average, there was a small surplus in the NIPA-based federal accounts in the 1950s and a small deficit in the 1960s. However, even the Vietnam build-up in defence spending and the beginning of Great Society social spending did not produce deficit to GNP ratios of more than 1.6 per cent in any year. The story changed again with the recession of 1974: since then deficits have reached a share of GNP previously matched only in wartime or during the Depression, and there has been no surplus since 1969. Deficits averaged 1 per cent of GNP in the early 1970s, over 2 per cent of GNP in the second half of the 1970s, and 3.9 per cent in the first half of the 1980s (table 5.1).

The budget numbers discussed above are defined according to the national income and product accounts (NIPA) basis for calendar years and as a result, the deficit measures the extent to which the federal government draws on national and international savings flows. In the United States, public discussion and legislative debates focus on what is called the unified budget for the fiscal year beginning 1 October. It is essentially a cash flow budget that includes net lending and is therefore not useful for measuring governmental effects on savings flows. It is, however, more convenient for discussing individual programmes. The unified and NIPA aggregates – outlays, receipts, and the deficit – tend to move together very closely. Both concepts are used in this paper with heaviest reliance placed on the NIPA definitions.

A better understanding of the causes of the deficit expansion can be gained by examining changes in unified budget outlays and revenues over the same period. By far the most important change occurred on the spending side as total on- and off-budget outlays increased between fiscal year 1960 and 1984 – from 18.5 per cent to 23.8 per cent of GNP. Payments to individuals grew at an even faster pace, rising from 4.9 per cent to 11.2 per cent. However, the difference between growth in outlays and growth in payments to individuals was more than made up

Table 5.1 *Federal deficit as percentage of GNP, 1950–84*

	Unified on- and off-budget deficit (fiscal years)	*NIPA deficit (calendar years)*
1950–59	0.4	−0.1[a]
1960–69	0.8	0.3
1970–74	1.2	1.2
1975–79	3.1	2.4
1980	2.9	2.3
1981	2.7	2.2
1982	4.2	4.8
1983	6.4	5.4
1984	5.2	4.8

[a] Surplus.

Sources: *Historical Tables, Budget of the United States Government Fiscal Year 1986*, US Department of Commerce, Bureau of Economic Analysis.

for by a long-term fall in defence from 9.7 per cent of GNP in 1960 to 5.9 per cent of GNP in 1984. (Defence had, however, fallen to as low as 4.9 per cent in 1979.) Interest payments grew from 1.4 per cent to 2.5 per cent of GNP and the off-budget category, which did not exist in 1968, amounted to 0.3 per cent of GNP in 1984. All other expenditures remained constant at 2.7 per cent. It is interesting to note that the 'other' category peaked between 1980 and 1981 at 3.4 per cent. To the extent that President Reagan and the Congress were able to exercise budget stringency, it focused on the 'other' category.

The increase in payments to individuals over the period is often associated with the development of the Great Society under President Johnson. However, 2.7 of the 6.3 percentage point rise (or 42 per cent) is associated with the expansion of Social Security, a New Deal rather than a Great Society programme. Traditional programmes such as unemployment insurance and civil service pensions account for another 5 per cent of the expansion. The most important Great Society health programmes – Medicare and Medicaid – account for 36 per cent. Other new welfare programmes created in the Johnson, Nixon and Ford administrations account for only 11 per cent of the increase. These include benefits for disabled coal miners; supplemental security income (SSI); food stamps; women, infants and children, and other nutrition assistance programmes, and new programmes for housing.

In the 16 years between 1960 and 1976, there was no significant trend in the average tax burden as measured by the unified budget receipts to GNP ratio. It stood at 18.6 per cent in 1960, fell to 17.7 per cent in 1965 after the Kennedy–Johnson tax cuts, and then rose to 20.5 per cent in 1969 with the imposition of the temporary Vietnam surtax. The ratio fell to 18.1 per cent in 1971 when the surtax was removed. After reaching a level of 18.2 per cent in 1976, the ratio began a strong five year upward trend as the legislated tax cuts of 1977 and 1979 failed to offset the bracket creep caused by inflation and the economic recovery. A post World War II record of 20.8 per cent was attained in 1981, not far below 1944's wartime record of 21.9 per cent. The implementation of the early stages of the Reagan tax cuts, along with the severe recession's impact on corporate profits, lowered the ratio to 18.6 per cent in 1984.

In fact, in the shorter run, a very large part of the rapid rise in the deficit between 1981 and 1983 was the result of the deep recession of 1982. During this period, however, the structural deficit was put on an upward course as well, and consequently, the deficit to GNP ratio responded very little to the vigorous recovery during calendar years 1983 and 1984. The structural deficit moved upwards partly because defence spending was put on a strong upward trend during the period and partly because the large cyclical component of the deficit indirectly raised the structural deficit as a result of its effect on the interest bill on the national debt.

Deficits to Gross Private Saving Ratio

Another way to see the extent to which federal deficits have grown in relative terms is to compare NIPA deficits to gross private saving. These data give us a better idea of the stress federal government borrowing has put on credit markets.

Table 5.2 shows the numbers are nothing short of astonishing. Government borrowing as a share of gross private savings has risen quite sharply over the last few years – from 12.5 per cent in 1981 to a high of 31.2 per cent in 1983.

Table 5.2 *Government deficit (NIPA) as a percentage of gross private saving (calendar years)*

Year	
1950–59	−0.8[a]
1960–69	1.7
1970–74	7.3
1975–79	13.7
1980	14.1
1981	12.6
1982	28.3
1983	31.2
1984	2.1

[a] Surplus.
Source: US Department of Commerce, Bureau of Economic Analysis.

Stability of the Debt to GNP Ratio

Public debt as a percentage of GNP fell until the mid 1970s. In 1974 the ratio reached its postwar minimum; it then rose a bit, flattened during the late 1970s and then accelerated rapidly during the 1980s (figure 5.1). Currently, the ratio continues to rise. The new budget plan would, however, imply that the ratio declines after fiscal year 1987.

Many economists argue that movements in the debt to GNP ratio provide a better indication of the long-term pressures imposed on

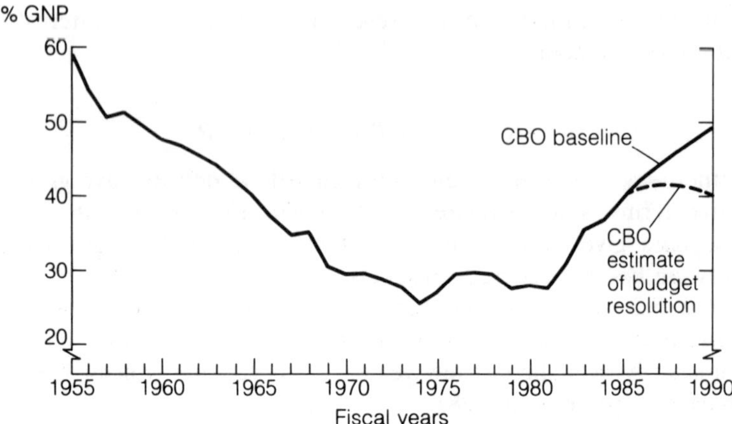

Figure 5.1 Federal debt held by the public (Source: Congressional Budget Office) Note: extrapolated by CBO in 1989 and 1990

interest rates than movements in the deficit to GNP ratio. (Ideally, a debt to wealth ratio should be used, but wealth data are unsatisfactory and here the debt to GNP ratio is used as a convenient proxy.) If true, this hypothesis represents bad news, because, as just noted, the debt to GNP ratio can be expected to rise through 1987 while the deficit to GNP ratio should start to fall in 1986.

The importance of the debt to GNP ratio has been particularly emphasized by Benjamin Friedman. In his paper 'Managing the U.S. government deficit in the 1980s' (Friedman, 1984) he found increases and decreases in federal debt to GNP have been accompanied by approximately offsetting changes in non-federal debt as a percentage of GNP. Similarly, Leeuw and Holloway (1983) showed in their paper, 'The measurement and significance of the cyclically-adjusted federal budget', that growth trends in the federal debt to GNP ratio appear to have been mirrored by opposite trends in the capital output ratio (see also Congressional Budget Office, 1984).

The empirical evidence on these matters is, however, very murky. Many studies fail to find statistically significant evidence of an interest rate impact of either the deficit or debt to GNP ratios (see Barth et al., 1984). Some theoreticians argue that there should be no relationship since the public may regard public debt as a perfect substitute for private debt and adjust their private saving behaviour accordingly (Barro, 1974). I believe it fair to say, however, that this represents a minority view in the economics profession.

Nevertheless, there is one aspect of a continually rising debt to GNP ratio that should be non-controversial. That is that there is a danger that the interest bill on the rising debt may become so large that it may become increasingly difficult to prevent the debt from exploding as it grows and feeds on itself. The probability of an interest bill explosion, of course, rises dramatically if interest rates rise as the debt to GNP ratio rises (Miller, 1983). To be more specific, if the nominal interest rate equals the growth rate of nominal GNP, then a deficit which is exactly equal to the interest bill implies a constant debt to GNP ratio. A deficit lower than this amount results in a falling debt to GNP ratio, while a deficit which is higher results in a rising debt to GNP ratio. If the interest bill begins to explode as a result of an exploding debt to GNP ratio, there is little choice but to begin financing government expenditures with money rather than debt creation. The end result must be hyperinflation.

At the beginning of 1984 CBO projections of the deficits, consistent with the policies then in effect, implied that the US was on an explosive path. This result occurred, in part, because nominal interest rates were projected to be close to GNP growth rates thus implying that stability required a deficit less than the interest bill. But deficits far higher than the interest bill, i.e. large primary deficits, were projected. Deficit reducing measures enacted during 1984 brought the system close to stability. Our most recent projection (August 1985) both lowered interest rates and showed that the policies planned for the fiscal year 1986 and beyond by the new budget resolution will eventually imply a significant primary surplus. Thus, it seems that we are well off the explosive path in the longer run.[2] But any one of a number of things could go wrong. Interest rates could be higher than expected; a severe recession could cause the primary deficit to shift from a surplus to deficit position; and Congress may not implement all of the deficit reducing measures implied by their most recent budget plan. In other words, there is not a significant margin of safety in our current fiscal policy and much remains to be done.

Net Saving and Investment Flows

One of the more interesting economic changes of the last five years has been the change in the components of saving (table 5.3; figure 5.2). Since 1950, net private savings in the US economy have averaged about 7.2 per cent of GNP. State and local governments also registered a small surplus in most years. Foreign investment was usually negligible until the 1980s. Federal deficits absorbed about 1.1 per cent of GNP on a national income accounts basis, leaving total private and public

Table 5.3 Net savings and investment flows as a percentage of GNP (NIPA basis)

	(1) Net private domestic savings	(2) State and local surplus	(3) Federal deficit	(4) Net domestic savings available for domestic investment (1)+(2)−(3)	(5) Net private domestic investment	(6) Net domestic savings shortfalls (5)−(4)= net foreign investment
1950–59	7.2	−0.2	−0.1	7.0	7.1	0.1
1960–69	7.8	0	0.3	7.5	7.0	−0.6
1970–79	7.2	0.8	1.8	6.3	6.4	0.1
1980–82	5.6	1.2	3.1	3.7	3.7	0.0
1983	5.9	1.3	5.4	1.8	2.9	1.0
1984	7.4	1.4	4.8	4.1	6.4	2.3
1985 (first half)	7.0	1.6	4.8	3.7	6.1	2.4
Average 1950–84	7.2	0.4	1.1	6.4	6.4	0.0

Details may not appear consistent with totals because of rounding.
Source: US Department of Commerce, Bureau of Economic Analysis.

saving available for domestic investment equal to about 6.4 per cent of GNP. In the 1980s, however, available domestic savings have fallen sharply, and a large part of domestic investment has been financed by net foreign investment. Net private domestic saving fell sharply during the recessionary period of 1980–82, but has since recovered. The surplus of state and local governments is much higher than its historical level. But these favourable movements are more than offset by the massive increase in the federal deficit, so that total net domestic saving dropped from a historical range of about 6 to 7.5 per cent of GNP to a 2 to 4 per cent range in the early 1980s. Net private domestic investment, after the end of the recession, recovered to close to its historical average. Thus net foreign investment, which had been on average an insignificant source of funds for domestic investment through 1979, rose to nearly 3 per cent of GNP in 1984 and early 1985.

Net Private Domestic Saving

Gross saving by American individuals and corporations increased in the early 1980s, and particularly during the first two years of recovery from the recent recession. The gross private domestic saving share of

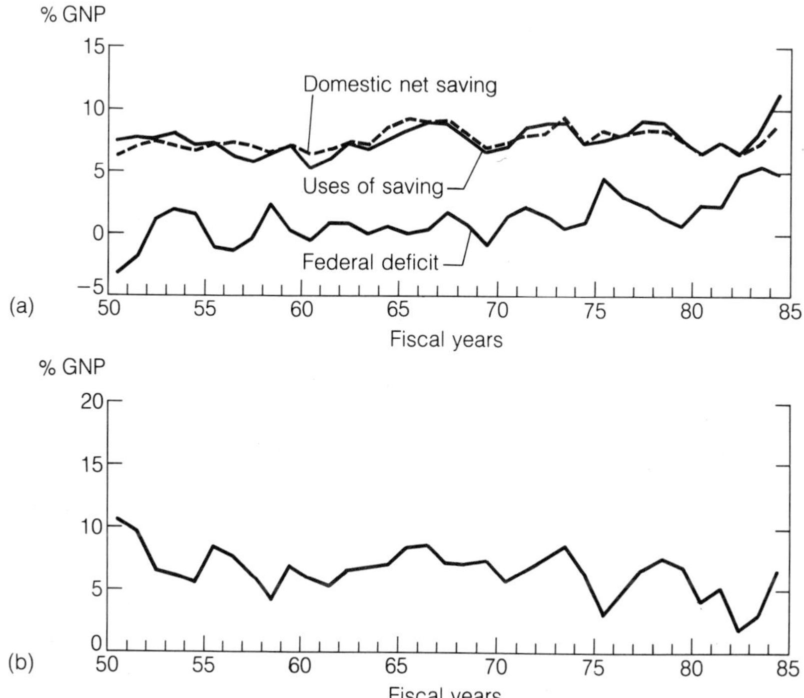

Figure 5.2 (a) Net savings and investment flows (b) net domestic investment (Sources: US Department of Commerce, Bureau of Economic Analysis, Congressional Budget Office)

Note: Domestic saving is net non-federal domestic saving (columns 1 and 2 in table 5.3). Uses of saving is net domestic investment plus the federal deficit (columns 3 and 5 in table 5.3). The difference between domestic net saving and the federal deficit is the amount of domestic savings left for private domestic investment.

GNP was nearly 19 per cent in mid 1984, a level previously exceeded only once. It has dropped sharply in the first half of 1985, but this may in part be a reflection of the unusual delay in processing personal tax refunds this year.

Net private savings – excluding economic depreciation – looks considerably less strong, as a result of the growth in capital consumption allowances in the late 1970s. Net private savings rates have for a long time been well below those of other major OECD countries (figure 5.3): in 1984 net private savings was only 7.4 per cent of GNP in the United states, as compared with 13.0 per cent in Canada, 13.2 per cent in Italy, 13.9 per cent in Japan, 8.5 per cent in West Germany and 9.1

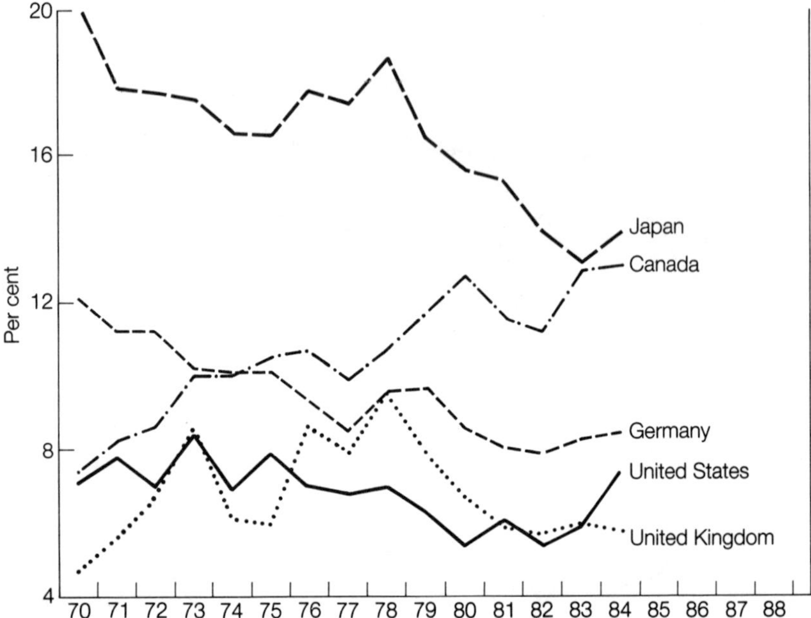

Figure 5.3 Net private saving as a percentage of GNP/GDP. (Sources: Wharton Econometric Forecasting Associates, Inc.,; International Monetary Fund; US Department of Commerce, Bureau of Economic Analysis)

per cent in France. Only the 5.8 per cent United Kingdom savings share was below that of the United States.[3]

Corporate saving has been an important support to the overall saving rate in recent years. The corporate tax cuts of 1981–82 reduced corporate tax collections, but dividend distributions did not increase in line with the increased after-tax cash flow: thus, corporate savings have increased by $119 billion, or 1.8 per cent of GNP, since the recession trough. Personal savings, on the other hand, do not show any clear effect of the incentives for personal saving that began with the 1981 legislation. The legislation included substantial cuts in marginal tax rates for all taxpayers spread over a three-year period and an immediate reduction in the top marginal tax rate on income other than wages and salaries income from 70 per cent to 50 per cent. Enhanced Individual Retirement Account provisions, and other incentives for savings were enacted. The results of this activity have been disappointing, either because the responsiveness of savings to changes in after-tax rates of return is very low, or because the tax changes were overwhelmed by other factors. It should be noted that American investors enjoyed large capital gains on bonds and stocks in the early 1980s and these are not reflected in the NIPA savings figures discussed above.

State and Local Surpluses

In the United States, state and local governments are independent entities not under the direct control of the federal government. In recent years their total expenditures (on a NIPA basis) have been a little more than half as large as those of the federal government. The federal government attempts to influence their behaviour with grants, tax concessions, and regulatory measures, but their response to such devices is not always predictable.

Recent large surpluses in state and local government budgets have helped offset both the federal deficit and the growing credit demands of business. Since every state except Vermont and all local governments are required to balance their budgets, the surpluses are certain to continue. The question is, can we count on state and local surpluses remaining large enough to significantly reduce the burden of federal deficits? The answer depends on several things, the most important of which is the performance of the economy as a whole. The fortunes of state and local governments have tended to fluctuate with business cycles, primarily because they have become more dependent on income and sales taxes for raising revenue. This cyclical tendency has been well illustrated in the last couple of years, during which we have seen the surplus go from $32.9 billion or 22 per cent of the federal budget deficit in 1982 to $53 billion or 30 per cent of the federal deficit in 1984 – a $20 billion jump from recession to recovery.

Another factor that influences the surplus to federal deficit ratio is of course the growth of federal deficit itself. It is revealing to note that even the 1984 figure represents a substantial decline from the 1970s when the average state and local surplus was 53 per cent of a considerably smaller federal deficit. Even with an improved federal budget outlook this ratio will not return to the average level of the 1970s until late in the 1980s.

To further understand the projected trends in state and local surpluses it is useful to break down the overall surplus into two parts: a trust fund surplus and an operating surplus. The trust fund surplus, which made up 80 per cent of the overall surplus in 1984, is primarily composed of pension fund reserves. These funds have been growing since the late 1950s (when good data on state and local governments first became available) and are expected to continue growing at least throughout this century. Much of the recent growth in reserves has been due to efforts by state and local governments to put their pension funds on an actuarially sound footing, so that the value of the funds is large enough to cover all outstanding liabilities owed to workers in the pension plan. The funds' major sources of income – earnings on investments and monthly employee contributions – have grown faster than benefits paid out to individuals. Whether or not trust fund surpluses should be considered as a means of financing the federal deficit is a matter of great controversy. Because they represent retirement assets they may simply substitute for private savings.

The other category, operating funds, is basically what is left over after pension funds are deducted. It will vary cyclically and there is no reason to expect a future upward trend relative to GNP.

Net Private Investment

Since the start of the current recovery, gross private domestic investment has risen substantially, and its share of GNP is high relative to historical averages. Business investment, moreover, did not decline as sharply during the recession as might have been expected: the fall in business investment was about in line with past recessions, though the recession itself was much deeper than average. Net private domestic investment, too, rose sharply in the recovery, but because a larger percentage of investment is now being used to maintain and replace existing capital than in the past, net investment is quite close to its historical average share of GNP.

Underlying the discrepancy between gross and net investment is a very rapid rise in the equipment share of gross investment, since capital equipment generally depreciates much more rapidly than structures. While real total gross private business investment has risen by 38.2 per cent from the recession trough (by far the best performance for investment at the current phase in expansion), real equipment purchases by business have risen even more, by 43.1 per cent. Growth was especially strong in purchases of office equipment and business vehicles. Such a rapid rise in the equipment share in the recovery phase of the cycle is not unusual since equipment spending can typically be adjusted more flexibly than construction in response to cyclical fluctuations in demand.[4] The recently rising equipment share is, therefore, not unusual (see figure 5.4). The equipment share has been rising since the early 1960s, and coincides with (and is in part caused by) a secular decline in the price of new capital equipment relative to that of new structures.

What remains to be explained, then, is that the rapid growth of private gross investment is disproportionately high relative to that of GNP, even at a time of historically high real interest rates. The changes in tax law in 1981–82, combined with the falling relative price of capital

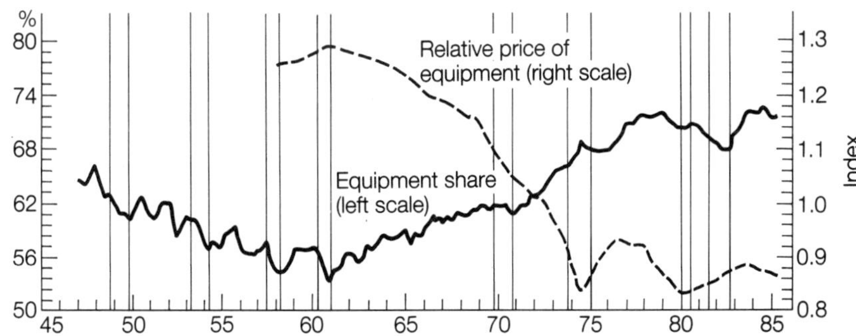

Figure 5.4 Trends in the equipment share of gross business investment

goods, approximately offset the high interest rates for the average equipment investment, though not for structures. Bosworth has recently shown that aggregate demand movements substantially underestimate investment in purchases of office machines and vehicles by businesses, and commercial structures during the recent recovery. Approximately 75 per cent of the growth in private gross investment since the recession trough is attributable to growth in these asset categories, plus residential investment.

Diverse reasons underlie the recent growth of these investment components.

Residential Fixed Investment Favourable demographic patterns and rising affordability aided the unprecedented expansion enjoyed by the residential housing sector. As the baby boom generation has matured, the rate of household formation has also increased. The availability of a wider array of mortgage instruments owing, in part, to financial deregulation, declining mortgage commitment rates and slower growth in house prices has enhanced affordability. Investment syndicates formed under limited partnership arrangements were accorded favourable tax status under the 1981–82 laws, and this has stimulated multifamily housing construction.

Office Machinery Equipment This sector is predominantly computers, and fared rather well in the recession. Given the widespread diffusion of computer-based technologies, the general business recovery necessarily led to a faster than average pick-up in investment in this asset category. Because of technical advance, therefore, it is to be expected that office machinery investment will continue stronger than in the past, despite the apparent slowing this year.

Commercial Structures The strength in residential construction has spurred investment demand in retail construction. Officc building construction cycles typically have longer periods than the cycle in general activity. While the office building boom that began in the late 1970s seems to be slowing as vacancy rates have risen, many have attributed the continuing strength in office building also to the popularity of limited partnerships that receive major tax benefits.

Net Foreign Investment

Rapid build-up of government debt together with the large demand for investment pushed up interest rates in the US during the early 1980s causing capital to be attracted from abroad. These large net capital inflows have resulted in high negative US current account balances, totalling $150 billion over the last three years. Currently, US net international assets are rapidly declining and the US very probably became a net debtor nation early this year.

Net capital inflows have clearly had a beneficial impact on interest rates in the United States. The related appreciation of the dollar has also reduced inflation rates. At the same time capital outflows abroad have drained capital away from foreign countries and forced up their interest rates. In 1983, we estimate that the US federal deficit absorbed about 20 per cent of the total net private savings of the seven major industrial countries. As a probable result, countries which have had falling deficits, such as Germany, have also faced high real interest rates. If the foreign interest rates remain high in future years, then private investment spending in the rest of the world may remain low, thereby freeing foreign private savings for other uses – such as investment in US assets.

Purchases of US assets by foreigners have been accompanied by disinvestment overseas by US residents. Contrary to popular belief, many US based institutions have chosen to curtail their investments abroad and invest more at home.

While I believe that the recent large capital inflow is, in large part, caused by large federal deficits, it is clear that other factors have also played a role. The US expansion and political stability has created a very attractive environment for investment. Different observers place different weights on these different factors. Nevertheless, the similarity in the movements of the federal deficit and the international capital account is quite remarkable as shown in figure 5.5.

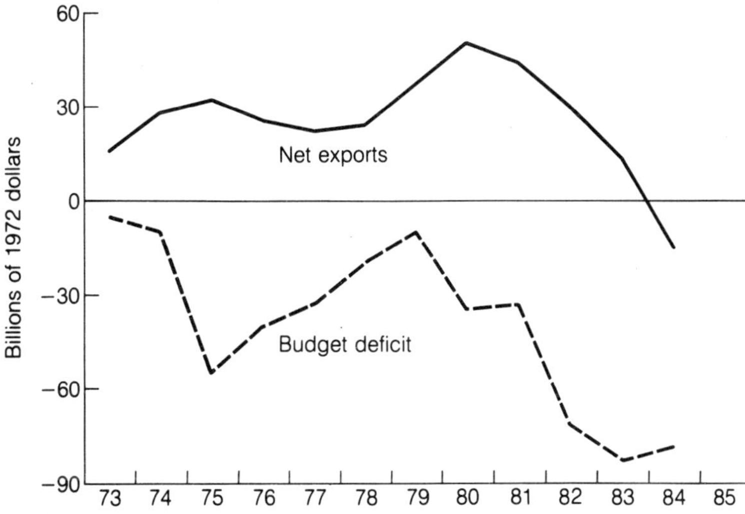

Figure 5.5 US budget deficit and net exports (Source: US Department of Commerce)

II SOME MANIFESTATIONS OF PRESSURES IMPOSED ON THE ECONOMY

Trends in Short and Long Interest Real Rates

As noted before, empirical studies of the relationship between government deficits and interest rates have been inconclusive, although economists generally support the view that large government deficits raise interest rates. The correspondence between rapidly mounting deficits and rising real interest rates over the last five years has tended to vindicate this point of view, and it is quite possible that the huge change in the deficit in the early 1980s will provide economists with the 'experiment' that they need to establish this relationship more conclusively (see table 5.4).

Recent Growth in the Value of the Dollar

As discussed earlier, much of the increase in credit demands in the past few years has been satisfied by capital inflows from abroad. These capital inflows have increased the demand for dollars causing the value to grow in both real and nominal terms since 1980 (figure 5.6).

Table 5.4 Average real short and long interest rates

	Average						
Interest rates (%)	*1960s*	*1970s*	*1980*	*1981*	*1982*	*1983*	*1984*
Treasury bill rate	1.5	−0.3	1.9	6.9	6.5	5.1	6.5
Corporate AAA bond rate							
Ex-post rate	2.2	1.0	5.9	9.9	10.6	8.4	8.6
Ex-ante rate	2.9	2.5	4.4	5.9	5.1	4.4	6.5

Real interest rates are not directly observable. Nominal rates are adjusted by inflation measures constructed from the personal consumption deflator as follows: for the real Treasury bill rate, the actual inflation rate for the three-month period following issuance; for the ex-post real corporate rate, the actual inflation rate for the three-year period following issuance; and for the ex-ante real corporate rate, a distributed lag on actual inflation where the weights are derived from a model of an optimal inflation forecast process.
Sources: Federal Reserve Board; Moody's Investor Services; Congressional Budget Office.

The rise in the dollar has tended to hold back sales, profits and prices in domestic industries that compete with imports domestically or that export products abroad. These effects are not readily apparent from the available data because changes in economic composition have occurred slowly and have been obscured by other important

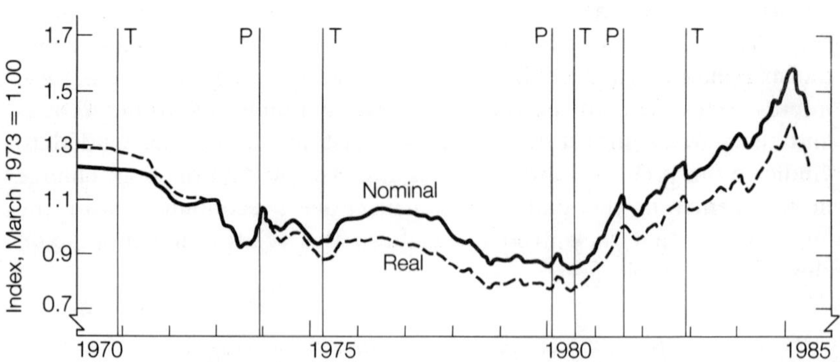

Figure 5.6 Exchange rate (Sources: Federal Reserve Board; International Monetary Fund; Congressional Budget Office)
Note: The nominal index is a trade-weighted average of bilateral dollar exchange rates. The real index adjusts the nominal index for relative movements in CPIs and is a measure of the relative prices of domestic and foreign goods and services.

developments such as the strong cyclical recovery and changes in federal spending, tax and regulatory policies. Thus, it is not surprising that the effects of the dollar's increase have only recently become evident in many sectors of the economy.

The most obvious impact of the rise in the value of the dollar has been the unprecedented deterioration of net exports. Real net exports have gone from around 3.4 per cent of GNP in 1980 to around 1.9 per cent of GNP in the first half of 1985. While not all of the loss can be directly attributed to the rise in the value of the dollar, it is clear that the high dollar played an important role.

Increases in the dollar's value do not affect all sectors equally. Industries producing tradables – primarily goods – are likely to fall as a percentage of GNP, both in terms of output and in terms of employment. Important suppliers to these industries also tend to lose out. On the other hand, industries using imports as inputs are helped by a high dollar.

Output and Employment

Several domestic factors – the recovery and cuts in personal taxes – have tended to increase purchases of goods and this increase in demand has, to some degree, offset the effects of rising imports on goods production. The purchases-based goods share of real GNP was until recently at its highest level since the 1950s. During the last year, however, growth of the purchases-based goods sector slowed dramatically, and fell in the first half of 1985, leading to an overall slowdown in GNP growth.

Employment data clearly show less strength in the goods sector than in the service sector of the economy. Until recently, this may have reflected the relatively strong productivity growth in goods production rather than the impact of the strong dollar and rising imports. Employment in non-farm goods industries is still below the peak reached in 1979, though total employment has increased by 8.4 per cent since then. Moreover, since the beginning of 1985, there has been no growth at all in employment in the goods sector, while manufacturing employment fell by 211,000. Slow growth of goods employment and a reduction of its share in total employment are typical of recessions. However, trend-adjusted manufacturing and mining employment is below its normal share of total employment for the middle of a business cycle expansion. Early in the recovery, manufacturing and mining employment appeared to grow slightly faster than usual, but as a result of losses in the past year it is now close to the level reached at the bottom of the recession.

Changes in the Composition of Domestic Production and Prices

Increased defence procurement since 1980 has added substantially to domestic demand for American produced goods, because of the general preference for domestic sources of defence purchases. Defence capital goods shipments rose from about 1.9 per cent of all manufacturing shipments in 1979 to 3.4 per cent in the first half of 1985.

Exports have dropped and imports have risen, causing domestic output to fall relative to domestic demand, despite the increase in defence procurement (see figure 5.7). But as shown above, the change in the broad aggregates of goods and services production has not been sharp enough to clearly distinguish it from cyclical factors affecting the economy in the current expansion. This is not surprising: imports account for only about 10 per cent of GNP, even after the recent surge.

It is clear that the changing trade balance affects some industries more than others. Even industries that have managed to avoid sharp import increases by cutting prices will have lost profits. The least affected producers will be those that are well protected by tariffs or quota restrictions or that make products for which there are no good foreign substitutes.

The capital goods industry is one sector that clearly seems to have been hit quite hard by the rising dollar. It is, with the exception of the

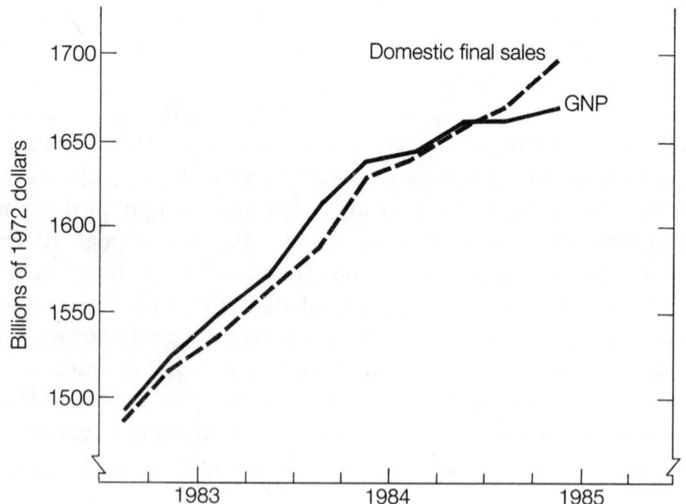

Figure 5.7 Domestic demand and GNP (Source: US Department of Commerce, Bureau of Economic Analysis)

Note: Domestic final sales is GNP less both inventory change and net exports.

auto industry, not well protected by tariffs or quotas. Demand for its products has been stimulated by the rapid growth in producers' durable equipment investment, particularly in high-tech products, yet this has not prevented the industry from losing a considerable part of its market share in the past few years. Domestic non-defence capital goods shipments, which in 1980 was about 90 per cent of the total supply of non-defence capital goods, fell to only about 84 per cent in mid 1984. Relative prices of broad categories of domestically produced machines have also fallen somewhat since 1980, in part reflecting a response to the pressure of foreign competition. Output in some specific industries – construction and allied equipment, metalworking machinery and recently electrical machinery – has fallen significantly relative to total production. The growth of domestic demand, combined with some apparent tendency to hold down price increases, has prevented severe damage to production aggregates in broad capital goods industry.

III CONCLUSION

When it became apparent in 1981 and 1982 that the US federal deficit had been put on a strong upward path, many American economists concluded that the subsequent economic expansion would see high real interest rates and relatively low investment while consumption expanded rapidly. The high real interest rates emerged, but the typical economic forecast of the early 1980s failed to anticipate that the high rates would attract massive inflows of international capital. This restrained the rise in US real interest rates and probably allowed the business tax cuts to promote a rapid rise in business capital spending. Thus it cannot be said that rising US budget deficits crowded out US capital formation.

That does not mean, however, that the deficits were painless. The rising dollar associated with the huge capital inflows depressed the export- and import-competing sectors of the economy. Crowding out occurred, but it afflicted the trading sectors of the economy rather than capital formation.[5] During 1983 and 1984 the effects of this phenomenon were obscured by the beneficial impact of the rapid economic recovery on the goods producing sectors. But in 1985 the adjustment of the composition of the economy became more apparent and more painful. While the confounding effects of the business cycle make it impossible to document a direct link between the budget deficit, high real interest rates, the capital inflow, the trade deficit and the dislocation of American industry, the coincidence of these events is highly suggestive of a causal relationship.

In the longer run, the huge foreign debt accumulated during the period of high budget deficits will have to be serviced. This will require the US to move to a higher net export surplus than would have otherwise been required. Because we shall be able to consume a lower proportion of our output, standards of living in the US will be diminished. Although the long-term cost to the US economy will be substantial, it will probably be lower than that which would have been imposed if our budget deficit had to be financed entirely from domestic saving. Then, domestic capital formation would have been lowered more substantially and future productivity and wage growth would have been more depressed. This is, of course, of no comfort to foreign nations who have lost much capital in the process.

NOTES

1 The 1985 deficit was artificially inflated by a change in the financing of certain housing programmes. This change amounted to $13 billion, but has little economic significance.
2 Technically, the debt to GNP ratio is unstable if the average interest rate on the debt is greater than the growth in GNP. The ratio will explode upward if the actual debt to GNP ratio is above its unstable equilibrium level and downward if the actual ratio begins below its unstable equilibrium. The distinction between a stable and unstable situation may, however, be overemphasized. If the debt to GNP ratio has a stable equilibrium but that equilibrium is very high, say 900 per cent, a country would be forced to resort to hyperinflation long before the stable equilibrium is approached. Thus, there may be little practical difference between the implications of a debt to GNP ratio that is rising rapidly along a stable path and one that is rising rapidly along an unstable path.
3 Figures for countries other than the United States are estimates from Wharton Econometric Forecasting Associates.
4 Many analysts have argued that the rise in the equipment share was caused by the shortening of tax lifetimes for equipment relative to structures mandated by the 1981–82 tax law changes. Recently, however, Bosworth (1985, 1–38) has pointed out that the overall bias of the tax changes towards favouring equipment investment were not at all relevant for the categories of equipment that grew most rapidly, as these assets happen to have been accorded relatively less favourable treatment under the new laws.
5 As an aside, it can be noted that the association between the growing budget and trade deficits deprives the former of much of its traditional Keynesian expansionary effects.

REFERENCES

Barro, R.J. 1974: Are government bonds net wealth? *Journal of Political Economy*, 82, 1095–1118.

Barth, J.R., Iden, G. and Russek, F.S. 1984: Do federal deficits really matter? *Contemporary Policy Issues*, September, 80.

Bosworth, B.P. 1985: Taxes and the investment recovery, *Brookings Papers on Economic Activity*, 1, 1–38.

Congressional Budget Office 1984: *The Economic Outlook*, February, Appendix B.

Friedman, B.M. 1984: Implications of the government deficit for U.S. capital formation, *The Economics of Large Government Deficits*, Federal Reserve Bank of Boston.

Leeuw, F. de and Holloway, T.M. 1983: Cyclical adjustment of the federal budget and federal debt, *Survey of Current Business*, 63, 25–40.

Miller, P. 1983: Higher deficit policies lead to higher inflation, *Federal Reserve Board of Minneapolis Quarterly Review*, 7, winter, 8–19.

Ornstein, N.J. 1985: The politics of the deficit. In P. Cagan (ed.) *Essays in Contemporry Economic Problems, 1985*, American Enterprise Institute, Washington, DC.

Italy

6

Fiscal Policy and Saving in Italy since 1860

FRANCO MODIGLIANI AND TULLIO JAPPELLI

I INTRODUCTION

In this chapter we use more than a century of Italian data to study the determinants of consumption and saving and, in particular, the extent to which they are affected by fiscal policy. More than ten years ago, Barro (1974) set forth the proposition – referred to hereafter as the Ricardian equivalence proposition (REP) – that the choice of financing a deficit by borrowing instead of by taxation is of no practical importance, since agents can be expected to incorporate in their budget equation the present value of all future tax liabilities implied by current deficits and therefore private saving will rise by exactly the same amount as the increase in deficit. As a consequence, national saving and the rate of capital accumulation are unaffected.

Completely different implications for the behaviour of national saving can be derived within the framework of the life cycle hypothesis (LCH), according to which consumption will in general respond to the way a given level of government consumption is financed. In particular, an increase in government deficit due to a switch from taxation to borrowing will reduce national saving because consumption will in general increase in response to a tax cut, so that private saving will not increase enough to compensate for the decrease in government saving.

Another related issue is whether crowding out of national saving can result also through inflation illusion – because the public regards as income some portion of government interest payments which represent an inflation premium, i.e. a compensation for the inflation erosion of the outstanding stock of government debt. Since government interest enters the private sector budget equation only as a component of net taxes, and since, under REP, net taxes have no effect whatever on consumption, it follows that inflation could also not affect saving, at least through this channel. But under the LCH, where net taxes have a major influence on consumption – given before tax income – if the inflation premium is regarded as part of perceived government interest income, and, accordingly, nominal interest transfers result in a fall in perceived net taxes, the outcome may very well be a significant rise in consumption and crowding out of capital formation at least for a while in the short run. Hence, testing for possible effects on consumption of the inflation premium component of nominal rates is of major interest both as a test of the relevance of REP and for an understanding of the consequences of inflation. Note that an effect of the inflation premium on consumption is sufficient to reject REP, but a lack of this effect requires only absence of inflation illusion, and hence is not inconsistent with the LCH.

While in this study we focus primarily on the determinants of saving, our empirical tests are based on a consumption function because consumption, as opposed to saving, can be measured independently from the definition of income, and thus permits testing for the effect of inflation.

In recent years a number of empirical tests have been performed to investigate these issues, mainly using US data. Although some (notably Kormendi, 1983;[1] Seater and Mariano, 1985) have found support for the neutrality proposition, most of the recent empirical analysis (for example Feldstein, 1982; Modigliani, 1984; Modigliani and Sterling, 1985) have rejected it and found evidence in favour of the LCH. In a recent study (Modigliani et al., 1985) we have used Italian postwar yearly data to test whether substituting debt for taxes has any effect on national saving and whether private consumption responds to the nominal portion of government interest payments. We found that the response of consumption to deficit has been fairly small in the Italian postwar experience; we also estimated that when one corrects for the effect of inflation and for government investment, the rise in deficit in recent years is small if compared to the change in the commonly quoted unadjusted deficit. However, due to multicollinearity of the data, we had to leave the issue of inflation illusion open for further research.

In this chapter we propose to carry out a similar test, but using a much larger data set that covers more than 100 years of Italian history which include wide variations in the rate of saving. Although the data that we have used before 1950 are undoubtedly less reliable, we hope that they constitute at least an approximation to the behaviour of the most important Italian economic variables, and that they can help to shed some light on the issues under investigation. We also feel that the present analysis of the consumption function, using an unusual set of data, can be of value in putting today's economic problems in a historical perspective.

The chapter is organized as follows: in section II we lay out the specification of the model to be estimated. Section III describes the data used in the estimation, sections IV and V report parameter estimates and tests of hypotheses. Finally, section VI utilizes the estimates to account for the historical behaviour of national saving.

II A GENERAL FORMULATION OF THE CONSUMPTION FUNCTON

In the standard model of intertemporal utility maximization, the problem of a consumer choosing a consumption plan that maximizes utility subject to a lifetime budget constraint, will lead to the following first order conditions:

$$C = a(H + W) \tag{6.1}$$

where H and W are human and non-human wealth respectively, and a depends on the rate of time preference, age, the rate of interest and the form of the utility function. Using the notion that human wealth can be expressed as the present discounted value of labour income net of the present discounted value of net taxes over the lifetime of the consumer, Sterling (1985) and Modigliani and Sterling (1985) have derived the following specification of the consumption function, in which expectational variables are expressed in terms of present and past values of observable variables:

$$\begin{aligned} C &= \sum_{i=0}^{-n} a_i (\text{NNP}_i - T_i) + bW + cD + \sum_{i=0}^{-n} d_i G_i \\ &= \sum_{i=0}^{-n} a_i \text{NNP}_i - \sum_{i=0}^{-n} (a_i + d_i) T_i + \sum_{i=0}^{-n} d_i E_i + bW + cD \end{aligned} \tag{6.2}$$

Here NNP is net national product, T is taxes net of all transfers (including government interest payments corrected for actual inflation), W is the stock of private wealth (inclusive of government debt D), G is the current account government deficit, and E is government expenditure. The second equality follows from the identity $G = E - T$.

The parameters

$$c \text{ and } \sum_{i=0}^{-n} d_i$$

depend on the age structure of the population, on the length of the planning horizon and on the personal discount and interest rates (see Sterling, 1985). One limiting case of equation 6.2 corresponds to the case when the planning horizon of the individual is infinite. In this case the coefficients

$$\sum_{i=0}^{-n} d_i$$

can be shown to be equal to the negative of the coefficient of income

$$\sum_{i=1}^{-n} a_i$$

and the coefficient of debt to equal the negative of that of wealth. As a result, the tax variable disappears, and equation 6.2 reduces to

$$C = \Sigma\, a_i\,(\mathrm{NNP}_i - E_i) + b(W - D) \tag{6.3}$$

But this limiting case is basically the one that underlies Barro's derivation of REP. He effectively assumes that individuals have an infinite planning horizon because in his model generations are connected by an infinite chain of intergenerational bequests. It is therefore not coincidence that equation 6.3 exhibits the basic characteristics of the REP: private consumption (a) depends on the physical product of the society net of the portion used up by the government; and (b) is independent of how E is financed. For the same reason that deficits do not affect consumption, government debt is not part of net wealth, since the infinite lived consumer correctly anticipates the future taxes that the government will raise in order to repay the principal and the interest on its obligations.

On the other hand, consider the case of a myopic consumer, whose planning horizon is effectively zero, and who therefore does not take into account the future taxes implied by current deficits; in this particular case, the coefficient of deficit (Σd_i) will be zero, as well as the coefficient c of government debt, so that the general model equation 6.2 reduces to

$$C = \Sigma\, a_i(\mathrm{NNP}_i - T_i) + bW \tag{6.4}$$

which is the standard specification of the consumption function.

It should by now be apparent that from the LCH perspective in which individuals are recognized to have a life planning horizon, Σd_i should fall between Σd_i and 0, i.e. consumption should depend on net taxes as well as on government consumption. In assessing the size of the deficit coefficient (Σa_i), the following considerations are paramount:

- the planning horizon of the individual is not likely to exceed greatly the average length of life, and it is possible that it is much shorter; this is true even allowing for bequests, as long as they are of limited importance, and the utility of the donor is not generally determined by that of the beneficiary (Modigliani, 1984);
- if some individuals are liquidity constrained, they will respond by increasing consumption one for one in response to a tax cut, and this will lead consumption, in the aggregate, to respond to deficit and taxes;
- in the presence of imperfect capital markets, and when the rate at which individuals can borrow exceeds the rate at which they can lend, the government can effectively change the budget constraint faced by individuals, by opening (or by rendering more favourable) the possibility of trading current for future consumption; in this case one should expect a tax cut financed by borrowing to increase current consumption and not only saving.

For these reasons, we expect that, although in principle consumption should respond negatively to the government deficit for a given level of taxes (or, equivalently, to government consumption as well as taxes), the coefficient Σd_i should be rather small in absolute value, and far from the negative of the coefficient of income implied by the infinite horizon REP. Similarly, the coefficient of government debt – once wealth is defined to include debt – might be negative, in that consumers probably respond at least partially to the future liabilities implied by the current outstanding debt, but well below the coefficient of wealth in absolute value.

To summarize, both the REP and the 'limited horizon' for inflation (LH–LCH) belong to the same LCH family and imply the same form of consumption function, namely equation 6.2. Both models imply that consumption should be reduced by a deficit, given taxes ($\Sigma d_i < 0$), or, equivalently, by taxes and government consumption. The difference lies in the relation between the coefficients of the variables that are assumed to affect consumption: REP implies that Σd_i should come close to minus the income coefficient Σa_i, while LH–LCH suggests a value much closer to zero so that taxes matter most. Similarly, REP implies that the coefficient of debt should equal minus that of wealth, while for LCH this coefficient should be around zero (or possibly somewhat positive, see below).

So far, we have neglected the second issue that we propose to investigate, namely the question of whether consumers suffer from inflation illusion or are instead capable of distinguishing that part of interest income (and deficit) that is purely a compensation for the inflation losses (gains) suffered in periods of inflation (deflation). This is because we have lumped in the definition of net taxes, T, all transfers (and therefore both the positive transfers represented by nominal interest payments (RD) and the negative transfers represented by the inflation loss on government obligations (pD)). Therefore, our definition of disposable income ($NNP - T$) and current account deficit have been both adjusted for inflation and do not correspond to the conventional measures of national accounts. This formulation implies that consumers are rational and therefore consumption responds to *real* interest payments, and that, in principle, the response is the same as to any other component of taxes and transfers. That response is given by the sum of the coefficients of income and deficit ($\Sigma a_i + \Sigma d_i$). However, since in periods of high and volatile inflation, consumers cannot instantly adjust for the current inflation rate which cannot be directly observed or reliably gauged, consumption might be expected to respond to some measure of expected inflation, or equivalently, to the expected real rate, rather than to the actual one. Moreover, one can think of the expected real rate as the sum of two components, the permanent rate, that should reflect very long-run expectations and be rather stable, and the transitory deviations of the expected real rate from the permanent one; it is for this reason that the propensity to consume out of current expected real interest payments may well be different (lower) than the propensity to consume out of other forms of (net) transfers and that debt might have a positive coefficient reflecting the 'permanent' real rate (cf. Modigliani et al., 1985, section 1). In addition, one should allow for the possibility that consumers suffer from inflation illusion and thus base their consumption decisions on the *nominal* interest earned on the national debt, largely disregarding the loss of principal due to inflation.

In order to assess the actual effect of inflation on consumption, we define net taxes ($T^* = T + (R - p)D = T - rD$) as the sum of direct and indirect taxes minus all transfers except interest, and denote by $r^eD = (R - p^e)D$ the expected real interest payments on government debt. We can then rewrite equation 6.2 as

$$C = \Sigma a_i(NNP_i - T_i^*) + bW + cD + \Sigma d_i G_i^* + fRD + hp^eD \qquad (6.5)$$

where $G^* = E - T^*$. We therefore propose to test for the presence of inflation illusion by decomposing the expected real interest bill in nominal interest payments and expected depreciation of the stock of public debt. Full rationality requires $f = -h$, while in the case of complete inflation illusion $h = 0$. Any significant value of h between zero and $-f$ would imply that all consumers suffer from *some* inflation illusion (or that some proportion is affected by complete inflation illusion while others still act rationally).

If, in addition, the response of consumption to the expected real interest income ($r^{e}D$) is the same as all other forms of income and taxes, then f could reach a value of $(\Sigma a_i + \Sigma d_i)$; as noted before, due to the variability of inflation, f may well be lower than $(\Sigma a_i + \Sigma d_i)$ and, in principle, even be negative if the substitution effect prevails over the income effect.

There are some straightforward implications that can be derived from the consumption function equation 6.5 for the behaviour of national saving; since the latter is defined as $S_T = \text{NNP} - C - E$, using the identity $E = G^* + T^*$ and turning equation 6.5 in an aggregate saving function, we obtain

$$S_T = [(\text{NNP} - T^*) - \Sigma a_i(\text{NNP}_i - T^*)] - (G_i^* + \Sigma d_i G_i^*) - bW - cD - fRD - hp^{e}D \quad (6.6)$$

From equation 6.6 it can be seen that under the REP hypothesis $\Sigma a_i = -\Sigma d_i$, $f = 0$, $c = -b$ and, presumably, $h = 0$, so that equation 6.6 reduces to

$$S_T = [(NNP - E) - \Sigma a_i(NNP_i - E_i)] - b(W - D) \quad (6.7)$$

and neither taxes, debt nor inflation are seen to affect the behaviour of the national saving rate which, accordingly, depends only on government consumption and on wealth other than government debt.

On the other hand, in the LH–LCH model one expects the sum of coefficients Σd_i to be negative, but fairly small, so that the effect of an increase in government deficit, given income net of taxes, is to crowd out saving by close to a dollar per dollar. If, in addition, there is complete rationality, $h = -f$ and the last two terms of equation 6.6 collapse in $-fr^{e}D$; if, instead, there is complete inflation illusion, $h = 0$ and S_T depends only on the nominal rate, fRD. Thus, the LH–LCH recognizes a significant role for each of these variables, deficit, government debt, government interest, and possibly, for inflation.

As mentioned above, in our previous paper, because of the collinearity of data and the limited number of observations, we were not able to establish conclusively whether the observed behaviour reflected rational consumers' response to the fluctuations of real interest rates or the irrational response of consumers suffering from inflation illusion. The present study, in which we make use of a much larger data set, was intended in part to provide more reliable evidence and more precise estimates of the parameters of interest.

III PRESENTATION OF THE DATA

As operational definitions, income $Y^*(= \text{NNP} - T^*)$ is defined as private disposable income net of real interest payments, deficit $G^*(= E - T^*)$ is the current account deficit net of real interest payments, consumption includes expenditure on durables, beginning of period net wealth includes the stock of government debt, interest payments do not include payments to foreigners.

The Appendix contains a detailed explanation of the definition and sources of the variables used in the estimation for the period 1862–1950 (except for wealth, available only after 1882); afterwards we have used the same data set as used by Modigliani et al. (1985), with the only exception of government debt, for which a newly published series, elaborated by Spaventa et al. (1984), has been used.

Although we have tried to preserve consistency among the different series and definitions, in many cases the variables are not strictly comparable; in fact, the major differences between them are:

- wealth is defined as the sum of the stock of capital and government debt from 1882 to 1950, whereas afterwards it includes also currency in circulation;[2]
- government debt, which ideally should result from the consolidated balance sheets of the central and local governments, before 1950 only includes the debt of the central government (net of government claims), but does not take into account – unless reflected in the balance sheet of the central government – the debt of local institutions, government agencies, social security funds and public enterprises (included in the series elaborated by Spaventa);
- similarly, government deficit, for which we have relied on the work of Repaci (1962) because it was consistent with the definition of disposable income provided by Ercolani (1969), only includes the deficit of the central government. However, a portion of these expenditures, such as those that financed investment of government enterprises, cannot be considered as current expenses. The issue is relevant because, according to REP, it is only current consumption expenditure (as opposed to capital investment) that reduces private consumption. Since it is not easy to assess the magnitude of these expenses, we rely on two definitions of deficit, the one measured by Repaci and another that excludes most capital expenses (G_I) from the government budget, but may exclude also some items that are truly government consumption.[3]

To summarize, it can be seen that the fiscal variables are all biased in the same direction (namely, they only consider the central government in the years preceding 1950). However, considering that local institutions and government agencies have grown in importance mostly within the last decades, we hope that our measures will not be seriously distorted.

In table 6.1 we present average values for the entire period and selected subperiods of a number of variables expressed as a percentage of private income as conventionally measured ($Y^* + RD$). Column (1) reports consumption; (2) wealth; (3) debt; (4) current account government deficit; (5) government investment; (6) nominal interest payments; and (7) inflation losses on government debt. In column (8) we also report the national saving rate (relative to NNP), and in columns (9) and (10) the consumption and the deficit to income ratio corrected for actual inflation loss (pD). Finally, in columns (11) and (12) we report the average inflation rate (measured as the rate of depreciation of the deflator of private consumption) and the average rate of growth of real NNP.

The swings of many of the variables (even though averaged over many years) are very remarkable, reflecting the length of the period of observations, the presence of two major wars and the succession of different regimes and economic and political institutions. The period that runs from 1862 until the turn of the century is essentially characterized by economic stagnation (with the exception of a period of moderate growth in the 1880s, followed by a deep depression). At the same time, there were government deficits (including public investments). The combined effect of these deficits, fuelled in part by high interest rates, plus the inheritance by the new Italian State of the old obligations of the pre-existing States, caused the burden of the public debt to increase enormously until the end of the century, by which time it had doubled since the beginning of the 1880s.

The years between 1897 and 1907 represented, in all respects, the period of most rapid growth that the Italian economy had experienced; following the growth in income, private saving increased for the first time above the average of 3.3 per cent of the previous period to an average of 10.2 per cent of disposable income in the first decade of the century.

The combination of balanced budgets at the beginning of the century, some inflation and income growth, in turn resulted in a substantial decline of the national debt to income ratio during the period immediately preceding the First World War (1908–14), a period which is similar in many respects to the previous decade of rapid growth and high propensities to save on the part of the private sector

Table 6.1

Periods	*C* (1)	*W* (2)	*D* (3)	G^*+RD (4)	G_I (5)	*RD* (6)	*pD* (7)	S_T/NNP (8)	*C/Y* (9)	*G/Y* (10)	*Inflation* (11)	*NNP Growth* (12)
1864–1896	96.4	—	1.03	0.1	1.8	4.8	0.8	3.3	96.7	−0.1	0.6	−0.1
1897–1907	91.4	14.0	1.12	−2.4	2.1	4.8	0.8	10.2	92.3	−3.3	0.9	2.4
1908–1914	89.7	3.6	0.80	−1.9	2.7	2.8	1.4	11.2	91.0	−3.3	1.9	1.3
1915–1918	80.7	2.7	0.58	22.5	1.5	2.3	12.8	−3.1	92.8	11.3	31.2	1.5
1919–1923	88.8	3.4	0.81	16.2	2.5	3.5	6.1	−4.7	95.3	10.2	11.6	0.0
1924–1939	91.4	4.1	0.93	2.8	3.1	4.5	0.2	5.2	91.8	2.3	0.9	0.1
1940–1945	90.7	3.6	0.76	28.1	1.7	3.6	24.8	−17.7	121.7	4.1	68.1	11.4
1946–1950	89.8	3.1	0.25	2.0	9.3	1.2	3.9	7.5	93.4	−2.0	24.0	11.0
1951–1963	84.0	3.1	0.22	−2.5	—	1.6	0.7	16.0	84.6	−3.2	3.4	6.5
1964–1982	78.9	3.2	0.35	3.8	—	3.7	3.7	15.0	82.0	0.2	10.9	3.5
1981–1982	79.1	3.7	0.51	10.2	—	8.9	7.7	9.5	85.7	2.7	17.8	1.0
1864–1950	93.2	2.9	0.92	1.4	2.7	4.2	0.8	5.0	94.2	0.4	2.9	0.6
1950–1982	81.3	3.1	0.30	1.4	—	2.8	2.4	15.2	83.0	−1.0	7.7	4.6
1864–1982	89.6	3.0	0.75	1.3	—	3.8	1.3	8.2	90.9	−0.2	4.4	1.7

Period average of: the propensity to consume (1), wealth (2), debt (3), deficit (4), government investment (5), nominal interest payments (6), and inflation losses on government debt (7) relative to income as conventionally measured in the national accounts (Y^*+RD). National saving ratio as a percentage of NNP (8), propensity to consume (9) and deficit income ratio (10) corrected for actual inflation (*pD*), average inflation (11) and average rate of growth of real per-capita NNP (12). The periods 1864–1950 and 1864–1982 exclude the war years.

At first glance it seems that the propensity to consume falls also in the years immediately following, corresponding to the First World War, characterized by huge deficits (column (4)) and high inflation (almost 300 per cent in the years 1916–20). But if one corrects income for *ex-post* inflation, the average propensity to consume actually rose moderately during the First World War and the period 1919–23. The inflation resulted in very large negative real rates which in turn contributed greatly to reducing the huge nominal deficits of column (4) – see column (10) – and to contain the fall in national saving (column (8)) and to reduce substantially the debt ratio (column (3)).

During the fascist period, and up to the Second World War, the propensity to consume continues to average around 90 per cent of disposable income, but because of huge government deficits – especially at the end of the 1930s in preparation for the Second World War – government debt climbs back to historically high levels, national saving falls back to the low levels of the previous century, while growth also shrinks to zero. With the Second World War, there is a large decline in output while the high inflation rate reduces drastically the debt to income ratio by about 75 per cent.

The 1950s and early 1960s are characterized by unprecedentedly rapid growth, accompanied by a high propensity to save, a decline in the wealth to income ratio, government surpluses and a stable (and low, from an historical point of view) relation of debt to income.

In the last period, beginning in the mid 1960s, the propensity to consume appears to decrease further and very substantially (to an average of 78.9 per cent), but if one looks at column (9) where consumption is divided by income corrected for the *ex-post* inflation loss, it appears that the reduction is really not striking, and that by the 1980s we actually observe an increase in the corrected propensity to consume. At the same time, the debt to income ratio started to rise again at the end of the 1960s and reached, at the beginning of the 1980s, a value more than twice as high as it was in the 1950s and at the beginning of the 1960s. Spaventa et al. (1984) have estimated that it has reached a value as high as 66.5 per cent of GNP in 1984 and could be as high as 80 per cent by 1988.

In some circumstances, the government was able to reduce the burden of the public debt by relying on the inflation tax through negative interest rates (as in the two postwar periods); in others, as at the beginning of the century, the debt to income ratio diminished because the economy was experiencing a period of fast and steady growth. Today the prospect of a rate of growth of the economy higher than the real interest rate is particularly uncertain. In addition to this fact, it seems that the government has lost its ability to obtain credit at substantially negative real rates.

This can best be seen by looking at figure 6.1(a) and (b), where we have plotted the nominal interest rate on government bonds together with the rate of inflation. What is particularly striking is the apparent stickiness of the nominal rate and its lack of responsiveness to the volatile inflation rates, up to the early 1970s. Indeed, throughout this period the nominal interest on government obligations remained close to the 5–6 per cent range, and seemed to be completely unaffected by the rate of inflation. Even during the two hyperinflations, the nominal rate did not move from its usual values. (Note that the hyperinflation periods are not drawn on the same scale.[4]) It was 5.39 in 1915, it then fell slightly to 4.87 in 1917, after which it rose again until 1920, but only to 5.68. During the second hyperinflation, prices started to increase in 1940, but the inflation was particularly high in the years 1944–46. The nominal interest rate on government debt was 5.66 in 1940, reached a peak of 8.22 in 1943, and then actually declined to 6.59 in 1944, 5.95 in 1945 and 5.85 in 1946.

As can be seen from figure 6.1(b), it is only in the last decade that nominal interest rates have started to increase, seemingly to compensate for inflation. But even this late behaviour might be rationalized as partly the result of significant recent innovations in the Italian financial markets. Thus, one might be led to conclude that some degree of inflation illusion, if not complete inflation illusion, must have characterized the behaviour of Italian consumers and investors in fixed assets, at least until the most recent period, when the persistence of substantial inflation initiated a learning process through which the Italian consumers have finally begun to shed their inflation illusion. This interpretation would, in practice, validate Fisher's law only in the latest period of our sample, and interpret the behaviour of the Italian economy as characterized by complete inflation illusion throughout the major part of its history.

However, as will be shown in section V, a quite different explanation is possible for the observed behaviour which is not inconsistent with Fisher's law and rational behaviour of consumers and investors throughout the period. We will also indicate why, in our view, this alternative provides a better and more credible explanation of the facts.

IV TEST OF THE BASIC MODEL

In table 6.2 we test the specification of the LCH model presented in section I. The variables used in the estimation are per caput and

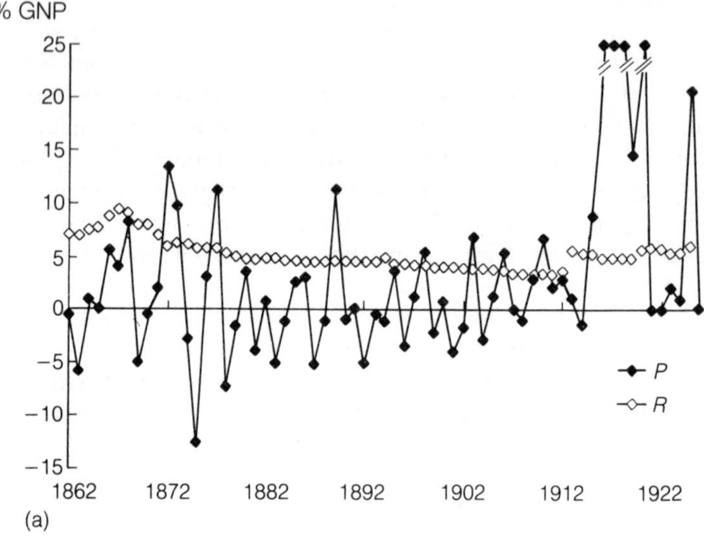

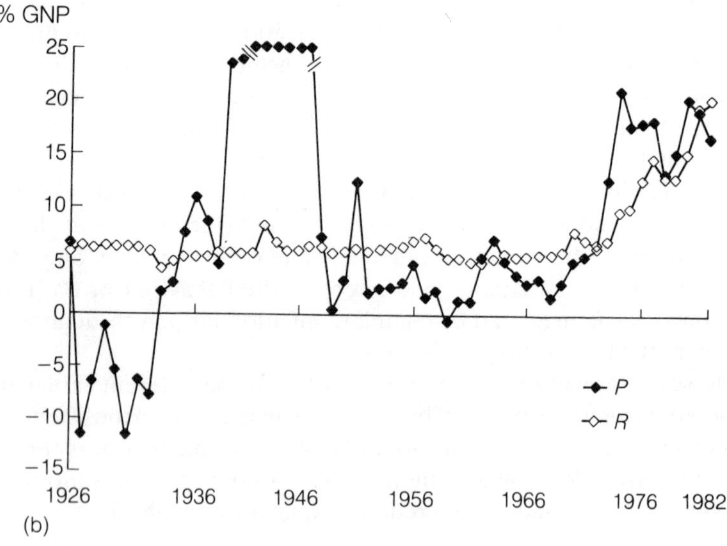

Figure 6.1 (a) Inflation rate (*P*) and nominal interest rate on Government bonds (*R*), 1862–1924 (b) inflation rate (*P*) and nominal interest rate on Government bonds (*R*), 1924–82.

expressed in thousands of 1970 lire through deflation by the implicit deflator of private consumption; they are described in the Appendix. Except for the net stock of capital available from 1882 to 1982, and an estimate of the value of land available from 1882 to 1950, all other variables are available from 1862 to 1982. To account for long-run expectations, we relied on current and lagged values of the income variable appearing in equation 6.2. It may be desirable to consider a higher number of lags on both income and the deficit; however, by adding a lag to the deficit, a second lag to all variables, or by using Almon polynomial lags, the sum of the coefficients of income and of the deficit was always very close to the sum of current and lagged coefficients of the income variable and of the current deficit, so that we feel that not much is lost by the specification that we have adopted.

Our strategy will be to present first in table 6.2 estimates of the basic model represented by equation 6.2 without taking into account the effect of real interest payments on public debt. This is fully justified if one is interested in testing the REP model against the LH–LCH, since, according to the REP, the coefficient of the deficit should offset that of net income. Consequently, interest, as well as all other taxes and transfers, should not affect consumption. In tables 6.3 and 6.4 we then proceed to analyse the effect of debt and interest on debt and try to assess the effect, if any, of inflation on consumption (equation 6.5).

In table 6.2 we begin by showing estimates for the postwar period (1950–82) for which the information is deemed to be substantially more reliable, and the results of previous studies, including our own (Modigliani et al., 1985) are available. We next give results for the earlier period beginning not later than 1882 but in some tests as early as 1862. Finally, results are given for the two periods pooled, including tests of homogeneity. All results omit the years of the First and Second World Wars (1915–18 and 1940–45, respectively), unless otherwise stated.

Regression (2.1) presents an estimate of the basic equation 6.2. We use the formulation of the first equality of equation 6.2 to insure the constraint that the effect of taxes and government consumption should add up to the income coefficient. The fit of the regression is quite good as the standard error is only about 2.0 per cent of the mean (2.3 per cent of the smallest value) of the dependent variable. The constant term is positive which is not strictly consistent with the predictions of both models that consumption should be independent of the absolute level of income, but fairly small (around 6 per cent of the mean of consumption over the period 1950–82) and not very significant.

The wealth coefficient is close to expectations and subject to small error. We note also that the coefficient of the deficit is only about one-

Table 6.2 *Estimates of the basic LCH model*

ID	*Period*	*C* (1)	Y^* (2)	Y^*_{-1} (3)	*W* (4)	G^* (5)	*RHO* (6)	*SE* (7)
2.1	1950–1982	34.0	0.48	0.20	0.029	−0.17	0.77	7.54
		(1.7)	(9.3)	(3.0)	(3.6)	(−1.6)	(6.8)	
2.2	1950–1982		0.45	0.28	0.032	−0.33	0.77	0.01196
			(8.2)	(5.7)	(3.5)	(−2.3)	(6.8)	
2.3	1882–1950	15.2	0.50	0.20	0.027	−0.30	0.85	4.03
	(*W* includes land)	(0.5)	(14.7)	(6.2)	(1.2)	(−5.4)	(12.3)	
2.4	1882–1950		0.51	0.20	0.035	−0.34	0.77	0.02165
	(*W* includes land)		(16.6)	(6.1)	(6.5)	(−5.0)	(9.3)	
2.5	1882–1950	30.6	0.51	0.19	0.028	−0.29	0.80	4.02
		(2.4)	(15.6)	(5.4)	(1.7)	(−5.2)	(10.2)	
2.6	1864–1950	34.7	0.49	0.21	0.020	−0.28	0.79	3.91
		(3.8)	(15.7)	(6.7)	(.1.7)	(−5.4)	(11.4)	

2.7	1864–1950 (G^* includes G_I)	31.1 (3.2)	0.52 (14.7)	0.22 (6.4)	0.019 (1.5)	−0.22 (−4.0)	0.77 (10.4)	4.20
2.8	1864–1982	33.1 (8.2)	0.48 (21.7)	0.20 (7.5)	0.028 (6.3)	−0.23 (−4.6)	0.76 (12.3)	5.08
2.9	1882–1982 (*W* includes land until 1950)	5.2 (0.7)	0.49 (20.3)	0.22 (8.3)	0.035 (5.7)	−0.27 (−5.2)	0.82 (13.9)	5.32
2.10	1882–1982 (*W* includes land until 1950)		0.51 (22.1)	0.22 (8.5)	0.033 (9.8)	−0.33 (−6.0)	0.78 (11.9)	0.0177
2.11	1864–1982 (includes wars)	31.6 (8.8)	0.49 (21.9)	0.21 (7.5)	0.025 (5.5)	−0.23 (−5.7)	0.78 (13.7)	5.33

t-statistics in parentheses. The mean of the dependent variable (in 1970 thousand lire) in the regressions estimated in level forms is 594 in the period 1950–1982, 204 in 1882–1950, 197 in 1864–1950, and 313 in 1864–1982 (always excluding the war years). Income (Y^*) and deficit (G^*) are net of real interest transfers. Regressions (2.2), (2.4) and (2.10) are estimated in ratio form. In regression (2.7) G^* includes government investment (G_I). Regression (2.11) includes the war years (1915–1918 and 1940–1945). Wealth excludes land unless otherwise stated.

quarter of that of income (Σa_i), and that the difference between the two coefficients is significantly different from zero beyond any reasonable level but broadly consistent with the predictions of the LH–LCH.

Regression (2.1) uses the linear specification. For an economy growing rapidly, such a specification might be questioned for lack of homoskedasticity. For this reason, regression (2.2) is estimated in ratio form; it can be seen that the estimates are not greatly affected except for the coefficient of the deficit which rises to 0.3 but remains broadly consistent with the LH–LCH and not with the REP. We are inclined to believe, however, that the results reported in row (2.2) are biased by the omission of the constant term, which, as explained below, may be proxying the value of land which is excluded from our definition of wealth.

Regressions (2.3) through (2.8) report the results for the earlier portion of our sample. The main features distinguishing this period from the one considered above are:

1 the rate of development of the economy, very slow to moderate in the period 1864–1950, and exceptionally vigorous during most of the later period, especially in the years of the 'miracle', though less so towards the end; and
2 the reliability of the data, which is unavoidably less in the earlier period.

In row (2.3) we present an estimate for the period 1882–1950, the only one for which we have available an estimate of the value of land to include in wealth. The results for the seven decades preceding the Second World War are remarkably similar to those for the postwar period considering the institutional developments, the large difference in the rate of growth and the enormous associated variation in the personal saving rate (or C/Y^*). This can be seen by comparing (2.3) with (2.1) in linear form where the only difference of any account is in the coefficient of the deficit; but even this difference disappears in comparing the ratio estimations (2.2) and (2.4). The only difference is then that the fit is considerably closer in the later period – the standard error is 1.2 per cent in (2.2) versus 2.2 per cent in (2.4) – which could readily be accounted for by the quality of the data. At the same time, the similarity of the two estimates justifies confidence also in the previous data.

The comparability is somewhat marred by the fact that land is included in the estimates of wealth for the prewar, but not for the postwar, years. To secure full comparability, in row (2.5) we have re-estimated (2.3) omitting the value of land from the definition of wealth. It is seen that the only appreciable difference is a rise in the value (and significance) of the constant term. This is understandable, since the constant term is presumably proxying the omitted value of agricultural land, which was, in fact, nearly constant – or moving very slowly – throughout this period. At the beginning of the 1880s, it was around one-half of the value of total wealth (inclusive of debt and land), but then declined to less than 30 per cent of the value of wealth at the beginning of the 1950s.

As noted before, our suspicion is that a similar mechanism could have been operating in the latest period of the sample (1950–82) – namely, that during the period of rapid industrialization the relative importance of land kept shrinking, making its omission less serious, but producing a moderately positive constant term.

In regressions (2.3) through (2.5), the estimates are for the period 1882–1950, because the wealth series was only available over this period. However, since the other variables are available over the entire period 1864–1982, we have extrapolated backward the value of the wealth series – excluding the value of land – by simply assuming that its behaviour could be described by the average rate of growth of real income in the period 1864–82. To test whether this rough approximation was at least unbiased, we have re-estimated regression (2.5) starting in 1864 and added a multiplicative dummy on wealth in the first period of estimation (1864–82). It was found that the dummy on wealth was rather small and completely insignificantly different from zero. On the basis of these results we have felt it worthwhile rerunning our basic equation for the entire period 1864–1950, dropping the dummy, with the results reported in regression (2.6).

It is apparent that the estimated coefficients in row (2.6) are nearly identical to those provided by row (2.5). However, one can also note, much as one would expect, (a) a further rise in the constant term (to 18 per cent of the mean of the dependent variable) since land is again omitted, and also (b) a reduction in the value of the coefficient of wealth, consistent with the poorer measurement of this variable.

We do not report a ratio estimate corresponding to (2.6) since we feel that the suppression of the constant is no longer justifiable, but that the comparison of (2.3) and (2.4) convincingly establishes that heteroskedasticity is not a problem in this period of very limited growth.

Regression (2.7) is similar to (2.6) but tests an alternative measure that adds government investment (G_I) to government consumption in computing the deficit. It is seen that this measure, that we regard as less appropriate, produces in fact a somewhat poorer fit and a lower and less significant coefficient of deficit.

The remaining four equations of table 6.2 are based on the pooled sample (1864–1982 or 1882–1982). Since in this case the problem of heteroskedasticity might be even more serious than in the two separate subperiods, a number of tests were conducted, but none found that the size of the squared errors was directly related to any of the independent variables, and particularly to the income variable.[5] The reason is that in the first part of the sample the change in real income – more appropriate than the actual level, since we always obtain high serial correlation of the errors – is characterized by a standard deviation about six times the mean, while in the second half of the sample the standard deviation is only about 1.7 of the mean. It would appear that the period of stability that characterized the 1950s and 1960s, as well as the presence in the postwar years of more effective stabilization policies, played an important role in explaining the absence of heteroskedasticity in the residuals of our equations.

It is seen that the pattern of the coefficients of (2.8) comes very close to those estimated in both the first part of the sample (row (2.6)) and the second one (row 2.1)). It is thus not surprising that a Chow test for structural break yields an *F* statistic of only 0.3, and one cannot reject the null hypothesis that the structure of the economy has remained stable over the entire period.

One troublesome aspect of (2.8) is that the constant term is highly significant. However, if we re-estimate (2.8) starting from 1882 instead of from 1864 and include land in the wealth variable, we obtain very similar coefficients and a fairly small and insignificant constant term (2.9).[6] A further test of heteroskedasticity can be made by estimating (2.9) in ratio form (row 2.10), where the results clearly show no appreciable change in the coefficients with respect to (2.9).

So far, all our estimates have excluded the two World Wars because these wars were of catastrophic proportions and involved huge government expenditure and deficits and quite high rates of inflation. In addition, the Second World War also resulted in large-scale destruction of private and public capital. These periods involve both extreme observations and may be non-representative of normal behaviour because of the unusual circumstances, including the role of patriotism in the First World War and that of price and related controls. It seems, none the less, of some interest to see how sensitive the estimates are to the inclusion of the wars. As can be seen by comparing (2.11) with (2.8), the change in the coefficient estimates is very small, although the standard error is increased by some 5 per cent, indicating, not surprisingly, larger shocks during war years.

We can summarize the results presented in table 6.2 by noting that the estimates of the basic model are remarkably stable over various sample periods, and lead to the conclusion that the main prediction of the REP, that private saving will completely offset any change in government deficit, is not supported by the data; the point estimate of G^* is in fact negative, as predicted by both models, but in absolute value is relatively modest – especially in the most recent period – as predicted by the LH–LCH.

V TESTS OF THE EFFECT OF INTEREST INCOME, DEBT AND INFLATION ON CONSUMPTION

In this section we turn to the second set of our tests, namely the effect of debt, interests on debt and inflation on consumption, that is, to tests of the specification of equation 6.5. Table 6.3 reports the results for each of the two subperiods, while table 6.4 presents estimates for the two periods combined. We begin again with the postwar period.

Regression (3.1) adds first the national debt D to the variables of row (2.1) in table 6.2. According to the REP, its coefficient should be the negative of that of wealth; according to LH–LCH, the coefficient should be zero, or possibly a small positive number, reflecting the effect of the long-run expected real rate. It is seen that the coefficient of debt is positive and very significant (the standard error of the regression is reduced from 7.6 to 6.7). This result points towards a clear rejection of the REP. To be sure, the coefficient of D is somewhat high even for LCH, but this could reflect the role of the interest, given a fairly constant long-term expected real rate. Indeed, when in (3.2) we further add nominal interest payments, the coefficient of D becomes small and insignificant. At the same time, the RD coefficient points to a clear-cut rejection of the REP, that transfers in the form of interest have no effect on consumption because it is seen to be highly significant, and to imply an effect on consumption that is quite close to that estimated for all other taxes and transfers, namely, 0.5 (the sum of the coefficients of columns (2), (3) and (5)) which is consistent with LH–LCH.

Row (3.3) reports a test of whether consumption responds to nominal or to real interest payments, i.e. to payments adjusted for the inflation-induced loss of purchasing power on claims against the government. To this end we should add to (3.2) a variable measuring this loss in purchasing power. However, as mentioned in section II, it must be recognized that the perceived loss cannot be identified with the *ex-post* loss due to actual inflation; rather it should properly be identified with the anticipated loss because the actual, simultaneous inflation loss cannot be fully known or reacted to instantaneously. We considered several alternative ways of estimating the unobservable expected inflation and tested a few. We report here the results of the approach

Table 6.3 *Test of the effect of interest, debt and inflation, 1950–1982 and 1864–1950*

ID	*Period*	*C* (1)	Y^* (2)	Y^*_{-1} (3)	*W* (4)	G^* (5)	*RD* (6)	P^eD (7)	*D* (8)	*RHO* (9)	*SE* (10)	*LL* (11)
3.1	1950–1982	56.2	0.43	0.22	0.018	−0.20			0.12	0.68	6.74	106.4
		(3.8)	(8.3)	(3.5)	(2.3)	(−2.0)			(2.9)	(5.2)		
3.2	1950–1982	45.5	0.45	0.26	0.009	−0.22	0.50		0.027	0.62	6.31	104.4
		(3.6)	(9.0)	(4.3)	(1.1)	(−2.4)	(2.2)		(0.5)	(4.5)		
3.3	1950–1982	40.2	0.44	0.27	0.015	−0.22	0.70	−0.30		0.63	6.13	103.4
		(3.9)	(9.3)	(4.5)	(1.7)	(−2.4)	(4.1)	(−1.4)		(4.6)		
3.4	1950–1982	40.2	0.44	0.22	0.03	−0.20	0.63	−0.46		0.66	6.32	104.4
		(3.4)	(9.1)	(4.2)		(−2.2)	(3.6)	(−2.3)		(5.0)		
3.5	1950–1982	35.5	0.43	0.24	0.030	−0.19	0.59			0.61	6.38	104.7
		(3.4)	(8.6)	(4.0)	(5.1)	(−2.0)	(3.4)			(4.4)		
3.5	1950–1982	46.5	0.42	0.22	0.03	−0.20	0.51	−0.47	0.043	0.68	6.37	104.7
		(3.2)	(7.9)	(4.1)		(−2.2)	(2.1)	(−2.3)	(0.8)	(5.2)		
3.7	1882–1950 (*W* includes land)		0.47	0.17	0.040	−0.32	0.28		0.031	0.78	0.0189	150.4
			(14.1)	(4.8)	(7.3)	(−5.1)	(2.8)		(1.4)	(9.6)		
3.8	1882–1950 (*W* includes land)		0.47	0.17	0.040	−0.32	0.28	0.01	0.030	0.78	0.0191	149.9
			(13.9)	(4.8)	(16.6)	(−4.6)	(2.7)	(0.1)	(1.4)	(9.6)		
3.9	1864–1950	31.8	0.48	0.21	0.038	−0.29	0.92		−0.07	0.75	3.74	210.7
		(4.1)	(14.9)	(6.7)	(2.9)	(−5.5)	(1.7)		(−3.0)	(9.9)		

t-statistics in parentheses. The periods 1864–1950 and 1882–1950 exclude wars. In regression (3.5) the variable *RD* is replaced with ($RD - p^eD$). Regressions (3.7) and (3.8) are estimated in ratio form. *W* excludes land unless otherwise stated. Column (11) reports the log of the likelihood function.

that appeared most satisfactory. It consists of obtaining estimates of expected inflation, p^e, by means of a rolling regression of the actual inflation on lagged inflation rates and using the estimated coefficients for each year to forecast that year's inflation. This approach is supported by a number of considerations. First, it is evident that in this period the nominal interest rate reflects inflation along the lines of Fisher's hypothesis since it is highly correlated with inflation; a regression of R^7 on p yields, in fact, a coefficient of p of 0.69 (with a t ratio of 7.4 and an R^2 of 0.64). Second, inflation was generated by a very persistent – and therefore predictable – process; indeed, our measure of expected inflation predicts actual p^e quite closely since the correlation between p and p^e is 0.86. One further test consists in regressing R on p^e and $(p - p^e)$. If p^e is a good approximation to expected inflation, it should be able to account for R, while $(p - p^e)$, representing unexpected inflation, should not contribute significantly to the explanation of R (under Fisher's hypothesis). It is found that p^e has a coefficient of 0.65 and highly significant t-ratio of 8.0. On the other hand, the coefficient of $(p - p^e)$, although it has a positive point estimate (0.3), has a standard error so large (0.16) that one cannot reject the hypothesis that the coefficient is zero, at the 5 per cent level of significance. Furthermore, a good portion of the positive effect of $(p - p^e)$ can be traced to the highly transitory Korean war inflation of 1951 which was, *per se*, unforecastable and generated no inflationary expectations as is apparent from the behaviour of R.

Thus, in (3.3) we add p^eD to (3.2); as a measure of the expected loss of purchasing, the results of the test, reported in row (3.3), cannot reject the null hypothesis of inflation illusion ($h = 0$), since the coefficient of p^eD, though negative, is not significantly different from zero. However, (3.3) and (3.2), as well as (3.1), run into another problem, namely, that the coefficient of wealth is unreasonably small compared with the results of table 6.2 (and also those of other investigations) which hover around 0.03 and reach as high as 0.04. In (3.1) and (3.3) the coefficient is half as high (and in (3.2) even less) although the difference is hardly significant in view of the very large standard error. This consideration suggests a strong likelihood of the presence of collinearity between W, RD, D and p^eD, making for large standard errors and erratic estimates. To test this hypothesis in row (3.4), we have constrained the coefficient of wealth to take the reasonable value of 0.03 and dropped the insignificant debt variable. The results are striking because: (a) the constraint imposed on the coefficient hardly reduces the fit and could not be rejected even at the 5 per cent level and higher, (b) the coefficient of p^eD becomes significant so that one can reject the hypothesis of complete inflation illusion, and (c) it is not very different from that of RD, as one would expect under full rationality (and supposing that p^e is a good approximation to perceived inflation).

We have actually carried out a formal test of 'rationality' by re-estimating (3.4) constraining the coefficients to be the same (that is, entering $RD - p^eD$ instead of RD and p^eD separately). The result given in (3.5) indicates that the hypothesis of complete rationality cannot be rejected either comparing the unrestricted (3.3) with (3.5), or (3.4) with (3.5) since the difference in the likelihood ratio test is 2.6 and 0.6 respectively, well below any customary level of significance. We also note that the coefficient of wealth turns out to be again of an order of magnitude consistent with our expectations and is also very significant.

The last regression that we report for the period 1950–82 (3.6) adds back to (3.4) the national debt D. To control for multicollinearity, we again constrain the coefficient of W to be 0.03. The coefficients of the other variables are hardly changed except that those of RD and p^eD move even closer. The coefficient of D is again positive, but is again so imprecisely estimated that one cannot meaningfully make any reliable inferences. The difficulty of assessing the effect of debt (which will be further taken up) derives from the fact that the coefficient of wealth is itself very small, so we are looking for small effects, and from the fact that, not surprisingly, there appears to be strong multicollinearity among wealth, debt D, nominal interest bill RD, and expected depreciation of the stock of public debt p^eD.

Proceeding next to the earlier subperiod, results are reported in the last three rows of table 6.3. In (3.7) the period of estimation is 1882–1950 and wealth includes the value of land. This regression should be compared with (2.4) and is estimated in ratio form on the grounds that the constant term can be dropped when wealth includes land. In (3.7) the coefficient of RD is significant and makes for a substantial reduction in the standard error (from 2.2 per cent in (2.4) to 1.9 per cent). As in the postwar period, the coefficient D is positive but imprecisely estimated.

In (3.8), we test for the effect of p^eD, having computed p^e by the same rolling regression method used in the second part of the sample. It is seen that this variable has no effect on consumption. One might interpret this result as providing evidence of inflation illusion in the prewar period. There is, however, an alternative and more subtle explanation which is suggested by the imaginative contribution of Barsky (1985). Relying on American and English historical data, he concludes that 'inflation evolved from essentially a white noise process in the pre-World War I years to a highly persistent, nonstationary ARIMA process in the post-1960 period' (p. 78). It turns out that the Italian experience mirrors quite closely his findings, as is readily apparent from figures 6.1(a) and (b).

During the period 1864–1914 inflation appears more or less as a white noise process and, indeed, a regression of p on p_{-1} yields a coefficient of zero (if also p_{-2} is included, inflation shows some moderate negative correlation). The period that follows the First World War (1919–39) shows some evidence of moderate positive correlation (a coefficient of p_{-1} of 0.4 with a t-statistic of 2.4). It follows that in the prewar period, to a first approximation, inflation was, by and large, unexpected, and the best predictor of inflation is a constant. This conclusion is consistent with the fact that in this period the nominal rate is independent of inflation, as can be verified from figures 6.1(a) and (b) and is confirmed by a zero correlation between R and p. Obviously, under these conditions, the *nominal* rate can be taken as a valid approximation of the *expected* real rate and the irrelevance of p^eD in (3.8) is consistent with rational behaviour.

Row (3.9) extends the period of estimation to 1864–1950 and drops land from the wealth variable. The result is a notable 'deterioration' of the estimates, as (a) the coefficient of RD is 0.9 – too high even from the LH–LCH perspective – and estimated with a large standard error, and (b) the coefficient of D turns out to be much too negative even for the REP. In view of the limitation of the data for the 18 added years, these results must be regarded as not very reliable.

In table 6.4 we present results for the whole period 1864–1982 and try to pin down the value of the critical coefficients (RD and p^eD) by relying on a greater number of observations. Regression (4.1) is one step in this direction, since the coefficient of RD is high and very significant. A Chow test comparing the subperiod regressions (3.2) and (3.9) with the restricted counterpart (4.1) yields an estimated F of 0.94 and indicates that the hypothesis that the structure is the same throughout the period cannot be rejected at the 5 per cent level of significance.

However, we have reason to believe that different subperiods differ considerably with respect to the role of p^e because, as we have seen, until the postwar period the nominal rate was unaffected by actual inflation, suggesting that inflation was largely unexpected; at least up to the First World War this hypothesis is supported by the fact that current inflation appears to be statistically independent of previous inflation. Accordingly, the overall p^eD was introduced with two multiplicative dummies, one for the years 1864–1914 and one for 1919–50. The result reported in (4.2) – where, as in table 6.3, we constrain the coefficient of W to control for multi-collinearity – confirms that the

Table 6.4 *Test of the effect of interest, debt and inflation, 1864–1982*

ID	*C* (1)	Y^* (2)	Y^*_{-1} (3)	*W* (4)	G^* (5)	*RD* (6)	p^eD_1 (7)	p^eD_2 (8)	p^eD (9)	*D* (10)	*RHO* (11)	*SE* (12)	*LL* (13)
4.1	38.8	0.49	0.23	0.014	−0.25	0.64				−0.02	0.74	4.57	320.4
	(14.9)	(24.0)	(9.2)	(2.8)	(−5.5)	(5.0)				(1.6)	11.4		
4.2	29.5	0.47	0.21	0.03	−0.26	0.56	0.36	0.46	−0.37		0.75	4.69	323.3
	(8.8)	(22.3)	(9.1)		(−5.4)	(4.4)	(2.0)	(3.0)	(−2.8)		(11.7)		
4.3	30.1	0.47	0.20	0.03	−0.25	0.56			−0.37		0.75	4.68	322.9
	(8.9)	(22.6)	(9.0)		(−5.4)	(4.4)			(−2.8)		(12.0)		
4.4	28.0	0.478	0.22	0.029	−0.24	0.48					0.72	4.75	324.6
	(9.5)	(21.8)	(8.5)	(7.4)	(−5.0)	(4.0)					(10.8)		
4.5	30.3	0.48	0.20	0.028	−0.09	0.45					0.71	4.97	329.5
	(9.6)	(11.8)	(4.9)	(6.9)	(−1.3)	(3.5)					(10.5)		
4.6	29.0	0.46	0.22	0.031	−0.23	0.53				−0.01	0.70	4.76	324.8
	(9.2)	(21.5)	(8.4)	(.6)	(−5.0)	(4.0)				(−0.8)	(10.4)		
4.7	31.3	0.48	0.21	0.026	−0.23					0.02	0.76	5.08	331.9
	(8.2)	(21.6)	(7.6)	(5.2)	(−4.6)					(0.9)	(12.1)		

t-statistics in parentheses. The period of estimation excludes wars. In regressions (4.4), (4.5) and (4.6) the coefficient of p^eD is constrained to be the opposite of that of *RD*. Regression (4.5) is estimated by instrumental variables.

'expected inflation' effect is important and close to the right magnitude for the postwar period, but is just about zero in the remaining two subperiods.[8] On this basis, we introduce in (4.3) a new measure of 'effective expected inflation' which is zero up to 1950 and p^e as defined earlier thereafter. The results are strongly supportive of the LH–LCH and contrary to the REP. This is true not only with respect to the deficit coefficient, but also in that interest income is very important, and so is the correction for effective expected inflation.

If, however, (4.3) is re-estimated without imposing the constraint on wealth, the coefficient of p^eD becomes smaller in absolute value and is estimated with larger error – a pattern of results similar to that observed in the postwar period – (cf. (3.3) and (3.4)). In view of our previous results (table 6.2) and the fact that the coefficient of wealth rises when we replace RD and p^eD with r^eD (cf. (3.5) and, below, (4.4)) we feel that the restriction is not inconsistent with the data, and that we can, on the basis of (4.3), reject the null hypothesis of inflation illusion ($h = 0$) in the entire sample.

To be sure, the coefficient of p^eD is a little smaller than that of RD, but as is shown by (4.4) – where RD is replaced by r^eD – the full rationality hypothesis calling for equal and opposite coefficients cannot be rejected even at the 5 per cent level. Note also that the results (4.4) are completely consistent with the constraint that the wealth coefficient be 0.03, as the unconstrained coefficient in (4.4) is almost the same (0.029 with a t-ratio of 7.4).

Finally we want to mention that our estimates could be criticized on the ground that they might be affected by simultaneity bias arising from the potential endogeneity of income and deficit. As shown by Feldstein (1982) and Seater and Mariano (1985) the problem is important and has to be carefully handled. Moreover, the potential bias of the deficit coefficient works in favour of the REP and against the LH–LCH, since, over the business cycle, lower income would lead to lower consumption and taxes and increase the deficit, thus inducing an upward bias in the deficit coefficient. When we tried to correct for the endogeneity of income and the deficit using instrumental variables, the results did not differ much from those presented. For this reason we only report the results that one obtains if (4.4) – the regression that we will use in the next section to account for the forces that have driven the national saving rate – is re-estimated by an instrumental variable procedure. In row (4.5) the instruments chosen are exports and government expenditure.[9] The differences from (4.4) are very small, with the exception that, as expected, the coefficient of the deficit comes closer to zero and is estimated with a larger error.

In the two final regressions of table 6.4 we try to come to grips with the separate effect of the stock of government debt. It is clear that we do not succeed. The point estimates are consistent with the LCH in both (4.6) and (4.7) where, fearing correlation between D and r^eD we have dropped the r^eD variable. But they are subject to such margin of errors relative to the reference wealth coefficient that no reliable conclusion would be justified.

VI THE EFFECT OF GROWTH AND FISCAL POLICY ON THE NATIONAL SAVING RATE

The empirical test of the model laid down in section II has shown that:

- the response of consumption to government deficits is negative, in accordance with the LCH, but rather small, as predicted by the LH–LCH;
- in constrast with the prediction of the REP, interest transfers have strong positive effects on consumption – roughly equal to that of all other forms of transfers; also, the evidence is not inconsistent with the hypothesis that consumers have taken into account expected real, rather than actual, nominal interest transfers, as called for by rational behaviour, although only in the latest years can we reject the null hypothesis of inflation illusion.

These behavioural characteristics can be used to account for the forces that have driven the national saving rate in the last century. For this purpose, we propose to rely on regression (4.4) of table 6.4 in which consumption responds to the expected real (rather than to the nominal) rate measured by the difference between nominal payments and expected inflation. Recalling equation 6.6 in section II, we can thus write:

$$S_T = [(NNP - T^*) - \Sigma a_i(NNP_i - T_i^*) - bW - cD - [(E - T^*) + \Sigma d_i(E_i - T_i^*)] - fr^eD \tag{6.8}$$

For the special case of regression (4.4) in which the maximum lag on income is one, there is no lag on the deficit, $\Sigma a_i + d = f$ and $c = 0$, we can rearrange the terms of equation 6.8 and divide by NNP to derive the following decomposition of the national saving rate:

$$\frac{S_T}{NNP} = (1 - a) + a_2\frac{\Delta NNP}{NNP} - a\,\frac{E}{NNP} - (\Sigma a_i + d_i)\frac{(G_i^* + r^eD_i)}{NNP} - \frac{bw}{NNP} - a_2\frac{\Delta E}{NNP} - \frac{k}{NNP} \tag{6.9}$$

$$= 0.31 + 0.22\frac{\Delta NNP}{NNP} - 0.69\frac{E}{NNP} - 0.23\frac{G^* + r^eD}{NNP}$$

$$- 0.22\frac{G^*_{-1} + r^eD_{-1}}{NNP} - 0.029\frac{W}{NNP} - 0.22\frac{\Delta E}{NNP} - \frac{28}{NNP}$$

where $a = a_1 + a_2$ is the marginal propensity to consume, $d_2 = 0$ and k is the constant term in regression (4.4).

From equation 6.9 it appears that the national saving rate:

- increases with the rate of growth of income;
- increases when the wealth to income ratio declines, and consumers reduce consumption in order to restore its long-run equilibrium value. The wealth to income ratio in turn should tend to decline with the rate of growth of income (Modigliani, 1975), providing one further reason for the association of growth and saving;
- decreases when there is a rise in government expenditure for a *given* deficit, that is, when there is a rise in tax financed expenditure. This is because the rise in taxes lowers disposable income and hence private saving by about 0.3 per dollar;
- decreases when there is a rise in the deficit expenditure held constant, that is when there is a fall in taxes, because of the resulting rise in disposable income and consumption; the effect is less than that via disposable income (Σa_i) to the extent that consumption decreases when there is a rise in deficit (d) and according to (4.4) the net effect is (0.69 – 0.24), or 0.45.

Since we find that consumers' behaviour is consistent with rationality and that the response to r^eD is similar to that of T^*, the same applies whenever expected real interest payments increase.

From equation 6.9 it can also be seen that fully anticipated inflation does not affect the national saving rate except in so far as it is systematically associated with the real rate itself. Otherwise inflation results in offsetting changes in R and p^e which leave r^e unaffected. If, however, inflation turns out to exceed the expectation, our results suggest that the private sector still consumes on the basis of the expected real rate and hence more than would be justified by the *ex-post* real rate. None the less, according to our results, unexpected inflation does not affect national saving, because, as is apparent from equation 6.9, the only way saving could be affected by inflation is through the deficit term – but this tends to depend on the perceived real rate and not on the *ex-post* realized one. Stated differently, both private consumption and, of course, public consumption E depend on r^e and not on actual inflation.

To summarize, our model predicts that the national saving rate depends on two factors: (a) a growth factor, that includes the effect of ΔNNP, of the wealth income ratio and of the constant term, to the extent that it is proxying for growth; and (b) a fiscal factor, that includes the effect of the rate of government consumption and of deficit financing.

In figures 6.2(a), (b) and (c), we have plotted the national saving rate and the forces that have been driving it.[10] The construction of these figures is most easily explained with reference to figure 6.2(c)

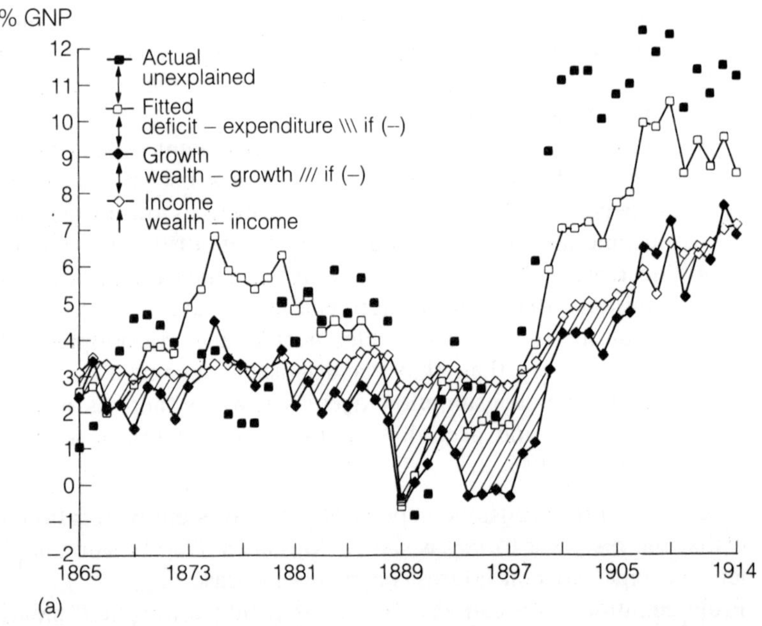

Figure 6.2 (a) National saving rate and its major determinants, 1864–1914
Note: Actual net saving rate relative to NNP (actual). The other variables are divided by NNP multiplied by the coefficient in regression (4.4) according to the decomposition (9) and subtracted from their mean (last row of table 6.5). Line *income* is the reciprocal term of (9). Line *growth* adds to income the growth factors (the variables W and ΔNNP multiplied by their coefficients in (9)). Line *fitted* adds to growth the fiscal factors (the variables E and $(G^* + r^eD)$ multiplied by their coefficients in (9)), and represents our fitted values. Each variable has been smoothed with a three-year moving average. The shaded area between fitted and growth indicates the negative contribution of fiscal policies to the fitted saving rate. The shaded area between growth and income is the negative contribution of the growth factor to the saving rate. The difference between fitted and actual is the *unexplained* residual, that includes also the autocorrelated component of the error term

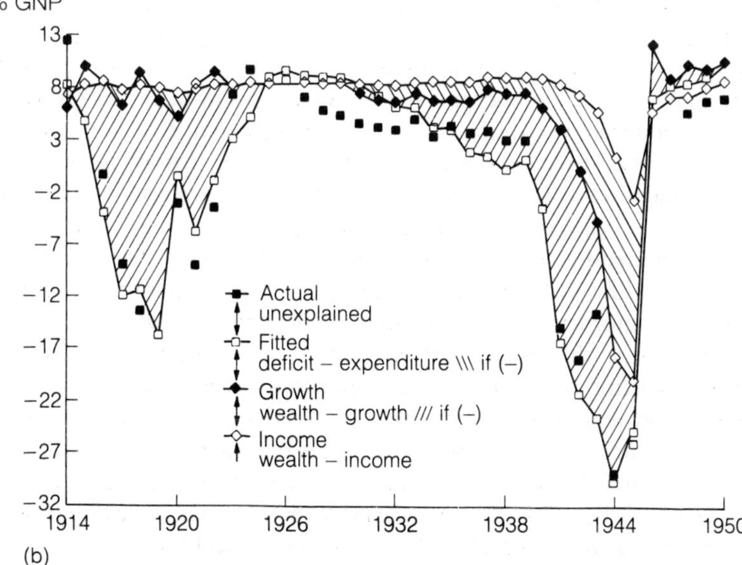

Figure 6.2 (b) National saving rate and its major determinants, 1914–50
Note: see note to (a). The variables for the war years, excluded in estimating (4.4), are actual values and are not based on moving averages

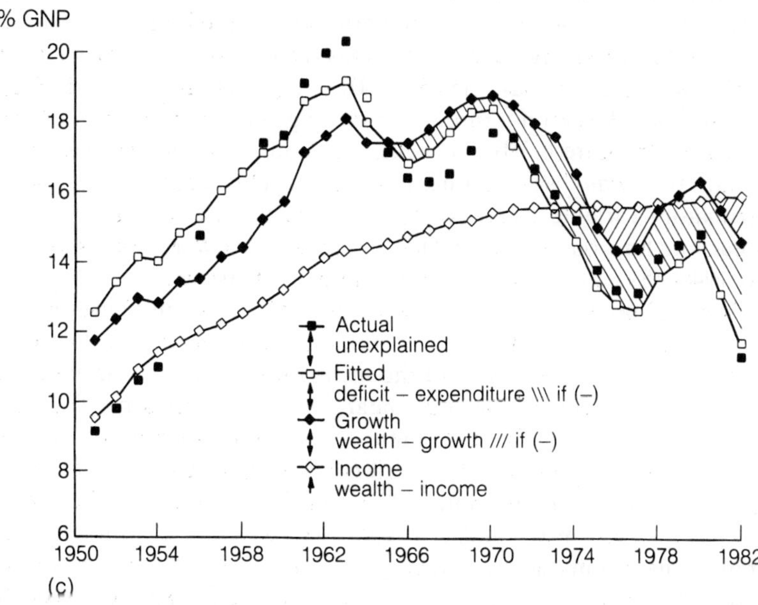

Figure 6.2 (c) National saving rate and its major determinants, 1950–82
Note: see note to (a)

and looking at the years around 1960. Three broken lines are identified; looking at the side, the point labelled 'Income' represents the constant term times the reciprocal of income. The second line, labelled 'Growth', is the sum of the income and the growth effect which consists of two components: the wealth income ratio and the rate of change of income, each multiplied by its coefficient. The growth effect itself is, of course, the distance between the income and the growth lines. It indicates a positive effect on saving to the extent that the growth line exceeds the income line, and a negative effect when it falls below. The third broken line labelled 'Fitted' represents the rate of national saving as computed from our empirically fitted equation. The area between it and the growth line is the remaining component of equation 6.4, the fiscal factor consisting of the expenditure and the deficit, both multiplied by their coefficients. To pinpoint the thrust of fiscal policy and growth on national saving, we have shaded the areas between Growth and Fitted, and between Growth and Income so that one can readily locate the year in which fiscal policy and/or growth make a negative contribution to the saving rate. Finally, the dots not joined by a line 'Actual' represent the actual value of saving so that the vertical distance from the fitted line measures the residual error. It should be noted that we regard as 'unexplained residual' not only the white-noise residual that we obtain from regression (4.4), but also the autocorrelated component of the error. Since we are interested primarily in the long-run behaviour of the national saving rate, rather than in its cyclical variations, the graphs in figures 6.2(a) (1865–1914), 6.2(b) (1914–50) and 6.2(c) (1950–82) are based on a three-year moving average of all the relevant variables. In figure 6.2(b), however, and only for the war years, we present the *actual* saving rate (as well as the actual values of the explanatory variables) and not the average because we are interested in learning how our equation (fitted *excluding* the war periods 1915–18 and 1940–45) actually performs in those brief episodes.

Table 6.5 provides an overview of the information in figures 6.2(a), (b) and (c) by giving, for each of nine selected subperiods, the mean of the national saving rate and the mean of the 'causal' variables, all in deviations from the overall mean, and multiplied by the coefficients in regression (4.4). In table 6.5 we have separately reported each of the components of equation 6.9 so that the fiscal effect in figure 6.2 is the sum of columns (3) and (4) of the table, the growth effect is the sum of (2) and (5), while the 'absolute income' effect is reported in column (6). Column (7) of the table reports the average of the difference between the Actual and the Fitted line over the selected periods. In choosing the benchmarks, we have tried to follow the swings of the saving rate, as well as to account for some of the

Table 6.5 *Breakdown of the national saving rate (S_T)*

Periods	*Actual* (1)	*W* (2)	$G^* + r^e D$ (3)	*E* (4)	NNP_{-1} (5)	*I* (6)	*Unexplained* (7)
1865–1881	−4.8	0.1	0.2	1.5	−0.7	−4.8	1.1
1882–1897	−5.1	−1.6	0.4	1.0	−0.7	−4.9	−0.7
1900–1914	3.2	−0.1	1.2	1.6	−0.2	−2.0	−2.7
1924–1929	−0.9	0.3	0.7	0.3	−0.4	−0.5	−2.3
1936–1939	−5.3	−1.4	−3.2	−3.1	−0.4	1.1	1.7
1948–1950	−1.0	0.8	0.4	−0.5	1.1	−0.8	−2.0
1961–1964	11.3	2.7	1.9	−1.1	1.1	6.1	−0.6
1976–1978	5.5	−0.5	0.3	−1.8	−0.4	7.6	0.3
1980–1982	3.2	−0.9	—	−3.0	−0.4	7.9	−0.4
1983	0.2	−2.1	−0.3	−4.0	−0.8	7.9	−0.5
1984	0.2	−1.6	0.5	−3.8	−0.2	7.9	−2.6
Mean 1865–1982	8.2	−10.1	−0.5	−3.2	0.5	−10.0	—

All variables are multiplied by their coefficient in regression (4.4) of table 6.4, subtracted from their mean (last row of the table) and divided by NNP. The period over which we have computed the mean (1865–1982) excludes the two war periods. The sum of the last row of the table is 8.2 (the average saving rate) up to the constant term $(1 - a)$, where a equals $a_1 + a_2 = 31.5$. In the years 1983 and 1984 we have used regression (4.4) to *forecast* the value of the net national saving rate; for these years column (7) thus represents the forecast error.

major events that have characterized the Italian economic history: the long period of stagnation until the end of the century, the ensuing first take-off until the First World War, the slowdown of economic activity and the war finance during the fascist regime, the economic boom of the 1950s and (after 1964) the beginning of a period of more moderate growth followed by the shocks of the 1970s.

The first two rows of table 6.5 and figure 6.2(a) show that in the first period (1865–97) the saving rate, after rising somewhat at the beginning of the 1880s (by some considered the first Italian industrial revolution), at the end of the century was back to levels similar to those prevailing at the beginning of the period. But it is important to note that its composition was substantially different: the government was in fact running balanced budgets at the beginning of the period, and surpluses by the end of the century, and, since these were only partially compensated by an increase in expenditure financed by taxes, gave a positive contribution to national saving in the 1890s. At the same time, the growth of the economy was so slow that the net saving of the private sector was very low throughout the period (around 3 per cent). One should also note that the fit of our equation yields large errors from 1865 to 1881 (first row of table 6.5) but improves somewhat from 1882 to 1897 (second row of table 6.5), due, presumably, to the better quality of data available since 1882.

It is at the turn of the century, in connection with a period of sustained and high growth, comparable with the 'miracle' of the 1950s, that the saving rate exhibited a very substantial increase (not fully accounted for by our equation) and remained high, reaching an average of 11.4 per cent of NNP in the period 1900–14 (second row of table 6.5). In fact, after the peak reached in 1907, the saving rate stabilized until the beginning of the First World War, mainly because of a reduction in government surpluses (reflected in a shrinking of the shaded area in figure 6.2(a)) and a slowdown of economic activity. It can be seen that during the period as a whole the fiscal variables contributed partly to the high saving as both the deficit and tax financed expenditure were distinctly below average. However, a significant factor accounting for the rise in saving rate of 8.1 percentage points turns out to be (unfortunately) the constant term (the Income line) that rises from an average of −4.9 to an average of −2.0, thus contributing 2.9 percentage points to the explanation; this result was to be expected in view of the large constant term and rapid growth, though as we have suggested, this effect could reflect at least partly the wealth effect of land omitted from wealth (see section IV).

In figure 6.2(b), we have plotted our variables for the period 1914–50. Note that the war periods were not included in our sample and that they are not smoothed with a moving average. After the First World War (discussed below) the saving rate reached, in the mid 1920s, levels not much lower than in the immediate prewar period, but by 1936–39 it had fallen by 5 per cent of NNP because of a very negative fiscal policy effect during the fascist period reflecting government expenditure and deficit (especially after 1934) to finance the Ethiopian war and to prepare for the Second World War. The distinctive feature of this period is in fact that the combined effect of expenditure and deficit contributes to substantially lowering the saving rate, as opposed to what we have observed in the pre-World War period.

It is immediately apparent from figure 6.2(b) how the movements in the saving rate during the two World Wars are entirely dominated by those of government expenditure and the extent of reliance on deficit financing. We have estimated that, contrary to the REP, government deficit crowds out national saving by roughly one-half and that expenditure reduces it by roughly 0.70. Clearly, these estimates, even though obtained by omitting the war years, explain the developments during the wars remarkably well. From figure 6.2(b) we also note that in the First World War the saving rate did not become negative until 1917, that it reached its lowest value in 1919, and that it only fully recovered to the prewar level in 1923. The reason is that both expenditure and deficits remained very large, due to the enormous burden of military outlays, until at least 1922.

The situation was somewhat different during the Second World War. In 1940 the saving rate was already substantially negative, and it declined further until the end of the war. But in the year immediately following the war, the economy recovered quickly as the deficit was brought nearly under control. Thus by 1946 the saving rate was already higher than in 1939, and in 1950 it was as high as it was in 1924.

In figure 6.2(c) it can be seen that in the period that followed (1951–63), characterized by unprecedented growth and economic stability, the saving rate continued to rise and reached a historical peak in 1963 (more than 20 per cent of NNP). The characteristics of this period (as well as the performance of our equation), are similar to the ones of the first decade of growth at the turn of the century. In both periods the impact of fiscal policy on national saving was positive but limited, in both the growth effect contributed substantially to national saving, but, in addition, the constant term effect also contributed appreciably to the rise in computed saving rate (Income line).

Finally, the last two decades (1963–82) have seen a decline in the saving rate (interrupted by modest improvement corresponding to the economic recoveries of the late 1960s and late 1970s) by about 9 per cent of NNP from the peak of 1963 to 1982. From figure 6.2(c) one can see that the performance of our equation is quite good in this period; from table 6.5 it appears also that all of our variables contribute to explain this decline. In particular, the combined effect of the fiscal variables is very strong, since they account for some 3.8 points of the decline of the saving rate; by observing the difference between Fitted line and Growth line, it can also be seen that the substantial positive fiscal effect of the early 1960s has turned to a negative one since the mid 1970s. The residual and important part of the change in the saving rate can be attributed to the sharp slowdown in the rate of growth of the economy. This slowdown is reflected in the difference between the Growth and Income lines, which is positive and growing until 1970 and declines rapidly afterwards, becoming small and even negative after the mid 1970s. This slowdown is reflected in a rise in the wealth to income ratio which contributes more than 3½ percentage points to the fall in the saving rate (cf. column (2) in table 6.5) and to a rate of change effect (column (5)) which contributes another 1½ points. The slowdown begins with the transitory episode of 1964 and ensuing monetary stringency but then resumes on a larger and more persistent scale with a series of real shocks. These include the second wage explosion of 1969 (the '*autunno caldo*') and subsequent years, the growing labour immobility, the oil crisis and the subsequent slowdown in world demand.

The last two rows of table 6.5 show that the decline in net national saving rate continues for the years 1983 and 1984 which are not included in our sample. They also show how well our equation performs when extrapolated to these years. The outcome is quite close in 1983 when the computed value is 8.9. The decline from the 11.4 value of the previous period is explained both by the continued slowdown and by both components of fiscal policy. The forecast for 1984 is appreciably worse, as it wrongly predicts a recovery of the saving rate by 2 percentage points as a result of improvements in both growth and fiscal stance not now visible in the data. But it should be noted that the error is still well within our standard error.

In discussing the postwar period we have mentioned that fiscal policy contributed significantly to the reduction in the national saving rate after 1970. This conclusion does not appear particularly novel and, indeed, is widely accepted by both experts and public opinion. It must be noted, however, that our analysis offers a rather different assessment of the magnitude and mechanism at work. The general perception is that the harm came from the rise of the total borrowing requirement (and, consequently, of the outstanding public debt) of the public sector, which reached the enormous level of some 15 per cent of NNP by the early 1980s and which, it was feared, would reduce national saving by a commensurate amount. The behaviour of this variable is depicted by the top line (B in the graph) of figure 6.3. However, our estimate of the effect of the deficit on national saving is only −0.5 (last row of table 6.5) in the early 1980s. There are three reasons that account for the fact that we obtain so small an estimate of the recent impact of the deficit on saving:

1 The first is that in this study we are concerned with the determinants of net national saving, and therefore we must subtract from the total borrowing requirement that part of the deficit that finances productive investment. We have thus concentrated on the current account deficit (line $G^* + RD$ in figure 6.3) on the assumption that national income accounts' distinction between public consumption and public investment is a meaningful one.
2 However, the line $(G^* + RD)$ measures the nominal deficit. In the presence of inflation one has also to take into account the depreciation of the stock of public debt. Conventionally, the deficit is corrected by subtracting pD (the *ex-post* inflation

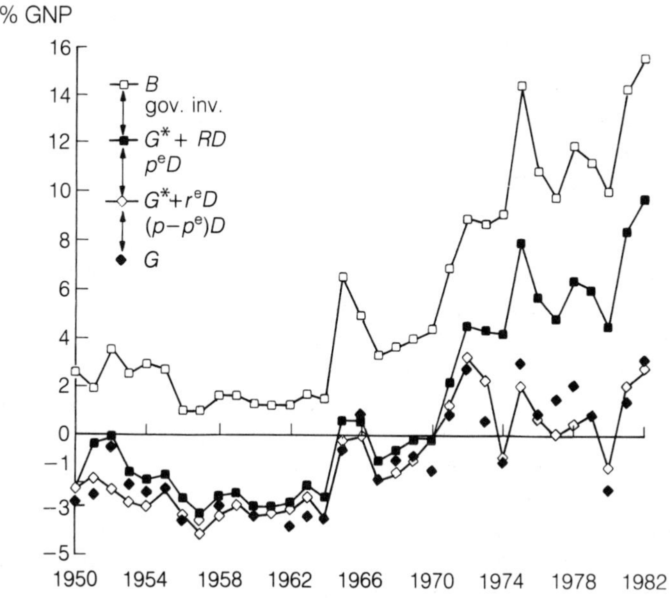

Figure 6.3 Four measures of government deficit, 1950–82
Note: Total government borrowing relative to NNP (B), government deficit as conventionally measured $(G^* + RD)$, corrected for expected inflation $(G + r^eD)$ and for actual inflation (G)

loss) from nominal interest transfers. This measure of the deficit is shown by the dots G in figure 6.3. But we have argued that, from the point of view of crowding out, what matters is the nominal deficit corrected for the *expected* depreciation of the debt – or p^eD (line $G^* + r^eD$ in figure 6.3). Since the difference between actual and expected inflation is modest and not systematic in the postwar period, the latter two measures of the deficit do not differ much from each other.

3 Finally, we have shown that deficits do not crowd out national saving one for one in that we estimate that the effect is roughly $0.5\ (\Sigma a_i + d)$, given, of course, the level of expenditure.

The main implication of these findings is that, contrary to the commonly held view, the deficit was not a major problem until the early 1980s, at least as far as national saving is concerned. Of course it is also true that the 'true' measure of deficit ($G^* + r^eD$) has increased very substantially since the 1950s and 1960s but mainly because substantial surpluses have turned into moderate deficits (from an averge of −3 per cent of NNP to 1 per cent of NNP in the early 1980s). Somewhat surprisingly, according to our calculations, the effect of the deficit is of the same order of magnitude of that represented by the rise in government expenditure (2 points of NNP) and described at the beginning of this section. Note also that in equation 6.9 expenditure reduces national saving via disposable income by a larger amount than the deficit (0.67 versus 0.45) and thus expenditure has increased by only about $\frac{2}{3}$ of the deficit in the last two decades.

In figure 6.4 the graph shows three measures of the saving rate. The first is the net national saving of figure 6.2 (S_T).[11] The second is the conventional measure of private saving (SPN = $Y^* + RD - C$). The third is the 'corrected' measure in which income includes expected real interest (SPC = $Y^* + r^eD - C$). To obtain S_T one can alternatively subtract from SPC the corrected measure of the deficit ($G^* + r^eD$ in figure 6.3) or from SPN the conventional measure ($G + RD$ in figure 6.3). It can be observed that until the early 1970s, the two measures of private saving do not differ much from each other. However, in times of inflation, the difference can be very substantial, as can be noted by the divergent paths of SPC and SPN since the turn of the 1960s. The reason is that SPN is *not* independent of inflation; on the contrary, it is positively correlated with inflation, while SPC and S_T are, as we have shown, independent of inflation provided the private sector does not suffer from inflation illusion and the expected real rate is independent of inflation. The high rate of inflation of the last decade

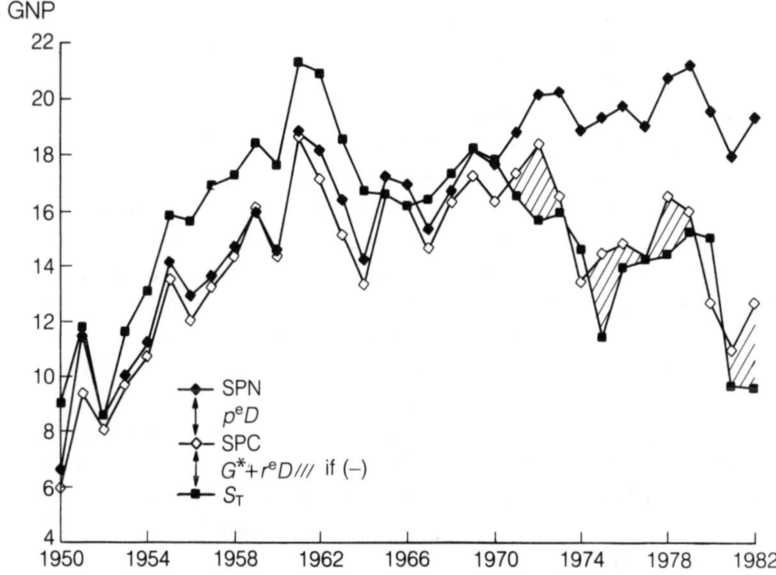

Figure 6.4 National and private saving rate, 1950–82
Note: private saving rate as conventionally measured (SPN = $Y^* + RD - C$), corrected for expected inflation (SPC = $Y^* + r^eD - C$) and net national saving rate (S_T). The shaded area between S_T and SPC indicates government deficits corrected for expected inflation

has swollen SPN, creating the false impression that Italy was continuing to enjoy uncommonly high private saving as during the golden period of the late 1950s and 1960s. In reality, saving, properly corrected, has declined rather dramatically, as a consequence of the severe slowdown of the economy.

VII CONCLUSIONS

In this chapter we have analysed the behaviour of the private consumption and national saving over the entire history of the Italian State, a period covering some 120 years. This experience is of notable interest as it covers a wide variety of circumstances, including persistent stagnation, moderate growth and unusually fast development, periods of stable prices and rapid inflation, orthodox fiscal policies and seemingly huge government deficits, especially in connection with two major wars, one of them catastrophic. This varied experience is reflected in the behaviour of the national saving rate. Previously available statistics on aggregate saving ratios, based mostly on developed countries, had created the impression that the ratio is a relatively stable number, at least within a given country; but in the case of Italy, net national saving has exhibited wild fluctuations, with extended periods of very little saving – as low as 3 per cent of NNP – while in other periods the rate hovered in the 17 to 20 per cent range.

Our analysis suggests that all of this varied experience can be explained, to a very large extent, by a life cycle type of consumption function and that, furthermore, the hypothesis that the coefficients of this function have *remained stable* throughout the period of well over a century cannot be rejected on the basis of standard statistical tests.

The consumption function we have used differs from earlier formulations in that it endeavours to take explicitly into account the role of fiscal variables. Once it is recognized that consumption depends on *expected* net-of-tax income, and account is taken of the intertemporal government budget equation, one finds that consumption is reduced not only by current taxes as in the conventional view, but also by expected taxes and government expenditure. Equivalently it responds positively to expected net income and negatively to government deficits. The quantitative effect of deficits turns out to depend on the length of the average planning horizon. If the horizon is infinite, as is effectively postulated by the proposers of the REP, then taxes matter not at all, while the response of consumption to government expenditure (or equivalently to deficit, given net income) would coincide with the propensity to consume. This of course implies that budget deficits have *no* effect on national saving, and the same would be true of any transfer, including payment of interest on national debt. These implications are the well-known essence of the Barro/RE proposition. By contrast, if the planning horizon is of the order of the length of remaining life, as postulated by the standard version of the LCH, then the coefficient of expenditure and deficit should be appreciably lower than the propensity to consume. It thus follows that the effect of deficits (including interest) on national saving will be large, not much lower than the propensity to consume.

The consumption function estimated for Italy appears to reject convincingly the REP and to be fully consistent with the life horizon LCH; specifically, we find: (a) that the estimated effect of the deficit on consumption is generally between $\frac{1}{3}$ and $\frac{2}{5}$ of the propensity to consume, and this seems to hold even in war periods, when the deficits are huge and hence their contribution can be estimated more reliably; and (b) that consumption responds to interest payment on national debt much as it responds to any other transfer, provided the interest payments are adjusted for the perceived loss of real principal due to expected inflation. One further possible test is, however, totally inconclusive – namely that relating to the effect on consumption of that component of private wealth that consists of government debt. Since our measure of wealth includes debt, and its coefficient is around 0.03, we can infer that, if debt is added to the equation, its coefficient should be around −0.03 for the REP and, say, between zero and around −0.01 for the LH–LCH. In fact, the coefficient estimated for the entire period is found to be precisely −0.01, but it is so poorly estimated (standard error −0.012) that no definite conclusion would be justified. For sub-periods, the results are equally inconclusive – for the postwar period as well as for the period 1882–1950, the coefficient is typically positive but again very imprecisely estimated. However, if one adds to the prewar period the 18 years 1864–81 for which the data are incomplete, then the coefficient becomes negative but too much so to be accounted for by the REP hypothesis. We conclude that the tests on the whole support LCH but by no means conclusively, and that a test of these implications does not look like a promising route for testing REP versus LH–LCH.

One significant result of our analysis is that while fiscal policy and, in particular, the deficit are important determinants of national saving (thereby playing an important role in domestic investment), their impact cannot be gauged from the behaviour of the current account deficit as conventionally measured. In the conventional measure the deficit includes the nominal service of the debt. We find instead that what affects consumption, and hence the deficit relevant to the estimation of the crowding out effect, is the *expected real* interest payment. This measure can be very much different from the nominal one under conditions of persistent, readily predictable inflation. Such conditions have prevailed since the early 1970s – though, apparently, not in earlier times.

Summing up, our empirical results indicate that the long swings in the saving ratio reflect primarily two forces – fiscal policies via expenditure and deficits, and variations in the growth rate of the economy, which manifest themselves in variations of the wealth to income ratio, in the rate of change of income effect and, presumably, in part, in the constant term. To illustrate, between 1936–39 and 1961–64, the national saving ratio increased $16\frac{1}{2}$ percentage points – from 3 to $19\frac{1}{2}$. The change explained by our equation is a little larger, $17\frac{1}{2}$. Of that change 7 points are attributable to fiscal policy – 5 of which are due to the swing in the budget from large deficit to a substantial surplus. Another $5\frac{1}{2}$ is attributable to the combined wealth and rate of change effect as the overall growth rate rose from zero to 6.5 per cent. The remaining

5 points are due to the constant term and presumably reflect in part a further wealth effect (via land) and possibly some absolute income effect.

As for the recent decline from the early 1960s to the early 1980s of some 8 percentage points (of which 7 are accounted for by the equation), we find that, contrary to a widely held perception, the major cause of decline is not the seemingly huge and highly visible deficit. Indeed, when the deficit is correctly measured it appears rather small even in the 1980s. Accordingly, fiscal policy accounts for less than half of the decline, and only half of that is due to the deficit. Furthermore the effect is not due to a substantial deficit *now* but, rather, to a substantial surplus *then*. The more important component of the decline in savings is related instead to the sharp drop in the growth of the economy, from 6.5 per cent to 1 per cent.

Finally, our analysis suggests that the observed variations in saving cannot be attributed to a systematic, direct effect of inflation. Indeed, that variable does not appear explicitly in our final equation, though it was tested on various occasions. This does not exclude the possibility of an indirect effect if, for example, (a) inflation had a systematic effect on the expected real rate (i.e. Fisher's law systematically fails to hold), and/or (b) taxation were, as a rule, adjusted to keep in balance the *nominal* budget. There is, however, little evidence that either of these two phenomena has played an important role in recent Italian history.

The LCH model suggests that other variables, in principle, should affect savings. These include in particular the demographic structure of the population and the social security system. While these variables are, by their nature, slowly changing, they could be important over the long span covered by our analysis. We have not so far found any satisfactory way to test for the presence of these effects but we do regard them as important topics for future research.

APPENDIX: SOURCES OF DATA

The sources of the data for the period 1950–82 (except for the series on government debt, that has been revised) can be found in the Data Appendix of Modigliani et al. (1985). From 1862 to 1950 we had to rely on a number of sources, of different quality and not always entirely consistent. Below we describe how each series has been constructed.

Private Consumption

Source: Ercolani (1969, p. 422, table 4.1.A). This variable, as well as consumption after 1950, includes expenditure on durables.

Disposable Income

Ercolani (1969, p. 427, table 4.4) provides an estimate of disposable income (gross of depreciation); we have computed the net disposable income of the private sector by subtracting depreciation. (Source: ISTAT, 1957.)

Wealth

Ercolani (1969, p. 418, table 3.3), provides an estimate of the stock of capital and of the value of agricultural land from 1882 to 1952. From 1861 to 1882 we have extrapolated this series backward, assuming the change in the stock of capital to be the same as the average rate of growth of disposable income. Finally, wealth is defined as the sum of the net stock of capital and government debt.

Government Debt

It is the only variable that has been revised from the one used by Modigliani et al. (1985), because a new series provided by Spaventa et al. (1984) was available at the time we started working on this paper. Essentially, Spaventa et al. (1984) have computed a series of the net debt of the public sector from 1960 to 1982, and improve upon previous available statistics because they subtract from the stock of debt of the public sector the amount of deposits of Central and Local Government to the banking sector. To preserve consistency, in the period 1950–60 we have rescaled the series on debt provided by Spaventa et al., assuming that the growth pattern of the public sector debt (unobservable from 1950 to 1960) could be approximated by the series on Central Government debt.

For the period 1864–1950 we relied on the following sources: from 1861 to 1900, Romani (1976, p. 268, table 12); from 1901 to 1935, ISTAT (1957, p. 173); from 1935 onward, United Nations, (1955, p. 89). The series from 1862 to 1950 excludes foreign debt but does not include the debt of local governments and public agencies, so that it is not readily comparable with the series provided by Spaventa et al., although one might argue that the importance of the debt of local governments and agencies has been growing in importance only in recent years.

Government Deficit

There are two estimates of government deficit over the period 1861–1950, the official one provided by ISTAT (1957) and another by Repaci (1962). Since the estimate of disposable income relies, among other sources, on the estimates done by Repaci, we have used the latter estimate of government deficit. It must also be noted that, as in the case of government debt, the deficit only refers to the Central Government.

Government Investment

Source: Ercolani (1969), series 'Servizi Economici' (p. 435, table 4.10). This series includes a number of different items, but generally refers to government investment for public services (electricity, railroads, etc.) and financing of public enterprises. The series is not entirely consistent with the definition of deficit elaborated by Repaci because it is based on the official statistics of the Central Government balance sheets.

Taxes

The sum of direct and indirect taxes. Source: Repaci (1962).

Nominal Interest Payments

Defined as interest paid by the Central Government to residents. From 1862 to 1900 the source is Romani (1978), from 1901 to 1935 ISTAT (1957) and from 1937 onward, United Nations (1955).

Inflation Loss on Government Debt

Defined as:

$$pD = (D/\text{defl})\,(\text{Defl} - \text{Defl}_{-1})$$

where p is the actual inflation rate, D is the beginning of period debt outstanding and Defl is the end of period deflator or private consumption.

Deflator of Private Consumption

Source: Ercolani (1969, p. 424, table 4.1.B).

Population

Source: Ercolani, p. 412, table 2.1.

Nominal Interest Rate on Government Obligations

(Used in figure 6.1) for the period 1862–1912, Romani (1976, p. 101, table 16); for the period 1926–50, Ercolani (1969, p. 456, table 5.2); for the period 1951–82, IMF, row 61b. For the period 1913–25 we had to rely on Spinelli (1979), who provides a series on the commercial paper rate.

NOTES

1 For a critique of Kormendi's approach, see Modigliani and Sterling (1985).
2 The way the variable is constructed also greatly differs among the two periods (see the Data Appendix in Modigliani et al. (1985), also Ercolani (1969)).
3 To give a feeling of the magnitude involved in the correction of government deficit for capital expenses, the item that we subtract from government deficit is about 10 per cent to 15 per cent of government expenses (except for the years following the Second World War, in which it reaches a peak of 46 per cent of government expenses). In terms of disposable income,

government investment usually is in the range of 2 per cent to 3 per cent, except for the postwar period in which it reaches a peak of 7.3 per cent of disposable income.

4 The actual rates of inflation in those years were 43 in 1916, 44 in 1917, 29 in 1918, 15 in 1919 and 41 in 1920. During the Second World War, inflation was 38.5 in 1942, 61 in 1943, 145 in 1944, 118 in 1945, 36 in 1946 and 73 in 1947.

5 We have conducted a Goldfeld test – assuming that the size of the errors was an increasing function of income – and the more general Park–Gleiser test; in no case did the errors appear to be heteroskedastic.

6 Regressions (2.9) and (2.10) have been estimated with multiplicative dummies on wealth and on the constant term, to account for the fact that wealth includes land until 1950 and that the constant term in (2.1) appears to be higher than in (2.3). Since the coefficients of the dummies were very small and never significant, we have dropped them and obtained the results reported in the table.

7 In the regression, we have used the market interest rate on medium-term government bonds. This measure of R is not entirely consistent with the RD variable, since RD is *not* the product of R and D, but is taken from the national account statistics. Thus, the implied R of our variable RD reflects the maturity structure of the public debt. It is, therefore, moving slower and is more serially correlated than the market rate. Since Fisher's law relates expected inflation to the market rate, we have used this latter variable in computing correlations among R, p and p^e.

8 A dummy on p^eD was introduced also in (3.7) to allow for a different coefficient in the period 1864–1914 and 1919–39. Since the dummy, as well as the coefficient of p^eD, was zero, we have not reported this regression.

9 To obtain consistent estimates in the presence of auto-correlated residuals, we have also added to the list of instruments the lagged dependent variable, the exogenous variables and all variables lagged once.

10 In plotting the variables as well as in computing the averages presented in table 6.5, we have been careful in carrying on the calculations based on the values of the coefficients of regression (4.4). Therefore, the coefficient of r^eD (0.53) is not assumed to be equal to $(\Sigma a_i + d)$. Equation 6.9 is for illustrative purposes only, although the differences with the actual values are negligible.

11 Note that S_T in figure 6.4 differs from S_T in figure 6.2 because the latter is smoothed with a three-year moving average.

REFERENCES

Barro, R. 1974: Are government bonds net wealth? *Journal of Political Economy*, 82, 1094–1117.

Barsky, R. 1985: Three interest rate paradoxes, MIT, Ph.D. Thesis.

Ercolani, P. 1969: Documentazione Statistica di Base. In Giorgio Fua (ed.) *Lo Sviluppo Economico in Italia*, Fronco Angeli Edibone, Milano, pp. 380–455.

Feldstein, M. 1982: Government deficit and aggregate demand, *Journal of Monetary Economics*, 9, 1–20.

ISTAT 1957: Indagine Statistica sullo Sviluppo del Reddito Nazionale dell'Italia dal 1861 al 1956, Rome.

Kormendi, R. 1983: Government debt, government spending and private sector behavior, *American Economic Review*, December, 73, 994–1010.

Modigliani, F. 1975: The life cycle hypothesis of saving twenty years later. In M. Parkin (ed.) *Contemporary Issues in Economics*, Manchester University Press, Manchester.

Modigliani, F. 1984: The Economics of Public Deficits, *Proceedings of the Conference on Economic Policy in Theory and Practices*, Israel, May.

Modigliani, F. and Sterling, A. 1985: Government debt, government spending and private sector behaviour: a comment (forthcoming in *American Economic Review*).

Modigliani, F., Jappelli, T. and Pagano, M. 1985: The impact of fiscal policy and inflation on national saving: the Italian case, *Banca Nazionale del Lavoro Quarterly Review*, June, 91–126.

Repaci, F.A. 1962: *La Finanza Pubblica in Italia nel Secolo 1861–1960*, Zanichelli, Bologna.

Romani, M. 1976: *Storia Economica d'Italia nel Secolo XIX, 1815–1914*, Vol. 2, Giuffre, Milano.

Seater, J. and Mariano, R. 1985: New tests of the life cycle and discounting hypothesis, *Journal of Monetary Economics*, 15, 195–215.

Spaventa, L., Artoni, R., Morcaldo, G. and Zanchi, P. 1984: *L'Indebitamento Pubblico in Italia: Evoluzione, Prospettive e Problemi*, Report prepared for the V Commission of the Chamber of Deputies, Rome, September.

Sterling, A. 1985: Public debt and private wealth: the role of anticipated taxes, MIT Sloan School of Management, April, Ph.D. Thesis.

7
Four Arguments for Fiscal Recovery in Italy

RAINER S. MASERA

What a government spends the public pay for. There is no such thing as an uncovered deficit. But in some countries it seems possible to please and content the public, for a time at least, by giving them, in return for the taxes they pay, finely engraved acknowledgements on watermarked paper. The income-tax receipts, which we in England receive from the Surveyor, we throw into the wastepaper basket; in Germany they call them bank notes and put them into their pocket-books; in France they are termed *rentes* and are locked up in the family safe. (J.M. Keynes, *A Tract on Monetary Reform*, Macmillan, 1923)

I INTRODUCTION

This chapter provides a brief survey of budget developments in Italy and focuses particularly on the question of sustainability. In sections II, III and IV, the issue is examined from different points of view, paying particular attention to the dynamic budget constraint.

First, the traditional stability analysis of the budget is revisited, with the emphasis on the relationships between interest and non-interest balances, on marginal and average debt interest rates and economic growth rates and on correction of the budget for inflation and the cycle. Second, the connection between deficits, debt, and financial assets is examined. Finally, the implications of the budget constraint for the

The views expressed are those of the author and do not necessarily reflect those of the Banca d'Italia. I am grateful to Paolo Baffi and to Emilio Barone, Cesare Caranza, Franco Cotula, Giampaolo Galli, Maria Teresa Pandolfi and Salvatore Rossi for their comments on earlier drafts of this paper. In addition, I derived much benefit from comments received during the discussion on the paper at the Conference. Any errors that remain are, naturally, my own.

creation of monetary base and money are reviewed. In this last section, the additional constraints and potential sources of instability, which arise in Italy because of the direct access of the Treasury to monetary base financing through its overdraft facility, are identified.

The various – mutually reinforcing – arguments confirm the need for fiscal adjustment in Italy. They lend support to the desirability of a gradual, but effective, programme of action to eliminate the disequilibrium in public finances. While the ultimate objective, in my opinion, should be a 'structural' balance, with constitutional guarantees, an intermediate target to be aimed at should be a zero deficit net of interest rate payments.

II GOVERNMENT DEFICITS AND THEIR SUSTAINABILITY

The Budget Deficit

In Italy, the structure of the public finances changed very significantly between the 1960s and the 1970s. The continued growth in expenditure and the deficit in the past decade was accompanied by monetization of the public sector borrowing requirement and by a tendency to reduce the real value of the debt through inflation. During the 1980s, with a gradual tightening of monetary policy, inflation fell and real interest rates rose; the deficit was largely financed by direct acquisitions of government paper by the household sector.

These developments[1] will be reviewed with reference to the budget constraint both at current and at constant prices. The public deficit has to be financed by issuing net financial debt (ΔDN), i.e. through the creation of monetary base, and/or by issuing interest-bearing debt:

$$G - T + iB = \mathrm{DEF} = \Delta\mathrm{DN} = \Delta\mathrm{BMT} + \Delta\mathrm{B} \qquad (7.1)$$

More specifically, final expenditure (G), on consumer and investment goods, on services and on wages and salaries of public employees, less taxes (T), net of all non-interest transfer payments, plus interest flows on the stock of interest-bearing public debt ($i \times B$, assumed to be one-period bills) generates the sector's financial deficit (DEF) which is financed by private sector acquisitions of new monetary base (ΔBMT) and/or securities (ΔB).

The factors which led to Italy's growing budget deficit are shown in tables 7.1 to 7.3.

Between 1960 and 1984 public sector revenues rose from 31.4 to 45.6 per cent of GDP, largely because of increases in direct taxes and social security contributions. Expenditure, however, rose from 32.4 to 60.3

Table 7.1 *Public sector revenues (percentage of GDP)*

	1960	*1970*	*1980*	*1981*	*1982*	*1983*	*1984*
Current revenues	31.1	32.1	38.2	39.9	42.6	45.5	45.4
direct taxes	(5.5)	(5.6)	(11.2)	(12.8)	(14.2)	(15.5)	(15.3)
indirect taxes	(12.1)	(11.2)	(10.1)	(9.7)	(10.1)	(11.2)	(11.3)
actual social security contributions	(8.3)	(10.7)	(12.9)	(13.1)	(14.1)	(14.5)	(14.4)
Capital account revenues	0.3	0.3	0.2	0.2	0.2	0.2	0.2
Total revenues	31.4	32.4	38.4	40.1	42.8	45.7	45.6

Table 7.2 *Public sector expenditure (percentage of GDP)*

	1960	*1970*	*1980*	*1981*	*1982*	*1983*	*1984*
Current expenditure	27.7	31.6	42.0	47.0	50.4	52.7	53.1
Operating costs	14.4	15.2	17.7	20.0	20.4	21.0	21.2
purchase of goods and services	(5.1)	(4.5)	(5.2)	(5.7)	(6.1)	(6.5)	(6.6)
wages and salaries	(9.3)	(10.7)	(12.5)	(14.3)	(14.3)	(14.5)	(14.6)
Interest payments	1.6	2.0	6.4	7.3	8.6	9.2	9.9
Transfer payments	11.7	14.4	17.9	19.7	21.4	22.5	22.0
to households	(9.8)	(12.4)	(15.8)	(17.7)	(18.7)	(19.6)	(19.5)
to firms	(1.1)	(1.2)	(1.4)	(1.3)	(1.7)	(1.8)	(1.7)
to international agencies and others	(0.8)	(0.8)	(0.7)	(0.7)	(1.0)	(0.7)	(0.8)
Capital account expenditure	4.7	4.8	5.2	5.7	6.1	6.7	7.2
Gross investment	4.1	3.5	3.9	4.3	4.6	4.8	4.8
Transfer payments	0.6	1.3	1.3	1.4	1.5	1.9	2.4
contributions to investment	(0.5)	(1.3)	(0.9)	(1.2)	(1.4)	(1.7)	(1.9)
other	(0.1)	(—)	(0.4)	(0.2)	(0.1)	(0.2)	(0.5)
Total expenditure	32.4	36.4	47.2	52.7	56.5	59.4	60.3

Financial items[a]	0.7	0.6	2.4	3.5	2.4	3.2	1.7
net credits and particular	(0.7)	(0.6)	(2.1)	(2.1)	(2.1)	(2.4)	(1.7)
variations in bank deposits	(—)	(—)	(0.3)	(1.4)	(0.3)	(0.8)	(0.0)
Grand total	33.1	37.0	49.6	56.2	58.9	62.6	62.0
Health care [bd]	3.1	4.7	6.0	5.8	6.1	6.2	6.1
Pensions[cd]	5.3	7.9	11.5	12.8	13.3	14.6	14.4

[a] *Source*: G. Morcaldo and P. Zanchi, *Un modello di previsione del bilancio pubblico per il breve-medio termine*, Proceedings of the Perugia Conference, February 1984.
[b] Total expenditure, in current and capital account, including the cost of administrative services.
[c] Including pensions (civil and war), payments to the blind, deaf-mutes and invalids.
[d] *Source*: ISTAT, *I Conti della protezione sociale*, Supplement to the Monthly Bulletin of Statistics, No. 28, 1983.

Table 7.3 Public sector deficit (percentage of GDP)

	1960–69	*1970–79*	*1980–84*	*1980*	*1981*	*1982*	*1983*	*1984*
Deficit on current account	−1.71	4.18	6.41	3.90	7.13	7.81	7.33	7.57
Deficit	2.68	8.64	12.20	8.95	12.63	13.74	13.88	14.73
Overall borrowing requirement	3.56	10.98	14.58	11.07	13.35	16.27	16.98	16.74
Interest payments	1.60	3.90	8.30	6.40	7.30	8.60	9.20	9.90
Borrowing requirement – interest payments	1.96	7.08	6.28	4.67	6.05	7.67	7.78	6.84

per cent, mainly because of rising transfer payments.[2] There was also a marked rise in financial transfer[3] – with corresponding changes in public sector financial assets.

The divergence between revenue and expenditure trends widened progressively through the 1970s and has persisted in the 1980s; though it now owes more to the size of interest rate payments as a result of both higher real rates and a growing debt/income ratio. The current balance, which averaged a surplus of 1.7 per cent of GDP in the 1960s, recorded a deficit of over 7.0 per cent from 1981 through 1984. At the same time, net indebtedness rose from 2.7 to 14.7 per cent and the total borrowing requirement from 3.6 to 16.7 per cent. The borrowing requirement net of interest payments was less than 2 per cent in the 1960s, but averaged around 7 per cent in the following 15 years.

Budget Instability

It is worth noting here that the conventional wisdom on the issue of non-convergence – which centres on the relationship between the average rate of interest on total outstanding government debt and the GDP growth rate – has recently been challenged. Blanchard et al. (1985) have argued that convergence requires that the balance net of interest should generally be positive.[4] The analysis in question rests, however, on the implicit assumption that – in equilibrium – the rate of growth of GDP is lower than the rate of interest. This need not be the case in the steady state.

Traditional stability analysis, with which I am in broad agreement, suggests instead that, given a net-of-interest deficit that is constant as a ratio of output, the debt to GDP ratio would reach a theoretical ceiling, provided that the rate of interest was less than the rate of growth of output. The ceiling is given by the ratio of (a) the deficit net of interest as a proportion of output to (b) the difference between the growth and the interest rate (see Appendix 1).

This conclusion rests on the assumption that government debt accumulation does not affect interest rates. Analytical considerations and empirical evidence on very recent experience, e.g. in the US and in Italy, suggest that, in spite of Barro's (1974) thesis, private saving will not automatically match increasing government deficits: interest rates, therefore, rise as a result of the growing deficit. With a given monetary policy, the dangers of a debt explosion are increased because both blades of the stability scissors work in a destabilizing way.

The outcome of these considerations, as applied to the present situation in Italy, suggests that the budget – from a technical point of view – is on the verge of instability. If the deficit, net of interest, is held at the average values recorded in the last 15 years (about 7 per cent), and assuming that the real rate of interest on the debt can be kept at present levels (about 2 per cent), with output growing at an annual rate of 3 per cent, then the theoretical equilibrium ceiling for the debt to income ratio would be 7% / (3% − 2%) = 7. It is evident that a ceiling of this level would pose problems of credibility and give rise to concern about the possibility of monetization. Quite apart from other considerations, the ensuing risk premium would tilt the relationship between growth and interest rates.

Analysis of the sustainability issue based on the direct comparison of real rates of interest and growth thus confirms that the situation is close to the limits of dynamic instability. It must be stressed here that the comparison is often – albeit wrongly – made between the rate on selected Treasury securities and the growth rate of output. If, instead, the average rate on the total debt is compared with the growth rate, the situation does not seem to be jeopardized (see table 7.4). While both in 1984 and in 1985 the yield on 6-month Treasury paper exceeded GDP growth by some 2 percentage points, the average rate on the debt was, respectively, 1.5 and 0.9 per cent below.

The figures reported in table 7.4 indicate, however, that the difference between the average rate and the marginal yield has been declining steadily: this is primarily the result of the disproportionate rise in government bonds. Time for adjustment is thus running very short, even allowing for the fact that the above calculations should be made with reference to the interest rate after taxation; in 1985 this would lower the average rate by about 0.8 percentage points.

The Effects of Inflation

As is well known the nominal budget position does not represent an accurate measure of the thrust of fiscal policy. For this purpose, suitable adjustments must be made for inflation and the economic cycle.

Starting with inflation, we can express (7.1) at constant prices:

$$\frac{G - T + iB}{P} = \Delta\frac{DN}{P} + \pi\frac{DN_{-1}}{P}$$

$$= \Delta\frac{BMT}{P} + \Delta\frac{B}{P} + \pi\frac{(BMT + B)_{-1}}{P} \qquad (7.2)$$

where π is the rate of inflation.

Solving (7.2) with respect to the change in the volume of net debt at constant prices, we find that it is equal to the deficit at constant prices adjusted for the change in buying power of the initial stock of

Table 7.4 *Interest payments by the public sector and ratios on the average stock of debt*

Years	Interest payments billions of current lire (1)	% GDP	Average stock of debt billions of current lire (2)	(3) = (1)/(2)	Rate on 6-month Treasury bills (4)	Inflation rate (5)	Real interest rates (6) = (3)−(5)	Real interest rates (7) = (4)−(5)	Growth rate of real GDP (8)	(9) = (6)−(8)	(10) = (7)−(8)
1980	21,525	6.4	208,993	10.3	16.0	21.2	−10.9	−5.2	3.9	−14.8	−9.1
1981	29,465	7.3	254,935	11.6	19.8	17.8	−6.2	2.0	0.1	−6.3	1.9
1982	40,592	8.6	321,304	12.7	19.4	16.5	−3.8	2.9	−0.5	−3.3	3.4
1983	49.845	9.2	407,695	12.2	17.8	14.7	−2.5	3.1	−0.4	−2.1	3.5
1984	60,335	9.9	507,726	11.9	15.3	10.8	1.1	4.5	2.6	−1.5	1.9
1985[a]	67,500	9.9	620,478	10.9	13.8	9.3	1.6	4.5	2.5	−0.9	2.0

Interest rate expenditure is net of interest payments by the Bank of Italy to the Treasury. The yield on 6-month Treasury bills is obtained as a weighted average of yields of fortnightly tenders. The rate of inflation is the yearly average increase in consumer prices.

[a] Estimates and forecasts kindly provided by Dr G. Salvemini.

debt over the period under consideration. The deficit at constant prices does not therefore generate a corresponding increase in real debt, whereas the deficit at current prices naturally creates a corresponding expansion in the nominal debt. The net change in the real debt is given by the deficit at constant prices less the monetary erosion (loss of purchasing power) of the initial stock of debt over the period under consideration.

The growing importance of monetary erosion from the early 1970s on is illustrated in figure 7.1, which traces trends in the nominal public

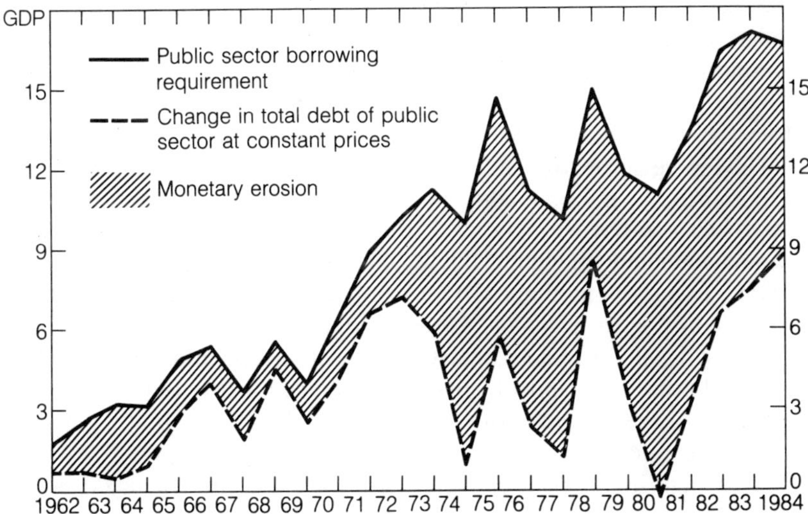

Figure 7.1 Public sector borrowing requirement (general government and autonomous agencies) and changes in total debt

Note: The public sector borrowing requirement can be broken down into two components for accounting purposes: the change in the corresponding gross debt at constant prices as a share of real GDP and the monetary erosion of the stock of debt at current prices at the beginning of the period as a ratio of nominal GDP.

$$\frac{FB}{Y} = \left(\frac{1}{y}\right) \Delta d + \left(\frac{1}{Y}\right) D_{-1}\pi \qquad (1)$$

where $FB = D - D_{-1}$ is the gross nominal borrowing requirement, Y is the nominal GDP, y is the real GDP, d is the gross debt at constant prices, D is the gross debt at current prices, $\pi = (P - P_{-1})/P$ is the inflation rate and p = GDP deflator. The demonstration of (1) can be obtained as follows:

$$\frac{FB}{Y} = \frac{\Delta D}{Py} = \frac{\Delta(Pd)}{Py} = \frac{\Delta dP + d_{-1}\Delta P}{Py} = \left(\frac{1}{y}\right)\Delta d + \left(\frac{1}{Y}\right)D_{-1}\pi$$

When the interest rate on the debt is equal to the rate of inflation (real rate equals zero), equation (1) shows that the change in real debt with respect to real GDP is equal to the borrowing requirement net of interest as a share of GDP: interest payments only restore the real value of the stock of debt eroded by inflation.

sector borrowing requirement and the corresponding change in real debt as a ratio to GDP. The note accompanying the figure explains that the area between the two lines represents monetary erosion, which increased from 1–2 per cent in the 1960s to 5–10 per cent in the 1970s and 1980s.

Table 7.5 quantifies both the monetary erosion and the 'inflation tax'[5] on the total net liabilities of the public sector. The 'inflation tax' has been calculated as the algebraic sum of monetary erosion and nominal interest payments on the debt.[6] In the 1960s for the most part there were net transfers, albeit small ones, from the public sector to the rest of the economy. Average real interest rates were positive. The inflation tax reached its highest levels in 1974, 1976, 1979 and 1980, amounting to respectively 5.9, 6.6, 4.6 and 5.1 per cent of GDP. Thereafter the tax first shrank and then swung back into net positive transfers in 1983 and 1984 of 0.7 and 2.9 per cent respectively.

Having reviewed the figures for inflation correction in the Italian experience, let me now add some words of caution on their use. This approach is often wrongly used to derive one-sided indications about the strength and the sign of the fiscal impulses imparted by the nominal budget at a given moment. To look only at the budget figures corrected for inflation is to make the same mistake as those who consider only the growth rate of real monetary balances to assess monetary impulses. As we know, this kind of error has often led at the outset of hyper-inflation to the conviction that monetary policy was actually playing a restrictive role!

That high inflation often significantly reduces the corrected budget deficit – or even turns it into a surplus – does not justify concluding that if there is a drop in inflation the budget will automatically return to balance. Apart from any other considerations, at least the trends that actually affect the items of the budget over a given period of time must be taken into account.

In the Italian case, for example, Morcaldo and Salvemini (1984a) used a model of public finances to project receipts and expenditures over a five-year period, on the assumption of gradual exogenous dis-inflation and relatively sustained real growth. They showed that the ratio of the nominal deficit to GDP would tend to stay at its present very high level, while the ratio of the public debt to GDP would continue to rise.[7]

The definition of the structural budget surplus or deficit should also take cyclical fluctuations into account. Moreover, for a small, open economy, like Italy's, reference to the concept of sustainable potential income would have to take the external constraint explicitly into account. Since present methodology is largely based on the US economy, it does not give this element the consideration it requires.

Table 7.5 Loss of purchasing power and inflation tax on net public sector financial liabilities: 1961–84

Year	Monetary erosion of net public sector liability	Interest payments by the public sector	Inflation tax (negative in sign)	Monetary erosion of net public sector liability	Interest payments by the public sector	Inflation tax (negative in sign)	Monetary erosion of net public sector liability	Interest payments by the public sector	Inflation tax (negative in sign)
	(billions of current lire)			(billions of 1980 lire)			(percentage of GDP)		
1961	264	395	131	1,389	2,078	689	1.02	1.53	0.51
1962	620	427	−193	3,116	2,146	−970	2.14	1.47	−0.66
1963	694	452	−242	3,245	2,113	−1,131	2.09	1.36	−0.73
1964	619	467	−152	2,733	2,062	−671	1.70	1.28	−0.42
1965	390	543	153	1,647	2,293	646	1.00	1.39	0.39
1966	322	692	370	1,330	2,857	1,528	0.76	1.63	0.87
1967	379	875	496	1,509	3,483	1,975	0.81	1.87	1.06
1968	161	957	796	632	3,759	3,127	0.32	1.89	1.57
1969	762	1,088	326	2,915	4,162	1,247	1.36	1.95	0.58
1970	1,108	1,268	160	4,041	4,624	584	1.76	2.02	0.26
1971	1,152	1,589	437	4,008	5,529	1,521	1.68	2.32	0.64
1972	2,185	1,943	−242	7,190	6,394	−796	2.90	2.59	−0.32
1973	4,421	2,532	−1,889	13,126	7,518	−5,609	4.93	2.82	−2.10
1974	10,169	3,691	−6,478	25,346	9,120	−16,147	9.18	3.33	−5.85
1975	6,276	5,285	−991	13,373	11,261	−2,112	5.01	4.22	−0.79
1976	17,731	7,439	−10,292	32,362	13,577	−18,784	11.32	4.75	−6.57
1977	13,690	9,664	−4,026	21,354	15,074	−6,280	7.20	5.08	−2.12
1978	14,099	13,360	−739	19,612	18,584	−1,028	6.34	6.01	−0.33
1979	28,430	16,046	−12,384	34,452	19,445	−15,007	10.52	5.94	−4.58
1980	38,705	21,525	−17,180	38,705	21,525	−17,180	11.43	6.35	−5.08
1981	40,394	29,465	−10,929	34,290	25,013	−9,278	10.06	7.34	−2.72
1982	47,346	40,592	−6,754	34,509	29,586	−4,923	10.06	8.63	−1.43
1983	46,336	49,845	3,509	29,457	31,688	2,231	8.00	9.25	0.65
1984	42,767	60,335	17,568	24,536	34,616	10,079	6.99	9.86	2.87

At any rate, even if the nominal adjustments for both inflation and the cycle are made, neglecting the caveats just formulated, the deficit of the Italian public sector remains exceedingly high, both in absolute terms – on average, about 6 per cent in the 1970s and also in the 1980–84 period – and compared with other countries, as can be seen for instance in table 7.6, prepared by the EC Commission.

Table 7.6 Budget balance, adjusted for cycle and inflation

	1971–80	*1981*	*1982*	*1983*	*1984*
B	−3.6	−8.4	−5.4	−5.5	−4.1
DK	1.3	−4.2	−7.3	−5.0	−2.5
D	−1.6	−3.7	−1.4	0.0	0.4
GR	—	−10.5	−8.2	−6.2	−6.2
F	−0.4	−1.3	−1.9	−1.4	−0.3
IRL	—	−11.1	−9.6	−6.1	−4.5
I	−6.3	−9.0	−7.7	−4.6	−6.2
L	−0.7	−6.8	−4.9	−2.0	−1.4
NL	−2.3	−5.7	−5.1	−3.5	−3.4
UK	−2.3	0.3	0.5	−1.7	−1.9
CE	−2.4	−3.8	−3.0	−2.3	−2.0

Source: Commission of the EC, *European Economy*, November 1984.

III GOVERNMENT DEBT ACCUMULATION AND CREATION OF FINANCIAL ASSETS AND CREDIT

We come now to a second set of considerations on the sustainability of budget deficits, hingeing on the analysis of the implications of the budget constraint for the creation of financial assets and monetary base.[8]

Domestic Financial Assets and Credit

The budget constraint in nominal terms ties the balance of expenditure and revenues to changes in the stock of debt. If we rewrite equation 7.1 in terms of the borrowing requirement (that is, with the inclusion of financial items) we get

$$G - T + iB = (\Delta D/D)D \qquad (7.3)$$

where F is the financial outflows and D is the gross public debt.

Using a flow-of-funds approach at current prices, it is possible to identify the links between total flows of financial assets and the channels of creation, one of which is the borrowing requirement.

$$\Delta \mathrm{AF} = \Delta \mathrm{AFI} + \Delta \mathrm{AFE} \tag{7.4}$$

$$\Delta \mathrm{AFI} = \Delta D + \Delta \mathrm{PFI} + \mathrm{BP} = \Delta \mathrm{CTI} + \mathrm{BP} \tag{7.5}$$

where F is the total financial assets, AFI is the domestic financial assets, AFE is the foreign financial assets, PFI is the domestic indebtedness of firms and households, BP is the balance of payments and CTI is the total domestic credit.[9]

Equations 7.3 and 7.5 show how the public sector borrowing requirement contributes to the creation of financial assets. This is detailed with reference to the Italian experience in table 7.7, which shows the increasing importance of the fiscal deficit in the creation of domestic financial assets.[10]

In the 1960s, while average annual increases of 5.8 and 4 per cent were recorded in real GDP and consumer prices, domestic financial assets expanded by an average rate of 13.4 per cent. The public debt grew at a rate of 8.6 per cent, and accounted for only one-fifth of the total expansion of financial assets. In the succeeding decade, growth in real product almost halved, dropping to 3.3 per cent, while consumer prices rose at an average rate of about 13.5 per cent, almost four times higher; financial assets recorded a growth rate of 18.9 per cent, five points up on the 1960s rate. Deficits pushed up the public debt at an average rate of 23.6 per cent, and accounted for about half the overall creation of domestic financial assets.

In the 5-year period from 1980 to 1984, domestic financial assets continued to expand at the rate recorded in the 1970s, while the public debt grew even faster, at an annual rate of close to 25 per cent. As a result of the latter and the growing weight of public debt on financial assets, the public deficit accounted for more than 70 per cent of the creation of domestic financial assets. A similar picture emerges from table 7.8, where the calculations just described are repeated for total domestic credit and the state's share.

An examination of the past 25 years makes it hard to argue against the view that the state takes the lion's share of financial resources.

Household Financial Savings

On average, between 1971 and 1980 the rapid growth of total financial assets was matched by corresponding increases in the adjusted monetary base and in nominal output. As a result, the ratio of the private sector's

Table 7.7 Domestic financial assets: growth rate and the share 'explained' by the state-sector debt

	1960–69	*1970–79*	*1980–84*	*1980*	*1981*	*1982*	*1983*	*1984*
	average growth rate throughout the period							
Domestic financial assets	13.36	18.94	18.44	15.79	17.83	18.95	20.54	19.08
State-sector debt	8.59	23.60	24.35	20.90	22.94	28.04	27.11	22.78
Share[a] due to state-sector debt	20.80	47.71	71.39	64.20	65.16	79.18	76.01	72.39
Memorandum items								
Real GDP	5.82	3.31	1.14	3.9	0.1	−0.5	−0.4	2.6
Nominal GDP	10.85	17.16	17.44	25.4	18.5	17.2	14.6	11.5
Consumer prices	4.04	13.48	16.20	21.2	17.8	16.5	14.7	10.8

[a] Proportion of change in domestic financial assets represented by the change in state-sector debt.

Table 7.8 *Total domestic credit: growth rates and share 'explained' by the state-sector debt*

	1960–69	*1970–79*	*1980–84*	*1980*	*1981*	*1982*	*1983*	*1984*
	average growth rate throughout the period							
Total domestic credit	13.60	18.90	19.67	18.55	18.10	20.85	20.66	20.19
State-sector debt	8.59	23.60	24.35	20.90	22.94	28.04	27.11	22.78
Share[a] due to state-sector debt	21.14	44.34	63.85	53.76	61.69	68.72	70.96	64.13

[a] Proportion of change in total domestic credit represented by the change in state-sector debt.

financial assets to GDP was roughly the same in the first and last years of the ten-year period.

At the turn of the 1970s, it gradually became obvious that the public had become aware of the inflation tax, and was reacting to the growth in prices by substantially reducing its rate of financial saving. This can be seen from table 7.9, which contains figures on both overall financial savings and households' disposable income, appropriately corrected for inflation (for a detailed analysis of the variables and of the correction procedure see Lecaldano, Marotta and Masera, 1985). The rate of net financial saving averaged 10.7 per cent during the 1970–72 period, i.e. before the inflationary wave. Between 1973 and 1978 the average rate was 2.5 per cent; in 1979 and 1980 it declined to −0.2 and −4.1 per cent respectively.

In these circumstances, it was only with a tightening of monetary policy that savers were enticed to return to financial saving, and notably to direct acquisitions of government bonds. The required portfolio shifts were made contemporaneously with progressively rising real rates of interest.

Table 7.9 *Households' gross saving, net financial saving and inflation adjustment (in percentages of households' gross disposable income)*

Year	Gross saving (A)	Net financial saving (B)	Inflation adjustment (C)	(A) − (C)	(B) − (C)
1970	22.4	12.4	4.5	17.9	7.9
1971	23.8	15.6	4.1	19.7	11.5
1972	24.8	19.7	7.0	17.8	12.7
1973	24.7	14.7	11.3	13.4	3.4
1974	24.0	13.0	20.5	3.4	−7.6
1975	26.4	17.8	9.0	17.4	8.8
1976	26.1	16.3	18.7	7.4	−2.4
1977	25.9	16.6	12.0	13.9	4.6
1978	27.2	18.5	10.3	16.9	8.2
1979	26.4	17.2	17.4	9.0	−0.2
1980	24.5	14.9	19.0	5.5	−4.1
1981	24.7	16.6	15.8	8.9	0.8
1982	24.6	17.6	14.9	9.7	2.7
1983	24.1	19.8	12.3	11.8	7.5
1984	24.3	20.3	9.7	14.6	10.6

Source: Lecaldano, Marotta and Masera (1985).

Theoretical analysis suggests the net impact of interest rates on saving is the result of substitution effects on the one hand and income and wealth effects on thc other, and they work in opposite directions. Empirical evidence on Italy over the last decade, obtained by adjusting both the disposable income and the final savings of the household sector for purchasing power losses on financial assets, suggests that changes in the real rate of interest on financial assets exerted a noticeable effect on financial saving. This effect is partly due to a reallocation of existing wealth between financial and non-financial assets and partly to the change in the allocation of new savings.[11]

As figure 7.2 shows, in 1980, when the average real yield on total financial assets held by the household sector was around −8 per cent, the share of disposable income devoted to financial saving was around 3 percentage points below that required to maintain the purchasing power of the initial stock of financial assets. By contrast, in 1984, when the average yield climbed back to positive values in real terms, the share of income allocated to financial asset accumulation was some 10 percentage points above that required to restore the initial purchasing power.

The high real yields on government paper (see figure 7.3) which emerged in the financial markets as a result of the pressure stemming from a very large demand for funds by the Treasury and a moderate growth in the adjusted monetary base, helped contain households' final expenditure by encouraging their accumulation of financial assets, and notably of government paper.

In the years 1973–74 some four-fifths of households' financial saving went into monetary (M_2) assets. In 1983–84, the proportion fell to less than two-fifths. Treasury and other medium- and long-term bonds, which ten years ago accounted for one-tenth of financial saving, now represent about one-half. The private sector's holdings of domestic financial assets rose as a ratio to GDP from 1.11 in 1981 to 1.26 in 1984, as shown in table 7.10, and was expected to increase further to 1.34 by the end of 1985. These two values are the highest recorded by this series, which dates back to 1960.

Here again, however, it is evident that the situation is not a stable one. The portfolio distortions implicit in a situation where savers are called upon to hold an increasing proportion (a) of their wealth in financial assets, and (b) of their financial assets in government bonds do not appear sustainable beyond the medium term. Higher yields on a growing proportion of financial assets generate the risks of dynamic instability already alluded to.

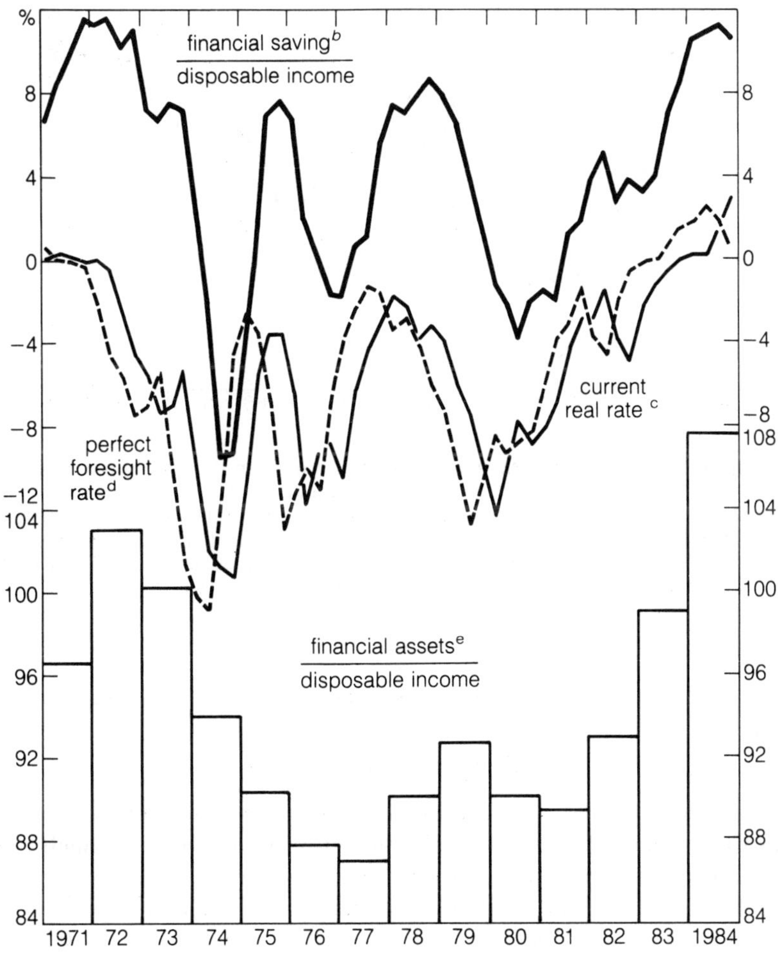

Figure 7.2 Financial assets, income and interest rates[a]

([a]Net of shares, participations, actuarial reserves, atypical securities and foreign assets. [b]Cumulative variations over four quarters, net of inflation-induced depreciation of financial assets. [c]Weighted average of mean quarterly rates of return, net of taxes, deflated by the annualized change in consumer prices in the six months under consideration. [d]Weighted average of mean quarterly rates of return, deflated by the annualized change in consumer prices in the two subsequent quarters. [e]Average of five quarterly figures.)

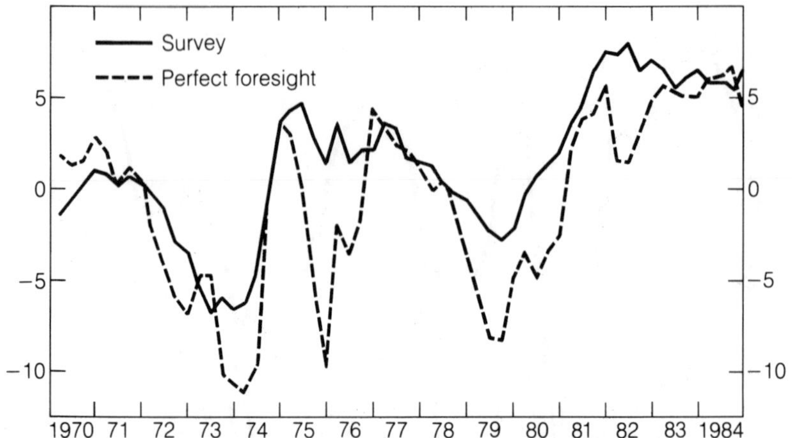

Figure 7.3 Expected real rate of interest on six-month Treasury bills[a] (Source: Bank of Italy)
([a]Until the third quarter 1975 weighted average rate for all TB issued. The perfect foresight rate of inflation (dashed line) is defined as the rate of change in the next six months of the consumer price index. Alternatively (heavy line) a survey-based six-month expected rate of change of consumer price index is used (see Visco, 1984))

IV THE BUDGET AND THE PROCESS OF MONEY CREATION

Creation of Monetary Base

As equations 7.1 and 7.3 show, the public sector borrowing requirement has to be financed either through interest-bearing debt or through the creation of monetary base. In principle, the central bank can control the Treasury's overall creation of monetary base by its net purchases of government securities (at issue or on the open market). Until the 'divorce' in 1980, this control was limited by the Bank of Italy's commitment to purchase all Treasury bills not sold at issue.[12]

The Italian system provides the Treasury with direct access to the central bank, via its current account overdraft facility. The amount of this facility is fixed by law (a ceiling of 14 per cent of each year's original spending estimates and subsequent modifications). Obviously, this legislative provision could easily be evaded if the Bank of Italy did not have full discretionary powers to decide on the amount of its purchases of government securities in order to keep the overall expansion of Treasury monetary base in line with targeted monetary and credit flows.

in parentheses)

	Gross domestic product		State-sector borrowing requirement		Funds to the non-state sector		Total domestic credit (A)+(B)			Financial assets of the private sector[a]			
											%		
Year	[b]	% growth	Billions of lire	(A)[c]	(B)[b]	% growth	[b]	% growth	% GDP	[d]	[e]	[f]	[g]
1970	62883	**12.5**	3222	3031	5237	**12.2**	8268	**13.8**	(13.1)	6376	**11.0**	(10.1)	(102.0)
1971	68510	**8.9**	4823	4293	7657	**15.9**	11950	**17.5**	(17.4)	10196	**15.9**	(14.9)	(109.0)
1972	75124	**9.7**	5910	5644	9875	**17.8**	15519	**19.3**	(20.7)	13525	**18.1**	(18.0)	(118.0)
1973	89746	**19.5**	7993	7242	13784	**21.1**	21026	**21.9**	(23.4)	19962	**22.5**	(22.2)	(118.0)
1974	110719	**23.4**	8960	8796	12547	**16.2**	21343	**18.4**	(19.3)	13279	**12.5**	(12.0)	(108.9)
1975	125378	**13.2**	16444	14218	16861	**18.7**	31079	**22.6**	(24.8)	24761	**20.7**	(19.7)	(115.2)
1976	156657	**24.9**	14867	14208	19753	**18.8**	33961	**20.1**	(21.7)	29549	**20.5**	(18.9)	(111.5)
1977	190083	**21.3**	22567	17973	17289	**13.9**	35262	**17.4**	(18.6)	34075	**19.5**	(17.9)	(110.0)
1978	222254	**16.9**	34305	31763	17498	**12.7**	49251	**20.7**	(22.2)	48780	**23.3**	(21.9)	(116.2)
1979	270198	**21.6**	30371	28531	25217	**16.5**	53748	**18.7**	(19.9)	58166	**22.5**	(21.5)	(117.5)
1980	338743	**25.4**	37017	34015	29256	**16.4**	63271	**18.6**	(18.7)	51655	**16.3**	(15.2)	(109.2)
1981[h]	401579	**18.5**	53296	45242	28092	**13.5**	73334	**18.1**	(18.3)	70453	**19.1**	(17.5)	(110.9)
1982[h]	470484	**17.2**	72653	68987	31404	**13.4**	100391	**20.9**	(21.3)	89555	**20.1**	(19.0)	(113.1)
1983	538998	**14.6**	88604	85541	35002	**13.1**	120543	**20.7**	(22.4)	108164	**20.3**	(20.1)	(119.0)
1984	612112	**13.6**	95351	91364	47112	**15.3**	138476	**19.5**	(22.6)	129179	**20.1**	(21.1)	(126.1)
1985[i]	669600	**9.4**	99900	94600	43000	**12.0**	137600	**16.2**	(20.5)	127000	**16.5**	(19.0)	(134.0)

[a] Domestic assets excluding shares, actuarial reserves and atypical securities.
[b] Level in billions of lire.
[c] Domestically financed.
[d] Annual flow in billions of lire.
[e] Annual flow % stock.
[f] Annual flow % GDP.
[g] Stock as % GDP (end-of-period stock).
[h] Funds to the non-state sector and total domestic credit are adjusted for non-interest-bearing deposits on payments abroad.
[i] Official targets.

Source Bank of Italy.

The Effect of the Treasury Overdraft Facility on the Monetary Base

The overdraft facility constitutes an important constraint on the conduct of monetary policy in Italy; it gives rise to day-to-day management problems and, ultimately, is a threat to the controllability of the monetary base.

This can be seen by looking at the following model, where it is assumed for simplicity's sake that the counterparts of the total monetary base (BM) are only credits to the Treasury in the form of the overdraft facility ($OD = E$) and securities in the central bank's portfolio (BCB).

$$BM = BMT = \alpha E + BCB \tag{7.6}$$

where $E = G + iB$ is the total government expenditure.

It is next assumed that the stock of money is related to the stock of high-powered money by means of the multiplier μ

$$M = \mu BM \tag{7.7}$$

It is assumed that the stock of government bonds held by the central bank is kept constant, and that monetary policy is aimed at achieving a rate of money growth equal to that of nominal output; we therefore have

$$G_{\text{BM}} = G_{\text{E}}\frac{\alpha E}{BM} \tag{7.8}$$

$$G_{\text{M}} = G\mu + G_{\text{BM}} \tag{7.9}$$

$$G_{\text{M}} = G_{\text{Y}} \tag{7.10}$$

$$\lim_{t \to \infty} \frac{E}{BM} = 1 \tag{7.11}$$

If the rate of growth of government expenditure systematically and significantly exceeds that of output, as has been the case in the past ten years in the Italian economy (29 against 19 per cent),

$$G_{\text{E}} = \beta G_{\text{Y}} \quad \beta \gg 1 \tag{7.12}$$

we obtain

$$G\mu = G_{\text{Y}}\left(1 - \beta\frac{\alpha E}{BM}\right) \tag{7.13}$$

if $\beta \gg BM/\alpha E$, $G\mu < 0$.

In these circumstances, to achieve dynamic equilibrium, if the currency to deposit ratio is constant, the reserve ratio has to be steadily *rising*, which, however, leads to disintermediation of the banking system.

Alternatively, we can assume that the multiplier remains constant, the burden of adjustment then falls on the stock of government debt held by the central bank. This can only be a medium-term solution, however, since the stock is finite and may not assume negative values.

To assess the importance this source of monetary base growth has acquired in the Italian context, it should be noted that at the end of 1984 the overdraft represented nearly 40 per cent of the total monetary base, as against 12 per cent ten years earlier. During the same year, the Treasury used the facility for a total of Lit. 18,554 billion, including the reimbursement of an extraordinary advance of Lit. 8,000 billion obtained in 1983. This is equivalent to 134 per cent of the creation of monetary base during the year. Even excluding the extraordinary advance, the overdraft accounted for 76 per cent of the total creation. Thus, in spite of a decline of some Lit. 3,400 billion in the stock of Treasury securities held by the Bank of Italy, the Treasury accounted for a Lit. 10,000 billion increase in the monetary base, compared with a total creation of 13,800 billion.

The data of table 7.11 show that, starting in the early 1970s, the Treasury has played a dominant role in the creation of monetary base; they also show that the central bank has enjoyed a significant degree of freedom since the 'divorce'.

Between 1960 and 1969, the average growth rate of the monetary base was 9 per cent (10 per cent when adjusted for changes in the compulsory reserve ratio).[13] The Treasury component grew at a slightly lower rate, accounting for 60 per cent of the growth of the total aggregate. In the following decade the average growth rate of the overall base almost doubled. The Treasury's growth rate reached 21 per cent: overall expansion was held below this rate by destroying monetary base through other channels. From 1980 to 1984, despite further increases in the budget deficit and the expansion of over 24 per cent in the public debt, the rate of growth of the monetary base slowed to 14.1 per cent (12.6 per cent on an adjusted basis).

It needs to be stressed that under present circumstances it would not be possible to reduce the short-term costs of the adjustment needed in the Italian economy by monetary accommodation of the deficits, i.e. by resorting to the inflation tax again. This might of course be a temptation because, as the experience of many countries shows, when inflation rises, real interest rates tend to decline, at least temporarily (see for instance Galli and Masera, 1983). Quite apart from any other considerations, the public debt has climbed, as a ratio to income, from 44 per cent in 1970 to close on 100 per cent in 1985; furthermore,

Table 7.11 *Monetary base: growth rates and the share 'explained' by the Treasury*

	1960–69	*1970–79*	*1980–84*	*1980*	*1981*	*1982*	*1983*	*1984*
	average growth rate throughout the period							
Monetary base	9.12	17.09	14.12	13.81	13.32	14.07	15.03	14.36
Treasury monetary base	8.40	20.97	17.80	23.47	27.83	19.48	5.88	12.34
Memorandum								
Adjusted monetary base	10.15	16.14	12.64	13.02	11.68	12.66	13.31	12.52
Share[a] due to the Treasury	57.59	116.86	96.07	123.77	164.75	122.63	35.81	72.42

[a] Proportion of the change in monetary base represented by the change in monetary base creaed by the Treasury.

nearly all government debt is now either short-term or at variable rates of interest. Finally, savers have become extremely alert to the real return on the assets in their portfolios. A renewed acceleration of prices would push them away from financial assets into housing, consumer durables and foreign assets. The experience of the 1970s (see table 7.12) would be repeated, with the risk of seeing the rate of price changes accelerate above the levels reached in that decade.

Table 7.12 Final domestic consumption of households and imports of goods and services (percentage change at an annual rate, seasonally adjusted data at 1970 prices)

	Households' consumption	Imports	Expected real rate on deposits (perfect foresight)	Expected real rate on loans (perfect foresight)
1972 IV–1973 II	7.0	50.9[a]	−5.96	−11.16
1975 III–1976 I	5.5	49.3	−5.17	−9.38
1979 II–1979 IV	7.0	24.9	−7.49	−5.26

[a] Changes from 1972 II–1972 IV, i.e. anticipated by six months.

V SUMMARY AND CONCLUSIONS

In this paper four arguments have been developed to substantiate the view that it is both urgent and vital that the budget should be redressed in Italy. For greater clarity, the various points have been kept distinct and treated in succession. It should be stressed, however, that they are not logically separate; rather, they should be taken to represent different facets of the same problem: the sustainability of government debt accumulation in a context of growth and disinflation.

Growth of Government Debt and of the Economy

To start with, attention was drawn to the question of budget sustainability from a technical point of view, by focusing on the relationship between the rate of interest on government debt and the rate of growth of the economy. It was shown that net-of-interest deficits, even for prolonged periods, do not necessarily imply that the debt to GDP ratio will grow without limit; but it was also shown that the present situation in Italy requires immediate action aimed at eradicating the deficit net of interest. This is so for two reasons. First, the ultimate theoretical ceiling is so high that it is utterly implausible that the rate of interest could remain below the rate of growth as the debt to income ratio stabilizes; this conclusion is reinforced when account is taken of the fact that doubts about the sustainability of the financial process are likely to be enhanced because government borrowing is used to finance public consumption, i.e. there is a markedly large deficit on current account. Second, the relationship between the average rate of interest and the rate of growth of the economy is rapidly moving towards an 'unstable' position, merely as a result of composition effects, since the rate of growth of interest-bearing debt is much higher than that of output. We can see from column (10) of table 7.4 that the yield on Treasury bills and Treasury credit certificates has already for many years been higher than the GDP growth rate.

These arguments are not altered if the budget is corrected for inflation and the cycle. As has been argued, such adjustments can be misleading for the evaluation of appropriate targets in programmes of financial stabilization, primarily because they are inflation-neutral and do not adequately take account of the external constraint. Moreover, the fact cannot be ignored that it is *actual* deficits that have to be financed and, therefore, that add to outstanding debt.

Government Debt and Domestic Assets

The second line of argument is based on the implications of the public sector borrowing requirement for the creation of domestic financial assets and credit. To recap, over the past fifteen years, government debt has grown at an average rate of nearly 25 per cent, compared with growth of real and nominal output of around 2 and 17 per cent, respectively. In view of government debt's increasing share of total domestic assets, the expansion of the debt over the last few years has accounted for about four-fifths of the growth of total financial assets. A similar picture emerges if the analysis is conducted on the credit side: in the past three years the borrowing requirement of the State has averaged nearly 70 per cent of total credit creation, which proceeded at an annual rate of around 20 per cent.

Leaving aside the question of direct crowding-out, if the private sector takes the view that government deficits which are financed through bond issues rather than taxes do not add to its net wealth, private savings will rise *pari passu* with bond-financed deficits. In this situation the additional supply of government debt is automatically matched by private demand, since the private sector discounts future tax liabilities and saves more: there is therefore no reason for interest rates to rise, and no indirect crowding-out.

I have always regarded this so-called 'ultra-rational' world as somewhat irrational, and argued, on analytical grounds, against the notion that an increase in government bonds in private portfolios represents a *zero* addition to perceived net wealth (Masera, 1979).

In my opinion, recent experience in major industrialized countries – and notably in the United States and Italy – refutes this extreme approach. Additional Treasury borrowing in credit markets, with unchanged money growth, exerted strong pressure on interest rates, thereby negatively affecting the volume and cost of credit flowing to the private sector.

Italian experience shows that household saving in financial assets is highly responsive to expected real yield differentials on alternative assets. During the 1970s, nominal yields on financial assets tended to increase, but with long lags with respect to price rises, especially when inflation peaked. In that decade changes in house prices – which roughly proxy the yield on the real assets of households, in view of the importance of saving and wealth in houses – exceeded the rate of consumer price inflation. In this situation, the rate of saving in financial assets adjusted for inflation declined rapidly and eventually became negative. In contrast, during the 1980s, real rates on financial assets increased substantially, while the rate of increase of house prices first declined and then became negative.

The pattern of saving changed dramatically; investment in housing declined, while the accumulation of financial assets and notably of government paper was stepped up, as indicated in section III. Here too, however, seeds of instability are evident, and point to the need for immediate adjustment. The current rates of expansion of government debt and its relative size mean that, even if all other sources of financial asset creation were made to dry up, total financial assets would still grow at rates of around 17 per cent – which is not consistent with medium-term financial equilibrium or price stability in an economy whose potential growth rate is about 3 per cent.

Brief mention needs to be made in this connection of the external repercussions of increasing bond-financed government expenditure. If this is not wholly offset by private savings the current account will deteriorate and interest rates will tend to rise in response to the intertemporal shift from future to present spending in the home country and to attract the necessary flow of foreign savings. This is likely to be accompanied by a temporary real exchange rate appreciation, which may in turn adversely affect the sustainable growth rate of the economy.[14]

Monetary Growth

The third argument – which is closely related to the previous one – refers directly to the question of monetary growth. If a relatively stable real demand for M2-type assets exists, even without accepting monetarist propositions it has to be admitted that a process of disinflation will require monetary growth to be gradually reduced to rates consistent with the desired targets of nominal income growth.[15]

During the 1970s the adjusted monetary base increased at an average annual rate of 16 per cent. During the period 1980–84 the adjusted base slowed to an average rate of 12.6 per cent, i.e. approximately half that recorded by total government debt. The very large shifts which took place in the portfolios of the private sector have been illustrated in sections III and IV.

The ratio of the growth rate of the 'adjusted' base to the growth rate of government debt, as a component of AFI, can be taken to represent an indicator of monetary 'friction' in portfolio accumulation. In the 1960s the ratio on average was 1.1, declining to 0.68 in the 1970s and 0.52 in the period 1980–84.

To assess the implications of the huge accumulation of public securities in private portfolios, it is necessary to use a model which integrates the flows of income and saving with the accumulation of wealth and the changes in the stocks of assets, i.e. an integrated model of the real and financial sectors.[16] Traditional demand-for-money models are based on the hypothesis that the return on money, considered primarily in its function as a means of payment, is exogenously fixed in nominal terms, in contrast with that on other financial aggregates. Money is a hot potato; changes in its supply cause adjustments exclusively in the returns on all alternative assets. By contrast, variations in the supply of any other financial asset bring about changes both in the yield of that asset and in those on all alternative assets.

When this dichotomy does not apply, because money earns an explicit market-determined yield, there is greater substitutability between money and other financial assets and, in general, a more homogeneous process of portfolio adjustment. In this context it is important to ascertain how the equilibrium structure of rates is affected by, say, an increase in the share of government bonds accompanied by a decline in the share of wealth held in monetary form.

If the substitutability of money for bonds is low, only sizeable increases in the yield of bonds will make operators economize on their monetary balances. This, *ceteris paribus*, leads to significant crowding-out. On the other hand, if the degree of substitutability between bonds and real capital (or titles to real capital) is relatively low, the private sector will not displace investment *pari passu* with the acquisition of government bonds. The relative yield of bonds must rise, but this does not entail full crowding-out, as would happen with perfect substitutability.[17]

It is worth noting in this respect that, even if favourable substitutability parameters obtain, the very large shifts in portfolio shares which characterize the Italian situation, given the present trends in public finances, are bound to make themselves felt on the equilibrium yield differentials, thus pushing the system towards unstable conditions.

This clearly indicates the dilemma confronting the monetary authorities. If monetary growth is gradually restrained in line with the objective of disinflation and deceleration in nominal income expansion, the absorption of government securities in private portfolios may well require increasing real rates of interest, with adverse effects on investment and income growth; ultimately, this policy may indeed prove ineffectual in containing aggregate demand because of the working of the income effect on consumer spending. But even before that critical point is reached, the balance between growth and real interest rates on the debt may be tilted towards instability. On the other hand, monetary financing of the deficit would make it impossible to pursue the goal of non-inflationary growth. And, as has been pointed out, the risks implicit in monetization are now much greater than during the 1970s.

We come again to the same – and by now obvious – conclusion: unless structural adjustments are made to public finances, the economy runs the risk of being tossed in the short term between the Charybdis of stagnation and the Scylla of inflation; beyond that the situation of public finances would anyhow be unsustainable.

The Treasury and the Monetary Base

The fourth argument deals with a specific question raised by the institutional setting in Italy, whereby the Treasury can directly create monetary base by drawing on its current account with the central bank. Since the credit line expands with budget expenditures, which have been growing at rates far in excess of those of nominal output, an additional problem of stability is encountered, this time in the very process of monetary creation, as indicated in section IV.

These problems are manageable for the moment, but the magnitude of the figures indicates that this question should also receive immediate attention. It must be stressed, however, that if government expenditure was appropriately restrained, a large part of the difficulties in this area would disappear.

CONCLUSIONS

It is not the purpose of this chapter to offer suggestions on the ways and means of redressing the Italian budget; specific and authoritative plans have been put forward and contain useful guidelines.[18]

Instead I would like to dwell on a number of 'methodological' aspects. Whatever measures are taken on the spending and/or the revenue side, it is of paramount importance that the incompatibility that has developed between the demands on the public sector and the available resources should be highlighted. The public should also be able to assess the cost of government directly.

Recent developments in fiscal theory – specifically the work of Buchanan (1983) and his 'Public Choice' school – have made it possible to take an analytical approach to the problem; it would be well to take this into account.

The conventional approach stresses the redistribution effect of taxation: the government majority imposes taxes and decides transfer payments. This would be a zero-sum game for the 'players' – in the sense that gains made by some are necessarily equal to the losses suffered by others without any scope for Paretian improvements – were it not possible to affect the 'quality' of existing transfers.

From this point of view it is not difficult in the Italian case to identify where changes could be made in the purely welfare nature of some transfers to firms and households which has impeded the creation of new productive jobs and still continues to do so.

Apart from this, however, an objective explanation of the 'excessive' upward push of expenditure and taxation – and therefore of the possibility for constitutional controls on the fiscal authorities – can be found in the interaction and synergy of explanatory models of a 'structural' nature with 'monopolistic' ones.

The former identifies sources of systematic distortion in the institutional structure which bias decision making in the direction of higher public spending. First of all, deficit financing of government expenditure, especially by creation of the monetary base, conceals the true cost of that expenditure for the collectivity. Furthermore, the progressive nature of taxation automatically generates extra revenues in a situation of rising real incomes and prices. Finally, since tax collection tends to be widespread, whereas transfers are made to specific groups, it is possible for power lobbies to bring strong pressure to bear on politicians.

These demand mechanisms, which ultimately depend on the non-transparent nature of many taxes, interact with supply mechanisms, according to which the government itself begins to act like a monopolist bent on maximizing the 'surplus' of revenues and on increasing the powers of the bureaucracy. These observations give us ground rules it would be well to follow while 'adjusting' imbalances in public finance. First, there is the need for timely and effective information on the immediate and medium-term impact of every piece of legislation and on the development of public finance balances; this is the premise for any theory of concrete 'financial programming'. Many technical solutions would meet this need: it is necessary, however, that the body designated be institutionally independent and report directly to Parliament.

The difficulties encountered in curbing the growth rate of expenditure and the accumulation of budget deficits would suggest that fiscal norms should be rewritten and inserted into the Constitution.[19] The first step would be the effective reinstatement of Article 81 of the Constitution and Law 468 of 1978.[20]

Finally, it is my opinion that, once the budget has been redressed, there should be a constitutional obligation that the 'structural' budget – net of monetary erosion and cyclical fluctuations – be in equilibrium. It should be noted in this respect that the monetary correction would have to be made with reference to the *target* rate of inflation – to be brought down gradually to zero or at any rate to the average for EMS countries. This *ex-ante* adjustment would overcome the problems which are encountered in the usual practice of *ex-post* correction. Reference to potential output in the calculation of cyclical fluctuations would explicitly allow for the external constraint.

I would like to take this opportunity to stress that I am by no means suggesting that this target should be pursued immediately. That the objective I am referring to is long term is implicit in the fact that it would require Constitutional amendments! Additionally, a structural budget balance, as defined here, would imply halving projected deficits for both 1985 and 1986. These huge adjustments could not take place without serious repercussions on growth and thus might trigger a vicious interest rate growth spiral.

An intermediate operational objective, against which the programme of basic medium-term adjustment could be set, is a rapid reduction to zero of the deficit net of interest,[21] as has been advocated, for instance, by the Governor of the Bank of Italy.

The easing of pressure on the credit markets could promote a reduction in real interest rates. Furthermore, the likely weakening of external inflationary impulses could help, in the short term, to lessen the Treasury's real interest burden, as traditionally defined (see Appendix 2). Thus a virtuous circle of forces able to trigger off and sustain a decline in public expenditure would be set in motion.

The two targets for public finance balances outlined here are naturally in response to different lines of argument: from the economic point of view, the compatibility between the two formulas is to be found in the proposed sequence. The gradual reduction to zero of the deficit net of interest is the operational goal for the 1980s. Once the primary borrowing requirement has again been brought under control, resolving thereby the present state of emergency, the equilibrium of the structural budget – as I have defined it – would become the long-term constraint. This constraint would be guaranteed by the Constitution and therefore shielded from discretionary powers.

Naturally, the 'traverse' from one formula to the other could well create quantitative problems. However, it is worthy of notice that, given the values of the relevant parameters, both approaches lead now to similar conclusions. For example, if the reduction to zero of the state sector structural borrowing requirement were taken as the target for 1985, given the parameters of the economic planning scenario – and, therefore, ignoring the feedbacks of the budget – the overall borrowing requirement would have to be adjusted to 63,000 billion.[22] The goal of reducing to zero this borrowing requirement net of interest, always ignoring the feedback effects of the measures taken, would have resulted in the establishment of a practically identical 'target' budget.

APPENDIX 1 NOTES ON BUDGET CONSTRAINT AND SUSTAINABILITY OF THE DEBT[23]

Let Y be nominal national income, D be nominal public debt outstanding, G be nominal public spending net of interest payments or outstanding debt, T be nominal tax revenue, net of transfers, I be interest payments on outstanding debt, $i_D = I/D$ and G_x be the rate of growth of the variable x. Then the budget constraint of the public sector can be written as

$$\dot{D} - i_D D = G - T \qquad (7.A1)$$

Hypothesis 1

Assuming for the sake of simplicity that the growth rate of income is constant ($G_Y = g$), in order to study the long-run implications of equation 7.A1 we begin with the hypothesis that the deficit to GDP ratio is held constant:

$$\frac{\dot{D}}{Y} = \delta = \frac{G - T + i_D D}{Y} \qquad (7.A2)$$

It can be shown[24] that the debt to income ratio tends towards a finite number whatever the relationship between the interest rate (i_D) and the growth rate of nominal output ($g = \pi + \gamma$).

$$\lim_{t \to \infty} \frac{D}{Y} = \frac{\delta}{g} \qquad (7.A3)$$

Note that in long-term equilibrium the growth rate of the debt is equal to the growth rate of income.

$$\frac{\dot{D}}{D} = \frac{\dot{D}}{Y}\frac{Y}{D} = \delta\frac{g}{\delta} = g \qquad (7.A4)$$

The burden of debt servicing then becomes

$$\iota = \frac{i_D D}{Y} = i_D \frac{\delta}{g} \qquad (7.A5)$$

The budget constraint can, therefore, be written as

$$1 - \frac{i_D}{g} = \frac{G - T}{Y\delta} \qquad (7.A6)$$

Assuming, for example, that the borrowing requirement to income ratio is stable at 15 per cent and the growth rate of nominal income is 10 per cent we get

$$\frac{D}{Y} = 1.5$$

If instead the growth rate of income was 3 per cent

$$\frac{D}{Y} = 5$$

Assuming that in both cases the interest rate and the growth rate are equal, we get from equation 7.A5

$$\iota = \delta = 0.15$$

Analytically, the above equations can be used to show how, in a stationary economy with a positive real interest rate, equilibrium can exist provided $\delta = \bar{\delta}$

If we assume that $i_D > g = \pi > 0$, we get, in the limit:

$$\frac{D}{Y} = \frac{\delta}{\pi}$$

and

$$\iota = i_D \frac{\delta}{\pi} > \delta$$

The debt burden is therefore greater than the deficit to GDP ratio.

In the case of $\pi = 0$ we get

$$\iota = \frac{i_D D_0}{Y_0} + i_D \delta t$$

For equilibrium δ must equal 0. We then get:

$$\frac{G - T}{Y} = -\frac{i_D D_0}{Y}$$

$$\iota = \frac{T - G}{Y}$$

Hypothesis 2

Let us assume now that it is not the total deficit to GDP ratio that is stable, but only that part which is net of interest payments:

$$G - T = \beta Y$$

Therefore equation 7.A1 can be written, as a ratio of income,

$$\dot{d} - (i_D - g)\,d = \beta \tag{7.A7}$$

If the condition $g > i_D$ is satisfied, we get:

$$\lim_{t \to \infty} d(t) = \frac{\beta}{g - i_D}$$

Now, let us suppose that $D = B + M$, where B is the interest bearing debt outstanding and M is the monetary base. The budget constraint can be rewritten as:

$$\dot{B} - iB = (G - T) - \dot{M} \tag{7.A1$'$}$$

where $i = I/B$. Assuming that M is a constant share (m) of Y, and denoting r the real rate of interest and γ the rate of growth of real income, the budget constraint in terms of ratios to Y can be rewritten as

$$\dot{b} = (r - \gamma)b + \beta - mG_M \tag{7.A2$'$}$$

Again, if the condition $\gamma > r$ is satisfied, we get

$$\lim_{t \to \infty} b(t) = \frac{\beta - mG_M}{\gamma - r} \tag{7.A8}$$

Equation 7.A8 shows that a stable ratio of debt to income requires neither a surplus net of interest payments ($\beta < 0$) nor a surplus net of interest payments and of the seignorage from the creation of the monetary base ($\beta - mG_M < 0$). In the special case where $\beta - mGM < 0$, b will tend to become a credit; otherwise, it follows that

$$\lim_{t \to \infty} G_B = g > i$$

B will tend to grow at a rate equal to that of nominal income, which is, by assumption, greater than the nominal rate of interest.

If instead $r > \gamma$, b would show in general an unstable path. To stabilize it, an appropriate value for $\beta - mG_M$ must be chosen: setting $b = 0$ in equation 7.A2 it is found that

$$\beta - mG_M = -(r - \gamma)b_0 < 0 \tag{7.A9}$$

Note that equation 7.A9 does not require that today's debt be matched by future surpluses. It simply requires that future deficits (net of interest payments) be less than the money seignorage. Only under the further assumption: $G_M \leqslant 0$, β must be negative. It is concluded that the condition $\beta < 0$ (which is the transversality condition of Blanchard et al., 1985) is required only when the real rate of interest exceeds the growth rate of the economy and money financing is precluded.

APPENDIX 2 REAL DEBT SERVICE BURDEN AT CHANGING INFLATION RATES

This Appendix serves to illustrate the changes in the debt interest burden in the face of changing rates of inflation, given constant real interest rates. It will be shown that in the 'traverse' phases associated with accelerating or decelerating prices the burden of interest payments as traditionally defined varies in response to changes in monetary erosion (loss of purchasing power) of the debt.

Inflation and the Debt Burden

Let the debt service burden at constant prices be

$$\mathrm{ON} = \frac{iD}{P} \tag{7.A10}$$

where i is the nominal interest rate on the public debt, D is the outstanding debt (one-period bonds) at current prices and P is the general price index. Let G be the growth rate of a variable, then we get from equation 7.A10

$$G_{\mathrm{ON}} = G_{\mathrm{i}} + G_{\mathrm{D}} - G_{\mathrm{P}} \tag{7.A11}$$

Taking now the following simplifying assumptions:

$$i = \pi + r \quad \text{Fisher's equation } (\pi \equiv G_{\mathrm{P}} > 0 \tag{7.A12}$$

$$r = \bar{r} > 0 \quad \text{constant real rate} \tag{7.A13}$$

$$G_{\mathrm{D}} = i \quad \text{deficit net of interest} = 0 \tag{7.A14}$$

Equation 7.A11 can be written thus:

$$G_{\mathrm{ON}} = G_{\mathrm{r}}\frac{r}{i} + G_{\pi}\frac{\pi}{i} + i - \pi = G_{\pi}\frac{\pi}{i} + r \tag{7.A11$'$}$$

It is evident from equation 7.A11′ that the debt burden measured at constant prices increases (diminishes) with the rise (decline) of the inflation rate. Only when inflation is stable ($G_\pi = 0$) will the debt burden stabilize at the level of the real interest rate.

Effect of Monetary Erosion on the Debt

The reason for this is not immediately obvious, but becomes evident as soon as account is taken of the existence of monetary erosion on the debt, and of the fact that nominal interest payments include a component entirely attributable to the restoration of the real value of the debt that would otherwise be eroded by inflation.

We begin with the definition of the budget constraint at current prices:

$$G - T + iD = dD \tag{7.A15}$$

where G is the nominal expenditure on goods and services, T is taxes net of transfers, excluding interest on outstanding debt, in nominal terms and dD is the change in nominal debt.

If equation 7.A15 is deflated with respect to prices, we get the constraint at constant prices

$$g - t + \frac{iD}{P} = dd + \frac{\pi D}{P} \tag{7.A16}$$

where g is the real expenditure on goods and services, t is net real taxes and dd is the change in real debt.

Using 7.A12 we can rewrite 7.A16 as

$$g - t + (r + \pi)\, d - \pi d = dd \qquad (7.\text{A}16')$$

Once more introducing assumptions 7.A13 and 7.A14, which becomes now $G_d = r$, we get

$$g - t - rd + [(r + \pi)d] + [-\pi d] = 0 \qquad (7.\text{A}16'')$$

It is clear from that 7.A16″ that in the face of changing inflation the budget constraint must be respected; and it is respected since, for example, there is a corresponding negative change of a compensatory nature in the real value of the debt

$$\left(\frac{\partial}{\partial \pi}\,[(-\,\pi d)] = -d)\right)$$

when a rise in the inflation rate increases the burden of real interest

$$\left(\frac{\partial}{\partial \pi}\,[(r + \pi)d] = d)\right)$$

The opposite is also true: if there is a decline in inflation, the real interest burden diminishes, becoming lower than the real rate of interest, in response to the slowdown in monetary erosion.

NOTES

1 On these points see also Spaventa (1984), Spaventa et al. (1984), Morcaldo and Salvemini (1984b).

2 Further to the data in tables 7.1–7.4, fuller and more satisfactory 'economic' aggregation would show up more clearly the marked increase in overall real transfer payments to enterprises, together with the soaring expenditures for pensions and interest. Simplifying somewhat, it can be maintained that most of Italy's public financial disarray is accounted for by these three items, the first two independently and the third induced by the rising debt. By aggregating current contributions to production, payments to the Wage Supplementation Fund, state assumption of certain employer social security contributions, capital account transfers to state-controlled companies and net financing to the non-state sector, we get the expenditure for private and public enterprises (see Alvaro, 1984). This increased from 2,980 billion lire in 1964 to 45,900 billion in 1983, and from 2.7 per cent to 9.7 per cent of GDP. For the most part, contributions to enterprises consisted of assistance to non-competitive older industries, which diverted resources from reorganization and technological modernization and slowed down the creation of productive new jobs.

3 The implications of this increase for financial analysis are not examined in this study. On this point see Monti et al. (1983).

4 Their 'restrictive' position appears odd, being presented in a paper which leads to policy suggestions of an 'expansionary' fiscal nature.

5 Keynes (1923, ch. 2) was the first to make a complete investigation of inflation as an instrument of taxation. Einaudi (e.g. 1944) concurred in this approach, which Baffi (1974) developed in an important analytical and empirical study (see also Masera, 1979; Cotula and Masera, 1980).

6 For a possible alternative procedure see, for example, Bank of Italy (1985).
7 On these points see Bank of Italy (1983, 294–97).
8 On this point see also Arcelli and Valiani (1981).
9 For an examination of this approach, see Cotula and de' Stefani (1979, ch. XXV), Caranza and Fazio (1983) and Vaciago (1983). In relating equations 7.3 and 7.5, the foreign indebtedness of the public sector has been left out for the sake of simplicity. This can be done in the case of Italy without loss of generality, in view of the relative unimportance of this item so far.
10 In conformity with total domestic credit accounting practices, table 7.7 and subsequent tables refer to the state sector deficit and debt.
11 On these points see Lecaldano et al. (1985).
12 See Capriglione (1984), especially on changes in the way Treasury bills have been issued.
13 See Zautzik (1982) on the adjustment of the monetary base in Italy.
14 For a review of the issues involved here see Masera (1985).
15 I dealt with these points, in the light of the Italian experience, in Masera (1984b).
16 On these points see, for instance, Tobin (1980). It should be noted in this respect that the models developed in Italy in the 1960s and 1970s – based on the simultaneous analysis of money, total financial assets, bank credit and total domestic credit and referred to in section III of this chapter – provide an important reference framework.
17 For a review of this theme see, for example, Blanchard et al. (1985).
18 See, for instance, the so-called 'Goria plan'; see also Bank of Italy (1983), also Giannone (1985) and Sylos Labini (1985).
19 See on this Pedone (1985) and Salvemini (1985). For a more general treatment see Carli and Capriglione (1981).
20 On this see Bank of Italy (1980).
21 The fact that a rapid decline of the deficit net-of-interest is a necessary condition for convergence of the debt emerges also from the medium-term projections given by Prometeia (1985).
22 I wish to thank Vieri Ceriani for his help in processing these data; the data were obtained by using his study on the problem of correcting budget data for cyclical effects in the Italian experience (Ceriani and Di Mauro (1985)).
23 On these points see Domar (1944), Johansen (1965), Masera (1984a) and Blanchard et al. (1986). In this Appendix, growth rates and interest rates are predetermined. As indicated in the text, this is a limit for the concrete analysis of stability. For an analytical study of these problems see, for example, Galli (1985).
24
$$D = D_0 + \frac{\delta Y_0}{g}(e^{gt} - 1)$$

$$\frac{D}{Y} = \frac{D_0}{Y_0 e^{gt}} + \frac{\delta}{g}(1 - e^{-gt})$$

REFERENCES

Alvaro, G. 1985: La finanza pubblica nel sistema economico italiano. In *La finanza pubblica in Italia: Stato e Prospettive*, Franco Angeli, Milano.

Arcelli, M. and Valiani, R. 1981: Il finanziamento del fabbisogno del settore pubblico, *Rivista di Politica Economica*, December.

P. Baffi, 1974: Il risparmio in Italia, oggi, *Bancaria*, 2, February.

Bank of Italy 1946: *Annual Report of the Bank of Italy for the year*, The Governor's Concluding Remarks.

Bank of Italy 1981: *Annual Report of the Bank of Italy for the year*, The Governor's Concluding Remarks.

Bank of Italy 1983: *Annual Report of the Bank of Italy for the year*, The Governor's Concluding Remarks.

Bank of Italy 1985: The inflation adjustment of financial balances, *Economic Bulletin*, October.

Barro, R.J. 1974: Are government bonds net wealth?, *Journal of Political Economy*, 82, 1095–1117.

Blanchard, O., Dornbusch, R. and Buiter, W. 1985: *Public Debt and Fiscal Responsibility*, CEPS Papers N. 22, Bruxelles, 1985.

Buchanan, J.M. 1983: I limiti alla fiscalità, *La Costituzione Fiscale e Monetaria*, CREA, Roma.

Capriglione, F. 1987: Buoni e Certificati di Credito del Tesoro, *Enciclopedia Giuridica*, forthcoming.

Caranza, C. and Fazio, A. 1983: L'evoluzione dei metodi di controllo monetario in Italia: 1974–1983, *Bancaria*, 39, 819–33.

Carli, G. and Capriglione, F. 1981: *Inflazione e Ordinamento Giuridico*, Milano, Giuffrè.

Ceriani, V. and Di Mauro, F. 1985: Finanza pubblica e politica fiscale: i risultati di alcuni indicatori, mimeo.

Commissione CEE 1984: *Economia Europea*, November.

Cotula F. and Masera, R. 1980: Private savings, public deficits and the inflation tax, *Review of Economic Conditions in Italy*, 3, October.

Domar, E. 1944: The 'Burden of the Debt' and the National Income, *American Economic Review*, 34, 798–827.

Einaudi, L. 1944: *I Problemi Economici della Federazione Europea*, Nuove edizioni di Capolago, Lugano.

Galli, G. 1985: Tasso reale, crescita e sostenibilità del debito pubblico, *Contributi del'Analisi Economica, Banca d'Italia.*

Galli, G. and Masera, R. 1983: Real rates of interest and public sector deficits: an empirical investigation, *Economic Notes*, 3.

Giannone, A. 1985: L'operatore pubblico in un sistema economico e sociale. In *La Finanza Pubblica in Italia: Stato e Prospettive*, Franco Angeli, Milano.

Goria, G. 1985a: *Politiche e Obiettivi per il Controllo della Finanza Pubblica*, Ministero del Tesoro, Rome.

Goria, G. 1985b: *Verso il rilancio dell'economia italiana: il risanamento della finanza pubblica*, Ministero del Tesoro, Rome, November.

ISTAT, 1983: *I Conti Della Protezione Sociale*, Suppl. al Boll. Mens. di Stat. 28.

ISTAT, *Relazione Generale Sulla Situazione Economica Del Paese.*

Johnansen, L. 1965: *Public Economics*, North Holland, Amsterdam.

Keynes, J.M. 1923: *A Tract on Monetary Reform*, Macmillan, London.

Lecaldano, E., Marotta G. and Masera, R. 1985: Households' saving and the real rate of interest: the Italian experience, 1970–1983, *Temi di Discussione*, Banca d'Italia.

Masera, R. 1979: *Disavanzo pubblico e vincolo del bilancio*, Edizioni di Comunità, Banca Comerciala Italiana, Milan.

Masera, R. 1984a: Monetary Policy and Budget Policy: Blend or Dichotomy? In *Europe's Money: Problems of European Monetary Coordination and Integration*, R. Masera and R. Triffin (eds), Oxford University Press, Oxford.

Masera, R. 1984b: Moneta, credito e prezzi: considerazioni sull'esperienza italiana, *Quale Politica Monetaria? Il Dibattito sul Monetarismo*, CREA, November.

Masera, 1985: Il coordinamento delle politiche economiche e i tassi di cambio: alcune considerazioni, speech delivered at the meeting of the Società Italiana degli Economisti, Roma, 6–7 November.

Monti, M., Siracusano, B. and Tardini, P. 1983: Spesa pubblica, finanziamento del disavanzo e crowding-out. In *Spesa Pubblica e Sviluppo dell'Economia*, Edizioni di Comunità, 1983.

Morcaldo, G. and Salvemini, G. 1984a: Il bilancio pubblico per il quinquennio 1984–88: alcune simulazioni. *Temi di Discussione*, Banca d'Italia, July.

Morcaldo G. and Salvemini, G. 1984b: Il debito pubblico: analisi dell'evoluzione nel periodo 1960–83 e prospettive, *Rivista di Politica Economica*, 74.

Morcaldo, G. and Zanchi, P. 1984: Un modello di previsione del bilancio pubblico per il breve-medio termine. In *Ricerche quantitative per la politica economica*, Banca d'Italia, Rome, pp. 207–263.

Pedone, A. 1985: Regole costituzionali in materia di finanza pubblica, *Politica Economica*, Il Mulino, 1, April.

Prometeia, 1985: Rapporto di previsione, March.

Salvemini, M.T. 1985: Costituzionalismo monetario e fiscale, *Politica Economica*, Il Mulino, 1, April.

Spaventa, L. 1984: The growth of public debt in Italy: past experience, perspectives and policy problems, *Banca Nazionale del Lavoro Quarterly Review*, June.

Spaventa, L. Artoni, R., Morcaldo, G. and Zanchi, P. 1984: L'indebitamento pubblico in Italia: evoluzione, prospettive e problemi, Report prepared for the Commissione Bilancio of the Camera dei Deputati, Rome, September 1984.

Sylos Labini, P. 1985: Intervento alla Tavola rotonda su *La Finanza Pubblica in Italia: Stato e Prospettive*, Franco Angeli, Milano.

Tobin, J. 1980: *Asset Accumulation and Economic Activity*, The University of Chicago Press, Chicago.

Vaciago, G. 1983: *La Programmazione Dei Flussi Finanziari*, Società Editrice il Mulino, Bologna.

Visco, I. 1984: *Price Expectations in Rising Inflation*, North Holland, Amsterdam.

Zautzik, E. 1982: Base monetaria aggiustata e sue interpretazioni: aspetti teorici e applicazione al caso italiano, *Contributi alla ricerca economica*, Banca d'Italia, 15, December.

8

Keynes on British Budgetary Policy 1914–46

N.H. DIMSDALE

I INTRODUCTION

Keynes was deeply involved in issues of economic policy from his entry into the Civil Service in 1906 until his death in 1946. Most of his writings on budgetary policy are to be found in his pamphlets, newspaper articles, evidence to government committees and official memoranda. The treatment which budgetary policy receives in his major academic works, *A Treatise on Money* (1930) and *The General Theory* (1936), is by comparison rather perfunctory.[1] This point can be appreciated now that the full scope of Keynes's work can be assessed from his *Collected Writings* edited by Donald Moggridge and Sir Austin Robinson for the Royal Economic Society.

Keynes's ideas on using fiscal policy for curbing unemployment and restraining inflation are clearly relevant to policy issues today. There has been a recent revival of interest in arguments against fiscal policy not unlike those which were advanced by the Treasury in the 1920s and 1930s. In addition Keynes was concerned with the problem of managing a substantial debt largely created by borrowing in wartime. The issue of balancing the budget was a matter of some concern to him both in the interwar period and in his plans for postwar economic policy.

The development of Keynes's views on budgetary policy, which is here taken to include some aspects of debt management policy in addition to fiscal policy in a narrow sense, falls into a number of distinct

I am grateful to participants at the Conference on 'Private Saving and Public Debt' for helpful comments on this paper, and in particular J.S. Flemming and R.S. Masera. The remaining errors are my own responsibility.

phases. The first phase, which includes the First World War and its aftermath, ends about 1924. Apart from *The Economic Consequences of the Peace* (1919)[2] Keynes's best-known work of this period is *A Tract on Monetary Reform* (1923). This is a collection of newspaper articles republished in book form. Keynes appears as an economist in the Marshallian tradition, using the quantity theory of money to analyse short period problems and emphasizing the connection between money, inflation and the consequences of government borrowing.

The second phase runs from about 1924 until the suspension of the restored gold standard in 1931. It includes Keynes's rather gradual move towards the firm advocacy of public works. In *Can Lloyd George Do It?*,[3] a pamphlet written in collaboration with Hubert Henderson, Keynes used the special case argument developed in the *Treatise* to support the Liberal campaign for the 1929 general election, which included a pledge to reduce unemployment through a programme of public investment. He developed this argument at greater length in his evidence to the Macmillan Committee (Committee on Finance and Industry) and elsewhere. He continued to lay the main emphasis on reductions in the long-term interest rate for stimulating large closed economies, such as the United States, but argued that public works were needed to promote recovery in the special conditions affecting the British economy.

The third phase begins with the suspension of the gold standard but from the point of view of fiscal policy the real starting point is the publication of *The Means to Prosperity*[4] in 1933. In this series of newspaper articles he argued for expansion of public investment programmes in both open and closed economies to stimulate revival from world depression. Keynes relied heavily on Kahn's multiplier theory to quantify the impact of increased public expenditure on both the level of income and the balance of the budget. The role of monetary policy was now reduced and its function became basically supportive to fiscal measures. Keynes provided the theoretical basis for his new approach to macroeconomics in *The General Theory of Employment, Interest and Money* (1936). He developed the implications of his theory for counter–cyclical policy in a series of newspaper articles and in his discussions on the Committee on Economic Information of the Economic Advisory Council.

In the fourth and final phase, which runs from 1940 to 1946, Keynes is occupied with the use of fiscal policy to mobilize resources for war and to create a framework for postwar policy. His views on wartime finance were set out in *How to Pay for the War* (1940) and he had a major influence on the design of wartime budgets, in particular the 1941 budget, which made extensive use of national income accounting techniques. Here more attention is given to his recommendations for the design of postwar fiscal and debt policy, rather than his advice on the war economy. His views were developed in the discussions which led up to the publication of the White Paper on Employment Policy (Cmnd 6527, 1944) and his evidence to the National Debt Enquiry of 1945. It is notable that his recommendations, which were substantially embodied in the White Paper, did not go as far as the younger generation of Keynesian economists would have wished.

By the time of his death, Keynes appeared to be relatively conservative in his advice to the Treasury, while showing considerable sympathy for the younger generation of economists who were engaged in exploring the implications of his own theory.

II THE FIRST WORLD WAR AND ITS AFTERMATH, 1914–24

Keynes was confronted with the problems of internal finance during his initial period of service at the Treasury in the First World War. He looked at war finance both from the point of view of mobilizing resources for war and of financing the requirements of the British government and its allies. His memoranda contain clear perceptions about the general problem of resource allocation. He pointed out that specific shortages should be treated as a symptom of overcommitment of resources and that it is necessary to consider each project as being at the expense of some other expenditure. For example, he argued that increasing the size of the army would be at the expense of other objectives, such as the production of munitions or financial assistance to the allies. He did not go far beyond recognizing the general nature of this basic problem but he measured resources in terms of manpower in assessing demands on the economy, a technique which was to be used much more extensively in the Second World War.[5]

When considering the problems of government finance he distinguished between finance through 'real resources', that is taxation and borrowing, and 'inflationist borrowing', that is increases in the money supply. Inflationism was a useful device and could be employed in so far as the public was willing to increase its holdings of money balances. If, however, the money was spent, there would be upward pressure on the price level and a weakening of the balance of payments, which could threaten the pegged exchange rate. Keynes recommended the issue of gilt-edged securities at regular intervals to mop up bank deposits in the hands of the public and urged greater reliance on taxation. He emphasized the need to reduce the living standards of the bulk of the population through taxation and a certain amount of inflation, while recognizing that pressing 'taxation beyond this extreme limit would defeat its own object by destroying the sources of revenue and loan through over-taxation'. Shortly after expressing these views in 1916 he was transferred to bear responsibility for external finance and the management of the exchange rate.[6]

Once the war was over, Keynes argued that the vigorous boom which had followed it should be curbed by a sharp rise in Bank Rate. He was prepared to see Bank Rate held at 10 per cent for up to 3 years, if that was necessary to dampen inflationary expectations.[7] On the budgetary side he favoured the elimination of wartime budget deficits and thought that serious consideration should be given to the introduction of a capital levy. This would provide a way of increasing tax revenues without raising marginal rates of income tax which could have adverse effects on incentives. He was concerned about the burden of servicing the debt accumulated as a result of wartime budget deficits in both Britain and Continental countries. One way of dealing with the problem was to let the currency depreciate, which he recognized as being inevitable in some economies. He preferred a capital levy as being less arbitrary in its incidence but accepted that it would be unlikely to be implemented in practice. One of the principal arguments which he advanced against returning to prewar exchange rates was that the real burden of the debt would thereby be increased. Keynes favoured stabilization of currencies at postwar levels which could be achieved in conjunction with measures to eliminate budget deficits. He was particularly critical of those who called for a return to the prewar parity in Britain and also refused to accept the case for a capital levy. This was a recipe for maximizing the burden of the dead-weight debt.[8]

While urging the need to reduce budget deficits, Keynes was also aware of the limitations of taxation. He returned to his earlier theme of the limits of taxable capacity in his discussion of the problems of extracting reparation payments from Germany in *A Revision of the Treaty* (1922), as pointed out by McIntosh (1977).[9] He also analysed the working of the inflation tax in *A Tract on Monetary Reform* and concluded that: 'What a government spends the public pay for. There is no such thing as an uncovered deficit'.[10]

Keynes was severely critical of the rise in Bank Rate in July 1923. He claimed that 'The raising of the Bank Rate to 4 per cent is one of the most misguided movements of that indicator which have ever occurred',[11] since the increase was not justified by the depressed state of the British economy. He attributed the sluggishness of the economy to the appreciation of the exchange rate and the associated tight monetary policies. An additional factor was the disorganization of the European economy.

The persistence of high unemployment was starting to engage his interest. He attributed it initially to the rise in real wages, particularly for unskilled labour, as compared with prewar levels and also to the rapid growth in the working population, but as a staunch free trader he was adamant that protection could not create employment.[12]

III THE MOVE TOWARDS PUBLIC WORKS, 1924–31

Arguments for Public Investment, 1924–29

Keynes first raised the issue of public works in 'Does Unemployment Need a Drastic Remedy?', a newspaper article which appeared in May 1924.[13] He argued that the economy needed a stimulus to get it out of a rut. Investment in public utilities was being discouraged by regulation which prevented attractive returns from being earned. Savings were tending to drift abroad because of lack of incentives to employ them at home. Keynes urged that 'the Treasury should not shrink from promoting expenditure up to (say) £100,000,000 a year on the construction of capital works at home'. The main source of finance for this expenditure was to be the Sinking Fund, the annual budgetary provision for the repayment of government debt. Keynes suggested that this be directed to the provision of new productive debt through the finance of 'state encouraged constructive enterprises at home'. The areas suggested for home investment were housing, road building and electric power transmission.

There was strong criticism of Keynes's alleged raid on the Sinking Fund. He sought to deny such suggestions, pointing out that he was proposing to use the Sinking Fund and not to suspend it. He rephrased his argument in terms of a bias in the capital market in favour of overseas issues and claimed that foreign lending did not necessarily raise the demand for British exports. To redress the balance the Treasury should offer guarantees for investment in domestic public utilities. The bias in the capital market was aggravated by the working of the Trustee Acts, which encouraged investment in foreign rather than home securities.[14] This issue was explored in a further article 'Foreign Investment and the National Advantage' and also in his evidence to the Colwyn Committee on National Debt and Taxation.[14,15] The case for public works had become sidetracked into a discussion about the merits of home versus foreign investment. When asked by Barbara Wootton about his proposals for public works, during his evidence to the Colwyn Committee, he stated that 'I do not mean to suggest that the Treasury should put this sum of money in directly, but that it should facilitate investment of some such sum in various ways.'[16] Keynes was, therefore, suggesting some assistance to home investment but not state financed projects. Keynes also informed the Committee that although he had been in favour of a capital levy in 1920 he no longer advocated such a tax, since he did not consider the burden of existing taxes to be excessive.[17]

There was then no further immediate discussion of public works as Keynes concentrated his attention upon the problems of the exchange rate and the restoration of the gold standard in 1925. This work culminated in *The Economic Consequences of Mr Churchill*, which first appeared in the *Evening Standard* having been turned down by *The Times* as being too controversial.[18] In October 1926 he called for the reimposition of the embargo on foreign lending which had been imposed at the time of the return to gold and subsequently relaxed. He noted that an expansion of domestic credit to promote recovery would merely encourage foreign lending unless overseas issues were restricted.[19] He returned briefly to the issue of public works in his review of the Report of the Colwyn Committee. He stated that he was only in favour of the provision of a larger Sinking Fund in the budget, if there were a large programme for investment in public utilities which could not easily be financed by the capital market. As for the burden of the debt, which was examined by the Committee, he pointed out that the policy of returning to the gold standard at the prewar parity had raised the burden by about one third but 'this is a subject on which the Committee have thought it better to preserve a discreet silence'.[20]

A call for public works to reduce unemployment was made in the report of the Liberal Industrial Enquiry *Britain's Industrial Future* which was published in 1928. Keynes was a member of the executive committee of the enquiry and was a keen participant in its activities, but it is not clear what contribution he made to the writing of the report other than the chapter on Currency and Banking.[21] The Liberal discussions did, however, give him an opportunity to raise again the issue of public works. In 'How to Organize a Wave of Prosperity'[22] he reviewed the progress of the economy since the publication of *The Economic Consequences of Mr Churchill* three years earlier. He criticized the authorities for deflating prices through overvaluation of the exchange rate and credit restriction. He urged the Bank of England to relax credit and to encourage European central banks to do the same. Credit relaxation should be combined with an expansion of public investment. He criticized the confusions of 'so-called "sound finance"' arguing that: 'When we have unemployed men and unemployed plant and more savings than we are using at home, it is utterly imbecile to say that we cannot *afford* these things. *For it is with unemployed men and unemployed plant, and with nothing else, that these things are done*.'[23]

Keynes defended the Liberal Party proposals for public works contained in the pamphlet *We Can Conquer Unemployment* (1930) as part of their programme for the 1929 general election in two articles in the *New Statesman and Athenaeum*.[24] The government took the unusual step of issuing a White Paper *Memoranda on Certain Proposals Relating to Unemployment* (Cmnd 331, 1929), which was intended to challenge the Liberal proposals and Keynes's defence of them. The White Paper set out the well-known Treasury view that a programme of public works would be at the expense of investment in the private sector or overseas. The Treasury argued that a reduction in overseas lending would reduce the demand for British exports. While it was admitted that public investment projects might have other merits, it was claimed that they could not contribute to the reduction of unemployment. The White Paper concluded that 'in these circumstances a very large proportion of any additional government borrowings can only be procured, without inflation, by diverting money which otherwise would be taken soon by home industry'.[25] The theoretical argument underlying the paper was drawn largely from Hawtrey, who claimed that expenditure on public works could not raise employment unless there was a simultaneous expansion of credit, since 'a credit expansion unaccompanied by any expenditure on public works would be equally effective in giving employment. The public works are merely a piece of ritual convenient to people who want to be able to say that they are doing something useful, but otherwise irrelevant' (Hawtrey, 1925, 38; see also Hancock, 1960, 311).

Hawtrey's argument had been challenged by Pigou in *Industrial Fluctuations* (1929, 318), who pointed out that the proposition would only hold if the velocity of circulation of money were fixed rigidly. Pigou noted 'that higher interest rates stimulate the public to transfer balances to businessmen against new issues of securities, thus increasing the stream of resources available to businessmen, while leaving the price level unaltered. It [Hawtrey's argument] also neglects the fact that the raising of discount rate stimulates lending (on deposit) to the banks.'

In *Can Lloyd George Do It?* (1929) Keynes and Henderson defended the Liberal proposals to reduce unemployment through a programme of public works as set out in the pamphlet *We Can Conquer Unemployment*.[26] They did not reject the Treasury view directly but merely pointed out that, if valid, the argument would apply to all investment projects. Thus any expansion by one firm must be at the expense of the employment of another firm. This would imply that there was insufficient capital to employ the labour force at a time when Britain was a substantial exporter of capital. Their pamphlet pointed to the sources from which finance for public expenditure might be obtained.

These included savings currently being used to support the unemployed, savings running to waste on account of a lack of credit and hence not being embodied in home investment, and savings which might come from a reduction in net foreign lending. The theory underlying these arguments was drawn from *A Treatise on Money* which was not published until the following year, and may well have been as unfamiliar to economists as to the general public.

Keynes and Henderson pointed out that monetary expansion would lead to a fall in interest rates in Britain relative to the rest of the world, causing a loss of reserves from the Bank of England and so forcing a contraction of credit. They argued that a public works programme should be accompanied by a gradual expansion of credit, which would leave interest rates unchanged. In this way the dangers of monetary expansion would be avoided and the crowding-out argument advanced by Hawtrey was bypassed. In their criticism of Treasury debt management policy the authors noted that: 'The capital market is an international market. All sorts of influences which are outside our control go to determine the gilt-edged rate of interest; and the effect which the British government can exert on it by curtailing or expanding its capital programme is limited'.[27] Under these conditions the scope for an independent monetary policy must be severely restricted.

Keynes and Henderson admitted that a programme of public works would cause some deterioration in the balance of trade and that this was the way in which the reduction in net foreign investment was likely to be brought about. It did, however, presuppose a reasonably secure initial surplus on the current account. This condition was perhaps satisfied in 1929, but the balance of payments was likely to constrain any major programme of public works.[28] In fact, the Liberal proposals were for a relatively modest exercise in pump-priming. The scheme was to cost £300 million spread over three years and the annual cost to the budget would be £18 million assuming a rate of interest of 6 per cent per annum and no return on the investment itself. Keynes and Henderson claimed that a scheme of this size would not create a serious burden on the budget. They suggested that nearly half the capital cost would be recovered by the Treasury within a year through savings on unemployment benefit and increased tax receipts.

They claimed that the Treasury view was not supported by other economists, citing in particular Pigou's *Industrial Fluctuations*. The authors might also have mentioned Robertson who also challenged the ineffectiveness of public works in *A Study of Industrial Fluctuations* (1915, 253–4). Keynes was by no means the first economist to advance the case for public works but his arguments attracted the widest publicity.

The Treatise *and Public Works, 1929–31*

According to the general case of *A Treatise on Money* (1930) an excess of savings over investment causes business losses and unemployment. Some of the excess savings is absorbed by the dissaving involved in supporting the unemployed. Equilibrium in the general case could be restored by a reduction in the rate of interest which would encourage higher investment, raising both business profits and employment. In an open economy an excess of savings could also be absorbed by increased overseas lending, which would be encouraged by a reduction in domestic interest rates relative to those ruling in the rest of the world.

Keynes emphasized that Britain did not fit the general case on account of its special circumstances. It was an old economy offering a lower rate of return on investment than more recently developed economies. There was, therefore, a tendency for British investors to lend heavily overseas. Foreign lending tended to exceed the current account surplus, which was weakened by a lack of competitiveness. This was attributable to high money wages in relation to productivity, following the return to the gold standard. The normal adjustment of money wages to restore competitiveness was prevented by the downward inflexibility of money wages.

Britain had a tendency for home savings to exceed home investment, but lack of competitiveness prevented the excess savings being absorbed by net foreign investment. If foreign lending exceeded the current account surplus, there would be a loss of gold which the Bank of England would resist by raising interest rates, so discouraging home investment.

The special case is outlined in the *Treatise* (chapter 37)[29] and was used as the basis of Keynes's evidence to the Committee on Finance and Industry (the Macmillan Committee, 1931) of which he was a leading member. He set out both his theoretical argument and his proposed remedies to the Macmillan Committee and also to the Economic Advisory Council, set up by the newly elected Labour Government in February 1930, and to its Committee of Economists. He also wrote privately to Montagu Norman, the Governor of the Bank of England, using similar arguments.[30]

The remedies which Keynes proposed for an economy which had an excess of home savings over home investment and net foreign investment, combined with an over-valued exchange rate and money wage inflexibility, were various. Net foreign investment could be raised by stimulating exports, which could be achieved by measures to improve competitiveness. These could take the form of a general agreement on a reduction in money incomes, an increase in efficiency through rationalizing industry, or industrial subsidies financed through general taxation. Net foreign investment could also be increased by a reduction in imports through the imposition of a tariff. The departure from free trade could be justified by the inflexibility of money wages which prevented the normal restoration of competitiveness. As devaluation was agreed to be ruled out, Keynes favoured a combination of an export subsidy financed by a general tariff on imports which would have equivalent effects. This recommendation appeared in the Minority Report of which Keynes was a signatory.

On measures to promote home investment, Keynes considered discrimination against foreign issues on the London capital market and the imposition of a special tax on interest from foreign bonds. He argued that the discouragement of foreign lending would encourage home investment more than it discouraged net overseas investment. Finally there were measures to promote home investment more directly. A reduction in interest rates was not likely to be effective because of the danger of a reduction in the gold reserves, but public works undertaken directly by the government or by granting subsidies to public utilities could be effective. This was the remedy favoured by Keynes in his evidence to the Macmillan Committee and in the discussions of the Economic Advisory Committee, but he admitted in his letter to Norman that he recognized the difficulty of organizing projects on a scale which would be adequate to make an effective contribution to the problem. Rather surprisingly Keynes did not give serious consideration to measures to encourage consumption.

Keynes's arguments based on the framework of the *Treatise* were discussed by the Committee of Economists of the Economic Advisory Council. The membership of the Committee was Pigou, Henderson and Robbins, with Keynes as chairman. His theory was not in general acceptable to other members of the Committee who each approached policy issues from their own distinctive point of view, as explained by Howson and Winch (1977, 59–76). Pigou, who was generally sympathetic to proposals for public works, questioned the notion of business savings running to waste and also the idea of secondary employment being generated from primary expenditure.[31] Robbins adopted a strongly independent theoretical position and remained resolutely opposed to any departure from free trade, while Henderson showed growing concern about the impact of the deteriorating world economy on the UK and an increasing lack of sympathy for highbrow theory, which was of questionable relevance to the current situation. It seems fair to conclude that, despite Keynes's massive effort of exposition, he had not succeeded in convincing his professional colleagues of the validity of the analysis which was derived from the special case of the

Treatise. Nevertheless there was some measure of agreement among the economists about individual policy issues, as described by Howson and Winch.

The debate between Keynes and the Treasury about the effect of public works on employment culminated in his exchange with Sir Richard Hopkins, the Permanent Secretary, when Sir Richard gave evidence to the Macmillan Committee.[32] The Treasury view as presented by Hopkins was more subtle than the arguments put forward in the White Paper *Certain Proposals Relating to Unemployment*. Hopkins did not withdraw the earlier argument that increased public investment must be at the expense of investment elsewhere in the economy, but he was ready to concede that savings on the cost of unemployment benefits could provide a limited source of finance. He considered that the general effects of public works in raising tax revenues and business profits were questionable and speculative. The Treasury were, however, mainly concerned about the problems of organizing projects and the selection of schemes which would be beneficial. The criterion of acceptability was not merely one of the expected yield on the investment, although that was important, since other factors such as the impact of the scheme on public opinion and business confidence had to be taken into account. The conclusion of the interview was less unfavourable to capital schemes than the earlier White Paper. The Treasury would be prepared to consider projects which satisfied their criteria for being good schemes and which did not divert capital from more useful employment in other sectors of the economy. They did not, however, share Keynes's enthusiasm for such schemes and remained unconvinced by his theoretical arguments. Keynes's final remark, 'I find, as a result of your evidence, Sir Richard, that the Treasury view has been gravely misjudged', seems entirely justified as well as the chairman's conclusion, 'I think we may characterise it as a drawn battle'.[33]

The balance of the budget was not a major feature of the debate between Keynes and Hopkins but it became an issue of growing importance as the economy slipped into the abyss of depression in 1930 and 1931. The issue was put forcefully to Keynes by Hubert Henderson in May 1930, when Henderson expressed doubts about their joint proposals for using public works to counter unemployment. He now saw unemployment as a long-term problem which would require a continuing programme of public works with an accumulating interest burden on the budget. The budget problem would be aggravated as less remunerative projects came to be selected and provision for servicing the cost of such a programme should be made without delay.[34]

Keynes accepted Henderson's argument for a new source of revenue to ease the budgetary problem in the form of a general tariff. But he continued to press for public works, since, in his view, the difficulty of balancing the budget arose from the high level of unemployment.[35]

Although accepting arguments for the tariff in private, Keynes did not publicly reject free trade until his article 'Proposals for a Revenue Tariff' appeared in the *New Statesman and Nation* in March 1931.[36] He pointed out that 'the *direct* effect of an expansionist policy must be to cause government borrowing, to throw some burden on the budget, and to increase our excess of imports'.[37] Objections to expansion arising from the instability of the international position, the state of the budget and lack of confidence could not readily be dismissed. A revenue tariff would help the balance of the budget and prevent a decline in confidence which a deficit might engender. It would also improve the trade balance and increase employment. However, after the suspension of the gold standard in September 1931, Keynes rejected a revenue tariff. He argued that it was no longer necessary in view of the fall in the exchange rate. He wrote a letter to *The Times* within a week of the departure from gold pointing out that the tariff issue had now given place to 'the currency question'.[38]

IV THE NEW THEORY AND FISCAL POLICY, 1931–39

In the period which immediately followed the suspension of the gold standard Keynes was preoccupied with the exchange rate policy or what he called 'the currency question'.[39] The next major event was the massive debt management operation to convert 5 per cent War Loan to a 3½ per cent basis which took place in 1932. The conversion operation was associated with a general reduction in interest rates in Britain, which Keynes greatly welcomed. He considered that the general benefits to be expected from lower interest rates in Britain and possibly in the rest of the world exceeded the advantage of the reduction in debt servicing costs brought about by the conversion. Keynes argued that the operation on War Loan was not just a publicity exercise but should mark a turning point in the course of interest rates.[40] He did not return to the case for public works until the publication of 'The Means to Prosperity' in 1933.[41] In this series of newspaper articles he used the Kahn multiplier (1931) to quantify the impact of increased public spending on employment. He also examined the consequences of such expenditure for the budget. On plausible assumptions he showed that additional expenditure of £100 would result in a saving of unemployment benefit of £33 and after a lag an increase in tax receipts of £20. Thus rather more than half of the additional expenditure would within a year be remitted to the budget in the form of reduced transfers and increased tax receipts, without taking account of any return on the investment itself.

Keynes's detailed exposition of the multiplier is not entirely straightforward. Fuller calculations appeared in the American version of the articles than those which were published in *The Times*. Further details were also given in an article in *The New Statesman*.[42] There appears to be an inconsistency in that Keynes apparently altered the size of the multiplier in the course of his calculation.[43] The issue was raised in private correspondence by Professor Giblin and Keynes promised to clarify the matter in his forthcoming book, *The General Theory*.[44] Little difference, however, is made to Keynes's main conclusion that 50 per cent of additional government spending could be offset by reliefs to the budget.

In 'The Means to Prosperity' he called for public investment to revive the depressed industrial economies. The case which he made was general and applied to the US as well as to the UK. This was in marked contrast to his earlier argument based on the *Treatise*. Previously he had recommended reductions in the long-term interest rate for promoting recovery in the US, as in the Harris lectures given in Chicago in 1931, while recommending public works for the UK, special case.[45] In 'The Means to Prosperity' the remedies in the two countries were broadly the same.

In his new analysis Keynes did not neglect monetary policy, since the provision of bank credit and the reduction in long-term interest rates were still necessary parts of a programme for recovery. Public investment was, however, to play the major role in providing the initial stimulus to recovery and should preferably be coordinated on an international basis. The new prescriptions formed the basis of Keynes's advice to President Roosevelt on the New Deal in a letter published in *The New York Times* in December 1933 and in subsequent correspondence in *The Times*.[46]

There was a noticeable pause in the flow of articles and correspondence as Keynes concentrated upon writing *The General Theory* published in 1936. He was, however, active in the discussion of fiscal policy on the Committee on Economic Information of the Economic Advisory Council as Howson and Winch (1977, ch. 5) have shown. The Treasury responded to Keynes's proposals for the British economy in 'The Means to Prosperity'. He had recommended a reduction in taxation of £50 million to be financed by suspension of the Sinking Fund, the finance of unemployment benefits by loan rather than taxation and loan financed public works of £60 million.[47] Although encountering initial opposition, the multiplier calculations did much to secure acceptance by the Treasury of public works, albeit on a small scale. Phillips, Under-Secretary at the Treasury, admitted that 'his [Keynes's] argument is no doubt valid for a moderate expenditure' (Howson and Winch, 1977, 130) while expressing doubts about both the multiplier and the adverse psychological effects of an unbalanced budget.

The General Theory greatly strengthened the theoretical cogency of Keynes's policy prescriptions. Keynes emphasized the role of public investment in sustaining aggregate demand in several passages.[48] He did not consider that fluctuations in the marginal efficiency of capital could readily be offset by rapid changes in long-term interest rates, hence stabilization of private investment using monetary policy alone would prove difficult. Economic stability would be improved by greater government participation in the investment process. He suggested that a co-ordinated programme of public and semi-public investment could provide a basis for maintaining full employment.

He developed his ideas on counter-cyclical policy in 'How to Avoid a Slump', a series of articles written for *The Times* in January 1937.[49] The British economy was then reaching a cyclical peak and Keynes argued that a further general expansion of demand was not likely to raise output. Additional production and a reduction in unemployment from its current level, then about 8 per cent, might be achieved by seeking a better regional distribution of demand. Keynes strongly opposed any attempt to raise interest rates to curb the boom. Dear money in a recovery 'must be avoided like hellfire' because of the difficulty of reducing long-term rates during the following recession. The interest rate should be kept continuously at its long-term optimum level and the burden of cyclical stabilization should fall largely on fiscal policy. The government should aim for a budget surplus to restrain demand in the boom and for a deficit to promote revival in a slump. Since public investment projects could not be organized at short notice, there should be a forward-looking public investment programme. Projects should be accelerated or slowed down according to the state of the economy. Trade policy should also be used to assist fiscal policy by discouraging imports in a slump and relaxing restrictions during a boom. A trade deficit in a boom should be accepted with equanimity. Similar recommendations were made by Keynes to the Committee on Economic Information. An active counter-cyclical policy on the lines which Keynes was advocating is recommended in the 18th and 22nd reports of the Committee. By 1937 it appears that the Treasury had moved a considerable way towards accepting Keynes's arguments.[50]

In terms of the analysis of stabilization policy developed by Poole (1970), Keynes was recommending that real disturbances be offset by fiscal and trade measures, whereas financial disturbances should be accommodated by varying the money stock, keeping the rate of interest constant. This view was contested by Robertson who argued that interest rates should be permitted to rise to choke off demand in a boom. Robertson did not object to the use of fiscal policy to stabilize demand but he considered that monetary policy should also make some contribution to the task by allowing interest rates to vary over the trade cycle (Howson and Winch, 1977, 140–1; see also Robertson, 1937).

Keynes examined the growing impact of defence expenditure on demand from 1937 onwards. In his earlier articles on avoiding a slump he had argued for financing defence through taxation rather than borrowing.[51] When the decision went the other way, he considered the consequences for the economy. In March 1937 he pointed to the increasing pressure on resources but concluded 'that the Chancellor's loan expenditure *need* not be inflationary. But, unless care is taken, it may be rather near the limit'.[52] There was an immediate problem at the peak of the cycle in 1937 but as the recession of 1938 gathered pace, defence expenditure would cushion the economy against the downturn.

During the approach to war, Keynes continued to argue for no increase in interest rates, urging that private expenditure be restrained through taxation and controls rather than the rate of interest. He was concerned about the level of demand in relation to the capacity of the economy and also about the balance of payments, but he was not concerned about the balance of the government's accounts. He argued that increased government expenditure would generate equivalent savings and the only issue was the form in which the increased public debt would be held by the public. He suggested that debt should be issued in appropriate maturities to meet the preferences of the public without disturbing the structure of interest rates.[53]

V FISCAL POLICY AND THE RESOURCES FOR WAR

War Finance, 1939–45

Keynes's proposals for war finance were set out in his pamphlet *How to Pay for the War*.[54] The original proposals were modified in the light of extensive comment and criticism. The pamphlet distinguished between the problem of resource allocation in wartime and the problem of internal finance. The government could obtain the resources required for the war effort through expenditure financed by taxation and borrowing. In carrying out its war expenditures, the government would generate private incomes and private demands on resources well in excess of the value of consumption goods which would be available. A financial problem arose from the need to match the demand and supply of consumer goods without undue inflation, which could reduce efficiency and aggravate social tensions.

During the First World War general taxation had been used sparingly and there had been heavy reliance upon borrowing at high interest rates. The excess demand for consumption goods generated as a result of high war expenditure had resulted in prices rising faster than wages, inflating profits and raising the yield of profits taxes. Keynes commended this form of finance in the *Treatise*, regarding inflation as a necessary part of the process.[55] When he offered a new scheme at the outbreak of the Second World War, he attached great importance to the control of inflation. This was to be achieved by a combination of taxes, mainly income taxes falling on the bulk of the population, and a proposal for deferred pay. Workers were to receive part of their wages in a deferred form to be released after the war at a time of the government's choosing.

In *How to Pay for the War* he argued that maximum reliance be placed on deferred pay to restrain consumers' demand. However, in the event much greater emphasis was placed upon conventional taxation and he accepted the reduced role of deferred pay.[56] With this major exception the 1941 budget broadly reflected Keynes's views on war finance, being based for the first time on the use of national income analysis. During the discussion of Keynes's proposals an effective criticism was made by Hicks, who pointed out that deferred pay favoured the rich.[57] They could run down their assets in wartime in the confident expectation that they would be restored when deferred pay was released after the war. Keynes regarded the argument as excessively actuarial but did not deny its validity.

Keynes showed considerable preference for taxation over rationing, expressing his aversion to rationing most vigorously.[58] He was, however, concerned about the possible disincentive effect of having a high standard rate of income tax with a generous system of allowances. Workers might get the impression that they were paying tax at the standard rate when their effective tax rate was considerably lower.[59] He was also keen to encourage personal savings, emphasizing the importance of primary saving out of income before the income is respent. His championing of thrift was in marked contrast to his previous questioning of that Victorian virtue.[60]

One area where his recommendations were fully accepted was the finance of wartime borrowing at a long-term interest rate of 3 per cent. This was achieved, as he proposed, by convincing the market that the yields on gilt-edged securities were not going to increase, and by offering investors a wide range of assets to purchase with savings arising from the high levels of incomes generated by government spending combined with rationing of consumer goods. Keynes was not concerned about the asset composition of private sector portfolios, for example the growth of bank deposits was not seen as a factor tending to raise consumers' expenditure.[61] Nor did he show concern about the possible wealth effects arising from persistent wartime budget deficits.

Postwar Budgetary Policy, 1942–46

From 1942 until his death in 1946 Keynes was a leading participant in the official discussions on postwar economic policy. The main focus for Keynes's views on budgetary policy were the discussions which preceded the publication of the White Paper *Employment Policy* (Cmnd 6527) in May 1944 and also his evidence to the National Debt Enquiry of 1945.

Keynes's wartime memoranda and comments on official papers provide good evidence of his views about the conduct of fiscal policy after the war. They also give some insight into the distinction which has been made between Keynes and the Keynesians. Keynes appears relatively cautious and financially orthodox in comparison with some of the younger generation of economists. He occupied a middle position between the Treasury and its economic section, where there was a concentration of economists. His ideas seem to have developed partly in response to discussions with James Meade who was in close touch with the thinking of the economic section.

Keynes anticipated that there would be a strong trade cycle in the postwar economy which would need to be offset by discretionary stabilization policy. His views on the design of counter-cyclical policy were a development of the ideas which he had put to the Committee on Economic Information from 1935 onwards. He favoured the use of fiscal measures, based on variations in public and semi-public investment, to offset the trade cycle. The budget should be divided into an ordinary or revenue account and a capital account.[62] The aim should be to balance the ordinary budget by varying the rate of public investment included in the capital account. Since the trade cycle would tend to give rise to a deficit in the revenue budget during a recession, he argued that the counter-cyclical expenditure in the capital budget would act in the opposite direction and so help to balance the revenue budget. He, therefore, contrasted his proposals with a policy of a running budget deficit in recession. He was ready to admit that a severe recession might force the revenue budget into deficit but it was not something which the Chancellor of the Exchequer should plan for.[63] An advantage of using public investment to stabilize aggregate expenditure was that there would be a return on it in addition to the increase of tax receipts due to the rise in national income. Both influences would benefit the revenue budget. He claimed that: 'The very reason that capital expenditure is capable of paying for itself makes it better budgetwise and does not involve the progressive increase of budgetary difficulties which deficit budgeting for the sake of consumption may bring about or, at any rate, would be accused of bringing about.'[64]

He was critical of the proposals of the economic section of the Treasury put to him by James Meade for cyclical variation in both direct and indirect taxes. He replied that 'A remission of taxation on which people could only rely for an indefinitely short period might have very limited effects in stimulating their consumption.'[65] He also mentioned the lags and inconvenience associated with changes in income tax. He did not favour changes in indirect taxes, since he did not feel that people should be encouraged to smoke and drink when they are out of work. His fundamental objection to varying tax rates appears to have been political: while governments would no doubt be willing to reduce taxes in recession, they would be reluctant to raise them during a boom.[66]

An additional reason for promoting capital expenditure in a slump was Keynes's view that the British economy suffered from a shortage of capital, which was likely to persist for 15–20 years after the end of the war. He argued that: 'It is better for all of us that periods of deficiency expenditure should be made the occasion of capital development until our economy is much more saturated with capital goods than it is at present.'[67]

Keynes did, however, strongly support Meade's proposal for varying the rate of social security contributions according to the percentage of unemployment. He argued that it was less objectionable than varying tax rates 'because it could be associated with a formula, and partly becaue it would be pumping purchasing power into the hands of the class which can most easily vary its expenditure without altering its general standards'.[68] He also supported the use of hire purchase restrictions as a way of influencing consumers' expenditure. Keynes concluded that: 'Capital budgeting is a method of maintaining equilibrium; the deficit budgeting is a means of attempting to cure disequilibrium if and when it arises.'[69] The Chancellor should be non-committal on other aspects of deficit finance than Meade's social security proposals.

He gave further details of the proposals for a capital budget in his evidence to the National Debt Enquiry.[70] He distinguished between an Exchequer Budget, a Public Capital Budget and an Investment Budget. The first included the capital expenditure of the central government, the second included also the capital programmes of the local authority and other branches of the public sector, and the third extended to include capital expenditure by the private sector. The Exchequer Budget would include the surplus or deficit of the unemployment funds and the sinking fund. An annual charge for the repayment of debt should be made against the Revenue Budget, which would also pay interest on the debt and receive interest earned by productive debt. Keynes envisaged the gradual repayment of non-productive debt through the sinking fund and its replacement by productive debt.

The Public Capital Budget would be the principal instrument for stabilizing the economy. It would be used to offset fluctuations in private investment and help to balance the Revenue Budget through dampening variations in income. Forward planning of public sector investment would be needed to achieve this obective as well as regular surveys of private sector investment intentions. The Treasury or National Investment Bank would have responsibility for co-ordinating investment plans as part of a policy of full employment.

The role of monetary policy in offsetting the trade cycle would be relatively minor.[71] The wartime technique of tap issues of gilt-edged securities should be continued, allowing the public to determine the distribution of debt between different maturities. No attempt should be made to lengthen the average maturity of the debt by funding, a Treasury policy which he had criticized in the 1930s. Long-term interest rates should be kept down but some variation in rates on shorter-dated securities might be permitted as an adjunct to counter-cyclical policy. While Treasury bill rates should be kept down to domestic holders, a special variable short-term rate might be paid on overseas funds attracted to London. Keynes apparently believed that much of the system of official control over financial markets which grew up under wartime conditions could be carried over into the postwar world.

While emphasizing the importance of increasing the capital stock in the medium term, Keynes envisaged a later era in which it would be necessary to encourage consumption through fiscal incentives and redistribution of income, because of a lack of outlets for investment.[72] His favoured solution to the problem of long-run capital satiation was a reduction in the length of the working week rather than the accumulation of budget deficits. He recognized that the problem had more immediate relevance to the United States than to the British economy.[73]

The 1944 White Paper on *Employment Policy* included Keynes's main proposals for the postwar conduct of macroeconomic policy. It recommended that:

1 Public investment expenditure be varied to offset fluctuations in the private sector.

2 Little emphasis be placed on varying consumption through taxation.
3 Social security contributions be varied over the cycle as proposed by Meade.
4 The budget, defined as Keynes's Revenue Budget, be balanced, if not annually, then over a number of years.
5 The maintenance of low and stable long-term interest rates.

The White Paper was criticized by some Keynesian economists for being a rather weak and disappointing document. Although closely reflecting the master's views, it was written in a flat-footed Treasury style, unlike Keynes's sparkling memoranda.

Little (1952, 165) commented on the White Paper in his chapter on 'Fiscal Policy':

> The actual proposals were fiscally pusillanimous. An undue reliance was placed on counter-cyclical public investment, implying cycles and unemployment to counter. The decline in insurance contributions with which it was proposed to reduce unemployment of quite severe incidence would have been a drop in the ocean.

He asserted that 'balancing the budget from year to year is a futile aim with nothing to recommend it. Even in the long run a continuous budget deficit is not to be feared.'[74] Keynes had anticipated the criticism that the emphasis on budgetary equilibrium in the White Paper was excessive and that more emphasis should be placed on unbalancing the budget in recession. He argued that since variations in both public capital expenditure and in social security contributions would fall outside the normal budget, there should be no conflict between balancing the budget and a forward employment policy. The criticism only becomes valid if a budget deficit is assumed to be the inevitable consequence of public works.[75]

Keynesian economists have generally had fewer reservations about deficit financing than Keynes. In *The Trade Cycle* Harrod (1936, 215) went beyond counter-cyclical fiscal policy. He envisaged an economy prone to excessive saving in which 'it may be necessary to maintain public works and public borrowing as permanent processes to be intensified from time to time when the determinants threaten a depression'. In his contribution to the *Economics of Full Employment* Kalecki (1944, 44–6) examined the problem posed by the use of deficit spending which would entail a continuous expansion of the national debt. He noted that the cost of servicing the debt need not be a problem if the growth of income is sufficiently high, a problem which was analysed more formally by Domar (1944). Kalecki also considered what should be done if the growth of the burden of interest payments on the debt exceeded the growth of nominal income. He proposed a capital tax to prevent a rise in income tax rates, which could have adverse effect on incentives. This argument is similar to Keynes's views on the case for a capital levy as a way of relieving the burden of taxation falling on incomes. As an alternative Kalecki proposed a modified income tax which could be allowable against capital expenditure. The cost of capital goods after tax woud be reduced by the same percentage as the rate of taxation falling on profit. Thus the post-tax rate of return on investment would be unaffected by the tax rate. Keynes wrote to Kalecki congratulating him on his succinct discussion of deficit finance and strongly commending the proposal for a neutral income tax, which Keynes suggested should be extended to include investment in working capital as well as fixed investment.[76]

Keynes wrote to Meade about Lerner's proposals for the conduct of finance policy according to 'Functional Finance': 'His [Lerner's] argument is impeccable. But, heaven help anyone who tries to put it across the plain man at this stage of the evolution of our ideas.'[77] While accepting the force of Lerner's logic, Keynes was reluctant to accept his specific proposals for the conduct of policy. Keynes's response to Lerner (1943) has been explored in more detail by Colander (1984).

While Keynes remained relatively cautious and conservative in his advice to the Treasury, he was also encouraging younger economists to develop new principles for policy. But he considered that any departure from well-established policy conventions should be gradual. This general statement is well illustrated by his more circumspect approach to budget deficits than that of his Keynesian followers.

NOTES

1 See Moggridge and Howson (1974) for a discussion of Keynes's views on monetary policy.

2 Keynes, *The Collected Writings of John Maynard Keynes* (hereafter referred to as JMK) Vol II.

3 JMK IX.

4 JMK IX.

5 JMK XVI pp. 110–15, 'The Alternative'.

6 JMK XVI pp. 117–25, 'The Financial Prospects of the Financial Year'; pp. 125–8, 'The Meaning of Inflation'; pp. 162–78, 'The Financial Problem', the quote is from p. 167.

7 JMK XVII pp. 180–1, Chamberlain's notes of an interview with Keynes. In treasury papers (T) 172/1384; and pp. 181–4, 'Memorandum on the Bank Rate'. See also Howson (1975) pp. 19–20.

8 JMK IV pp. 53–60; JMK XIX pp. 33–76, Lectures to the Institute of Bankers, 22 November–5 December 1922.

9 JMK III p. 59.
10 JMK IV pp. 52–3.
11 JMK XIX pp. 100–6, 'Bank Rate at Four Per Cent', *The Nation and Athenaeum*, 14 July 1923. 'Bank Rate and the Stability of Prices – A Reply to the Critics,' *The Nation and Athenaeum*, 21 July 1923.
12 JMK XIX p. 78, Speech to the Annual Meeting of the National Mutual Life Assurance Society, 31 January 1923; pp. 79–80, Letter to *The Times*, 14 February 1923; pp. 113–18, 'Currency Policy and Unemployment', *The Nation and Athenaeum*, 11 August 1923. JMK XIX pp. 147–56, 'Free Trade', *The Nation and Athenaeum*, 24 November and 1 December 1923.
13 JMK XIX pp. 219–23, 'Does Employment Need a Drastic Remedy?' *The Nation and Athenaeum*, 24 May 1924. The quotes are from p. 222 and p. 223.
14 JMK XIX pp. 223–31, Letter to *The Times*, 28 May 1924 and 'A Drastic Remedy for Unemployment: A Reply to the Critics', *Nation and Athenaeum*, June 1924.
15 JMK XIX pp. 275–88, 'Foreign Investment and the National Advantage', *Nation and Athenaeum*, 9 August 1924 and 'Home Versus Foreign Investment', *Manchester Guardian Commercial*, 21 August 1924. JMK XIX p. 297, Evidence to the Committee on National Debt and Taxation, 1 October 1924.
16 JMK XIX p. 322, Q 40223. JMK XIII pp. 22–3, Keynes also argued in an early draft of the *Treatise* that to be effective public works should be accompanied by an expansion of credit, otherwise they could actually do harm by diverting working capital from other uses.
17 JMK XIX pp. 840–1, Evidence to the Committee on National Debt and Taxation, 6 May 1925.
18 JMK IX pp. 207–30.
19 JMK XIX pp. 568–74, 'The Autumn Prospect for Sterling: Should the Embargo on Foreign Loans be Reimposed', *Nation and Athenaeum*, 23 October 1926.
20 JMK XIX pp. 675–94, 'The Colwyn Report on National Debt and Taxation', *Economic Journal*, June 1927. The quote is on p. 694.
21 JMK XIX p. 731. See also Harrod (1951, 393).
22 JMK XIX pp. 761–6, 'How to Organize a Wave of Prosperity', *Evening Standard*, 31 July 1928. The quotation is on p. 765.
23 JMK XIV p. 765.
24 JMK XIX pp. 804–12, 'Mr. Lloyd George's Pledge', *Evening Standard*, 19 March 1929 and 'A Cure for Unemployment', *Evening Standard*, 19 April 1929.
25 'Memoranda on Certain Proposals' pp. 50–1.
26 JMK IX pp. 86–125. See also Keynes's review of the White Paper, JMK XIX pp. 819–24.
27 JMK IX p. 122.
28 The current account surplus in 1929 was +£76 million, falling to +£15 million and −£114 million in 1930 and 1931 respectively (Sayers, 1976).
29 Keynes (1930) Vol II pp. 376–7.
30 JMK XX pp. 94–157, Evidence to the Macmillan Committee on 28 February and 6 March 1930. pp. 350–6, Letter to Montagu Norman, 22 May 1930. pp. 370–84, 'Economic Advisory Council: The State of Trade', answers to the Prime Minister's questions. See also Howson and Winch (1977, 51–9) and Moggridge and Howson (1974).

31 JMK XX pp. 420–1, Letters from Pigou, 26 and 27 September 1930.
32 JMK XX pp. 165–79, Evidence of Sir Richard Hopkins to the Macmillan Committee. See also Kahn (1984, 77–90).
33 JMK XX p. 179.
34 JMK XX pp. 357–61, Letter from Henderson, 30 May 1930, and Keynes's reply of 4 June 1930.
35 JMK XX pp. 360–1, 364–6.
36 For example Howson and Winch (1977, 76) in addition to the correspondence with Henderson cited. JMK IX pp. 231–8, 'Proposal for a Revenue Tariff', *New Statesman and Nation*, 7 March 1931; also JMK XX pp. 489–506, 'Put the Budget on a Sound Basis: A Plea to Lifelong Free Traders', *Daily Mail* 13 March 1931 and correspondence in the *New Statesman and Nation*.
37 JMK IX p. 234.
38 JMK IX pp. 243–4, Letter to *The Times* 29 September 1931.
39 JMK XXI pp. 16–32, 'Notes on the Currency Question'.
40 JMK XXI pp. 114–25, 'A Note on the Long-Term Rate of Interest in Relation to the Conversion Scheme', reprinted from *Economic Journal*, September 1932.
41 JMK IX pp. 335–66, *The Means to Prosperity*. The version reprinted is the American edition giving fuller discussions of the multiplier.
42 JMK XXI pp. 171–8, 'The Multiplier', *New Statesman and Nation*, 1 April 1933.
43 JMK XIII pp. 414–19.
44 JMK IX pp. 345–7. Keynes's calculation of the budgetary consequences of an increase in loan financed expenditure on public works appears to be as follows: of the initial expenditure of £100 only £66 raises domestic incomes, the remainder leaks into imports, running down of stocks, etc., and the marginal propensity to consume is assumed to be 0.75 which appears to include a leakage into taxation. The leakages at each round of the multiplier are $(0.75)(0.66) \simeq 0.5$ and the expenditure series is then $£66(1 + \frac{1}{2} + \frac{1}{4} \ldots) = 132$, implying a multiplier for an increase in gross loan financed expenditure of 1.32. The employment multiplier is 2, since expenditure of £66 is assumed to generate $\frac{1}{3}$ of a man-year of primary employment, making the total increase in employment $\frac{2}{3}$ of a man-year for a rise in income of £132. Since the annual cost of keeping a man on the dole is taken to be £50, the saving to the Treasury is $\frac{2}{3} \times £50 = £3$ per annum.

When calculating the rise in income to derive the increase in tax receipts, Keynes uses an income multiplier of 2. The rise in income for gross expenditure of £100 is £66 $(1 + \frac{2}{3} + \frac{4}{9} \ldots) \simeq 200$. The marginal rate of tax is assumed to be 0.10, so that tax receipts rise by £20 and the total contribution to the budget is £53. If the same leakages are assumed as in the calculation of the saving on the dole, the rise in tax receipts is £13.2, making a total contribution to the budget of £46.2.

The reworking of Keynes's calculations does not undermine his general conclusion that the eventual saving to the budget will be about half of the increase in public expenditure. But the saving is slightly less than half rather than 'a little more than half of the loan expenditure' which he claims. For a discussion of the multiplier see Patinkin (1982).
45 JMK XIII pp. 343–67, 'An Economic Analysis of Unemployment', Harris Foundation Lectures, Chicago, June 1931. See in particular pp. 364–7.

46 JMK XXI pp. 289–97, Letter to *The New York Times*, 31 December 1933; pp. 297–304, 322–32, Letters to *The Times*, on 2 January, 11 June and 22 June 1934.
47 JMK IV pp. 364–5.
48 Keynes (1936) pp. 164, 220–1, 320, 325, 349, 377, 380–1.
49 JMK XXI pp. 384–95, 'How to Avoid a Slump', *The Times*, 12–14 January 1937.
50 Howson and Winch (1977) pp. 134–48 and 18th and 22nd Reports of the Committee on Economic Information reported there as pp. 319–53. See also Peden (1979) pp. 61–3 who suggests that the Treasury's conversion to Keynesian economics before the Second World War was far from complete.
51 Keynes urged the finance of defence expenditure chiefly through taxation, JMK XXI p. 390, but explored loan finance in his letter to *The Economist* of 2 February 1937, JMK XXI p. 398–400.
52 JMK XXI p. 408, 'Borrowing for Defence, Is it Inflation: A Plea for an Organized Borrowing Policy', *The Times*, 11 March 1937.
53 JMK XXI pp. 509–18, 'Crisis Finance: An Outline of Policy', *The Times*, 17 and 18 April 1939; pp. 551–64, 'Borrowing by the State High Interest or Low: A Recommendation', *The Times*, 24–25 July 1939.
54 JMK IX pp. 367–439, and Keynes (1940). For further discussion of the finance of the Second World War see Moggridge (1975) and Sayers (1956).
55 Keynes (1930) Vol I pp. 170–6; see also JMK XIX pp. 781–95, 'National Finance in War'.
56 JMK XXII pp. 205–12, and pp. 234–40.
57 JMK XXII pp. 107–10, Correspondence over deferred pay, 28 February–13 March 1940.
58 JMK IX p. 410, JMK XXII p. 43, p. 263, 'Supplementary Note on the Dimension of the Budget Problem'.
59 JMK XXII p. 209, 'Notes on the Budget III'.
60 JMK XXII pp. 300–1, pp. 307–8, pp. 322–3, 'Notes for the Budget Statement 1941'.
61 JMK XXII p. 291, 'The Theory of the "Gap"'.
62 JMK XXVII pp. 277–80, 'Budgetary Policy'.
63 JMK XXVII pp. 356–7, 'Maintenance of Employment'.
64 JMK XXVII p. 320, Letter to J.E. Meade, 25 April 1943. See also pp. 326–7, Letter to J.E. Meade, 27 May 1943.
65 JMK XXVII p. 319, Letter to J.E. Meade, 25 April 1943; also pp. 323–4, 'The Long Term Problem of Full Employment'; and p. 326, Letter to J.E. Meade, 27 May 1943.
66 JMK XXVII pp. 319–20, Letter to J.E. Meade, 25 April 1943; and pp. 350–1, letter to Josiah Wedgwood, 7 July 1943.
67 JMK XXVII p. 320, Letter to J.E. Meade, 25 April 1943; and also p. 324, 'The Long Term Problem of Full Employment'.
68 JMK XXVII p. 319, Letter to J.E. Meade, 25 April 1943. See also p. 353, Letter to Sir Wilfrid Eady, 10 June 1943; p. 365, 'Post War Employment: A Note by the Steering Committee'.
69 JMK XXVII pp. 352–3, 'Maintenance of Employment: The Draft Note for the Chancellor of the Exchequer'.
70 JMK XXVII pp. 405–13, 'National Debt Enquiry: The Concept of a Capital Budget'.
71 JMK XXVII pp. 396–400, 'National Debt Enquiry: Summary by Lord Keynes of His Proposals'.

72 JMK XXVII pp. 320–5, 'The Long Term Problem of Full Employment'; see also pp. 359–61, Letter to Sir Wilfrid Eady and others 9 July 1943.

73 JMK XXVII p. 350, Letter to Josiah Wedgwood, 7 July 1943; p. 384, Letter to T.S. Eliot, 5 April 1945.

74 Little (1952, 165). He then qualifies this statement: 'In the now almost unimaginable circumstance in which the required deficit made the rate of growth of the national debt greater than that of the national income, the appropriate policy would normally be to reduce the rate of interest on new debt until the circumstance had ceased'.

75 JMK XXVII pp. 376–7, 'White Paper on Employment Policy'.

76 JMK XXVII pp. 381–3, Letter to M. Kalecki, 30 December 1934.

77 JMK XXVII p. 320, Letter to J.E. Meade 25 April 1943.

REFERENCES

Colander, D. 1984: Was Keynes a Keynesian or a Lernerian? *Journal of Economic Literature*, 22, 1572–5.

Committee on National Debt and Taxation (Colwyn Committee) 1927: *Report*, Cmnd 2800, London.

Committee on Finance and Industry (Macmillan Committee) 1937: *Report*, Cmnd 3897, London.

Dimsdale, N.H. 1975: Keynes and the Finance of the First World War. In M. Keynes (ed.) *Essays on John Maynard Keynes*, Cambridge.

Domar, E.D. 1944: The 'Burden of the Debt' and the National Income, *American Economic Review*, 34, 798–827.

Hancock, K. 1960: Unemployment and the economists in the 1920's, *Economica*, 27, 305–21.

Harrod, R.F. 1936: *The Trade Cycle*, Oxford University Press, Oxford.

Harrod, R.F. 1951: *The Life of John Maynard Keynes*, Macmillan, London.

Hawtrey, R.G. 1925: Public expenditure and the demand for labour, *Economica*, 5, 38–48.

Howson, S. 1975: *Domestic Monetary Management in Britain 1919–1938*, Cambridge University Press, Cambridge.

Howson, S. and Winch, D. 1977: *The Economic Advisory Council 1930–1939*, Cambridge University Press, Cambridge.

Kahn, R.F. 1931: The relation of home investment to unemployment, *Economic Journal*, 41, 173–98.

Kahn, R.F. 1984: *The Making of Keynes' General Theory*, Raffaele Mattioli Foundation, Cambridge.

Kalecki, M. (ed.) 1944: *The Economics of Full Employment*, Blackwell, Oxford.

Keynes, J.M. In Sir Austin Robinson and Donald Moggridge (eds) *The Collected Writings of John Maynard Keynes*, Macmillan, London [JMK].

Vol. II, *The Economic Consequences of the Peace* (1919) [1971] London.

Vol. III, *A Revision of the Treaty* (1922) [1971] London.

Vol. IV, *A Tract on Monetary Reform* (1923) [1971] London.

Vol. IX, *Essays in Persuasion* (with additional essays) (1931) [1972] London.

Vol. XIII, *The General Theory and After: Part I, Preparation* [1973] London.

Vol. XVI, *Activities 1914–19: The Treasury and Versailles* [1971] London.

Vol. XVII, *Activities 1920–22: Treaty Revision and Reconstruction* [1977] London.

Vol. XIX, *Activities 1922–9: The Return to Gold and Industrial Policy*, Parts I and II, [1981] London.
Vol. XX, *Activities 1929–31: Rethinking Employment and Unemployment Policies*, [1981] London.
Vol. XXI, *Activities 1931–9: World Crises and Policies in Britain and America*, [1982] London.
Vol. XXII, *Activities 1939–45: Internal War Finance*, [1978] London.
Vol. XXVII, *Activities 1940–6: Shaping the Post-War World: Employment and Commodities*, [1980] London.

Keynes, J.M. 1930: *A Treatise on Money*, Vols I and II. Macmillan, London. JMK published by Macmillan for the Royal Economic Society.

Keynes, J.M. 1936: *The General Theory of Employment, Interest and Money*. Macmillan, London.

Keynes, J.M. 1940: *How to Pay for the War*. Macmillan, London.

Lerner, A.P. 1943: Functional finance and the federal debt, *Social Research*, 10, 38–51.

Liberal Industrial Enquiry, 1928: *Britain's Industrial Future*, Benn, London.

Liberal Party, 1929, *We Can Conquer Unemployment*, Cassell, London.

Little, I.M.D. 1952: Fiscal policy. In D. Worswick and P. Ady (eds) *The British Economy 1945–1950*. Oxford University Press, Oxford, pp. 159–87.

McIntosh D.C. 1977: Mantoux versus Keynes: a note on German income and the reparations controversy, *Economic Journal*, 87, 765–7.

Ministry of Labour 1929: *Memorandum on Certain Proposals relating to Unemployment*, Cmnd 331.

Ministry of Reconstruction 1944: *Employment Policy*, Cmnd 6527.

Moggridge, D.E. 1975: Economic Policy in the Second World War. In M. Keynes (ed.) *Essays on John Maynard Keynes*, Cambridge University Press, Cambridge.

Moggridge, D.E. and Howson, S. 1974: Keynes on monetary policy, 1910–1946, *Oxford Economic Papers*, 26, 226–47.

Patinkin, D. 1982: *Anticipations of the General Theory*, Blackwell, Oxford.

Peden, G.C. 1979: *British Rearmament and the Treasury 1932–1939*, Scottish Academic Press, Edinburgh.

Pigou, A.C. 1929: *Industrial Fluctuations*, 2nd edn, Macmillan, London.

Poole, W. 1970: Optimal choice of monetary instruments in a simple stochastic macro model, *Quarterly Journal of Economics*, 4, 147–216.

Robertson, D.H. 1915: *A Study of Industrial Fluctuations*, King, London.

Robertson, D.H. 1937: The trade cycle: an academic view, *Lloyds Bank Review*, September.

Sayers, R.S. 1956: *Financial Policy 1939–45*, HMSO and Longman, London.

Sayers, R.S. 1976: *The Bank of England 1891–1944*, Appendices, Cambridge University Press, Cambridge.

9

Deficit Financing: Keynes, the Keynesians and the New Approach, with Special Reference to the UK

M.J. ARTIS

I INTRODUCTION

There are many definitions of Keynesianism and many interpretations of the *General Theory* (Keynes, 1936). But it may be widely agreed that Keynesianism is identified with a commitment to the effectiveness of budgetary policy and more specifically with the potential virtues of deficit financing. US critics of Keynesianism have viewed the deficits of the Vietnam war period as evidence of the success of a Keynesian revolution (Buchanan and Wagner, 1977); a UK observer (Tomlinson, 1981, 1982) has viewed the modesty of UK deficit finance as evidence of the absence or at least the weakness of the Keynesian revolution. An immediate paradox in all this is the contrast between the identification of Keynesianism and budgetary policy and the almost total lack of discussion of budgetary policy in the *General Theory* itself.[1] In the next section of this chapter I comment on this issue further, drawing in part on Kregel's recent investigation of Keynes's thoughts on the matter of deficit financing (Kregel, 1985). Perhaps nowhere more than in the UK did practical Keynesianism become associated with the fine tuning of aggregate demand through fiscal policy, post mortems on which – generally of an unfavourable character – have aroused some controversy. Reviewing this field of endeavour we add a further contribution to the pile of stylized facts in section III. The post mortem examination of fiscal policy raises questions about the nature and comparability of measures of fiscal policy or fiscal stance commonly available and in section IV we take the opportunity to comment on this issue. The decline from favour of Keynesian fiscal policy gave way, in the UK at least, to a mistaken experiment in deficit fiscal targeting. Now it has become fashionable to advocate 'coarse tuning' of the fiscal deficit. In the last section of the chapter I review these issues.

II KEYNES AND DEFICIT FINANCING

Keynesianism has been widely identified as placing budgetary policy at the centre of an active policy of demand management. In particular, it has been identified with justifying deficit financing in this context, and for some this is the essential ingredient. Indeed, in a recent controversy conducted by Tomlinson and other workers[2] in the pages of *Economy and Society*, the protagonist argued that there had not been a Keynesian revolution in policy making in the UK because full employment had not been maintained – in the years when this condition prevailed – by recourse to deficit financing (see Matthews, 1968), whilst in the years (post 1973) when such recourse was needed to maintain full employment, deficit financing did not occur, or did not occur on a sufficient scale, to restore this condition. Tomlinson's point is that the truly revolutionary aspect of Keynesian budgetary policy lies in its positive advocacy of deficit financing in appropriate circumstances and that we have not seen the success of this advocacy. From a perspective which is at the opposite end of the political spectrum, Buchanan and Wagner (1977) could nevertheless be read as implying substantial agreement with Tomlinson's test, but with a different outcome, namely that in the United States there was – on the evidence of the Federal deficits of the 'Great Society' and Vietnam war period – a successful Keynesian revolution. These assessments introduce a further paradox: is it plausible that the US has had, and the UK has not had, a Keynesian revolution?

Clearly there is something wrong about these 'tests' for the presence of a Keynesian revolution. It is understandable that deficit financing should receive a special emphasis, but its presence or absence is no good indicator of the Keynesian character of the policy regime or the success of a Keynesian revolution (otherwise one would be obliged to subscribe to the theory of a super-Keynesian revolution in the Reagan years!). Rather, the issue is, as Lerner (1943) himself pointed out, whether the deficit follows from the precepts of 'functional finance'.

Lerner's doctrine of functional finance asks that budgetary policy should be made and judged by the criterion of whether it stabilizes the economy; the planned balance in the budget should be endogenous to the achievement of target inflation and unemployment rates – this is why he advocated the use of the term 'functional finance'. Budgets are not to be drawn up on the basis of any other rules than those that emerge from the use of budgetary policy to stabilize the economy and are functional in this sense. On this basis, it is clear that Keynesian policy makers will not plan for (additional) deficits when employment is already high and/or inflation is a threat; if deficits nevertheless emerge in such conditions they cannot be ascribed to a Keynesian revolution. Thus, as Schott (1982) points out, Tomlinson's (1981) use of Matthews' famous 1968 paper to prove his case is beside the point, and the post-1973 refusal to endorse greater deficit spending may equally be rationalized as an instance where inflation constrained this action on good functional finance grounds.[3] In the same way Buchanan and Wagner cannot – as they themselves admit (1977, 50) – consistently argue that the deficits of the Great Society–Vietnam war period are Keynesian in inspiration. What they say on this point is that the preceding Keynesian revolution had fatally weakened the attraction of the balanced budget principle and thus allowed in (non-Keynesian) forces making for growing deficits (but Keynesian economists are nevertheless castigated for not foreseeing this consequence of their success).

Keynes's own attitudes to deficit financing are fully discussed elsewhere in this volume in the chapters by Dimsdale. He elaborates and, in doing so, largely confirms the impression given by Kregel (1985) in his earlier exegesis. Kregel draws attention to Keynes's conservative statements on the subject, noting that 'Keynes himself did *not* ever directly recommend government deficits as a tool of stabilization policy – this came rather in Lerner's concept of functional finance . . .' (Kregel, 1985, 32). Yet Lerner's concept cites Keynes as the originator of functional finance, which he describes as being 'first put forward in substantially complete form by J.M. Keynes in England'. The dissonance produced by the juxtaposition of these two quotations is mirrored by the contrast in Keynes's writings between his overtly conservative statements of position on fiscal deficits and the 'radicalism' towards fiscal policy implied in most readings of the *General Theory*. Can the 'conservative' Keynes who viewed budget deficits with what Kregel has described as a 'clearly enunciated lack of enthusiasm' be reconciled with the Keynes who in the *General Theory* was not averse to recommending such 'wasteful' activities as the promotion by governments of mining to recover pound notes in bottles buried in disused pit shafts? Part of the answer indicated by Labini (1985) is that Kregel's account gives heavy weight to qualifications to deficit spending introduced by Keynes in writings outside the *General Theory*, and that the occasions for these comments were provided by a context of postwar reconstruction. It would not be surprising therefore to find a 'medium-term' emphasis in such comment. Moreover, Kregel neglects to mention Keynes's *How To Pay For The War* (Keynes, 1940). From the viewpoint of finding out what Keynes thought about deficit financing in conditions of unemployment the omission is inconsequential. From the viewpoint of finding an example of functional finance and an application of the new principles of demand management, the omission would be critical, for this is what *How to Pay For the War* is. As Christopher Dow explains (Dow, 1964, 180) 'The idea that the level of taxation should be adjusted to bring total demand into balance with total supply, was, however, applied very boldly and simply to the problem of *How To Pay For the War*. There, as it happens, the emphasis has remained'.

The upshot of all this is that the key Keynesian policy principle is that of 'functional finance', and that this is foreshadowed in the *General Theory*, applied clearly in *How to Pay For the War* and – of course – most directly enunciated by Lerner. It is true that direct references to *deficit* finance for the purpose of maintaining employment are surprisingly scarce in Keynes's writings. But a narrow search for reference to deficit finance, like the attempt to test for Keynesianism by reference to the presence or absence of deficits, is capable of being highly misleading. The key intellectual inheritance is the principle of functional finance. In certain circumstances the application of this principle will lead to the advocacy of deficits; in others, it will not.

III THE EFFECTIVENESS OF BUDGETARY POLICY

The application of the rules of functional finance led to the era of demand management and fine tuning. In the United Kingdom, perhaps more than elsewhere, the conscious management of aggregate demand, primarily through taxation policy, became the centre-piece of economic policy. As already noted, the *General Theory* was not strong on budgetary policy generally, but most of what it had to say referred to government expenditure rather than taxation,[4] so the actual development of 'Keynesian' fine tuning belied the prospectus of the *General Theory* in this way too. The aim of functional finance, as of stabilization policy generally, was to secure internal and external balance. Nevertheless, most attempts to assess the effectiveness of these policies have focused on the record with respect to output.

Dow began a controversy, as much because his methodology was left unclear as because of the conclusion itself, by terminating his examination of postwar British demand management with the statement that 'As far as internal conditions are concerned, then, budgetary and monetary policy failed to be stabilizing, and must on the contrary be regarded as having been positively destabilizing' (Dow, 1964, 384). Later investigations by different authors, for periods that only partly overlap, come to different conclusions. Bristow (1968) found in favour of a stabilizing influence for his period (1955–65), whilst Artis (1972) found against for his (1958–70 and 1965–70). Hansen's, the most well-known study (Hansen, 1969), found policy to have been destabilizing over the period 1955–65. All these studies focus on GDP and (with modifications) identify success (failure) in stabilization with a reduction (increase) in the variance of GDP around its trend. As Kennedy (1985) has correctly emphasized, however, exclusive concentration on such a measure of stabilization for a single objective of policy runs foul of the criticism that the authorities themselves consciously varied from time to time the rate of GDP potential use, in order to attain more closely the other goals of policy. Moreover, the effect of policy on the trend can easily be more important than its effect on quarter-by-quarter stability.

Recognition of these points requires that the policy effects on the trend and stability of the whole range of policy goals should be calculated[5] or that the test itself should be modified to take account of the planned deviation from trend in GDP which the authorities consciously undertook to create. Kennedy (1985) takes the latter route and by comparing estimates of the effects of policy with estimates of the authorities' actual target for output comes to the conclusion that over the whole period from 1952 to 1974 policy was on average stabilizing in the sense of moving the economy closer to the authorities' target.

The alternative route was taken by Artis and Green (1982) in a study of the period 1974–79 and an extension is reported here (table 9.1) for a later period 1979–82. The extension is based on the paper by Artis et al. (1984), in which two econometric models of the UK economy (those of the National Institute of Economic and Social Research (NIESR) and of HM Treasury) were used to provide estimates through simulation methods of the fiscal (and also monetary) policies undertaken in the period. The method (described in more detail below) is conditional on the model employed and the assumptions used to describe a neutral benchmark for policy against which to measure activism; however, the estimates did not reveal a great difference as between the two models employed in this particular exercise and the stabilizing measures reported in table 9.1 rely on the policy effects produced by just one of these models (that of the NIESR). The measure of policy effects has been used to generate a series of 'policy off' values for GDP, the balance of payments, inflation and unemployment. Semi-log regressions were then fitted to the resultant 'policy off' series, as also to the 'policy on' (actual) series and the detrended coefficients of

Table 9.1 *Effects of fiscal policy 1979–82*

A Quarter-to-quarter stability	*GDP*	*Unemployment*	*Current account balance*[a]	*Inflation*
Coefficients of variation				
1 With policy[b]	0.01	0.07	0.91	0.23
2 Without policy[c]	0.01	0.07	1.64	0.33
3 *F* ratio of residual variances[d]	0.77	0.84	1.07	1.54
B Mean change (per quarter)	%	000s	£million	% points
4 1979–80	−0.17	10.26	57.51	2.83
5 1981–82	−2.91	324.44	621.49	1.00
6 Whole period	−1.63	177.82	358.30	1.85

[a] Taken as cumulative for purposes of part A of the table.
[b] i.e. actual series.
[c] Hypothetical series.
[d] Calculated from semi-log trend regressions, as the ratio of 'policy on' to 'policy off' detrended residual variances.
Source: Statistics are calculated from data quoted in the study by Artis et al. (1984).

variation for each of the two consequently calculated. These are shown in the top half of table 9.1 with, in the third row, the *F*-ratio of the residual variances: none of these appears to be statistically significant at any of the conventional levels. However, it seems clear that the information provided in the lower part of the table comes closer to intuition about what is meant by stabilization. The slice of time considered is especially unflattering to the governmental authorities in this case, the computed effect of its fiscal policies raising both unemployment and inflation at the same time.

These measures of the stabilizing effect of policy depend on a modelling of fiscal policy of a more or less sophisticated character. Despite the availability of such models, there is nevertheless a great deal of interest in summary indicators of fiscal policy or fiscal stance. Most of these are variations on the theme of the balance in the budget, an issue which recurs in the next section.

IV MEASURES OF FISCAL POLICY AND FISCAL STANCE

The focus on fiscal policy as a short-term stabilizer brought with it a number of measures proposed as indicators or measures of policy. To the extent that these are based on the balance in the budget, as most of them are, they may also be related to normative rules for the medium-term setting of fiscal policy as explained in the next section. But this is a distinct role from that played by these measures as indicators of fiscal policy impact in the short run.

The relationship between the conventional summary measures and a model-based measure such as the one implemented by Blinder and Goldfeld (1976) may be clarified by resort to a primitive IS/LM model:[6]

$$Y = C + I + G \tag{9.1}$$

$$C = C(Y - T) \quad C_Y = -C_T > 0 \tag{9.2}$$

$$T = T(Y, \tau) \quad T_Y > 0, T_\tau > 0 \tag{9.3}$$

$$I = I(R, \alpha) \quad I_R < 0, I_\alpha < 0 \tag{9.4}$$

$$R = R(\bar{M}, Y) \quad R_{\bar{M}} < 0, R_Y > 0 \tag{9.5}$$

where, all variables being in real terms, Y is aggregate income, C is private consumption, I is private investment, G is government spending, T is income tax revenue, R is the rate of interest, $\bar{M}$ is the quantity of money, τ is the real income tax rate and α is the autonomous component of private investment. The model is standard, except for the inversion of the money demand function in equation 9.5. It solves as

$$Y = C[\bar{Y} - T(Y, \tau)] + I[R(\bar{M}, Y) + \alpha] + G \tag{9.6}$$

and in differential form

$$\mathrm{d}Y = \frac{\mathrm{d}G - C_Y T_\tau \mathrm{d}\tau}{1 - C_Y(1 - T_Y) - I_R R_Y} + \frac{I_\alpha \mathrm{d}\alpha + I_R R_{\bar{M}} \mathrm{d}M}{1 - C_Y(1 - T_Y) - I_R R_Y} \tag{9.7}$$

The conventional measures of fiscal policy, in first difference form, are:

$$\text{Actual budget surplus} = \mathrm{d}T - \mathrm{d}G$$
$$= \mathrm{T}_Y \mathrm{d}Y + T_\tau \mathrm{d}\tau - \mathrm{d}G \tag{9.8}$$

$$\text{Leverage} = (\mathrm{C}_Y \mathrm{d}T - \mathrm{d}G)(1 - C_Y)^{-1}$$
$$= (C_Y T_Y \mathrm{d}Y + C_Y T_\tau \mathrm{d}\tau - \mathrm{d}G)(1 - C_Y)^{-1} \tag{9.9}$$

'Structural' (full employment) budget surplus

$$= \mathrm{d}T(Y^{\mathrm{F}}, \tau) - \mathrm{d}G$$
$$= T_\tau(Y^{\mathrm{F}}, \tau)\mathrm{d}\tau - \mathrm{d}G \tag{9.10}$$

Weighted full employment budget surplus

$$= C_Y \mathrm{d}T(Y^{\mathrm{F}}, \tau) - \mathrm{d}G$$

$$= C_Y T(Y^{\mathrm{F}}, \tau)\mathrm{d}\tau - \mathrm{d}G \qquad (9.11)$$

Weighted standardized surplus $= C_Y \; T_\tau \mathrm{d}\tau \; - \; \mathrm{d}G$ (9.12)

Simulation-based measure

$$= \mathrm{d}Y(\mathrm{d}G, \mathrm{d}\tau) - \mathrm{d}Y(\mathrm{d}\hat{G}, \mathrm{d}\hat{\tau})$$

$$= \frac{\mathrm{d}G - C_Y T_\tau \mathrm{d}\tau}{1 - C_Y(1 - T_Y) - I_R R_Y} \text{ iff } \mathrm{d}\hat{G}, \mathrm{d}\hat{\tau} = 0 \qquad (9.13)$$

Most of these are self-explanatory. The leverage measure is Musgrave's (1964) suggestion for evaluating the contribution of government by taking the difference between the economy with, and without, the entire government sector. The full employment budget measures (equations 9.10 and 9.11) ask that tax revenues be normalized at 'full employment' levels. The weighted standardized surplus is the measure which Blinder and Solow (1974) favoured in the conclusion of their well-known survey. Distinct from the normalized measures, it is evaluated at actual income levels.[7] A simulation measure, of the kind implemented by Blinder and Goldfeld (1976) for the US and by Artis and Green (1982) for the UK could be expressed as shown in equation 9.13, as the difference between the change that would have occurred at assumed 'benchmark' or 'neutral' values of dG and dτ, indicated as dG and dτ. If, as would be natural in this simple model, these are taken as zero, then equation 9.13 is simply the measure 9.12 with sign reversed and weighted by the model multiplier.

On this view of things there is a strong family resemblance between the set of measures discussed. However it may be argued in favour of the simulation-based measure that it is in practice free from some of the criticisms levied against the summary measures (for a wide-ranging set of criticisms, see, for example, Bean and Hartley (1978)); contrary to the summary measures, the simulation method is not unidimensional: it can be scaled in terms of any endogenous variable, not just output. The simulation method is also precise about timing, where summary measures are often unclear and is sensitive to initial conditions and the instrument settings of other policies (e.g. monetary policy). However, it may be argued in favour of the traditional summary indicators that they are in some sense broader than simulation measures; they measure fiscal 'stance' rather than policy *per se*. And it may be argued that they are, though only in a very weak sense, less model dependent.[8]

'Stance' versus 'Policy'

How forceful is the distinction between fiscal 'stance' and fiscal 'policy', and measures respectively thereof? As constructed, measures of fiscal stance (the budget balance measures) are certainly different from simulation-based measures of fiscal policy. (The recent UK data in table 9.2 illustrate the point.) But it is a moot point whether the differences are *per se* desirable or should be regarded as measurement error; the National Institute's recently published view (Biswas et al., 1985) inclines to the former, my own to the latter, as the simple algebraic set-up introduced earlier suggests. Buiter (1983) also suggests that the standard budget balance-related measures are only valid in 'a static, rather old-Keynesian and expectations-innocent model' and declares his preference for a simulation-based measure. This is a particular (strong) example of the view that the standard measures are policy measures manqué, one that (too harshly) makes no allowance for the economy of computation costs afforded by the summary measures. It must be admitted, though, that if the standard measures are supplemented by

Table 9.2 *Fiscal policy: comparison of a model-based measure and a summary indicator*[a] (per cent GDP)

	A *Cyclically adjusted weighted deficit*[b]	*B* *Model-based*
1980/1	0.16	0.16
2	0.02	0.33
3	1.34	−0.19
4	−1.36	−0.62
1981/1	−1.33	−2.02
2	−1.17	−2.83
3	−2.37	−3.33
4	−2.36	−2.04
1982/1	−1.30	−0.55
2	−1.29	−0.28
3	−0.95	0.49
4	1.50	−0.36

[a] The figures are the fourth-quarter difference in the cyclically adjusted weighted deficit with sign reversed (column A) and the fourth-quarter difference in the model-estimated fiscal policy effect on GDP (column B). Column A indicates an implied increase in deflationary impact.

[b] Biswas et al. (1985, Table A3), 2 per cent trend assumption.

[c] Artis et al. (1984).

an inflation adjustment, the result is to drive a large wedge between the measures of stance and the measures of policy. The augmented measures of stance will vary not only with policy, but also with inflation. However, the balance could be restored by specifying that the benchmark for fiscal policy in the simulation approach is discretionary action (on taxes or spending) sufficient to neutralize precisely the inflation tax; as the benchmark for tax policy has long since moved to embrace indexation as the norm, this further step might not seem particularly large nor altogether unreasonable: surely no more so, at any rate, than the practice of augmenting the traditional measures.[9]

Table 9.2 compares a measure of the fiscal stance with a policy measure drawn from the study by Artis et al. (1984). This measure takes the fourth difference of the effect on output of fiscal policy as estimated using the National Institute model, as a percentage of actual output for comparison with the fourth differenced measure of stance, given by the weighted, cyclically adjusted deficit (with sign reversed), as recently calculated by Biswas et al. (1985).

The agreement between the two series is surprisingly good considering the scope for difference. In particular, the measure of stance (column A), like the model-based measure (column B), shows the deflationary impact of policy peaking in 1981. Unfortunately, there are no consistent model-based measures available over a longer period to permit a more detailed comparison. (However, see Artis and Green (1982) for an earlier subperiod comparison.)

V THE LONGER RUN

So far we have discussed the evolution of short-term, fine-tuning fiscal policy with special reference to its effectiveness in the UK and to the construction and use of some familiar summary indicators. This is all traditional Keynesian matter, the meat of functional finance in a demand management setting.

The dominance of fiscal policy evaluation by the principles of functional finance was indeed more or less complete, at least in the United Kingdom, in the 1950s and 1960s, but during the 1970s various developments occurred which prompted the search for new ways of looking at fiscal policy. In particular, as Odling-Smee and Riley (1985) have pointed out, policy makers became concerned with the connection between money creation and fiscal deficits, in the context of a desire to pursue monetary targets, whilst at the same time the deceleration of economic growth gave rise to concern for the structural implications of deficit financing.[10] On the intellectual plane, these developments were paralleled by the extension of short-run Keynesian models to incorporate the dynamics of asset accumulation, the rise of monetarism, and the challenge of new classical macro economics and the various responses it has evoked.

One result has been an episode of deficit targeting, which has been widely criticized as mistaken. The principal limitations of this form of fiscal policy are, and were, readily deducible from the principles of functional finance and standard 'old Keynesian' theory: it means switching off the built-in stabilizers, amplifying the effects on output of both demand and supply shocks (though, by the same token, better control of prices may result). The asset accumulation extension of IS/LM analysis adds a further consideration: a deflationary demand shock arising from an increase in the private sector's desired financial wealth to income ratio will be dampened if the automatic stabilizers are switched on, as this mechanically provides an added supply of financial assets. With the stabilizers switched off, this dampener is removed and the rise in the desired wealth to income ratio is likely to be met by a fall in income (whereas it could be met in principle by a rise in investment, the income decline is likely to discourage this, cf. Currie (1985)). Moreover, a principal reason for such targeting, at least as understood in the design of the United Kingdom's Medium Term Financial Strategy (MTFS), was to assist the realization of monetary targets at given interest rates. But not only was the initial statement of this connection badly flawed;[11] empirically, it has received no support. Moreover, in a world of capital mobility, interest rates in Britain cannot be expected to be closely determined by British budget deficits, so the government will have all too little to show for its policies of fiscal restraint by way of lower interest rates, as the painful experience of 1984 brought home.

The overriding of the principles of functional finance in favour of deficit targeting has thus been strikingly unsuccessful unless one is to apply to this episode, as has been applied by Fforde (1983) to monetarism generally, the rationale that it was a policy designed to distract attention from prior discussion of the costs of deliberate disinflation. This is not to deny that the budget is a prime source of financial wealth to the private sector. The literature built around recognition of the government budget constraint affords ample recognition of this; and, whilst the deficit targeting associated with the episode of monetary disinflation has been justly criticized (see, for example, Buiter, 1983; Currie, 1985), this insight supports the argument for targeting a ratio of public sector debt to (trend) output (on which, more below).

New classical macro economics would, if accepted, also provide a reason for overriding the Keynesian demand management approach to fiscal policy. Indeed, a full information equilibrium provides no occasion for the use of stabilization policy. However, both in its specific applications to fiscal policy (of which Barro's (1974) paper is the most outstanding example) and in its application to macro economics more generally, the full-blown new classical approach has been widely questioned.[12] Indeed, the alternative 'macro-disequilibrium' paradigm commands significant attention. Whilst the nature of the factors that bring about significant and long-lasting departures from full employment equilibrium is becoming increasingly understood, it is equally clear that the relative weights of the different arguments and their precise implications are not; the result is bound to be a qualitatively taxonomic state of affairs – if the requirements for a full information equilibrium are met, the Ricardian results apply; if not, they don't. The result is certainly an unsatisfactory state of affairs: on the one hand, the emphasis on the forward-looking character of expectations, and their relevance for current behaviour, demands that policy makers should construct, and pay attention to, medium-term criteria in setting fiscal policy; on the other hand, the severity of lapses from full employment robs such medium-term criteria of decisive purchase on the short run. A way forward is suggested by the notion of innovation-contingent rules. If the principal rule is described in such a way as to build in a degree of automatic stabilizing, so much the better, for this limits the amount of contingent override that needs to be separately specified. But there is a difficult trade-off here. On the one hand, the appeal of a simple rule is that it makes an unambiguous commitment which may have the desired effect of reassuring markets that medium-term criteria are not being lost sight of. On the other hand, if such a rule is implausible in the degree of sacrifice of welfare that it promises in the event of untoward occurrences, no one will believe it anyway. A more complicated rule would be better. Yet complication itself may only produce the accusation of chicanery.

Little practical progress has actually been made towards designing contingent rules, but the emphasis in drawing up rules that meet medium-run criteria has been to choose formulae that permit some degree of built-in stabilizing. Examples are: public sector debt to GDP ratios, full employment budget surplus to GDP ratios, public sector net worth ratios. As will be seen, all three permit the automatic stabilizers to work. But none of these suggestions has been accompanied by an indication of the principles on which the medium-term target might itself be altered for short-run reasons; and although the formulae go one better than the crude current deficit targeting described earlier, they nevertheless err in the same direction.

Of the three suggestions, that for targeting a ratio of public debt to output has the distinction of being advocated (in the UK) by a possible future policy maker (the Shadow Chancellor of the Exchequer, Mr

Hattersley). The suggestion appears to be more formal than the generalized call for reductions in the public sector debt to GDP ratios put about recently by the OECD and the IMF. The suggestion appears to be to target a ratio of public sector debt to trend nominal GDP. This means that the target deficit, as a percentage of trend (nominal) GDP, can be expressed as the product of the growth rate of trend nominal GDP (= trend real growth + target inflation) and the target ratio of debt to trend nominal GDP. Clearly, this allows the actual deficit to GDP ratio to rise as GDP deviates from trend in a downward direction, and requires a reduction if the deviation should be upward, thus 'turning on' the stabilizers. The principles on which the target ratio should be chosen have not been made clear and the ratio itself has varied widely in recorded history; Odling-Smee and Riley (1985) show that it has varied from a low point of about 30 per cent, in the UK in the year before the First World War, to over 200 per cent in the Second World War, from which peak it has declined to a level of about 40 per cent today. Additionally, the proposal embeds the stabilizer response in a particular (1 : 1) 'trade off' of prices against real output. The stabilizer response treats a deviation in prices in the same way that it treats a deviation in real output. Nevertheless, the proposal has the merit of being more flexible than the current deficit targeting, whilst being at the same time comparatively clear and easy to understand.

Discussion of the movement of the structural (full employment) deficit is now a commonplace of international discussion of fiscal policy (as, for example, in the publications of the OECD and the IMF). Targeting it explicitly was a suggestion associated with the early use of the concept in the United States; then the target was supposed to be zero, a concession to balanced budget ideas with no justification. Zero need not be the correct figure. Recently, the targeting of full employment budget deficits has been advocated by Steinherr (1984) in the setting of an EEC-wide co-ordination of fiscal policy. He advocates the targeting of full employment deficits calculated from inserting trend values of the external balance and private sector savings surplus into the basic equation of sectoral balance (viz. $(S - I) = (G - T) + (X - M)$. This also allows for the operation of the stabilizers as actual output deviates from 'full employment', but no further conjunctural relationship is advocated (the contrary in fact, for Steinherr places a premium on co-ordination across countries and whilst he sees this as being facilitated by the simple full employment budget rules he advocates, he considers that it would be far more difficult to specify coherent rules for fine tuning across countries.

Depending on how the prices dimension of the problem is treated, the public sector debt to GDP ratio and the full employment budget deficit to GDP ratio could in equilibrium be regarded as the same thing, differently expressed. However, the public sector debt ratio target is an integral control version of the full employment deficit measure, and so out of continuous steady state has the additional property of automatically correcting for past deficit overruns and shortfalls. Moreover, the public sector debt ratio measure, as already explained, embodies an inflation target and a trade-off of prices and real output in the stabilizer function. By contrast, the full employment deficit measure has usually been expressed in a way which accommodates deviations from target inflation (i.e. it is initially calculated in real terms). Thus the ratio measure does embody some desirable features, and if adhered to, would imply a coarse tuning of demand in the light of its stabilizing features, whilst at the same time making an appeal as a long stop on fiscal excesses. Its most obvious weakness is that its coarse tuning is still limited. The response of its advocates to this criticism might be that any attempt at finer tuning would be self-negating as agents would interpret added flexibility as fiscal excess. This is essentially unproven (either way), but one of the effects of promulgating targets such as these is to give them more credibility than they would otherwise command. The authorities, in announcing such a target, would therefore be tying their hands behind their backs in more senses than one. Not only are they formally committing themselves to no more coarse tuning than is implied by the formula; simultaneously they raise the cost of breaking the rule. Of course, much the same thing can be said of monetary targets, where experience has led to calls for innovation contingent rules and in practice has produced a series of modifications increasing the authorities' discretion and importing a degree of (albeit implicit) conditionality.

An alternative, though related, suggestion has been put forward by Buiter (1983). This is to calculate and target the ratio of the government's 'net worth' to GDP. Corresponding to this is the notion of the 'permanent deficit', estimated as the difference between the government's current consumption and its permanent income (the value of consumption consistent with a permanently constant share of public consumption in trend output). Actually, as Buiter notes, the term 'permanent deficit' is an abuse of language since by construction a deficit so measured is in fact unsustainable. The permanent deficit calculation can be presented, as Buiter shows, as a correction of the current deficit. The important corrections involve deducting from the current deficit the public sector's capital formation, and adding back the cyclical excess of tax revenues over their 'permanent' value (at current tax rates), the excess of current over permanent natural resource right earnings and the permanent value of the 'inflation tax'.

The exercise is undoubtedly an instructive one, and with further work the large scope for measurement error may be significantly narrowed.

The calculation makes operational the criterion that a sustainable fiscal plan promises a constant ratio of public sector net worth to GDP (hence a 'permanent' deficit of zero). Nevertheless, the criterion provides no immediate guide to action. An unsustainable deficit can be corrected by, for example, an increase in tax rates, but there is nothing to say when or at what rate this should be done, nor is there anything in the calculation itself which suggests a particular target value for the ratio of the public sector's net worth to trend GDP. So, whilst it is true that the conventional measures of fiscal impact (full employment budget surplus and the like) do not give any indication of what is sustainable, the permanent deficit does not give any indication of how long the unsustainable should be sustained. Nevertheless, we may suppose that on some criterion a target ratio is calculated and agreed. Up to the point at which this is reached permanent deficits are permitted if the initial ratio is below target, surpluses if the initial ratio is above target. Thereafter permanent deficits and surpluses are not sustainable. Once again, the proposal incorporates a degree of stabilizing influence, since the target is cast in terms of a ratio to trend (full employment) GDP, so deviations from trend permit variations of the actual deficit in appropriate directions.

The attraction of the measure is that it is careful about the composition of the items on either side of the government's balance sheet, the heterogeneity of which is denied by our simple-minded textbook practices (to their great detriment). It is therefore not the same as a full employment budget deficit or the public sector debt ratio criterion, and would only be comparable if in fact all government spending were of the wasteful variety usually assumed. There is a penalty to be paid for the additional complexity: the room for error in measuring heterogeneous items to a common basis. For this reason, it is perhaps less likely to command support than the public sector debt measure, even though it appears conceptually superior, for example in offsetting only the *permanent* value of the inflation tax (instead of the current period tax as in the public sector debt ratio, or not at all as in the full employment deficit approach), automatically adjusting for changes in the scope of the government sector (nationalization and privatization) and for changes in the composition of government expenditure. But over short (but not too short) periods, these differences can be normalized away and both measures share desirable stabilizing and integral control properties and an appeal to what seems like a sensible long-run norm. Like the public sector debt ratio to GDP measure, the net worth measure provides only for coarse tuning; the considerations that go into its construction do not suggest that the target ratio should itself be altered for 'conjunctural' reasons.

The new approach to fiscal policy now being suggested comes after successive periods of fine tuning and closed-loop rules each of which has seemed to attract a large quota of problems; perhaps not surprisingly, what the new approaches seem to attempt is a compromise of the flexibility of the fine-tuning approach and the rigidity of the closed-loop rule. They do so by adopting targets which provide for a built-in degree of flexibility, though falling well short of an innovation contingent rule. Simplicity is one of the desiderata inherited from the era of monctary targets and seems to be reflected in the fiscal policy rules now being suggested. It may also prove to be an important source of weakness as the next decade or so could reveal.

NOTES

1 Christopher Dow remarked on this in his pioneering and classic work on British demand management policy: 'It may nowadays be forgotten that the use of budgetary policy had practically no place among the proposals for action suggested in the *General Theory* (Dow, 1964, 179).
2 See Tomlinson (1981, 1982), Smith (1982) and Schott (1982). Tomlinson's recent book (Tomlinson, 1985) revives a similar but more circumspect line of argument.
3 I nevertheless have some sympathy with Tomlinson in the second of the exhibits of his case. An argument can be sustained (see Steindl, 1985) that it was the *incompleteness* of the Keynesian revolution on the *international* level, rather than domestic inflation, which was the undoing of domestic Keynesian policies.
4 There is a reference (Keynes, 1936, 95) to taxation affecting the 'aggregate propensity to consume'.
5 There is no reason to limit the set of goals only to those which the *authorities* considered significant.
6 This treatment is taken from Artis and Green (1982). The model is for a closed economy, but can easily be adapted for the open case.
7 As the measure is constructed in first differences the problem that normalization is designed to overcome (endogenization of tax revenues to income) does not arise and, as against the normalized measure, the weighted standardized surplus provides security from the error which arises if a tax measure is implemented which has a substantially different impact at actual as opposed to full employment levels.
8 Cf. Biswas et al. (1985). Clearly all the measures depend on a model of a kind – the decision whether or not to weight, and the choice of weights are modelling decisions. The simulation method merely goes further in supplying variable dynamic multiplier values.
9 Some nervousness about recognizing the inflation tax adjustment has arisen, partly because of the range of possible adjustments which might reasonably be made (see Miller, 1985) and partly because of the implicit identification

by observers of the budget balance measures with policy measures, and a consequent reservation about calling the non-offsetting of the inflation tax a deflationary policy (which is, after all, what is implied).

10 Despite the American example, which is (we assume) from this viewpoint a 'mistake', the supply-side concern to reduce the size of government has in itself no necessary implications for the size of the deficit, but rather for both sides of the balance sheet.

11 The Treasury (HM Treasury, 1980) appeared to overlook that a growth in GDP would require a positive deficit for any given debt to GDP ratio to be preserved, and to this extent overstated the need to control the budget deficit in order to control the money stock. They also appeared insufficiently sensitive to argument that the targets for a secularly declining PSBR to GDP ratio should be adjusted for the cycle. (See Budd et al., 1985.)

12 The Barro paper showed, in the context of an overlapping generations model with bequests, that bond issues would be treated as deferred taxation, and that bonds could not, therefore, be treated as wealth. The requirements that have to be satisfied for this result to go through, however, are very restrictive indeed, as Tobin (1980) among others has shown, and plainly are not remotely satisfied 'in the real world'.

REFERENCES

Artis, M.J. 1972: Fiscal policy for stabilization'. In W. Beckerman (ed.) *The Labour Government's Economic Record*, Duckworths, London.

Artis, M.J. and Green, C.J. (1982), Using the Treasury model to measure the impact of fiscal policy'. In M.J. Artis, C.J. Green, D.G. Leslie and G.W. Smith (eds) *Demand Management, Supply Constraints and Inflation*, Manchester University Press, Manchester.

Artis, M.J., Bladen-Hovell, R., Dwolatsky, B. and Karakitsos, E. 1984: The effects of economic policy 1979–1982, *National Institute Economic Review*, 108, 54–67.

Barro, R. 1974: Are government bonds net wealth?, *Journal of Political Economy*, 82, 1095–1117.

Bean, C. and Hartley, N. 1978: The standardized budget balance, *Government Economic Service Working Paper*, No. 1 (*Treasury Working Paper* No. 1).

Biswas, R., Johns, C. and Savage, D. (1985), 'The measurement of fiscal stance', *National Institute Economic Review*, 113, 50–64.

Blinder, A.S. and Goldfeld, S.M. 1976: New measures of fiscal and monetary policy 1958–73, *American Economic Review*, 66, 780–96.

Blinder, A.S. and Solow, R.M., 1974: Analytical foundations of fiscal policy. In *Economics of Public Finance*, Brookings Institute, Washington, D.C.

Bristow, J.A. 1968: Taxation and income stabilization, *Economic Journal*, 78, 299–311.

Buchanan, J.M. and Wagner, R.E. 1977: *Democracy in Deficit*, Academic Press, New York.

Budd, A., Dicks, G. and Keating, G. 1985: Government borrowing and the financial markets, *National Institute Economic Review*, 113, 89–97.

Buiter, W.H. 1983: Allocative and stabilization aspects of budgetary and financial policy, Centre for Economic Policy Research, Discussion Paper Series, No. 2.

Currie, D.A. 1985: The conduct of fiscal policy, *National Institute Economic Review*, 113, 81–8.
Dow, J.C.R. 1964: *The Management of the British Economy*, Cambridge University Press, Cambridge.
Fforde, J. 1983: Setting monetary objectives, *Quarterly Bulletin of the Bank of England*, June.
Hansen, B. 1969: *Fiscal Policy in Seven Countries, 1955–65*, OECD, Paris.
HM Treasury 1980: Memorandum to the House of Commons Select Committee on the Treasury and Civil Service.
Kennedy, M.C. 1985: The stabilizing effectiveness of demand management, mimeo, Manchester University.
Keynes, J.M. 1936: *The General Theory of Employment, Interest and Money*, Macmillan, London.
Keynes, J.M. 1940: *How To Pay For The War*, Macmillan, London.
Kregel, J. 1985: Budget deficits, stabilization policy and liquidity preference: Keynes' post-war proposals': In F. Vicarelli (ed.) *Keynes's Relevance Today*, Macmillan, London.
Labini, Paolo Sylos 1985: The *General Theory*: critical reflections suggested by some important problems of our time. In F. Vicarelli (ed.) *Keynes's Relevance Today*, Macmillan, London.
Lerner, A.F. 1943: Functional finance and the federal debt, *Social Research*, 10, 38–51.
Matthews, R.C.O. 1968: Why has Britain had full employment since the war?, *Economic Journal*, 78, 555–69.
Miller, M.H. 1985: Measuring the stance of fiscal policy, *Oxford Review of Economic Policy*, 1, 44–57.
Musgrave, R.A. 1964: On measuring fiscal performance, *Review of Economics and Statistics*, 46, 213–20.
Odling-Smee, J. and Riley, C. 1985: Approaches to the PSBR, *National Institute Economic Review*, 113, 65–80.
Schott, K. 1982: The rise of Keynesian economics 1940–64, *Economy and Society*, 11, 292–316.
Smith, K. 1982: Why was there never a Keynesian revolution in economic policy? A comment, *Economy and Society*, 11, 223–8.
Steindl, J. 1985: J.M. Keynes: society and the economist. In F. Vicarelli (ed.) *Keynes's Relevance Today*, Macmillan, London.
Steinherr, A. 1984: Convergence and coordination of macroeconomic policies: some basic issues', *European Economy*, 20, 69–110.
Tobin, J. 1980: *Asset Accumulation and Economic Activity*, Basil Blackwell, Oxford.
Tomlinson, J. 1981: Why was there never a Keynesian revolution in economic policy?, *Economy and Society*, 10, 72–87.
Tomlinson, J. 1982: The 'Keynesian Revolution': a response, *Economy and Society*, 11, 229–31.
Tomlinson, J. 1985: *British Macroeconomic Policy since 1940*, Croom Helm, Beckenham, Kent.

PART III
Empirical and Theoretical Issues

10

Deficits, Public Debt, Interest Rates and Private Saving: Perspectives and Reflections on Recent Analyses and on US Experience

MICHAEL J. BOSKIN

I INTRODUCTION

The relationship between budget deficits, public debt and other economic variables has sparked a tremendous debate. Various strands of thought argue that deficits (a) are inflationary, (b) help the recovery, (c) shift the composition of output away from investment and net exports, (d) raise interest rates, (e) do not matter, (f) curtail private saving, and (g) raise private saving.

Obviously, all of the arguments mentioned above cannot be true simultaneously. Since it is clear that the US is running very large deficits, and is projected to do so for the foreseeable future, it is important to understand when each argument makes sense. Are deficits so serious that we need to do something about them *soon*? My evaluation of the evidence is that deficits sometimes do matter for various economic outcomes. Nevertheless, their impact is more subtle and less severe than the recent hysteria would suggest.

The deficit is the difference between spending and taxes. Thus, a deficit could be created either by keeping the level of government spending constant and cutting taxes, or by raising government spending. Further, the spending may be for current consumption or public investment. Thus, different policies could lead to the same deficits, but to very different economic outcomes.

The question of whether deficits matter is really several questions rolled into one.

First, which economic variables do deficits affect? Interest rates? The inflation rate? Real GNP? The composition of output? Second, under what economic conditions do deficits have these effects? Third, what is the mechanism by which deficits affect the economy? Is it through an impact on interest rates, disposable income, inflation expectations, or the behaviour of the federal reserve? Fourth, does the source of the deficit (increased spending or decreased revenues) matter? Finally, what are the likely magnitudes of these effects?

An exhaustive review of the role of the budget deficit in the economy is beyond the scope of this chapter; nevertheless, the questions above provide a guiding framework for analysing several key aspects of the relationship between deficits and the economy. When the economy is at substantially less than full employment, a tax cut or spending increase can produce *some* stimulus in aggregate demand and income. However, this effect is much less than traditional textbook Keynesian models predict. This occurs for several reasons, the most important of which is that we live in a much more open economy (to both trade and capital flows) than the textbook models suggest. This severely limits the possibility of substantial fiscal stimulus. A deficit may produce a slight rise in interest rates, attract foreign capital, appreciate the dollar, curtail exports and stimulate imports. The fact that 47 per cent of the decline in real GNP in the 1981–82 recession was in net exports highlights the importance of this effect.

The potential effect of the deficits on interest rates will also be slightly offset by increased private saving. The rise in interest rates, if sustained over a long period of time, should increase saving. Statistical results indicate that this effect will be important, but neither large enough nor rapid enough to offset the direct dissaving induced by the deficit.[1]

It is arithmetic that at full employment, continuing substantial deficits *eventually* would lead to monetization of the debt by the federal reserve and to acceleration of inflation. This would occur because there is an upper bound to the amount of government bonds the private sector and the rest of the world is willing to hold. Eventually, even the dollar holdings of foreigners will reach a saturation point, and we will not be able to finance our deficits abroad forever. There are only two alternatives: (a) the Fed buys the bonds, reigniting inflation, or (b) we change our fiscal policy. This result, however, would require substantial deficits run over many years to guarantee an inflationary outcome. There is no necessary short-term relationship between deficits and inflation whether through monetization by the federal reserve or otherwise. (In the high inflation of the late 1970s, the Fed monetized very little of the deficit.) Moreover, there is not much evidence that they must lead to higher inflation in the next year or two.

While the empirical evidence is hardly overwhelming, it is very likely that deficits do contribute to high interest rates both directly through increased demand in credit markets, and indirectly through uncertainty premia over their likely economic effects and how they will be resolved (i.e. since economists cannot agree on their economic effects, we cannot expect private investors to think and act with certainty). We should distinguish the effect on interest rates of the US federal deficit from the *combined* fiscal deficit of *all* government units in the United States and the fiscal deficits of the other advanced countries. The combined US fiscal deficit, including the state and local government *surplus*, is matched by a corresponding aggregate fiscal deficit in the United Kingdom, Italy, France, Japan and Germany combined. Thus, the economic effects of a change in the US fiscal deficit, say by one percentage point of GNP, is substantially less than if all of these governments simultaneously reduced or increased their deficit by one percentage point of their respective GNP.

The purpose of this chapter is to provide some reflections on the current US fiscal dilemma and recent analytical and statistical studies on the relationship of public debt and private saving. In order to do so, section II discusses some measurement, forecasting and accounting problems concerning deficits and the national debt in the United States. It indicates that beyond the current short-run federal deficit, substantial additional problems remain in the unfunded liabilities in our social insurance programmes. It also reminds us that deficits – even properly measured – may be a very poor guide to government saving or dissaving. Government saving is simply the difference between tax revenue and government consumption, and we cannot know the extent of government saving until we decompose government spending into consumption and investment.

Section II also discusses some simple analyses of the relationship of deficits and debt. In a growing economy, of course, deficits may be consistent with a *decline* in the ratio of national debt to national income. It is only when the ratio of the deficit to GNP exceeds the growth rate of the economy that the ratio of the national debt to GNP will grow. If real interest rates exceed the growth rate, a deficit will explode as the interest component of the budget grows. In the usual case with the growth rate exceeding the real rate of interest on government securities the pattern of the growth of the national debt will depend upon the size of the primary deficit and the relationship between growth and interest rates. We discuss briefly two recent historical episodes in the

United States to indicate the potential inability to sustain large fiscal deficits and their ultimate inflationary consequences.

Section III discusses several avenues by which national fiscal policies can affect private saving: the structure of taxation, redistribution from rich to poor, differential public and private propensities to consume and the growth of implicit and explicit public debt, or what I prefer to call intergenerational redistribution. The saving rate in the United States has declined substantially in recent years, and the discussion in section III indicates that it is unlikely that the first three types of policies could have been the primary reason for the decline in the saving rate. However, the growth of explicit and implicit public debt may well be a major cause of the decline.

In section IV, I discuss various tests and estimates of alternative modes of saving behaviour, focusing on the intergenerational altruism model of Barro and the pure lifecycle model of Modigliani. I reject both as a sufficient explanation of saving behaviour in the United States, although there is undoubtedly a substantial amount of lifecycle saving going on. I also discuss some recent studies of the interest elasticity of saving.

Finally, in section V, I conclude that public debt policies are likely to have a deleterious impact on private saving, because of their intergenerational redistribution of the command over resources. This effect is undoubtedly mitigated by some intergenerational altruism and some potentially modest response of private saving to increases in real rates of return due to large deficits and growing debt to GNP ratios.

II MEASUREMENT AND ANALYSIS OF DEFICITS AND THE NATIONAL DEBT

Before discussing the potential economic effects of deficits and the national debt, it is important to realize that measuring, let alone forecasting, deficits and debt in the US is not an easy task. For example, large numbers of items are excluded by law from the federal budget, various other federal government accounting procedures are not consistent with the general notion of accrual accounting, separate capital and current services accounting, and adjusting from par to market valuations (see Boskin, 1982; 1987). Thus, for example, when we had a large defence build-down under President Carter, it was partially disguised by the fact that new investment in military hardware was falling far short of the depreciation and obsolescence of the existing capital stock. Or, note that in 1980 the $59 billion nominal federal government deficit was offset by a still larger decline in the inflation-adjusted value of the previously issued national debt held by the public! Further, it is often the case that the combined state and local government sector of the United States runs a substantial surplus. While it cannot be the purpose here to go through a complete reworking of federal budget accounting concepts, suffice it to say that care must be taken in interpreting even historical deficit figures, let alone in forecasting future ones.

Further, deficits do *not* measure government dissaving. Government saving, S_g, is the difference between tax revenue, T, and government consumption, C_g. Thus,

$$S_g = T - C_g \tag{10.1}$$

If government consumption (including consumption of government durables) falls short of total government spending by a sufficient amount, government saving could be positive despite a deficit, e.g. there could be substantial government investment.[2]

With this proviso in mind, we turn, in table 10.1A, to the Congressional Budget Office's estimates of deficits for the next few years.

Table 10.1A CBO budget projections baseline[a] (by fiscal year), at time of conference

	1983 actual	*1984 base*	*1985*	*1986*	*1987*	*1988*	*1989*
Total deficit,[b] $billions	208	185	210	212	229	243	264
Deficit as % of GNP	6.4	5.2	5.5	5.1	5.1	5.1	5.1
Debt held by public as % of GNP	35.4	36.7	39.6	41.9	43.9	45.8	47.5

[a] Assumes no change in laws governing taxes or entitlement spending.
[b] Includes off budget deficit of $15 billion or 0.3 per cent of GNP per year.

Table 10.1B Revised CBO budget projection, 2/86

	1985 actual	*1986 base*	*1987*	*1988*	*1989*	*1990*	*1991*
Total deficit, $billions	212	208	181	165	144	120	104
Deficit as % of GNP	5.4	5.0	4.0	3.4	2.8	2.1	1.7
Debt held by public as % of GNP	38.4	41.0	42.2	42.7	42.3	41.4	40.2

The administration in presenting its budget to Congress and the Congressional Budget Office (CBO) are required to present budget forecasts for five years. While it is undoubtedly correct that the economic assumptions upon which such budget forecasts are made are both difficult to make precisely, and subject to political manipulation (see Penner, 1981), it is clear that for the first time in post Second World War history, the United States entered a period of substantial budget deficits as a fraction of gross national product, even at full employment.

In other episodes of substantial deficits, events usually change to eliminate them. Large deficits were usually associated with wars or recessions. They quickly vanished thereafter. However, for the first time, we are faced with the prospect of sustained large deficits which will not vanish purely on the basis of an economic recovery. Thus, unless we have a sustained period of much more rapid economic growth than is prudent to forecast, large deficits will continue. That is, they will remain *unless* fiscal policy is changed either to reduce spending or to raise revenue. We shall see below that some such changes have begun in the US.

Let us place these numbers into perspective. The CBO estimates show deficits continuing to rise both in terms of dollars and as a percentage of GNP through 1990. Administration estimates show a downward trend to one-half the 1989 CBO estimate, but most of the difference rests on an administration forecast of interest rates falling to 5 per cent. They continue to run about 5 per cent of GNP, which is also about the same size as our net private saving pool (to be discussed below). Deficits of this magnitude are not uncommon. As noted above, the federal government of the United States has run deficits of this order of magnitude in the depths of recessions (for example, the one in 1975), and much larger in wartime. Many other countries have run deficits of this magnitude or larger, relative to the size of their economy. Some important economies are running larger deficits today (see table 10.2).

What is unique for the United States running deficits of this order of magnitude is to expect them to continue, despite a strong recovery, and to see the ratio of the national debt to GNP rise substantially. CBO estimates that this ratio will increase by more than one-third over the next few years, under current policies.[3]

The deficits have been blamed for the 1981–82 recession, have received credit for the 1983–84 recovery, or have been alleged to raise real interest rates, to increase private saving, not to matter, and/or to scare Congress into cutting spending or the federal reserve into inflationary money growth. The single most important thing to note about these deficits is undoubtedly their size. Even if we had relatively

Table 10.2 The worldwide fiscal deficit (deficit in $billions combined for all levels of government)

	US	Japan	West Germany	France	UK	Italy	Canada
1978	−4.3	43.5	15.1	9.7	14.2	30.4	6.1
	(−0.2)	(5.5)	(2.5)	(1.9)	(4.2)	(9.7)	(3.1)
1979	−14.6	42.9	16.4	6.7	13.8	42.2	4.1
	(−0.6)	(4.8)	(2.7)	(1.1)	(3.2)	(9.5)	(1.8)
1980	31.6	52.0	12.8	−1.0	18.9	53.4	6.2
	(1.2)	(4.5)	(3.1)	(−0.3)	(3.5)	(8.0)	(2.5)
1981	26.6	45.7	15.0	13.7	13.4	69.4	3.1
	(0.9)	(4.0)	(3.9)	(1.9)	(2.8)	(11.7)	(1.1)
1982	116.8	46.5	14.1	13.3	8.9	69.2	15.4
	(3.8)	(4.1)	(3.5)	(2.6)	(2.0)	(11.9)	(5.3)
1983	120.1	39.0	20.1	16.1	10.8	37.9	17.3
	(3.8)	(3.4)	(3.1)	(3.4)	(2.7)	(12.0)	(5.7)
1984	123.5	30.6	12.8	16.3	9.4	36.4	15.0
	(3.7)	(2.5)	(2.1)	(3.8)	(2.3)	(12.5)	(5.1)

Numbers in parentheses are percentages of GNP.
Source: Organization for Economic Cooperation and Development.

precise estimates of the economic impact of changes in smaller deficits, it is uncharted water in which we are navigating and it would not necessarily be wise to extrapolate such estimates to a situation with much larger deficits.

The spectre of such deficits and their potential economic effects caused major changes in congressional legislation in the US. First, Congress adopted a 1986 budget resolution that assumed zero real defence spending growth in 1986 and 3 per cent in the next two years rather than 5 per cent real growth previously forecast (which was below administration requests). Actual 1986 appropriations were less than the 1986 budget resolution target (i.e. 1986 real defence growth was negative). Further, the CBO now projects zero real growth in defence in the future rather than the 3 per cent real growth assumed in the 1986 resolution. This reduces projected *defence* spending by $78 billion in 1990. Further cuts already enacted and Gramm–Rudman–Hollings (balanced budget act) committing the Congress and the President to large deficit reductions imply reduced interest rates resulting in interest savings of $51 billion in 1991.

Thus, the assumed zero real defence growth and the associated decrease in interest costs are the primary reason why the new CBO deficit projections, presented in table 10.1B, show a declining pattern to under 2 per cent of GNP. Clearly, the budget decisions required for this outcome will be difficult to enforce. Perhaps it would be most prudent to suggest that there is likely to be a smaller deficit in future years than originally forecast, but great uncertainty as to the amount of the decrease.

Some Simple Analyses

Ultimately, at full employment, large deficits, net of the interest component (the so-called primary deficit), run continuously for a very long period *must be inflationary*. If the US runs primary deficits of several per cent of GNP for a very long period of time, some strange things are going to happen. To analyse that, examine table 10.3 and the following equations which indicate where the ratios of *privately* held national debt are headed if we continue large deficits as a share of GNP (net of the interest component) and run the real interest rates and growth rates that are being forecast.

Let D represent the debt to GNP ratio, d the deficit (net of interest) to GNP ratio, r the real interest rate, g the growth of real GNP. Then, by definition

$$\dot{D}_t = d_t + (r_t - g_t)D_t \tag{10.2}$$

For a fiscal programme with constant d, and constant r and g, D will evolve towards an equilibrium D_e (if $g > r$) of

$$D_e = \frac{d}{g - r} \tag{10.3}$$

Table 10.3 Some US fiscal episodes

	1975–79	*1984–89*	
D_0	23.4%	37%	37%
		CBO baseline	Administration
d (average)	3.7	1.8	1.4
g (average)	3.5	3.8	4.0
i (net of monetization)	6.0		
GNP deflator	7.2		
r	−1.2	3.6	2.4
$g - r$	4.7	0.2	1.6
D_e	79%	900%	88%

D_t declined steadily from the Second World War to 1974.
Source: M. Boskin, Conceptual and Measurement Issues in the Analysis of Deficits and Debt, paper presented at the NBER Taxation programme meeting, Palo Alto, CA, March 1983.

The ratio of the federal government debt to GNP evolves through time depending upon this primary deficit and the relation between the real rate of interest and the growth rate. For example, if we start out with a positive national debt, and the real interest paid on the national debt exceeds the growth rate, then the interest payments will grow more rapidly than the GNP, and if nothing else has changed, eventually the interest payments will consume all of the budget, then all of GNP, then all of national wealth in an explosive pattern. In the more usual case of the growth rate exceeding the rate of interest the ratio of debt to GNP will evolve according to the equation above.

Table 10.3 presents some estimates of two recent major fiscal episodes in the United States. First, we see the substantial increase in the equilibrium debt to GNP ratio towards which we were headed if fiscal policy had not been changed, in the 1975–79 period, a period generally regarded as the beginning of the increase of the ratio of debt to GNP after the substantial postwar decline in this ratio. The second, and more important for our purposes, is where we are headed now. We can see that under current projections, the ratio of debt to GNP is heading towards an equilibrium which is many times, not only current GNP, but the ratio of the entire value of the capital stock of the United States to GNP. This latter number is around 3, so it is clear that either the private sector will have to increase its wealth to income ratio by an enormous increase in saving, or the rest of the world will have to buy up the Treasury bills that the United States floats, or if neither of these alternatives is available and we persist in our current fiscal policies for the indefinite future, the federal reserve will have to buy up the bonds as the lender of last resort, thereby reigniting inflation. Can we reasonably expect foreigners to continue to finance our deficits *ad infinitum*? It would be imprudent of us to operate on the assumption that this was possible, let alone desirable. Eventually, foreign firms and individuals will have a progressively higher fraction of their wealth in dollar-denominated assets, which will mean that further increases in dollar-denominated assets will be even riskier for them. Thus, we can expect the flow of foreign capital into the United States, *ceteris paribus*, to slow down. Neither do I foresee such a huge increase in our saving rate as to increase the capital to output ratio by such a large amount. In short, the current fiscal policy, if continued, is either inflationary or unsustainable.

III GOVERNMENT FISCAL POLICY AND NATIONAL SAVING

In considering the government's potential impact on saving one might ask whether the total (federal, state and local) government consumption to NNP ratio has increased. It has, but the increase has been fairly modest. Government consumption averaged 21.4 per cent of net national product in the 1950s, 23.0 per cent in the 1960s, 23.5 per cent in the 1970s, and 23.1 per cent in the period 1980–84. If, during the last five years, government consumption had remained at the 21.4 per cent of the 1950s rather than 23.1 per cent of NNP and if private consumption as a share of NNP had not changed, the net national saving rate would have averaged 6.5 per cent rather than 4.7 per cent (see table 10.4). Assuming that private consumption is invariant to changes in government consumption seems, however, highly unrealistic. At one extreme, government consumption may substitute perfectly for private consumption (proposed by Bailey 1962) and discussed, but rejected by David and Scadding (1974)). In this case the 1.7 percentage point increase in the ratio of government consumption to NNP between the 1950s and early 1980s would, abstracting from issues of tax distortions and redistributions, have been completely offset by a 1.7 percentage point decrease in the ratio of private consumption to NNP, leaving the net national saving rate unchanged. With government consumption a perfect substitute for private consumption, the private sector's ultimate disposable income is simply NNP; and the private saving rate would coincide with the net national saving rate. From this perspective, the key question is why private sector saving behaviour changed such that total consumption, private plus government, rose as a share of NNP.

At the other extreme, government consumption might not enter private utility functions at all, or might enter separably. In choosing its consumption level one would expect the private sector in this case to view NNP−G, where G is government consumption, as its ultimate disposable income, since current government consumption must ultimately be financed by the private sector.[4] In the 1950s the private sector saved 10.9 per cent of this definition of disposable income. In the 1980s the corresponding saving rate has been only 6.1 per cent. Had the private sector maintained its 1950s' 10.9 per cent rate saving out of NNP−G, the rise in the ratio of government's consumption to NNP would have generated only a 4.5 per cent decline in the net national saving rate between the 1950s and 1980s, rather than the 46.6 per cent drop actually observed. From this perspective the increase in the government's rate of consumption out of NNP contributed, at most, a small amount to the decline in the net national saving rate. Again, the real question is why an appropriately defined private saving rate fell during this period.

A second accusation that could be levelled at government policy is that the use of distortionary taxes to finance both its consumption and

Table 10.4 *US net saving and investment, 1951–84*

	1951–60(%)	*1961–70(%)*	*1971–80(%)*	*1981(%)*	*1982(%)*	*1983(%)*	*1984(%)*
Total net saving	6.9	7.5	6.1	5.2	1.6	1.8	4.0
Net private saving	7.2	8.0	7.1	6.1	5.4	5.9	7.4
Personal saving	4.7	4.7	4.9	4.6	4.4	3.6	4.3
Corporate saving	2.5	3.3	2.2	1.4	1.0	2.3	3.2
State-local govt surplus	−0.2	0.1	0.9	1.3	1,1	1.3	1.4
Federal govt surplus	−0.2	−0.5	−1.9	−2.2	−4.8	−5.4	−4.8
Total net investment	7.0	7.5	6.3	5.4	1.6	1.8	3.8
Net foreign investment	0.3	0.5	0.1	0.2	−0.2	−1.0	−2.6
Private domestic investment	6.7	7.0	6.2	5.2	1.8	2.9	6.4
Plant and equipment	2.7	3.5	3.0	3.1	2.0	1.5	4.8
Residential construction	3.2	2.5	2.5	1.3	0.6	1.8	
Inventory accumulation	0.8	1.1	0.7	0.9	−0.9	−0.4	1.6
Memoranda: Capital consumption	8.9	8.5	9.9	11.2	11.7	11.4	11.0
Gross private saving	16.1	16.4	17.0	17.2	17.1	17.3	18.4

Data are averages (except for 1981–84) of annual flows, as percentages of gross national product. Total net saving and total net investment differ by statistical discrepancy. Detail may not add to totals because of rounding.
Source: US Department of Commerce.

transfer expenditures has reduced incentives to work and save. While there was some increase in average marginal taxes on labour earnings, the increase was modest and seems unlikely to account for the decline in the US saving rate. A recent article by Barro and Sahasakul (1983) suggests that the average marginal tax on labour income was 22 per cent in the 1950s, 22 per cent in the 1960s, and 27 per cent in the 1970s.[5]

These marginal tax figures exclude social security's payroll tax. However, there is reason to believe that inclusion of social security's tax and benefit provisions in the analysis would reduce rather than raise estimated marginal labour taxes particularly in the 1970s. Blinder and Gordon's (1981) analysis suggests that social security's tax and benefit provisions constitute a sizeable subsidy to labour earnings of married males and others, leaving net effective marginal taxes on labour earnings for these groups quite low. Boskin and Hurd (1984) confirm the significant size of the Gordon effect. Crediting the public with the perspicacity and knowledge required to assess correctly the marginal social security return on the marginal tax contribution may be unrealistic; but the opposite assumption, that workers believe they receive no return at the margin for marginal social security tax payments, seems equally implausible. If one takes an intermediate view that workers view marginal social security taxes as providing marginal social security benefits of equal present value, then the post 1950 rise in the average marginal tax on labour income is adequately captured by Barro and Sahasakul's estimates.

Marginal saving incentives are also determined by capital income taxes. Several studies argue that effective capital income taxes, at least on corporate source income, rose substantially in the 1970s (e.g. Feldstein and Summers, 1979). But in contrast to this popular belief that such taxes rose between 1950 and 1980, extensive calculations contained in King and Fullerton (1984) suggest a small decline in effective marginal taxes on capital income over this period. The 1981 Economic Resources Tax Act (ERTA) lowered effective marginal capital income taxes more significantly. Based on a 10 per cent pre-tax return to capital and the prevailing inflation rate King and Fullerton calculate that the overall effective marginal capital income tax rate was 48 per cent in 1960, 37 per cent in 1980, 26 per cent in 1981, and 32 per cent in 1982. In combination with the figures just cited for marginal taxes on labour income, these findings suggest that the distortive effects of government fiscal policy cannot explain the drop in the US saving rate over the last 35 years.

Another type of policy that could potentially be blamed for the saving decline is intragenerational redistribution from the rich to the poor. The poor may have a higher rate of time preference than the rich. Alternatively the poor may be liquidity constrained. In either case the poor within any age group will have larger marginal propensities to consume than their better-endowed contemporaries; and intragenerational transfers from the rich to the poor will lower saving. Emily Lawrence (1983) recently examined the potential effect of intrageneration redistribution on saving using a life cycle simulation model. Lawrence considered very substantial differences in time preference rates between the rich and poor as well as liquidity constrained consumption by the poor. She found that even very significant intragenerational redistribution, such as that characterizing US welfare programmes, has only minor effects on saving in life cycle models.

The explanation for these small changes in the case of differences in time preference rates is simply that neither the associated differences in marginal consumption propensities across the two groups nor the size of the simulated transfers are sufficiently large to have much impact on the economy's total wealth accumulation. In the case that the poor are liquidity constrained, their marginal consumption propensities are unity; but the change in disposable income multiplying their unitary propensities is only current transfers. For rich, unconstrained transferers, the reduction in current consumption equals their much smaller marginal propensity to consume multiplied by the present value of transfers, which is typically a much larger number than simply the current payment. The reduced consumption of the rich offsets to a significant extent the increased consumption of the liquidity constrained poor producing only a small reduction in national saving despite a quite substantial program of intragenerational transfers. We conclude from this and related models that intragenerational redistribution is probably not a major determinant of the decline in the US saving rate since 1950.

A fourth channel by which government policy may have reduced saving is by transferring resources from younger and future generations to older generations. Intergenerational transfers towards older generations, which is referred to here as debt policy, can be and have been conducted in quite subtle ways. The unfunded financing of the US Social Security System is by now a well understood, if none the less quite subtle, debt policy (Feldstein, 1974). Less well-understood debt policies are changes in the tax structure that shift the burden of taxation from older to younger age groups (Summers, 1981a; Auerbach and Kotlikoff, 1983a) and changes in tax provisions that raise market values of financial assets and, thereby, transfer resources to older age groups who are the primary owners of such assets (Feldstein, 1974; Summers, 1981b). An example of the former type of policy is switching from income taxation to wage taxation. An example of the latter policy is reducing investment incentives (Auerbach and Kotlikoff, 1983b). Since investment incentives in the US are effectively provided only to new investment, old capital, capital that has been fully or partially written off, sells at a discount reflecting the differential tax treatment. A reduction in investment incentives means a smaller discount and a capital gain to owners of old capital. Younger and future generations are worse off as a result of such policies because they must now pay a higher price to acquire claims to the economy's capital stock.

In addition to these more subtle mechanisms of transferring to older generations, governments can engage in debt policies by reducing taxes levied on current generations and raising taxes levied on future generations. Intergenerational redistribution of this variety may eventuate in larger officially reported deficits. An example in which even this more obvious form of redistribution does not necessarily alter official calculations is when such tax cuts and tax increases are coincident, respectively, with equivalent reductions and increases in the level of government consumption.

The fact that very significant intergenerational redistribution can be run without its ever showing up on government books suggests that officially reported deficits are at best a very poor indicator of underlying economic debt policies.[6] This proposition notwithstanding, there has been an enormous public interest, especially in recent years, in officially reported deficits. Curiously, public attention has focused only on a subset of official liabilities of the federal government and has essentially ignored both the official assets of the federal government as well as the official assets and liabilities of state and local governments. As discussed by Boskin (1982; 1987), Eisner and Pieper (1984) and the *1982 Economic Report of the President*, the market value of the US federal government's official assets may currently equal if not exceed the market value of its official liabilities.

In the light of the very significant, if not overwhelming, difficulties of gauging the extent of true debt policies from official reports, it seems safer to assess postwar US debt policy by asking the following question: were the lifetime budget constraints of older generations expanded significantly in the postwar period as a consequence of government policy at the expense of contracted budget constraints for young and future generations? One might point, in this context, to the enormous expansion of the social security system which greatly increased the budget opportunities of the elderly. The problem, however, with considering any one component of government policy is that it may have been instituted to offset some other component; i.e. the postwar redistribution through social security to the elderly may simply represent the government's way of compensating the elderly for higher income taxes over their lifetimes or for their contribution to the nation during the Second World War. Just as there is no single correct way to measure official deficits, there is no single correct way of posing counter–factuals about observed government transfer policies. To put this point differently, intergenerational redistribution must always be assessed relative to some benchmark, and the choice of a benchmark seems inherently subjective. The implication of this point is that any calculation of the magnitude of postwar intergenerational transfers will be arbitrary.[7]

Having conceded this point we believe that at least one interesting, if arbitrary, counter-factual to pose with respect to postwar US debt policy is an economy with either a very small unfunded social security programme targeted towards the elderly poor or a larger, but fully funded social security system. The US social security system's unfunded liabilities appear to range between 4 and 6 times the size of the US government's official liabilities (see table 10.5). The growth of this programme was coincident with the decline in the net national saving rate. The social security system appears to represent the only (potentially) discrete postwar intergenerational transfer policy capable of producing a major drop in the national saving rate. Simulation studies of the potential savings impact of unfunded social security suggest a possible reduction in long-run savings of 20 to 25 per cent (Kotlikoff, 1979; Auerbach and Kotlikoff, 1983c).

To summarize this section, we have identified four stylized features of fiscal policy, namely government consumption, the extent of distortionary taxation, intragenerational transfers and intergenerational transfers, each of which can affect a nation's saving behaviour. We have tried to argue, although hardly exhaustively, that of these four features of fiscal policy, intergenerational transfers are the most likely

Table 10.5 *The long-term social security and Medicare deficit: effect of 1983 amendments on actuarial balance of OASDI and HI – alternative assumptions, 75-year period (% of taxable payroll)*

	Pre-1983 amendments	*1983 amendments intermediate assumptions*	*Indexing of taxable amounts or dissipation of surplus*	*Indexing and dissipation of surplus*
OASDI	−1.80	0.02	−0.60	−1.20
HI	−5.21	−5.21	−5.21	−5.21
Total	−7.01	−5.19	−5.81	−6.41

Source: Author's calculations plus 1983 Annual Report of the Trustees of the Social Security Administration.

to have generated a decline in the US saving rate over the last three and a half decades.

IV STUDIES OF THE IMPACTS OF DEFICITS

Deficits and the Composition of Output

While a pro-deficit policy may be slightly expansionary during a recession and ultimately may rekindle inflation, the single most likely impact of deficit, as opposed to tax, finance as the economy gets close to full employment, is a likely rise in interest rates which will crowd out interest sensitive activities such as investment and net exports. The traditional argument is portrayed in figure 10.1(a), where the additional demand for capital by the federal government borrowing drives up the total demand for capital to D_{Total}, which in turn drives up interest rates from i_0 to i_1. This picture is drawn for a closed economy, ignoring foreign capital imports, and with a supply of capital curve that responds slightly to increases in interest rates, allowing for additional private saving, but not so much as to finance the deficit itself. If this was the end of the story, we would ask ourselves to what extent interest sensitive activities would be curtailed, i.e. we would look at the interest elasticities of the demand for investment, residential construction, state and local government capital expenditures, and the interest sensitivity of exports and imports. Each of these categories appears to be quite sensitive to interest rates, holding other things constant (such as the level of real economic activity, inflationary expectations, etc.).

Thus, a substantial tax cut and shift to deficit finance could lead to some increase in consumer spending, and in the traditional analysis, shift the composition of output to less investment and net exports. This simple analysis in a closed economy setting has led many economists and policy makers to conclude that the recovery must be unbalanced, and the deficits responsible for the very high real interest rates. While real interest rates have been falling recently, they are still quite high, averaging (on short-term Treasury offerings) over 4 per cent, double the historic average. Longer-term securities are yielding several percentage points more, but the differential is due to extra risk and the expectations of higher inflation than we are currently experiencing. Certainly, the high real interest rate in the United States has contributed to the sharp overvaluation of the dollar. There are certainly other causes, such as the fact that the United States is a relatively safe haven, but the sharp overvaluation of the dollar (about 25 to 30 per cent on a trade-weighted basis) has caused a substantial increase in our foreign trade deficit. That deficit is exceeding $100 billion per year. While this partly reflects

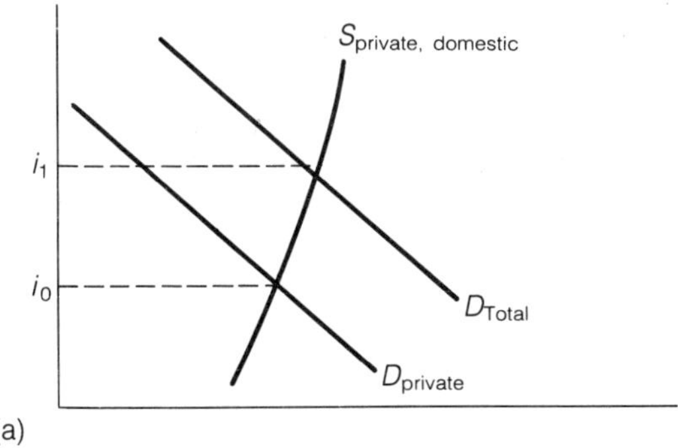

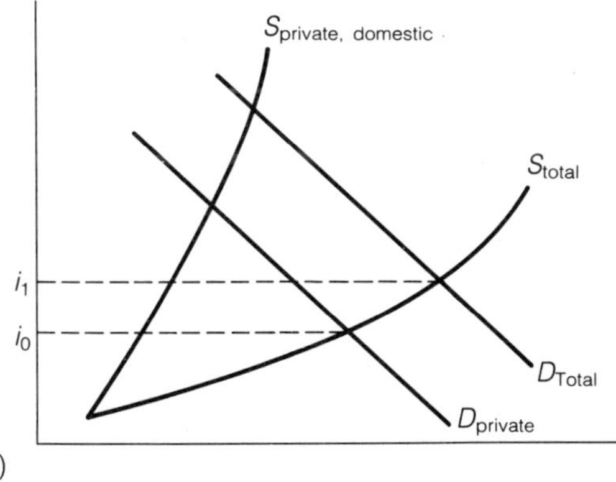

Figure 10.1 Government borrowing and interest rates in closed and open economies

the more rapid and quicker recovery of the US economy, and thus our proclivity to purchase imports, it also heavily reflects the price disadvantage due to the overvalued dollar making our exports much more expensive and our imports much less expensive, than their competitors.

Private domestic investment, however, has rebounded *more* rapidly than in typical postwar recoveries. This is largely because the investment incentives in the 1981 Tax Act have offset the effects of high real interest rates. Thus, for a while, the effective cost of acquiring new capital, while driven up by higher real interest rates, was on balance slightly lower than several years ago.

More important, real interest rates have not risen, but actually fallen, although much less than have nominal interest rates. Nominal interest rates have fallen from over 20 per cent to the 10 to 12 per cent range, whereas real interest rates have fallen from 10 per cent to 4 or 5 per cent. Part of the reason why real interest rates have crept down and not reaccelerated despite the very large and growing deficits, has been the substantial inflow of foreign capital. Figure 10.1(b) 'opens up' the economy to capital inflows and outflows. Just as we added the federal government demand for funds to the private sector demand for funds (D_p), so now we add the potential flow of capital from abroad to the available net private saving. The flow of capital from abroad is very sensitive to interest rates, and, therefore, the aggregate available short- to medium-term supply of saving is much more 'elastic'. Following the above line of reasoning, the extra demand for funds from federal government borrowing drives up interest rates much less because of this elastic supply of funds from abroad. Were these funds to be quickly withdrawn, interest rates would rise rapidly, but there is no reason to believe that the flow of such funds will abate instantly. It is likely that the net capital inflow is likely to continue for some time, but ultimately at a slower rate.

Thus, the federal government fiscal deficit has largely been offset by the state and local surplus and capital inflow from abroad. Table 10.4 highlights these effects. In the 1950s, 1960s, and 1970s, net private saving averaged between 7 and 8 per cent of GNP. This has fallen to 5 or 6 per cent in the last few years. State and local governments which had run roughly balanced budgets in the 1950s and 1960s moved into surplus, beginning in the 1970s, and have more or less remained so ever since. Our federal government, which more or less ran balanced budgets in the 1950s and 1960s, and averaged slightly under 2 per cent of GNP for its deficit in the profligate 1970s, is projected to run a deficit for 1985 of about 5 per cent. This leaves us with net national saving, the sum of what the private sector saves, state and local government save or borrow, and the federal government saves or borrows, of about half the levels of the 1950s through 1970s. Were this the end of the story, our net investment would have fallen still further. While gross investment has rebounded, our net investment still remains at historically low levels. Fortunately, one-third of it is being financed by a net capital inflow from abroad. The United States has changed from being a net exporter of capital in the 1950s and 1960s to a large net importer of capital in the last couple of years. This large *net* import of foreign capital has two salutary effects: it prevents interest rates from rising still further, and provides funds for badly needed domestic investment.[8]

Thus, it is likely that, in the short run, deficits pose only a small threat of increased interest rates, or of accelerating inflation, but eventually we cannot rely on continued net capital inflows and large state and local surpluses to bail us out. We must get our fiscal house in order prior to a sharp downward slowdown of capital imports and/or the state and local government surplus to avoid a sharp rise in interest rates. This in turn would put enormous pressure on the federal reserve to reaccelerate money growth and abandon its anti-inflation fight, and therefore would not augur well for future inflation, investment, net exports, and productivity and growth.

We must reiterate that the effect of a deficit on the composition of output depends heavily on the nature of the spending and taxes whose difference comprises the deficit. The impact, for example, on productivity might differ substantially if the spending was on government investment, e.g. on roads, airports, etc., than if it was on government consumption. Likewise, the *net* impact on private saving will be different if much of the deficit is financing interest payments to US citizens who are likely to reinvest the interest than if it is on transfer payments to individuals with a low propensity to save. Thus, there is no specific answer to the question 'What is the impact of *the* deficit?' without specifying the nature of the taxes and spending.

Statistical Evidence on the Effects of Deficits on Interest Rates

From the discussion above, it is clear that the potential effects of deficits on interest rates depend upon many factors, including the nature of the spending and the taxes whose difference generates the deficit, monetary policy pursued both here and in the rest of the world, and undoubtedly worldwide fiscal deficits. In fact, as table 10.4 indicates, the combined fiscal deficits of several of the other large industrialized countries were as large as the US fiscal deficit in total, and several of them were running larger deficits as a fraction of GNP.[9] Thus, the effect of a change in our deficit on interest rates depends in part upon the reaction of monetary and fiscal policy in the rest of the world, the time horizon being considered (Is it long enough for net inflows of capital to slow down?), etc. It is not surprising, therefore, that available statistical studies of the effect of deficits on interest rates tend to come to a wide range of conclusions, depending upon the sample period covered, the specification of the other variables assumed to effect interest rates, etc. It is worth noting, however, that a substantial number of recent studies update and improve the earlier work done by Feldstein and Eckstein (1970) and on balance conclude that increases in deficits do indeed lead to an increase in interest rates. A careful reworking of some of these studies by Barth et al. (1984) concludes that a more careful specification of the deficit variable into its structural and cyclical components, and a variety of other adjustments, tend to reinforce these findings.

It should be clear that such studies can only give us a rough idea of the average historical impacts, holding various measures of other impacts on interest rates, such as expected inflation, constant. Two somewhat less direct avenues for examining the potential impact of deficits on interest rates are to examine their impact on the demand for money and on aggregate demand. Again, recent evidence suggests that increases in the federal debt do have a positive impact on the demand for money which is therefore likely to lead to higher interest rates. Finally, the results of Eisner and Pieper (1984) and Feldstein (1982) suggest that deficits, particularly when adjusted for measurement problems such as those due to inflation, lead to an increase in aggregate demand and real GNP. While I have mentioned above several caveats to this story limiting the likely size of the impact of a pro-deficit tax cut on real GNP, it is important to point out that some fiscal stimulus still remains after one has made all these adjustments. Further, it should be realized that the debt neutrality hypothesis assumes a given level of government spending. An increase in government expenditures is likely to raise total aggregate demand somewhat (the extent depending upon the nature of monetary policy) and therefore can affect interest rates in this way as well.

In summary, it should not be surprising that there are many avenues by which deficits, government spending, and various forms of taxes can affect interest rates and the composition of GNP, as well as the level and growth rate of nominal GNP and its division into real and inflation components. However, the alleged 'bang-for-the-buck' in fiscal stimulus is undoubtedly much less than had been supposed by the Keynesian fine tuners who dominated economic policy making in the 1960s and 1970s.

It is instructive to examine the likely effects of federal government deficits on the composition of GNP by examining the actual correlation between changes in the deficit and various components of GNP. Since the federal government deficit is just the difference between federal government spending and taxes, it must equal the sum of private saving, net foreign investment, the state and local surplus or deficit, less domestic investment. Simply put, if the level of GNP is held constant (the deficit may affect the level of GNP but we are concerned here with its composition), increases in the deficits must crowd out something. Will they lead to an increased private saving and increased net foreign investment, changes in state and local surpluses and/or decreases in domestic investment? A provocative, but very rough study by Summers (1984) suggests that budget deficits call forth increased private savings of about 30 cents per dollar of deficit. This results from a combination of extra savings for future tax liabilities resulting from the deficits, the sensitivity of savings to higher real interest rates caused by deficits and/or the crowding out of consumer durable expenditures due to higher interest rates. In addition, he estimates that deficits crowd out net exports by attracting foreign capital, in this case, about 25 cents on the dollar. He also estimates about a 5 cents increase per dollar of deficit in state and local surpluses, and a 40 cents per dollar decrease in net investment. Further, of course, the net investment must be separated from residential investment which crowded out at about 20 cents on the dollar. These estimates are highly preliminary and subject to many statistical problems. They are discussed here merely to point out the fact that the impact of the deficit on the composition of GNP is almost certainly not to crowd out business investment in plant and equipment, dollar for dollar. The total crowding out of investment is likely to be much less than this, and only some of the investment which is crowded out will be business investment in plant and equipment. Recall that the exact mix of what gets changed by the federal government deficit will depend not only on the size of the change in the deficit, but on the nature of the spending and taxes.

Some Recent Studies Testing Theories of Private Saving Behaviour

The two leading theories of private saving behaviour are the pure life cycle theory of Modigliani and Brumberg (1954) and Modigliani and Ando (1957) and the intergenerational altruism model of Barro (1974). In the Barro model it is unclear whether the government can affect national saving, since the private sector will seek to undo any change in government saving or borrowing. While problems exist with the Barro model, were it correct, the long-run saving rate would approximate optimal utilitarian rates if current savers had accurate information about the parameters, there were no capital market restrictions (e.g. non-negative net worth), etc. The life cycle model provides no automatic mechanism for individual households to account for the fact that future generations will be richer except by issuing greater public debt. There is no bequest motive and the average propensity to consume over the lifetime is one.

Various studies have attempted to demonstrate that life cycle behaviour can explain several important phenomena concerning aggregate wealth accumulation in the United States (see Tobin, 1967). More recently, there has been an attack on the pure life cycle model (no bequest, average propensity to consume over the lifetime of one) by a variety of authors. For example, Kotlikoff and Summers (1981) conclude that life cycle saving can account for only about 20 per cent of the aggregate wealth in the United States. Unfortunately, a mathematical error in their derivation of the formulae is part of the explanation for their result, and corrected, the numbers would be about 50 per cent. This is still a telling indictment of the extreme version of the life cycle hypothesis.

There have also been a number of studies attempting to examine the extent of dissaving after retirement. For example, Darby (1979) demonstrated, using longitudinal household data, that there was surprisingly little dissaving post-retirement, and concluded these results were incompatible with the pure life cycle hypothesis. Mirer (1979), David and Menchick (1980) and King and Dicks-Mireaux (1982) also find either no dissaving or too little dissaving after retirement to be consistent with the pure life cycle model.

In recent work, Bernheim (1984) and Diamond and Hausman (1984), using panel data, do observe dissaving after retirement. In an important study just completed, Hurd (1986) makes several methodological and data improvements (e.g. a ten-year longitudinal panel study rather than a cross-section or shorter panel), and his conclusion is that the dissaving pattern of the elderly is quite consistent with the pure life cycle model. Further, tests for a bequest motive show no evidence of one.

Rejection of the pure form of the life cycle model should not be taken to mean that there is no consumption smoothing over the life cycle, or that the propensity to consume is independent of age. It is the rejection of the assumption that the average propensity to consume over the lifetime is one, and that there is no bequest motive (even accounting for the fact that an uncertain date of death may require very slow dissaving in the absence of actuarially fair annuities).

A variety of studies presume the pure form of the life cycle theory in analyses of public policy. I shall comment on several below, but it is important to point out that one of the major conclusions from the pure life cycle model is that public debt – explicit or implicit – crowds out private saving, and ultimately, therefore, capital formation. In an alternative model proposed by Barro, extending the work of Bailey (1961), and dating all the way back to Ricardo, a Say's law of public finance is developed in which increases in the supply of public debt call forth an increased demand for it. The argument is simply that in a world where there are intergenerational altruism and operative bequest motives – as well as many other assumptions such as lump sum finance, etc. – the private sector can undo the government's attempt to redistribute resources across generations.

Many studies have tried to analyse the effect of some measure of deficits or public debt on consumption (e.g. Feldstein (1982) and the numerous studies cited therein, and Barth et al. (1984) and the studies cited therein) or of unfunded liabilities in social security on the consumption/saving choice (see Feldstein, 1974; Barro, 1978; Feldstein and Pellechio, 1979; among many). The conclusions are somewhat mixed. I believe that an accurate summary of the econometric literature is that Feldstein's original dollar for dollar estimate of the substitution of unfunded social security liabilities or public debt for private saving has been revised to 25 to 50 cents on the dollar.

Since concepts such as deficits, public debt and unfunded social security liabilities are subject to vagaries of accounting procedures, more *direct tests* of the intergenerational altruism model are possible. To see this, note that in the intergenerational altruism model *aggregate* consumption depends only on *aggregate* resources, not on their age distribution. This forms the basis for the test developed by Boskin and Kotlikoff (1985). We develop a finite approximation to the intergenerational optimization problem for Barro-type behaviour under earnings and rate of return uncertainty, and demographic change, for the US economy, and test whether, given the level of consumption predicted by this model, variables measuring the age distribution of resources influence actual consumption. Data on the age distribution of resources are obtained from the annual Current Population Surveys. The results, presented in a variety of forms using various measures of the age distribution of resources, reject the hypothesis that aggregate consumption is independent of the age distribution of resources. They therefore cast considerable doubt on the pure intergenerational altruism model and on the contention that government debt policy – explicit or implicit – does not affect the consumption/saving choice.

Thus, neither the pure life cycle model nor the pure intergenerational altruism model seems *sufficient* to explain aggregate saving behaviour or the effects of policy on saving. Undoubtedly, different people in the economy could be described in their saving behaviour by different models, including a Keynesian liquidity constraint consumption/saving model, and the convex combination that results in aggregate saving is some complicated combination of these models.

I do believe that it is important to realize, however, that there are substantial differences in the propensity to consume by age, some lifetime smoothing and substantial bequests in aggregate capital formation. Thus, elements of both the bequest model and the original pure life cycle model are important in explaining saving behaviour, despite the fact that each of the models in its most pure form is rejected in the data.

Another important controversy has arisen over the extent to which changes in the real after-tax rate of return affect private saving. If deficits or debt drive up real rates of return, how will private saving respond? Denison's law – the apparent constancy of the gross private saving rate at times of full employment through the mid 1970s – was often taken to suggest that tax policy did not affect aggregate private saving, but only its composition between the household and corporate sectors. Since there has been substantial controversy about structural tax policy and its effects on effective tax rates on capital income, renewed interest has focused on this issue.

The article by Boskin (1978) sparked a substantial amount of controversy. In that work, I consistently found estimates of the real net rate of return elasticity of private saving of about 0.4. While hardly enormous, such a modest interest elasticity has important implications for public policy. For example, the social opportunity cost of public funds to be used in cost-benefit analyses of government programmes is substantially lower than the private marginal product of capital since some of the funds freed from the private sector by either taxation or borrowing and made available to the government come at the expense of additional private saving, rather than just forgone private investment. Were saving unresponsive to rates of return, all of the funds raised, for example, by government borrowing, would come from private investment, whose social opportunity cost is the (before-tax) marginal product of capital. Also, the intertemporal efficiency losses in our tax system are large and swamp the atemporal inefficiencies due to misallocation of the capital stock among assets and industries (see Fullerton et al. (1983) who use my estimates).

There are substantial difficulties in defining, estimating, and interpreting an interest elasticity of saving.[10] First, one must be careful in defining the conceptual experiment to decide whether one is holding a stream of income constant or wealth constant when one changes the real after-tax rate of return, e.g. by debt or tax policy. Is a change caused in the future after-tax stream of capital income which is exactly matched by a reduction in the rate at which it is discounted, thereby leaving financial wealth unchanged, but perhaps affecting the valuation of future expected earnings, and through this change in human wealth affecting consumption and saving? While numerous studies of the interest elasticity of saving abound, greater clarity on the exact questions being posed and the conceptual experiment being analysed is highly desirable. I confess to having been all too brief in my 1978 paper on this issue. Recent work has tended on the one hand either to confirm my earlier results or suggest that the rate of return elasticities are still larger (see Summers, 1981a; 1984), or on the other hand to cast doubt on these results (see, for example, Howrey and Hymans, 1980). A stylized finance model with labour earnings in period 1 and consumption out of interest income and assets in future periods yields the result that, as risk aversion rises, the response of saving to the rate of return eventually becomes negative. While adding uncertainty to the model is a step forward, we should be careful in reading too much into this result. First, with many periods, including subsequent periods of earnings, the result is unclear; second, as noted above, in aggregating households to determine the response of total saving to rates of return, surely much of saving is done for longer term reasons, and examining behaviour towards risk in portfolio allocation among the wealthy may be misleading.

While I do not think the issue is at all settled, I would like to share with you the preliminary results of a major study of postwar US consumption that I have just concluded with my colleague, Lawrence Lau. The major innovation in our study is the use of annual Current Population Survey information on cross-tabulations of household characteristics, especially age of head of household, with income, and the building of age cohort-specific wealth accounts with which to analyse the share of wealth consumed in goods and as leisure. We build the simplest possible model that is a legitimate candidate for exact aggregation from individual behaviour. The individual household's current period consumption and leisure are functions of the spot prices of current period consumption and leisure and forward prices of future period consumption and leisure, wealth of the individual households, and the household's attributes. Under assumptions about stationarity of expectations, we define the forward prices at each point in time, and since time series data on individual households are not available, we use aggregate data on current consumption and leisure expenditures which satisfy necessary conditions for exact aggregation. They are consistent with 'no money illusion' and thereby impose various restrictions on the parameters. The estimated equations for the US postwar period perform remarkably well, predicting the share of wealth consumed with but small deviations. We then decompose the growth in consumption in the postwar period into its components. The approximate 3 per cent average annual percentage change in consumption is decomposed into the total change due to changes in wealth, wage rates, rates of return, population growth, the age composition of households, wealth by age of the household, changes in female labour force participation and the vintage of the household defined as whether or not the household head was born after or prior to 1939 and thus experienced the Great Depression first hand.

Several intriguing results emerge from that study. For the purpose at hand, suffice it to say that the estimated interest elasticities of saving are larger than from my previous studies, and are estimated relatively precisely. Thus, if anything, I would argue that my earlier results of positive elasticities tend not only to be confirmed, but that the interest elasticity is probably in the range 0.5–2.0 for persons aged 45–54. These elasticities expressly include the revaluation of wealth due to the changes in the rates of return. The elasticity of consumption expenditures with respect to wealth is about 1.0. Finally, we note not only that the propensity to consume varies with age, but that there is an intriguing difference both in the elasticity of consumption with respect to wealth, and in the shares of wealth consumed, as well as the interest elasticity of saving in the vintages of households born pre-1939 and post-1939. We find that *at the same age*, households born post-1939 have a higher propensity to consume out of their wealth than households born prior to 1939, but on the other hand, they are somewhat more responsive to changes in rates of return. I mention this study only to indicate that substantial refinements are possible in analysing saving behaviour and integrating various types of data despite the absence of full-blown panel studies providing accurate balance sheets on individual households.

I do not mean to suggest that the real net rate of return elasticity of saving is a closed theoretical or empirical issue, but my own judgement – as devoid of personal bias as possible for someone who has spent much time working on the problem – is that despite the numerous difficulties in such estimation, my work, and the work of Summers, even adjusted for the criticisms noted above, still lead me to believe that there is at least a modest positive interest elasticity of private saving in the United States.[11]

V CONCLUSION

Recent empirical results combined with the analysis above generate several implications for the analysis of fiscal policy, such as structural changes in tax policy, changes in unfunded social security obligations or the public debt. They suggest that a good working hypothesis is that unfunded social security obligations and public debt do crowd out some private saving, but this is likely to be substantially less than dollar for dollar. The age distribution of resources does matter for aggregate consumption in the economy, and changes in the age distribution brought about by age-specific fiscal policy – such as increases in public debt or changes in the age structure of social security benefits and taxes – are likely to change saving behaviour.

The size of these variables – a true measure of real public debt plus unfunded social security obligations (including those projected in

Medicare) – is quite large (Boskin, 1987). The unfunded liabilities in OASDI in present value terms were as large as the privately held national debt prior to the 1983 Social Security Amendments. Various tax increases, the projected building of a very large surplus in the period 1990–2015 (i.e. approximately one-third to one-half of GNP!) and gradual increases in the age of eligibility for retirement benefits reduce this estimated present value of the unfunded liabilities in OASDI approximately to zero. However, it would be naïve to assume that the exempt amount in the income taxation of social security benefits will remain unindexed once half of the benefits of the middle class become taxable, and/or that we will passively accrue a surplus many times that of what social security has been able to accrue in the past. It is more likely that the surplus will be dissipated to pay part of the *even larger* deficit that is projected in the Hospital Insurance part of Medicare (see Boskin, 1986). Thus, even a partial offset of social security's unfunded liabilities, and/or the growing public debt, on private saving is likely to be the most compelling problem for those concerned about raising the saving rate.

It is my belief that while we still have substantial structural tax problems, inefficiently allocating the existing capital stock, and (while inefficiently subsidizing some types of investment) on balance curtailing saving and investment via our system of income taxation, that these effects have been mitigated substantially. The growth of employer provided pension benefits, Individual Retirement Account (IRA) and Keogh accounts, and the recent reduction in effective marginal tax rates in the corporate tax are part of the reason. Also, there is a controversy over whether effective marginal tax rates on capital income really rose as much in the 1970s as has been suggested by some (e.g. by Feldstein and Summers (1979), but see the contrary view of King and Fullerton (1983)). Thus, we have been moving in a very haphazard way towards a consumption tax, as opposed to an income tax, system. Much more could be done in this regard, but I do not believe that the structural nature of the tax system is sufficient to be the culprit by itself in the decline of our saving rate. I believe that the efficiency losses are large and that a substantial fraction of saving is done at the after-tax, not the before-tax, rate of return (e.g. approximately half of IRAs are at the limit allowed). Thus, the study of the interest elasticity of saving remains relevant for these efficiency issues, but I do not believe that the increases in capital income tax rates in the 1970s plausibly can be estimated to have been large enough in combination with reasonable interest elasticities of saving to suggest that they are the *primary* reason for the decline in net saving. They probably contributed something, and may well combine with our intergenerational transfer policies to have reduced our net national saving rate.

Recent proposals to reduce tax rates and broaden the tax base have sometimes carried with them the notion that they would stimulate saving and investment. Of paramount importance is how the base is broadened. If depreciation allowances are slowed down, tax free savings vehicles limited, etc., it is likely that the inclusion of more investment income in the tax base will more than offset any lowering of the rates in the net effect on tax rates on saving and investment. Only broad-based consumption or consumed income type taxes among the reform proposals are likely to have a positive impact on US saving. The reforms moving us closer to pure income taxation will likely do the reverse as they extend the double taxation of saving substantially (albeit at somewhat lower rates).

I might add that casual analyses of recent saving behaviour have tended to suggest that the 'supply-side' tax incentives did not work. While the investment boomlet we experienced in 1984 may well be in part a reaction to the tax incentives in ERTA/Tax Equity and Fiscal Responsibility Act, private saving has only rebounded slightly, and net private saving is still quite low. While there has been a substantial flow into IRAs, much of this comes from already existing assets, and only part is from accumulation of new wealth. Thus, some people see the sharp increase in real interest rates and the apparent modest response of saving as suggesting that there is not a very large interest elasticity of saving. I would rather suggest that an important institutional factor has been overlooked in these data. As pointed out by Bernheim and Shoven (1985), there is virtually an automatic negative interest elasticity in the personal saving rate because defined benefit pension plans will reduce their contributions substantially with increases in the interest rates assumed by actuaries which reflect historic experience in the economy. Thus, there was a decrease in 1984 of almost 30 billion dollars in contributions to private defined benefit pension plans. It is rather remarkable that net private saving actually increased as much as it did in 1984 in spite of this mechanical short-run automatic negative response of the defined benefit contribution of private saving to these rates of return. Further, increased real interest rates may curtail durables purchases – an important part of saving correctly measured – and increase consumption out of the existng stock of durables by increasing the opportunity cost of holding them.

I conclude therefore that public policies can and do affect private and national saving, and that, by virtue of their magnitude and likely response, intergenerational redistribution policies – explicit and implicit public debt – are probably quantitatively more important than capital income taxation, but that the latter certainly plays some role. In any event, federal government dissaving is currently swamping any likely increase in private sector saving that could be produced by structural changes in tax policy in the near future. In order to increase our net national saving rate, we will have to decrease government dissaving.

NOTES

1 Barro and others have argued that the prospect of future taxes to pay higher future interest payments on the larger debt will lead to increased saving to pay those future taxes. This analysis is intriguing, and probably partially correct, but the conditions for it to hold are quite restrictive and there is little empirical support for it (witness the current low saving rate). Also, Keynesians argue that if GNP expands, saving should increase. But to offset the deficit this would require a much larger expansion in GNP and people to save a much larger fraction of their increased disposable income than our historical experience suggests.

2 Table 10.5 highlights the role of government and household investment in durables as saving in adjusting the US traditional National Income and Product Accounts saving data. Government saving is positive in the US despite large deficits. The point is even more extreme in Japan, where government saving is enormous, despite larger fiscal deficits.

3 As this chapter was written, the US Congress passed a budget resolution which, *if implemented*, would cut the deficit in half by 1990. Unfortunately, there is considerable uncertainty on whether reductions this large will actually occur.

4 This assumes the economy is below the golden rule.

5 Barro and Sahasakul (1983), table 2, post 1980s, column 2.

6 Boskin (1982; 1985) and Kotlikoff (1984) provide extensive discussions of the failure of officially recorded debt to measure underlying redistribution to older generations.

7 One might argue that zero intergenerational transfers is an objective benchmark. First, distinguishing negative intergenerational transfers from taxes required to finance government consumption is completely arbitrary. Second, past intergenerational transfers imply (require) offsetting current or future intergenerational transfers. Hence, taking zero intergenerational transfers as the benchmark requires considering a world in which intergenerational transfers in the past had always been zero.

8 Ultimately, of course, the returns to the investment by foreigners will be expatriated abroad. It would be better if we were generating our own private saving to finance this investment.

9 These are not cyclically corrected deficits. In fact, in many of these countries, the 'full employment' budget was in surplus. As noted, however, a properly measured pro-deficit policy is unlikely to increase GNP enough, even in a deep recession, to increase saving. This would require a 'multiplier' and marginal propensity to save far higher than is plausible.

10 This has led some people to search for 'deep structural parameters' using the Euler equation approach to estimating parameters of intertemporal consumption and has often led to a commingling of time preference and risk aversion parameters. While I am sympathetic to the Lucas critique that changes in the macro environment might alter not only the stability of consumption or saving functions but their interpretation as well, the Euler

equation work has been done in a very restrictive single-equation framework, usually assuming additively separable utility of a representative consumer. Such assumptions are extremely restrictive, and it is unclear that this approach introduces fewer problems than it solves. Hopefully, further research along these lines will improve our understanding of intertemporal consumption behaviour.

11 The US is an open economy in the short run at least, and thus, in the short run, the supply of savings from the rest of the world is quite elastic.

REFERENCES

Auerbach, A.J. and Kotlikoff, L.J. 1983a: National savings, economic welfare, and the structure of taxation. In M. Feldstein (ed.), *Behavioral Simulation Methods in Tax Policy Analysis*, University of Chicago Press, Chicago, pp. 459–93.

Auerbach, A.J. and Kotlikoff, L.J. 1983b: Investment versus saving incentives: the biggest bang for the buck and the potential for self financing business tax cuts. In L.H. Meyer (ed.), *The Economic Consequences of Government Deficits*, Kluwer-Nijhoff, Boston, pp. 121–54.

Auerbach, A.J. and Kotlikoff, L.J. 1983c: An examination of empirical tests of social security and savings. In E. Helpman, A. Razin and E. Sadka (eds), *Social Policy Evaluation: An Economic Perspective*, Academic Press, Chicago.

Bailey, M. 1962: *National Income and the Price Level*, McGraw-Hill, New York.

Barro, R. 1974: Are government bonds net wealth?, *Journal of Political Economy*, 82, 1095–1118.

Barro, R. 1978: *The Impact of Social Security on Private Savings*, American Enterprise Institute, Washington.

Barro, R. and Sahasakul, C. 1983: Measuring the average marginal tax rate from the individual income tax, *Journal of Business*, 56, 419–52.

Barth, James R., Iden, G. and Russek, F.S. 1984: Do federal deficits really matter?, *Contemporary Policy Issues*, III, 79–95.

Bernheim, D. 1984: Dissaving after retirement, *National Bureau of Economic Research Working Paper*, No. 1409, July.

Bernheim, D. and Shoven, J.S. 1985: Pension funding and saving, *National Bureau of Economic Research Working Paper*, No. 1622.

Blinder, A., Gordon, R.H. and Wise, D.E. 1980a: Social security, bequests and the life cycle theory of savings: cross-sectional tests, *National Bureau of Economic Research Working Paper*, No. 619.

Blinder, A., Gordon, R.H. and Wise, D.E. 1980b: Reconsidering the work disincentive effects of social security, *National Tax Journal*, 3, 431–42.

Boskin, M.J. 1978: Taxation, saving, and the rate of interest, *Journal of Political Economy*, 86, 3–27.

Boskin, M.J. 1982: Federal government deficits: some myths and realities, *American Economic Review*, 72, 296–303.

Boskin, M.J. 1986: *Too Many Promises: The Uncertain Future of Social Security*, Dow Jones-Irwin, Homewood, IL.

Boskin, M.J. 1987: *The Real Federal Budget*, forthcoming, Harvard University Press, Cambridge, Mass.

Boskin, M. and Hurd, M. 1984: The effect of social security on retirement in the early 1970s, *Quarterly Journal of Economics*, 99, 767–90.

Boskin, M. and Kotlikoff, L. 1985: Public dept and U.S. saving: a new test of the neutrality hypothesis, *Carnegie-Rochester Conference Series*, Summer.

Darby, M.R. 1979: *The Effects of Social Security on Income and the Capital Stock*, American Enterprise Institute, Washington.

David, M. and Menchik, P. 1980: The effect of income distribution and redistribution on lifetime saving and bequests, *University of Wisconsin Institute for Research on Poverty Discussion Paper*, No. 582.

David, P.A. and Scadeling, J.L. 1974: Private saving: ultrarationality, aggregation and Denison's law, *Journal of Polical Economy*, 82, 225–50, March.

Diamand, P. and Hausman, J. 1984: Individual retirement and savings behavior, *Journal of Public Economics*, 23, 81–114.

Eisner, R. and Pieper, P.J. 1984: A new view of the federal debt and budget deficits, *American Economic Review*, 74, 11–20.

Feldstein, M. 1974: Social security, induced retirement, and aggregate capital accumulation, *Journal of Political Economy*, 82, 905–26.

Feldstein, M. 1982: Government deficits and aggregate demand, *Journal of Monetary Economics*, 9, 1–20.

Feldstein, M. and Eckstein, O. 1970: The fundamental determinants of the interest rate, *Review of Economics and Statistics*, 52, 363–75.

Feldstein, M. and Pellechio, A. 1979: Social security and household wealth accumulation: new microeconomic evidence, *Review of Economics and Statistics*, 61, 361–8.

Feldstein, M. and Summers, L. 1979: Inflation and the taxation of capital income in the corporate sector, *National Tax Journal*, 32, 445–70.

Fullerton, D., Shoven, J.B. and Whalley, J. 1983: Replacing the U.S. income tax with a progressive consumption tax: a sequenced general equilibrium approach, *Journal of Public Economics*, 20, 3–24.

Howrey, E.P. and Hymans, S.H. 1978: The measurement and determination of loanable-funds saving, *Brookings Papers on Economic Activity 3*. Also in J.A. Pechman (ed.) 1980: *What Should Be Taxed: Income or Expenditure?*, The Brookings Institution, Washington.

Hurd, M. 1986: Savings and bequests, *National Bureau of Economic Research Working Paper*, No. 1826, January.

King, M.A. and Dicks-Mireaux, L. 1982: Asset holdings and the life cycle, *Economic Journal*, 92, 247–67.

King, M.A. and Fullerton, D. 1983: *The Taxation of Income from Capital: A Comparative Study of the U.S., U.K., Sweden and West Germany*, National Bureau of Economic Research, University of Chicago Press, Chicago.

Kotlikoff, L.J. 1979: Testing the theory of social security and life cycle accumulation, *American Economic Review*, 69, 396–410.

Kotlikoff, L.J. and Spivak, A. 1981: The family as an incomplete annuities market, *Journal of Political Economy*, 89, 372.

Kotlikoff, L.J. and Summers, L. 1981: The role of intergenerational transfers in aggregate capital accumulation, *Journal of Political Economy*, 89, 706–32.

Lawrence, E. 1983: Do transfers to the poor reduce savings?, mimeo.

Mirer, T.W. 1979: The wealth–age relations among the aged, *American Economic Review*, 69, 435–43.

Modigliani, F. and Brumberg, R. 1954: Utility analysis and the consumption function: an interpretation of cross-section data. In K.E. Kurihara (ed.), *Post-Keynesian Economics*, Rutgers University Press, New Brunswick NJ.

Modigliani, F.and Ando, A. 1957: Tests of the lifecycle hypothesis of saving. *Bulletin of the Oxford Institute of Economics and Statistics*, 19, 99–124.

Penner, R. 1981: Forecasting budget totals: why can't we get it right?, *AEI Economist*.

Summers, L.A. 1981a: Capital taxation and accumulation in a life cycle growth model, *American Economic Review*, 71, 533–44.

Summers, L.A. 1981b: The after tax return does affect private savings, *National Bureau of Economic Research Working Paper*, No. 1351.

Summers, L.A. 1984: The asset price approach to the analysis of capital income taxation, *NBER Working Paper*, No. 1356.

Tobin, J. 1967: Life cycle saving and balanced growth. In W. Fellner (ed.), *Ten Essays in Honor of Irving Fisher*, John Wiley, New York.

11

Debt Neutrality and Fiscal Illusion: Theoretical Underpinnings and Empirical Studies. A Comment

MICHELE BAGELLA

I INTRODUCTION

If the 1970s were characterized by the debate on the role of inflation in stabilization policies, the 1980s began with a new controversy concerning the role of the public debt and the budget deficit (Kotlikoff, 1984; Tobin and Buiter, 1980a). In this case too, the theoretical work provided the background for empirical studies – studies, in this instance, of the effects of changes in the stock of government bonds on the market for consumer goods. The basic issue addressed is whether – and to what degree – private savings are influenced by changes in these stocks and, if so, whether such changes bring about changes in the rate of interest and thereby the level of investment. The question is, in other words, does the issue of bonds or money to finance an increase in the budget deficit have effects on the rate of interest, or is it, in this respect, absolutely 'neutral'?

Keynesians tend to believe that such effects *do* exist, whilst those of a neoclassical persuasion typically do not. These conflicting views can be traced back to the basic points of contention lying at the heart of the Keynesian-monetarist controversy, namely the issues of 'neutrality' and 'illusion', both monetary and fiscal (Tobin and Buiter, 1980b).

As was the case in the now classic monetary debate that preceded it, the current debate has centred largely around empirical studies. This paper focuses on some of these studies, not so much with the intention of evaluating the extent to which each provides support for one or other of the theoretical positions, but more with the aim of showing that – to the extent that the estimates are reliable – many questions remain unanswered. Regarding the issue of the interpretation of the estimates, it is sufficient to note, at this stage, that they lead to different conclusions, depending on the time period covered and on the different definitions employed.

So, the first part of this chapter aims to show that the difference of opinion that exists on the issues of neutrality and fiscal illusion has its roots in the more general difference of opinion between Keynesians and neoclassicists about the theoretical underpinnings of their respective 'systems'. The second part of the chapter is concerned with the interpretation of some of the most recent empirical results.

II INTEREST RATES AND THE STOCK OF MONEY

As has already been mentioned, the concept of neutrality in postwar macro-economic theory has typically been interpreted in terms of *money* neutrality. This stems from the revolutionary treatment of money in the *General Theory* (Keynes, 1962), where the demand for money was argued to be interest elastic and where the rate of interest was treated as a monetary phenomenon. This view went against one of the most fundamental tenets of classical monetary theory, namely that the rate of interest is a real variable and is invariant with respect to changes in the stock of money. The notion of a proportional relationship between the stock of money and the general price level was thus seriously challenged and with it the idea of 'neutral money'.

Subsequent studies served to place the question firmly at the centre of the theoretical debate. Patinkin's papers (in particular Patinkin, 1965) helped to clarify the issues involved. The Walrasian thesis – that the demand and supply of goods are determined solely by relative prices and are invariant with respect to the general price level – was rejected on the grounds that if money represents private sector net wealth, changes in the general price level alter the level of demand by changing the real value of the stock of money. The subsequent development of the 'real balance effect' served to specify more precisely the limits of this argument and therefore those concerning the neutrality of money. These limits have been shown to derive from the now standard basic assumptions underlying the neoclassical macro-economic model employed to analyse the workings of the real balance effect. These include perfect flexibility of prices and wages and perfect information (or equivalently perfect certainty regarding the future values of the relevant variables determining supply and demand in each of the various markets). Against a background such as this, in which the phenomenon of uncertainty is ruled out, increases in the stock of money leave the rate of interest unaffected, since the real balance effect manifests itself in the form of an equiproportional increase in the demand for goods and for bonds. The conclusion was, then, that any influence of the quantity of money on the rate of interest could only come about as the result of a particular type of behaviour on the part of agents tending to result in their favouring bonds rather than goods.

Indeed, in evaluating this theory, one should not lose sight of the fact that – in the analytical framework proposed – only behaviour based on *money* rather than *real* values is considered irrational. Thus, whenever the stock of money and prices grow proportionally, there is no reason for agents to change their degree of liquidity, save in the case where preferences change. By contrast, the analytical framework proposed by the *General Theory* was – as has been noted – based on expectations of an uncertain future. In this case any tendency on the part of agents to increase their liquidity in the face of falling rates of interest would stem from expectations of higher future 'normal' rates and from the need to increase money holdings in the face of an increasing value of the stock of bonds.

Further insights into this result have been obtained using the theory of portfolio selection (Tobin, 1969). But it was with Brunner's 'wealth approach' that it was confirmed that any tendency for interest rates to fall in the face of an increase in the stock of money can only be temporary, since the demand for goods would increase. In terms of the IS–LM paradigm an increase in *M* would move the LM curve to the right, but would do the same also to the IS curve, whilst interest rates, after an initial decline, would start rising again. With full employment the money stock increase would thus have purely inflationary effects. The expansionary role of monetary policy would be denied, while the neutrality of money would be reasserted.

III INTEREST RATES, PUBLIC DEBT AND THE BUDGET DEFICIT

If these are, very briefly, the arguments in support of the invariance of interest rates with respect to money stock changes, they are not different from those in support of the same invariance with respect to changes in fiscal variables such as the public debt and the budget deficit. Neoclassicists argue (a) that the mode of financing the budget deficit is of no relevance from the point of view of changes in the interest rate (bond finance included), and (b) that for this reason studies attempting to analyse the differential effects of financing the deficit through the issue of new bonds as compared to the issue of new money do not have a sound theoretical rationale. Thus the financial instrument is considered to be neutral and therefore to have no effects on the rate of interest or on private savings (Barro, 1974).

The main arguments in support of this conclusion rest on various assumptions typical of the neoclassical position. Under conditions of full employment a budget deficit brought about by a reduction in the tax rate in the absence of any change in government spending can be financed either by issuing government bonds or by printing money. In the first case there would be no effect on the rate of interest since the cut in tax rates would provide precisely the increase in disposable income required to fund the bond purchase. The cut in the tax rate will also leave demand unchanged because agents are assumed to realize that the bond issue will have to be financed in the future by increased taxes equal to the amount of the bond issue plus interest. Foreseeing this, agents will refrain from spending the extra income and will instead increase their savings, thereby offsetting the new bond issue. In other words, it is as if the Government granted a tax credit and agents, realizing this, refrain from performing any action that could render them insolvent in the future (Tobin and Buiter, 1980b).

There is, however, an additional assumption that needs to be made explicit in order to complete the picture, namely that since agents are not able to predict when this credit will expire – whether during their life or after their death – it is assumed that they do not leave debts of this type to their successors. One assumes, in other words, that they do not reduce their bond holdings during their life, but rather they transfer their bonds to their heirs in order that, when the time comes, they can cope with the increase in taxes necessary for their repayment. For these agents, therefore, the acquisition of these bonds would not represent net wealth (Barro, 1974), simply because their life is effectively assumed to be infinite on account of the chain of heirs they wish to protect. In this way, even if they enter private sector portfolios, the Government bonds would represent only the present value of a tax debt that the private sector has toward the state. Thus the new bond issue would have no effects on the interest rate, in part because, at the moment of the bond issue, the new bonds would be offset by increased savings brought about by higher disposable income and in part because it is assumed that bondholders have a propensity to consume with respect to this type of wealth equal to zero.

The same argument applies to the issue of new money. In this case the increase in demand would push prices up, assuming full employment. This would increase money income, but this increase – foreseen rationally by agents – would induce them to set aside an additional sum (more than proportional), thereby causing the level of disposable income to return to its initial level. The sum set aside would be equal to the tax reduction plus an amount deriving from the propensity to save out of disposable income prior to the tax reduction. Consequently, even if the deficit is financed by the issue of money, it would have no net effects on demand. Its initial increase would be absorbed by inflation whilst the tax cut would be neutralized by the expectation of its eventual reversal. Once again the rate of interest would remain unaffected.

IV INCOME AND DEMAND

The opposing school of thought expresses doubt as to the significance of (a) the hypothesis concerning the evaluation and the expectations regarding the role of the variation in the value of the stock of Government bonds, (b) the effects of inflation on Government stocks and (c) the assumption of full employment.

Regarding (a) it has been noted that the tendency to consider the behaviour of agents as uniform – as if one were dealing with only one agent – conflicts with reality. In particular, agents do not always concern themselves with their heirs. Moreover, even if they do, it is not to say that the anticipation of the moment in which the new taxes will have to be paid is such as to prevent the present beneficiaries of the tax cut from taking some advantage, even if only momentarily. In other words, ensuring 100 per cent fiscal solvency of heirs implies *certainty* about the moment in which the State will levy new taxes, implying therefore that at the date when the bonds expire, the debt accumulated to finance the deficit will not be continued by the Government. It also implies that the heirs will not benefit from such increases in income as would provide them with the means to pay for the new taxes (Tobin and Buiter, 1980b).

Moreover, the idea of not considering the devaluation of the stock of bonds and its effects, whenever the monetary funding of the deficit results in inflation, would undermine the rationale of the whole argument. It is true that the fall in the value of the Government bonds results in a reduction in the value of the tax debt, but it is also true that it does not have to be the case that those in possession of these bonds are those who have underwritten them. In other words, if one admits the existence of a secondary financial market where bonds already in existence are exchanged, it is natural to conclude that any fall in their value would have effects on the rate of interest. To assume that there are no such effects is to assume that such a market does not exist.

Given these premises, Keynesians claim that the effects of an increase in disposable income are completely different from those described by the advocates of debt neutrality. In particular, it is assumed that an increase in disposable income increases demand and thereby consumption and investment. It is also maintained (Modigliani – Life-cycle Hypothesis) that if the quantity of money remained constant, the pressure on liquidity would cause the interest rate to rise. Though this might facilitate the sale of Government bonds, it would have the effect of deterring new investment. Looking at the problem in another way, it is assumed that with the rise in income and financial wealth in the form of bonds, there would also be a wealth effect tending to add to money holdings. From this would follow an equal tendency for the interest rate to rise with the result that investment would be crowded out (Arcelli and Valiani, 1979). In conditions of underemployment, real income would increase but not by an amount that would have been called for by the increase in demand in the absence of an increase in the rate of interest. If, on the other hand, the economy is in conditions of full employment, an increase in demand will cause prices to rise and subsequently the rate of interest as well. If, however, an increase in demand had to be sustained by an increase in the amount of money in circulation in the case of a money-financed deficit, then the rate of interest would tend to fall and the demand for bonds representing real capital (shares) would tend to increase, whether by a fall in the value of fixed-interest bonds or by their indexation against inflation (Tobin and Buiter, 1980a). The increase in demand will bring about a reduction in saving, but within it the monetary and fixed-interest components would be penalized.

V THE NEOCLASSICAL VERSUS THE KEYNESIAN HYPOTHESES

The conclusion that appears to follow from all this is that the differences in the effects can be explained in terms of two key hypotheses concerning agents' behaviour. The first – the neoclassical – ascribes to agents a total ability to predict the future, including what will happen to future generations. Therefore, the neutrality of deficit financing is simply the result of the assumptions of 'certainty' and 'transparency'.

The Keynesian hypothesis, on the other hand, ascribes to agents a less than total ability to predict, allowing for the presence of some degree of uncertainty and, for this reason, accords a special place to the short-run effects. Thus the *full* discounting to the present of future tax burdens is not considered plausible, in part because it is viewed as unrealistic, and in part because of the expectation that an increase in the public debt would have a direct effect on savers' behaviour through the extra uncertainty it will generate. In the case of a non-monetary deficit funding, an increase in the interest rate is considered to be a consistent result. This is due partly to the fact that the increase in demand reflects a desire on the part of agents to take immediate advantage (if only partially) of the higher disposable income and partly to the view that, despite the agents' desire to protect fiscally their heirs, this protection can hardly be total since they do not have the ability to foresee exactly when the major taxes will be levied by the Government. From an analytical point of view, therefore, the stock of bonds is *not* 'frozen'. On the contrary, transactions may take place and – in the view of agents – bonds may become part of their financial wealth. In other words, it is concluded that the distribution of bonds amongst agents and changes in this distribution are important when evaluating their effects on the rate of interest – whether they come about as a result of price increases or through changes in the quantity of bonds in circulation or through increases in real income and of other forms of wealth.

One is therefore dealing, as mentioned above, with two different types of analyses where each agent's behaviour is conditional on the information available to him. There is, therefore, no inconsistency in the view that bonds are to be considered as a form of wealth, at least in the sense of the word as it is used in neoclassical analysis. Such a view is the result of the assumption of uncertainty regarding both future policy on mode of repayment (new bond issue versus new taxes) and trends in the real income of heirs.

As in the traditional Keynesian–neoclassical debate, the divergence of opinion can be traced back to the different hypotheses about agents' behaviour: 'certainty or uncertainty' or, with regard to the working of the system, 'transparency or opaqueness'. Given that neither hypothesis can be dismissed merely on a priori grounds, the debate has moved towards empirical tests aiming at discriminating between the approaches on the basis of their ability to explain observed phenomena.

VI EMPIRICAL RESULTS

Table 11.1 summarizes the results of some recent estimates of the consumption function in which fiscal variables – such as the budget deficit – are included. All the estimates are based on United States data and are widely known, having generated a good deal of debate.

Table 11.1 *United States: effects on consumption of $1 increase in budget deficit, public debt and tax burden*

	Koklin *1952–71*	*Yavitz and Meyer* *1953–69*	*Tobin and Buiter* *1949–76*	*Tanner* *1947–78*
Budget deficit	−0.22		−0.25	−0.29
Public debt		0.05		
Fiscal pressure			−0.33	

$$CND = 5.56 + 0.283Y_t - 0.224DEF + 0.643CND_{t-1} \quad (11.1)$$
$$C_t = 0.75Y_t + 0.03W_{t-1} + \mathbf{0.05B_{t-1}} \quad (11.2)$$
$$CND = -133.139 + 0.224PIB - 0.337PF - 0.254DEF + 0.798CND_{-1} \quad (11.3)$$
$$CND = 0.718Y + 0.204Y_{t-1} + 0.256RE + 0.327U.Y. - 0.13DUR_{t-1} + 0.028K_{t-1} - 0.014GDEB_{t-1} + 0.291TSUR \quad (11.4)$$

CND is non-durable consumption
Y is household's disposable income
DEF is federal budget deficit
C is total consumption
W is household net wealth less public debt at market value
PIB is national income
B is public debt at market values
PF is total fiscal pressure
RE is corporate retained earnings
U.Y. is a composite variable
DUR is household stock of consumer's durables at beginning period
TSUR is public sector budget surplus (state, local, federal)
GDEB is federal bonds at market value
K is net stock of fixed non-residential business capital and residential housing

They are included in the table to emphasize their conflicting results concerning the key question of debt neutrality (Kessler and Levigne, 1984).

Equation 11.1 from Kochin (1974) is estimated for the period 1952–74. The author argues that the negative sign of the coefficient of the budget deficit variable indicates a tendency for consumption to decrease following an increase in the budget deficit, regardless of the mode of finance. In equation 11.2 (Yawitz and Mayer, 1976) the fiscal variable is the public debt: according to the parameter estimates it exerts no statistically significant influence on consumption. This result would seem also to support, therefore, the hypothesis of neutrality. It should be noted, however, that for the period chosen (1953–69), the effect of family real wealth is also insignificant (Kessler and Levigne, 1984).

Equation 11.3 (Tobin and Buiter, 1980b) estimates real per capita consumption as a function of two fiscal variables – the federal budget deficit and the fiscal burden, both per capita. This is a more sophisticated test of the hypothesis of neutrality. Tobin and Buiter claim that if the deficit is perceived by the holder as a tax, the variable DEF (see legend accompanying the table) would have a coefficient equal in magnitude to that on the other fiscal variable, namely the tax burden. However, the results of the regression over a period longer than those previously studied (1949–76) show coefficients which, although of the same sign, are significantly different from one another in size.

The final regression in the table is equation 11.4 (Tanner, 1979). Once again it shows an insignificant relationship between consumption and the public debt. It also shows a statistically significant negative effect of the budget deficit on consumption, since the relationship between consumption and the budget surplus is positive and significant. This regression would also, therefore, seem to lend support to the hypothesis of neutrality.

Different results are presented by Holcombe et al. (1981), who use savings as the dependent variable and estimate the equation for the period 1929–76. Their results imply that an increase in the US budget deficit leads to an increase in savings of only 20 per cent, the difference going to an increase in consumption.

Finally, with different variable definitions, and for the period 1865–84, Evans (1985) has obtained results which suggest that even substantial increases in the budget deficit do not affect the rate of interest. In other words, notwithstanding the comments of, for example, Feldstein (1983), the rate of interest does not, according to Evans' results, rise following an increased budget deficit. This implies that, not only is demand not affected but – on the contrary – such deficits are considered by savers to be anticipated taxation. Indeed, Evans' results for subperiods with relatively high budget deficits suggest that the impact of an increase in the budget deficit on the rate of interest may – at such times – actually be *negative*. Evans argues that these results lend support to Boskin's (1978) hypothesis that an increase in the budget deficit increases the propensity to save due to a total anticipation of future taxes (gross of interest).

VII CONCLUSIONS

Some general conclusions can be reached from the aforementioned empirical studies. Firstly, the results in support of or against neutrality are generally only *indirect*. A negative relationship between the rate of interest and the size of the budget deficit is viewed as evidence in favour of the neutrality hypothesis, as is an observed positive relationship between consumption and the size of the budget surplus. If, on the other hand, the coefficients on the budget deficit and the tax burden in the consumption equation have negative signs, but the tax burden coefficient is larger in absolute size (as in the case of Tobin and Buiter's results), the hypothesis of neutrality is considered to be rejected. So, to the extent that these estimates are reliable, they appear to give rise to yet more uncertainty about the validity of the claims of the two opposing schools of thought (Spaventa, 1984).

In addition to this, there is also the problem that the periods covered are frequently too long for one to be able to assume safely that the relationships have remained structurally stable over time. One cannot rule out, therefore, the possibility that the results are due to structural changes rather than to the validity of the behavioural hypotheses.

A final remark, more specific to the debate on neutrality, would seem to be in order. If Barro's hypothesis is considered to be an accurate description of behaviour, the budget deficit appears to have *no impact* on the working of the financial markets and of the economy as a whole. But for many countries – not only for Italy – the problem of the sustainability of the public debt (Valiani, 1985) is of great practical importance for their economic policy, as was emphasized also by Eltis (1984) in a recent conference. It seems, therefore, somewhat surprising that advocates of neoclassical principles should claim, albeit with differing motives, that the rise in public debt, connected to the budget deficit, is of little relevance to the level of economic activity, whether in terms of its effect on the rate of interest or on the rate of growth. These ideas, in fact, risk contributing towards raising it even more.

REFERENCES

Arcelli, M. and Valiani, R. 1979: Il crowding out: alcune riflessioni per la politica economica, *Economia Italiana*, no. 2.

Barro, R.J. 1974: Are government bonds net wealth?, *Journal of Political Economy*, 82, 1095–1117.

Boskin, M.J. 1978: Taxation, saving and the rate of interest, *Journal of Political Economy*, 86, 3–27.

Eltis, W. 1984: *President Reagan's Deficit or Mrs Thatcher's Balanced Budget: which makes more Sense?*, The Bank Credit Analyst Conference, New York.

Evans, P. 1985: Do large deficits produce high interest rates?, *The American Economic Review*, 75, 68–87.

Feldstein, M. 1983: A summary of the theoretical models. In *Inflation, Tax Rules and Capital Formation*, NBER, ch. 2.

Holcombe, R.G., Jackson, J.D. and Zardkooni, A. 1981: The National Debt Controversy, *Kyklos*, no. 2.

Kessler, D. and Levigne, A. 1984. Public Debt and Household Savings, Saving for Development, *Report of the 2nd Symposium on the Mobilization of Personal Savings in Developing Countries*. United Nations, New York.

Keynes, J.M. 1962: *The General Theory of Employment, Interest and Money*, Macmillan, London (reprint).

Kochin, L.A. 1974: Are future taxes anticipated by consumers?, *Journal of Money, Credit and Banking*, 6, 385–94.

Kotlikoff, L.J. 1984: Economic impact of deficit financing, *International Monetary Fund Staff Papers*, Sept.

Modigliani, F. and Ando, A. 1957: Tests of the life cycle hypothesis of saving, *Bulletin of the Oxford Institute of Economy and Statistics*, 19, 99–124.

Modigliani, F. and Brumberg, R. 1954: Utility analysis and the consumption function: an interpretation of cross-section data. In K.E. Kurihara (ed.) *Post-Keynesian Economics*, Rutgers University Press, New Brunswick, N.J.

Patinkin, D. 1965: *Money, Interest and Prices*, Harper and Row, New York.

Spaventa, L. 1984: La crescita del debito pubblico in Italia: Evoluzione, prospettive e problemi di politica economica, *Moneta e Credito*, no. 147.

Tanner, J.E. 1979: An empirical investigation of tax discounting, *Journal of Money, Credit and Banking*, no. 2, 214–18.

Tobin, J. 1969: A general equilibrium approach to monetary theory, *Journal of Money, Credit and Banking*, 1, 15–29.

Tobin, J. and Buiter, W. 1980a: Fiscal and monetary policies, capital formation and economic activity. In G.M. von Furstenberg (ed.) *The Government and the Capital Formation*, Ballinger, Cambridge, Mass.

Tobin, J. and Buiter, W. 1980b: Debt neutrality: a brief review of doctrine and evidence. In G.M. von Furstenberg (ed.) *Social Security versus Private Saving and the Capital Formation*, Ballinger, Cambridge, Mass.

Valiani, R. 1985: What solutions are there to Italy's public debt? *Review of Economic Conditions in Italy*, no. 1, Banco de Roma, pp. 75–95.

Yavitz, J.B. and Mayer, L.M. 1976: An empirical investigation on the extent of tax discounting, *Journal of Money, Credit and Banking*, 8, 247–54.

12

Public Debt, Private Savings and Supply-side Policies

LUIGI PAGANETTO

I INTRODUCTION

The size of the public-sector deficit in relation to national product in many industrialized countries and its tendency to increase, combined with the belief that there is a critical point beyond which a deficit gives rise to instability in the economic system, has led to the view that public-sector deficits are always harmful and must therefore be contained.[1] If the deficit therefore is financed mainly through the issue of public debt, the question assumes greater immediacy and becomes one of containing the debt,[2] since this can, in excess of certain levels, generate expectations rendering it impossible for the monetary authorities to control. The importance of these problems, increased by the pressure of events, has had the effect of pushing the medium-term impact of budgetary policies into the background. At the same time, economists' knowledge of the effects of the public-sector deficit on income, inflation and the allocation of resources tends to lag behind, owing – in Buiter's view (Buiter, 1984) – to the long-standing separation between the theoretical bases of Keynesian stabilization policies and the micro-economic analyses of public finance. If account is taken of the confused state of macro-economic theory and the related policies, even if one does not share Tobin's view that the situation is discouraging,[3] one can certainly find further justification for the difficulties in satisfactorily analysing the overall interaction between public-sector deficits and the economy.

Even if the macro-economic models predominating today tend increasingly to deal with the operations of the public sector, from direct and indirect taxation to transfers and subsidies, debt and the deficit, the resulting economic policy proposals differ widely. The reason naturally lies in the particular nature of the assumptions – one has only to think, in this connection, of the hypothesis of rational expectations which is the basis of the new neoclassical macro-economics[4] – incorporated in turn in the various models. In this context it is undoubtedly very difficult to evaluate the economic policies actually followed and implemented if an attempt is made to show their analytical bases. Supply-side policies have been treated with a certain condescension [5] by many economists, who have pointed to the weakness of the theoretical formulation and above all, leaving aside easy criticism of the Laffer curve, the lack of reference to a coherent analytical system. Even if one has to agree with this assessment, the emphasis of supply-side policies on the substitution and allocation effects of prices, which has undoubtedly been stimulated by the trend of economic events, has certainly found fertile ground in the crisis of macro-economic theory, which may be said today to be in search of its micro-economic foundations. In addition, to the extent that supply-side economics emphasizes the role of relative prices, and in particular interest rates, in determining the level and allocation of savings in competition with public debt, devoting particular attention to the medium-term aspects of these phenomena has the effect of posing a series of theoretical questions which, leaving aside whether or not one accepts the economic policy proposals bound up with them, call for careful analysis. It is interesting to note that, whilst concern for the immediate effects of an increase in the public-sector deficit naturally remains, it is not central, and is at any rate tied in with the medium-term trend of the economy.

I A CURRENT US TREASURY ANALYSIS

A recent US Treasury document (US Department of the Treasury, 1985) contains the assertion that although the administration is keeping a careful watch on the level of the deficit, as an indicator of excessive government expenditure crowding out private expenditure, any reduction of the deficit obtained by means of an increase in taxation would not produce growth stimuli. The idea that every available means should be used to reduce the deficit is regarded as mistaken because an increase in taxation would have the effect of reducing savings.[6] Savings can only be stimulated by a reduction in total public expenditure which, by leaving room for private expenditure, has the effect of allowing an increase in savings. In view of the fact that the more the government succeeds in raising through taxation, the more it tends to spend, any increase in taxation would end up by increasing expenditure rather than restricting the deficit.

Public-sector spending should therefore be contained because it crowds out private expenditure, but not at the cost of increasing taxation. Indeed, and this is in fact what is happening at the moment in the USA, the stimulus exerted by tax cuts is regarded as so substantial as to make an actual increase in the public-sector deficit temporarily acceptable. According to the same document, the stimulus associated with tax cutting derives from the change it produces in relative prices rather than from an increase in total demand.[7] Conditions being equal, it increases the propensity to supply labour and, above all, savings. In the absence of a reduction in government expenditure, tax cutting does not produce an increase in expenditure if it is offset by equivalent public-sector borrowing. Hence the conclusion that the attention due to the public debt must not turn into an 'hysterical' preoccupation (US Department of the Treasury, 1985, 14). It is the recession, and not tax cuts, which creates the problem of the deficit, since according to supply-side economists deficits are reduced by economic growth (Bartlett, 1985; Wanniski, 1978). The deficit, moreover, has little or no influence on interest rates, which are dependent on monetary policy. In addition to controlling inflation, a restrictive monetary policy in the end reduces nominal interest rates and at the same time, by these means, ensures conditions of monetary stability.[8]

In a period in which interest rates remain high they are not, in any case, an obstacle to growth. Investment in fact depends essentially on the after-tax return on capital and if fiscal incentives have increased that return by the right amount, the negative effect of high interest rates is not felt. At the same time the profit outlook is improved by the lower cost of labour derived from reduced taxation of incomes. If those supplying labour want to at least keep their after-tax pay unaltered, despite inflation, demands for wage adjustments will be lower with a lower level of income taxation.[9]

This summary of how a government document incorporates the main supply-side policy recommendations is intended to provide a framework for subsequent verification of the extent to which these are supported by a theoretical foundation, particularly as regards the question of the effects of the public-sector deficit on economic activity, which, even if it is presented reductively as a less important problem, is in reality the most important question of all.[10]

As we have already seen, in supply-side economics an increase in the deficit has the effect of crowding out private expenditure only to the extent that it is accompanied by an increase in public expenditure. According to a well-known study of this subject, since government expenditure has the effect of using resources which could otherwise have been used for investment, the reduction in investment which occurs with high interest rates cannot be regarded as the consequence of the financial situation. The reduction in investment reflects the allocation of resources determined by public expenditure competing with private expenditure at times of scarce resources. Credit is by nature scarce, so that even if the government was completely absent from the capital market, there would always be some potential borrower at every level of interest rates who would be 'crowded out' – perhaps an entrepreneur whose expected rate of return on the proposed investment would be less than the interest rate or a consumer who postpones his consumption in response to the high level of interest rates. If, however, the scarcity of credit is reduced by an increase in savings, room is created for the consumption and investment expenditure previously crowded out (US Department of the Treasury, 1984).

Alongside these considerations it is clear, however, that the government's position as a borrower is peculiar in at least two respects: the remarkable insensitivity its demand to changes in interest rates and the fact that government loans mostly finance activities that do not generate increases in productive capacity. If, however, an increase in government borrowing were to finance tax cuts, this would generate increased cash flow for enterprises and therefore, conditions being equal, reduced demand for credit. In addition, since the supply of savings increases when the interest rate rises, the amount of credit lost by potential private borrowers will be smaller than the increase in public debt. The conclusion is therefore that the deficit does not necessarily crowd out private expenditure. The problem of the increase in the deficit which can arise from this approach is met by the consideration that the question of its sustainability only emerges in the long term and that this cannot at any rate be defined a priori, but will depend on: (a) the responsiveness of the supply of labour and savings to net rates of return, (b) the productivity of the capital, (c) the average marginal rate of taxation, and (d) the proportion of productive expenditure, and therefore of public investment, to total expenditure.

From the theoretical point of view, it is hard to determine whether these propositions with regard to the deficit and its relationships with private activity are acceptable, not least because of the particular period through which macro-economic theory is passing.

III THE STANDARD KEYNESIAN APPROACH AND BARRO'S CONTRIBUTION

According to the 'standard' Keynesian approach an increase in the public-sector deficit, if financed by the issue of public debt, has the effect of increasing output even if it results in a certain crowding out of investment. Adopting the IS/LM diagram, in fact, the increase in demand brought about by the expansion of the deficit results, unless the money supply is boosted, in an increase in interest rates which produces a reduction in investment for a given return on capital and at the same time causes a fall in liquid balances so that the increased demand can be financed with available money. Even looking at a more sophisticated model, in which account is taken of the increase in private wealth which occurs following the subscription of public debt securities, the crowding-out effect in respect of private expenditure is confirmed. The increase in wealth also increases consumption and therefore reduces savings and the consequences, if not the magnitude, of the resulting phenomena are similar to the preceding ones.

Contrary to the view held by the British Treasury in the 1920s, whereby an increase in the deficit crowded out private investment but did not boost the level of activity, in the Keynesian analysis crowding out is the price that has to be paid for an increase in output. This representation of events no longer holds good if, like Barro, we assume that public debt securities are not net wealth (Barro, 1974). This conclusion derives, as is well known, from an intergenerational model where economic agents consider a utility function in which the preferences include not only the (differing) options for each period of the individual's life, but also those relating to his descendants and the position that they will have in relation to the legacies they receive. The consumer's horizon tends therefore to shift from a finite perspective to an infinite one, in which the increase in public debt is perceived as an indicator of future taxation[11] and therefore generates an amount of savings equal to that needed in due course to meet increased taxation. Rational operators therefore, concerned to achieve intertemporal maximization of their utility functions, will not reduce their savings, regarding their net wealth as unchanged. The sharp criticism of this approach (see, for example, Tobin, 1980, 64 *et seq.*) derives from awareness that the new neoclassical macro-economics, in so far as one accepts Barro's analysis, demonstrates the irrelevance of Keynesian-type fiscal policies. Not only do consumers not modify their savings with the issue of government securities, they do not modify them in the event of monetization of the deficit either. In this case it is rising prices which reduce the value of money stocks and therefore stimulate their holders to reconstitute them by an equal amount. The conclusion is that no effect can be looked for from the manner in which the deficit is financed; the effect that public expenditure has on the economic system depends entirely on its level and structure, and not on the consequences of the wealth effect and the corresponding crowding-out effects.[12] Opponents of Barro's theory basically point out the difficulty of reconciling his assumptions with the necessary empirical support: it does not seem possible that maximizing behaviour with an infinite horizon in which each individual adopts an intergenerational objective can be generalized to all economic agents. In addition, although the debt may be regarded as an indicator of future taxation, it is not easy to assess its incidence, not least in relation to the need to produce a reliable forecast of when the taxation will actually occur. In the light of the fact that the results of the econometric analyses aimed at verifying Barro's hypothesis do not lead to unambiguous conclusions, the prevailing view is that the hypothesis has not been demonstrated.[13]

VI THE SIGNIFICANCE OF FELDSTEIN'S ANALYSIS

In addition to its analytical merits, the relevance of Barro's model lies in the fact that it has focused attention once again on the long-term effects of fiscal policy. These, though always borne in mind in the debate, had undoubtedly received less attention, not least because of the central position assigned by Keynesian policies to management of the cycle. Nevertheless, albeit in the context of a somewhat different perspective (that of the effects of public indebtedness on the incomes of future generations), neoclassical synthesizing models have, as is well known, studied the long-term effects of fiscal policies. These models, by analysing the influence of public debt on the process of economic development, arrive at the general conclusion that the debt absorbs private savings and reduces long-term accumulation. The existence of the social security system is regarded as tending to have the same effect as the debt since the prospect of income from a pension also tends to reduce private savings and long-term accumulation. The question has been taken up in the models representing the most thorough endeavour to provide supply-side policies with a satisfactory theoretical basis. Particularly in the work of Feldstein, there is an attempt to combine the indications of the importance of an increase in the savings ratio for growth with the attendant consideration of the effects of the public-sector deficit.[14] The general idea on which this research is based is that, in inflationary situations, the traditional Keynesian policies for increasing the level of activity and the proportion of investment to income are not applicable. They in fact lead to recommendations for the use of a restrictive fiscal policy as a means of containing demand, and thus inflation, and a permissive monetary policy to sustain investment demand. The experience of recent years, in which Keynesian policies have prevailed and inflation rates have been high and investment rates low, leads Feldstein to believe that, in the context of economies relatively close to full employment, such an economic policy mix can operate only in conjunction with a public-sector surplus. Where there is such a surplus the government will be able to reduce its borrowing, and individuals, in their turn, will be able to replace government securities with private-sector securities and therefore the accumulation of private capital can increase. Considering, however, that a deficit is the norm, and furthermore that its size is increasing, the government is obliged to issue public debt continuously. In the presence of a permissive monetary policy, which keeps interest rates relatively low, private individuals will therefore, in the meanwhile, reduce their savings and then shift their investments from real capital to consumer durables and housing. In this situation an alternative strategy would be a restrictive monetary policy to combat inflation and a fiscal policy that would sustain savings and investment. The increase in interest rates which occurs as a result of a restrictive monetary policy is already, in itself, a stimulus to saving; this can be reinforced by tax reductions on interest income, just as investment can be supported by reductions on capital income (Feldstein, 1983, 13–14). Within this general presentation the use of a steady-state model makes it possible to show how the presence of a growing public-sector deficit gives rise to inflationary effects and/or crowding-out effects in respect of private investment with a consequent reduction of long-term accumulation. Account also needs to be taken of the tendency of monetary authorities, faced with a major deficit, to make this easier to finance through a policy of constant real interest rates, and of the simultaneous trend of yields on real capital to fall in the presence of inflation. For, since depreciation is carried out at historic and not replacement cost, it follows that the cost calculation is less than it should be. Real profits consequently decline and this encourages private individuals to hold public debt rather than securities representing private capital. The outcome is a decline in capital intensity, which occurs unless the effect of inflation on the demand for money is greater than the effect it has in increasing the demand for securities. But this does not seem likely, in view of the greater substitutability between securities and capital than between capital and money. The increase in the deficit will at the same time generate higher inflation unless the interest rate rises enough to absorb the greater quantity of public debt in circulation, simultaneously reducing the demand for liquid balances by the necessary amount.

The conclusion is, therefore, that if accumulation is not to be allowed to fall and increased inflation is to be avoided, the deficit must not increase. Since, however, a deficit is hard to control, the same results can be obtained even with a growing deficit. If private saving is responsive to them, the higher interest rates, accompanied by measures to reduce the propensity to spend on consumer durables, housing and the like, can encourage the accumulation of productive capital (Feldstein, 1983, 26). The overall picture that emerges from this representation of the long-term trends of the economy is undoubtedly the most complete theoretical justification of supply-side policies. It brings out the central role played by savings in the process of accumulation, its dependence on the interest rate (interpreted as an expression of the return on the savings in question), the importance of measures aimed at ensuring an increasing supply and, lastly, the limited relevance of the public-sector deficit. The scant attention and limited importance given to the trend of the deficit by supply-side economists is tempered, in this interpretation, by a more qualified evaluation of the role of the deficit. In the long term, an increase in the deficit inevitably results in reduced capital intensity and/or higher inflation, unless balanced by an increase in savings. The difficulty of controlling the public-sector deficit, which is clear from the experience of almost every industrialized country, leads to the economic policy conclusion that it is necessary to act on the determinants of saving so as to boost the latter because the result will be an increase in accumulation and the rate of growth. Since this automatically increases government revenue, the public-sector deficit should thereby decrease as progress is made along the 'virtuous' path created by the increase in savings. These conclusions are a synthesis of what, in this view, is the combined effect of the deficit and inflation. According to Tobin (1965) inflation, by bringing about an increase in the nominal rate of interest, in the long term produces a higher opportunity cost of holding liquid balances and shifts investment towards real capital. Tobin's conclusion that capital intensity increases as a consequence of inflation alters if we take account, with Feldstein, of the effects of taxation and the responsiveness of savings to the interest rate. If these relations are relevant, savings will be stimulated whenever, in a period of inflation, the percentage rate at which interest income is taxed is lower than that for firms' capital income. In this case, in fact, the real net rate of return received by savers increases on the basis of the following simple relations. If the net return is

$$r_n = (1-t_r)i-\dot{p}$$

where t_r is tax on interest and $\dot{p}$ is inflation since

$$i = p_k + \frac{\dot{p}}{1 - t_s}$$

where p_k is the productivity of capital per person and t_s is tax on the income of companies. Then

$$r_n = (1-t_r)\, p_k + \frac{t_r - t_s}{1 - t_s}\dot{p}$$

This conclusion is reinforced if account is taken of the effect of calculating depreciation by the historic cost method rather than that of replacement cost. In times of inflation, this method of calculation implies a nominal depreciation value which does not take account of the increased cost of replacement, and therefore a depreciation sum smaller than should otherwise be calculated. The consequence is a nominal profit in excess of the real one and, *de facto*, implicit higher taxation, and therefore once again a smaller real net return on capital invested. The capacity of inflation to influence capital intensity is linked in this view to the manner in which yields vary for those supplying savings and those demanding them, taking into account the incidence of taxation and the methods of calculating depreciation. Whenever the rate of taxation has a greater impact on the real returns of those offering savings than it has on those borrowing them, there is a decline in accumulation; the same phenomenon may also be observed when, although the situation as regards yields is the reverse, methods of calculating depreciation have the effect of offsetting the greater nominal return on capital. The public-sector deficit in its turn has the above-mentioned effects on capital intensity, within the framework of a long-term steady-state model involving three different assets: money, public securities and real capital. Contrary to Tobin's conclusion, referred to above, an increase in inflation does not modify the propensity of holders of wealth in favour of real capital, but rather brings about an increase in the holding of public debt. The monetary policy adopted and the structure of taxation are, in their turn, at the root of the way in which the deficit causes inflation and a reduction in capital intensity. In particular, a monetary policy that keeps the real interest rate stable produces a fall in capital intensity as inflation changes, because inflation reduces the real net return on capital through the depreciation mechanism. At this point holders of assets find it to their advantage to acquire more public securities if the real net return on such securities is kept deliberately constant. At the same time inflation increases because – since it is linked with per capita growth of money and securities $(m + b)$ – without a change in the real interest rate it is impossible to shift demand towards securities by more than the decline in the demand for money, and the value of $(m + b)$ must therefore increase.

It should be pointed out that the increase in the deficit produces inflation and a reduction in capital intensity to the extent that it at the same time changes the proportion of public expenditure to national income. In steady-state conditions this proportion does not, by definition, change. But if one assumes, with Feldstein (1980, 636 *et seq.*), that a constant fraction of national income is constituted by the interest on public debt, it follows that each increase in expenditure on interest, as well as increasing the deficit, also brings about a change in the proportion of public expenditure to income, and therefore produces inflation and/or a reduction in capital intensity. This emerges from a combination of the following relations:

$$a = (\dot{p} + n)(m + b)$$
$$m = f(i)\, y$$
$$S_d = S_s$$

where a is the per capita deficit, n is the natural rate of growth, y is the per capita output, $S_{d,s}$ is the savings demanded and supplied and in which securities (b) are demanded as a function of the real net return on capital and the real net interest rate while savings are supplied in relation to disposable income, the variation in the real value of money and securities and changes in the amount of interest on the public debt, and held in the form of real capital, money and securities. The most interesting aspect of this whole construction is that if, for whatever reason, there is excess saving, it can, contrary to the Keynesian belief, be absorbed. This can occur principally where it is possible to reduce the inflation rate, but where this is not possible, recourse could be had to an increase in the deficit accompanied by a reduction in the interest rate. The lower rate of interest would prevent the lower return on capital from leading to a decline in capital intensity and enable the increased savings to be absorbed – provided of course that there was no change in inflation which, together with the larger deficit, allows the absorption of the increased money and securities made necessary by the fall in the interest rate.

The same result would be achieved with a reduction in the rate of taxation. Such a reduction would, to a probably even greater extent, avoid the decline in the net rate of return on capital connected with the excess saving and would therefore permit an increase in capital intensity. The latter assertion seems to be of central importance as a theoretical justification of supply-side policies, in view of the attention they devote to the influence of relative prices on the level of activity. It would appear to provide confirmation of the idea that, by enhancing the return on invested capital through tax concessions and increasing available savings by intervention to boost the real net return, increased growth would be obtained without higher inflation where a restrictive monetary policy was in operation to keep it under control. Although the construction is attractive, careful attention needs to be paid to a series of questions calling for discussion. First of all it is clear that the distinctive nature of its conclusions is to a large extent due to being linked to specific fiscal mechanisms – those, naturally, of the USA. In particular, the deductibility of loan interest paid out of the income of companies is not something which applies everywhere, and similarly, although it is indeed true that depreciation at historic cost increases the nominal income, it is also true that in many countries assets are periodically revalued to take account of inflation. The importance of this point is clear since, as is well known, models in which it is assumed that taxes do not alter the net rate of return on capital lead to very different, and in some cases quite opposite, results.[15]

Leaving aside these remarks, there is a question of substance with regard to the problem of depreciation in general. It is possible, and indeed probable, that at times of inflation the historic-cost method of calculation has an influence. However it is also true that on the basis of experience the need to consider higher depreciation allowances is connected with the incidence of rapid technological change rather than with inflation. That is why, in recent years, productive combinations have seen a high rate of change in which the processes of substitution as between capital and labour have been accompanied by even more important phenomena, such as the alteration of production cycles. The speed of technological change, more than inflation, seems in general to have resulted in a reduction in the average life of machinery and consequently a need to reckon on increased depreciation charges. The considerations with regard to capital intensity would certainly have to be revised if account were taken – contrary to what is the case with a steady-state model – of the fact that the rate of growth of the labour force has varied considerably in recent years. The possibility should consequently be borne in mind that the observed fall in capital intensity may be connected with variations in the supply of labour rather than with inflation.[16] Then again, the technological process is also reflected in a change in the quality of the capital and labour employed in productive combinations, which certainly cannot be described in a steady-state world in which labour is measured in efficiency units.

These considerations with regard to the adequacy of the model in relation to experiential data are certainly familiar to anyone using a steady-state model to describe the long-term trends of the economy. Naturally the decisive observation remains that such models are among the few theoretical instruments available to economists, although it should be remembered that they were neglected for many years under the influence of neo-Ricardian criticism. Today, although awareness of the limits on the internal cohesion of aggregate growth models has – not least in this way – increased, they are again being taken up and used (not only by supply-side economists). This is probably because the importance and urgency of public finance problems and their discussion in the context of macro-economic stabilization policies call for immediate responses relating not only to short-term but also to medium- and long-term trends. Even if the scope of the discussion is to be restricted in this manner, the most striking aspect of the supply-side economists' presentation is the decisive role attributed to savings decisions. This position, which is widely reflected in official economic policy documents in the USA, is based on the idea that, whatever the level of saving, the economic system is always able to absorb it and transform it into increased investment. Hence the encouragement of savings through appropriate increases in the rate of return, in the conviction that the savings ratio responds to variations in the interest rate. Opinions on this point differ, as is well known, although due credit should be given to Boskin[17] for having reopened an important question. His views, which are however confirmed by subsequent research,[18] have been criticized because they have proved highly sensitive to changes in the period of estimation.[19] Even where analysis of the behaviour of the consumer (saver) has been carried out within a general consumption model like that of the life cycle, the debate has continued because it has become clear that in this case different savings elasticities are compatible with various assumptions on the nature of consumers' preferences.[20] The main question is still, however, whether or not saving is central to accumulation and what effect the public-sector deficit has on accumulation in an inflationary environment. We have already seen that a decisive factor here is the way in which one looks at the effects of the public debt on net wealth.

V A KEYNESIAN ADDENDUM

In Feldstein's model the hypothesis is that an increase in public debt produces an increase in net wealth. Interestingly, this coincides with the models seeking to evaluate the effects of a deficit financed by the issue of securities from a Keynesian angle.[21] Barro's hypothesis is therefore excluded and it is assumed that issues of securities increase the net wealth of the public.[22] At the same time, however, it is assumed that people will adjust their behaviour perfectly to changes in the rate of inflation. As may readily be seen, even in a model with only two assets (securities and real capital), an unexpected change in inflation can have cumulative effects which on the other hand are not taken into account by Feldstein. What is more important, however, is that the conclusion that savings are automatically absorbed appears closely linked with the fundamental lack of an investment behaviour function, since investment does not appear to be dependent on a certain minimum level of profit. If on the other hand, in a steady-state model, it is assumed that investors wish to achieve a profit slightly higher than the current interest rate, i.e. regard their rate of return as a premium on that interest rate, then the conclusion is that there is no longer a continuous relationship between capital intensity and public debt. In this case, if the aim is to maintain price stability and full employment, there will be only one public-sector deficit compatible with the return desired by entrepreneurs.

The only economic policy capable of influencing accumulation and income under these circumstances is one in which the rate of return demanded by entrepreneurs is modified by interest rate management.[23] Thus, as always, economic policy conclusions may vary considerably with reference to different hypotheses. What needs to be stressed, however, leaving aside these formal aspects connected with the characters of steady-state models, is the fact that belief in the decisive importance of the savings ratio ends up by forming the basis of a whole theoretical construction. The importance attached to the savings ratio in the debate on economic policy options is demonstrated by the amount of research devoted to it by scholars of widely differing views.[24] But it is certainly difficult to accept the idea that excess saving is necessarily reflected in an increase in accumulation in the sense of an increase in plant and machinery. In this connection it has been pointed out[25] that if we are thinking of how a monetary economy works, the constraints on the expansion of production are, for reasons of technology and preference, linked to monetary rather than real factors. Experience suggests that every production unit is rigidly linked to the characteristics of the project from which it derives. The level of production corresponding to the minimum cost is therefore, for each unit, determined strictly in relation to the relative price structure of the factors of production. If this changes, so necessarily do the production levels at which optimum plant utilization can be achieved. In this sense there is always, when relative prices change, a certain degree of unutilized productive capacity in the economic system or, to put it differently, a 'natural' level of production. This can be altered, not by a change in the savings ratio but by altering the return expected by entrepreneurs so as to make new investment attractive.

What becomes a central factor in the long term is the position of the banking system, seen as a group of economic agents maximizing profit.

In this case, if we assume with Keynes that the financing of investment – 'the finance motive'[26] – is no more than a special instance of financing of the production process, although it has the distinguishing characteristic of being subject to particular fluctuations, the banking system's liquidity preference becomes decisive. The increase in liquidity required by firms' planned investments – where there is an excess of demand over the supply available from private savers – may bring about an increase in the interest rate, which discourages investment if new securities are issued. If on the other hand, given the banking system's liquidity preference, there is scope for the expansion of credit, the interest rate does not increase and the planned investments can accordingly be made.[27]

VI CONCLUSIONS

The conclusion is therefore that the banking system has the effect of influencing investment decisions through its system of preferences. Different levels of investment can be financed, for a given level of savings, when these preferences change. Leaving aside the observations to which these reflections lead, what should be pointed out is that the monetary root of Keynesian analysis is significant for its capacity to demonstrate the functioning of the economic system with reference to the concrete structure of production processes. Such processes require financing in order to start up, as well as when a decision is taken to expand them. Savings and investment decisions should therefore be seen in this context rather than in one of a system of atemporal exchanges[28] or steady-state growth in an aggregate growth model. Consideration of the monetary aspects of production processes is the way in which Keynesian theory, using a level of analysis which 'chooses' to base itself on postulates that are 'limitative' in relation to those of the theory of general economic equilibrium, succeeds in maintaining a considerable explanatory capacity in respect of reality.[29] This capacity is obviously something different from its empirical checks. These are legitimate where they are conducted, bearing in mind the assumptions of the theory and the phenomena it attempts to explain. This is obviously true of all the 'coherent' theoretical systems the economist has at his disposal.

In the Keynesian case when, as in the last few years, events occur to which the theory does not seem applicable, it is necessary to consider the extent of its validity, or better, the extent of its explanatory capacities. If this method of interpretation is adopted, it becomes more difficult to take opposite sides in support of one theoretical approach or the other. Nor is it particularly sensible to ask oneself whether Keynesian policies have failed and should be replaced by other policies, whether monetarist or not. The question can be tackled more correctly at the methodological level – leaving aside more or less faithful interpretations of Keynes's suggestions[30] – by checking the adequacy of the assumptions and limitative postulates with regard to the reality to be represented. Where such a check leads to a negative conclusion, the problem is not necessarily one of referring to a different theoretical paradigm. What is certainly still relevant in Keynes today, to use another of Tobin's expressions and leaving out of consideration for a moment the specific iterations between the variables in his theoretical model, is the decision to develop analysis of the functioning of the economic system taking into account its structural characteristics. It is precisely this 'pre-analytical' circumstance which accounts for the importance given, in the Keynesian order, to investment decisions seen as the 'motor' of the system. If this aspect is disregarded it is easy to arrive at the opposite conclusions (cf. Feldstein, 1981) and attribute a decisive function in accumulation to savings. If, however, we bear in mind that the changes that have for some time been taking place in the industrialized economies are connected with a process of transition from one technological path to another, with inevitable consequences for the allocation of resources, it may also be thought that the increase in public-sector deficits is not necessarily and exclusively linked to generalized adoption of Keynesian policies but is also in part a reflection of the complex situation with regard to the adjustment and reallocation of production. Supply-side policies take account of this aspect when they emphasize the importance of growth in reducing the deficit and refer to basic instruments for the reallocation of resources, such as the price of factors of production, but not when they give prominence to the function of savings in accumulation. Whilst the immediate problems of the public debt remain urgent and should therefore be tackled, there is a considerable amount of work to be done at both the theoretical and applied levels on the problems of economic stabilization in the medium term.

NOTES

1 This, for example, is the view of the prestigious International Monetary Fund; its managing director believes that in the present economic situation the public-sector deficit has definitely negative effects which should be mitigated by spending cuts or increases in taxation (Larosière, 1982).

2 The importance and urgency of this question for Italy has given rise to considerable discussion on the advisability of a degree of monetization of the public debt (cf. Spaventa, 1984; 1985; Arcelli, 1985; Valiani, 1985).

3 Tobin (1985). Similar conclusions are reached by Phelps (1982) who, in drawing attention to the crisis in demand-side policies, also points out the limitations of the monetarist approach and therefore the state of crisis in macro-economic theory.

4 The hypothesis of rational expectations, which has received its most carefully worked out and thorough application in the work of Lucas (1981), is essentially a theoretical tool for eliminating at the root the implicit assumption of instability of the economic system that is the basis of the Keynesian order. If, as Modigliani (1977) maintained, the difference between monetarists and Keynesians ultimately lies in their opposing views on the intrinsic stability of the economic system, there is no doubt that Lucas's work constitutes a convincing attack on Keynesian theory (cf. Spaventa, 1982; Vercelli, 1983; Vicarelli, 1985).

5 Tobin (1985) comments temperately that supply-side economics has been identified with a number of absurd theories and forecasts. Qualitatively what is involved is a renewed emphasis on earlier themes: the importance of incentives and rewards for savings and labour. For a comprehensive evaluation of supply-side economics see Cozzi (1982).

6 This view tallies with the studies on the responsiveness of savings to the return offered on them begun in the work of Boskin (1978). Similar results are to be found in the recent work of Summers (1984).

7 Lindbeck (1983) expresses his opposition to tax increases as a means of controlling the deficit from an entirely different standpoint. He believes that increased taxation has the effect of triggering off wage increases and subsequently inflationary pressures.

8 Indeed, a restrictive monetary policy, with its consequence of high interest rates, is regarded as appropriate by Mundell because of the positive effects of an appreciation of the exchange rate in relation to domestic prices. At the same time an expansionary fiscal policy implemented by means of tax cuts would allow the increase in demand needed to increase income (Mundell, 1975).

9 The effect of reducing taxation on employment and income is examined by Corden (1981).

10 It is sufficient in this connection to cite, for example, the quantity of public debate on the subject (see, for example, Federal Reserve Bank of Boston, 1983a, 1983b; Conference Board, 1983).

11 This view is opposed on the same front by both Keynesians and the supporters of complete crowding out, such as Buchanan and Wagner (1977).

12 An extension of this position consists in regarding intergenerational maximizing behaviour as having the effect of cancelling out even the crowding-out effects of social security on private savings (cf. Aaron, 1982).

13 The main studies on the subjects are by Kochin (1974), David and Scadding (1974) and Kormendi (1983). A critical examination of some of these studies is given by Tobin and Buiter (1979) and Tobin (1980, ch. 3). The theoretical debate on Barro's theorem is still extremely lively – among the most recent contributions are those by Carmichael (1982) and McCallum (1984).

14 His most important research has recently been collected together in one volume (Feldstein, 1983).

15 In Tobin and Buiter's (1980) model the conclusion is that an increase (not a reduction) in the tax rate promotes the formation of capital, even if it is inflationary. The question of the long-term effects of fiscal policy is taken up by Tobin (1979; 1980, ch. 3).

16 On the empirical adequacy of the models of supply-side economics, see Thurow (1983).

17 Boskin (1978). In this work Boskin shows a significant responsiveness of consumption in relation to total disposable income (net of tax), wealth and unemployment rate, as well as to the interest rate (net of tax), for the period 1934–69. In particular, according to his calculations, a 1 per cent increase in the interest rate implies a 1 per cent increase in the savings ratio.

18 Gylfason (1981). Gylfason finds a very similar effect to that of Boskin, with reference to data up to 1970 (see also Feldstein and Tsiang, 1968).

19 This is the theory of Howrey and Hymans (1978).

20 This is the conclusion reached by Evans on Summers' results (see Summers, 1981; Evans, 1983).

21 The assumption that the issue of securities increases net wealth has different consequences depending on whether the public, in an attempt to adjust its portfolio, reacts by increasing its stocks of money or real capital. In the Keynesian case securities and real capital are assumed not to be close substitutes for each other; the result is a crowding-out effect which, however, allows income to increase (by virtue of the increased expenditure associated with income received in the form of interest) (cf. Blinder and Solow, 1973). In the monetarist case, the increased volume of securities gives rise to increased demand for liquid balances which, for a given supply of money, produces a fall in income. Friedman (1978) pointed out that the question is linked to empirical checking of the extent to which money and/or real capital are the closest substitutes for public debt.

22 David and Scadding (1974) reached the same conclusions as Barro on the basis of the constancy of savings *vis-à-vis* GNP. If the savings ratio remains constant while the proportion of public expenditure to GNP has increased, private individuals must have increased their savings. Evidently they consider that public investment is in fact replacing private investment.

23 These relations are set out in a simple form by Solow (1970), on the basis of a function which links the debt to income ratio (m) to the capital to output ratio (v) and of a demand for debt which is a function of the capital to output ratio and the rate of return on capital, less the real cost of loans. In this case if h is public consumption and g is the natural rate of growth, then:

$$m = \frac{(1-h)s}{(1-s)g} - \frac{v}{1-s}$$

At the same time:

$$m = m(v, r - i + p)$$

For a certain desired v^* (which corresponds to the return sought by entrepreneurs) there will be a single value of m compatible both with it and price stability.

24 An interesting survey, with particular reference to economic policy questions, is given by Bosworth (1984).

25 This point is mentioned by Kregel (1984).

26 The debate between Keynes, Ohlin and Robertson on the 'finance motive' in the *Economic Journal* of 1937 brings out that it is at all events the

banking system which has to provide the increase in liquidity necessary to business activity. This point is made by Kregel (1984, 148).

27 A somewhat different view of this problem is taken by Asimakopulos (1983) and Graziani (1983; 1984) who distinguish between a circuit relating to savers and enterprises and one relating to banks and enterprises.

28 In this sense and in this respect it may be thought that Keynesian analysis does not tie in very well with the approach involved in the theory of general economic equilibrium, as suggested by disequilibrium analyses. This naturally does not imply that the Keynesian system is not a system of interdependences (cf. Paganetto, 1982).

29 The expression 'limitative' postulates is to be understood in the sense of Hempel, as the adoption of a series of propositions which, by reducing the universality of certain propositions within the same theoretical body, have the effect of permitting a connection with experiential data which can be difficult or impossible for a completely axiomatized system (Hempel, 1952).

30 It is, however, interesting to note on this point, as has recently been emphasized, that support for global demand was, for Keynes, above all support for investments (cf. Cozzi, 1983, 21 *et seq.*; Kregel, 1985).

REFERENCES

Aaron, H. 1982: *Economic Effects of Social Security*, Brookings Institution, Washington DC.

Arcelli, M. 1984: Deficit pubblico e svolta monetaria, *Economia Italiana,* Supplemento, no. 2, June, 29–44.

Arcelli, M. 1985: Public deficit and monetary course change in Italy since 1981, *Zeitschriftfuer Wirtschafts und Sozialwissenschaften*, 2–3.

Asimakopulos, A.1983: Kalecki and Keynes on finance, investment and saving, *Cambridge Journal of Economics*, 7, 221–34.

Barro, R. 1974: Are government bonds net wealth?, *Journal of Political Economy*, 82, 1045–1117.

Bartlett, B. 1985: Supply-side economics: theory and evidence, *National Westminster Bank Quarterly Review*, February.

Blinder, A. and Solow, R. 1973: Does fiscal policy matter?, *Journal of Public Economics*, 2, 314–37.

Boskin, M. 1978: Taxation, saving and the rate of interest, *Journal of Political Economy*, 86, 3–27.

Bosworth, B.P. 1984: *Tax Incentives and Economic Growth*, Brookings Institution, Washington DC.

Buchanan J. and Wagner, R.E. 1977: *Democracy in Deficit*, Academic Press, New York.

Buiter, W.H. 1984: *Allocative and Stabilization Aspects of Budgetary and Fiscal Policies*, Inaugural Lecture, London School of Economics.

Carmichael, J. 1982: On Barro's theorem of debt neutrality: the irrelevance of net wealth, *American Economic Review*, 72, 202–13, March.

Conference Board 1983: *Towards a Reconstruction of Federal Budgeting.*

Corden, M.W. 1981: Taxation, real wage rigidity and employment, *Economic Journal*, 91, 309–30.

Cozzi, T. 1982: La 'supply-side economics', *Rivista di Politica Economica,* June 1982, 583–613.

Cozzi, T. 1983: Keynes su disoccupazione, inflazione e spesa pubblica. In *Keynes*, Piemonte vivo ricerche.

David, P.A. and Scadding, J.L. 1974: Private saving: ultrarationality, aggregation and Denison's law, *Journal of Political Economy*, 82, 225–50, March.

Evans, O.J. 1983: Tax policy, the interest elasticity of saving and accumulation: numerical analysis of theoretical models, *American Economic Review*, 73, 398–410.

Federal Reserve Bank of Boston 1983a: *Conference on Government Deficits and the Economy*, Boston.

Federal Reserve Bank of Boston 1983b: *Conference on the Trend and Measurement of the Structural Deficit*, Boston.

Feldstein, M. 1980: Fiscal policies, inflation and capital formation, *American Economic Review*, 70, 636–50.

Feldstein, M. 1981: The retreat from Keynesian economics, *Public Interest*, 64, 92–105.

Feldstein, M. 1983: *Inflation, Tax Rules and Capital Formation*, University of Chicago Press, Chicago.

Feldstein, M. and Tsiang, J.C. 1968: The interest rate, taxation and the personal savings incentive, *Quarterly Journal of Economics*, August.

Friedman, B. 1978: Crowding out or crowding in? Economic consequences of financing government deficits, *Brookings Papers on Economic Activity*, 3.

Graziani, A. 1983: Aspetti monetari della teoria di Keynes. In *Keynes*, Piemonte vivo ricerche.

Graziani, A. 1984: Note sull'efficacia della politica monetaria. In *Moneta ed economia nazionale*, Piemonte vivo ricerche.

Gylfason, T. 1981: Interest rates, inflation and the aggregate consumption function, *Review of Economics and Statistics*, 63, 232–45.

Hempel, C. 1952: *Fundamentals of Concept Formation in Empirical Science*, University of Chicago Press, Chicago.

Howrey, E. and Hymans, S. 1978: The measurement and determination of loanable funds savings, *Brookings Papers on Economic Activity*, 3.

Kochin, L.A. 1974: Are future taxes anticipated by consumers?, *Journal of Money, Credit and Banking*, 6, 385–94.

Kormendi, R.C. 1983: Government debt, government spending and private sector behavior, *American Economic Review*, 73, 994–1011.

Kregel, J.A. 1984: Constraints on the expansion of output and employment: real or monetary?, *Journal of Post Keynesian Economics*, 2, 134–52.

Kregel, J.A. 1985: Budget deficits, stabilization policy and liquidity preference. In F. Vicarelli (ed.) *Keynes' Relevance Today*, Macmillan, London.

Larosière, J. de, 1982: Restoring fiscal discipline. A vital element for economic recovery, *International Monetary Fund*, Washington DC, March.

Lindbeck, A. 1983: Budget expansion and cost inflation, *American Economic Review, Papers and Proceedings,* no. 2, May, pp. 285–90.

Lucas, R.E. Jr. 1981: *Studies in Business Cycle Theory*, MIT Press, Cambridge, MA.

McCallum, B.T. 1984: Are bond financed deficits inflationary? A Ricardian analysis, *Journal of Political Economy*, 92, 123–35.

Modigliani, F. 1977: The monetarist controversy, or should we forsake stabilization policies?, *American Economic Review*, 67, 1–9.

Mundell, R. 1975: Inflation from an international viewpoint. In D. Meiselman and A. Laffer (eds) *The Phenomenon of Worldwide Inflation*, American Enterprise Institute, Washington DC.

Paganetto, L. 1982: *La teoria generale e i post-keynesiani*, Liguori, Napoli.

Phelps, E.S. 1982: Cracks on the demand side: a year of crisis in theoretical macroeconomics, *American Economic Review*, 72, 2, 378–81.

Solow, R. 1970: *Growth Theory. An Exposition*, Oxford University Press, Oxford.

Spaventa, L. 1982: Una svolta a U nella teoria economica. In *Scritti in onore di I. Gasparini*, Giuffrè, Milano.

Spaventa, L. 1984: The growth of public debt in Italy: past experience, perspectives and policy problems, *Banca Nazionale del Lavoro Quarterly Review*, June.

Spaventa, L. 1985: Adjustment plans, fiscal policy and monetary policy, *Review of Economic Conditions in Italy*, Banco di Roma.

Summers, L.H. 1981: Capital taxation and accumulation in a life-cycle growth model, *American Economic Review*, 71, 533–44.

Summers, L.H. 1984: The after-tax rate of return affects private savings, *American Economic Review*, 72, 249–53.

Thurow, L. 1983: *Dangerous Currents. The State of Economics*, Random House, New York.

Tobin, J. 1965: Money and economic growth, *Econometrica*, 33, 671–84.

Tobin, J. 1979: Spending and crowding out in shorter and longer runs. In H. Greenfield (ed.) *Economic Theory for Economic Efficiency. Essays in Honor of A.P. Lerner*, MIT Press, Cambridge, MA.

Tobin J. 1980: *Asset Accumulation and Economic Activity*, Blackwell, Oxford.

Tobin, J. 1985: La teoria macroeconomica in discussione, *Bancaria*, 1, 13.

Tobin, J. and Buiter, W. 1979: Debt neutrality: a brief review of doctrine and evidence. In G.M. von Furstemberg (ed.) *Social Security Versus Private Saving*, Ballinger, Cambridge, MA.

Tobin, J. and Buiter, W. 1980: Fiscal and monetary policies, capital formation and economic activity. In G.M. von Furstemberg, (ed.) *The Government and Capital Formation*, Ballinger, Cambridge, MA.

US Department of the Treasury 1984: *The Effects of Deficits on Prices of Financial Assets: Theory and Evidence*, Washington DC.

US Department of the Treasury 1985: *The Reagan Economic Program*, Washington DC, February.

Valiani R. 1985: What solutions are there to Italy's public debt? *Review of Economic Conditions in Italy*, Banco di Roma, 1.

Vercelli A. 1983: Anti-Lucas, ovvero la 'Nuova economia classica' e la rivoluzione keynesiana. In *Keynes*, Peimonte vivo ricerche.

Vicarelli, F. 1985: Leggi di natura e di politica economica: considerazioni sui fondamenti della nuova macroeconomia classica, *Politica Economica*, 1, 7–36.

Wanniski, J. 1978: *The Way the World Works: How Economics Fails and Succeeds*, Basic Books, New York.

13

Some Implications of Deficit-financed Tax Cuts: These Will Always Increase Demand, but Will They Reduce Supply?

WALTER ELTIS

I INTRODUCTION

It was widely argued in the 1970s and the 1980s that macro-economic policies would function more effectively in a country which was enjoying the benefits of falling taxation, than in one where taxes were rising.[1] It is uncontroversial that tax cuts with parallel reductions in public expenditure to produce a neutral overall effect on the budget should have some favourable effects on supply. But some supporters of supply side economics have gone further and argued that taxes can be cut as an element in macro-economic policy, even in the absence of parallel reductions in public expenditure.[2] They believe that tax cuts which produce an initial deterioration in the budget may involve no widening of the deficit in the medium term if their eventual favourable effects on supply are sufficient.

There is the additional and distinct possibility that tax cuts might be an ideal element in policies to expand an underemployed economy towards its equilibrium employment rate without the accelerating inflation that Keynesian policies might otherwise involve, because the inflationary impact of their tendency to raise effective demand may be counterbalanced by their favourable impact on the rates at which wages and prices increase,[3] for if tax rates are cut, wages and prices will be able to rise less and still provide workers and companies with the growth of net of tax incomes that they have come to expect.

The key question which must be answered before the viability of such short-term tax cutting policies to reduce unemployment can be assessed is the nature of any beneficial long-term effects on supply. If these are sufficient, then tax cuts which expand an economy rapidly in the short term might not produce unsustainable deficits in the medium term. The next section of this chapter will therefore be concerned with the long-term effects of tax cuts on supply. After that the question of whether deficit-financed tax cuts can be used to provide an expeditious cure for unemployment without adverse long-term real and financial effects will be considered. The United States cut taxes sharply after 1980, and then raised employment rapidly and reduced inflation at the same time, but a variety of adverse pressures are now emanating from the consequent structural deficit. The chapter will conclude with a few words about the possible relevance of the argument to the American case.

II THE LONG-TERM BENEFITS FROM LOWER TAXATION

As this section is concerned with the *long-term* influence of lower taxation, an economy with the labour market continually in equilibrium and unemployment therefore always at the natural rate will be assumed. Initially it will also be supposed that the budget is balanced so that the favourable supply-side effects of lower taxation are not being partly offset by unfavourable crowding-out effects from the higher interest rates that might accompany extra government borrowing.

Lower rates of taxation will have a variety of possible effects on supply in a fully employed economy with a balanced budget, and there is an enormous range of literature which bears on this subject.[4] Lower taxation will influence the supply of labour and capital and of other factors of production. It will influence the efficiency of resource allocation, and attitudes to risk. Out of these, attention will be focused here on the influence of lower rates of taxation on the supply of labour and capital, and through these on the level of capacity output and therefore the long-term tax base. Other influences, on the efficiency of resource allocation, on risk taking, and on the supply and quality of entrepreneurship may matter more in the longest of long runs, but they are exceedingly difficult to model. The effects of taxation on the supplies of labour and capital are in contrast mainstream problems which have received a great deal of attention.

It will be assumed that there is a uniform rate of tax of T on all incomes,[5] a uniform elasticity of labour supply of N_s and a uniform elasticity of demand for labour of N_d if employment is always at its equilibrium rate, and the (growing) capital stock is given at each point of time. N_d will be close to but not equal to the elasticity of substitution between labour and capital. With these assumptions, the formula for $E_{L/T}$, the elasticity of equilibrium employment with respect to percentage point changes in the rate of taxation is[6]

$$E_{L/T} = -\frac{1}{1-T}\,\frac{1}{1/N_s - 1/N_d} \qquad (13.1)$$

This may be positive or negative depending on whether the elasticity of labour supply is positive or negative; that is, lower taxation may be associated with a higher or lower equilibrium level of employment. N_d, the elasticity of demand for labour, will always be negative, and $E_{L/T}$, the elasticity of equilibrium employment with respect to the rate of taxation, is certain to be negative (that is, lower taxation will be associated with higher employment) if N_s, the elasticity of supply of labour, is positive. Recent United States evidence appears to indicate that the elasticity of supply of male workers may be close to zero while the supply of female workers reacts positively to net of tax real wages with the result that the overall elasticity of supply of labour, N_s, may perhaps be of the order of +0.15.[7] If the elasticity of demand for labour is −0.75 (values of the elasticity of substitution between labour and capital of between 0.5 and 1.0 have been widely found,[8] then $E_{L/T}$, the elasticity of employment with respect to the rate of taxation will be $-0.125[1/(1 - T)]$, so that a 1 percentage point tax cut will raise the equilibrium level of market sector employment by only 0.14 percentage points where the rate of tax is 10 per cent, and by just 0.21 percentage points where it is 40 per cent, in which case a 5 percentage point tax cut would raise the supply of labour a mere 1 per cent. Thus the rate of tax will generally have little influence on the economy via increases in the equilibrium supply of labour at full employment – unless N_s is far larger than recent empirical work suggests.

There is one qualification to this negative result which may sometimes be important. At very high rates of taxation, for instance 90 per cent, even modest elasticities of labour supply, of the kind so far assumed, will have quite considerable effects. Thus at 90 per cent taxation, a 1 percentage point tax cut will raise the supply of labour by as much as 1.25 per cent, even if the elasticity of supply of labour is only +0.15. Average tax rates are rarely as high as 90 per cent, but marginal tax rates may often be as high as this in a complex tax and social security system, so there may indeed be instances where reductions in such extremely high rates have significant supply side effects. With the present arithmetic, a 5 percentage point tax cut from 90 to 85 per cent would raise equilibrium employment by over 6 per cent which is by no means an insignificant effect. But, in general, the supply-side benefits from lower taxation will be modest so far as the supply of labour is concerned. What of the supply of capital? Are larger benefits to be expected there?

The most straightforward assumptions to make about aggregate saving are that all net saving is private, and that this depends on permanent private incomes and upon the real rate of interest that savers receive. It can be assumed for simplicity that permanent incomes will be reduced, *pari passu*, by proportional taxation at rate T which is expected to be levied indefinitely, and that where the budget is balanced the level of T will not influence the net of tax rate of interest that savers receive.[9] Then total saving as a ratio of the national income, s, will always equal $(1 - T)s_p$, where s_p is the propensity to save permanent incomes.[10] If an economy has an exogenously given long-term or 'natural' rate of growth of g_n, its capital to output ratio will always tend towards s/g_n which equals $(1 - T)s_p/g_n$.[11] As the capital to output ratio will therefore be proportional to $(1 - T)$, any tax cuts which reduce T will raise the equilibrium capital to output ratio correspondingly.

With the customary neoclassical assumptions, if the elasticity of output with respect to the real capital stock is α (that is, if a 1 per cent increase in the capital stock raises output α per cent), then a 1 per cent increase in the capital stock will raise the capital to output ratio $(1 - \alpha)$ per cent. Thus a rise in the capital to output ratio of 1 per cent, that is, a rise in $(1 - T)s_p/g_n$ by 1 per cent, will be associated with a rise in the capital stock of $1/(1 - \alpha)$ per cent. It follows from this that the formula for $E_{K/T}$, the elasticity of the capital stock with respect to percentage point changes in the rate of tax is

$$E_{K/T} = -\frac{1}{1-T}\frac{1}{1-\alpha} \qquad (13.2)$$

If α is 0.33, then the elasticity of the capital stock with respect to the rate of taxation will be $-1\frac{1}{2}[1/(1 - T)]$, so that a 1 percentage point cut in the rate of tax will raise the capital stock 1.67 per cent where the rate of taxation is 10 per cent, by $2\frac{1}{2}$ per cent where it is 40 per cent, and by 15 per cent where it is 90 per cent. The assumption that the elasticity of output with respect to the capital stock is 0.33 is in no way ambitious or controversial, and it will be evident that this suggests an elasticity of the capital stock with respect to the rate of tax which is quite considerable. Thus, at 40 per cent taxation, it appeared that a 1 percentage point tax cut might raise the supply of labour by only around 0.2 per cent, but it might well raise the capital stock in due course by as much as $2\frac{1}{2}$ per cent.

Equation 13.1 showed the elasticity of employment with respect to the rate of tax, and equation 13.2 the elasticity of the capital stock with respect to this. But what is of most interest is the elasticity of the equilibrium level of *output* with respect to the rate of tax, because this will show the full supply-side effects from the increase in both the labour force and the capital stock which are consequent on lower rates of taxation. The elasticity of real output with respect to percentage point changes in the rate of tax, $E_{\mathrm{Y/T}}$, as a consequence of the tendency of tax cuts to raise both the capital stock and the labour force, will be α, the elasticity of output with respect to the capital stock times the increase in this, plus β, the elasticity of output with respect to the labour force times the increase in this. Thus, using equations 13.1 and 13.2

$$E_{\mathrm{Y/T}} = -\frac{1}{1-T}\left[\frac{\alpha}{1-\alpha} + \frac{\beta}{1/N_{\mathrm{s}} - 1/N_{\mathrm{d}}}\right] \qquad (13.3)$$

With a constant returns production function β will be 0.67, that is, a 1 per cent increase in the labour force will raise output 0.67 per cent, if α is 0.33; and if N_{s} is +0.15 and N_{d} is −0.75, the elasticity of output with respect to the rate of tax will become $-0.5825[1/(1-T)]$. It is to be noted that with these assumed values which are intended to be plausible, the contribution of extra labour to output as a result of the supply-side effects of lower taxation is $0.0825[1/1-T)]$, while the contribution of extra capital is six times as great at $0.50[1/(1-T)]$, the combined effect of both together being to raise output by $0.5825\,[1/(1-T)]$ per cent for each percentage point cut in the uniform rate of tax. The assumptions about the elasticities which produce these results are of course arbitrary, but few would wish to assume the far greater elasticity of labour supply which would be needed to disturb the result that the supply-side benefits from lower taxation as a result of the larger capital stock this should induce will be of an altogether greater order of magnitude than those from a larger labour force.

The implications of the proposition that lower taxation should be associated with higher equilibrium output, mainly because there will be a larger capital stock, but also because there will be an increased labour force, are important. This is because all increases in output raise the economy's tax base, for taxation can be levied on the extra wages and profits that result from additions to output. A percentage point tax cut may raise output by something like $0.5825\,[1/(1-T)]$ per cent if the values of the various elasticities are close to those suggested, and the supply-side benefits of tax cuts can indeed produce more extra revenue in due course than the tax cuts themselves cost initially. In the present example, if the rate of tax is cut from 75 to 74 per cent, output will grow by 2.33 per cent from say 100 to 102.33, and 0.74 times 102.33 – 75.72 which exceeds 0.75 times 100, so once the supply-side effects of cutting taxation from 75 to 74 per cent are taken into account, it emerges that the government will actually obtain more revenue with 74 per cent taxation than with 75 per cent.

It can be said in general that if there are any supply-side effects at all, a 1 percentage point tax cut will always reduce the real resources available to governments by less than 1 per cent of the national income, while a 1 percentage point tax increase will always bring in less extra revenue than 1 per cent of the national income at the time the tax increase was imposed. The general relationship between tax rates and total tax revenues can be derived very straightforwardly from $E_{Y/T}$, the elasticity of the real national income with respect to the rate of taxation. Thus

$$Y = Y_0(1 - T)^{-(1-T)E_{Y/T}} \tag{13.4}$$

where Y_0 is the real national income with employment at the natural rate and zero taxation. Total tax revenue, R, will be T times Y, so that

$$R = TY_0(1 - T)^{-(1-T)E_{Y/T}} \tag{13.5}$$

These equations allow the real national income and total tax revenues to be estimated at different rates of tax for any given value of $E_{Y/T}$.

In table 13.1 these are set out for an elasticity of real output with respect to the rate of tax of $-0.5825[1/(1 - T)]$, the value of this that results when the values of the elasticities are those previously assumed.

Table 13.1 *The rate of tax, real national income, total tax revenue and the national income net of taxation where $\alpha = 0.33$, $\beta = 0.67$, $N_s = +0.15$ and $N_d = -0.75$*

Rate of tax %	*National income* $(\times Y_0)$	*Tax revenue* $(\times Y_0)$	*Income net of tax* $(\times Y_0)$
0	1.0000	0	1.0000
10	0.9404	0.0940	0.8464
20	0.8779	0.1756	0.7023
30	0.8122	0.2436	0.5686
40	0.7423	0.2969	0.4454
50	0.6674	0.3337	0.3337
60	0.5860	0.3516	0.2344
62.5	0.5643	0.35269	0.2116
63.16	0.5585	0.35275	0.2058
64	0.5510	0.35266	0.1983
70	0.4954	0.3460	0.1486
80	0.3911	0.3129	0.0782
90	0.2610	0.2349	0.0261
95	0.1742	0.1655	0.0087
99	0.0681	0.0674	0.0007

It will be seen that with these assumed values, total tax revenue rises at first as the rate of tax is increased, and reaches a maximum when the rate of tax is 63.16 per cent, after which it begins to fall.

The relationship which the table describes, where increases in rates of tax first increase and then reduce total tax revenue, and where all actual revenues apart from maximum revenue can be obtained with two alternative rates of tax (for instance, a revenue of 25 per cent of Y_0 can be obtained with either a tax rate of approximately 30 per cent, or one of around 88 per cent) is of course the Laffer curve.[12]

There will be a Laffer relationship of the kind illustrated in the table with all possible values of the elasticities (provided that the elasticity of labour supply is positive and not negative), and it follows from equations 13.3 and 13.5 that the formula for the revenue maximizing rate of tax is

$$\frac{\delta R}{\delta T} = 0 \quad \text{where } T = 1 \Big/ \left(1 + \frac{\alpha}{1-\alpha} + \frac{\beta}{1/N_s - 1/N_d}\right) \qquad (13.6)$$

This will always be less than 1 provided that N_s is positive and N_d negative, and with the present assumed values of α, β, N_s and N_d, the formula produces a revenue maximizing tax rate of 63.16 per cent. If the only supply-side benefits from lower taxation were those that follow from the favourable effects of lower taxation on the supply of labour, and N_s was indeed as low as +0.15, then the revenue maximizing rate of tax would be as high as 92.31 per cent (found by making α zero in the formula). If attention is focused instead on the far more important tendency for lower taxation to raise the savings ratio and thus to increase capital per worker and the capital to output ratio, while the effect of lower taxation on the supply of labour is ignored then the revenue maximizing rate (found by making β zero) will be 66.67 per cent. The two supply-side effects in combination produce a revenue maximizing tax rate of 63.16 per cent.

Two aspects of these conclusions must be emphasized. The first is that these results have rested on the assumption of the continuous achievement of equilibrium output with unemployment always at the natural rate, and in addition balanced budgets. Nothing has been said about the time required to obtain the full supply-side benefits from lower taxation. It may in fact take many generations before the capital to output ratio settles at the s/g_n which has been assumed, for this is the capital to output ratio in a steady state, and full adjustment of the capital to output ratio to the savings ratio will be a slow process.[13] The labour supply should adjust quite rapidly to higher net of tax incomes, but the principal supply-side benefits from lower taxation arise via the capital to output ratio where adjustment may be gradual. Therefore all that can be said is that where comparisons between steady states are made, which is what the table illustrates, economies with higher rates of tax will not enjoy extra real government revenues in anything approaching the same proportion. Economies with higher tax rates may only enjoy slightly higher real revenues, while market financed spending will often be vastly lower. But this will only be the case in long-run comparisons.

The second important caveat is one which follows from the assumption of balanced budgets. Countries will not be able to obtain the full long-term benefits from lower taxation by merely cutting rates of tax. A country on the second stage of the Laffer curve, with a tax rate in excess of the revenue maximizing one, will actually obtain a 'free lunch' by cutting taxation. In this situation reductions in tax rates will raise total tax revenues, so the budget can actually be improved while real government spending is increased and net of tax real incomes are raised. But in general, and in most economies, taxation will be below the revenue maximizing rate. So if the balanced budget assumption is to be retained, a lower rate of tax will only be feasible if real government spending is reduced at the same time.

As will be shown in detail in the next section where the long-term implications of *deficit-financed* tax cuts will be analysed, any attempt to reduce taxation without corresponding expenditure cuts will only produce a fraction of the supply-side benefits which have been set out. This is because they will raise the supply of labour *but reduce the supply of capital*. If there is lower taxation at full employment and these lower tax rates are expected to continue indefinitely, permanent private incomes will be higher with the result that private consumption will expand, and if consumption rises while the capital stock is at first unchanged, aggregate saving must fall. More marketed output will be consumed, but with an unchanged capital stock (and only the slight increase in labour supply that the previous argument suggests) little extra marketed output will be produced, so less marketed output than before will be saved and invested. In consequence the savings ratio in the economy's market sector will fall with the result that capital per worker, output per worker and the capital to output ratio will all become lower than they would have been in the absence of deficit-financed supply-side tax cuts. As the strongest favourable supply-side effects of lower taxation appear to follow from its tendency to raise the savings ratio, it follows that tax cuts unaccompanied by expenditure reductions will generally reduce aggregate supply and therefore the long-term tax base.

This does not mean that deficit financed tax cuts have no role to play in supply-side policies. Tax cuts financed through budget deficits may be handicaps so far as long-term growth is concerned, but they may be important for the rapid achievement of full employment.

III THE USE OF SUPPLY-SIDE TAX CUTS TO ACCELERATE TRANSITIONS TO FULL EMPLOYMENT WITHOUT ADVERSE EFFECTS ON INFLATION

Supply-side reflationary policies seek to make use of tax cuts with two objects in mind. In so far as these reduce prices, full employment may be approachable without the acceleration of inflation that is otherwise to be expected. In addition, tax cuts should raise effective demand in the traditional Keynesian manner (though less so than equal increases in public expenditure). The combined influence of a moderation of inflation and a stimulus to real demand can obviously be extremely helpful to the pace and sustainability of economic recovery.

Because their advocates expect supply-side policies to reduce inflation, they believe there is no accompanying need to raise the rate of growth of the money supply, so they hope to avoid this vulnerable aspect of traditional Keynesian policies. These lines of argument will now be developed.

To focus particular attention on the supply-side effects of the tax ratio, it will be assumed that real public expenditure grows at the economy's natural growth rate, g_n, and that the budget will be balanced at full employment at a uniform rate of tax of T_n. Total public expenditure is therefore T_nY_n, where Y_n is the national income with employment at the natural rate. It is assumed that there is initially unemployment in excess of the natural rate, and inflation in excess of p^*, the target inflation rate, but the tax ratio is assumed to be T_n, the ratio that would produce a full employment balanced budget. This means that if the initial national income (Y_0) is below Y_n, then there will be a budget deficit because taxation will amount only to T_nY_0 which is bound to be less than public expenditure which is always T_nY_n. However, there is no structural deficit because taxation would equal T_nY_n at the existing tax rate of T_n if employment was actually at the natural rate so that output was Y_n.

It can now be supposed that in order to implement supply-side policies to achieve full employment at the target inflation rate, the government reduces the uniform rate of tax by one percentage point in each successive year, and that it maintains an unchanged rate of growth of the money supply, namely the rate calculated to sustain the target inflation rate at full employment.

These successive reductions in the uniform rate of tax will have three main influences upon the economy. First they will reduce the inflation rate by up to 1 per cent in each successive year, in relation to what it would otherwise have been. Second, the expenditure effects of the tax cuts will raise real demand in each successive year. Third, each year in which the tax cutting policy persists will open up a full employment budget deficit of 1 per cent of the national income, so if it takes J years to reach full employment and the target inflation rate, the structural deficit at the end of that period will be J per cent of the national income.

The beneficial effect on the rate of inflation could amount to as much as a full 1 per cent per annum reduction in this with adaptive expectations wage and price equations.[14] If, for instance, there is a wage equation of the general form

$$w = {}_{e}P + {}_{e}q + \delta T_{d} + f_{1}(U_{n} - U) \quad f_{1}' > 0 \tag{13.7}$$

where w is the annual rate of wage increases, ${}_{e}p$ the expected rate of inflation, ${}_{e}q$ the expected rate of increase in *net of tax* living standards, and δT_{d} the annual increase in direct taxation (expressed as a ratio of the national income at factor cost), while U_{n} is the natural rate of unemployment and U actual unemployment, workers will bargain for increases in excess of expected inflation plus the rate of increase in real living standards to which they have become accustomed where unemployment is less than the natural rate, and they will accept less than this where unemployment exceeds the natural rate. A corresponding price equation can be set out as

$$p = w - a + \delta T_{i} + f_{2}(U_{n} - U) \quad f_{2}' > 0 \tag{13.8}$$

where, when unemployment equals the natural rate, p, the rate of price inflation, equal annual money wage increases, *less* a, the annual rate of productivity growth, *plus* δT_{i}, the change in indirect taxes (expressed as a ratio of the national income at factor cost). The simplest adaptive expectations assumption for the expected inflation rate is that this is the actual inflation rate of the previous period, so that ${}_{e}p = p_{-1}$; while for the expected growth of workers' real living standards, it can be supposed that they have previously been able to raise these in line with annual productivity growth, and that this is therefore the rate of increase they have come to expect, so that, ${}_{e}q = a$. With these substitutions

$$p - p_{-1} = \delta T_{d} + \delta T_{i} + f(U_{n} - U) \tag{13.9}$$

so that inflation will accelerate, either if unemployment is below the natural rate which is well known, or (which is less well known) if direct or indirect taxation increases (when previous rises in taxation have not already depressed ${}_eq$, the increase in real living standards which workers have come to expect, below a, the increase which productivity growth actually allows the economy to deliver).

With these equations, annual tax cuts *which are unexpected* will conversely produce deceleration in the rate of inflation. Thus if direct or indirect taxes are reduced by 1 per cent of the national income per annum, workers' real incomes will be able to advance 1 per cent faster than they have come to expect. As a result, money wages will be able to rise 1 per cent less in the next period, and this will mean that prices will rise 1 per cent less which will permit a further cut in the pace of wage increases.

Table 13.2 is an example of the sequence which could follow successive reductions in the uniform rate of tax of 1 per cent per annum. There will be some extra tendency for inflation to fall, because throughout the process set out in the table, unemployment is presumed to exceed the natural rate, and any such excess will have an additional tendency to reduce the annual rate of wage and price increases. Table 13.2 abstracts from this effect and merely outlines the tendency of a succession of supply-side tax cuts to reduce inflation by 1 per cent per annum above such reductions as excess unemployment is producing at the same time.

In table 13.2 it is assumed that productivity growth, a, is a steady 2 per cent per annum, and δT_i the annual change in indirect taxation is -1 in years 1, 2, 3, 4 and 5, the years in which indirect taxes are cut by 1 per cent of the national income, while rates of direct taxation are unchanged. The result is that p, the rate of inflation, falls from an initial 10 per cent in year 0 to 5 per cent in year 5. If direct taxes are

Table 13.2 *The influence of successive annual reductions of 1 per cent of the national income in the rate of indirect taxation*

	Annual percentage increases			
Year	*Increase in wages* $w = p_{-1} + {}_eq$	*Increase in productivity* a	*Increase in taxation* δT_i	*Increase in prices* $p = w - a + \delta T_i$
0	12	2	0	10
1	12	2	−1	9
2	11	2	−1	8
3	10	2	−1	7
4	9	2	−1	6
5	8	2	−1	5
6	7	[illegible]	0	5

reduced instead by 1 per cent of the national income in each of years 1, 2, 3, 4 and 5, while indirect taxation is unchanged, the deceleration of wage and price inflation will be as set out in table 13.3.

Many would consider the sequence of events set out in table 13.2, where it is indirect taxation that is reduced, considerably more plausible. There is widespread agreement that changes in indirect taxation will have a short-term impact on the price level, and that this will have some influence on the expected rate of inflation and therefore on subsequent wage negotiations. The one-for-one impact of indirect tax cuts on inflation set out in table 13.2 is of course no more than a limiting case, but there would be general agreement that there may be effects of this nature. There would be less assent for the view that direct tax cuts would immmediately reduce inflation in anything approaching the parallel extent set out in table 13.3. Analytically there should of course be an eventual symmetrical response to changes which affect workers' real incomes equally, so it is tempting to predict similar results from the two kinds of tax reduction, but tax cuts are likely to reduce inflation more immediately where it is indirect taxation that is being reduced, and that is what will be assumed from now on.

With inflation reduced by up to 1 per cent per annum, but an unchanged rate of growth of the nominal money supply, the growth of the real money supply will accelerate by up to 1 per cent per annum, which will help to produce an accelerating rate of growth of real effective demand. This will also be raised by the demand stimulating effects of the tax cuts themselves.

These will raise real disposable income by 1 per cent of the initial national income, Y_0, in the first year after taxes begin to be reduced,

Table 13.3 *The influence of successive annual reductions of 1 per cent of the national income in the rate of direct taxation*

	Annual percentage increases			
Year	Increase in direct taxes δT_d	Increase in wages $w = p_{-1} + {}_eq + \delta T_d$	Increase in productivity a	Increase in prices $p = w - a$
0	0	12	2	10
1	−1	11	2	9
2	−1	10	2	8
3	−1	9	2	7
4	−1	8	2	6
5	−1	7	2	5
6	0	7	2	5

and this increase will boost both consumption and investment. Consumption will depend partly on the propensity to consume permanent incomes and partly on the propensity to consume transient incomes, and some of the beneficiaries of tax cuts will regard these as permanent while others will consider them transitory. Those who regard the tax cuts as permanent will increase their consumption in so far as their net wealth and hence their permanent incomes are raised. Barro has suggested in his well-known equivalence theorem (which follows Ricardo) that deficit financed tax cuts may have a zero net effect on wealth because new obligations on taxpayers and their heirs to finance consequent increases in the national debt will reduce private net wealth to precisely the degree that tax cuts themselves increase it.[15] Many taxpayers will, however, base their consumption on their expected incomes over merely their own lifetimes or else some still briefer time span, and, as Tobin has pointed out, the net wealth and permanent incomes of these taxpayers will rise as taxes are reduced. Clearly the actual rise in consumption that accompanies tax cuts will depend quite considerably on the extent to which they are regarded as permanent, and the extent to which those who regard them as permanent actually believe that their net wealth has risen.[16]

As those who benefit from tax cuts raise consumption, real incomes will rise which will increase the desired capital stock, and this will incline companies to increase investment. They will also raise investment in so far as this is favourably influenced by any rise in net of tax profits that is consequent upon reductions in taxation. The result is that both real investment and real consumption will rise as rates of taxation are reduced.

There are a number of ways in which the effects of successive reductions in taxation upon consumption and investment could be set out, and the simple propositions that follow outline the nature of some of the possible interrelationships. It will be assumed that the overall marginal propensity to consume extra net of tax incomes is c, and that this takes into account that some beneficiaries of tax cuts regard these as permanent and wealth increasing, while others consider them transitory, or else wealth neutral. Consumption will then rise by c per cent of the previous 'year's' natural income in the first year in which taxes are reduced by 1 per cent of the national income, if it is assumed (for simplicity) that consumption decisions are not revised (upwards or downwards) in the course of the year.

It will be supposed for simplicity that gross investment at an unchanged rate of interest is always determined by an investment function of the general form $I_t = vY_{t-1} - dK_{t-1}$, where v and d are constants, so investment will only start to be favourably influenced by tax cuts in the 'year' after these begin. Thus in the year in which taxes are first reduced, there will be no addition to investment and their sole effect will be to raise consumption by c per cent of the national income, so in the first year δY, where this is regarded as the direct influence of the tax cuts upon investment and consumption via their influence on real disposable incomes, will merely be c.

In the second year, consumption will rise by c per cent of the previous year's national income as a result of the second 1 per cent cut in taxation but this will not be the sole increase in real demand. The rise in the national income by c in the previous year will produce extra induced investment of v times this, and the fact that incomes are c per cent higher as a result of the growth of the previous year will produce extra consumption of $c(1 - T)$ times these higher incomes of the previous year. The total rise in demand as a consequence of the growth of the previous year will therefore be $v + c(1 - T)$ times the growth of that year. This means that the total growth in demand in the second year will be $c[1 + v + c(1 - T)]$. The investment function, $I_t = vY_{t-1} - dK_{t-1}$, assumes that investment, as well as being favourably influenced by the growth of the previous year, is unfavourably influenced by the rise in the capital stock in that year. For simplicity the negative effect of the growing capital stock in this brief tax-cut-induced recovery is neglected, so that sole influence on investment of which account will be taken is the increase in the national income of the previous year. These simplifications suggest that demand will rise by c in the first year of the tax cutting programme, and by $c[1 + v + c(1 - T)]$ in the second year. In the third year the immediate effect of the tax cuts will again be to raise consumption by c, but the secondary effect, a rise in consumption and investment by $[v + c(1 - T)]$ times the growth of the previous year will now produce extra demand of $c[v + c(1 - T)]$ plus $c[v + c(1 - T)]^2$. Hence the total rise in demand in the third year of the tax cuts is

$$c\{1 + [v + c(1 - T)] + [v + c(1 - T)]^2\}$$

Similarly, the growth of real demand in the nth year will be

$$c\{1 + [v + c(1 - T)] + [v + c(1 - T)]^2 + \ldots + [v + c(1 - T)]^{n-1}\}$$

Thus the multiplier and accelerator effects of the tax cuts will produce an accelerating rate of growth of real demand if the rate of interest is unchanged. If, for instance, c is 0.5, T is 0.4, and v is 1.1, the growth of real demand will be 0.5 per cent in the first year, 1.2 per cent in the second, 2.18 per cent in the third, 3.55 per cent in the fourth, and so on. Other assumed values for c, v and T would produce different results but they would all produce a considerable acceleration in the rate of growth of real demand. The expansion of demand only accelerates with conventional multiplier–accelerator interactions if the value of v exceeds some critical value, but those results which Hicks (1950, ch. 6) has categorized depend on the assumption that expansion is triggered off by a single impluse; here expansion is more powerful because the government repeatedly injects extra demand into the economy in a succession of tax cutting budgets. That the growth of demand is bound to accelerate is extremely helpful because it was shown above that the tendency of successive tax cuts to reduce the rate of inflation by up to 1 per cent annum could raise the rate of growth of the *real* money supply by up to 1 per cent per annum so that this would rise by an extra 1 per cent in the first year, 2 per cent in the second, 3 per cent in the third, and so on. Thus the real money supply and the rate of growth of real demand will both have a tendency to accelerate in each year in which taxes are cut, so there will be an accelerating rightward movement in both the Hicksian LM and IS curves, though not of course at parallel rates. If the tendency of the real money supply to accelerate is greater than that of the multiplier–accelerator interaction, the LM curve will tend to move rightwards faster than the IS curve with the result that interest rates will tend to fall in so far as these are determined by the relationships discussed up to this point. Interest rates will of course tend to rise if the multiplier–accelerator interaction advances more powerfully than the real money supply. There will be a strong acceleration of growth in either case, and the excess of unemployment over the natural rate should gradually be eliminated, while inflation should at the same time fall towards the target rate.

It may be that employment will reach the natural rate before inflation falls to the target rate. In that event, the joint policies of control of the nominal money supply and continuous tax cuts could be differently balanced. Monetary growth could be tighter for instance, so that employment grew less, while inflation fell somewhat faster because it took employment longer to reach the natural rate. Conversely, if it appeared that the inflation target would be reached before the employment target, more emphasis could be placed on the tax cutting programme, and less on reductions in the rate of growth of the money supply.

If the joint policies succeed in achieving both targets after J years, growth can proceed from that point with employment at the natural rate and inflation at the target rate, but the budget will have a structural deficit of J per cent of the national income. This will have implications which will be the subject of the next section.

IV THE LONG-TERM CONSEQUENCES OF THE STRUCTURAL BUDGET DEFICIT THAT RESULTS FROM THE USE OF TAX CUTS TO EXPAND TO FULL EMPLOYMENT

The first consequence of the structural deficit is that real interest rates will need to be higher than if employment had reached the natural rate with a balanced budget. With the present assumptions, the share of consumption in the national income will be higher by cJ per cent (at unchanged real interest rates) than if taxes had not been cut by 1 per cent of the national income in J successive years. Interest rates will therefore need to be sufficiently above the rate they would reach if the natural rate of employment was attained with a balanced budget to raise the share of private saving in the national income or else to crowd out investment by cJ per cent of the national income. If 1 per cent higher interest rates raise the share of saving by A per cent of the national income, and cut the share of investment by B per cent, real interest rates will need to be higher by $cJ(A + B)$ percentage points. At these higher real interest rates the share of investment in the national income will be lower by $[B/(A + B)]cJ$ per cent of the national income, so if private saving and investment were previously s per cent of the national income, the fraction,

$$\frac{B}{A+B}\frac{cJ}{s}$$

of private investment will now be crowded out. In the fullness of time the capital to output ratio will also be lower to this extent. If the elasticity of output with respect to capital is α, this means that equilibrium output will eventually be lower by the fraction

$$\frac{\alpha}{1-\alpha}\frac{B}{A+B}\frac{cJ}{s}$$

than it would have been if growth with employment at the natural rate had been achieved with a balanced budget.

There is another adverse effect which many consider still more serious. If there is a budget deficit of J per cent of the national income when employment reaches the natural rate, then Domar has shown that if this deficit persists, the national debt will converge upon J/g_n per cent of the national income.[17] Financing the interest on this debt will require future taxation of iJ/g_n per cent of the national income where i is the real interest rate which the government will have to pay finance continuous annual borrowing of J per cent of the national income.

If borrowing is to be held indefinitely at J per cent of the national income, that is if the deficit that is required to expand up to the natural rate of employment is sustained indefinitely after this, then a simple proposition follows. The interest cost of the resulting deficit of J per cent of the national income will need to be financed through extra taxation and this will build up towards an eventual iJ/g_n per cent of the national income. Taxes can be reduced by J per cent of the national income along the initial expansion path to full employment, but after this they will gradually need to be raised by iJ/g_n per cent of the national income to finance the interest on the gradual accumulation of debt. If taxes are first cut by J and subsequently increased by iJ/g_n per cent of the national income, they will end up higher than their initial level if i exceeds g_n. Thus if the real rate of interest at which the government has to borrow exceeds the long term rate of growth, governments will end up levying higher rates of taxation than the initial level before the tax cutting policies were adopted. If, conversely, the real rate of interest on government debt is less than the long-term rate of growth, then the government will be able to levy lower taxation indefinitely, because debt interest will always require less extra taxation to finance it than the J percentage points by which tax rates were cut initially. The critical real interest rate at which supply-side tax cuts produce lower rates of taxation in the distant future as well as the immediate present is therefore the interest rate that equals the long-term rate of growth. If governments can borrow at interest rates below this in the very long run, then they can reduce taxation indefinitely and follow a quick road to full employment at the same time. If, on the contrary, they have to pay real interest rates (net of such taxes as they receive back on the interest they pay out) which exceed the rate of growth, then supply-side tax cutting policies will only allow tax rates to fall in the short term and they will eventually entail larger anti-supply-side tax increases.

There are a number of qualifications and amplifications to this relatively simple proposition. It has been assumed in what has been said so far that the government ceases to expand borrowing after the equilibrium level of employment is reached. It thus acquires a structural deficit of J per cent of the national income in order to reach full employment expeditiously, but expands borrowing no further after that. The result is that it has to raise the rate of taxation in order to pay debt interest which builds up towards iJ/g_n per cent of the national income. This debt interest could be financed through further increases in borrowing, which would raise real interest rates further, crowd out yet more investment, and continually reduce capital and output per worker. If debt interest was financed through further borrowing instead of taxation, there would be all these unfavourable effects, but there would be no accompanying need to raise taxation so this would remain J percentage points below its initial level. But as debt interest and extra borrowing to finance it built up, a point would eventually be reached where governments could not continue to expand their debt to national income ratios further. The price of postponed tax increases would then be an eventual financial crisis with unpredictable consequences.[18] It will be assumed here that governments will not embark on policies which involve *indefinite* increases in debt, so they will only finance a growing deficit through borrowing instead of taxation if specific short-term benefits are attainable, and the borrowing ratio needed to attain these is *limited*. That is the case with the use of supply-side tax cuts to reach full employment expeditiously, when the effect on the structural deficit should be containable, but it is not the case if there is further borrowing to pay consequent debt interest, because this would involve an indefinite increase in the debt to income ratio and an inevitable financial breakdown in the end.

The second qualification to the relatively simple result that borrowing will reduce eventual taxation where the rate of interest is less than the long-term rate of growth, and raise it if the rate of interest is higher than this, is the assumption which has been implicit so far that the economy has no previous debt. It has been assumed that there was formerly a balanced budget at full employment with the result that the structural deficit rises from zero to J per cent of the national income as a result of the adoption of new expansionary policies. If there is already debt amounting to the fraction, D, of the national income, the interest cost of financing this will gradually increase as interest rates rise. The additional borrowing of J per cent of the national income that is consequent upon the adoption of supply-side tax cutting policies will raise real interest rates by the time full employment is reached by $J/(A + B)$ per cent of the national income. This rise in interest rates will have to be applied to the previous debt of D as soon as the interest on this comes up for renegotiation, and extra interest costs of $[J/(A + B)]D$ per cent of the national income will then have to be incurred.[19] Tax rates will have to be raised by $[J/(A + B)]D$ per cent of the national income to pay this extra interest if an indefinite growth of debt is to be avoided, so a country which has already incurred debt will cut taxes in recession by J per cent of the national income in order to trigger off a supply-led recovery, but it will then have to raise them again by $[J/(A + B)]D$ per cent of the national income soon after full employment is reached. This subsequent increase in taxation will exceed taxation will exceed the initial tax cuts if $D/(A + B)$ exceeds unity, and it will in any case amount to a considerable fraction of the initial tax cuts if D is at all significant.

Many countries finance their borrowing through short-period debt instruments where interest rates have to be renegotiated with considerable frequency, and such countries could easily find that most of the hoped for benefits from new borrowing were largely absorbed into extra obligations to pay interest on existing debt. This would be entirely the case once a country's debt reached $1/(A + B)$ per cent of its national income. Thus is $(A + B)$ totals $1\frac{1}{2}$ for instance (which means that an increase in government borrowing of $1\frac{1}{2}$ per cent of the national income will raise real interest rates 1 per cent at full employment), and borrowing is actually raised by $1\frac{1}{2}$ per cent of the national income, then if existing debt totals $1\frac{1}{2}$ times the national income, 1 per cent extra interest on this will cost the budget $1\frac{1}{2}$ per cent of the national income, precisely the amount by which borrowing is being increased. This means that a country with existing debt which has reached $(A + B)$ per cent of its national income can gain no extra resources as a result of further increases in borrowing. Any further borrowing will merely raise interest costs sufficiently to absorb all or more than the increment that is borrowed. Obligations to pay interest will rise as fast or faster than increases in the national debt. Once a country has reached this point, it will be unable to make any rational use of extra borrowing for any purpose, including of course, borrowing to finance supply-side policies. Any tax cuts along the path to full employment will need to be reversed once this is attained, and the anticipation of these future tax increases (or else a future monetization of debt) may mean that there will not even be transitional benefits. The weaknesses and failures of Keynesian debt-financed expansions in the 1970s and the 1980s may have resulted in part because by then their previous successes had led some countries to push their existing debt to levels where further borrowing was significantly absorbed into extra obligations to pay interest.

If past debt is not so high that extra interest almost immediately absorbs all the extra funds a government obtains from additional borrowing, there will of course be opportunities to reduce rates of taxation immediately, even if they will eventually need to be increased. Domar's well-known result that taxation will have to rise in the end if the real rate of interest at which the government borrows exceeds the economy's long-term rate of growth is demonstrable for an *infinite* time horizon, but government do not commonly look so far ahead.

If, for instance, the government borrows in order to pursue supply-side tax cutting policies, and the real interest rate rises to $1\frac{1}{2}$ times the natural rate of growth *after* this, and if this is the first government borrowing the country in question has embarked on and g_n is 3 per cent per annum, then it can be shown that debt interest will build up so that it equals the borrowing ratio after 37 years. If, however, the country had previous government debt amounting to say $\frac{1}{2}(A + B)$ as a ratio of the national income, then interest payments will catch up with the government's further borrowing after just 23 years. In these cases therefore taxes will be lower for a few decades, but after this the interest on accumulated borrowing will push them up above their levels before the supply-side policies were adopted.

Proponents of supply-side tax cutting policies would argue that such calculations miss the main point of their strategy. They advocate supply-side policies precisely because they believe the economy will function more effectively with lower taxation – that is after all what the expression supply-side policies is intended to convey. They expect these policies to lead to a higher level of output and to a faster long-term rate of growth, with the result that future tax revenues will rise to produce benefits which the above calculations ignore. If the level of the national income is actually higher *when the economy reaches full employment* than it would have been in the absence of supply-side tax cuts, then that larger national income will produce more tax revenue than has so far been supposed. But will deficit-financed tax cuts actually raise the level of Y_n, the real national income with employment at the natural rate?

It was shown in the first section that lower rates of taxation will be associated with higher full employment output, because there are likely to be increased supplies of both labour and capital. But those results depended on the assumption of a balanced budget. In the present analysis of the use of tax cuts to take an economy rapidly to full employment, the budget is in continuous deficit, with the result that interest rates will be higher when the economy reaches full employment than they would have been with a balanced budget.

This will not affect the analysis of the influence of lower taxation upon the full employment supply of labour because that will depend only on rates of taxation, and not at all on the rate of interest. However, the analysis of how lower taxation will raise saving and therefore the capital stock will be seriously affected. Lower taxation with unchanged government spending is certain to raise the share of consumption in the full employment national income, so it is bound to reduce the full employment share of investment. Therefore far from raising investment and capital per worker, as tax cuts were bound to do at full employment with a balanced budget, deficit financed tax cuts will actually have the opposite effect: because they will inevitably raise the share of consumption, they are certain to have an unfavourable influence on the share of investment.

Worse still, it emerged that where budgets are balanced, tax cuts have a stronger impact on long-term supply potential via their tendency to raise capital per worker, than through their favourable impact on the size of the labour force. With plausible values for the various elasticities, it appears that the eventual favourable effects of tax cuts on potential supply resulting from a larger equilibrium capital stock might be about six times as great as those that could be expected from a larger labour force. It is therefore disturbing that deficit-financed tax cuts will actually reduce the capital stock. The worrying probability appears to be that they will be supply reducing and not supply increasing.

It is of course only in the longest of long runs that a country will suffer the full disadvantages of a lower savings ratio. According to Sato (1963), the full neoclassical transition to a lower capital ratio may take 90 years in an economy permanently at full employment, so it may take this long for the full adverse effects on the capital stock of higher consumption and a higher rate of interest to come through, while the benefits from lower taxation upon the supply of labour which were one-sixth as great in the first part of this chapter will be enjoyed immediately. It is therefore likely that as a policy of deficit financed tax cuts is embarked upon, the favourable effects on labour supply will be the greater influence at first, but the unfavourable effects via the influence of higher consumption and higher interest rates on the capital stock will gradually come to outweigh them, and the initial favourable effects will be extremely slight if the elasticity of labour supply is as modest as recent empirical work suggests.

The question that immediately arises after this disappointing analysis is whether an economy which uses supply-side policies to reach full employment and the target inflation rate can avoid the adverse long-term effects by correcting the deficit as soon as full employment is reached. Could this allow an economy to enjoy the benefits of a rapid transition to full employment without adverse long-term effects? In order to correct the structural deficit, taxes would have to be increased by the J per cent of the national income by which they were cut in the rapid transition to full employment. Suppose they are raised by 1 per cent of the national income in each of the J years after the natural rate is first reached. Will this undo all that was achieved in the favourable transition to this?

On the face of it, the previous favourable results should be precisely reversed. The gradual tax increases would then lead to an annual acceleration of inflation of 1 per cent per annum if the previous wage and price equation still applied, and this would reduce the rate of growth of the real money supply by 1 per cent per annum. At the same time the reduction in disposable incomes that followed the tax increases would reduce effective demand at an accelerating rate, so that the economy gradually drifted into recession, and quite possibly a stagflationary recession in which inflation accelerated as employment declined. Are there possible asymmetries which might allow this dismal conclusion to be avoided?

A possible assumption that would rescue the case for deficit financed tax cuts is that productivity growth might rise faster at full employment which would allow workers to continue to enjoy their accustomed rate of growth of real living standards, despite subsequent tax increases which gradually removed the deficit. There is a wide range of theories which suggest that if the long-term rate of productivity growth is not an exogenously given constant, then it will tend to vary with aggregate investment or else the rate of capital accumulation.[20] If there is force in these lines of argument, then there will actually be unfavourable long-term effects on productivity growth if an economy is run with a structural deficit, because this will always reduce the long-term share of investment in relation to what it would have been with a balanced budget.

The only case where these policies may actually raise the long-term rate of productivity growth will arise if an economy simply cannot otherwise attain the natural rate of employment. If the alternative is that full employment will never be reached, or else that the average level of employment will be significantly lower, then an economy which adopts supply-side policies may achieve a level of output that averages out closer to full employment output (Y_n). Suppose an economy with a structural deficit of J per cent of its national income thereby manages to achieve a level of output that averages 98 per cent of Y_n, then its share of investment will average $0.98\{s - Jc[B/(A + B)]\}Y_n$. Suppose another economy with a structurally balanced budget has a level of output which averages only $0.92Y_n$, but invests a full s per cent of this lower average national income because private saving is at no point diverted to finance government borrowing. Then the economy willing to pursue supply-side policies would invest more in the long term if $0.98\{s - Jc[B/(A + B)]\}Y_n$ exceeded $0.92sY_n$. That would require an extraordinary average output gain as a result of the pursuit of deficit financed full employment policies, because $\{s - Jc[B/(A + B)]\}$ will often fall short of s by one-quarter or one fifth, but the average output gain from using tax cuts to get closer to full employment can hardly amount to more than between one-twentieth and one-tenth of the national income at the utmost. There should then be few cases where aggregate investment will actually be higher over the cycle as a whole in economies where deficit financed tax cutting policies are pursued, which means that there will be few countries where these policies actually lead to faster productivity growth. Slower productivity growth because investment is lower seems far more probable in most cases.

The sad conclusion is that deficit financed tax cuts should indeed take an economy rapidly to full employment, but there will almost invariably be a price to pay. The share of investment will be lower at full employment and productivity growth therefore slower, with the result that such economies will almost always have an inferior long-term tax base. Worse still, any attempts to reverse tax cuts and rebalance the budget as soon as full employment is reached seem likely to reverse the beneficial effects on employment and inflation that expanded the economy so rapidly in the first place. Hence this particular line of policy, like several others, can only be expected to produce short-term benefits at a considerable long-term cost.

Moreover, this new variant of Keynesian policies will be entirely impractical over a series of cycles. If the structural deficit is raised by J per cent of the national income in each recession, the cumulative deficit will rise, with the result that the diversion of saving to consumption will all the time increase to produce a growing loss of capital per worker. In addition, the ratio of debt to the national income will rise in each successive cycle, and higher interest rates will need to be paid to finance extra borrowing on each occasion. These higher rates will need to be paid on previously incurred debt, which will absorb growing fractions of the extra sums that governments attempt to borrow, with the result that the time will come when no part of an increase in borrowing will actually be available to finance tax cuts. Because of the cumulative tendency of extra borrowing to raise the rate of interest, it may well be that countries will only be able to take advantage of a tax-cut-induced recovery once or twice or at most on perhaps three occasions. After that the ratio of structural borrowing to the national income is likely to reach a point where further attempts to increase borrowing will simply be absorbed into extra interest on previously incurred debt.

There is, however, one case where costless tax-cut-induced recoveries may still be feasible, and this may be one of the practical policy options that Keynes himself envisaged. It has been assumed so far that borrowing in recession will always lead to a structural deficit when full employment is reached. But what if a country has rates of taxation in recession that would actually produce a budget surplus at full employment? The public expenditure ratio might be the fraction T_n of full employment output, but tax ratios in excess of T_n could produce deficits in recession. This means that rates of taxation could then *be cut to* T_n in order to expand the economy in all the ways which have been set out, and still produce a balanced budget when full employment is reached. There are no long-term difficulties with supply-side recoveries which do not involve *a structural deficit*, so a country with *a structural surplus* would have the opportunity to cut taxes in order to accelerate economic recovery without painful consequences afterwards. But that appears to be the only case where the rapid attainment of full employment via tax cuts would be costless.

V CONCLUSION

There may well be parallels between the financial problems of the United States and the adverse effects of deficit financed tax cuts in the above argument. The United States apparently had a small budget surplus in 1979 on a cyclically adjusted basis. Unemployment was at the low rate of 5.8 per cent and the budget deficit (including on and off budget items) was about 1½ per cent of the national income. However, inflation of around 10 per cent per annum was reducing the real value of government debt, then 30 per cent of the national income, by perhaps 3 per cent of the national income. As new borrowing was adding 1½ per cent of the national income to government debt, and inflation was removing 3 per cent, this was falling on balance by 1½ per cent of the national income. In 1985 with unemployment again low, the nominal deficit is perhaps 5½ per cent of the national income, and the real deficit around 4 per cent: since 4 per cent inflation is cutting government debt of 35 per cent of the national income by 1½ percentage points. This suggests that the real structural deficit has widened by 5½ percentage points from −1½ per cent to +4 per cent, while the nominal deficit has widened 4 percentage points from 1½ to 5½ per cent.

In the earlier argument a 5½ percentage point widening of the structural deficit was entirely associated with lower tax rates, but in the American case less than one-third appears to be due to supply-side tax cuts, while over two-thirds is the result of increased government spending. The higher expenditure and the tax cuts were concentrated into the period 1981–84, in which the economy achieved a rapid recovery from recession while inflation fell simultaneously in the manner supply siders predict.

But it is entirely plausible that the larger structural deficit is now producing adverse financial effects of the kind set out in this chapter. Part of the 5½ per cent percentage point increase in borrowing is being financed internationally, so domestic saving has not had to be crowded in or investment crowded out to this full extent, but extra foreign borrowing has raised interest rates and real United States rates are now high by historical standards.

It would be interesting to know if the share of private investment in the national income and the rate of productivity growth are lower than when the economy previously achieved high employment: preliminary data suggest that higher real interest rates may already be producing adverse effects on productivity growth of the kind neoclassical analysis predicts.

United States net of tax real interest rates are considerably higher than the rate of growth, and the ratio of government debt to the national income is rising in the manner economic analysis suggests, from around 30 per cent in 1979 to a predicted 50 per cent in 1989 (see Congressional Budget Office, 1984, Pt. III, p. 4). It will converge on more than 100 per cent of the national income, according to Domar's formula, if the *real* deficit remains 4 per cent of the national income, and the long-term rate of growth approximates to the post Second World War average of 3½ per cent.

Adverse long-term effects on interest rates and capital investment can only be prevented from becoming continually more severe as the debt to income ratio rises towards and beyond 100 per cent, if taxation is now increased or expenditure reduced by around 3 per cent of the national income. This would cut the structural deficit to the 1 per cent which is compatible with a stable public debt to national income ratio of 30 to 35 per cent, at which there should be no new adverse financial pressures. But the argument of this chapter would suggest that tax increases might reverse some of the favourable effects on inflation and employment which were achieved in 1981–84.

The United Kingdom was not tempted towards a tax-cut-induced recovery after the Conservative election victory in 1979, and it has been estimated that the British budget was then in structural balance on an inflation adjusted basis so there was no genuine opportunity for this. But Mrs Thatcher's government may have forgone a genuine opportunity to take advantage of a tax-cutting 'free lunch' a few years into her first term when the economy was in deep recession, for it has been estimated that there may have been a structural surplus of over 4 per cent of the national income in 1981.[21] It might therefore have been possible to cut taxes faster than they were actually reduced from 1982 onwards to produce a tax-cut-led recovery of the kind set out in the tables without adverse long-term effects of the kind the United States is experiencing. Whether this was a genuine opportunity obviously depends on the assumptions on which the estimates of the full employment structural surplus are based, and these have often been overoptimistic in the past.

A key conclusion appears to be that there is only a clear case for tax-cut-led recoveries from a starting point of structural surplus. The United States probably had a small structural surplus in 1981 so it could have cut taxes slightly in the absence of simultaneous expenditure increases. Britain may well have had a larger structural surplus by then, so a series of supply-side tax cutting budgets might have been feasible in the years after 1981 without significant adverse effects on the ratio of government debt to the national income.

NOTES

1 See, for instance, Canto et al. (1983), Evans (1980; 1983), Laffer (1979; 1981), Roberts (1978), and Bacon and Eltis (1976).

2 This has been argued especially by Laffer (1979; 1981), but see also Fullerton (1980), and Canto et al. (1983).

3 See especially, Perkins (1979), Corden (1981) and Bacon and Eltis (1976).

4 Musgrave and Musgrave (1976) provide a comprehensive analysis of the various and disparate influences of taxation.

5 A uniform rate of indirect taxation which takes the fraction T of all value-added will have a similar effect, because it will remove approximately the fraction T of the purchasing power of wages. An important difference is, however, that indirect taxes such as value-added tax leave saving untaxed, so they are associated with a greater incentive to save at equal real revenues. Potential savers would allow for the need to pay the uniform value-added tax as soon as they sought to consume their accumulative saving, but they would still gain because the (untaxed) real interest rate at which saving accumulated would be higher.

6 In the absence of taxation, a supply of labour schedule of uniform elasticity can be written as $S_L = L_0 W^{N_s}$, while a demand for labour schedule can be written as $D_L = D_0 W^{N_d}$, where W is the cost of labour. As a uniform income tax at rate T reduces the net of tax wage on which labour supply is based by the multiple $(1 - T)$, this will modify the supply of labour schedule to $S_L = L_0[W(1 - T)]^{N_s}$. The labour market will be in equilibrium where $S_L = D_L$, that is, where $W^{(N_s - N_d)} = (D_0/L_0)\ (1 - T)^{-N_s}$. Hence, $(1/W)(\delta W/\delta T) = [1/(1 - T)][1/(1 - N_d/N_s)]$. The elasticity of equilibrium employment with respect to T which is shown in equation 13.1, will be this proportional rise in the cost of labour with respect to T times N_d, the elasticity of demand for labour with respect to the real cost of labour.

7 Some recent econometric evidence on the elasticity of labour supply is summarized by Fullerton (1980). See also Hausman (1981).

8 The evidence is summarized by Sato (1970).

9 A higher rate of tax will have two broad influences on the steady state net of tax rate of return that savers receive, and therefore on the rate of return that can be expected to influence their saving decisions. First, in so far as a higher rate of tax reduces the economy's savings ratio, it will reduce the

steady state capital to output ratio in the same proportion, and *raise* the marginal product of capital and therefore the rate of profit (with competitive assumptions) by $1/\sigma$ times the rise in the capital to output ratio (where σ is the elasticity of substitution between labour and capital). Second, a higher rate of tax will *reduce* the net of tax rate of return that is associated with any particular rate of profit before tax. The tendency of a higher rate of tax to raise the rate of return because it raises the marginal product of capital, and to reduce it because savers receive a lower fraction of this, will precisely cancel out if $\sigma = 1$ and the economy's savings ratio is $s_p(1 - T)$ at a constant rate of interest. (This is because the elasticity of the net of tax rate of return with respect to T is then $[1/\sigma - 1][1/(1 - T)]$, which is zero if $\sigma = 1$.) It will obviously much simplify the analysis if the possibly complex effects of the rate of taxation on the savings ratio via their influence on the rate of interest are neglected, as they safely can be where the two effects offset each other.

10 The effect of taxation on saving is analysed by Boskin (1978), and Ture (1980) offers a general neoclassical analysis of the supply-side effects of lower taxation. The interconnection between taxation and investment has been most thoroughly analysed by Feldstein, and an important example is Feldstein (1980).

11 The classical account of the neoclassical growth model where this result is derived is provided by Solow (1956).

12 Arthur Laffer reputedly first drew the curve on a napkin while he was explaining the case for tax cuts to an aide to President Ford in 1974 (Wanniski, 1978: chapter 6 is devoted to an exposition of the Laffer curve). Its derivation is set out rigorously by Canto et al. (1983).

13 The time period required for this neoclassical adjustment has been investigated by Sato (1963).

14 The use of wage and price equations like those set out below is justified by Eltis (1983). There are quite similar equations given by Grubb et al. (1982), but in their analysis accelerating inflation is due to disappointment with the rate of growth of real incomes as a result of slower productivity growth and not unexpectedly higher taxation.

15 See, in particular, Barro (1974) who is following Ricardo (1817, ch. 17).

16 The relevance of the equivalence theorem to the influence of deficit spending in actual twentieth century economies has been criticized along these lines by Tobin (1980, ch. 2).

17 This formula was first derived by Domar (1944).

18 See Sargent and Wallace (1981) for a well-known account of the consequences of indefinite increases in borrowing.

19 By the time this higher rate of interest has to be paid on previously incurred debt, its ratio, D, to the national income will have fallen, because growth in the *money* national income continuously reduces the ratio of past debt to this. Hence, D has a persistent tendency to fall in the absence of new borrowing.

20 See Arrow (1962), Conlisk (1969) and Kaldor (1957). These are restated and developed by Eltis (1971).

21 See, for instance, Miller (1985) who reports two studies which estimate that the United Kingdom's cyclically adjusted budget was in surplus by over 4 per cent of the national income in 1981.

REFERENCES

Arrow, K.J. 1962: The economic implications of learning by doing, *Review of Economic Studies*, 29, 155–73.

Bacon, R. and Eltis, W. 1976: *Britain's Economic Problem: Too Few Producers*, Macmillan, London.

Barro, R.J. 1974: Are government bonds net wealth?, *Journal of Political Economy*, 82, 1095–1117.

Boskin, M.J. 1978: Taxation, saving, and the rate of interest, *Journal of Political Economy*, 86, 3–27.

Canto, V.A., Jones, D.H. and Laffer, A.B. 1983: *Foundations of Supply-Side Economics: Theory and Evidence*, Academic Press, New York.

Congressional Budget Office 1984: *A Report to the Senate and House Committees on the Budget*, US Government Printing Office, Washington.

Conlisk, J. 1969: A neoclassical growth model wih endogenously positioned technical change frontier, *Economic Journal*, 79, 348–62.

Corden, W.M. 1981: Taxation, real wage rigidity and employment, *Economic Journal*, 91, 309–30.

Domar, E.D. 1944: The 'burden of debt' and the national income, *American Economic Review*, 34, 798–827.

Eltis, W. 1971: The determination of the rate of technical progress, *Economic Journal*, September, 502–24.

Eltis, W. 1983: The interconnection between public expenditure and inflation in Britain, *American Economic Review*, 73, 291–6.

Evans, M.K. 1980: The bankruptcy of Keynesian econometric models, *Challenge*, January–February.

Evans, M.K. 1983: *The Truth About Supply-Side Economics*, Basic Books, New York.

Feldstein, M. 1980: Fiscal policies, inflation and capital formation, *American Economic Review*, 70, 636–50.

Fullerton, D. 1980: Can tax revenue go up when tax rates go down? United States Department of the Treasury, Office of Tax Analysis, Paper 41 (Washington).

Grubb, D., Jackman, R. and Layard, R. 1982: Causes of the current stagflation, *Review of Economic Studies*, 49, Special Issue.

Hausman, J.A. 1981: Labor supply. In H.J. Aaron and J.A. Pechman (eds) *How Taxes Affect Economic Behaviour*, Brookings Institution, Washington, DC.

Hicks, J.R. 1950: *A Contribution to the Theory of the Trade Cycle*, Oxford University Press, Oxford.

Kaldor, N. 1957: A model of economic growth, *Economic Journal*, 67, December, 591–624.

Laffer, A.B. 1979: An equilibrium rational macroeconomic framework. In N.M. Kamrany and R.H. Day (eds) *Economic Issues of the Eighties*, Johns Hopkins, Baltimore.

Laffer, A.B. 1981: Government exactions and revenue deficiencies, *Cato Journal*, 1, Spring.

Miller, M. 1985: Measuring the stance of fiscal policy, *Oxford Review of Economic Policy*, 1, 44–57.

Musgrave, R.A. and Musgrave, P.B. 1976: *Public Finance in Theory and Practice*, 2nd edn, McGraw Hill, New York.

Perkins, J.O.N. 1979: *The Macroeconomic Mix to Stop Stagflation*, Macmillan, London.

Ricardo, D. 1817: *On the Principles of Political Economy and Taxation*, Reprinted Cambridge University Press, Cambridge (1951).

Roberts, P.C. 1978: The breakdown of the Keynesian model, *The Public Interest*, 52, Summer.

Sargent, T.J. and Wallace, N. 1981: Some unpleasant monetarist arithmetic, *Federal Reserve Bank of Minneappolis Quarterly Review*, Fall.

Sato, R. 1963: Fiscal policy in a neo-classical growth model: an analysis of time required for equilibrating adjustment, *Review of Economic Studies*, 30, 16–23.

Sato, R. 1970: The estimation of biased technical progress and the production function, *International Economic Review*, 11, 179–208.

Solow, R.M. 1956: A contribution to the theory of economic growth, *Quarterly Journal of Economics*, 70, February.

Tobin, James 1980: *Asset Accumulation and Economic Activity*, Blackwell, Oxford.

Ture, N.B. 1980: The economic effects of tax changes: a neoclassical analysis. In Congress of the United States Joint Economic Committee, *Special Study of Economic Change* (vol. 4: *Stagflation*), Government Printing Office, Washington, DC.

Wanniski, J. 1978: *The Way the World Works*, Basic Books, New York.

14
The Neoclassical Theory of Public Debt and the Theory of a Long-run Full-employment Deficit

STEFANO GORINI

I INTRODUCTION

The purpose of this chapter is a critical assessment of the nature of a steady state government deficit as it is embedded in the established neoclassical theory of public debt, and a comparison of such concept with the alternative Keynesian concept of a long-run full employment deficit. The latter may equally be defined within the same analytical framework, but after having relaxed the standard neoclassical assumptions of a long-run equilibrium and saving–investment identity and of the associated long-run stability of the real output market.

As the established neoclassical theory of public debt we shall take the model of monetary growth in its very simplest form, such as has been outlined by Tobin (1955; 1965), Solow (1970, chs. 4 and 5) and Feldstein (1980) in their well-known contributions to the subject. Their models, apart from variations in emphasis and disaggregation, share the same fundamental concepts, assumptions and structure. In the first stage of our discussion we set out a slightly generalized version of Feldstein's three asset model. Our generalization consists essentially of the following points: the introduction of the monetization ratio of the deficit and debt as an explicit policy variable; the definition of more general portfolio balance equations for money and government bonds; the identification of the *adjusted* deficit (the deficit adjusted for inflation, i.e. diminished by the monetary erosion of government debt, or *inflation tax*) as the key variable in terms of which the basic relationships of the model are defined; the explicit treatment of the associated key variable of the so-called primary deficit (the non-adjusted deficit less the debt interest payments); the specification of real growth in terms of gross investment and gross output, in order to include the limiting case of zero growth with positive income. We shall refer to this generalized version as the Tobin–Solow–Feldstein (TSF) model. It is a relatively simple one, and it lends itself to a straightforward geometric representation.[1]

The purpose in the first part of our discussion is to provide an overview of the main structural steady state relationships between such variables as non-adjusted, adjusted and primary deficit, real growth rate, saving rate, monetization, inflation, capital intensity and real interest. Such a comprehensive view, besides being interesting in its own right, is particularly useful for highlighting the differences in the steady state nature and role of an adjusted deficit under purely neoclassical and under more Keynesian assumptions.[2] Following Feldstein we confine ourselves to comparative steady state dynamics, without dealing properly with the likely dynamics of transition and with stability properties. However, there is one aspect of the transition and stability problem which does enter, at least implicitly, into our authors' reasoning, and plays an important role in our own discussion, because on it rests the possibility of defining the Keynesian concept of a long-run full employment deficit. We are referring of course to the controversial assumption of a long-run equilibrium and stability of the real output market. In this first part we shall consider the long-run working of the TSF model under what we may call the pure neoclassical assumption of a long-run saving–investment identity irrespective of the real interest level. Under such an assumption the steady state level of the adjusted deficit turns out, predictably, to be determined only by the requirement of equilibrating the assets market. We may thus speak of a long-run 'portfolio equilibrium' deficit in a neoclassical self-adjusting fully employed economy. We take the adjusted deficit as our key variable here, thus departing from Feldstein's emphasis on the non-adjusted deficit, because it is again the net deficit which will be the relevant variable when introducing the Keynesian alternative.

There is a special departure from the pure neoclassical assumption of a long-run saving–investment identity irrespective of the real interest level, which consists in the introduction of the concept of a critical differential between the return on real assets and the real return on government bonds (the real interest rate). When the actual differential falls below that critical value, real investment demand tends to fall to zero. When it exceeds it, real investment demand tends to become indefinitely high. In Solow's terminology this is the 'target rate of return' hypothesis, while Feldstein calls it the 'safety trap' case. This special hypothesis is indeed a step in the direction of separating long-run saving from investment, and of giving thereby to the adjusted deficit also a possible role in equilibrating the real output market. In the second part of our discussion we shall begin by showing the steady working of the TSF model under this special hypothesis, and we shall see that the step is in fact a very limited one. It allows the saving–investment identity assumption still to play the decisive role in ensuring equilibrium and stability in the real output market, while no real room is made for an equilibrating role of the deficit in that market. The natural thing to do is therefore to make the further step of separating saving from investment behaviour in a more general way, and we do so by introducing the simplest possible investment function. In the resulting 'Keynesian' version of the TSF model the steady state level of the adjusted deficit is no longer determined by the requirement of equilibrating the assets market, but also, and separately, by that of equilibrating the real output market. We may thus speak of a long-run 'full employment equilibrium' deficit in a Keynesian excess saving economy. In order to more fully clarify the consequences of such change in the nature of the deficit we briefly consider the main steady state structural relationships of this Keynesian version and the underlying instability of the output market.

In closing we shall mention certain aspects of the long-run theory of public debt, which are raised by the analysis of the TSF model, but which cannot be dealt with properly within the model itself. Also, we try to step back from the more analytical aspects of the comparison between the two contrasting approaches, and suggest some reflections on the assessment of their comparative validity in a truly long-run perspective.

II THE STRUCTURE OF THE TOBIN–SOLOW–FELDSTEIN (TSF) MODEL AND THE CONCEPT OF A LONG-RUN 'PORTFOLIO EQUILIBRIUM' DEFICIT IN A NEOCLASSICAL FULLY EMPLOYED ECONOMY

In this section we set out what we have called the generalized TSF model, and discuss its steady state working under the pure neoclassical assumption of a long-run identity between saving and investment, irrespective of the real interest level. The key variable in terms of which the basic relationships of the model are defined will be the ratio of the adjusted government deficit to GNP.

Let us summarize a few standard definitions. We adopt the usual notational convention of capital letters for nominal values and small letters for real values, and of a dot for the time derivative and a cap for the time rate of change. P is the price level and π the rate of inflation. $d = D/P$ is real government debt, divided into non-interest bearing real money, $m = M/P$, and interest bearing bonds, $b = B/P$, with $d = m + b$.[3] g is real government expenditure on goods and services, t is real net tax revenue (tax revenues net of non-interest transfer payments) and R is the nominal interest rate.

The real non-adjusted, adjusted and primary deficits are defined as follows. By definition the real non-adjusted deficit, i.e. the nominal deficit divided by the price level, ndf, is given by

$$\begin{aligned} \text{ndf} = g - t + bR = \frac{\dot{D}}{P} &= d\hat{D} \\ &= m\hat{M} + b\hat{B} \end{aligned} \tag{14.1}$$

Let us define the full real monetary erosion of government debt, namely $d\pi = (m + b)\pi$, as the real inflation tax. The real adjusted deficit, i.e. the real deficit adjusted for inflation, adf, is then the real non-adjusted deficit less the real inflation tax:[4]

$$\begin{aligned} \text{adf} = \text{ndf} - d\pi &= d(\hat{D} - \pi) \\ &= m(\hat{M} - \pi) + b(\hat{B} - \pi) \end{aligned} \tag{14.2}$$

with ndf = adf when $\pi = 0$. The real primary deficit, pdf, is simply the real non-adjusted deficit net of real debt interest payments:

$$\begin{aligned} \text{pdf} = g - t &= d\hat{D} - bR \\ &= m\hat{M} + b(\hat{B} - R) \end{aligned} \tag{14.3}$$

Writing y for real gross output (GNP), and δ, η and ϵ respectively for the ratios of the above deficits to GNP we repeat their definitions as

$$\begin{aligned} \delta = \frac{\text{ndf}}{y} &= \frac{d}{y}\hat{D} \\ &= \frac{m}{y}\hat{M} + \frac{b}{y}\hat{B} \end{aligned} \tag{14.1'}$$

$$\begin{aligned} \eta = \frac{\text{adf}}{y} &= \frac{d}{y}(\hat{D} - \pi) \\ &= \frac{m}{y}(\hat{M} - \pi) + \frac{b}{y}(\hat{B} - \pi) \end{aligned} \tag{14.2'}$$

$$\begin{aligned} \epsilon = \frac{\text{pdf}}{y} = \frac{g - t}{y} &= \frac{d}{y}\hat{D} - \frac{b}{y}R \\ &= \frac{m}{y}\hat{M} + \frac{b}{y}(\hat{B} - R) \end{aligned} \tag{14.3'}$$

In steady state the expressions for δ, η and ϵ are further simplified. If γ is the long-run growth rate of real gross output and π the long-run rate of inflation, then in steady state we shall have

$$\hat{D} = \hat{M} = \hat{B} = \gamma + \pi \tag{14.4}$$

Thus the steady state ratios of the non-adjusted, adjusted and primary deficits to GNP become, respectively,

$$\delta = \frac{d}{y}(\gamma + \pi) = \frac{m+b}{y}(\gamma + \pi) \tag{14.1''}$$

$$\eta = \frac{d}{y}\gamma = \frac{m+b}{y}\gamma \tag{14.2''}$$

$$\epsilon = \frac{g-t}{y} = \frac{m}{y}(\gamma + \pi) + \frac{b}{y}(\gamma - r) \tag{14.3''}$$

where $r = R - \pi$ is the real rate of interest.

In defining real private disposable income y_{d}, we adopt, like our authors, the traditional convention of subtracting from the GDP the balance of all actual transfers between the private sector and the government. By this definition the expression for y_{d} becomes

$$y_{\mathrm{d}} = y - g + \mathrm{adf}^{5} \tag{14.5}$$

Writing $\theta = g/y$ for the ratio of government expenditure to GNP, and using $\eta = \mathrm{adf}/y$, equation 14.5 becomes

$$y_{\mathrm{d}} = (1 - \theta + \eta)y \tag{14.5'}$$

Real gross output, y, real physical capital, k, and 'effective' employment (employment in efficiency units), l, are linked by a standard constant return production function, which, following Solow's usage, we express in labour intensive form

$$q = f(z) \tag{14.6}$$

where $q = y/k$ and $z = l/k$ (effective labour intensity).

The Harrod–Domar (H–D) condition for steady state growth under the pure neoclassical assumption of a long-run saving–investment identity is simply redefined to take account of the inclusion of the adjusted deficit into the definition of disposable income. With a given natural growth rate the H–D condition generates a function associating to each level of the adjusted deficit an increasing steady state level of the output to capital ratio, and thereby of labour intensity. What we do is simply to extend, to the present generalized TSF model, Solow's treatment of this point in his own two asset model, except that we use the adjusted deficit as the key variable, and define accumulation in terms of *gross* investment and output, so as to allow the limiting case of zero growth with positive net income and output to appear in the picture.

Let γ be the long-run growth rate of effective labour force. If we assume long-run constancy of the natural rate of unemployment, γ is also the long-run growth rate of effective labour supply, and, therefore, the natural growth rate of real output. Let ν be the constant rate of depreciation of real capital and i real gross investment, so that

$$i = \nu k + \dot{k} \quad \text{and} \quad \frac{i}{k} = \nu + \hat{k} \tag{14.7}$$

Assuming long-run coincidence of actual and natural rates of unemployment, γ is also the growth rate of effective employment. Therefore the condition for steady state constancy of effective labour intensity is that $\hat{k} = \gamma$, or

$$\frac{i}{k} = \nu + \gamma \tag{14.8}$$

Let σ be the long-run propensity to save out of long-run disposable income as we have defined it, so that $s = \sigma y_{\text{d}}$, where s is real gross private saving. Assuming gross private saving less the adjusted deficit to be identically equal to gross investment, we have

$$s - \text{adf} = [\delta(1 - \theta) - (1 - \sigma)\eta]y = i^{6} \tag{14.9}$$

Dividing by k and using equations 14.6 and 14.8 we get the pure neoclassical H–D condition in terms of the adjusted deficit and gross investment:

$$[\sigma(1 - \theta) - (1 - \sigma)\eta]q = [\sigma(1 - \theta) - (1 - \sigma)\eta]f(z) = \nu + \gamma \tag{14.10}$$

In figure 14.1, equation 14.10 is shown by the intersection of the rising curve $[\sigma(1 - \theta) - (1 - \sigma)\eta]f(z)$ with the horizontal straight line at height $\nu + \gamma$, and it identifies the steady state value of the output to capital ratio and of effective labour intensity. With given values of γ, θ, ν and σ, as the adjusted deficit rises the curve rotates downwards, its intersection with the horizontal line shifts rightwards, and the steady state output to capital ratio and labour intensity rise, while the saving–investment identity ensures long-run equilibrium in the real output market, and convergence of labour intensity towards its changing steady state level. The H–D condition (equation 14.10) may be rewritten as

$$q = \frac{\nu + \gamma}{\sigma(1 - \theta) - (1 - \sigma)\eta} = \varphi(\eta) \tag{14.10$'$}$$

This gives the steady state output to capital ratio as an increasing function of η, and is shown in figure 14.2(a). As the adjusted deficit

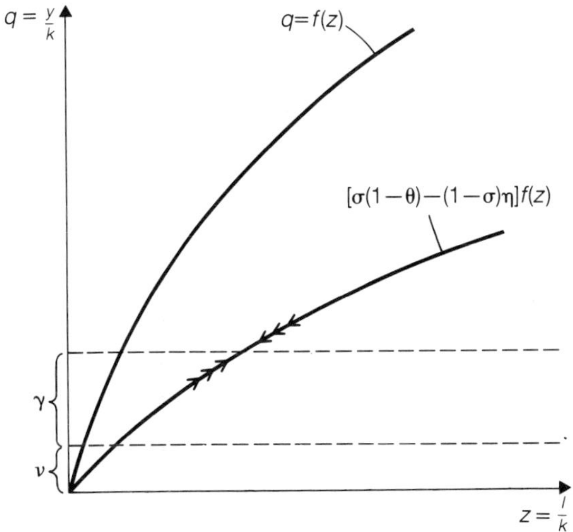

Figure 14.1 Saving-less-adjusted deficit and investment: the pure neoclassical case.

tends to its limiting value $\sigma(1 - \theta)/(1 - \sigma)$ the steady state output to capital ratio and labour intensity increase indefinitely. As the adjusted budget becomes balanced the output to capital ratio becomes $(\nu + \gamma)/[\sigma(1 - \theta)]$, and it decreases further when an adjusted surplus arises. Similarly, as γ decreases the curve $\varphi(\eta)$ shifts downwards, becoming more concave and tending to coincide with the thick line as the growth rate becomes negative and approaches $-\nu$.

As just shown, as far as the H–D condition is concerned, we may consider not only the case of a growing or stationary economy, and of a non-negative adjusted deficit, but also that of a declining economy, and of an adjusted surplus. Instead, as far as the steady state relationships between the non-adjusted, adjusted and primary deficit, and debt, ratios to GNP are concerned, we shall for simplicity consider only the case of non-negative real growth and adjusted deficit. In particular, dealing with steady states we shall see that the zero growth case is qualitatively different from the non-zero one.

Consider first the non-zero growth case. Using equation 14.2″ above we may express both the steady state debt and non-adjusted deficit ratios as functions of the adjusted deficit ratio

$$\frac{d}{y} = \frac{m+b}{y} = \frac{1}{\gamma}\eta \qquad (14.11)$$

$$\delta = \left(1 + \frac{\pi}{\gamma}\right)\eta \text{ [7]} \qquad (14.12)$$

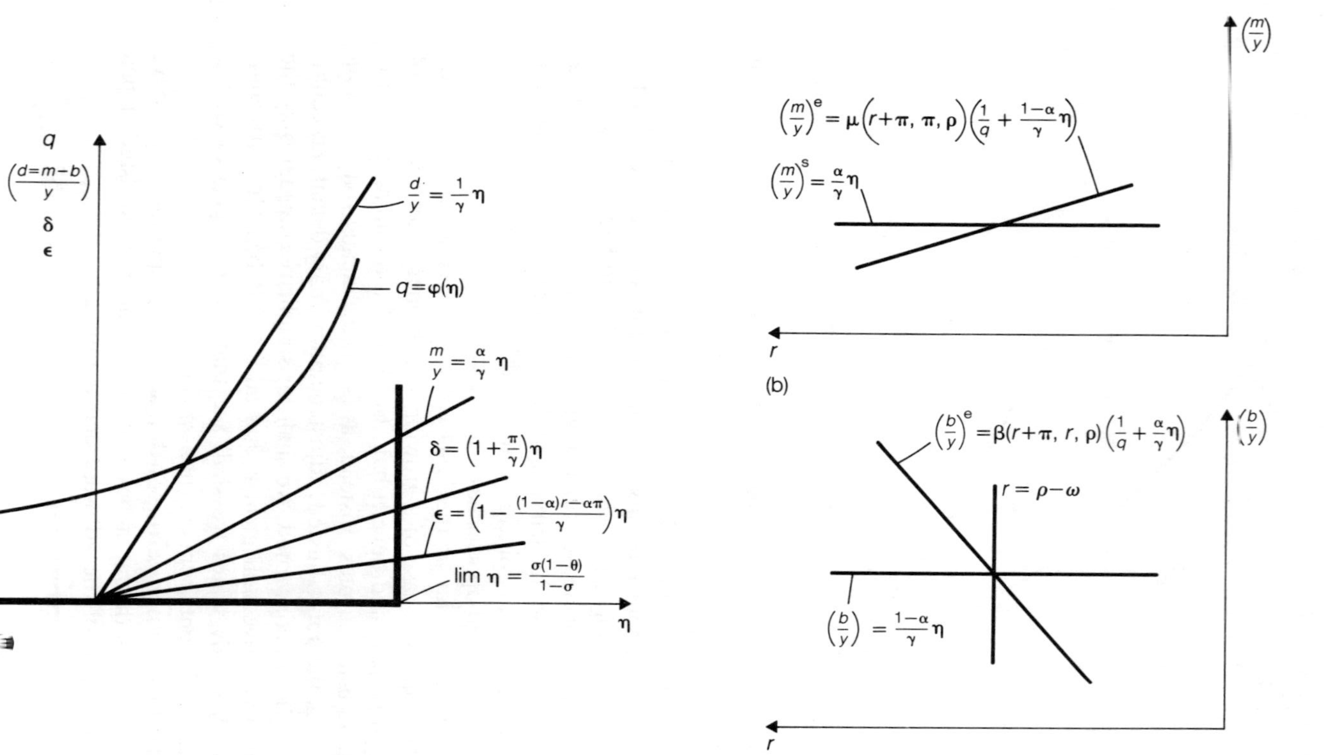

Figure 14.2 The TSF model of long-run debt: the steady state relationships (a) the output market: output to capital, debt to income and deficit to income ratios (b) the money market (c) the bonds market

As for the splitting of the debt into its components, in steady state the monetization ratios of non-adjusted and adjusted deficits and of debt are one and the same. If $0 \leqslant \alpha \leqslant 1$ is such monetization coefficient, then by accordingly splitting equation 14.11 we express both the steady state money and interest bearing debt ratios as functions of the adjusted deficit ratio and the monetization coefficient:

$$\frac{m}{y} = \frac{\alpha}{\gamma}\eta \qquad (14.13)$$

$$\frac{b}{y} = \frac{1-\alpha}{\gamma}\eta \qquad (14.14)$$

By substituting these two ratios into equation 14.3″ we may express also the steady state primary deficit ratio as a function of η

$$\epsilon = \frac{g-t}{y} = \left[1 - \frac{(1-\alpha)r - \alpha\pi}{\gamma}\right]\eta \qquad (14.15)$$

All such functions of η are represented by the corresponding straight lines out of the origin, drawn in figure 14.2(a).

Concerning the lines for d/y, m/y, b/y, δ, the obvious thing to notice is that as γ decreases they rotate upwards (but recall that if $\pi = 0$ then δ simply coincides with η) and tend to become vertical as γ tends to zero. With a given positive adjusted deficit ratio the steady state debt ratio increases indefinitely as the long-run real growth rate decreases towards zero. Another point which is worth noticing is that, according to the present model, for a monetary economy a steady state with non-zero growth is incompatible with a zero adjusted deficit, or, in other words, that in the long run a balanced adjusted budget is incompatible with a growing monetary economy. This would seem to be a peculiar result, and indeed it is simply due to the fact that in the present model the only available money is that generated through the monetization of the government deficit. If one allowed also for some different process of money creation, then a long-run balanced budget would be perfectly compatible with a growing monetary economy. However, the result underlines an important point concerning the role of a government deficit and debt in a pure neoclassical view. In its extreme form such a view would indeed indicate that the only conceivable proper 'economic' function of a government deficit would be precisely that of providing money for a growing economy. With alternative institutional devices for the creation of money one could, and should, dispense with long-run unbalanced budgets altogether.[8]

Concerning the line for the primary deficit ϵ, we see that given r, α and π, as γ decreases towards zero the line rotates downwards tending to become negatively vertical. Alternatively, with α, γ and π given, there is a critical value of the real interest rate. If r is lower than that, then the steady state primary deficit is positive. This means that in steady state a higher primary deficit (e.g. a lower taxation with a given expenditure ratio) is associated with a higher adjusted deficit. Instead, if r is higher than that level, then the steady state primary deficit is negative, i.e. it is a primary surplus. This means that in steady state it is a higher primary surplus (e.g. a higher taxation with given expenditure ratio) which is associated with a higher adjusted deficit. The critical level of r is obtained by equating to zero the coefficient of η in equation 14.15:

$$r = \frac{\alpha}{1-\alpha}\pi + \frac{1}{1-\alpha}\gamma \tag{14.16}$$

When r is at this level, the steady state primary budget is always balanced, irrespective of the adjusted deficit level. This is so because when r reaches such level, in steady state the adjusted deficit ratio becomes identical to the average real interest burden of the debt, i.e. the burden of the real interest on bonds $(b/y)r$, less the monetary erosion on money debt $(m/y)\pi$. An increase in the adjusted deficit by a one percentage point of GNP would be matched, in steady state, by exactly the same percentage increase in the average real interest on the debt.[9]

All the above curves, and their movements as induced by changes in the various parameters, represent diagrammatically the conventional results about the steady state relationships between output growth, non-adjusted, adjusted and primary deficit, and debt, ratios, monetization, inflation, real interest and labour intensity, in so far as the real output market equilibrium of a growing economy is concerned. We shall refer to them as the output market side steady state relationships.

As for the zero growth case, the conventional, and intuitive, result is that a zero growth steady state is incompatible with any positive adjusted deficit, because a positive adjusted deficit would generate a debt to GNP ratio rising asymptotically to infinity. The steady state relationships described by equations 14.11–14.15 above would vanish, and would have to be replaced by

$$\delta = \frac{d}{y}\pi \tag{14.1'''}$$

$$\eta = 0 \tag{14.2'''}$$

$$\epsilon = \frac{m}{y}\pi - \frac{b}{y}r \tag{14.3'''}$$

with any arbitrary level and decomposition of d/y.[10]

The assets market side of the TSF model consists of the markets for money and government bonds. We assume the equilibrium ratio of real money to real total private wealth, $m/(k+b+m)$, to be a function of the nominal interest, R, the inflation rate, π, and some index, ρ, of the profitability of holding real assets.[11] An increase in $R = r + \pi$, with given π and ρ, increases the opportunity cost of holding non-interest bearing money relative to interest bearing bonds. An increase in π with given R and ρ increase the opportunity cost of holding non-interest bearing money relative to holding real assets and also, since money is required as a medium of exchange, relative to real expenditure. An increase in ρ with given R and π increases the opportunity cost of holding money relative to holding real assets. By rearranging terms and dividing through by y this equilibrium ratio of real money to real wealth is transformed into a portfolio balance equation for money as a ratio to GNP:

$$\left(\frac{m}{y}\right)^{e} = \mu(r+\pi, \pi, \rho)\left(\frac{k+b}{y}\right) \tag{14.17}$$

with μ decreasing in each of its arguments, $R = r + \pi$, π and ρ. The condition for steady state equilibrium in the money market, which is represented in figure 14.2(b), becomes therefore

$$\frac{\alpha}{\gamma} = \mu(r+\pi, \pi, \rho)\left(\frac{1}{q} + \frac{1+\alpha}{\gamma}\eta\right)^{12} \tag{14.8}$$

As to the bonds market, we assume the equilibrium ratio of real bonds to real total private wealth, $b/(k+b+m)$, to be a function of R, r and ρ. An increase in $R = r + \pi$ with given r and ρ increases the advantage of holding bonds relative to non-interest bearing money. An increase in r with given R and ρ increases the advantage of holding bonds relative to real assets. An increase in ρ with given R and r increases the opportunity cost of holding bonds relative to real assets. Proceeding in the same way as for money we obtain a portfolio balance equation for bonds as a ratio to GNP:

$$\left(\frac{b}{y}\right)^{e} = \beta(r+\pi, r, \rho)\left(\frac{k+m}{y}\right) \tag{14.19}$$

with β increasing in $R = r + \pi$ and r, and decreasing in ρ, and the condition for steady state equilibrium in the bonds market, which is represented in figure 14.2(c) becomes

$$\frac{1-\alpha}{\gamma}\eta = \beta(r+\pi, r, \rho)\left(\frac{1}{q} + \frac{\alpha}{\gamma}\eta\right) \tag{14.20}$$

Putting the output and assets market equilibrium conditions together we have thus the following three equations:

$$q = \frac{\nu + \gamma}{\sigma(1 - \theta) - (1 - \sigma)\eta} \tag{14.21a}$$

$$\frac{\alpha}{\gamma}\eta = \mu(r + \pi, \pi, \rho)\left(\frac{1}{q} + \frac{1 - \alpha}{\gamma}\eta\right) \tag{14.21b}$$

$$\frac{1 - \alpha}{\gamma}\eta = \beta(r + \pi, r, \rho)\left(\frac{1}{q} + \frac{\alpha}{\gamma}\eta\right) \tag{14.21c}$$

They describe synthetically the steady state behaviour of the TSF model in the non-zero growth case.[13]

The three parts of figure 14.2 are an intuitive picture of the structure of the model 14.21. They provide an overview of the nature and role of a steady state government deficit, and a broad insight into the steady state comparative dynamics of the model. They are set out in such a way as to show the key role of the adjusted rather than the non-adjusted deficit. It is in fact the adjusted deficit η which determines directly the steady state levels of the output to capital ratio (and thereby of labour intensity) and of the supply of real debt and money. In steady state the effect of η on these variables embodies in turn the decisive, magnifying influence of the real growth rate.[14]

In a neoclassical fully employed economy we have defined steady state adjusted deficit as a 'portfolio equilibrium' deficit, meaning by this that in such an economy the steady state level of the adjusted deficit is determined only by the requirement of equilibrating the assets market, and not also by that of equilibrating the output market. This is so because by definition a neoclassical fully employed economy is one exhibiting long-run identity between saving-less-adjusted deficit and investment, and therefore long-run equilibrium and stability in the output market, with long-run full employment growth (although with possible short-run fluctuations in labour intensity, unemployment and inflation), irrespective of the adjusted deficit and real interest levels.

In order to visualize in figure 14.2 the way in which a steady state level of the adjusted deficit is determined only by the requirement of equilibrating the assets market, we perform an excercise in the 'operational' interpretation of model 14.21. The model consists of three equations. We may consider γ, θ, ν, ρ and σ as exogenously given parameters. We are then left with five other variables: q, r α, η and π. Of these we may consider α, η and π as policy variables, each of which may in principle be determined by the government. With given α and η the government may determine π by determining, through the non-adjusted deficit δ, the long-run growth rate of the nominal money supply $\hat{M}$. With given α and π the government may determine η by adjusting the primary deficit and the debt ratio. Finally, with given η and π the government may of course determine the monetization ratio α. Suppose we start with given, feasible levels of the exogenous parameters. Then, provided the basic functional relationships have the appropriate shape and position (as may generally be assumed), the equilibrium values of the remaining five variables may be determined with two degrees of freedom. If the government sets freely the values of two of the three policy variables, then the other three variables, including the remaining policy variable, are uniquely determined by the equilibrium conditions. Suppose the government fixes a pair of feasible values for α and π. With all parameters and also α and π given, the level of η determines the position of the money and bonds supply and portfolio balance schedules. Suppose we start off with a value of η such that the real interest r_m required to bring the money market in equilibrium exceeds the real interest r_b required to bring the bonds market in equilibrium: $r_m > r_b$. It is then easily seen that an increase in η would move the money and bonds supply and portfolio balance schedules in such a way as to decrease r_m and increase r_b. An increase in η would therefore drive r_m and r_b together until they meet at some portfolio equilibrium real interest $r_p = r_m = r_b$. Thus, at such level of η the equilibrium values of r and q would also be determined.

By way of example, notice that if the government fixes a pair of feasible values for, say, η nd π, then the equilibrating role in the assets market would have to be played by the policy variable α. Suppose we start off with some value of α such that again $r_m > r_b$. It is easily seen that an increased monetization reduces both r_m and r_b. If we assume that it would reduce r_m faster than r_b, then a sufficient increase in monetization would restore equilibrium in the assets market at some lower steady state real interest. Under the opposite assumption monetization would have to be reduced, bringing a higher steady state real interest.

Carrying our exercise one step forward, we may consider the direction in which changes in certain policy variables would move an original steady state equilibrium. Suppose that, starting from an equilibrium, the government increases the adjusted deficit leaving α and π unchanged. We have just seen that such an increase increases r_b and reduces r_m. We may ask how should inflation change in order to restore equilibrium. If we assume ρ to be unaffected by inflation, then with our assumptions about the portfolio balance functions μ and β we can easily see two things. First, an increase in inflation reduces both r_m and r_b. Secondly, it would reduce r_m faster than r_b, i.e. it would actually widen their gap. Thus a increased adjusted deficit with unchanged monetization would require, for the restoration of a steady state equilibrium, a *lower inflation* and a *higher real interest*. Capital intensity would be lower (through equation 14.21a), while the change in the non-adjusted deficit would be uncertain (higher η but lower π).[15]

These and similiar comparative steady state results are important, and retain as such their full economic meaning. However, it is worth remembering that their 'operational' interpretation in terms of an even loosely conceived causation should be regarded as highly uncertain.[16]

III THE 'TARGET RATE OF RETURN' AND THE CONCEPT OF A LONG-RUN 'FULL EMPLOYMENT EQUILIBRIUM' DEFICIT IN A KEYNESIAN EXCESS SAVING ECONOMY

In the previous section we have outlined what appears to be the basic nature of the deficit in a neoclassical fully employed economy, working under the pure neoclassical assumption of a long-run saving–investment identity, independently of the real interest level. In such an economy the steady state deficit is determined only by the requirement of equilibrating the assets market. In this section we complete the analysis of this stylized picture of the long-run theory of public debt by introducing the possibility of a steady state deficit determined *also* by the requirement of equilibrating the output market. This amounts to introducing the possibility of a long-run saving–investment divergence, and we do so by introducing the simplest possible investment function, namely that the long-run ratio of gross investment to GNP is a decreasing function of the real interest (or in the limit a constant). By consequence the real interest acts simultaneously as an equilibrating variable in the two separate markets for assets and for output, and this reduces the degrees of freedom of the TSF model.[17]

The possibility of excess saving is actually dealt with by our authors. Solow speaks of a 'target rate of return on real capital', while Feldstein speaks of a 'safety trap', but they are really the same thing, which can be viewed as part of the orthodox neoclassical theory of public debt, and may therefore be called the neoclassical treatment of excess saving. Our present extension may also be regarded as a generalization of such neoclassical treatment, but in fact it produces the important qualitative change just mentioned. Inserting the neoclassical treatment of excess saving into the TSF model does not reduce the number of its degrees of freedom, the structural relationships remain broadly unchanged, and the steady state deficit remains determined only by the requirement of portfolio equilibrium. The reason is that although the neoclassical treatment makes a special assumption about investment as distinct from saving behaviour, it does not really separate the two in a general way, so that in the end the long-run saving–investment identity continues to play the decisive role in the output market, with no role left in it for the adjusted deficit. It seems therefore justified, without ideological pretensions, to call our extension in this section a Keynesian treatment.

Formally, the neoclassical treatment of excess saving consists in changing drastically the shape of the portfolio balance function for bonds (equation 14.19). It is assumed that there is a certain critical differential, $\omega > 0$, between the return on real capital ρ and the real rate of interest (or real return on bonds) r. If the actual difference is lower, then private demand for bonds tends to absorb all private wealth, after allowing for the demand for money (as long as there is positive wealth and income there will be some positive demand for money, because money is supposed to be indispensable for transaction purposes). At the same time private demand for holding real assets and for real investment tends to be zero. If the actual difference between ρ and r is higher, then private demand for bonds tends to be zero, while private demand for holding real assets tends to absorb all private wealth (after allowing for some demand for money), and private demand for real investment tends to become indefinitely high. When the actual differential coincides with the critical one, then people will be indifferent between holding their wealth in bonds or real assets, and real investment demand will be identically equal to real saving (less the adjusted deficit).

What we have to do in system 14.21 is to substitute 14.21c with

$$r = \rho - \omega = \rho(q) - \omega \quad \omega > 0 \qquad (14.21c')$$

The last statement of this equation would be in order if we were to follow the usual convention of making real assets profitability an increasing function of labour intensity. In figure 14.2(c) this state of affairs would be represented by cancelling the portfolio balance schedule for bonds, and by substituting to it a vertical line at $r = \rho - \omega = r_b = r_{fe}$, where r_b is as before the bonds market equilibrium real interest, while r_{fe} stands for the full employment real interest (assuming ρ to increase with q, an increase in η, by increasing q, would shift the vertical line to the left; otherwise the latter's position would be fixed by ρ and ω, and η would not affect it.) If actual r is to the left of $r_b = r_{fe}$, then by our present definitions there is excess demand for bonds, and excess saving because real investment demand collapses. There will thus be excess aggregate supply and deflation, and no increase in the adjusted deficit could fill the deflationary gap. Effective labour intensity and the output to capital ratio will continue to grow, and effective real wages to decline, or else actual unemployment will continue to rise. The opposite happens if actual r were to the right of $r_b - r_{fe}$. There would be excess supply of bonds, and insufficient saving because real investment demand tends to become indefinitely high. There will thus be excess aggregate demand and inflation and no decrease in the adjusted deficit could cancel the inflationary gap. Effective labour intensity and the output to capital ratio will continue to decline, and effective real wages to rise, or else actual unemployment will shrink to nil. When actual r coincides with $r_b = r_{fe}$ the demand for bonds will be identically equal to supply, and real investment will be identically equal to saving less the adjusted deficit. The output market will be in equilibrium with any level of deficit. Effective labour intensity, real wages and the output to capital ratio will be stable, or converge to their steady state level, with long-run full employment.

Performing the same exercise as that of the previous section, suppose the government fixes a pair of feasible values for α and π. Then the steady state level of the net deficit is still determined only by the requirement of equilibrating the assets market. If we start off with a value of η such that $r_m > r_b = r_{fe}$, then, by increasing η, r_m would decrease, while $r_b = r_{fe}$ are unchanged (or increase, if ρ increases with η). The increase in η will thus drive r towards $r_b = r_{fe}$ until they meet. The real difference between this 'target rate of return case' and the pure neoclassical case does not lie in the role of the steady state deficit, but in the stability of the output market. If the actual real interest coincides with $r_b = r_{fe}$, then the output market obeys the pure neoclassical identity assumption, and it remains in a fundamentally stable equilibrium with whatever level of η. By contrast, if the actual real interest differed from $r_b = r_{fe}$, then the output market would be in a fundamentally unstable disequilibrium, and no level of η could stabilize it.

While keeping the assumption of a constant saving ratio, the simplest separation of investment from saving behaviour is to assume an independent gross investment ratio to GNP as some decreasing function of the real interest (or as some constant):

$$\frac{i}{y} = j(r) = j_0 - ur \quad (14.22)$$[18]

Because the condition for steady state constancy of effective labour intensity, previously defined in terms of the saving-less-adjusted deficit propensity, was assumed to be identically equal to the investment propensity, it must now be defined in terms of the independent investment propensity, and it becomes

$$\frac{i}{k} = j(r)f(z) = \nu + \gamma \tag{14.23}$$

(by equations 14.6, 14.8 and 14.22). The condition is represented in figure 14.3 by the intersection of the curve $j(r)f(z)$ with the horizontal line $\nu + \gamma$. As r increases, the curve rotates downwards. Reproducing in figure 14.3 the saving-less-adjusted deficit curve of figure 14.1 (from equation 14.10) shows how changes in η may be required to bring the two curves into coincidence. As far as the output market is concerned, if the two curves coincide we have simply the fundamental neoclassical stable equilibrium. But if, say, the saving-less-adjusted deficit curve were higher than the investment curve, then the assumption of long-run output market stability cannot be maintained without strong qualifications. There would be excess aggregate supply, and by standard reasoning two contrasting tendencies would operate: a stabilizing one, due to excess saving, for the real interest to decline, thereby raising the investment propensity, but at the same time a destabilizing one, due to the 'knife edge' effect, for the investment propensity to decline even with constant real interest. The first tendency would push in the direction of closing the excess supply gap, while the second would push straight in the opposite direction. In our oversimplified world it would seem that unless the knife edge effect were negligible the second tendency would be stronger than the first. Thus, as a first approximation, one may say that the excess aggregate supply associated with

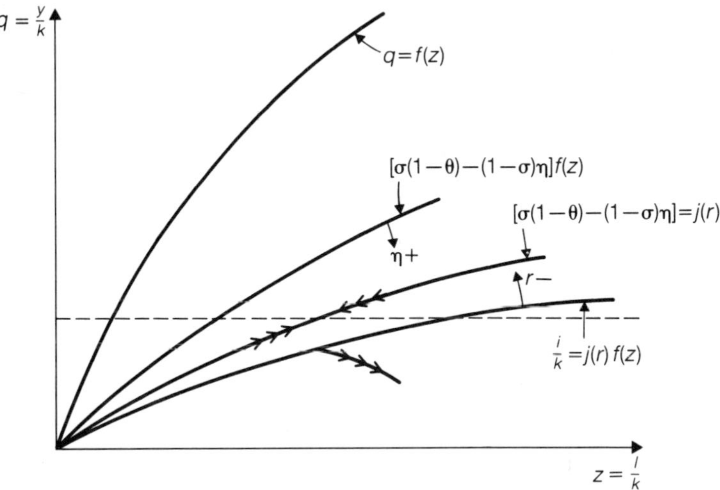

Figure 14.3 Saving-less-adjusted deficit and investment: the Keynesian excess saving case

a long-run saving-less-adjusted deficit curve higher than the long-run investment curve would generate instability in the output market.

The condition for long-run output market equilibrium (zero aggregate supply) requires that the saving-less-adjusted deficit propensity be equal to the investment propensity. By our definitions so far the condition is given by

$$\sigma(1-\theta)-(1-\sigma)\eta=j(r)=j_0-ur \qquad (14.24)$$

which may be rewritten showing r as a simple function of η

$$r=\frac{j_0-\sigma(1-\theta)+(1-\sigma)\eta}{u} \qquad (14.24')$$

and is represented in figure 14.4. The system representing the present Keynesian extension of the TSF model is thus obtained simply by adding equation 14.24′ to the three equations 14.21. The adjusted deficit adds to its equilibrating role in the assets market an equilibrating role in the output market, because as the real interest rises, widening excess supply, the adjusted deficit must also rise in order to maintain output market equilibrium. With reference to this fact we may speak of a long-run 'full employment equilibrium' deficit. With the previously chosen set of exogenous parameters (γ, θ, ν, ρ and σ) the pure neo-classical TSF model, consisting of the three equations 14.21, had two degrees of freedom. The Keynesian extension, consisting of the same

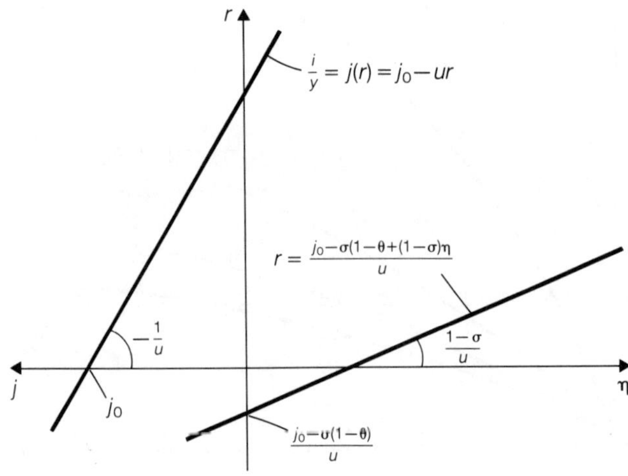

Figure 14.4 Investment propensity, real interest and full employment adjusted deficit ratio

three equations plus equation 14.24, will have only one, reflecting the two independent roles of η.

In order to visualize, under the present additional constraint and with the help of figures 14.2 and 14.4, the double equilibrating role of the adjusted deficit we may repeat the 'operational' exercise of the previous section. Suppose the government fixes a pair of values for α and π, and let us start off with some low level of η, such that it generates three different equilibrium real interest rates for the three markets (money, bonds and output), say $r_m > r_b > r_{fe}$. If η rises, r_m and r_b are drawn together until they meet at some intermediate r_p (portfolio equilibrium real interest). As η rises also r_{fe} rises, but there is no reason why, when the portfolio equilibrium is reached, r_{fe} should coincide with r_p. Suppose it will be $r_p > r_{fe}$. This means that if the actual interest were at r_p, then there would be excess saving and output market instability. In order to bring the output market into equilibrium the adjusted deficit would have to rise further. But this would throw the assets market into disequilibrium. Since the system has only one degree of freedom, in general with α and π fixed the adjusted deficit will not be capable of satisfying simultaneously its two equilibrating roles. Similarly there will not be in general a steady state equilibrium if the government fixed a pair of values for, say, η and π, letting α act as the equilibrating variable. In general one may fix some feasible value for only one policy variable. It could be for instance π. The other policy variables α and η would then both be determined uniquely by the equilibrium conditions. If we continued from the previously reached position with $r_p > r_{fe}$, a steady state equilibrium would require a change in *both* α and η. If a reduced monetization increases r_m faster than r_b, the graphical analysis suggests that there should be either a decrease in α and an increase in η, or vice versa, depending upon the relative sensitivity of r_m, r_b and r_{fe} to such changes. In the first case the steady state would require a higher adjusted deficit and a lower monetization, with a higher real interest. In the second case it would require a lower adjusted deficit and a higher monetization, with a lower real interest. Alternatively, if a feasible value for η were chosen, then both the steady state values for α and π would be determined uniquely by the equilibrium conditions.

The fundamental differences between the neoclassical and the Keynesian long-run theories of public debt, as derived within the framework of the present TSF model, are thus two, representing two faces of the same phenomenon, the separation between saving and investment behaviour. One difference is that, in the Keynesian theory, the adjusted deficit has the two independent equilibrating roles we have been describing. The other is that such a theory suggests the possibility of output market instability when the adjusted deficit does not satisfy the requirement of output market equilibrium.

In closing our discussion we would like to mention two points which in our view are important for placing it into a proper perspective. First we want to recall certain methodological limitations of the type of model we have discussed, which are particularly relevant for the specific subject of debt theory and policy. One limitation lies in the fact that the TSF model is a model of monetary growth where the only available money is, or at any rate requires, a form of government debt. This implies, quite simply, that if we want to have a growing economy we must also have a government deficit. In a pure neoclassical view this may not be so important, because the provision of money could in principle be thought of as precisely the only purpose of the government deficit. Instead, in a Keynesian view, the government budget has also a demand role, and while the case of excess saving would require a long-run deficit, the case of insufficient saving would require a long-run surplus. For the sake of generality it would therefore be necessary to allow for a mechanism of money creation not so completely dependent upon the existence of a government deficit. The other important limitation is the exogenous nature of the real growth rate. For simplicity, in our analysis of the budget we have not distinguished between public consumption and investment. We could have done so, even without changing the analytical framework, but the treatment of the really important issue, which seems to be the possibility of affecting, positively or negatively, the long-run growth rate through the budget, would instead have required significant methodological changes.

Our second point is in a sense more fundamental. Taking the analytical framework as it stands, it concerns the assessment of the comparative validity of the two outlined approaches. The idea that the saving behaviour by people obeys different rules and purposes from the investment behaviour by businesses, and that therefore in the macro-economy the propensity to save may very well differ from the propensity to invest, is an established concept of economics. On the basis of this, one might be inclined to regard the Keynesian version of the TSF model as more realistic than the pure neoclassical one, and indeed to regard the latter as fairly unrealistic *tout court*. The reflection we want to suggest here is that this conclusion is after all not so obvious. In so far as we remain in a short or medium run perspective, the possibility of a divergence between saving and investment propensities is indeed, and should be, largely accepted. But if we move on into a truly long-run perspective, then such a possibility seems to us to be much less convincing. Whatever the elements upon which the saving and investment ratios depend in the short run, if for some reason such elements should not change over a very long period, then it seems to us to be reasonable to think that the two ratios would tend to converge, sooner or later, into coincidence, through a progressive adjustment in attitudes, expectations and general patterns of economic behaviour on the part of people and businesses. If this were true, or at any rate likely, and if this is what may be really meant by the assumption of a long-run saving–investment *identity*, irrespective of the real rate of interest, then the pure neoclassical version of the TSF model, provided it is not removed from its own ground, might claim to have greater 'scientific' validity than the Keynesian conventional wisdom would be prepared to recognize.

NOTES

1 The neoclassical theory of taxation and debt in a growing economy has been developed in other theoretical directions, particularly in the context of life-cycle type saving assumptions, among others by Modigliani (1961), Diamond (1965), Phelps and Shell (1969). Such developments, briefly dealt with also by Atkinson and Stiglitz (1980, ch. 8), would clearly enrich our analysis. However the simpler conceptual framework provided by the TSF model contains all the basic features required for our present limited purposes.

2 As a by-product it will also contribute to a better understanding of the nature and limitations of Feldstein's type of analysis, while preserving the same methodological approach. A wider criticism of the general philosophy underlying the orthodox methodology can be found in Thurow's review article (1983) of Feldstein's book (1983). Thurow's critique is relevant and important, but of course it does not undermine the usefulness, however limited, of orthodox methodology.

3 For simplicity, and following Feldstein (1980), we do not distinguish between monetary base as a government liability, and money as a medium of exchange generated out of monetary base through the credit multiplier by the banking system. The distinction, which could be introduced at the cost of some complications, would not really affect the very general interdependencies to which we shall confine ourselves.

4 This is a slightly unconventional definition of the inflation tax. Others define it as the difference beween the average nominal interest paid on government debt and the latter's monetary erosion. The tax may then also be negative, when there is a sufficiently high nominal interest or a sufficiently low inflation (see for instance Masera, 1984).

5 GNP less the balance of all actual transfers means GNP less net tax revenues, plus nominal interest on government debt, less the inflation tax (which is an implicit but none the less actual transfer): $y_d = y - t + Rb - d\pi$. By 14.1 $t = g + Rb \quad d\hat{D}$. Substituting this into y_d above we obtain expression 14.5: $y_d = y - g + d(\hat{D} - \pi) = y - g +$ adf. Contrary to this approach, the 'rational' view of public debt, in its admittedly extreme form, suggests that in a long-run perspective there is no such thing as a public

deficit, because all public expenditure is correctly perceived as being precisely covered by taxation, either actual (explicit or implicit, via the inflation tax) or in the form of the present discounted value of future taxes required to repay the principal and interest of present borrowing. The adoption of such a view would considerably alter all our present arguments. Although there are perfectly good reasons for disputing such an extreme 'neutrality' view, it nevertheless represents the most serious challenge to the conventional treatment of fiscal policy. For an authoritative overview of the issue and its implications see Tobin and Buiter (1979, 1980).

6 From $S = \sigma y_d$, $y_d = (1 - \theta + \eta)y$ (equation 14.5′) and adf $= \eta y$ (equation 14.2′).

7 Equation 14.11 is the same as equation 14.2″. Equation 14.12 is obtained by substituting equation 14.11 into equation 14.1″. Notice again that when $\pi = 0$ then $\delta = \eta$.

8 In the words of Congdon (1984), 'what is the point of perpetuating the national debt? In a long run steady state the only beneficiaries of deficit financing are tax inspectors (who have to collect taxes to pay the interest), gilt-edged stockbrokers (who receive commission on transactions in the debt instruments) and macroeconomists (who pontificate on the pros and cons of particular fiscal policies)'.

9 By substituting equation 14.1 into 14.2 and dividing by y we obtain

$$\frac{\text{adf}}{y} = \eta = \frac{g - t}{y} + \frac{br - m\pi}{y}$$

In steady state, when r reaches the critical level 14.16, $(g - t)/y = \epsilon$ becomes zero (by 14.15), and our expression becomes $\eta = (br - m\pi)/y$, which says precisely that the adjusted deficit ratio is equal to the average real interest burden. As already explained, we consider only the steady state (long-run equilibrium) relationship between deficits and debt ratios. For a discussion of the serious instability problems which may arise in the dynamics of the debt ratio when real growth, real interest and primary deficit ratio are given independently, see the chapter by Masera in this volume (and the neat analysis of the case, given in its Appendix 1).

10 Equations 14.1‴, 14.2‴ and 14.3‴ are obtained by putting $\gamma = 0$ into equations 14.1″, 14.2″ and 14.3″. Furthermore, introducing the monetization coefficient α we would have $m/y = \alpha(d/y)$ and $b/y = (1 - \alpha)/(d/y)$, and 14.3‴ would become $\epsilon = (\alpha\pi - (1 - \alpha)r)(d/y)$. The arbitrariness of the values of d/y and α would obviously cease when the assets market is also brought into the picture.

11 We prefer to avoid identifying it with the marginal productivity of real capital, and to regard it rather as an exogenous parameter, with no specified link with capital intensity.

12 The steady state supplies of money and bonds as ratios to GNP have already been given by equations 14.13 and 14.14:

$$\left(\frac{m}{y}\right)^s = \frac{\alpha}{\gamma}\eta$$

(see also note 3) and

$$\left(\frac{b}{y}\right)^s = \frac{1 - \alpha}{\gamma}\eta\,.$$

$1/q$ is the capital to output ratio k/y. Equation 14.18 is obtained by equating $(m/y)^s$ to $(m/y)^e$ and substituting these expressions into such equation.

13 Equation 14.21a is 14.10′, 14.21b is 14.18 and 14.21c is 14.20. We omit to similarly put together the corresponding set of equations for the zero growth case. This can easily be done by taking equations 14.1‴–14.3‴ above and the associated expressions given in note 10, and by then following the same procedure as in the non-zero growth case.

14 The non-adjusted deficit, taken by Feldstein as his key deficit variable, may have greater operational meaning, but in a long-run steady state framework this may not be so important. As is evident from figure 14.2, the non-adjusted deficit δ has as such no direct link with the other variables entering into the determination of the overall long-run equilibrium. In particular it has no direct link to capital intensity, which is another key variable in Feldstein's analysis.

15 The first effect of increased inflation is shown immediately by figures 14.2(b) and (c). An increase in π moves the $(m/y)^e$ schedule downwards and the $(b/y)^e$ schedule upwards. In order to see the second effect one has to view the $(m/y)^e$ schedules as expressed in terms of the *nominal* interest R, writing $\mu(R, \pi, \rho)$ and $\beta(R, R - \pi, \rho)$, and measuring R on the horizontal axis. An increase in π moves both the $(m/y)^e$ and $(b/y)^e$ schedules downwards, reducing R_m and increasing R_b. This implies that the increase in π widens the gap between the equilibrium real interest rates r_b and r_m. This exercise would suggest that the validity of some of the Feldstein's (1980) results about the long-run effects of an increased deficit may not be so general. Specifically, his result that an increased non-adjusted deficit accompanied by a policy aimed at maintaining a constant real interest 'causes' both increased inflation and reduced capital intensity depends precisely, as he himself states, on the assumption that the positive effect of inflation on the demand for bonds be large enough to outweigh its negative effect on the demand for money implied by keeping the real interest unchanged. Assuming inflation to have either a sufficiently weak adverse effect on ρ, or a sufficiently strong *independent* adverse effect on the demand for money, or both, an increased non-adjusted deficit with constant real interest would more likely 'cause' a lower than a higher inflation. The view of a strong adverse effect of inflation on the return on real capital, through increased tax liability, is actually a central contention in much of Feldstein's recent work (1983). On the other hand Feldstein (1980) disregards the existence of an *independent* adverse effect of inflation on the demand for money, while the possibility that such an independent effect may not be negligible is largely accepted.

16 See Solow's comments on this difficult point (1970, pp. 70ff.)

17 The subjection of the original neoclassical approach to monetary growth to Wicksell–Keynesian criticism has led to the development of a large, sophisticated literature (see, among others, Rose, 1966; 1973; Stein, 1982, especially ch. 5). However, our simpler exercise seems sufficient for the purpose of dealing with the basic qualitative change in the nature of a steady state deficit.

18 The standard extension would be to let also the saving ratio increase with r and ρ, and decrease when the ratio of private wealth to private disposable income increases and to let the investment ratio increase with ρ. But for our present purposes the simplest way will do. In this context it is worth mentioning that the inclusion of private wealth in the determination of the

private saving propensity, together with the conventional view of public debt as private wealth, introduces an element of stability into the non-steady state behaviour of an excess saving economy. The classical statement of the implicit stability of a deficit spending policy for full employment, through the wealth effect of public debt, goes back to Lerner (1943) (see also Dernburg (1962), and again the elegant discussion in Dernburg and Dernburg (1969, section 7.3).

NOTATION

B, b	nominal and real interest bearing government bonds
$\left(\frac{b}{y}\right)^e$	portfolio balance for bonds
$\left(\frac{b}{y}\right)^s$	supply of bonds
D, d	nominal and real total government debt (= money plus bonds)
adf	real adjusted deficit (the real deficit adjusted for inflation, i.e. diminished by the real inflation tax)
g	real government expenditure on goods and services
i	real gross investment
j	ratio of gross investment to GDP
k	real capital
l	'effective' employment
M, m	nominal and real money
$\left(\frac{m}{y}\right)^e$	portfolio balance for money
$\left(\frac{m}{y}\right)^s$	supply of money
ndf	real non-adjusted deficit (the real deficit, without deduction of the inflation tax)
P	price level
pdf	real primary deficit (the real non-adjusted deficit diminished by the real debt interest payments)
$q = \frac{y}{k}$	output to capital ratio
R	nominal interest rate
$r = R - \pi$	real interest rate
r_b	bonds market equilibrium real interest
r_e	output market equilibrium (full employment) real interest
r_m	money market equilibrium real interest
r_p	portfolio equilibrium real interest
s	real gross private saving
t	real net tax revenues (real tax revenues less real non-interest transfer payments)
y	real gross output (GNP)
y_d	real (gross) disposable income
$z = \frac{l}{k}$	'effective' labour intensity

α	monetization ratio of deficit and debt
γ	'natural' growth rate of real output
δ	gross deficit ratio to GNP
ϵ	primary deficit ratio to GNP
η	net deficit ratio to GNP
θ	government expenditure ratio to GNP
ν	depreciation rate of real capital
π	inflation rate
ρ	index of real assets profitability
σ	propensity to save (out of disposable income)
ω	critical differential between return on real assets and real interest (rea return on bonds)
dot ($\dot{}$)	time derivative
cap ($\hat{}$)	time rate of change

REFERENCES

Atkinson, A.B. and Stiglitz, J.E. 1980: *Lectures on Public Economics*, McGraw-Hill, London.

Congdon, T. 1984: The analytical foundations of medium-term financial strategy. In M. Keen (ed.) *The Economy and the 1984 Budget*, Institute of Fiscal Studies, London.

Dernburg, T.F. 1962: A note on productivity, wealth and fiscal policy, *National Tax Journal*, 15, 327–9.

Dernburg, T.F. and Dernburg, J.D. 1969: *Macroeconomic Analysis*, Addison-Wesley, Reading, MA.

Diamond, P.A. 1965: National debt in a neoclassical growth model, *American Economic Review*, 55, 1125–50.

Feldstein, M. 1980: Fiscal policies, inflation and capital formation, *American Economic Review*, 70, 636–50.

Feldstein, M. 1983: *Inflation, Tax Rules and Capital Formation*, University of Chicago Press, Chicago.

Lerner, A.P. 1943: Functional finance and the federal debt, *Social Research*, 10, 38–51.

Masera, R.S. 1984: Monetary policy and budget policy: blend or dichotomy?. In R.S. Masera and R. Triffin (eds) *Europe's Money: Problems of European Monetary Coordination and Integration*, Oxford University Press, Oxford.

Modigliani, F. 1961: Long run implications of alternative fiscal policies and the burden of the national debt, *Economic Journal*, 71, 730–55.

Phelps, E.S. and Shell, K. 1969: Public debt, taxation and capital intensiveness, *Journal of Economic Theory*, 1, 330–46.

Rose, H. 1966: Unemployment in a theory of growth, *International Economic Review*, 7, 260–82.

Rose, H. 1973: Effective demand in the long run. In J.A. Mirrlees and N.H. Stern (eds) *Models of Economic Growth*, Macmillan, London.

Solow, R.M. 1970: *Growth Theory*, Oxford University Press, Oxford.

Stein, J.L. 1982: *Monetarist, Keynesian and New Classical Economics*, Blackwell, Oxford.

Thurow, L.C. 1983: The elephant and the Maharajah, *The New York Review of Books*, XXX, No. 20, December.

Tobin, J. 1955: A dynamic aggregative model, *Journal of Political Economy*, 63, 103–15.

Tobin, J. 1965: Money and economic growth, *Econometrica*, October 1965.

Tobin, J. and Buiter, W.H. 1979: Debt neutrality: a brief review of doctrine and evidence. In G.M. von Furstemberg (ed.) *Social Security versus Private Saving*, Ballinger, Cambridge, MA.

Tobin, J. and Buiter, W.H. 1980: Fiscal and monetary policies, capital formation and economic activity. In G.M. von Furstemberg (ed.) *The Government and Capital Formation*, Ballinger, Cambridge, MA.

15
Debt and Taxes in War and Peace: The Case of a Small Open Economy

JOHN S. FLEMMING

I INTRODUCTION

This chapter examines the role of budget deficits and surpluses in smoothing tax rates in a stochastic model. It is argued that interesting cases require that the stochastic variable should have some limited degree of serial correlation. The examples used involve stochastic transitions between two states where the probability of moving from one state to the other does not depend on how long it has persisted – nor is it affected by any economic variable such as the level of public expenditure. Two types of shock are considered: a random demand for public goods and a random real wage.

The model differs from those of Barro (1979) and Lucas and Stokey (1983) in that the costs of distorting taxes are explicit and the endogeneity of both the tax base and optimal level of public expenditure are fully recognized. This enables us to address questions not only relating to the role of debt but also to the choice of tax base – in particular between consumption and wage income.

Lucas and Stokey concentrate particularly on problems of time inconsistency – as also have Persson and Svensson (1984). These problems are not addressed here because the possibility of consumption and wage taxation enormously increases the range of the problem. It will always be tempting for a government to confiscate private wealth by an unanticipated increase in the consumption tax rate with its distorting effects on labour supply offset by a reduced wage tax. In effect we restrict

This chapter has had a long gestation period. Comments from Mervyn King have been helpful throughout. Jim Mirrlees was also of assistance at an early stage and Maurice Scott, Torsten Persson and Lars Svensson at a late one.

ourselves to policies to which a government might commit itself. Currie and Levine (1985) argue that in a stochastic world a (long-lived) government will have an incentive to retain its credibility – an argument which should apply in this case. We do, however, briefly consider state contingent capital market instruments which were also considered by Lucas and Stokey. In the context of our model these can be used to eliminate any need for varying tax rates or for budget deficits in an open economy.

The structure of the chapter is as follows: section II considers the limitations of Barro's (1974) 'Ricardian equivalence' of debt and taxes, also the issue of the openness or closedness of the economy (the exogeneity of factor prices), and a role for debt in a deterministic model in which, optimally, expenditure and the tax base grow at different rates. In section III this role is eliminated, by equating the interest and time preference rates so that, given a constant real wage, nothing is chosen to grow. Alternative stochastic specifications are also considered. Section IV examines the profiles generated by optimal consumption and wage taxation respectively, in the absence of contingent debt, when the shocks are discrete and Markovian as described above. It is shown that tax rates rise through 'bad' high tax states and vice versa. It is also suggested that the consumption tax is likely to prove superior to a wage tax when confronting either type of shock considered here. Finally state contingent bonds, as well as capital levies on adverse transitions, and the 'postwar credits' adopted by Britain on Keynes's suggestions in the Second World War are discussed in a brief section V. The arguments of sections II–V all relate to a small open economy in which factor prices are exogenous and unaffected by 'war'.

II THE ROLE OF DEBT IN PUBLIC FINANCE

What is the proper role of debt in public finance? Barro's (1974) 'Ricardian equivalence theorem' suggests that debt offers no additional opportunities if lump-sum taxes are available. The conditions for this result are very strong: the following are sufficient:

1 intergenerational transfers are all at interior optima (qualified by Bagwell and Bernheim, 1985);
2 there are no taxes elsewhere in the system with non-constant marginal rates;
3 there is no uncertainty.

The first of these requires either a homogeneous population and/or perfect capital markets. If the population is sufficiently heterogeneous some transfers will be from parent to child and some from child to parent. If the degree of identification between generations is less than 100 per cent there will be some cases in which no transfer is planned and none would be planned in response to small changes in the relative position of the parties. Such corner solutions can also be induced by capital market imperfections. In either case transfers by the authorities may not be welfare neutral as they are not offset by private transfers. Intergenerational transfers are a form of public debt, if made through a social security agency.

Even if the change in question relates to lump sum taxes, if there exist non-linear taxes on wealth, bequests, inheritance, property income, or savings, then the attempt by households to offset the effect of a changed sequence of lump sum transfers will involve changing the 'tax prices' they face and a full offset will not occur (Abel, 1985b). If the future lump sum taxes are uncertain, non-neutralities may arise as future tax payments are discounted for risk; even poll taxes may be effectively stochastic if the birth and death process is random; the number of my grandchildren liable to redeem the debt issued to finance a cut in my poll tax matters to me but is uncertain (Abel, 1985a).

If any of these conditions fails to hold, a role can be found for debt even in a world of lump-sum taxes. Perhaps more interesting, however, is to relax the assumption of lump-sum taxation, as Barro did in his 1979 paper. If only distorting taxes are available there may be a role for debt to 'smooth' tax relates if optimization subject to continuous budget balance implies erratic movements in rates. This could arise if either the constrained optimum expenditure profile, or that of the tax base, were lumpy. The presumption that the optimal path for tax rates is smooth follows from the fact that the deadweight burden of taxes typically rises more than proportionately with the tax rate. Moreover even if the profiles were smooth the path for the tax rate implied by continuous budget balance might well not be optimal for instance in the example below where a constant tax rate is optimal.

If, for this or other reasons, a role is found for debt, the consequences differ significantly between open and closed economies. In a small open economy a case can be made for taking the marginal product of capital, and hence the rate of interest, to be independent of the level, or rate of change, of the public debt, or of the size of the capital stock. This enormously simplifies the analysis and will be assumed in all of what follows although extension to a closed economy is clearly called for as state contingent bonds enable a small open economy to insure all the relevant risks on the world capital market (see section V).

Consider the special case in which the representative consumer's utility is made up of three additively separate elements:

$$U = U_1(C) + U_2(L) + U_3(G)$$

where C is private consumption, L is labour supply and G is the quantity of some public good. Suppose that consumption is subject to tax at a rate θ, and that U_1 is isoelastic in C (i.e. $U_1 = (1/\gamma)C^{\gamma}$). It is then fairly easy to see that, if borrowing is allowed, the optimal rate of consumption taxation is constant. This is demonstrated formally in the Appendix, but is a straightforward application of a result due to Atkinson and Stiglitz (1972).

With a constant tax rate the optimal growth rate of private consumption (g_C), and thus of revenue (g_R), is $(r - \rho)/(1 - \gamma)$ where r is the exogenous real interest rate and ρ is the rate at which consumers discount utility, while if U_3 is also isoelastic (i.e. $U_3 = (1/\epsilon)G^{\epsilon}$) the optimal growth rate of public expenditure (g_G) is $(r - \rho)/(1 - \epsilon)$. Only if $\gamma = \epsilon$ do both expenditure and revenue optimally grow at the same rate; and only in this case will the ratio of public debt to private, and public, consumption be constant.

What would the optimal borrowing strategy be? If $r > \rho$ both growth rates are positive, while if $\rho/r > \gamma, \epsilon$, the present values of consumption and public expenditure are both bounded (i.e. g_C, $g_G < r$). If, in this case, the growth (g_G) of public expenditure exceeds that ($g_C = g_R$) of the tax base (private consumption) and thus, at the constant tax rate, of revenue, in the limit as time goes to infinity revenue covers a negligible proportion of expenditure. The balance must come from interest accruing on negative debt (positive claims by the government on other sectors); in the limit the (negative) public debt and expenditure both grow at the same rate.

This case is illustrated in figure 15.1. In figure 15.1(a) the government is initially in debt, while in figure 15.1(b) it starts with excess net worth (i.e more than sufficient to endow the first-best supply of the public good) which it is assumed to be constrained to run down by resorting to a consumption subsidy (with distorting effects symmetrical to those of taxation) as well as to excess supply of the public good. Figures 15.1(c), (d) and (e) illustrate the case in which $\gamma > \epsilon$ and consumption and revenue rise faster than expenditure which, in the limit, becomes a negligible fraction of it, the balance being absorbed by debt service obligations.

Thus far we have identified two possible roles for public debt; an intertemporal redistributive role if lump-sum taxes are available but the other conditions for Ricardian equivalence are not met; an intertemporal resource allocation role if these conditions are met but the available taxes distort. In neither of these cases was the issue of 'lumpy' revenues or expenditures directly confronted. Deterministic lumpiness of expenditure translates directly into an enhanced role for debt. Similarly if some factor made it optimal for consumers to vary their consumption, but not its elasticity, then the optimal tax rate will remain

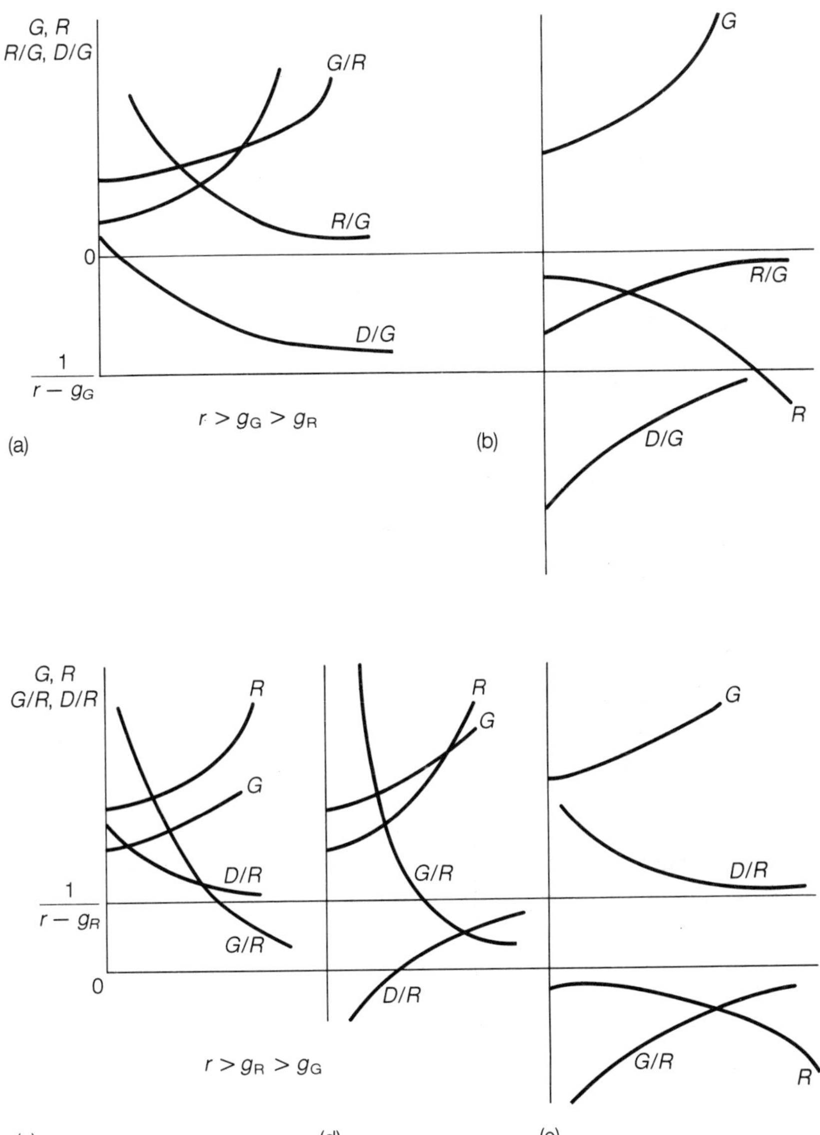

Figure 15.1 (a) Initial debt above long-term ratio (b) initial debt below (public sector net worth above) first-best level; negative distorting taxes necessary (c) initial debt above long-term ratio (d) initial debt below long-term ratio (public sector net worth possibly positive) net positive distorting taxes necessary (e) initial debt below (public sector net worth above) first-best level; negative distorting taxes necessary

constant and variation in the tax base will feed through directly into revenue and the deficit/surplus position.

III STOCHASTIC SPECIFICATIONS

More interesting questions arise if the variations in expenditure or revenue are less than perfectly predictable; it is these cases which are the principal subject of this chapter. In order to focus attention on the effects of randomness other sources of variation in tax rates will be (virtually) eliminated, not by the very special assumptions on the structure of the utility function necessary to make their optima constant, but by removing any tendency of the economy to grow. In a deterministic economy, assuming $r = \rho$ would suffice in the absence of interest taxation – which we also assume. In a stochastic environment risk may itself provide a reason for accumulation in which case the equality has to be adjusted by the addition of a suitable risk premium. Furthermore, although we do not assume that optimal tax rates would not vary if the economy were to grow, we do assume that the elasticities which determine them vary continuously if at all.

Relevant shocks might in principle occur in three different ways: they could shift the production function and thus the tax base, they could shift demand between public and private goods and thus the revenue requirements, or they could shift demand between private goods thus affecting the elasticity of supply of labour or consumption and the behavioural response to taxes. In what follows we consider only the first two types of shock; i.e. shifts in demand for public goods, and in the real wage – perhaps reflecting shifts in the terms of trade.

The formal specification is as follows. The representative individual's welfare function is of the form

$$W = \int_0^\infty e^{-\rho t}[U(C,L) + \tilde{s}P(G)]dt$$

The consumer maximizes $U(C, L)$ subject to

$$\dot{F} = rF + (1 - \tau)\tilde{w}L - (1 + \theta)C$$

where F is his financial wealth, τ the wage tax rate and θ the consumption tax rate. National income $Y = rK + \tilde{w}L$ and the public debt, all of which is indexed to the general price level, $D = F - K$, evolves as

$$\dot{D} = rD + G - \tau\tilde{w}L - \theta C$$

while the nationally owned capital stock, K, evolves as
$\dot{K} = rK + \tilde{w}L - C - G.$
The two random variables, $\tilde{s}$ and $\tilde{w}$, are indicated by tildes.

Not all random variations of $\tilde{s}$ and $\tilde{w}$ lead to interesting results. Suppose that each is generated by a 'white noise' process, i.e. the value in each period is drawn from the same distribution. Even if the drawing is made before taxes and expenditures are set, the optimum will be associated with a random budget deficit or surplus. The next period's problem differs from the first only by the larger or smaller debt and capital stock resulting from the previous period's realization, and the solution will differ only to the extent that it depends on these two state variables which now follow some form of random walk – as also will the optimal taxes and expenditures. For small real interest rates the variance of the tax rate process will be small relative to that of the white noise processes generating $\tilde{s}$ and $\tilde{w}$; that of expenditure will also be small except where it is reacting directly to shocks to $\tilde{s}$.

Secondly, suppose that $\tilde{s}$ and $\tilde{w}$ themselves follow random walks; in this case the best guess about the future is that it will be like the present. Taxes and expenditures should thus to a first approximation be based on assuming that $\tilde{s}$ and $\tilde{w}$ will permanently retain their present values. Assuming, as we have, that taxes and expenditures are constant in a deterministic optimum implies that the budget thus planned will balance. Thus in this case the debt will be constant while taxes and expenditures follow (possibly modified) random walks of variance of the same order as those of $\tilde{s}$ and $\tilde{w}$.

To generate more interesting results requires that shocks be in some way serially correlated – though not cumulating as in a random walk. In this sense they must follow stochastic 'cycles'. This will ensure a substantial role for debt. Note, however, that though the shocks may be cyclical the economy is one in which all markets clear continuously: there are no Keynesian cycles of alternating 'boom' and 'slump' in economic activity.

As the treatment of a general specification of such shocks is intractable, in this chapter I consider cases in which the economy switches between two states according to a Markov process. That is, the probability, per unit time, of moving to the other state is constant – though it will generally differ between the two states. Thus the shift in demand for public goods might represent the discrete transition from peace to war – which I assume to be characterized by a greater demand for public goods (the analogy is not close, the probability of transition to peace is unaffected by expenditure, the war does not interfere with trade or factor flows, the end of the world is no nigher). The real wage is perhaps less likely to change discretely – though it is affected by the terms of trade which OPEC has shifted twice – but for symmetry it may be appropriate to have an illustrative 'technical' shift as well as one of demand.

Our purpose is twofold; first to characterize fairly generally, though not rigorously, the optimal dynamic paths of expenditure, revenue, debt and tax rates in the face of such shocks when the only source of revenue is a distorting proportional tax. No attempt is made to rationalize the resort to distorting taxes by modelling the informational or distributional constraints on optimal lump-sum taxes. Nor do I address the time inconsistency problem raised by a consumption tax when there is private wealth which could be confiscated by raising the consumption tax and offsetting its effect on labour supply by a wage subsidy. (In the context of wage and inflation taxes, and with, like Barro, exogenous expenditure and tax base, this issue has been addressed by Lucas and Stokey (1983) and Persson and Svensson (1984).)

Subject to these limitations the second objective is to assess the relative merits of consumption and wage income as the base for the proportional tax. We know that the two candidates are equivalent in deterministic stationary states and that the implied non-taxation of interest income characterizes the optimum for a subset of cases involving separable and isoelastic utility functions (Atkinson and Stiglitz, 1972). Our arguments point to the superiority of the consumption base for coping with these particular shocks. It is also noted that a consumption tax which changes discretely when transitions occur changes the consumption value of private wealth. This could also be achieved by issuing a 'state contingent bond' (Lucas and Stokey, 1983) such as the (non-marketable) postwar credits in which, under Keynes's influence, forced savings were made in the UK during the Second World War.

IV OPTIMAL CONSUMPTION AND WAGE TAXATION

The government's problem is to select four functions $T_i(K,D)$, $G_i(K,D)$ where i indexes the state and $T = \tau$, θ depending on the tax base chosen. The government's choice is conditioned by the behaviour of private agents who also choose four functions $C_i(F, T)$, $L_i(F, T)$ in the knowledge of the government's tax rules. Given the separability assumption, public expenditure does not affect private decisions. Expectations of both parties are rational in the sense that the identity of the stochastic variable, which is generally observable, and the parameters of the process by which it is generated, are generally known; the government knows the consumers' optimizing response to taxes and the consumers know the government's tax rules.

In a static context we would expect the wage tax rate to rise both with the level of debt D and of the capital stock K; the first because greater debt increases servicing obligations; the second, in an open economy, because, with given population and exogenous wages, more capital raises potential income and demand for a normal public good; in both cases F rises reducing labour supply and the base of the wage tax (in a closed economy there might be some offset from extra capital raising the real wage). With a consumption tax the effect of debt is again to raise the required tax rate even though the greater debt adds to F and thus to private consumption – the extra revenue must be less than the extra interest due. The effect of greater capital is ambiguous as it increases private consumption, and thus raises revenue at an unchanged tax rate, as well as raising demand for the public good.

As in the deterministic case of the Appendix, the optimal value of the tax rates τ and θ can be expressed in terms of the shadow prices (λ, ν) attached to K and D in the government's problem and that (μ) attached to F in the private problem. If $r = \rho$ these shadow prices are all constant in the deterministic case and, loosely speaking, follow random walks in the stochastic case. This implies that the optimal tax rate T will also approximate a random walk:

$$\begin{aligned} T^* &= T^*(\lambda, \mu, \nu) \\ E_t(T^*_{t+h}) &= T^*_t(\lambda_t, \mu_t, \nu_t) + T^*_\lambda E\Delta\lambda + T^*_\mu E\Delta\mu + T^*_\nu E\Delta\nu \\ &\quad + (T_{\lambda\lambda}\sigma_{\lambda\lambda} + T_{\mu\mu}\sigma_{\mu\mu} + T_{\nu\nu}\sigma_{\nu\nu} \\ &\quad + 2(T_{\lambda\mu}\sigma_{\lambda\mu} + T_{\lambda\nu}\sigma_{\lambda\nu} + T_{\mu\nu}\sigma_{\mu\nu}) \end{aligned}$$

Where $E(\cdot)$ is the expectation operator and σ_{ij} the covariance between changes in variables i and j. Though $T(\lambda, \mu, \nu)$ is non-linear its curvature is uncertain as therefore is the deviation of $E(\Delta T)$ from zero which is the value used in the following argument.

If the unconditional expectation of the tax rate change $E(\Delta T) = 0$, then, although there are *ex-post* tax rate changes, behaviour is never affected by anticipation of change. Consumers/taxpayers may save in 'good' (low tax) states, providing a stock to be drawn down in the event of a 'bad' (high tax) state occurring, but anticipated tax rate changes do not have the dramatic intertemporal substitution effects of which expected changes are capable; indeed the argument reflects the fact that such temporary substitution effects involve welfare losses.

Consider a point in time at which the economy has just switched from a good to a bad state; at unchanged tax rates, revenue will have fallen more than expenditure, or expenditure risen; and at a positive interest rate this will also be true of their present values. Thus to restore expected present value budget balance, which must always hold, and assuming that revenues are not already maximal, tax rates must rise discretely. This is consistent with unconditional expectations prior to the shock that the tax rate would be unchanged, if tax rates would have fallen had the shock not occurred. This is turn is consistent if in the good state the budget was in surplus so that the debt would have fallen; the arguments for tax rate smoothing imply that the step rise in the tax rate on the adverse transition would not be sufficient to prevent the budget moving from surplus to deficit. As a result of the deficit, debt and the tax rate must rise throughout the duration of the bad state; as the marginal cost of revenue rises with the tax rate in this model the optimal provision of the public good will fall through bad states and rise through good ones. Thus by the end of a long 'war' the level of public expenditure may have fallen below that at the end of the preceding peace – but it will fall further when s reverts to its peacetime value.

Before illustrating these arguments more fully it is useful to establish the first-best responses to the shocks we consider, in the context, for example, of a single-member society. These responses may act as a benchmark by which to assess alternative second-best policies. In bad states (high s, low w) private consumption is lower than in good states; its marginal utility is therefore higher (given $U_{cc} < 0$) and therefore capital will be accumulated in good states and run down in bad ones. Thus, in good states, capital and consumption of both C and G rise if they are normal goods, and labour supply falls if leisure is normal – and vice versa in bad states. These features are reflected in figures 15.2(a) and (b) which differ only in that G and L are both high in the bad state in figure 15.2(a) (high $\tilde{s}$) and in the good state in figure 15.2(b) (high $\tilde{w}$); the former in response to temporarily greater need, and the latter to temporarily greater opportunity. In principle the labour response in figure 15.2(b) is ambiguous: in the limit as the transition probabilities go to zero the ambiguity is that of the static response to higher wages. The figures shows a positive response as being more likely by virtue of the temporary nature of the wage shift which also moderates the consumption response.

Consider now a multi-member society with distorting taxes and stochastic demand for public goods. If $\tilde{s}$ rises we have already seen that both G and the tax rate (T) will rise initially and, although G subsequently falls, T rises further as debt accumulates. Thus whether private consumption or wage income is taxed, C and G will vary qualitatively in the second-best case as in the first.

The same is not necessarily true of labour supply which can be written quite generally as

$$L = L\left[\frac{(1-\tau)\tilde{w}}{1+\theta}, \frac{rF}{(1-\tau)\tilde{w}}\right]$$

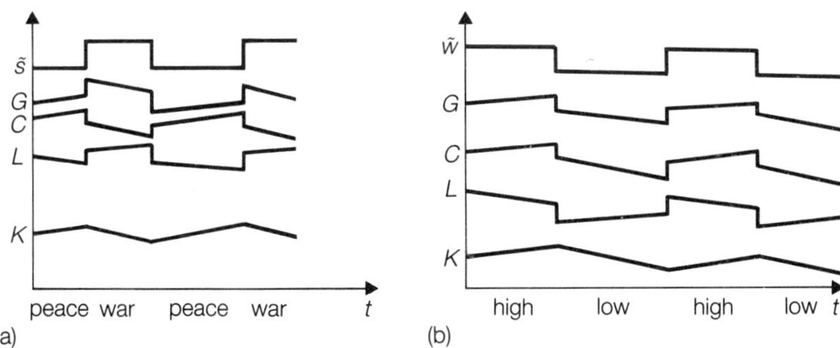

Figure 15.2 First best

where the first argument is the consumption purchasing power of the net wage, and the second is the amount of leisure that can be 'bought' with property income. While this second term has an unambiguously negative (income) effect on labour supply, that of the first term is uncertain. If it has a positive effect the pattern of labour supply will be the opposite of that in figure 15.2(a). If it has a negative effect the situation is more complicated for in this case a consumption tax stimulates labour supply while a wage tax might also do so if the effect were strong enough. Figure 15.3(a) is drawn on the assumption that consumption taxation stimulates labour supply while wage taxation reduces it – both for positive non-labour income.

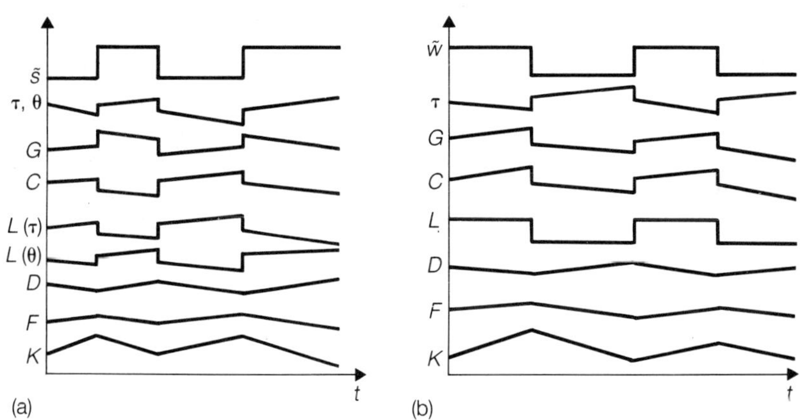

Figure 15.3 Second best

Given $rF > 0$, a wage tax is somewhat more likely to reduce labour supply than is a consumption tax, and to the extent that this diverges qualitatively from the first-best response it appears to be the inferior instrument when confronting stochastic demand for public goods. Notice also that in good states the public debt falls while private wealth rises, so that the productive capital stock K could be said to be crowded out (in) more than one-for-one by the fiscal deficit (surplus).

If the random variable is not $\tilde{s}$ but $\tilde{w}$, it is not clear that the rate of consumption taxation would have to rise even in the bad (low wage) state. When w falls so does the present value of future national income (assuming $r > 0$) and both C and G should also fall. It is possible that revenue and planned expenditure might fall *pari passu* and no deficit or surplus be opened up. This would be less likely if there were positive initial debt or if the income elasticities of public and private consumption differed. Nevertheless, it is possible that the expenditure tax rate could be constant and the picture for G, C, L and K be as in figure 15.2(b). In this case the budget is balanced throughout and K and F move together one-for-one.

If, however, $\tilde{w}$ is random and $\tilde{w}L$ is the tax base, the story is rather different. Optimal permanent-income-related-public-expenditure G is most unlikely to fall anything like as much as do earnings in response to a temporary fall in wages – a fall aggravated by the rise in the rate of wage taxation.

Again in figure 15.3(b), G and C are qualitatively as in figure 15.2(b). The jumps in labour supply in figure 15.2(b) are quite likely to be larger than their first-best level. Within each phase, labour supply is subject to possibly offsetting effects. In the good state, wealth is accumulated which tends to reduce labour supply as in figure 15.2(b) but the falling tax rate raises the net wage. As this might well tend to raise labour supply it is shown as flat.

The argument suggests that, where $\tilde{w}$ is random, the variations both within and between states in the wage tax rate would be greater than the (possibly negligible) variation in the rate of consumption taxation. Although this is not an adequate index of expected welfare losses it is suggestive of a superiority of a consumption tax base when the wage is stochastic as well as, for the reasons given earlier, when the demand for public goods is random.

V CONCLUSIONS

The conclusion I am tempted to draw from the argument so far is that the best way to cope with the shocks analysed above is to vary the rate of consumption taxation keeping the unconditional expected change in the rate close to zero and alternating between periods of low and falling tax rates with a budget surplus and periods of high and rising tax rates accompanied by a deficit.

In the case of shocks to the demand for public goods we know that this policy calls for step changes in the consumption tax rate when changes of state occur. Such changes alter the immediate consumption value of wealth and thus have something in common with wealth levies and distribution on, e.g. the outbreak of war and peace respectively. It is also the case that the consumption return on holding government debt for any period is contingent on the occurrence and timing of changes of state between the two dates. If I give up one unit of consumption at time t when the state is $i(t)$ and the tax rate is $\theta_{i(t)}(K(t), D(t))$ the amount I can consume at time $(t + h)$ is

$$\frac{(1 + r)^h[1 + \theta_{i(t)}(K_t,D_{it})]}{1 + \theta_{i(t+h)}(K_{t+h}, D_{t+h})}$$

Some of this effect could perhaps be achieved by explicit levies and subsidies on capital when states change, or by introducing bonds paying state contingent coupons. How would these affect our analysis?

A capital levy on the outbreak of war and its restitution on transition to peace is unlikely to contribute to social welfare. Because the levy occurs only on changes of state there can be no offset to the expectation of a positive levy in good states and a negative one in the bad state. To this extent the measure would distort intertemporal choice, amounting as it does to an *ex-ante* interest tax in the good state and a corresponding subsidy in bad states. The cost of this distortion would probably not be offset by the reduced variation of the consumption (or wage) tax as the government's debt fell by the amount of the levy at the start of a bad state.

Certainly a levy would be no part of an optimum arrangement in the small open economy considered here, as it, and varying taxes, are dominated by a state contingent bond. Suppose that in place of bills or bonds paying r in all states of the world, the government issues perpetual bonds paying r_1 in state 1 and r_2 $(< r_1)$ in state 2. We assume that such bonds can be sold for their expected discounted value on the world capital market – certainly if they did not eliminate variation in tax rates they would not appeal to residents and would never be held by them in any quantity.

In effect the government can insure on the international capital market against the incidence of, for example, war expenditures. At the time of the issue of contingent bonds the government has a debt of market value D_0. It issues a number N of contingent bonds which have a price in the current state i of P_i where $NP_i = D_0$. r_1 and r_2 and the constant tax rate T^*, and the two values of public expenditure G_1^* and G_2^*, are chosen so that $r_iN + G_i^* = R_1(T^*)$, $i = 1, 2$, where $R(T^*)$ is the revenue generated by the invariant tax T^* in state i (in the case of random s these functions are identical).

Full insurance is possible in the model where $\tilde{s}$ is random with all uncertainty shifted onto the world capital market. On the outbreak of war the government finds its debt service obligation falling by $(r_1 - r_2)N$ which is exactly the additional amount that it wants to spend $(G_2^* - G_1^*)$ where the marginal benefit of expenditure is equal to the marginal cost of financing it by raising the tax rate T^* which rate does not vary between states. The government budget then balances in every period and no new issues of debt take place.

The story is again slightly different where $\tilde{w}$ is stochastic, as private agents would also like to insure against changes in $\tilde{w}$. While, assuming positive debt and revenues varying with the wage, the optimal contingent government debt would pay more in good states than in bad, its citizens, holding positive wealth, would like to hold an instrument which paid more in bad states than in good. In fact if private utility were separable between consumption and leisure, and if the private sector had fully insured, it would consume at a constant rate through all contingencies and a constant consumption tax would finance an optimal constant level of public goods supply without the government resorting to the issue of contingent bonds. This is in contrast to the case in which s is stochastic where the optimal use of contingent public debt restores indifference between consumption and wage taxation.

The only example of contingent debt with which I am familiar is the British postwar credits, though I believe that Israel has also used similar vehicles for forced savings. At Keynes's suggestion, part of wartime income taxation took the form of a cash deposit to be released after the war. The balances did not bear interest so that their present value was conditional on the expected duration of the war and on the inflation rate. Part of the thinking behind them related to fears of a re-emergence of inadequate aggregate demand after the war which did not in fact occur. Inflation pressures were such that the credits were not released immediately and were eroded by inflation before being finally released. Being non-marketable, and having no implication for the profile of debt service, postwar credits are a closer approximation to a time varying consumption tax than to a state contingent bond. Starting from an income tax system they did, however, represent a small step in the direction suggested by the arguments of this chapter. Nicholas Dimsdale's contribution to this volume (Keynes on British Budgetary Policy) documents a number of relevant aspects of Keynes's thought including his own arguments for smoothing tax rates.

As mentioned above the scope for state contingent bonds is reduced if not eliminated in a closed economy. Further work on this, not reported here, suggests that the results of section IV would not change much in the closed economy in which of necessity greater reliance has to be placed on taxes than 'insurance'.

APPENDIX 1 STRUCTURE OF THE GENERAL MODEL

The model is of a small open economy in which trade in goods, or the mobility of factor, is sufficient to make the real wage (w) and the real return (r) on capital (K) exogenous. Without loss of generality we assume that the national debt is domestically held, thus national income

$$Y = rK + wL \tag{15.1}$$

where L is labour supply.

Taxes can be levied on either wage income (wL) or consumption (C). Thus the consumers' budget constraint is

$$\dot{F} = rF + (1 - \tau)wL - (1 + \theta)C \tag{15.2}$$

where F is private wealth, made up of the national debt D, and the nationally owned capital stock K (which could be negative), i.e.

$$F = D + K \tag{15.3}$$

τ is the rate of wage taxation and θ that of consumption taxation. As the tax rates are not necessarily constant the exclusion of explicit interest taxation is immaterial. If $\tau = -\theta$ and

$$\frac{1}{1+\theta}\frac{\mathrm{d}(1+\theta)}{\mathrm{d}t}$$

is constant the effective net interest tax is equal to the proportionate rate of increase of the tax-inclusive cost of consumption $(1 + \theta)$. Tax revenue

$$R = \tau wL + \theta C \tag{15.4}$$

enters the government budget constraint under which

$$\dot{D} = rD + G - R \tag{15.5}$$

where G is government expenditure. Equation 15.2, 15.3, 15.4 and 15.5 imply

$$\dot{K} = rK + wL - G - C \tag{15.6}$$

It is crucial to the simplicity of the subsequent results that govenment expenditure should enter separably into the relevant utility functions. The government maximizes an intertemporally additively separable objective function

$$\psi = \int_0^{\infty} \mathrm{e}^{-\rho t} W(t)\mathrm{d}t \tag{15.7}$$

where

$$W = U(C, L) + P(G) \tag{15.8}$$

but because government expenditure is a pure Samuelsonian public good, consumers effectively ignore the last term even though $P(G)$ accurately reflects their own valuation of the public good. Thus consumers maximize

$$\phi = \int_0^\infty e^{-\rho t} U(C, L) \tag{15.9}$$

subject to equation 15.2 and their initial wealth F_0.

The most questionable assumption is that all consumers are identical. The problem about this is that it makes the assumption of proportional taxation essentially arbitrary. It might be possible to appeal to consumers who differ only by an unobservable scale factor as shown by Mirrlees (1971) but this procedure is open here as elsewhere to the objections of Hahn (1973). The economy functions perfectly, in the sense that the labour market always clears and consumers face a perfect capital market. We abstract from any monetary aspects and assume that all the debt D takes the form of indexed bonds bearing the constant exogenous real rate r.

A potential problem in this kind of dynamic optimization exercise is that of time inconsistency (Kydlard and Prescott, 1977). Can we be sure that the path for taxes chosen at time t_0 for dates after t_1 will continue to be optimal at time t_1? In particular, is there any scope for a government to induce people to accumulate assets which can effectively be confiscated in an unexpected way? In general the answer to the second question is positive. Lucas and Stokey (1983) have emphasized the scope for confiscation by unexpected inflation. While this is not possible in our model, a capital levy could be imposed by an unexpected increase in the consumption tax θ, with its effects on future labour supply offset by a corresponding reduction in the wage tax τ. This would generate revenue with present value at time t of $(\theta_t - \theta_0)F_t$ if the consumption tax were raised from θ_0 to θ_t at that time.

This means that if F_0 exceeds the present value of the level of public expenditure which would be chosen if taxes did not distort, it would be feasible to finance this 'first-best' programme by an appropriate choice of θ (and $\tau = -\theta$). In what follows we assume no such capital levy is made, i.e. that the taxes are those a government would choose to commit itself to were such commitment possible. As Lucas and Stokey argue, this problem can only be avoided by eliminating all durable goods and financial assets.

The Hamiltonian associated with the private problem (equation 15.9) is

$$H_p = \int^\infty e^{-\rho t} U(C, L) + \mu F \, dt \tag{15.10}$$

Where μ is the shadow price of wealth, and

$$\dot{\mu} = \frac{\partial H_p}{\partial F} = -r\mu \rightarrow \mu = \mu_0 e^{-rt} \tag{15.11}$$

while differentiating with respect to the control variables C and L implies

$$U_C = (1 + \theta)\mu e^{\rho t} = (1 + \theta)\mu_0 e^{(\rho - r)t} \equiv (1 + \theta)\hat{\mu} \tag{15.12}$$

and

$$U_{\mathrm{L}} = -(1 - \tau)w\hat{\mu} \tag{15.13}$$

Thus, each of C, L and R can be expressed as a function of τ, θ, w and $\hat{\mu}$.

The Hamiltonian associated with the government's problem (equation 15.8) is

$$H_{\mathrm{g}} = \int^{\infty} \mathrm{e}^{-\rho t}[U(C(\tau, \theta, w, \hat{\mu}), L(\tau, \theta, w, \hat{\mu})) + P(G)]$$

$$+ \lambda\dot{D} + \nu\dot{K}\mathrm{d}t \tag{15.14}$$

where λ is the (negative) shadow price of debt and ν the (positive) shadow price of capital

$$\dot{\lambda} = -\frac{\partial H_{\mathrm{g}}}{\partial D} = -\lambda r \rightarrow \lambda = \lambda_0 \mathrm{e}^{-rt} \tag{15.15}$$

and

$$\dot{\nu} = -\frac{\partial H_{\mathrm{g}}}{\partial D} = -\nu r \rightarrow \nu = \nu_0 \mathrm{e}^{-rt} \tag{15.16}$$

while differentiating with respect to the government's control variables θ, τ, G implies, using equations 15.5 and 15.6

$$U_{\mathrm{C}}C_{\theta} + U_{\mathrm{L}}L_{\theta} = \hat{\lambda}R_{\theta} + \hat{\nu}(C_{\theta} - wL_{\theta}) \tag{15.17}$$

$$U_{\mathrm{C}}C_{\tau} + U_{\mathrm{L}}L_{\tau} = \hat{\lambda}R_{\tau} + \hat{\nu}(C_{\tau} - wL_{\tau}) \tag{15.18}$$

and

$$P = \hat{\nu} - \hat{\lambda}$$

From equation 15.4

$$R_{\theta} = C + \theta C_{\theta} + \tau w L_{\theta} \tag{15.20}$$

while

$$R_{\tau} = wL + \theta C_{\tau} + \tau w L_{\tau} \tag{15.21}$$

Using these, together with equations 15.12 and 15.13, equations 15.17 and 15.18 can be rewritten as

$$C_{\theta}\,[(1 + \theta)\hat{\mu} - (\theta\hat{\lambda} + \hat{\nu})] - wL_{\theta}[(1 - \tau)\hat{\mu} + (\tau\hat{\lambda} - \hat{\nu})] = \hat{\lambda}C$$

and

$$C_{t}[(1 + \theta)\hat{\mu} - (\theta\hat{\lambda} + \hat{\nu})] - wL_{\tau}[(1 - \tau)\hat{\mu} + (\tau\hat{\lambda} - \hat{\nu})] = \hat{\lambda}wL$$

respectively.

APPENDIX 2 DEBT DYNAMICS WITH ISOELASTIC UTILITY AND CONSTANT TAXES

To make progress the utility function needs to be made more specific. If $U(C, L)$ is additively separable in its two arguments, so that $U = U_1(C) + U_2(L)$ it is easy to see that equations 15.12 and 15.13 imply

$$C = C(\theta, \hat{\mu})$$

while $L = L(\tau, w, \hat{\mu})$ so that $C_\tau = L_\theta = 0$ and equations 15.22 and 15.23 reduce to

$$C_\theta[(1 + \theta)\hat{\mu} - (\theta\hat{\lambda} + \hat{\nu})] = \hat{\lambda} C \qquad (15.24)$$

and

$$L_\tau[(1 - \tau)\hat{\mu} + (\tau\hat{\lambda} - \hat{\nu})] = \hat{\lambda} L \qquad (15.25)$$

In the isolastic case

$$U_1(C) = \frac{1}{\gamma}C^\gamma \qquad \gamma < 1 \qquad (15.26)$$

$$U_2(L) = -\frac{1}{2 - \partial}L^{2-\partial} \quad \partial < 1 \qquad (15.27)^1$$

$$P(G) = \frac{1}{\epsilon}G^\epsilon \qquad \epsilon < 1 \qquad (15.28)$$

then from equations 15.12 and 15.13

$$C = [(1 + \theta)\,\hat{\mu}]\left(\frac{-1}{1-\gamma}\right) \qquad (15.29)$$

$$L = [(1 - \tau)w\hat{\mu}]\left(\frac{-1}{1-\partial}\right)$$

so that

$$C_\theta = -\frac{1}{1 - \gamma}\frac{C}{1 + \theta} \qquad (15.30)$$

and

$$L_\tau = -\frac{1}{1 - \partial}\frac{L}{1 - \tau} \qquad (15.31)$$

whence from equation 15.24

$$\theta = \frac{\hat{\nu} - \hat{\mu} - (1 - \gamma)\hat{\lambda}}{\hat{\mu}\gamma\hat{\lambda}} \qquad (15.32)$$

while from equation 15.25

$$\tau = \frac{\hat{\mu} - \hat{\nu} - (1 - \partial)\hat{\lambda}}{\hat{\mu} - (2 - \partial)\hat{\lambda}} \qquad (15.33)$$

Since all the shadow prices grow at the same rate $(\rho - r)$, both θ and τ are constant along the optimal path. This result is an example of a general theorem due to Atkinson and Stiglitz (1972) which rests on the separability and iso-elasticity properties.

NOTES

1 This utility function, and those used below, places no upper bound on labour supply which is a monotonically function of the net real wage.

REFERENCES

Abel, A.B. 1985a: Keynesian effects of lump-sum fiscal policy under altruism, mimeo., Harvard.

Abel, A.B., 1985b: The failure of Ricardian equivalence under progressive estate taxation, mimeo, Harvard.

Atkinson, A.B. and Stiglitz, J.E. 1972: The structure of indirect taxation and economic efficiency, *Journal of Public Economics*, 1, 97–119.

Bagwell, K. and Bernheim, D. 1985: Is everything neutral? mimeo, NBER.

Barro, R.J. 1974: Are government bonds net wealth? *Journal of Political Economy* 82, 1095–1117.

Barro, R.J. 1979: On the deterioration of the public debt, *Journal of Political Economy*, 87, 940–71.

Currie, D. and Levine, P. 1985: Credibility and time inconsistency in a stochastic model, Queen Mary College, London, Research Paper No. 36.

Hahn, 1973: On optimum taxation, *Journal of Economic Theory*, 6, 96–106.

Kydland, F.E. and Prescott, E.C. 1977: Rules rather than discretion: the inconsistency of optimal plans, *Journal of Political Economy*, 85, 473–92.

Lucas, R.E. and Stokey, N.L., 1983: Optimal fiscal and monetary policy in an economy without capital, *Journal of Monetary Economics*, 12, 55–94.

Mirrlees, J.A. 1971: An exploration in the theory of optimum income taxation, *Review of Economic Studies*, 38, 175–208.

Persson, T. and Svensson, L.E.O. 1984: Time consistent fiscal policy and government cash flow, *Journal of Monetary Economics*.

Persson T. and Svensson L.E.O. 1985: International borrowing and time consistent fiscal policy, *Scandinavian Journal of Economics*, 14, 365–74.

PART IV OVERVIEW

16
A Survey of the Debate

MICHAEL V. POSNER

I INTRODUCTION

Before I arrived at Alghero, and began to read the papers, I took a rather arrogant and in some crucial respects superficial view of the arguments. The building in which I now work is very tall. From it I can survey not merely the whole of London, but also a long stretch of the Thames, and I can with an effort of imagination extend my field of vision by some miles to cover the river estuary. I sometimes feel that, suitably for a man of my years, I can see from my tower not just London but the ebb and flow of the tides of economic doctrine. These tides are Atlantic rather than Mediterranean in character – they rise and fall by large amounts. As the tide of textbook Keynesianism swept in after the war, there were submerged first the quantity theory of money, then the concept of the burden of the national debt, then the influence of factor prices on employment, and finally the only piece of dry land left was the pure theory of effective demand. In the last decade, that tide has in its turn ebbed, and a new one appeared, running in different channels. The ebb and flow disturbed, as it were, the lie of the sandbanks that make up the estuary, and every few months new landmarks appear, as the old ones are swirled away by the tides of history (ably assisted by anomaly arbitrage operations in the City).

As the new tide began to flow, we watched first the money supply, whatever that was; then the fiscal balance, in its UK guise as the public sector borrowing requirement; now it is the ratio of the national debt to the national income.

It has appeared at times that some economists were taking intellectual jumps, so to speak, from sandbank to sandbank as these became exposed by the run of the tide; and it did occur to me that they might be engaged in an effort to keep their feet dry rather than in an intrepid intellectual exploration of exciting new territory. I even admit to awaiting, from my eighteenth floor window, one or two big splashes as my friends take an undesired swim. Now that I have read the papers in this volume, I find that, although some of the apparently firm ground revealed by successive tides turns out indeed to be composed of insubstantial shifting sands, there is rather more secure ground there than I had supposed. Indeed, some of the ground exposed by today's tidal flows is composed of solid rock, and was there to stand on some decades ago if we had only paid proper attention. Other newly emerging patches of terra firma seem destined, moreover, to become more permanent topographical features of our estuary, and are worth exploring in some detail.

The difficulty of exposition is that each of the pieces of solid ground – the genuine discoveries or 'true propositions' – have contiguous 'shifting sands' or errors attached to them. Abandoning the metaphor, many of the chapters in this volume report undoubted truths, of practical importance; but some of them also can be interpreted in ways that lead to exaggeration, and hence distortion.

II THE BASIC CAUSE FOR ALARM

The Domar proposition (Domar, 1944) provides the simplest and most striking cause for alarm. If the rate of interest is higher than the rate of growth of the economy, if government spending in aggregate is not so invested as to yield a financial return, then any primary deficit (that is, a deficit before taking account of interest payments) will lead eventually to an explosive rise in the size of the national debt. Bispham, who displays in his chapter the basic algebra, also shows that in plausible cases it might nevertheless take decades for the debt to income ratio to reach, say, 1 : 1; the time bomb might tick for a long time.

Intuitive acceptance of this proposition may be more easily attained if two analytical refinements are added. First, the relevant interest rate is the (inflation adjusted) interest on government debt minus tax payments on that interest; in most countries there are some debtholders who receive government interest payments without tax liability, but marginal holders pay significant tax. Interest net of tax is smaller than interest gross; this consideration makes the Domar condition bite less fiercely.

Secondly, are there grounds for expecting, a priori, any particular relationship between the interest rate and the growth rate of the economy? It would be very comforting, in the present context, if interest rates were expected, on general grounds, to be below growth rates – Domar instability would disappear. But all one can say, generally, is that in some growth models, the two rates are brought towards each other by fundamental forces; and that a state of affairs in which real interest rates are, for a run of years, much below per capita growth rates seems likely to lead to increasing investment and a rise in interest rates. However, a stable world *could* exist where the interest rate was above per capita growth rates but, because population was growing, below the growth rate of national income. It is nevertheless *not* possible to assert that this is a generally highly probable outcome. Once again, the Domar fears can be to some extent allayed, but not entirely banished!

What does the Domar proposition demonstrate? It warns us that an alleged Keynesian cure for steady state secular stagnation – deficit spending without limit, on unproductive capital projects – may not be sustainable. Financial markets, watching the behaviour of finance ministers in particular countries, will be concerned not so much with the ultimate explosive phase of such borrowing behaviour, they will be concerned also with the path of interest rates in the shorter term, and the temptations that will beckon governments towards the inflationary policies that alone can save them from the consequences of the irresponsibility of their predecessors. Therefore if there emerges a general assumption that, within any one country, the budget deficit is 'structural', that there are no natural tendencies for it to shrink and the policies required to contract it are politically implausible; and interest rates are above growth rates; then problems of maintaining the national debt in illiquid form may become rapidly insoluble.

This is the basic fear of fiscal irresponsibility which finance ministers do need to keep at the front of their minds. It is not a temporary insecure sandbank, but a piece of solid rock, dangerous for passing vessels, a secure foundation on which analysts can stand. But the implications of this basic proposition must be looked at individually and sceptically.

Note an important and even firmer piece of ground, much explored during the conference. Again, it is most easily seen in Bispham's chapter. Even if Domar instability is avoided, because the growth rate is in excess of the interest rate, a permanent primary deficit can lead to a large, although finite, increase in the debt to income ratio. Orders of magnitude here are important: a not implausible example might be of a country whose present debt to income ratio is around 0.5, but might, if present tendencies continued for a few decades, arrive at a position where the debt to income ratio was three or four times bigger – say around 2.0. A similar debt to income ratio might perhaps be reached by a country which starts from a position of Domar instability, but manages eventually to bring its structural budget deficit under control, by fierce containment of spending or rises in taxation. Such a process might take decades; during that time, there might be a large increase in the debt to income ratio.

The fear here is that the interest rate on the debt would similarly increase, at least by the same factor as the debt to income ratio itself increased; so that the cost of servicing the national debt could go up, say fourfold. The implications of this for the tax burden need not be grave if we start with a very low debt to income ratio, and a very low ratio of taxation to the national income (because the budget itself is small relative to the national income). But if the starting point of the story is a very high tax ratio – say 60 per cent – then an increase of that by another 10 percentage points to pay an extra interest burden would reduce personal disposable income by one-quarter; as Eltis pointed out in discussion, a proposition which was a mere *curiosum* when public expenditure was a small part of national income becomes striking and worrying when public expenditure (and taxation) become a very large part of national income. So even the non-explosive version of the Domar relationship can have severe implications for the viability of current government policies in many OECD countries, and worse implications no doubt amongst the LDCs.

It was this fear, less than Domar instability, but still a cause of considerable concern, that might been titled 'the Sardinian proposition' – the name being chosen to denote the site of the conference, not the alleged practices of the Sardinian fiscal authorities!

How much Weight will the Basic Propositions Stand?

Although there is solid ground here, it will not bear unlimited weight. First, who would want deficit spending to go on forever? Only an extreme version, almost a *reductio ad absurdum*, of Keynesian doctrine would suggest that full employment savings would be *permanently* in excess of investment, and hence should be offset by permanent government dissaving: it is suitable for us to remind ourselves that unless such recommendations assume negative interest rates they carry inherently unstable implications. Cozzi, Dimsdale and Artis all reminded us of Keynes's own preference for deficit spending to be for investment purposes rather than current expenditure, thus limiting the deadweight aspects of the debt thereby generated. Now I think we have very considerable experience to show that the use of public investment expenditure as a *counter-cyclical* device is highly ineffectual – the various time lags between decisions and outcomes are too long. (Whether tax variations over the cycle would be any more successful raises Barro–Ricadian issues which we discuss below.) This contention, however, does not dispose of the case for correcting quasi-permanent underemployment equilibrium with a quasi-permanent deficit, all of it directed to interest earning projects. To the extent to which this is successfully practised, neither the Domar nor the Sardinian alarm bells need ring.

Even if the stream of investment which is financed by the deficit is not commercially profitable, it could still expand the tax base. For instance, health service expenditure which materially improves the resistance of British wage earners to respiratory disorders, or African workers to malarial infection, could effectively shift the supply curve of labour and lead to the generation of more income, an expanded tax base, thus generating, at constant tax rates, the revenues necessary to service the increment in public debt floated to finance the health service expenditure. And it is even conceivable that public expenditure on improving the environment, although it will be without any impact at all on monetary flows of personal incomes, would so raise psychic incomes that politicians would judge that higher tax rates on cash incomes would be tolerable, thus reducing the primary deficit and limiting the Sardinian effect; Laffer-curve effects, as examined in Eltis' paper, might still reduce the supply of effort in the cash sector of the economy, but that sector would have a small weight.

Secondly, while Domar instability, even for a short number of years, may stimulate large interest rate rises at home and even, at least for small countries, the collapse of confidence from international investors, Sardinian effects are easier to accommodate and can in principle be reversed. There is no reason why periods of increases in the debt to income ratio cannot, as a matter of practice, be followed by periods of falls in that ratio. Fluctuations of this sort have occurred over long periods; the analytical issue is whether such fluctuations are merely mistakes, or could be, on some assumptions, optimal. Flemming's analysis, simplified for expositional purposes into his parable of periods of 'war' followed by periods of 'peace', suggest that long period fluctuations of this sort may at least be rationally explicable.

Thirdly, counter-cyclical manipulation of the budget, by varying tax rather than expenditure, is not in any way excluded by Domar or Sardinian considerations. True, a country which already has a high and growing debt to income ratio, and, *a fortiori*, a country caught in a Domar trap, may find it difficult to sell counter-cyclical devices to sceptical financial markets, and consequently difficult to sell bonds to the same markets in a more literal sense. Periods of virtue (Flemming's peacetime periods) need to precede periods of fiscal looseness (Flemming's wars). These tactical considerations are important, but do not constitute a solid case against fiscal activism.

Those who seek a convincing argument against all deficits in all circumstances, are tempted to rely on the so-called Barro–Ricardian hypothesis (Barro, 1974) which can be loosely expressed by saying the sum of all agents, including the public authorities, would, in a rational market economy, adopt much the same behaviour, much the same level and intertemporal pattern of spending, irrespective of whether its government financed the whole of its normal expenditure out of taxation, or instead chose to finance, say, a tenth of it by borrowing. Periods of government dissaving would be matched by simultaneous excess saving from the private sector, and vice versa. On this hypothesis, short periods of deficits in public finance might be possible without disaster, but would have no first order effects.

For the vulgar economist with a broadly Keynesian training, as for many more sophisticated observers, this proposition is extremely easy to disbelieve. Admittedly, in countries like the UK, where institutional investors (with time horizons which extend well beyond the likely life expectation of particular individuals) are the major holders of bonds and equities, it is plausible to ascribe to them long-term motivations, and long-term judgements about future rates of taxation forced upon governments with debt service obligations. But even pension funds rationally have finite horizons – bounded by the life expectancies of the dependants of their youngest members – although their trustees sometimes talk as if they have to look to the interests of subsequent generations as well. And although there are some truly 'perpetual' funds – defined as those for whom their own survival is an important component of the fund's objective function – their overall weight in the market is not great. Therefore, although one day all markets may behave in ways consistent with the Barro hypothesis, they do not do so yet, as the paper by Modigliani and Jappelli suggested for the Italian economy, and as informal discussion suggested for the United States economy. One and a half cheers for counter-cyclical fiscal policy might still therefore be raised, although many of the difficulties of timing, and judgement, and 'overspill' from small economies in an international setting provide, as is well known, formidable constraints on governmental action in this regard.

Fourth, it is sometimes suggested that governments may escape Domar or Sardinian problems by inflation. Indeed, there is a well-known newspaper article by Keynes which seems to recommend precisely such a solution to French debt problems in the 1920s [illegible] several participants in the conference drew attention to it. In my own review article (Posner, 1973) of the Moggridge volume of the Keynes papers containing that article I noted it in passing, as a rather irresponsible *curiosum*. I still so regard it. Such an approach to the problem of a large national debt is not a *solution*, it merely manifests the central and most evil *consequence* of the problem. I just do not believe that in modern times, in any moderately wealthy country (which I define as a country where errors in economic policy are not matters of life or death for the mass of citizens), any government official or minister or adviser has consciously chosen a path of inflation to wipe out interest rate burdens. And I would warn any colleague who plans to offer such advice that the debt-destroying consequences of a burst of inflation are the greater, the more unexpected and abrupt the rise in prices, and the longer the maturity structure of the debt when the episode begins: such a combination of secrecy, confident holding of long debt, and inflationary irresponsibility is hard to envisage.

This is not to say that there are no ways to modify the dangers of Domar instability, or ease the pain of the Sardinian squeeze. We were reminded that Keynes, in *How to Pay for the War* (1940), essentially relied on money illusion (and patriotic fervour) to permit negative real interest rates. And, in modern times, an obstinately stagnant underemployed economy might be coaxed into activity by pump-priming expenditure financed by frank expansion of the monetary base: money under the bed is the ultimate form of zero-interest public debt. Agreed, this could work only for short term pump-priming; and, agreed, there might be ultimate once-for-all effects on the price level; but the pump-priming image – the language of Roosevelt's New Deal rather than of Keynesian theory – suggests that we compare the *permanent* flow of water through the successfully primed pump, with the burst of original deficit spending and the burst of consequential price increases both of which are *temporary*, once-for-all.

In general, this approach invites us to trade off two once-for-all effects. For a time in the 1950s and 1960s, many economists believed that a Phillips curve trade-off between inflation rates and employment levels was permanently possible: few of us believe that now. Some commentators now seem to suggest that all inflationary consequences are permanent – inflation rates are raised forever – while employment effects are temporary. The convenience of concentrating attention on debt to income ratios is that this enables a comparison to be made between two quantities that share common dimensions: finite effects (which may be zero or positive) on income levels, for a finite period; and finite effects on debt to income ratios which would last forever, but could be reversed.

Dimsdale, in his comments on Eltis, made this trade-off point explicitly. It seems to me hard to resist. Of course the trade-off may be good, may be bad; policy action could conceivably improve the trade-off choice; some people might not wish to trust politicians to make a trade-off; other people (including I myself in 'normal' times) might fear that the various time lags and deficiencies of information flows are so large that the game is not worth playing at all; but yes, sometimes it might.

We called this in the conference 'fiscal coarse tuning', as distinct from fine tuning. Asked to define 'coarse', I took refuge in quoting (British) English linguistic usage – coarse fishing, coarse Rugby Football, etc. My Italian friends seemed to understand me very well, though some North Americans were less sympathetic.

Indeed, some of the alarm that is generated on this issue stems from what is almost a formal fallacy – the acceptance that 'what happens today happens forever'. Recall the period during which electricity demand was expanding fairly steadily at 7 per cent a year, while GDP grew at less than 3 per cent a year; it was right for wise observers, and particularly for Treasury economists, to point out that this could 'not go on forever'. It did not, because the objective circumstances changed, and the manifestation of those circumstances – differential growth rates – also corrected themselves. This example leads to the following simple points: that under appropriate circumstances debt to income ratios can go on expanding from a relatively low base for a good number of years without causing rational dismay; that the acceptable rate of change in those ratios depends in part on the structure of ownership (public sector versus private sector), and on the sectoral balances of savings and investment; that even over the longer run one needs to take a view first on the likely change through time in the accumulation of gross debt instruments in the economy as a whole before registering alarm at the national debt component.

Over the medium term, a 'coarse tuner' needs to consider the necessary interrelationship between the institutional facts of the distribution of industry between public and private sectors, the institutional habits of issuing debt and equity in the private sector, the role of investment banks in the provision of finance, the way in which pension and retirement funds are organized: these factors change but slowly, but the accumulation of debt and changes in the debt to income ratio are themselves not instantaneous, as Bispham's simulations demonstrate.

Finally, there are a set of important considerations, stemming originally from Tobin, which Gorini deploys in his chapter. Government debt, whatever the form or shape in which it is held, is part of the portfolio of assets held by financial institutions and others; in some ways it is part of the money stock, in other ways it underpins the money stock. I recall that when in the early 1970s we in the UK first began tentatively to discuss the concept of 'an optimum fiscal deficit' it was in a Tobin rather than a Domar framework. The Gorini argument was insufficiently pressed at Alghero; it may turn out to have a longer life than some of the other strands of argument.

Are there other Solid Propositions?

Here are some possibilities.

The Burden of National Debt One dog which did not bark during the conference was the burden of the national debt: there was no explicit discussion of this concept, and I suspect that most participants thought it too well understood to be worthy of attention. I did ask at one point, which burden was greater, domestic debt or debt held overseas? The answer, from Boskin I think, was that undoubtedly it is better to sell debt overseas, because the world capital market has a more elastic supply of funds than the home market, and hence the real interest charge on foreign held debt will be less for tomorrow's taxpayers.

I was brought up instead on the naïve view that domestically held debt imposed no burden on future generations, because the payment of interest and the taxes required to finance such payments were self-balancing transfer payments. We always recognized that there might be a public finance problem, but were inclined to emphasize the root of that problem in the non-optimality of the tax system: a well-devised tax system could be readily milked, without effective constraint, at virtually zero cost to incentives and all that, at least to a first approximation.

By contrast debt held by foreigners imposed a primary burden which had necessarily to be paid by future generations. To make warplanes in 1940 we could either reduce whisky consumption in 1940, thus forcing the adult citizens then alive to pay for the war; or we could sell the UK owned portfolio of Wall Street stock, thus reducing the real wealth handed down to the children. Moreover, if we borrowed from foreigners and had eventually to repay, our terms of trade would be in consequence lower – this secondary burden, the transfer problem, might not be small.

There are two reasons for rejecting the old view: neither on its own is conclusive, but taken together they are powerful. First, as we have already noted, disincentive effects of marginal increases in taxation when tax levels are already high may be more onerous than we believed in the old easy-going days: the internal public finance problem therefore looms larger. Secondly, public borrowing financed by sales of paper to domestic holders may crowd out private investment rather than private consumption – it is not whisky consumption that is cut, but industrial or housing investment: to the extent to which this happens, future generations face a burden (a lower capital stock) even when the debt is internally held, and the interest charges are costlessly transferred from one group to another. It is this second point which Conference participants seemed to have in mind. The US is building its capital stock faster by attracting inflows from abroad. Foreigners may be investing less. If part of the incremental return from capital formation is appropriated by other factors of production, then the country with the inflow is a net gainer, taking all generations together.

Of course, to the extent to which an increment in spending, financed by borrowing, has Keynesian effects in expanding output, that is a gain which would help to offset *any* burden of debt, whether held domestically or by foreigners. I concede, however, that action taken today which will result in a larger debt to income ratio tomorrow, does impose some burden on a future generation, even if the debt is internally held; that burden may be compensated in some manner and to some extent by the benign consequences of the additional government spending that generates it; but the net remaining increment in burden *may* be larger when the debt is held internally than when it is held externally.

Rate of Accumulation of Debt and Rate of Interest Is there a relationship between the rate of the accumulation of debt and the rate of interest? As a proposition about capital accumulation generally, it would require a set of special assumptions to conclude that, comparing two alternative steady states, the one with the higher rate of capital accumulation would have a higher rate of interest. It is a little easier to build a set of assumptions that will lead to the conclusion that the rate of interest paid by any one borrower will be larger, the larger the proportion of total national savings which he appropriates: the larger is government borrowing, the higher may be the interest rate on government debt. It is even easier to argue that, in conditions of relatively full employment, a government which obstinately and persistently fails to raise sufficient taxes to finance its ordinary expenditure, and thereby accumulates extra deadweight debt, will find the rate of interest which it faces, and probably the rate of interest throughout its domestic capital market, rising against it.

The strength of all these relationships, and their reliability, has something to do with how monetary policy is conducted, something to do with the country's standing in the world financial community, a lot to do with the institutional facts about who holds the debt and what part such debt typically plays in their balance sheets – for instance, if banks build a credit multiplier on holdings of public debt, or if pension funds insist on holding fixed proportions of public debt, then the relationship between volume and price may be more elastic. As a general proposition about policy, it seems sound that government should be advised that 'more borrowing may mean significantly higher interest rates'. If there is a large stock of debt outstanding, at effectively a floating rate of interest (because of short maturity dates), then a small increase in annual borrowing could under some circumstances have a large effect on total annual interest charges on the whole volume of debt: conceivably, for instance, an increase of borrowing in any one year could be entirely exhausted by an increased annual interest charge. (In the UK, the recent government publication Cmnd 9189 of 1984, paragraphs 54–55, seems to suggest such a relationship.) But this, although it may hold in some circumstances for some countries, is rather an extreme case of a general proposition: the general proposition is solid land on which to rest, the extreme possibility is perhaps more shifting sand.

Optimal Fiscal Deficit Is there an optimal fiscal deficit? As a proposition in general equilibrium welfare economics, on all the usual assumptions, it may be optimal for all economic agents to make intertemporal decisions based on probable flows of wealth and needs into the foreseeable future. Even 'governments' (viewed in a liberal way as mere managing agents employed by the citizens) should, it can be argued, behave in such a way. For instance, a government presented with a lump of revenue that will last for a short finite time period (e.g. rent from a national natural resource) 'should' spend that revenue over a longer period of time, rather than using it all (in extra government consumption or lower tax take) over the short period during which it accrues: it should 'capitalize' the windfall gain, and use only the annual revenue from the capital to cut taxes or increase current spending, not the capital sum itself (see Odling-Smee and Riley, 1985, 65 *et seq.*).

This proposition, deceptively 'practical' or even 'plain man' in shape, nevertheless carries important implications, and arises from a fecund analytical principle. If there is a 'proper way' for a government to treat a windfall gain, then is this not part of a far more general proposition, that there is a uniquely 'proper way' for it to determine its general stance on borrowing? If there is an optimal impact on the borrowing requirement of a given set of events in the North Sea, then surely the cumulation of the whole set of such events in history will generate an optimal borrowing requirement in aggregate?

My answer to this rhetorical question is – yes, *ceteris paribus*. In very much the same way, a corporation in the private sector, having determined a financial plan for the sources and use of funds over the next five years, might have to adapt that plan to deal with an unexpected event; and yes, in principle, if the analysis of a marginal change enables one to identify a unique optimal adjustment, that suggests that there may be a generalized optimal solution for a representative corporation in long-run equilibrium. But of course the actual pattern of sources and uses of funds by actual corporations in the real world varies sharply from case to case and from time to time; and the level of actual borrowing in any particular time period will be determined by a host of special factors.

For this reason, I prefer to put the argument in a more familiar, if less striking manner. I am prepared to make, for the sake of argument, all the same simplifying assumptions as would the proponents of the notion of 'an optimal fiscal deficit' – basically the neoclassical assumption of zero involuntary unemployment. The government now has windfall revenue from a North Sea profits tax, which is likely to last, say, for five years. One way of handling the problem would be to use the whole of the windfall tax revenue to reduce the current burden of ordinary taxation, leaving the flow of government borrowing unchanged from its previously determined path. Rational individuals, noting this reduction in their tax burden, and recognizing the transitory nature of the windfall, might themselves treat a large proportion of the tax cut as a capital item, essentially saving it rather than spending it; and, in a closed economy, this would work through to reduce the interest rate in the normal way. But the government, as the original recipient of the windfall, may well have knowledge about its size and future expected path that is denied to its citizens, and it might be best therefore if (instead of cutting taxes) the government took the original 'savings' decision on behalf of the public, using a large proportion of the windfall to retire parts of the national debt, cutting the annual flow of new borrowing accordingly. This reduced flow of gilt-edged sales by the government could lead to a lower interest rate, and possibly therefore to a higher rate of capital accumulation (including higher capital expenditure by parts of the public sector, which would to that extent mitigate the effect which we are investigating). The higher rate of capital accumulation, if it could be achieved, would be the natural and desirable mechanism, for society as a whole, of transferring into the future some of today's windfall profits; and bringing this about by changing the flow of government borrowing might ensure that a large element of the extra investment decisions are made in the private sector, according to private sector stimuli. Such a preference for fluctuations in the flow of government borrowing rather than fluctuations in the burden of taxation is reinforced by the consideration that welfare losses from tax rises are likely to be larger than the gains from symmetrical tax cuts (see Flemming, p. 545).

There are a lot of conditionals here, but all the considerations advanced are worthy of attention. They are unlikely to lead to a firm conclusion on the deficit to aim for in any one year.

Looking at all this out of my eighteenth floor window, I note wryly that some very modern economists prefer to use the notion of 'optimal public sector borrowing' to arrive at the sort of conclusion that could be arrived at by traditionalists in a more familiar way, standing, in terms of my initial metaphor, on different ground, of a more solid foundation.

Government Expenditure Expenditure by the government can displace (crowd out) other expenditure. At full employment, any one use of resources displaces, at the margin, some other resource use. That proposition holds however the new claim on resources is financed – whether by borrowing, taxation, a deliberate cut in some other expenditure, or inflation ('printing money'). This widely recognized elementary proposition led, some decades ago, to insistence on appropriate tests for the social or economic desirability at the margin of public investment projects – although the long-standing academic argument about the appropriate rate of time discount has, in the UK at least, deprived government economists of the widespread academic support which they would have needed to make that regime really work.

In conditions of unemployment, if I may grossly simplify an argument which has fortunately subsided, but which when active had heavy political overtones, the degree to which extra government spending would displace existing private spending depends not on the way it is financed, but on the source of unemployment. If the unemployment reflects a failure of markets to generate output at the price level which the authorities are prepared to validate, then crowding out will be the rule; but more generalized Keynesian demand deficiency can in principle be remedied by extra spending provided that the demand and supply for loanable funds are pretty elastic.

However, and it is for this reason that I list this proposition as a 'truth' rather than an 'error', much depends on timing. Public spending decisions take a long time to decide, to implement, to bring to fruition. A lag of three years between decision and the main flow of resource commitment to a new spending project is probably typical. A project costing X million decided upon in the middle of year one will generate spending at a rate of one-fifth of X per year for five years, centring on year four. Counter-cyclical public expenditure in that sort of industry does not make much sense, unless the authorities have perfect foresight.

A good practical rule of thumb for public sector resource planning must therefore be that resources are *continually* scarce at the margin.

Crowding out must be the standard philosophy of any effective mechanism for public sector expenditure control. Even though those responsible for stabilization policy may sneer at their slow-moving colleagues, and assert indeed that in a sluggish recovery from recession private spending may be crowded in by extra public spending, their pleas will necessarily fall on deaf ears. In Britain, this discovery was made by a distinguished civil servant, Sir Richard Clarke, a quarter of a century ago; he drew the conclusion that *expenditure* should follow a path of medium-term stability. It is typical of the odd process of the ebb and flow of the tides of economic doctrine that this proposition has now been rediscovered, upside down so to speak, by the present tide of fashion. None the worse for that! A stable (and therefore necessarily significantly lower than might *conceivably* be optimal) path for public expenditure is an aim that has a more durable and familar feel under our feet than the somewhat more novel and shifting argument about optimal fiscal deficits.

III THE FISCAL DEFICIT, THE BALANCE OF PAYMENTS, AND THE EXCHANGE RATE

This topic came up several times in the course of the conference. I mentioned it in my original paper, it is raised inferentially in Boskin's chapter, and in Penner's it appears explicitly throughout, particularly in figure 5.5. Outside our conference, the argument is also raging, as seen for instance in an excellent series of articles in the first number of the 1985 Brookings Papers.

The proposition that the government deficit raises the exchange rate is part of the system of striking paradoxes which often seem to characterize modern economics. The most puzzling question used to be 'if the money supply is reported as having risen unexpectedly quickly, is the result a rise or a fall in the rate of interest?' The new puzzle is 'if a government's fiscal deficit rises unexpectedly fast, does this lead to a rise or fall in the exchange rate?' The answer to both paradoxical questions starts in much the same way, 'provided that the authorities are known to have a firm and immutable policy for the long-term growth of the money supply, and that they are known to be able and willing to enforce it, then the answer to the first question is that the interest rate will go up, and the answer to the second question is that the exchange rate will go up'.

In the well-known particular case of the US economy over the last few years, for instance, it is widely believed that the high present and expected Federal deficit, together with a moderately restrictive monetary stance by the Federal Reserve Board, have generated high interest rates on US government debt, which has attracted high capital inflow from abroad; and this in turn has required an accommodating current account deficit, for which a loss in competitiveness through an appreciation of the US dollar was in turn a necessary condition. Despite some special factual grounds for a degree of scepticism about this story – for instance, the Federal debt on its own much overstates the total US public sector deficit; and a large component of the turnaround of the US capital account has been a decline in US capital outflow rather than an increase in the inflow – it is hard to deny the force of this new orthodox doctrine.

We should, however, be wary of one other institutional point of importance, and one overriding analytical caveat. The institutional fact is that not all countries are like the United States. If in either Britain or Italy, in some hypothetical future, there were to be deliberate government action sharply to increase the fiscal deficit, whatever well-intentioned remarks were made about maintaining a stern monetary policy, it is hard to believe that there would then be a resulting currency appreciation, in either country. The degree of separation of fiscal authority from monetary authority is much greater in Washington than in most other countries, and that is part of the relevant institutional fact. Another aspect of the uniqueness of the United States' experience is the sheer size and dominance of the US in the world's financial markets. Whereas most portfolio managers would have a very elastic demand for US securities at an interest rate only slightly in excess of the world rate, the same flood of finance is unlikely to be available to a very small OECD country.

The analytical warning is more complicated. I have already assumed, at the beginning of this section, that the market 'rationally believes' that monetary policy will follow its previously determined path. Whatever the market *believes*, moreover, to ensure that the mechanism works as described, it is necessary that, as a matter of fact, the fiscal expansion (of which the increase in borrowing is the consequence) does not have the Keynesian *result* of strongly increasing activity at home. If it did have that effect, then the expansion would, through the foreign trade multiplier, worsen the current account of the balance of payments, and to that extent accommodate the capital account inflow without any necessity for an appreciation of the dollar. In the present American case, the strong rise in the dollar seems to demonstrate the truth of the new orthodoxy. The current account has certainly worsened. But the question is whether that current account deficit is the result of a chain of causation which leads from fiscal deficit through high interest rates, capital account inflow, and appreciation of the dollar, or, instead, of a third 'mixed' mechanism. In this mechanism, the rise in the interest rate is the end result of a process; it occurs to the extent necessary to suck in the capital account counterpart of the current account deficit. And the force which helps to generate this increased interest rate is, in part, the Keynesian rise in economic activity in the face of a non-accommodating monetary policy.

One aspect of this argument is the light which it throws on the 'crowding out' hypothesis. The stronger is the direct causal link between borrowing, capital account inflow, and the exchange rate, the stronger is the stubborn resistance of the system to any form of interventionism by the authorities. Just as the Barro–Ricardian argument suggests that private saving rises to offset government dissaving, so, in the new orthodox story, a reduction in net exports will appear to offset whatever expansionary stimulus remains.

The strength of the dollar – which is a key explicand of the new orthodox story – does not appear in the second story, and is not stressed in the third story.

Rather than pursue further theoretical, a priori argument, it might be preferable to consider the empirical evidence. It is not simple to set up an 'experiment' that will adequately distinguish degrees of explanatory power. In discussion, Penner reported the studies made by his staff, and suggested that the major element in the decline in US net exports was due to a price effect, via the exchange rate, rather than an income effect, through the income propensity to import. The simultaneity of the pattern in the two curves on figure 5.5 of Penner's chapter (p. 119) seemed to me a little hard to account for if price effects are the main motor, since in the UK at any rate we are accustomed to fairly large time lags between price signals and quantity outcomes. (However, I do concede that in recent years, with competitive sourcing of intermediate goods for assembly operations, very quick shifts of suppliers can take place, and there is some suggestion that the short-term reactions to, for instance, the change in the dollar/sterling rate during 1983/85 have speeded up considerably compared with what was evident a decade ago.)

Because the rise in the dollar (and the beginning of its fall?) were much in our minds at the conference, there was a strong disposition in the minds of most participants to accept that the new orthodox doctrine had much to tell us. My own conclusion, in advance of further empirical investigation, and much modified by discussion at the conference and afterwards (and not least by the editors of this volume), is that the observed rise in the dollar must have been 'caused', to a large extent, by the US fiscal deficit; but that does not deny that the fiscal deficit also had an expansionary effect on economic activity in the US. It does seem, moreover, that the burden of the evidence is that the large swing in the US fiscal deficit has not reduced US private capital formation, and that its effect on US interest rates has been much mitigated by the inflow of funds from abroad.

Whether this story would be effectively repeatable for other countries, even if in principle they are following similar monetary policies, must be more doubtful, as I pointed out at the conference. United States debt instruments are already held far more widely than those of a typical medium-sized country, who would face a narrower market and consequentially lower ratings. Moreover, the dollar is held for reasons quite unconnected with normal capital market portfolio balance – for currency reasons, for reasons of international liquidity, for political reasons.

Indeed, many observers have held from time to time in the last two decades that the accumulation of overseas holdings of dollars might be becoming unstable; and if it were really still true that the path of the US fiscal deficit was risking Domar instability, then even in the case of the United States the mechanism I have described might be on the verge of breaking down. On the whole, the US participants at the conference were reasonably confident that the federal deficit was now coming under control, and the risks I have just sketched are therefore less cogent; but it is well to remind ourselves that the paradox 'a high fiscal deficit leads to a rising exchange rate' is far from universally true for all countries at all times.

A Target Fiscal Deficit?

It is sometimes suggested that it is more important to stick to a numerical target for the fiscal balance than to argue endlessly which target is the right one. Others would suggest that this is a good way of training dogs, a dubious principle for bringing up children, but a rule for practical economic policy that is so open to barbarian attack that the barbarians, as they put the defenders to fire and sword, should be slightly ashamed of so easy a victory.

The argument is well known and can be sketched as follows. Output and employment are given by the long-run forces of technology and the supply curves of the factors of production (supply 'prices' are in real units). Similar real forces (including real thriftiness) determine growth rates. The overall price level is exogenous, determined by monetary factors, which in turn (because of the institutional rules and conventions of banking) are linked to fiscal flows. The precise relationship between trends in the 'money supply' and trends in the price level is complex and hard to predict, but that relationship is constant or changes slowly. The absolute price level will need, no doubt, time to adjust itself to pre-set monetary and therefore fiscal conditions, and as soon as that once-for-all adjustment is made, the price level will track the desired path.

If we chose a high $\dot{M}$, the system will eventually give us a high $\dot{P}$; if we choose a lower $\dot{M}$, we shall get a lower $\dot{P}$. Any reasonably plausible stable $\dot{M}$ will give us non-accelerating inflation; and any reasonably stable fiscal deficit (in *nominal* terms) will give us a stable $\dot{M}$. We have a steady fiscal policy in order to maintain a moderately steady monetary policy. If the trouble in the past has been an unstable (in particular, an accelerating) $\dot{P}$, choose any moderately low fiscal balance, and *stick to it*. It is not real output which will respond, just the (rate of change in) the price level.

There are many problems in specifying the mechanism which must be assumed to exist by those who support this slogan. There are of course frictions and time lags and costs of adjustment – but that is true also of alternative mechanisms that might moderate or stabilize inflation rates. The *particular* problem with this approach is that it assumes that all paths of adjustment are equally attainable and do not differ in the degree of difficulty they present. Such an assumption is not plausible, and in my judgement is not true. To decelerate inflation slowly may be less difficult than to do it fast (although this is by no means always true); different circumstances, history, accompanying disturbances, will require different action. To assume that *any* path of adjustment is at least as easy as any other path is to assume away all relevant facts.

What, in any case, are we up to with all this targetry? Particularly *long*-term targetry? There are three different classes of reasoning which, in many countries, have driven statesmen of different parties to adopt policies for the money supply, or the fiscal balance, or for the debt to income ratio.

1 If there are no targets, economic managers cannot be judged by objective tests – the wish to enable 'management by objectives' has wended its way through the corridors of the business schools to the heights of government, in my view inappropriately. Despite my scepticism, however, many people like this approach. Since it is also widely believed that one or other of these nominal variables is a necessary intermediate step towards the control of inflation, and also that each of them is a manipulable or controllable variable, a general wish has emerged to treat one or other of them as management targets

2 Secondly, many commentators (particularly those who have been exposed to American intellectual thinking), profoundly distrust all politicians, as a breed, and hold that it is only by impaling governments on visible targets that they can be stopped from doing other things which the electorate would not wish if they had been asked. I hold a different position on political science; for me politicians are all men of wisdom and benevolence, amongst whom I choose from time to time at elections, and who I wish would do their best for the country using their own judgement as to how to act as events unfold between elections. I would not want them to be bothered by particular series of statistical information in between elections, except in so far as they would like to see such numbers to help in their job of running the country.

3 The third – and to my mind most compelling – reason for targetry is the alleged psychological effect on myriads of decision makers elsewhere in the economy. These people have to assume *something* about government policy; it would be best if they all assumed the same thing, and that their expectations were systematically satisfied. Secondary and higher order uncertainty would hence be removed. Internal consistency of decisions would be assured.

It is targetry of this third sort which can be fairly indifferent about the numerical niceties – any target is OK provided that the authorities stick to it; steady state driving around the Washington or Paris beltway can be as safe at 60 mph as at 50 mph, provided all observe the limit precisely, and inter-car separation is larger at the higher speed (to handle stochastic shocks).

I would comment that this is a rather crude, two-dimensional, cardboard cut-out mechanical psychology. Maybe it worked first time, just as any classroom trick does; as cynicism and experience accumulates, the distinction between more sensible and less sensible targetry begins to be debated, and willingness to accept any old numerical target about any old conceptual variable is much diminished.

Some commentators will even begin to ask whether the links between all possible intermediate targets and the final targets are strong enough to be relied upon; and whether other final targets than those first chosen begin to be of importance. I would summarize by saying that, yes, some *impasse fiscale* is a good idea, but it does matter which cul-de-sac you get stuck in, and how far up.

IV CONCLUSION

Quite a lot of the ground revealed by the swirl of the tides of economic fashion in London over the last decade is fairly solid, and those who have found these standpoints have important new things to tell us; they can see the flow of the water at certain points more accurately, and can understand whirlpools and eddy currents better. But there are insecure sandbanks, too. And even the solid ground will not stand excessive weight – you have to tread delicately, perceptively, not putting too much emphasis on fragile footholds. The topography may already be changing as the next tide flows.

The main criticism I would make of those who have tried to re-establish old footholds on the sandbanks labelled 'public borrowing' is that they are perhaps excessively preoccupied with long-term regularities without investigating the shifting institutional and economic foundations underneath; and that they are a little too agile, but I expect in the outcome not quite agile enough, as they leap from sandbank to sandbank, seeking always to keep their feet dry while still staying on the map grid reference points where they started. There is some truth in most of the propositions they advance, but no universal truth in any.

REFERENCES

Barro, R.J. 1974: Are government bonds net wealth?, *Journal of Political Economy*, 82, 1095–1117.

Domar, E. 1944: The 'burden of debt' and national income, *American Economic Review*, 34, 798–827.

Keynes, J.M. 1940: *How to Pay for the War*, Macmillan, London.

HM Government 1984: *The next ten years: public expenditure into the 1990s*, Cmnd 9189, HMSO, London.

Oddling-Smee, J. and Riley, C. 1985: Approaches to the PSBR, *National Institute of Economic Review*, 113, 65–80.

Posner, M.V. 1973: Review of D. Moggridge's edition of Keynes's works, *Economic Journal*, 83(329), 111–19.

Index

Aaron, H., 313
Abel, A.B., 375
absolute income effect, 156, 166
accelerator effect, 331–2
adjusted deficit, 347–8, 350–3, 355–6, 358–66
  see also non-adjusted deficit
Agtmael, A.W. van, 76
Almon polynomial lags, 139
Alvaro, G., 204
Ando, A., 275
Arcelli, M., 205, 292, 312
Argentina, 77, 82, 99
ARIMA process, 148–9
Arrow, K.J., 344
Artis, M.J., 238, 241, 243, 249
Asimakopulos, A., 315
assets
  domestic, 182–3, 184, 194–5
  household, 183, 185–8, 189, 195
  market, 347, 349, 357–62, 364–5
Atkinson, A.B., 367, 376, 380, 391
Auerbach, A.J., 267–8, 269
Australia, 28, 29–31, 33–4, 35–7
Austria, 20, 29–31, 33–4, 35–7

Bacon, R., 343
Baffi, P., 204
Bagehot, W., 82
Bagwell, K., 374
Bailey, M., 264, 276
balance of payments, 183, 210, 222
  fiscal deficits and, 408–411
Bank of England, 75, 213, 215, 216
Bank of Italy, 188, 191, 205
Bank Rate, 211
banking systems, 77, 82, 86–8, 310–11
Barro, R., 8, 9, 266
  intergenerational altruism, 250, 258, 275, 276, 302–3
  private savings, 110, 176, 277, 283, 290, 296, 309
  Ricardian equivalence, *see* Ricardian equivalence
Barsky, R., 148
Barth, J.R., 110, 273, 277
Bartlett, B., 300
Bean, C., 241
Belgium, 21, 29–31, 33–4, 35–7
Bernheim, D., 276, 282, 374
Biswas, R., 242, 243, 249
Blanchard, O., 176, 202, 205
Blinder, A.S., 240, 241, 266, 314
Boskin, M.J., 258, 266, 268, 277–8, 281, 283, 295, 309, 313, 344
Bosworth, B., 117, 124, 314
Brainard, W.C., 5
Brazil, 82–4, 99
Bresciani-Turron, C., 72, 97
Bristow, J.A., 238
Britain, 17, 72, 75, 86, 261, 342–3
  deficit financing, 234, 235–49
  postwar credits, 374, 380, 386
  savings/investments, 29–32, 34, 35–8
  see also budgetary policy (Britain)
broad money, 86, 87

Brookings Papers (1985), 407
Brumberg, R., 275
Buchanan, J.M., 198, 234, 235–6
Budd, A., 250
budget constraint, 172, 200–2
  assets creation, 182–8, 194–5
  money creation, 188–93, 195–7
budget deficits
  costs/benefits, 95–9, 105, 123–4
  current account, 7, 34–6, 409–10
  Domar instability, 396–401, 411
  federal, 115–16, 118, 409
  -financed tax cuts, 325–32
  impacts (studies), 270–80
  inflation and, 72–89, 256–8, 262
  interest rates and, 256–7, 262–3, 273–5
  measurement and analysis, 258–63
  nature of, 7–10
  optimal, 405–7
  private savings and, 256, 258, 280–3
  propositions, 396–408
  public debt and, 255–8, 280–3
  saving/investment behaviour, 3–12
  stability analysis, 171, 176–7, 193–4
  structural, *see* structural deficits
  sustainability, *see* sustainability (budget deficits)
  trends/effects (USA), 106–12, 115–16, 118–24
  see also debt; deficit financing
budgetary policy (Britain)
  effectiveness, 237–9
  Keynes' views, 208–28, 235–6
  see also functional finance
built-in stabilizers, 7, 8, 51, 58, 60, 64, 244, 245–7
Buiter, W.H., 3, 5, 242, 244, 247, 287, 290–2, 294–5, 298, 368
Burns, T., 90
business cycles, 106, 123, 151

Canada, 19, 29–32, 36–8, 261
Canto, V.A., 343, 344
capacity utilization, 7–8, 10
capital
  accumulation, 303–5, 309, 339, 404, 406
  budgeting, 224, 225–6
  equipment, 116–17
  formation, 123–4, 276
  goods, 122–3
  inflows, 105, 111, 118–19, 123
  insurance on, 377, 387–8
  intensity, 304–8, 310, 360
  market, 213–15, 376–7, 387–8
  output ratio, 321–2, 324–5, 333, 335, 338, 352–4, 358, 361–2
  supply, 319–22, 325, 337–8
capital stock, 98–9, 101–2
  tax cuts and, 321–2, 325, 330–1, 337
Capriglione, F., 205
Caranza, C., 205
Carli, G., 205
Carmichael, J., 313
Carter administration, 85, 258
CBO projections, 110–11, 259–61, 342
Ceriani, V., 205
Chow test, 144, 149
Clarke, Sir Richard, 408
closed economy, 375, 381, 387, 406
coarse-tuning, 235, 248, 402
Colander, D., 228
Colwyn Committee, 212–13, 229
commodity markets, 10
compensation, 98
Congdon, T., 90, 368
Congressional Budget Office, 110–11, 259–60, 261, 342
Conlisk, J., 344
consumption
  determinants, 126, 152–65
  government, 4, 263–4
  inflation and, 139, 145–52
  leisure and, 279–80
  private, 4, 166, 168, 264
  subsidy, 376, 385
  tax, 373–4, 376, 378, 380–6
  tax cuts and, 330–1, 337–8, 340
consumption function, 127–32, 164–5
  debt neutrality and, 293–6
  see also life cycle hypothesis
contingent debt, 374, 375, 380, 385–7
Corden, W., 90, 313
corporate sector, 12–19, 21, 23–4, 26–8, 37–8, 114
Cotula, F., 204, 205
Cozzi, T., 313, 315
credit, 213, 214, 215
  counterparts identity, 86–7, 88
  creation, 182–3, 184, 194–5, 199
crowding-out, 275, 276, 407, 408, 410
  supply-side, 9, 65, 299–302, 304
  tax cuts and, 98, 123, 333, 334–5

current account
  deficits, 7, 34–6, 408–9
  surplus, 215, 216
Current Population Surveys, 277, 279
Currie, D.A., 244, 376
cyclical trends, 7–8, 180, 182, 199
  counter-cyclical devices, 399–400, 408

Darby, M.R., 276
David, M., 264, 276, 313, 314
debt
  accumulation rate, 44–7, 404–5
  contingent, 374–5, 380, 385–7
  effect on consumption, 145–52
  income ratios, 78–82, 335, 340, 342–3, 396–9, 401–2
  neutrality, 287–96
  ratio dynamics, 42–53, 56–7, 60–2, 67–70, 392–3
  Ricardian equivalence, *see* Ricardian equivalence
  role (in public finance), 374–8
  service burden, 202–4
  see also budget deficits; deficit financing; public debt
debtor nations, 99–100
defence spending, 106–8, 122, 159, 261
deferred pay, 223
deficit financing
  budgetary policy and, 237–9
  fiscal policy measures, 239–49
  Keynes and, 234, 235–7
  Ricardian equivalence, *see* Ricardian equivalence
  sustainability, *see* sustainability (budget deficits)
  targeting, 235, 243–7
  tax cuts, 325–32
  see also adjusted deficit; non-adjusted deficit; permanent deficit; primary deficit; structural deficits
deflation, 139, 168
demand, disposable income and, 291–2
demand management, 235, 237, 243–4, 249
Denison's law, 278
Denmark, 22, 29–31, 33–4, 35–7
depreciation, 306, 308
  ratios, 12 28
Dernburg, T.F., 370
developed and developing countries (contrasts), 72–89
Diamond, P., 276, 367
Dicks-Mireaux, L., 276
DiMauro, F., 205
disinflation, 48–53, 55, 96, 196–7, 244
  inflation and (USA), 97–8, 99
disinvestment, 118
dissaving, 216, 256–7, 276, 283, 398, 400, 410
dollar appreciation, 96, 99, 100, 118, 119–21, 123, 256, 270–1, 409–11
dollarization, 77
Domar, E., 205, 227, 333, 336, 342, 344
  Harrod-Domar condition, 351, 352–3
  instability proposition, 396–401, 411
domestic assets, 182–3, 184, 194–5
Dornsbusch, R., 103
Dow, J.C.R., 237–8, 249

Eadie, Sir Wilfrid, 231, 232
Eckstein, O., 273
econometric models, 114, 124, 238, 303
Economic Advisory Council, 209, 216, 217, 220
economic growth, *see* growth rate
Economic Resources Tax Act (1981), 266, 271, 282
economic theories
  causes for concern, 396–408
  fiscal deficit proposition, 408–14
economy, structure of, 9–10
Edwards, S., 88
Einaudi, L., 204
Eisner, R., 268, 274
Eliot, T.S., 232
Eltis, W., 296, 343, 344, 398
employment, 103, 121–3, 401–2
  White Paper, 210, 226–7
  see also full employment deficits; labour; unemployment
equilibrium debt ratio, 59–60
equipment share, 116–17
Ercolani, P., 133, 166–7, 168
Eshag, E., 90
Euler equation, 283–4
Europe, 100–3, 182, 246
  public sector debt, 40–1, 53–62, 66
Evans, P., 295, 314
excess saving, 216, 360–7, 400
exchange controls, 77, 78

exchange rate, 10, 62, 120, 210–11, 213, 219
fiscal deficit and, 408–11
exports, 100, 122, 123, 216–17, 256
net, 119, 121, 124, 410

factor prices, 374, 395
Fazio, A., 205
federal deficit, 115–16, 118, 257, 409
Federal Reserve Board, 409
Feldstein, M., 34, 127, 151, 266, 273–4, 314, 344, 369
analysis (significance), 303–9
on unfunded liabilities, 267, 277, 281
see also Tobin–Solow–Feldstein model
Fforde, J., 244
finance motive, 311
fine-tuning, 237–43, 249, 274, 402
Finland, 23, 29–31, 33–4, 35–7
fiscal
illusion, 287–96
recovery (Italy), 171–204
retrenchment, 40, 51–3, 59–60, 62–5, 67
stance, 65–6, 242–3
stimulus, 65–6
fiscal deficit
exchange rate and, 408–11
impacts, 270–80
optimal, 405–7
private savings and, 255–8, 280–3
target, 411–14
fiscal policy
counter-cyclical, 399–400
functional, 228, 235–7, 243–4
inflation and, 51–2, 72–3, 80–6, 208
Italy, 152–63, 165–6
Keynesian, 208–9, 219–28, 234–5, 239–49
national savings and, 258, 263–70
supply-side policies, 303–4
USA, 95–103, 263–70
see also coarse-tuning; fine-tuning
Fisher's law, 137, 147, 166, 169
Flemming, J.S., 70
flow-of-funds approach, 5–6, 183
Ford administration, 108
foreign sector, 4, 6, 183
investment, 212, 214–17
investment (net), 105, 111, 118–19, 123, 265
loans, 78, 83, 89
France, 16, 29–32, 35–7, 261
free trade, 212, 217, 219
Friedman, B., 3, 8, 110, 314
full employment deficits
impact, 256, 260, 262
Keynesian, 235, 241, 245
target rate of return, 248, 360–7
targeting, 235, 245–7
tax cuts, 326–41
TSF model, 347–67 *passim*
Fullerton, D., 266, 278, 281, 343
functional finance, 228, 235–7, 243–4

Galli, G., 191, 205
Germany, 15, 29–32, 35–7, 72, 86, 97, 261
Giannone, A., 205
Giblin, Professor, 220
GNP
composition, 273–5
growth, 42–61
public debt ratio, 57–61, 67–70
real, deficits and, 256–60, 262–3
US budget deficit ratio, 104, 106–12
gold standard, 209, 213, 219
Goldfeld, S.M., 240, 241
Goldfeld test, 169
goods sector, 121–3
public, 373, 378–9, 382, 384–6
Gordon, R.H., 266
Gordon, R.J., 8
'Geria plan', 205
government
bonds, 8, 9, 137–8, 291–3, 347–50, 354, 356–7, 359
consumption, 4, 263–4
deficit, *see* deficit financing
dissaving, 256, 276, 283, 398, 400, 410
expenditure, 248, 350–1, 407–8
investment, 167–8, 209, 212–21, 265, 407
government debt, 167, 168
accumulation, *see* sustainability (budget deficits)
domestic assets and, 182–4, 194–5
growth, 172–82, 193–4
see also budget deficits; deficit financing; public debt
Gramm–Rudman–Hollings, 261
Graziani, A., 315

Great Depression, 106–7, 279
Great Society, 106, 108, 235, 236
Green, C.J., 238, 241, 243, 249
growth rate
budget sustainability and, 172–82, 193–4
debt/income ratio and, 78–80
interest rate and, 396–7
national savings and, 152–63, 165–6
Grubb, D., 344
Guarantees Committee, 72
Gylfason, T., 314

Hancock, K., 214
Hansen, B., 238
Harrod, R.F., 227, 229
Harrod–Domar condition, 351, 352–3
Hartley, N., 241
Hattersley, Roy, 246
Hausman, J., 276, 343
Hawtrey, R.G., 214
Hempel, C., 315
Henderson, H., 209, 214–15, 217–18, 230
heteroskedasticity, 143–4
Hicks, J.R., 223, 332
Hoel, M., 103
Holcombe, R.G., 295
Holloway, T., 110
homoskedasticity, 142
Hopkins, Sir Richard, 218
Horioka, C., 34
household sector, 12–19, 21, 23–4, 26–8, 37–8
financial savings, 183, 185–9, 195
housing, 117, 195
Howrey, E.P., 278, 314
Howson, S., 217, 220–1, 222, 228, 229, 230, 231
Hurd, M., 266, 276
Hymans, S.H., 278, 314
hyperinflation, 97, 137, 180

IMF, 168, 246, 312
imports, 122, 123, 217, 218–19
incentives, 114–15
investment, 96–9, 268, 271, 282
income
-debt ratios, 78–82, 335, 340, 342, 343, 396–9, 401–2
disposable, 167, 291–2
effect, 132, 156, 165, 166, 186, 410
Individual Retirement Account, 281

inflation, 40, 168, 202–4, 210
budget deficits and, 72–89, 262, 265–8,
consequences, 400–2
decelerating (USA), 84–6, 96–7
fiscal policy and, 51–2, 72–3, 80–6, 208
illusion, 126–7, 131–2, 137, 147–8, 151–2
interest rate and, 47, 56, 62, 64–6
LCH model, 126–7, 131–2, 137–9, 144–53, 161–3, 166
limited horizon, 130, 132, 139, 142, 145, 149, 151–2, 164–5
output and, 270–3
supply-side policies, 303–9
sustainability issue, 171–2, 177–82
target, 246, 247
tax, 180–1, 185, 191, 211, 247–8, 347, 350
tax cuts and, 318–19, 326–32, 338–9
see also disinflation; hyperinflation
insurance (capital), 375, 385–6
interest elasticity of saving, 258, 270, 272, 278–80, 281–2
interest rates, 41, 110–11, 118, 168, 396, 404–5
budget deficits and, 256–7, 262–3, 273–5
debt ratio dynamics, 42–53, 56–7, 60–2, 67–70
debt service burden, 202–4
inflation and, 47, 56, 62, 64–6
LCH model, 131–2, 136–7, 138–41, 145–52, 164–5
money stock and, 288–91
output and, 176–8, 200–2, 270–3
real, 47–8, 53–9, 78–80, 397–8
supply-side, 304–7, 309–11
tax cuts and, 332–7, 342
intergenerational transfers, 98, 266–9, 281–2, 374–5
altruism model, 129–30, 258, 275–7
investment
budget deficits and, 3–12
crowding-out, *see* crowding-out
foreign, 212, 214–17
foreign (net), 105, 111, 118–19, 123, 265
government, 167–8, 265
incentives, 96–9, 268, 271, 282
private, 12–28, 30, 34–8

private (net), 111–12, 116–18, 265
public, 209, 212–21
-savings identity, *see* savings
supply-side policies, 310–12
tax cuts and, 330–1, 333, 337–40, 342
unemployment and, 209, 212–19
IS/LM model, 240, 244, 302, 332
Israel, 77
ISTAT, 167, 168
Italy, 18, 29–32, 35–8, 261
fiscal policy and savings, 126–66
fiscal recovery, 171–204

Japan, 14, 29–32, 34, 35–8, 261
Johansen, L., 205
Johnson, E., 91
Johnson administration, 108
Jones, D.H., 343

Kahn, R.F., 230
Kahn's multiplier theory, 209, 219–21
Kaldor, N., 76, 344
Kalecki, M., 227–8, 232
Kennedy, M.C., 238
Kennedy administration, 108
Keogh accounts, 281
Kessler, D., 294
Keynes, J.M., 380, 400–1
on budgetary policy, 208–28
deficit financing, 234–7
neoclassical theory and, 287–93, 296
Keynesian economics, 81–2, 287–93, 296
long-run debt, 347–9, 360–7
supply-side policies, 301–3, 309–12
Keynesian revolution, 72, 234–7
King, M.A., 266, 276, 281
knife edge effect, 48, 71, 363
Kochin, L.A., 294, 313
Kormendi, R., 127, 313
Koskela, E., 3
Kotlikoff, L.J., 267–9, 276–7, 283, 287
Kregel, J., 234, 236–7, 314–15
Kydland, F.E., 388

Labini, P.S., 236
labour
intensity, 351–3, 356, 358, 361–2
markets, 10, 11
labour supply, 97, 308
tax base and, 382–4
tax cuts and, 319–20, 322, 324–5, 337–8

Laffer, A.B., 343, 344
Laffer curve, 299, 324, 325, 399
land value, 142–4, 148, 149, 158, 166, 167
Larosière, J. de, 312
Latin America, 73, 77, 82–4, 85–6, 88–9, 99
Lau, Lawrence, 279
Lawrence, E., 267
Lecaldano, E., 185, 205
Leeuw, F., 110
leisure, 279, 382–3, 386
Lerner, A.P., 228, 235–6, 237, 370
Levigne, A., 294
Levine, P., 374
life cycle hypothesis, 126, 292
consumption function, 127–32, 164–5
data, 133–7, 138
limited horizon, 130, 132, 139, 142, 145, 149, 151–2, 164–5
national savings and, 152–63, 164
pure model, 258, 275–6, 277
test (basic model), 137, 139–45
tests, 145–52
limited horizon (inflation), 130, 132, 139, 142, 145, 149, 151–2, 164–5
Lindbeck, A., 313
liquidity preference, 311
Little, I.M.D., 76, 227
living standards, 327–8, 339
Lucas, R.E., 313, 373, 381, 388

McCallum, B., 3, 5, 8, 313
McIntosh, D.C., 211
McKinnon, R., 87
Macmillan Committee, 209, 216, 217, 218, 229
macro-economic theory, 106, 298–9, 301, 302, 318
Mariano, R., 127, 151
Markovian shocks, 374, 381
Marotta, G., 185
Masera, R., 185, 191, 195, 204, 205, 367
Matthews, R.C.O., 235, 236
Mayer, L.M., 294
Meade, J., 224, 225, 227–8, 231–2
Medicaid, 108
Medicare, 108, 269, 281
Medium Term Financial Strategy, 244
Menchick, P., 276
Mexico, 82, 83, 99
micro-economic analysis, 298–9

Miller, M.H., 249, 344
Miller, P., 111
Mirer, T.W., 276
Mirrlees, J.A., 388
Modigliani, F., 127, 128, 130, 131, 133, 139, 153, 166, 167, 313
  life cycle model, 258, 275, 292, 367
Moggridge, D., 91, 208, 228, 229, 231, 400
monetarism, 244, 287–8, 312
monetary
  base, 172, 188, 190–3, 195–8
  erosion, 179–81, 199, 203–4, 347, 350, 356
  growth (TSF) model, 347–60, 366
monetary policy, 409–12 *passim*
  inflation and, 49–50, 86–8
  interest rates and, 273–4, 289, 300
  Keynes' views, 209, 215, 226
  supply-side and, 303–4, 306, 308
monetization, 312, 347, 355, 359–60, 365
money, 73–5
  creation, 172, 188–93, 195–7, 355, 366
  illusion, 279, 401
  neutrality, 288–9
  quantity theory, 209, 395
  supply, 86–8, 326, 332, 339, 412
Monti, M., 90, 204
Morcaldo, G., 180, 204
Muller, P., 60, 70
multiplier, 209, 219–21, 230
  effect, 331–2
Mundell, R., 103, 313
Musgrave, R.A., 241

narrow money, 87–8
national accounting framework, 4–7
national debt
  burden, 395, 403–4
  deficits, 257, 258–63
  see also debt; deficit financing; public debt
National Debt Enquiry, 210, 224, 225
National Institute of Economic and Social Research, 238, 242, 243
neoclassical theory, 287–93, 296, 299, 302, 303
  of excess savings, 360–7
  of long-run debt, 347–67
net national product, 128–9, 131–2, 134–5, 152–4, 157–9, 161–2, 164, 264
Netherlands, 24, 29–31, 33, 35–7
neutrality issue, 287–96
New Deal, 220, 401
NIPA data, 106–7, 109, 112, 115
Nixon administration, 108
non-adjusted deficit, 348, 350–3, 358–60
Norman, M., 216, 217, 229
Norway, 25, 29–31, 33–4, 35–7

OASDI, 281
Odling-Smee, J., 243, 246, 405
OECD, 3–38, 113, 114, 246, 261
office buildings/equipment, 116–18
oil prices, 3, 12, 29, 31, 34, 35
open economy, 10, 373–91
operating surplus, 115
Ornstein, N., 106
output
  capital ratio, *see* capital
  composition, 270–3
  employment and, 121–3
  growth, 176–8, 200–2
  market, 347–9, 352–4, 356, 358, 360–5
  see also productivity
overdraft facility, 172, 188, 190–3

Paganetto, L., 315
Park-Gleiser test, 169
Patinkin, D., 230, 288
peacetime, 106, 382, 383, 385, 399–400
Peden, G.C., 231
Pedone, A., 205
Pellechio, A., 277
Penner, R., 260
pension funds, 115–16, 400, 402
permanent deficit, 247, 248
Persson, T., 373, 380
Phelps, E.S., 103, 313, 367
Pieper, P.J., 268, 274
Pigou, A.C., 214, 215, 217
planning horizon, 129–30, 164
politics and politicians, 413
Poole, W., 221
population data, 168, 277, 279
portfolio, 289
  equilibrium, 347–8, 357–9, 361, 365
Posner, E., 70, 401
postwar budgetary policy, 209–10, 224–8
postwar credits, 374, 380, 386
Prescott, E.C., 388
Price, R.W.R., 60, 70

price
  effect, 123, 299, 410
  factor, 374, 395
  formation, 10–11
  levels, 96, 98, 328–9, 411–12
  shadow, 381, 389, 391
primary deficit, 262, 348, 350–3, 355–6, 359, 396, 397
private sector
  investment, *see* investment savings, *see* savings, private
production, 122–3, 310, 351
productivity, 121, 339, 340, 342
Prometeia, 205
propensity to consume, 134–5, 136, 164
propensity to save, 136
public choice, 198
public debt
  budget deficit and, 255–8, 280–3
  disinflation and, 48–53
  explosion, 44–7
  -GNP ratio, 57–61, 67–70
  income ratios, 78–82
  neoclassical theory, 347–67
  neutrality, 287–96
  performance implications, 53–61
  policy dilemma, 60, 62–6
  private savings and, 255–8, 280–3
  ratio dynamics, 42–53
  role (in public finance), 374–8
  supply-side policies, 298–312
public finance, debt in, 374–8
public sector
  borrowing requirement, 172–6, 179–80, 182–3, 188, 194, 199–200
  indebtedness, *see* public debt
  savings/investment, 12–31, 34, 36–8
  spending, 248, 350–1, 407–8
public works, 209, 212–19, 220–1, 407
pure lifecycle model, 258, 275–6, 277

Quantity theory, 209, 394

rates of return, 278–9
  target, 348, 360–7
rational expectations, 299
rationality hypothesis, 148, 149, 151, 153
rationing, 223–4
Reagan administration, 84–5, 108
recession, 51, 55
  tax cuts and, 339, 340–1
  USA, 106, 108, 111, 112, 114–17, 121, 256, 260
regression coefficients, 29, 30–3
Repaci, F.A., 133, 167, 168
Reparations Commission, 72
resources, wartime, 209, 222–4
retrenchment policies, 40, 51–3, 59–60, 62–5, 67
revenue tariff, 218–19
Ricardian equivalence, 38
  Barro's, 5, 126–7, 129–30, 132–3, 139, 142, 144–5, 151–2, 159, 164–5, 245, 330, 400, 410
  limitations, 374–8
Ricardo, D., 276
Riley, C., 243, 246, 405
risk, 75, 82, 86, 88–9, 375, 378
Robbins, L., 217
Roberts, P.C., 343
Robertson, D.H., 215, 222
Robinson, A., 208
Rodriguez, C., 103
Romani, M., 167, 168
Rose, H., 369

Sachs, J., 34, 103
'safety trap', 348–9, 360
Sahasakul, C., 266, 283
St John-Stevas, N., 90
Salvemini, G., 180, 204, 205
Sardinian proposition, 398, 399–401
Sargent, T.J., 344
Sato, R., 338, 343
savings
  budget deficits and, 3–12
  excess, 216, 360–7, 400
  interest elasticity of, 258, 270, 272, 278–80, 281–2
  -investment identity, 5, 347–9, 351, 361–7
  ratio, 321, 324, 325, 338
  sectoral, 3–38
savings, national, 95, 106, 112, 257
  consumption function, 128–32, 164–5
  determinants, *see* lifecycle hypothesis; Ricardian equivalence
  fiscal policy and, 152–63, 165–6, 258, 263–70
savings, private, 95, 106, 109
  behaviour theories, 258, 275–80
  measured, 102–3
  net, 105, 111–15

public debt and, 255–8, 280–3
tax cuts and, 333, 340
Say's law, 276
Sayers, R.S., 231
Scadding, J.L., 264, 313, 314
Schott, K., 236, 249
Seater, J., 127, 151
services sector, 121–2
shadow price, 381, 389, 391
Shell, K., 367
Sherwell, C., 90
shocks, random
demand for public goods, 373, 378–9, 382, 384–6
real wage, 373, 378, 379–380
Shoven, J.S., 282
simulation models, 41, 60, 62–6, 241–3, 401
Sinking Fund, 212, 213, 220, 226
Siracusana, B., 90
Smith, K., 249
social security, 257, 266, 268, 303
unfunded, 267, 269, 277, 280–1
Söderström, H., 38
Solow, R.M., 241, 314, 344, 347, 369
see also Tobin–Solow–Feldstein model
'sound finance', 89, 213
Spain, 26, 29–31, 33, 35–7
Spaventa, L., 133, 136, 167, 204, 296, 312–13
Spinelli, 168
stability analysis, 171, 176–7, 193–4
stabilization policies, 144, 221–2, 224, 236, 237–8, 298, 408
see also built-in stabilizers
steady state debt, 347–8
excess savings, 360–7
TSF model, 349–60
Stein, J.L., 369
Steindl, J., 249
Steinherr, A., 246
Sterling, A., 127, 128, 129
Stiglitz, J.E., 367, 376, 380, 391
stochastic model, 373–91
debt dynamics, 390–1
specifications, 378–80
structure of model, 387–9
Stokey, N.L., 373, 380, 388
structural budget balance, 172, 180, 182, 197–200
structural deficits, 7 8, 34, 319, 332–42, 397, 398
structural surplus, 341, 342–3
substitutability, 10, 196
substitution effect, 132, 186, 381
Summers, L., 266–8, 274, 276, 278, 280, 281, 313, 314
supply-side policies, 9, 298–312
see also taxation cuts
surplus, 112, 115–16, 341, 342–3
sustainability (budget deficits), 171, 173–81, 296
budget constraint, 182–8, 194–5
debt interest burden, 202–4
financial programming, 172, 197–200
money creation process, 188–93, 195–7
notes on, 200–2
Svensson, L.E.O., 373, 380
Sweden, 5, 27, 29–31, 33, 34, 35–7
Sylos Labini, P., 205

Tanner, J.E., 295
Tanzi, V., 71
tap issues, 226
target fiscal deficit, 411–14
target rate of return, 348–9, 360–7
targeting, deficit, 235, 243–7
Tax Act (1981), 266, 271, 282
taxation, 7, 8, 54, 198, 398
consumption, 373–4, 376, 378, 380–6
consumption function, 128–32, 168
incentives, 96–9, 268, 271, 282
inflation, 180–1, 185, 191, 211, 247–8, 347, 350
lump-sum, 376–8, 380
marginal, 264, 266, 281
shocks, 376, 373–80
supply-side, 299–303, 305–8
and taxable capacity, 75–6, 78, 211
wage, 373–4, 380–4
wartime, 222–5, 228, 237
taxation cuts, 96–9
deficit-financed, 325–32, 338–43
for full employment, 326–43
long-term benefits, 319–26
Thatcher government, 342
Thurow, L., 314, 367
Tobin, J., 3, 5, 205, 250, 275, 287, 289–92, 294–5, 298, 305–6, 313, 330
Tobin–Solow–Feldstein model, 347–8
Keynesian, 360–7
neoclassical, 349–60, 365–7
Tomlinson, J., 234, 235, 236, 249

trade cycle, 224–5, 226, 227
transfer payments, 176, 198
  see also social security
  Treasury, 172, 190–3, 195, 197
  bills, 82, 186, 188, 194, 226, 263
  indexed bonds (ORTNs), 82
trust fund surplus, 115–16
Trustee Acts, 212
Tsiang, J.C., 314
Ture, N.B., 344

uncertainty, 292–3, 296, 373, 413
unemployment, 41, 99, 102, 208
  public works and, 209, 212–21, 407
  tax cuts and, 318–19, 324, 326–7, 328, 332, 341
unified budget, 107, 108
United Nations, 167, 168
United States, 41
  budget deficits, 72, 84–6, 88–9, 105–24
  deficits, 257–63, 270–80
  federal deficits, 115–16, 118, 257, 409
  fiscal deficit, 255–8, 270–83, 409–11
  fiscal policy, 95–103, 263–70
  Keynesianism in, 234, 235
  savings/investment, 13, 29–32, 35–8
  taxation cuts, 96–9, 341–3
  Treasury analysis, 299–301
  see also dollar appreciation

Vaciago, G., 205
Valiani, R., 205, 292, 296, 312
Vercelli, A., 313
Vicarelli, F., 313
Vietnam War, 234, 235–6
Viren, M., 3
Visco, I., 188

wages, 10–11, 96–7, 223
  tax, 373–4, 380–4
  tax cuts and, 327–8, 329
Wagner, R.E., 234, 235–6
Wallace, N., 344
Walras, L., 288
Wanniski, J., 97, 300
War Loan, 219
wartime, 144, 147, 158–9, 399–400
  defence spending, 106–8, 122, 159, 261
  postwar budgetary policy, 209–10, 224–8
  postwar credits, 373, 380, 386
  resources for, 209, 222–4
  time deficits, 260, 261
  see also Vietnam War; World War I
wealth, 5, 101–2, 289, 309
  effect, 8, 9, 166, 186, 292
  LCH model, 128–30, 133–5, 139, 141–4, 147–9, 151–2, 158, 160, 165, 167
Wedgwood, Josiah, 232
Wharton Econometric Forecasting Associates, 114, 124
white noise process, 148–9, 156, 379
White Paper on Employment Policy (1944), 210, 226–7
Winch, D., 217, 220–1, 222, 229–31
windfall revenue, 405–6
Wootton, Barbara, 212
World War I, 209, 210–12

Yawitz, J.B., 294

Zautzik, E., 205

Indexed by Jacqueline McDermott